Integrating Psychotherapy and Psychophysiology

Integrating Psychotherapy and Psychophysiology

Edited by

Patrick R. Steffen and Donald Moss

OXFORD
UNIVERSITY PRESS

Great Clarendon Street, Oxford, OX2 6DP,
United Kingdom

Oxford University Press is a department of the University of Oxford.
It furthers the University's objective of excellence in research, scholarship,
and education by publishing worldwide. Oxford is a registered trade mark of
Oxford University Press in the UK and in certain other countries

© Oxford University Press 2024

The moral rights of the authors have been asserted

All rights reserved. No part of this publication may be reproduced, stored in
a retrieval system, or transmitted, in any form or by any means, without the
prior permission in writing of Oxford University Press, or as expressly permitted
by law, by licence or under terms agreed with the appropriate reprographics
rights organization. Enquiries concerning reproduction outside the scope of the
above should be sent to the Rights Department, Oxford University Press, at the
address above

You must not circulate this work in any other form
and you must impose this same condition on any acquirer

Published in the United States of America by Oxford University Press
198 Madison Avenue, New York, NY 10016, United States of America

British Library Cataloguing in Publication Data

Data available

Library of Congress Control Number: 2023950103

ISBN 978–0–19–888872–7

DOI: 10.1093/oso/9780198888727.001.0001

Printed and bound by
CPI Group (UK) Ltd, Croydon, CR0 4YY

Oxford University Press makes no representation, express or implied, that the
drug dosages in this book are correct. Readers must therefore always check
the product information and clinical procedures with the most up-to-date
published product information and data sheets provided by the manufacturers
and the most recent codes of conduct and safety regulations. The authors and
the publishers do not accept responsibility or legal liability for any errors in the
text or for the misuse or misapplication of material in this work. Except where
otherwise stated, drug dosages and recommendations are for the non-pregnant
adult who is not breast-feeding

Links to third party websites are provided by Oxford in good faith and
for information only. Oxford disclaims any responsibility for the materials
contained in any third party website referenced in this work.

Patrick R. Steffen: For my wife Monica and children Alexander, Cecilia, William, and David

Donald Moss: I dedicate this book to Nancy Moss, who for forty years supported my professional pursuits, and to our chapter authors, who contributed so much to the richness of this book

Foreword

Stephen W. Porges

Contemporary psychotherapy is progressively moving from a cognitive model to a more integrated model respecting bodily reactions and embracing the importance of the nervous system in diagnosis and treatment. During the past decade, as the impact of the body and nervous system on mental health has been acknowledged, there has been a dramatic shift in psychotherapy (van der Kolk, 2014). Many forms of psychotherapy, explicitly or implicitly, now integrate an understanding of the nervous system and bodily state in their treatment models. Research on psychotherapy has been increasingly documenting the role that the client's nervous system plays in treatment (e.g., Cozolino, 2017; R. A. Lanius et al., 2010; U. F. Lanius et al., 2014; Payne et al., 2019). The publication of *Integrating Psychotherapy and Psychophysiology* is a timely response to this trend. This volume, edited by Patrick R. Steffen and Donald Moss, includes chapters by pioneers who explore this integration and provide insights into the future of psychotherapy as it embraces an appreciation for the psychophysiological bridge between neurophysiological regulation and mental health.

Complementing the empirical literature are clinically relevant theoretical models that link neurophysiological function to mental and physical health such as the Neurovisceral Model (Thayer & Lane, 2000) and Polyvagal Theory (Porges, 1995). These theoretical mind–body and brain–body conceptualizations, frequently referenced within this book, have resulted in the psychotherapy community rethinking mental health disorders and treatments. As an increasing number of psychotherapists recognize the connection between mental processes and bodily function, rather than disparate symptoms leading to co-morbidities, these will be re-interpreted as a more systemic adaptive reaction to threat (see Porges, 2022).

The processes involved in the regulation or disruption of physiological states, which covary with thoughts and behaviors, are dynamically adjusting and adapting. Whether we focus our therapies on thoughts or behaviors, there is a physiological substrate that is dynamically adjusting with the simple pragmatic objective to optimize survival. This is true not only from the perspective of the individual, but also with respect to relationships. Thus, the co-regulation that occurs between individuals reflects an embodied relationship involving two nervous systems signaling each other with an agenda to mitigate threat within psychological, behavioral, and neurophysiological domains.

From a neuroscientific perspective, challenges to survival (e.g., trauma, adversity) functionally permeate into the survivor's nervous system, retuning it from a dynamic state that supports sociality and homeostatic functions (i.e., health, growth, and restoration) to a chronic state that supports defense (e.g., fight, flight, shutdown). Thus, we witness how adverse experiences become physiologically embedded, altering the optimal trajectory of a flexible and resilient nervous system, and profoundly disrupting the development of the experience of self and others.

Reframing trauma from an event to a psychophysiological response transforms our understanding of the consequences of "traumatic" events. From this perspective, the traumatic event is viewed as being capable of overwhelming the survivor's neuroregulatory capacity to support underlying physiological homeostasis and observable resilient and flexible behavior and thinking. The consequence is a general breakdown in the client's physiological and emotional regulatory capacity within themselves and in relation to the world around them. Treatment becomes a gradual work of repairing these ruptures, involving a therapeutic framework that elevates a sense of safety as a necessary substrate for the homeostatic functions (i.e., health, growth, restoration, and sociality), which serve as an essential neurobiological platform for transformation and healing.

A central message from a psychophysiological perspective is that psychotherapy can be efficiently delivered only if the therapist is trained to detect the cues of safety and threat that are broadcast by clients. Even in the absence of physiological monitoring, psychophysiologically informed therapists learn to infer the client's autonomic state from overt markers (e.g., facial expressions, vocal intonation, muscle tension, and gestures) linked to the neural regulation of our viscera.

In addition, therapists need to be aware of their own bodily reactions (i.e., interoception) to their clients, and to appreciate that clients are responding to subtle changes in physiological state that may be observable in their facial expressions, muscle tension, and vocal intonation. Thus, therapy will be most effective when the therapist's nervous system is "broadcasting" signals of safety and trust, while the client's physiology welcomes and supports it as a part of a co-regulatory relationship. Hypothetically, therapy will be more efficiently delivered if the nervous system of the client is accessible and places the client's physiology in a state of safety and not a state of defense. Although this is a precarious path for therapists and clinical researchers, it is a path that can be illuminated through the process described by the title of the volume, *Integrating Psychotherapy and Psychophysiology*.

In writing this foreword I have been reminded of my early research interests. When I entered graduate school in the fall of 1966, psychophysiology was emerging as a new discipline bridging psychology and physiology. It was a discipline with a scant literature. Few books and articles on the topic had been published. Only two years earlier, a new journal, *Psychophysiology*, was founded to provide a home for peer-reviewed research in this area and only six years earlier the Society for Psychophysiological Research had been founded. I was attracted to the potential of psychophysiology as a discipline that moves subjective experience into objective measures of physiological function. For me, psychophysiology was the portal to study mind–body relationships and move subjective experiences into the realm of objective measurement. One of my personal interests was to apply physiological monitoring to track a psychotherapy session. I wondered if the physiological indices would accelerate the therapeutic progress and improve outcomes. Although I never did this type of research, I did develop a device called a PhysioCam (Davila et al., 2017). The PhysioCam detects the pulse wave from a person's face and accurately quantifies beat-to-beat changes in heart rate to stream online values of heart rate, heart rate variability, and respiration. The technology embedded in the device received a patent and a startup company is now piloting a version that can be used in clinical settings that informs the therapist of shifts in the client's physiology (see https://televagal.com). Thus, illustrating how psychotherapy and psychophysiology can seamlessly be integrated.

As I read this volume, I had a deep appreciation of the challenging journey towards enhanced treatments in mental health that researchers and clinicians have been on during the past fifty years. As measurement of neurophysiological processes has become available via inexpensive sensors and monitors, the active integration of psychotherapy and psychophysiology is now accessible to clinicians outside of well-equipped research laboratories. This volume provides a bold step forward by showcasing the pioneering research and theory development that actively integrates a nuanced knowledge of neurophysiology in building the therapeutic models to integrate psychophysiology with psychotherapy with a goal of providing more effective and efficient therapeutic treatments.

References

Cozolino, L. (2017). *The neuroscience of psychotherapy: Healing the social brain (Norton Series on Interpersonal Neurobiology)*. W. W. Norton & Company.

Davila, M. I., Lewis, G. D., & Porges, S. W. (2017). The PhysioCam: A novel non-contact sensor to measure heart rate variability in clinical and field applications. *Frontiers in Public Health*, 5, 300. https://doi.org/10.3389/fpubh.2017.00300.

Lanius, R. A., Vermetten, E., & Pain, C. (2010). *The impact of early life trauma on health and disease: The hidden epidemic*. Cambridge University Press.

Lanius, U. F., Paulsen, S. L., & Corrigan, F. M. (2014). *Neurobiology and treatment of traumatic dissociation: Towards an embodied self*. Springer Publishing Company.

Payne, H., Koch, S., & Tantia, J. (2019). *The Routledge international handbook of embodied perspectives in psychotherapy: Approaches from dance movement and body psychotherapies*. Routledge.

Porges, S. W. (1995). Orienting in a defensive world: Mammalian modifications of our evolutionary heritage. A polyvagal theory. *Psychophysiology*, 32(4), 301–318. https://doi.org/10.1111/j.1469-8986.1995.tb01213.x.

Porges, S. W. (2022). Polyvagal theory: A science of safety. *Frontiers in Integrative Neuroscience*, 16, 871227. https://doi.org/10.3389/fnint.2022.871227.

Thayer, J. F., & Lane, R. D. (2000). A model of neurovisceral integration in emotion regulation and dysregulation. *Journal of Affective Disorders*, 61(3), 201–216. https://doi.org/10.1016/s0165-0327(00)00338-4

van der Kolk, B. (2014). *The body keeps the score: Brain, mind, and body in the healing of trauma*. Penguin.

Contents

Contributors	xiii
Editors' Introduction: Integrating Psychotherapy and Psychophysiology *Donald Moss and Patrick R. Steffen*	1

SECTION I THEORY IN PSYCHOPHYSIOLOGICAL PSYCHOTHERAPY

1. **An Evolution- and Compassion-Informed Biopsychosocial Approach to the Challenge of Building an Integrated Science for Psychotherapy** *Paul Gilbert*	13
2. **Neuroscientific Principles Underlying Psychotherapy** *Rebekka Matheson*	53
3. **Heart Rate Variability in Mental Health and Psychotherapy** *Julia Wendt and Julian F. Thayer*	75
4. **Brain Plasticity and Prediction of Response to Psychotherapy** *Sadie J. Zacharek, John D. E. Gabrieli, and Stefan G. Hofmann*	101
5. **Affect as a Foundation for How We Know and Understand the World: A Framework for Integrating Psychotherapy and Psychophysiology** *Travis Anderson and Patrick R. Steffen*	127

SECTION II ASSESSMENT IN PSYCHOPHYSIOLOGICAL PSYCHOTHERAPY

6. **Approaching Psychopathology from a Psychophysiological Perspective: Using Dimensional Diagnostic Approaches as Frameworks to Integrate Psychotherapy and Psychophysiology** *Dawson Hedges and Patrick R. Steffen*	153
7. **The Biology of Personality and Stress: Cardiovascular Reactivity as Central to Human Coping** *Brian M. Hughes, Siobhán Howard, and Aisling M. Costello*	171
8. **Using the Research Domain Criteria Framework to Conceptualize and Assess Personality: A Model of Personality for Psychotherapy/Psychophysiology Integration** *Patrick R. Steffen and Joseph A. Olsen*	189

SECTION III IMPLEMENTATION: INTEGRATING PSYCHOPHYSIOLOGICAL INTERVENTIONS INTO PSYCHOTHERAPY

9. Therapist Flexibility: Why a Psychophysiological Component in Psychotherapy is Important 221
   Paul M. Lehrer

10. Compassion as an Integrative and Integrating Therapeutic Process 243
    Paul Gilbert

11. An Interpersonal Perspective on the Physiological Stress Response: Implications for Therapeutic Interventions in Coronary Heart Disease 277
    Timothy W. Smith and Jenny M. Cundiff

12. As I Lay Dreaming: A Case Study in Psychophysiological Psychotherapy 311
    Donald Moss

13. *The Most Beautiful Man:* The Integration of Hypnosis and Biofeedback 323
    Donald Moss

14. Integrating Heart Rate Variability Biofeedback into Acceptance and Commitment Therapy (ACT) 337
    Richard N. Gevirtz

15. Breathing, Heart Rate Variability, and Their Application in Psychotherapy 351
    Inna Khazan

16. Compassionate Bodies, Compassionate Minds: Psychophysiological Concomitants of Compassion-Focused Therapy 373
    Nicola Petrocchi and Cristina Ottaviani

17. Compassion Focused Therapy and Heart Rate Variability 391
    Chase S. Sherwell and James N. Kirby

18. Ethical Principles and Practice Standards in Psychophysiological Psychotherapy 413
    Donald Moss

Index 423

Contributors

Travis Anderson, Department of Philosophy, Brigham Young University, Provo, Utah, United States

Aisling M. Costello, Department of Psychology, University of Limerick, Limerick, Ireland

Jenny M. Cundiff, Department of Psychology, University of Alabama, Tuscaloosa, Alabama, United States

John D. E. Gabrieli, Professor of Health Sciences and Technology and Cognitive Neuroscience, McGovern Institute for Brain Research, Massachusetts Institute of Technology, Boston, Massachusetts, United States

Richard N. Gevirtz, California School of Professional Psychology, Alliant International University, San Diego, California, United States

Paul Gilbert, Centre for Compassion Research and Training, College of Health and Social Care Research Centre, University of Derby, Derby, United Kingdom

Dawson Hedges, Departments of Psychology and Neuroscience, Brigham Young University, Provo, Utah, United States

Stefan G. Hofmann, Department of Psychology, Philipps University Marburg, Germany

Siobhán Howard, Department of Psychology, University of Limerick, Limerick, Ireland

Brian M. Hughes, School of Psychology, University of Galway, Galway, Ireland

Inna Khazan, Harvard Medical School, and Boston Center for Health Psychology and Biofeedback, Boston, Massachusetts, United States

James N. Kirby, Compassionate Mind Research Group, School of Psychology, The University of Queensland, Brisbane, Australia

Paul M. Lehrer, Professor Emeritus, Rutgers Robert Wood Johnson Medical School, Piscataway, New Jersey, United States

Rebekka Matheson, Neuroscience Center, Department of Psychology, Brigham Young University, Provo, Utah, United States

Donald Moss, Professor and Dean, College of Integrative Medicine and Health Sciences, Saybrook University, Pasadena, California, United States

Joseph A. Olsen, FHSS Research Center, Brigham Young University, Provo, Utah, United States

Cristina Ottaviani, Associate Professor, Department of Psychology, Faculty of Medicine and Psychology, Sapienza University of Rome, Rome, Italy

Nicola Petrocchi, Compassionate Mind Italia, Rome, and Adjunct Professor, Department of Psychological and Social Sciences, John Cabot University, Rome, Italy

Stephen W. Porges, Distinguished University Scientist, Indiana University, Bloomington, Indiana; Professor of Psychiatry, University of North Carolina, Chapel Hill, North Carolina; Professor Emeritus, University of Illinois at Chicago and University of Maryland, College Park, Maryland, United States

Chase S. Sherwell, Compassionate Mind Research Group, School of Psychology, The University of Queensland, Brisbane, Australia

Timothy W. Smith, Department of Psychology, University of Utah, Salt Lake City, Utah, United States

Patrick R. Steffen, Department of Psychology, Brigham Young University, Provo, Utah, United States

Julian F. Thayer, Department of Psychological Science, University of California, Irvine, California, United States

Julia Wendt, Biological Psychology and Affective Science, University of Potsdam and Oberberg Clinic Potsdam, Potsdam, Germany

Sadie J. Zacharek, Department of Brain and Cognitive Sciences, Massachusetts Institute of Technology, Boston, Massachusetts, United States

Editors' Introduction

Integrating Psychotherapy and Psychophysiology

Donald Moss and Patrick R. Steffen

This book introduces research and clinical approaches to the integration of psychotherapy and psychophysiology. The book highlights concepts in neuroscience and autonomic physiology which illuminate what is happening in therapeutic transformation. The authors emphasize that interventions that impact our brain and nervous system can accomplish much that we expect from psychotherapy. For example, both compassion training and heart rate variability training not only impact autonomic regulation but also impact sub-cortical brain systems. Integrating such interventions as preparation for psychotherapy or as an integral part of therapy, can enhance therapeutic benefits.

This book provides both a theoretical framework supported by current research in neuroscience and psychophysiology, and a practical guide for mental health practitioners in the clinic, who seek to utilize mind–body interventions in psychotherapy. The theoretical framework includes an emphasis on an embodied unitary concept of affect and cognition, an evolutionary approach, and an integration of interpersonal, affective, relational, and biological perspectives.

Section I: Theory in Psychophysiological Psychotherapy

Chapter 1 introduces an integrative framework for understanding psychotherapeutic change. Paul Gilbert's approach is informed by evolutionary models, attention to physiological and neurophysiological mechanisms, and the central role of compassion. Gilbert emphasizes compassion, because of his belief that "all other motives, emotions, and beliefs are regulated and directed through caring compassion motives." Gilbert highlights reciprocal pathways linking heart rate variability, compassion, and self-compassion. In Gilbert's model, one of the central tasks of psychotherapy is to enable the individual to transcend threat-processing and responding systems and to activate "caring for" and "being cared for" as a primary orientation in living. This is as much a physiological task as a psychological one, with the role of the vagus nerve, the parasympathetic nervous system, and the hormone oxytocin paralleling the move to a caring relational orientation.

In Chapter 2, Rebekka Matheson introduces a neuroscience-based non-dualistic approach to mind and body. She advocates for a biological understanding of psychotherapy and psychotherapeutic interventions. She suggests we understand anatomy as structure and behavior as the process resting on the structure and in turn transforming the structure. As she writes, "Muscle is not movement; it executes movement and is changed by that movement." Currently, healthcare is pervaded by dualism. Neurology and psychiatry are separated, with neurology treating identified brain disorders. Yet, neuroplasticity is the foundation for psychiatric and psychological disorders and their therapies. Every psychotherapeutic intervention addresses disordered neuroplasticity. She provides a number of clinical examples illustrating this unified neuro-behavioral understanding of both behavioral disorders and their treatment, for example, presenting cognitive behavioral therapy as a biological intervention, "changing functions of mind *because* it changes functions of brain."

In Chapter 3, Julia Wendt and Julian F. Thayer provide an overview of the phenomenon of heart rate variability (HRV) and its relevance to mental health and psychotherapy. Extensive research shows a correlation between poor mental health and impaired HRV. The authors review the physiological basis for HRV in the parasympathetic/vagal system and the close interface between respiration and cardiovascular regulation. They highlight the evidence that higher vagally mediated HRV indicates greater inhibitory controls in the brain and greater adaptive responses to environmental demands. Specifically, they show that vagally mediated HRV serves as an index of prefrontal cortex functionality, with important effects on subcortical structures such as the amygdala. Lower HRV and deficient prefrontal cortical function lead to chronic feelings of stress and chronic negative affect. For this reason, Wendt and Thayer argue that HRV is a transdiagnostic marker for psychopathology. The lower the HRV, the greater presence of psychopathology. This relationship holds true for disorders as diverse as psychosis, the addictions, and anxiety. Overall, the authors regard lower HRV as a *general vulnerability factor* for psychological disorders.

In Chapter 4, Sadie J. Zacharek, John D. E. Gabrieli, and Stefan G. Hoffman examine the brain processes that accompany all psychological change. They open the chapter by proposing that all beneficial changes in thoughts, feelings, and behavior, whether they are induced by medication or psychotherapy, are mediated through brain plasticity. They briefly review the tools of neuroimaging, highlighting their role in measuring neuroanatomy, neurophysiology, and neurochemistry. The chapter then addresses two major topics: First, they examine research evidence on specific brain systems that mediate psychotherapeutic changes, including the amygdala, the insula, the anterior cingulate cortex, prefrontal cortical areas, non-prefrontal cortical areas, and hippocampal areas. They draw primarily on neuro-imaging studies of the application of cognitive behavioral therapy to the anxiety disorders. Second, they review current evidence on biomarkers that predict response to psychotherapy. Given that most behavioral health treatments benefit only about 50 percent of patients, it would be valuable to identify predictive markers that would assist in optimal selection of treatments. This is the dream of *precision* or *personalized* medicine, the design of individualized treatment plans, optimally assisted by artificial intelligence, based on each patient's baseline characteristics. The authors examine potential biomarkers including neuroimaging of prefrontal regions, the basal ganglia and cerebellum, the amygdala, the visual cortex, along with multi-modal predictions based on multiple brain measures. The authors acknowledge the limitations in practical prediction of optimal treatments in research to date, yet emphasize that, to date, neuroimaging biomarkers outperform demographic, clinical, and genetic predictors. They end the chapter by describing the kinds of research needed to further develop a reliable basis for precision medicine.

In Chapter 5, Travis Anderson and Patrick R. Steffen explore the key role of affect—the emotional domain—in human experience and behavior. They call on the philosophers Baruch Spinoza (1632–1677) and Martin Heidegger (1889–1976) for a conceptual framework to combat the implicit Cartesian dualism that separates thinking and feeling in psychological science. Spinoza offered a non-dualistic, unified view of mind and body, emphasizing that cognition and emotion are interconnected. The authors review current models of perception and cognition in neuroscience and argue that a non-dualistic unified understanding of mind and body is supported by current research. The authors also cite the philosopher Heidegger, who emphasized that understanding is always rooted in the human being's mood and attunement to a current situation. They discuss the work of the neuroscientist Antonio Damasio and others, who show that human perception is active and affective, not passively objective or purely rational. Anderson and Steffen suggest that a unified understanding of affect and cognition is critical in understanding the process of psychotherapy. The authors also recommend integrating into psychotherapy an emphasis on affect as a foundation for healthy functioning.

Section II: Assessment in Psychophysiological Psychotherapy

In Chapter 6, Dawson Hedges and Patrick R. Steffen review difficulties in the categorical approach to psychopathology, as exemplified by the widely used *Diagnostic and Statistical Manual* (DSM-V) (American Psychiatric Association, 2013). The categorical approach introduces artificial distinctions between disorders that share significant numbers of behavioral symptoms, ignores psychological and neurophysiological commonalities shared by discrete disorders, and introduce an all or nothing diagnostic mindset, that ignores the large numbers of individuals who exhibit subsyndromal levels of disturbance, yet do not qualify for current diagnoses. The authors propose instead that both researchers and clinicians adopt a dimensional approach to conceptualizing psychopathology, and review two current dimensional approaches, each with significant research support: the Research Domain

Criteria (RDoC) and the Hierarchical Taxonomy of Psychopathology (HiTOP). They review research on each approach, and demonstrate that the dimensional approaches are more holistic, acknowledging the integral involvement of psychophysiological, mind–body pathways to disturbance, and including conceptualizations of both health and disease. Further, the dimensional approaches more easily integrate psychophysiological and neuroscience research findings, which generally show common neurophysiological mechanisms contributing to a variety of categorical disorders.

In Chapter 7, Brian M. Hughes, Siobhán Howard, and Aisling M. Costello propose that the psychological response to stress is an inherently biological phenomenon. They highlight the cardiovascular stress response, which closely mirrors the current emotional state. Hughes and colleagues examine the cardiovascular stress response as an "evolved psychophysiological coping resource," that is, a critical component in the human response to stress. They highlight the extensive research on the reactivity of heart rate and blood pressure to stress, and the complex interactions between elevated cardiovascular reactivity and personality traits such as neuroticism, which are relatively persistent over decades. Optimal stress responding, on the other hand, is an adaptive response to stress that is time-limited and subject to habituation. Hughes and colleagues also discuss promising approaches within psychotherapy to reduce the psychological and physiological impact of stress.

In Chapter 8, Patrick R. Steffen and Joseph A. Olsen further examine the RDoC, which was introduced in Chapter 6. They propose that the RDoC provides a useful framework for a unified model of personality, facilitating the integration of psychopathology and psychotherapy. The dimensional approach of the RDoC emphasizes moderate responding on each dimension as adaptive, with pathological functioning occurring at both extremes of a dimension, such as fear. The ideal point in this dimensional model is in moderate responding and moderate levels of affect. Steffen and Olsen conceptualize personality as the basis for evolutionary adaptation and survival, maintaining well-being and affective states around a set point, as the environment changes and presents challenges over time. They discuss psychological flexibility as the basis for optimal personality functioning, and intraindividual variability (or reactivity) as the basis for neurotic adjustment. They examine personality dimensions such as approach/avoidance that are based in evolution and frequently serve as frameworks in psychophysiological and neurobiological research. They examine a number of dimensions in personality that can be conceptualized in a fruitful way with the RDoC, such as negative and positive valence systems, cognitive and social systems, and arousal and sensorimotor systems. Finally, they examine challenges in measuring and assessing personality, including the non-linear and sometimes curvilinear relationship between personality and impaired and maladaptive functioning. They examine a number of efforts to statistically map this non-linearity, and briefly propose a quadratic unfolding model, to map this non-linearity.

Section III: Implementation: Integrating Psychophysiological Interventions into Psychotherapy

In Chapter 9, Paul Lehrer provides a brief history of non-drug therapies in healthcare, and highlights in particular the relative lack of emphasis on the psychophysiological component in therapies. Lehrer advocates for the therapeutic benefit of integrating psychophysiological interventions such as progressive muscle relaxation, autogenic training, and various forms of biofeedback. He recommends a broader education in psychophysiological approaches and therapies in psychotherapy training.

In Chapter 10, Paul Gilbert returns to the theme of compassion-focused therapy (CFT) as an integrated and integrative therapeutic process. CFT is first a vehicle for integrating psychophysiological understandings into psychotherapy, accessing the physiological mechanisms of threat regulation and positive affect generation. Gilbert conceptualizes CFT as a cross-disciplinary biopsychosocial approach integrating elements of many other psychotherapy techniques. In this chapter he examines two sets of competencies active in CFT, many with origins in other forms of psychotherapy. The first six competencies facilitate the client's compassionate engagement with distress and suffering; the second six competencies facilitate the client's movement from empathic attention into actions supportive of others. Gilbert views these competencies as the means by which CFT enables the client to develop a compassionate mind, open to the experience of others, and to translate compassionate understanding into compassionate behavior.

In Chapter 11, Timothy W. Smith and Jenny M. Cundiff introduce an interpersonal perspective on the physiological stress response. The authors highlight the significant contributions of interpersonal events to the onset of the stress response and emphasize that interpersonal events can produce either heightened risk or improved resilience to stress. They utilize the example of coronary heart disease to illustrate the impact of psychosocial factors on physiological mechanisms, for example, increased cardiovascular reactivity and elevated cortisol levels. They introduce interpersonal strategies to enhance resilience and reduce the impact of stress on cardiovascular function and they argue for inclusion of both stress-management and specific interpersonal strategies in any intervention program for individuals with coronary heart disease.

In Chapter 12, Donald Moss provides a case narrative illustrating the use of psychophysiological monitoring and mind–body interventions in psychotherapy. The patient is a seventy-five-year-old man, Jacob, whose sleep was disturbed by vivid dream encounters with sexual partners. The therapy included relaxation training, home relaxation practice, and monitoring of several physiological systems during therapy sessions. The physiological monitoring supported a behavioral desensitization process and diminished the individual's physiological and emotional reactivity to relationship cues. Through this psychophysiological approach, the quality of Jacob's sleep improved as did the quality of his current marital relationship.

In Chapter 13, Donald Moss provides a second case narrative, that introduces several specific mind–body practices—including mindful breathing, hypnosis, heart rate variability biofeedback (HRVB), and an affective journal—along with physiological monitoring, to address the problems of Marguerite, a thirty-six-year-old woman with post-partum depression and dissociative features. Marguerite benefitted from eighteen months of psychotherapy, augmented by the mind–body practices, with measurable decreases in depression and anxiety, and a sense of "living more fully again."

In Chapter 14, Richard N. Gevirtz introduces an approach integrating HRVB with Acceptance and Commitment Therapy (ACT). ACT is one of the most popular "third wave" therapies, integrating features of mindful acceptance with a general cognitive approach to therapy. Gevirtz discusses both Steven Porges' polyvagal theory and Julian Thayer and Richard Lane's neurovisceral integration theory as theoretical frameworks useful in understanding the physiological basis and therapeutic impact of HRVB (Porges, 2009; Thayer & Lane, 2000). Gevirtz also reviews core principles of ACT. Finally, he presents a case narrative of Judith, a forty-one-year-old woman employed as a medical receptionist, to illustrate the integration of HRVB with ACT. Judith presented with shoulder and arm pain, aggravated by work stress. A major irritant for Judith involved her frustration with co-workers who seemed indifferent to patients' well-being. Using a combination of HRVB and ACT skills, Judith was able to de-sensitize her physiological stress reactions to images of the work setting. At follow-up, she reported only occasional pain and stiffness, and she was able to manage these moments with a combination of muscle release and paced breathing.

In Chapter 15, Inna Khazan provides a detailed introduction to the psychophysiology of respiration and the therapeutic value of breath training. She confronts a number of widely held misconceptions about breathing and points out that misguided breath training can exacerbate physiological dysregulation. Maladaptive breathing patterns can contribute to the onset or amplification of generalized anxiety, panic disorder, phobias, chronic pain, and posttraumatic stress disorder. Correcting breath patterns can enhance emotional self-regulation, increase resilience, reduce medical and psychological symptoms, and improve HRV. This chapter provides step-by-step instructions for breath training as well as for HRVB training. Physiologically informed breath training and HRV training provide useful therapeutic interventions in themselves and useful adjunctive interventions in combination with psychotherapy.

In Chapter 16, Nicola Petrocchi and Cristina Ottaviani apply an evolutionary perspective to compassion and compassionate motivation. They emphasize the *eusocial* features of the human brain, suiting humans for extended periods of caregiving and engaging in complex compassionate and affiliative relationships with others. The authors introduce a discussion of Steven Porges' polyvagal theory, which proposes that the myelenated vagal nerve system provides structural support for human engagement and compassion. They conclude that HRV is associated with a number of psychological and behavioral variables that are usually the target of psychotherapy. They propose that practices that increase HRV, such as compassion-focused practices that can increase HRV will directly move the process of psychotherapeutic transformation forward. They highlight the regulatory power of the compassion state. Increasing heart rate variability enhances the emotional state of safeness and also increases positive emotions related to calmness and sooothing.

In Chapter 17, Chase S. Sherwell and James N. Kirby explore the links between compassion and physiology, along with examining the efficacy of compassion-focused therapy for improving physiology. They discuss compassion from an evolutionary perspective originating with mammalian caregiving. The extended period of caregiving and heavy parental investment in mammals serves as the basis for attachment bonds and compassion for a wider circle of others. The authors draw on Steven Porges' polyvagal theory to explore the physiological basis of attachment and compassion, with emphasis on vagally mediated HRV as a basis for prosocial behavior. They highlight the reciprocal relationship between HRV and compassion. Just as higher HRV may influence increases in compassion, research also shows that higher compassion increases HRV. This reciprocal relationship has immediate relevance for psychotherapy. The authors review the research to date showing that compassion training can increase HRV, as well as the emerging research on combining HRV biofeedback training into compassion-focused therapy. The research findings are mixed so far, and the authors propose directions for further research.

In Chapter 18, Donald Moss provides a brief overview of ethical principles and practice standards in psychophysiological psychotherapy. The chapter emphasizes that the psychotherapist who utilizes physiological monitoring and physiological skills training remains a psychotherapist. A key element in all psychotherapies is the therapeutic relationship, with elements of empathic rapport, compassion, communicative attunement, and personal empathy. There is an added challenge, to orient and educate the patient to the purpose and process of physiological methods, such as physiological monitoring. Educating patients about the mechanisms and specific steps in the new specialized interventions is a priority, so that patients better understand the electrode placement and how physiological monitoring or feedback training is relevant for addressing their presenting problem. Persons who understand the intervention and have a sense of ownership in the treatment plan, develop more active participation in the treatment.

Integrative Summary

The authors in the present volume provide a variety of perspectives important for the understanding of psychotherapy and enhanced practice of psychotherapy. The fundamental take home message of the book is that human emotion and cognition are embodied—they are integral mind–body processes, indivisible, and not capable of being understood by any dualistic Cartesian model. Anderson and Steffen show that cognition is never an isolated process separate from the body and from affect. Rather, drawing on the philosophers Spinoza and Heidegger, they argue that cognition is always grounded in our mood and attunement to concrete situations.

Human development shows the acquisition of human affect and sociality in evolutionary steps, for example with the major transition to mammalian life, the extended caregiving of the mammalian infant, and the attachment bonds that emerge with caregiving.

Two neurophysiological models—the polyvagal model of Steven Porges (2009) and the neurovisceral integration theory of Julian Thayer and Richard Lane (2000) illuminate the psychophysiological basis of attachment and compassionate engagement. Porges' polyvagal theory ascribes importance to the evolutionary emergence of the myelinated vagal nerve, as the basis for affiliation, attachment, and prosocial behavior. Thayer and Lane's neurovisceral integration model presents a model integrating processes in autonomic, attentional, and affective systems that illuminate the processes of self-regulation and adaptation.

Both models emphasize that the vagal system and vagally mediated HRV are essential processes in the emergence of human attachment. Vagally mediated HRV also correlates with inhibitory controls in the prefrontal cortex and greater adaptive responses to environmental demands. Increases in HRV are associated with positive changes in a number of psychological and behavioral variables that are targeted as goals of psychotherapy.

Several authors in the present book highlight HRV as a critical factor in understanding what happens in psychotherapy and as a factor that should be utilized to enhance psychotherapy outcomes. Petrocchi and Ottaviani highlight the reciprocal relationship between HRV and compassion. Increased levels of HRV increase measured levels of compassion, and compassion training in turn increases measured levels of HRV. Attention to this reciprocal relationship is promising for taking psychotherapy to the next level.

Authors in the intervention section uniformly advocate for greater attention to psychophysiology to augment the effectiveness of psychotherapy. The chapters in this section propose a science and practice of clinical intervention, applying research-tested tools, ranging from compassion training to compassion-focused training to direct training of respiration and HRV. Tools and psychotherapeutic approaches proposed in the intervention chapters range from compassion-focused therapy to acceptance and commitment therapy to interpersonal interventions to physiological monitoring during psychotherapy to breath training to biofeedback to hypnosis.

References

American Psychiatric Association. (2013). *Diagnostic and statistical manual of mental disorders* (5th ed.). American Psychiatric Association. https://doi.org/10.1176/appi.books.9780890425596.

Porges, S. W. (2009). The polyvagal theory: New insights into adaptive reactions of the autonomic nervous system. *Cleveland Clinic Journal of Medicine, 76* (Suppl 2), S86–S90. https://doi.org/10.3949/ccjm.76.s2.17.

Thayer, J. F., & Lane, R. D. (2000). A model of neurovisceral integration in emotion regulation and dysregulation. *Journal of Affective Disorders, 61*(3), 201–216. https://doi.org/10.1016/s0165-0327(00)00338-4.

SECTION I
THEORY IN PSYCHOPHYSIOLOGICAL PSYCHOTHERAPY

1
An Evolution- and Compassion-Informed Biopsychosocial Approach to the Challenge of Building an Integrated Science for Psychotherapy

Paul Gilbert

Biopsychosocial approaches are not new and can be traced back to the Greek physicians Hippocrates and Galen (Gilbert, 1984, 2020a; Pilgrim, 2002; Sperry, 2008). However, the last twenty years have seen a flourishing of biopsychosocial approaches to psychotherapy rooted in our rapidly expanding science of "body, brain and mind" (Cozolino, 2017; Porges, 2021; Schore, 2019; Schotte et al., 2006; Siegel, 2020; Van der Kolk, 2014). This chapter argues for developing better evolution-informed, biopsychosocial models of the mind, linked to one of the most important motivational systems for emotion and self-regulation: the "caring system" (Cassidy & Shaver, 2016; Gilbert & Simos, 2022; Mayseless, 2016). This caring system also links to prosocial behavior and well-being (Gilbert, 2015b; Wu & Hong, 2022).

There are a number of different dimensions to the science of psychotherapy integration (Žvelc & Žvelc, 2021). Castonguay et al. (2015) suggest four areas of integration: theory, technical, common, and assimilative. There is also now a specialist *Journal of Psychotherapy Integration*. However, integration refers not just to integrating different schools of psychotherapy but also to developing an integrated approach to the science of mind and in particular the complex interactions between biological, psychological, social, and ecological contexts that give rise to complex brain states. Historically the origins of Western systematic psychotherapeutic approaches to mental health problems were rooted in evolution-informed biopsychosocial approaches. The early psychodynamic theories of Freud, Jung, Adler, and Reich emerged in the immediate post-Darwinian era and focused on how their ideas of evolved motivational processes played out in a human mind partly regulated by social approval and sanction (Ellenberger, 1970, pp. 280–281). In contrast in Russia, Ivan Pavlov won the Nobel Prize in physiology in 1904 for showing how the environment could *directly* change physiological processes (Moore, 2012). It became known as Pavlovian or classical conditioning and provided a key focus for the study of the interplay of the brain with the environment. It led directly to several forms of behavior therapy. More recently, the Pavlovian model also contributed to the conclusion that psychotherapies need to be aware of the conditioning body states, as in Van der Kolk's (2014) work on "the body keeps the score." Both the psychodynamic and Pavlovian approaches were rooted in ideas on how evolution had shaped the nature of our minds and bodies, the need to understand their basic evolved functions and psychophysiological regulators.

For Pavlov, the body becomes regulated through associated learning, whereas in the 1890s, Freud worked on what he called "the project" that sought a physiological basis for his concepts of id, ego, and superego. He abandoned the project when he realized that the science of the brain simply was not there at the time (Ellenberger, 1970). It was nearly one hundred years before this challenge was taken up again (Cozolino, 2017). From the 1920s, Adolf Meyer regarded psychiatry as having become too mechanical and that mental states were the products of conscious minds and social relationships. Meyer, along with Engel, introduced the first systematic approaches to biopsychosocial science (Eisenberg, 1977; Pilgrim, 2002). Over the last one hundred years we have learned much about how social relationships influence physiological systems, health, and well-being, and impact epigenetics, with a greater appreciation of the importance of relationships and social contexts in the shaping of our minds (O'Donnell & Meaney, 2020; Slavich, 2020). This chapter explores these processes and how we can map the mind in a way that facilitates integration of basic sciences. It also indicates the psychophysiological integrative properties of care and compassion motivation, which can be central for change (Gilbert, 2000a, 2014; Gilbert & Simos, 2022; Žvelc & Žvelc, 2021). We begin with the concept of consilience proposed by Wilson (1999) and discussed by Gilbert (2019).

The sociobiologist Edward Wilson (1999) highlighted the fact that many sciences today have become overly specialized with little integration or cross-fertilization between them. He called for a *consilient approach*, meaning a cross-disciplinary orientation that integrates scientific insights from a range of different disciplines. Hence, the first form of integration would be to adopt a *consilient approach* to the science of mental health and therapy, involving (for example) the sciences of anthropology, sociology, psychology, physiology, neuroscience, and epigenetics (Gilbert, 1989, 1995, 2019; Gilbert & Simos, 2022). Brain states of distress and suffering are the result of multiple processes: from the phylogenetic (evolved dispositions) through to the way culture impacts child-rearing practices, social development, and economic opportunities, all of which shape bodies, values and behaviors. What is also important for integration is that it is not just bringing different elements together, it is the recognition that *in their interaction* they give rise to the emergence of different unique patterns, which have feedforward and feedback effects (Johnson, 2002). Many mental health problems (e.g., anxiety, depression, paranoia) and social ones (e.g., racism, sexism, and callousness) can be understood as multidimensional, inviting us to explore how different "sciences" can contribute to their understanding and prevention.

Hence, a major dimension of integration is *biopsychosocial* processes, where the focus is on the *emergent properties* and *new patterns of functioning* arising from interactions of the biological, social, and psychological. Figure 1.1 offers an overview of a basic biopsychosocial model (Gilbert, 1995, 2005). Biopsychosocial processes are contextualized within their local, historical, and ecological contexts, that can be relatively benevolent or hostile. Benevolent relationships that have profound effects on all three biopsychosocial dimensions (Wu & Hong, 2022) emerged from the evolution of care motivation with core physiological systems underpinning it (for reviews see Gilbert, 2017; Gilbert & Simos, 2022; Seppälä et al., 2017) and is regulated and shaped through different domains of social relating. These interacting processes are depicted in Figure 1.1. Individuals, families, and social communities are not ecologically decontextualized beings but exist and seek to pursue their life goals and challenges within a variety of helpful and harmful ecologies (Siegel, 2020). These have profound effects on the interactions of our biopsychosocial mind. War, poverty, racism, sexism, and stigmatizing all play a role in how brains and bodies come to mature in the way they do and lay down vulnerabilities to enacting harmful behavior, as well as physical and mental health problems.

For some clients, it is important that they are able to contextualize their difficulties as emerging from these processes (Abel & Clarke, 2020; Bornemann et al., 2016). In addition, therapies need to be impactful on all three dimensions (Slavich, 2020; Wu & Hong, 2022). We need therapies that impact our biological states, psychological processes, values, and motivations, and impact our social behavior to move us toward empathy and compassion for self and others (Gilbert, 2019). This chapter outlines different types of integration using the compassion-focused therapy (CFT) approach as an example of integrating psychotherapy and psychophysiology

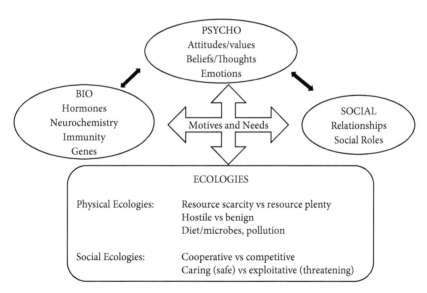

Figure 1.1 A biopsychosocial and ecological interactions model.
Note: Adapted from Gilbert (2005). © Paul Gilbert

(Gilbert, 2000a, 2014, 2020a; Gilbert & Simos, 2022; Petrocchi & Cheli, 2019; Žvelc & Žvelc, 2021).

Four Functions of Evolved Minds

Psychotherapy integration starts with the obvious fact that all lifeforms, from simple cell organisms to the most complex humans, are created from deoxyribonucleic acid (DNA). DNA is composed of two polynucleotide chains that coil around each other to form a double helix structure and provide genetic instructions for building proteins, cells, and organisms. Sequences of DNA molecules make up genes. We now know that genetically provided information can be regulated through "tags" like "on/off" switches (called methylation), which can be influenced by life experiences. This is called epigenetics. Problematic versus caring childhoods have different epigenetic effects (Cowan et al., 2016), along with the many physiological systems that mature and grow and are influenced by experience (O'Donnell & Meaney, 2020). Given these biopsychosocial realities, there is increasing awareness that the future development of psychotherapies will need to work on these processes, finding ways to have potential epigenetic effects (Kumsta, 2019; O'Donnell & Meaney, 2020; Slavich, 2020).

One way to start a journey into biopsychosocial integration is to map out the mind in terms of its evolved functions according to our current scientific understandings (Davey, 2018). Psychological science has suggested four basic functions of mind: motives, emotions, competencies, and behaviors, with various subdivisions possible (Davey, 2018). While some therapies tend to focus on only one or two functions, such as cognitive or emotion-focused processes or behavioral contingencies, ideally, we need to map *all the main* functions of the mind *and their interactions and emergent brain states*. For example, how do evolved motives interact with socially and culturally formed beliefs? How do emotions interact with motives; how do direct behavioral interventions impact beliefs and motives? How does improving mind(ful) awareness impact all functions? And so forth. Figure 1.2 presents a coordinated and integrated approach to these evolved psychological functions, recognizing that patterns of neural firing represent the interaction of such multiple processes within the brain.

Life Tasks and the Four Functions of the Mind

The sections that follow explore each of the four functions. In this model, evolved motives are primary drivers and organizers of the biopsychosocial processes of our minds. Motives evolve because they offer potential solutions to the life tasks of "survival and reproductive challenges and problems" (Buss, 2019). They guide organisms to pay attention to, and act on, salient stimuli in the environment that are linked

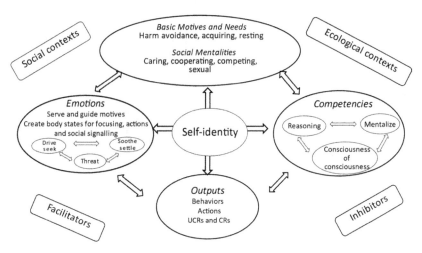

Figure 1.2 Four basic psychological functions.
Note: From Gilbert (2022a) © Paul Gilbert

to survival and reproduction. There are three major classes of motives that have specialist feature-detectors for detecting environment-appropriate information and orientating organisms to notice and then pay attention to:

1. *Threat and harm* in their domains of existence. This motive system evolved stimulus/feature-detectors for threats that trigger threat emotions (e.g., anger and anxiety) and actions (e.g., attack and retreat). Looked at another way, it is a basic protection and safety-seeking system. Threat systems can be very easily triggered and conditioned and tend to work on a "better safe than sorry" principle, making it easy for us to learn particular fears and threats (Gilbert, 1993; LeDoux, 2022; Nesse, 2019). This is sometimes called a "negativity bias" but is better thought of as a "threat bias" that operates in many domains (Baumeister et al., 2001). Threat system processing also estimates (for example) the probability of a threat, the short- and long-term impact of a threat, its controllability, frequency, and (likely) duration (Perrez & Reicherts, 1992) and its approach path, labelled *looming* (Riskind et al., 2021).
2. *Resource seeking.* Clearly, to sustain life and reproduce, animals must explore the environment and secure life-sustaining resources, such as finding and consuming food, locating or creating shelter, seeking out sexual partners, and (for some) living in groups. Hence, resource-seeking motives will have feature-detectors for that resource, such as being able to detect/identify food sources, potential mating partners, and one's own offspring. Threat arises from blocks to acquire these resources. Thus, the threat system is activated not only by the presence of a threat, but also the absence of, or inability to acquire control of a needed resource. This has major implications when the resource, in a species like humans, is the love and affection of early caregivers. Hence, evolved needs,

resource acquisition efforts and threat are interlocked processes. The simple fact that animals need resources to survive and have brains that will be seeking them and responding with threat to their absence, means that *needs,* especially social needs, should be a key process for psychotherapy.

3. *Safety, safeness, and satisfaction.* It is important that threat systems are not activated when they do not need to be and therefore the detection of *the absence of threat* or its controllability is a salient assessment for animals. In CFT, this is referred to as "safety," different from safeness (Gilbert, 2020a, see below). However, central too is that resource-seeking activities use up energy, and not being able to secure them is a threat. Accordingly, when *they are secured*, then the body can: (a) calm drive and threat activation, and (b) move into different patterns (for example of the autonomic nervous system) that facilitate settling and resting. Hence, the fulfilment of basic needs and the acquisition of essential sources enables rest and digest states, which are essential for body repair and recuperation, regeneration, and positive affect.

When resources are easily available, including access to helpful caring others, individuals *are safe* from threat *and* need. When the individual experiences being embedded in caring relationships with others who will help in times of need or stress, this stimulates psychophysiological systems that downregulate threat and are associated with positive affect (Gilbert, 1993, 2020a; Porges, 2021). As noted, some time ago, the physiological systems and feature-detectors that tune in to signals of helpfulness and safeness are different from those that tune in to the presence or absence of threat (Gilbert, 1989, 1993). So important are experiences of safeness, particularly within attachment and caring relationships, that "seeking and responding to safeness" is a fundamental motive that works through different affect regulation systems than safety seeking (Armstrong et al., 2021; Gilbert, 1993).

The two branches of the autonomic nervous system (ANS), the sympathetic and parasympathetic, are orientated for these different functions (Gibbons, 2019; LeBouef et al., 2021; Petrocchi & Ottaviani, in press; Petrocchi et al., 2022). The sympathetic component is linked to arousal for action. For threat this can be "fight or flight." For resource-seeking (e.g., food, sexual opportunities), this is explorative behavior (e.g., chasing prey, grazing). In contrast, the parasympathetic nervous system is designed for "rest and digest" and functions to partly regulate the sympathetic nervous system. It operates "without conscious control throughout the lifespan of an organism to control cardiac muscle, smooth muscle, and exocrine and endocrine glands, which in turn regulate blood pressure, urination, bowel movements, and thermoregulation" (LeBouef et al., 2021, p.1). The balance between these two branches of the ANS system is important for well-being and can be influenced via caring behavior. This balance is a potential target for compassion-focused therapies (Gilbert, 2000a, 2010; Gilbert & Simos, 2022; Kirby, 2016; Petrocchi & Cheli, 2019; Petrocchi & Ottaviani, 2024; Petrocchi et al., 2022; Porges & Dana, 2018; Steffen et al., 2021). Indeed, there is growing evidence that the vagus nerve and its impact on heart rate variability (HRV) play a significant role in caring and compassionate processing and behavior (Di Bello et al., 2021).

Algorithms of the Evolved Mind

Motives and emotions operate via "*if A, then* do *B*" stimulus-response (S-R) algorithms. These are the elements of information-flow that guide survival and reproductive behaviors. For example, the algorithm for threat would be: *if* a threat is detected, such as a predator, *then* activate the defense menu of responses, which operates through, for example, the hypothalamic-pituitary adrenal axis and the amygdala. Potential threats can be picked up by detecting movement, sound, and smell. The selected behavior may be to run, hide, or fight, or do nothing depending on context and how that threat is processed in terms of its likely impact/seriousness and controllability, the availability and adequacy of coping skills (Perrez & Reicherts, 1992), and the availability of help (Gilbert, 1993, 2020b). *If,* on the other hand, a stimulus indicates food, *then* this activates the physiology appropriate for eating/engaging approach-behaviors and preparing for consumption. That algorithm operates via a very different set of physiological systems involving the hypothalamus differently than when it is responding to threat. If the signal is one of sexual opportunity, then again, the triggered physiological system will be quite different. Having an algorithm-based understanding of motives enables us to think about the S-R algorithms underpinning caring and compassion and, in doing so, to identify their evolved physiological infrastructures. Hence, we can identify processes that link to the stimulus detection of and engagement with (move toward) suffering and distinguish them from the response-functions of the motive.

The S-R algorithm approach to care and compassion gives rise directly to the definition of compassion. Compassion has the stimulus properties of (a) "sensitivity to suffering in self and others" and (b) the response-properties of being committed to "seeking to relieve and prevent suffering" (Gilbert, 2014, 2020a; Mascaro et al., 2020). Although compassion is not usually labeled as an evolved algorithm, most definitions, old and new, clearly separate out these functions and processes of (a) how we engage, pay attention, and process suffering, with courage and wisdom that enables us to tolerate distress associated with moving toward suffering and understanding its causes, and (b) how these interact with the separate process of how we develop insight into what is likely to be helpful and take action. Sometimes that action can also be threatening and stressful (e.g., a firefighter), again requiring courage and wisdom. Neuroscience has revealed that developing insights into the nature and causes of mental states is different from those processes involved in planning and taking action; and this is the case with compassion (Di Bello et al., 2021; Kim et al., 2020) and other psychophysiological processes. One can be very sensitive to suffering but not know what to do or behave in ways that make suffering worse. Gilbert and Mascaro

(2017) found that sensitivity to suffering without knowing what to do is positively associated with depression and anxiety scores. Empathic sensitivity by itself is not necessarily helpful. Indeed, like all motives with algorithms, if one cannot enact the appropriate response, then the motive is frustrated and thwarted, creating potentially high levels of stress (Gilbert, 2001). The remainder of this chapter explores the basic functions of mind: motives, emotions, competencies, and behaviors. Each of these is discussed in turn.

Motives

The crucial aspects of motivation have been studied for many years, with a number of different theories linked to issues such as instincts, drives, desires, and needs (Davey, 2018); archetypes (Stevens, 2002); "have to do" (externally driven) *vs* "want to do" (internally driven) (Ryan & Deci, 2000, 2017); as well as conscious and unconscious awareness of motives (Bargh, 2017). Ryan and Deci (2000, 2017) noted that people could be motivated to do things because of internal or external reasons. They argued that *autonomous* motivation was generated from within, linked to personal values and feelings of control over one's own behavior. *Controlled* motivation generated behaviors such that people felt they had to conform in order to avoid negative consequences and external pressures. *Amotivation* is a third category referring to people who felt they had no reasons to engage in particular behaviors. These are clearly dimensions that vary according to personal values and context. Some forms of caring behavior can be linked to external pressures and a sense of duty or conformity, while other forms are more autonomous. Important for this chapter is the finding that self-criticism tends to be linked to controlled motivation, with lower positive affect and higher negative affect (Clegg et al., 2022). Hence, one of the goals of CFT will be to shift individuals to more autonomous motivation for compassion for and with self.

These variations have significant implications for psychotherapy. For example, people may have many desires that they do not act on, sometimes for good reasons, whereas unfulfilled needs can have serious consequences. Individuals can have motives and desires that are harmful (e.g., overeating, use of substances, harming others). Some motives are very distantly related to evolved motives. For example, the fashion industry is rooted in motives for status and social conformity. Religion is linked to motives for status regulation, attachment, and group belonging. People can be motivated to sacrifice themselves for a highly symbolic abstract set of ideas, believing this to be a caring or compassionate act. Motivation therefore is multi-textured and layered. In addition, people can engage in motivated behaviors, like caring, for many different reasons (Böckler et al., 2016), including to be liked or wanted (Catarino et al., 2014). We do things for mixed motivations; therefore, any particular caring act can have multiple determinants. Motives also branch into many culturally created sub-motives.

For example, human competitive resource-seeking and control motives propel individuals to go to school, acquire skills, pass exams, get careers, find status in the world, and have access to resource control and wealth in culturally scripted ways. The more motivated we are to pursue status and wealth, the stronger our emotions will be shaped by success or failure. Competitive motives come with their own physiological infrastructure and are quite different from caring motives. Upsetting somebody you are competing with, or have vengeful motives for, can be associated with positive emotions but if your motivation is to care for that person then your emotions will be distressing. Indeed, it is often the interplay of these two social motives that are a focus in CFT (Gilbert, 1989, 2019, 2022a).

Social Motives as Social Mentalities

CFT highlights the distinctions between social and non-social focused processes (Gilbert, 1989, 2022a). Non-social motives include harm avoidance, feeding, shelter, and so forth. Social motives have been called *social mentalities* because they require complex feature-detectors and processing systems for operating in dynamic, reciprocal interactions with other reciprocating minds (Gilbert, 1989, 2019, 2022a). As an example, the evolution of attachment means that parent and child actively seek out each other and create certain kinds of dynamic, reciprocal interactions that are mutually physiologically regulating (Cassidy & Shaver, 2016; Nguyen et al., 2020). The seeking functions of the motive carry within them some ideal or representation of what is being sought; this is called an archetypal image or value (Knox, 2003; Stevens, 2002). The ideal is partly genetic and partly socially created. For example, interacting with individuals that have at least some degree of the ideal qualities, such as the ideal parent, sexual partner, or friend provides inputs/signals that stimulate physiological systems underpinning positive affect. Social mentalities evolved to pursue biosocial goals, creating dynamic, reciprocal, interacting roles in the process (Gilbert, 1989, 2017). In other words, social mentalities—such as for sex, cooperation, competing, and parenting—require a social partner with a similar type of brain (Gilbert, 1989, 2000a, 2019; Gilbert & Simos, 2022). In some ways we can see this as different physiological systems, interacting in sender and recipient, becoming attuned or miss-attuned with physiological consequences.

Because social mentalities depend on reciprocal dynamic communication, they have to *co-evolve*. Hence, social mentalities create forms of role-sensitive, psychophysiological synchronies between participants. Courting behavior is an example of complex physiological, co-regulating social exchanges and behaviors between sexual partners. At any point in the dance of these dynamic, reciprocal interactions, one partner may switch out of sex and into threat, and attack or run away. When reciprocal relationships are in harmony, sensitive and care-focused participants generally create positive affect, but when communications and motives become conflictual, the pursuit of the biosocial goal and role can be compromised and trigger the threat system (Gilbert, 2019; Gilbert & McGuire, 1998).

The motive to be caring of one's offspring must co-evolve with processes in the infant that can detect and respond to signals of being cared for, and the caregiver must be able to detect and attune to the infant's needs. Reptiles do not respond to soft voices or stroking the way that human babies do. It is important then that the caregiver "knows" how and when to (say) use soft voices, strokes and hugs, feed or provide warmth. The infant must then have the physiological detectors to respond to such stimuli. One system (care giving) cannot evolve without the other (care receiving). In the attachment context, the reciprocal, dynamic interactions between infant and parent create psychophysiological synchrony (Nguyen et al., 2020).

Looked at in this way, we can see that psychotherapy is engaged in the exchange of role-guiding social signals that can be experienced as caring, uncertain, or threatening, thereby stimulating the appropriate systems within the client. For clients who come from threatening backgrounds and have not internalized the sense of secure base or safe haven from others, such signals can be registered as a threat (Gilbert, 1989, 1993; Gilbert et al., 2011; Kirby et al., 2019; Van der Kolk, 2014). For such clients, the care-receiving systems and their underpinning processes, such as secure base and safe haven (e.g., vagus nerve, and neurocircuits that detect and respond to care), are not functioning particularly well. Lacking access to these physiological regulators, they can find it difficult to feel a sense of safeness or care from others, including the therapist.

Social mentalities then, evolved with the abilities to *detect* a signal, *send* a signal, and *respond* to a signal that is role-specific (to create caring, cooperative, sexual, and competitive reciprocal roles and to create dynamic reciprocal dances of communication). This has important implications for psychotherapy. Psychotherapy is essentially a process of creating an interplay of social roles where different psychophysiological systems are being turned on and off by the interplay. For example, certain kinds of care-seeking or distress signals from a client can stimulate the care-provisioning mentality in the therapist, whereas a hostile, competitive client can stimulate defensive counter (transference) competitive behavior or submissive anxiety and avoidance. A mindful therapist is cautious of their own psychophysiological responses, noticing their body shifting to anxiety in this encounter, irritation in another encounter, or sense of confusion in another. They may notice that their background physiological state impacts these interactions. Maybe they are physiologically responding differently today because they have a virus, are very tired, just won a large lottery, or are suffering from a serious hangover. These dances of our brain states can be accompanied and shaped by cognitive processes but equally the cognitions may be responses from shifts in physiology which are not necessarily conscious (Bargh, 2017). Mindful therapists must be cautious of automatic activation of impulses: on the one hand, an activation of sympathetic concern and an urge to jump in with "rescuing" behavior, or on the other hand, if the client criticizes the therapist, becoming overly defensive. CFT helps both clients and therapists to become mindful of the subtle interplay of their social mentalities and "interpersonal dances" (e.g., to compete, cooperate, care, back down) that are being played out moment-by-moment. We can become observers of what these algorithms are doing within and between our minds.

Self-to-Self Relating
Given that social mentalities evolved competencies to both send a signal and respond to specific role-focused signals, we can stimulate social mentalities for relating to ourselves. For example, we can stimulate our sexual arousal by purposefully generating a sexual image or signal, then responding to it. We can also engage in a hostile, competitive dominant-subordinate relationship in which we self-critically attack ourselves and then experience a submissive, or even a defeated, response to our own attacks (Gilbert, 2022c, 2022d). Indeed, the point of a dominant attack is to stimulate fear and compliant behavior in the subordinate; that becomes our inner interplay. For people who hear voices, there seems to be a problem in the identification of signal origin; in other words, hostile self-criticism can be experienced as an external "hostile dominant other" signal. Voice hearers can experience submissive fear as if they are under attack but misidentify the attack as external, not as self-generated. One of the reasons for this may be because, whether it is an external signal or an internal signal, it is operating through the same social mentality that evolved for conflict in social competition (Gilbert et al., 2001; Martins et al., 2020). So, for example, if fear of being hurt by others is triggered or is a background texture, then arousal of feeling under threat orientates the mentality to create the expected signal. Basically, if an emotion cannot be explained we fill in the blanks and will create that which we perhaps are most frightened of. The social mentality can generate both the attack-signal and the submissive-behavioral response (Gilbert, 2000b; Gilbert et al., 2001). Hence, CFT works with voice-hearers in conversational and relational frameworks, enabling a differentiated experience of how, for example, hostile signals to self are being generated from one's own fears or an external threat that creates a self-attacking dominating system (Gilbert, 2000a; Heriot-Maitland, 2022; Heriot-Maitland et al., 2019). Indeed, we found that depressed people hearing hostile self-critical thoughts and people hearing critical voices experienced them in relatively similar ways but identified their origins differently (Gilbert et al., 2001). In regard to self-compassion, we can detect physical and emotional pain and then respond to those signals with efforts to alleviate and prevent them. Hence, voice hearers can be invited to explore the motivation behind their voices and also to consider what compassion-motivated voices would sound and feel like, and how they could develop a compassionate sense of self that can interact with hostile voices (Heriot-Maitland, 2022; Heriot-Maitland et al., 2019; Mayhew & Gilbert, 2008; see King's Cultural Community, n.d.).

The ways our social mentalities are cultivated for relating to others and to the self, and for "role forming," are linked to experienced relationships. For example, if we have grown up in families where we have been regularly criticized and made to feel

24 Building an Integrated Science for Psychotherapy

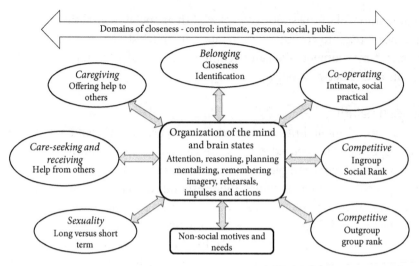

Figure 1.3 The organizing functions of motives and social mentalities.
Note: From Gilbert, (2022a) © Paul Gilbert

inferior or a failure, it will be very easy for us to adopt "that relationship" with ourselves. In contrast, if we have grown up feeling loved, valued, and cared for, our caregiving mentality will mature in such a way that we can have that relationship with ourselves; we are sensitive to our distress and motivated to address it with appropriate caring behavior.

Social Motives Organize Biopsychosocial Processes

Figure 1.3 offers a representation of how different social mentalities (motives) organize our attention, reasoning, and behavior orientations, and multiple physiological systems. For example, in caring motivation, we pay attention to suffering, but if in a competitive motivation, we may callously disregard it. When caring, we feel relieved by reducing suffering. When competing, we may feel excited by increasing suffering. What is rewarding and what is threatening and punishing, what is facilitated and what is inhibited, what is inspiring and what is depressing are linked to motives.

In regard to social relationships, there is a dimension that runs from *close and intimate relating through to distant and more public relating*. For example, we are motivated to care for our own children far more than for unknown children in foreign lands, even when we know they may be starving while ours are flourishing. We forgive people we know and like much more easily than people we don't know or like. Compassion is distributed very unevenly according to the closeness and likeability of individuals we relate to. The same is true with compassion for ourselves. Self-compassion is relatively straight forward for problems we are not ashamed about, but difficult for those we are ashamed of.

It has been known for a long time that our minds are not patterned by some unitary self-process but by a range of conflicting motives, emotions, and beliefs (Bargh, 2017; Gilbert, 2000a; Stevens, 2002). These in turn are linked to different psychophysiological processes. Hence, CFT therapists seek to help clients gain insight into their complex and possible conflicts in the pattern of motives, emotions, and beliefs.

Competing for Resources versus Sharing and Caring
That humans can be helpful to others or (self-focused) competitive and exploitative has been recognized in many spiritual traditions and the psychological sciences for a long time (see Gilbert, 2021, for a review). At the root of the evolutionary process is competition for survival and reproductive resources. Interspecies competition takes many forms where what is successful for one individual can be a disaster for another. Predator success means death for its prey. The life progress of viruses, bacteria, and parasites can harm their hosts; locusts can devastate food sources; when humans take over ecologies, we can drive other species to extinction; we can fish out the seas and damage the planet through climate change.

Intraspecies competition also takes various forms. Common trans-species strategies involve suppressing subordinates' resource seeking and control through intimidation and aggression. These remain common in areas such as human bullying, domestic threats, and violence (including to children), criminal gangs. These strategies are utilized by many leaders around the world today. They are associated with the "dark triad traits" of Machiavellianism, psychopathy and narcissism, which share dimensions of manipulative callousness (Jones & Figueredo, 2013). Groups can also behave in these oppressive exploitive ways (Pratto et al., 2013). Individuals subjected to such oppression from others have a range of physiological difficulties such as overdriven threat systems, with a lowered sense of social safety and safeness (Armstrong et al., 2021; Gilbert, 1993, 2000b; Slavich, 2020; Slavich et al., 2023). These consequence of oppressive trauma are targets for many psychotherapeutic interventions (Lee, 2022).

Even without aggressive conflict, elites can manipulate resource control to ensure that they have greater access to resources with the "least able" being pushed into "narrow limited resource domains" that we call poverty; the poor have less claim on power to secure resources (Wilkinson, 2020). These variations in wealthy versus poor environments have profound effects on a range of physiological systems (Busso et al., 2017; De France et al., 2022). Moreover, social and economic inequalities are known to directly affect physical and mental health, and criminality (Wilkinson, 2020).

Although group competition can be a source of violence and great tragedy (e.g., war) and economic inequalities that create many mental health problems, psychotherapy more typically focuses on how individuals navigate the "within group" competitive challenges of life. This relates to the way their own competitive motive is organized; for example, how they judge themselves in regard to status, opportunity, social comparison; the degree of component assertiveness or narcissistic entitlement to resources; or their fear of inferiority and treatment of others (Basran et al., 2019).

The competitive, social ranking (motive) mentality by itself, that evolved to seek power and resource control, when unregulated by concerns with compassion and fairness, can be callous, very harmful, and play major roles in a range of mental health problems and anti-social behaviors. Forms of unfavorable social comparison, submissive behavior, fear of authority, depression, shame displays, and social anxiety are all linked to how individuals experience themselves as "lower ranking" and vulnerable to criticisms, rejection, and having reduced claim on resources including being cared for and about (Gilbert, 2009, 2020b). This is captured with experiences of feeling disconnected from others and of low social worth. However, we have found that depressed people tend to feel inferior only when it comes to competing for resources. If you ask them about whether they see themselves as helpful, supportive, or trustworthy (care motive competencies) they do not regard themselves as inferior (McEwan et al., 2012). Hence, it is the competitive and social rank mentalities, with their concerns with inferiority, shame, and being self-critical, that are transdiagnostic in many mental health problems and represent the opposite of compassion (Gilbert & Simos, 2022).

An unregulated competitive social mentality causes serious problems at the other end of the spectrum. Some individuals experience themselves as high-ranking, accompanied by a sense of entitlement and narcissism, and at times, with contempt for those lower in rank. Indeed, as individuals become more powerful in organizations, they can lose interest in subordinates' needs (van Kleef et al., 2008). Another form of dysregulated social competition and ranking motivational systems can be seen in bipolar disorders. Here, individuals can move into hyper manic states of feeling successful, talented, more able, and special compared to others but then collapse into experiences of feeling worthless, defeated, and inferior when depression strikes. Helping clients understand the rank mechanisms can be very useful in helping them switch to compassion-focused motives (Gilbert et al., 2022).

Yet another variant on the dominant submissive competitive and social rank system is paranoia. Here, individuals can feel that others are attending to them to identify reasons to attack them—the perception of malevolent intent. Rank-based paranoia takes two forms (Gilbert et al., 2005). First, down rank arises as fear that a dominant individual is keeping an eye on them and will attack them if they step out of line (Gilbert et al., 2005). The second is up rank where dominant individuals are fearful that subordinates are planning a takeover in some way (Gilbert et al., 2005). Stalin was a classic in this regard and engaged in reigns of terror as forms of self-protection. Indeed, insecure dominant primates will regularly attack subordinates to ensure they are in a fearful non-challenging state (Gilbert & McGuire, 1998). A third form of paranoia arises from the perceptions of group attack and stigma.

The Profound Importance of the Evolution of Caring Behavior

In contrast to self-focused competitiveness, the evolution of caring behavior encouraged the opposite behavior, that is behavior that supports, provides for, protects, and shares with another. Although this caring behavior evolved in the context of infant caring, which is linked to competition for gene survival, its impact on how brains and bodies were built for conspecific inter-relating was profound. The evolution of caring as an attachment process not only facilitated a range of physiological systems (see below), but also eventually enabled the benefits of social communication (language) and cooperation, which supported the evolution of human intelligence (Camilleri et al., 2023). As it evolved over millions of years in different species, it created contexts for new competencies, such as for empathy and social reasoning (Decety & Ickes, 2011).

There are different evolutionary pathways for caring behavior that interact but can also be seen as separate processes. One pathway appears to evolve from rescuing behavior and caring for the injured. Kessler (2020) reviewed rescuing behavior in many species. She noted, for example, that termites and ants will carry injured colleagues back to the nest where other conspecifics will lick their wounds and help them recover. Spikins (2015) highlighted how the archeological record shows that humans were highly sensitive to helping sick and injured individuals within their groups. For the most part, other species, like chimpanzees, avoid sick or injured individuals (Goodall, 1990). Humans are very different. They are easily moved to engage in rescuing behavior and there are many professions dedicated to rescuing and healing others, including strangers, even at risk to oneself (e.g., firefighting, mountain and sea rescue, various medical and social professions). Importantly, however, individuals orientated to rescuing behavior or a rescue profession will not necessarily be empathic and compassionate in other contexts, such as in close intimate relationships. Compassion has different pathways and should not be seen as one process but as a variety of processes associated with context and underpinned by caring motives.

A second evolutionary pathway to caring was the warm-blooded reproductive behavior of "infant caring." Reproductive success in many species of fish and reptiles like turtles, depends on creating hundreds of offspring, only a few of which will survive to become reproducing members. However, small changes in how a parent relates to the infant had fundamental impacts. With warm-bloodedness and live birth came, not just protection, but the beginning of provisioning food and warmth. To provide this, infant and parent needed to be in close contact and they, therefore, each evolved evolutionary motives and feature-detection to operate and maintain close proximity to each other.

Indeed, proximity maintenance was one of the key themes for the evolution of attachment, as described by Bowlby (1969, 1973, 1980; Cassidy & Shaver, 2016). Research has revealed how the evolution of hormones like oxytocin and the endorphins (Carter et al., 2017; Depue & Morrone-Strupinsky, 2005; Kucerova et al., 2023) and adaptations to the autonomic nervous system, particularly the vagus nerve (Porges, 2021), along with various neurocircuits (Ashar et al., 2021; Vrtička et al., 2017), have come to play fundamental roles in the co-evolved caregiving and care-receiving social mentality and relationships. With these adaptations, parent and offspring evolved capacities for physiological and emotional co-regulating synchrony (Nguyen et al., 2020). In addition to a range of physical resources such as food, thermal regulation, and shelter, attachment theorists highlighted the important psychological resources for the infant, in terms of providing a secure base and save haven (see Chapter 10). A secure base provides a place where the infant is relatively safe, does not need to be vigilant to threat, and can explore their environment under the guidance of the parent. Play and the sharing of positive emotions is very important, particularly for humans. A secure base supports activation and engagement with the world. The safe haven provided a place to return to when needs emerged, the infant had become fatigued, threatened, or over-aroused. The function of the parent here is primarily to calm, soothe, and facilitate resting. With evolution, these two key functions resulted in an explosion of caregiving and care-receiving behavior in avian and mammalian species.

A third pathway for the evolution of caring and compassion was the shift from aggressive, dominant hierarchical forms of living to egalitarian, hunter gatherer group living (Boehm, 1999). In this context status and helpful social engagement depended upon altruistic caring and sharing behavior (Barkow, 1989; Gilbert, 2021). These evolved pressures generated what became called the social brain with its expanded frontal cortex primarily orientated for social relating (Camilleri et al., 2023). One consequence of this was that a sense of social connectedness and safeness (which have major psychophysiological effects; Slavich, 2020) emerges from feeling one can contribute to others' welfare, and is valued and appreciated (Gilbert, 1989, 2022b). Mental health problems associated with perceptions that one does not matter to anybody, cannot contribute, and loneliness are linked to major psychophysiological effects including epigenetic effects (Cacioppo et al., 2014).

Given that motives have profound effects on organizing psychophysiological processes, switching motivational focus and orientation can be a central concern for psychotherapy. Individuals who have become overly orientated through the competitive social mentality are prone to see themselves and relate to others in certain ways (for a review see Gilbert, 2020b). There is now considerable evidence that seeing oneself as inferior, others as more powerful, as judging and potentially rejecting, and using submissive strategies, creates vulnerability to depression and social anxiety while seeing oneself as superior and entitled is linked to narcissistic presentations (Gilbert, 2020b.) A therapeutic maneuver therefore is to help clients shift out of an overly competitive focus into a caring social mentality because this changes multiple psychophysiological processes associated with these different social mentalities (Gilbert et al., 2022).

Figure 1.4 depicts how various processes are transformed in the shift from competitive to compassionate social mentality, along with examples of measures in the different mentalities.

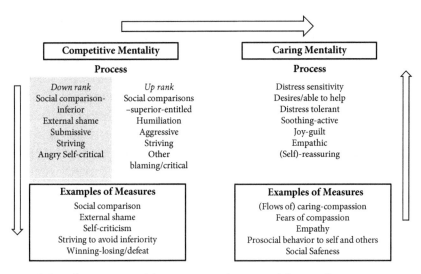

Figure 1.4 Shifting from a competitive to compassionate social mentality.
Note: From Gilbert (2022a) © Paul Gilbert

Emotions

Another crucial function of the mind is emotion. While our "guiding" motives (to avoid harm and seek resources and contexts of safeness) are constantly with us, emotions are different. This is because they are short-term changes in psychophysiological state that focus attention and prime specific behaviors in the pursuit of motives (Davey, 2018; Gilbert, 2015a, 2015b; Keltner et al., 2018; Nesse, 2019; Panksepp, 1998); they are very susceptible to social shaping (Keltner et al., 2018; Klimecki, 2015). As indicated in Figure 1.2 (and depicted in more detail in Figure 1.5), the

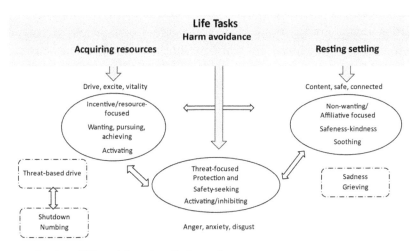

Figure 1.5 The three "life task functions" of emotions.
Note: Adapted from Gilbert (2010, 2022a). © Paul Gilbert

three very different life tasks (motives) have co-evolved three very different types of emotion attuned to dealing with: (a) threats, (b) resources seeking and acquiring, and (c) opportunities for rest and calming the body under conditions of safeness.

Figure 1.5 indicates how the different life tasks have given rise to different types of emotion because they require us to pay attention to different types of stimuli and events and prepare the body for different forms of action. Because different emotions have different functions, there are different routes to the triggering, regulation, amplification and attenuation, and "passing" of emotions. LeDoux (2022) suggests that emotions are primarily derived from lower-brain motor programs and evolved to be activated quickly, whereas *feelings* are complex textures of emotions patterned by high-level cognitive and social processes (see below in section on *competencies*). For example, in the state of anxiety, we may deliberately choose not to run away but to face it, or when angry, not to act out aggression. Compassion-focused processing of these emotions is particularly important at these decision points. As indicated above and in the diagram, we can distinguish the functions of threat-emotions from two types and functions of positive emotions.

Threat Emotions

Typical emotions for threat are anxiety, anger, and disgust, with various combinations linked to more complex ones such as envy, shame, and guilt (Gilbert, 1993; Keltner et al., 2018; LeDoux, 2020; Nesse, 2019). Each emotion can have different functions and profiles. For example, it is important to distinguish individuals who experience low frustration-tolerance from those who experience their anger in the context of vengeance, shame, or envy. The compassion-engagement will be different because the roots of anger are different. It is also well-known that there are many different forms and functions of anxiety and disgust.

Threat-emotions can also be associated with activating (as in running away) and deactivating, demobilizing, or inhibiting as in faint, freeze, helplessness, and submissive inhibition. Some threat-emotions are short-lived and settle when the threat is dealt with. However, keeping with the idea of the algorithm of emotions (stimulus activation and response), the learned helplessness research has shown that the activation of a threat-defense (emotion), such as anxiety, first generates efforts to escape. However, if these escape efforts are blocked and escape is impossible, the defense system changes to helplessness-demobilization. In CFT, we call this process *arrested defenses* and it applies to any defensive emotion when the appropriate behavior cannot be executed (Dixon, 1998; Gilbert, 2001). For example, someone trapped in an abusive marriage may have a strong escape arousal, but escape is impossible. Individuals who experience high levels of anger but fear expressing it, can go into states of arrested anger which can be linked to self-harm (Clarke et al., 2016). Abbass (2015) has shown how arrested anger can affect smooth muscle and striatal muscle giving rise to various somatoform disorders. Individuals who have experienced trauma can experience a tonic raising of the threat threshold, such that anger or anxiety can be triggered more easily and intensely but also inhibited (Lee, 2022; Van der Hart et al., 2006; Van der Kolk, 2014).

Shutdown and Entrapment States

Nearly fifty years ago, Seligman (1975) showed that when animals are subjected to uncontrollable stresses, they will at first struggle, motivated to escape the stressor (threat-based activation), but with successive failure they go into shutdown/helplessness (demobilized) states. This is the situation when the individual cannot escape or control threats and stresses. Struggles that fail have also been described as "defeat states" (Gilbert, 1992; Gilbert & Allan, 1998; Gilbert et al., 2002; P. J. Taylor et al., 2011). What is particularly toxic to experiences of defeat is to feel trapped and unable to escape the situation; move on to new contexts. Research has revealed that states of defeat and entrapment are strongly linked to problems such as depression, anhedonia, anxiety, self-harm, suicidality, and posttraumatic stress disorder. In addition, defeat and entrapment are significantly linked to prognosis (see Siddaway et al., 2015, for a major meta-analysis and overview).

As reviewed by Lee (2022), Terpou et al. (2019), Van der Kolk (2014), and others, different types of trauma caused by different types of events and individuals (familiars versus strangers), over various lengths of time and with different options for coping, can result in quite different defense profiles. For example, while some people show heightened fight-flight and sympathetic arousal presentations, others show a response profile associated with dissociation and shutdown (Gilbert, 1984, 1992; Porges, 2021). These states, however, can fluctuate, which makes them different from the chronic anhedonia of severe depression. Clearly then, compassion-motivation, and the physiological systems that come with it, will have to do quite different jobs depending on whether the issue involves over-sensitivity in the sympathetic arousal or shutdown states. There are different types of shutdown states—some involve fatigue and sleep disturbance, while others link to a blunting of positive emotion.

A different control-and-defeat problem from that of not getting away from a threat (e.g., aggressive other) is trying but failing to gain access to needed resources, such as helpful, caring others. Bowlby (1969, 1973) outlined how the parent acts as a constant stimulus that down-regulates threat-processing via offering a secure base and safe haven. While the parent is accessible and available, infants can be in states of safeness. They do not need to be vigilant to threat, their needs are met, and they can play and explore (Cassidy & Shaver, 2016). However, with separation, those "safeness signals" are removed, releasing the threat system from inhibitory control (Cassidy & Shaver, 2016; Gilbert, 1993, 2020a, 2022b). That is important because, without a protector, the infant must be put on high alert. A mammalian infant in the wild, without the protection or provision of a parent, will be dead quite quickly. The defensive response is triphasic, mirroring the learned helplessness profile of activation, deactivation/demobilization, and then recovery when the threat has passed. This sequence, as linked to attachment separation, Bowlby (1973, 1980) called *protest-despair-repair*. In protest, infants engage in anxious searching-behavior and distress-calling. However, this will draw attention to itself as a defenseless "meal." If reunion is not forthcoming, the defense becomes one of shutdown, demobilization, hiding, and having to "wait or hope for rescue" (Gilbert, 2022b). For the infant, this is safer in the short-term, and will not attract predators. These brain states involve down-regulating the positive affect, resource-seeking, and explorative behavior (Gilbert, 1992, 2020b). Such shutdown states are quite different from the short-term "play dead" shutdown defenses that have been noted under trauma-threat.

Another way defeat-states can arise and lead to being overwhelmed and shutdown, can develop when behavior is oriented to seeking resources to avoid harms. This can be called *threat-based drive,* partly because it involves seeking resources. For example, we may pursue a particular job opportunity because we really want to work in that company, it would give us a sense of meaning and opportunity, and we would enjoy the activity. However, it is also possible that we pursue the same job, not because we like it or want to do it for pleasure, but because we need the money to eat or look after the family. CFT distinguishes doing things that we want to do—voluntary *behaviors*—from *involuntary behaviors,* having to do things (seek resources) in a way that we really do not want to (but the consequences of not doing them are losses and harms; Gilbert, 1989, 2000a). The voluntary-involuntary dimension that links to social rank behaviors (Gilbert, 1992) is also very in tune with Ryan and Deci's (2000, 2017) distinction between autonomous (intrinsic) and controlled motivation (extrinsic) (see Gilbert, 2014, p. 13, for discussion).

In summary, we can focus on the relatively short-term emotions, such as anxiety or anger, and their regulation. However, we can also see the importance of long-term changes and brain states of activation and deactivation. Loss of control, entrapment, and defeat are often associated with long-term changes of states and mental health problems, and have different textures (Gilbert & Allan, 1998; Gilbert et al., 2002; Siddaway et al., 2015). People can be trapped in aversive, toxic situations and relationships, or trapped in lifestyles they have pursued to maintain their life or just survive. Some people get trapped in loneliness because of lack of access to supportive relationships (Gilbert, 1992, 2001).

Numbing

Threat and threat-based drive shutdowns can be different from states of numbing, where people have been subjected to traumas or are entrapped in traumatizing environments and *actively try to prevent "feelings"* (see Terpou et al., 2019 for reviews). This is brilliantly captured in the Pet Shop Boys' song "Numb," which can be shared and discussed with clients who display this difficulty (Pet Shop Boys, 2009). Numbing is different from the anhedonic shutdown states of depression, where people can feel "lost, alone, hopeless, cut off, and inwardly dead." Depressed anhedonic clients are not wanting to shut down feelings; indeed, they wish they could feel something rather than a sense of inner-coldness, deadness, and emptiness. Numbness is linked to, but different from, the experience of being emotionally frozen. Emotional freezing can occur in individuals who have experienced neglect (Music, 2022) or who have arrested grief that may derive from feeling unloved and unwanted as a child (Gilbert, 2023; Gilbert & Irons, 2005; Music, 2017, 2022). One client who experienced profound grief over her adoption into a rather cold family, described how she had not realized how detached she was from emotions for most of her life until therapy which facilitated working through intense yearning to have felt the emotional caring warmth of a mother. She said, "it was like I was living in a world of shades of gray and then I began to notice there is color in the world." There is nothing categorical about these brain states and they blend into each other, however they require different empathic engagements and compassion-strategies of intervention. More research is needed on these important subtle differences that link to different types of entrapment and escape orientations. Sometimes, for anhedonia, the focus is cultivating explorative and seeking-based motives whereas for trauma-based numbness, issues are more rooted in the safeness system (Craske et al., 2019; Gilbert & Simos, 2022; Lee, 2022).

Sadness and Grief
Sadness can be a passing state of mind or part of a long process of grieving. Sadness and grief are normal reactions to major losses, and grieving individuals go through various stages including anger and anxiety, as well as sadness. A grief process is not just part of threat-processing because it also facilitates regeneration and restoration. Facilitating grief processes is often central for working with more complex individuals who have come from traumatic early life backgrounds and may be in shutdown states. Grieving in CFT can include grieving for what one had and lost, but also grieving for what one needed but did not have (Gilbert, 2023). For example, in the process of helping clients work with their caring motivational system, the therapy engages with their traumas and losses coded in terms of care motive systems. This involves recognition that humans evolved to seek out caring attachments and later in life to experience being valued by making a contribution (Gilbert, 2022b). Our brains and bodies use those inputs, of being cared about and being valued by others to help us develop a competent, confident, and caring sense of self. Not receiving inputs for evolved systems does not mean they just go away, but they can be frozen or distorted (Gilbert, 2020a, 2022a; Gilbert & Irons, 2005). Helping clients get in contact with that underlying yearning for "caring connections" can be important for healing the fractures in the care motivational systems. Therapists can explain the issue of how social mentalities and archetypes are "seeking systems," and if unfulfilled can leave us in a state of yearning or compensation. Clients are offered a language that de-pathologizes states of mind that might be linked to inner feelings of loneliness, grief, and yearning.

Clients who are seeking social connections, who want to be cared about, valued, and experience themselves as "a good and lovable person", can struggle with coping with inner hostile emotions. As the therapist begins to help them with unprocessed rage, via gradual exposure, they can experience themselves as becoming more unloveable, shame worthy, and in the short term can feel worse. However, facilitating anger tolerance, with a compassionate orientation to it, and at times as part of a grieving process, also facilitates the ability to become more assertive and confident.

Two Types and Functions of Positive Emotions

Emotions that support resource-seeking require different attentional-focus and body-orientation to that of threat or resting. Positive emotions have two very different functions. One is to be activated (move in the environment), explore, seek out resources and experience (positive reward) emotions that increase the chances of repeating the behaviors (Keltner et al., 2018). A different function and form of positive emotion is linked to having achieved, consumed, and turned off threat and drive, to enable rest and digest (Depue & Morrone-Strupinsky, 2005). Emotions that are linked to resource-seeking and acquisition include interest, pleasure, joy, and excitement (Keltner et al., 2018). An extreme example would be winning a multi-million-dollar lottery that would change our (dopamine) physiological state for some days and (assuming we were not multi-millionaires before) put us into a mild hypomania of joy and excitement. It could be difficult to control, in that our minds would constantly be coming back to this reality, and we would probably find it difficult to sleep. In the usual course of events, however, activation will over time exhaust the body. States for rest and digest are important for replenishment and recuperation. Emotions linked to rest and digest tend to include calmness, relaxation, and contentment, which have different emotional textures from those of excitement and drive.

CFT highlights the importance of distinguishing these two very different types of positive affect and not assuming they follow the same regulators. In depression, for example, some clients benefit enormously from focusing on an increase in explorative behavior and acting in ways that have the potential to stimulate dopamine and reward systems (Craske et al., 2019). However, in addition many clients need to feel safe and be able to utilize many of the psychophysiological systems that link to the rest and digest system (not just drive ones), which in turn can be linked with supportive relationships (Porges, 2021). In a factor analysis, Gilbert et al. (2009) found that different types of positive affects could be distinguished: (a) excitement and activated positive affect, (b) relaxed positive affect, such as feeling calm, and (c) feelings of safeness and contentment. The strongest predictor of depression was safeness. There have now been studies exploring these specific emotions that seem to constitute safeness, contentment, and social belonging, with increasing evidence that they form an emotion system in their own right (Armstrong et al., 2021).

Differences in positive affect, and their underlying psychophysiological regulators such as dopamine and oxytocin, have also been linked to differences in social mentalities and social motives. Mapping on to distinctions between caring and competitiveness, Depue and Morrone-Strupinsky (2005) distinguish emotions linked to affiliation and social bonding from what they call "agency" that is focused on achievement and status seeking. These distinctions are important because flourishing depends upon a balanced portfolio of social mentalities. Keeping in mind that compassion is how we (wisely and courageously) are sensitive to and seek to prevent suffering (including being a cause), then agency, achievements, and status seeking need to be textured by compassion in order not to be callous, narcissistic, or exploitative. Affiliate bonding needs compassion for it not to become harmful dependency, controlling, or overly submissive.

How Attachment Changed Threat Regulation and Positive Affect

A central focus of CFT is how the evolution of attachment and other forms of caring effected: (a) the regulation of threat processing and responding; (b) the seeking system, such that social relating is a source of joy, excitement, and meaning; (c) the soothing systems, such that relationships are a source of soothing, grounding, and safeness (Gilbert, 1989, 2014). Put simply (unlike species such as turtles) mammals give birth to infants who cannot protect, feed themselves, or keep warm. Any activation of need (e.g., for food), fear, or danger has to recruit the parent. Not only have mammalian parents evolved to protect against external threats and provide resources, but also to regulate the internal arousal process of the infant (Bowlby, 1969; Cassidy & Shaver, 2016; Music, 2017). In addition, the parent is able to stimulate calmness in the infant by activating the vagus nerve and other processes (Brown & Brown, 2015; Gilbert, 1989, 1993; Mayseless, 2016; Porges, 2021). In attachment theory, this is linked to what is called *secure base and safe haven* respectively (Bowlby, 1969; Cassidy & Shaver, 2016; Music, 2017, 2022). The parent provides a secure base by provisioning infants with what they need, such as food, shelter, warmth, a protected environment to explore and develop, and sources of stimulation and guidance for learning. For the most part, these are energizing and activating functions. However, infants and children are unable to emotionally regulate themselves in the first instance. Hence, the parent provides a safe haven such that when a child is distressed or dysregulated, they return to the parent who then behaves in soothing ways (Cassidy & Shaver, 2016). This balances the infant's central and autonomic nervous system, which has a calming, balancing effect. This means that attachment gave rise to the evolution of a very different form of threat regulation, and a different source of joy and sense of safeness. This is outlined in Figure 1.6.

On the left-hand side of Figure 1.6 are the processes and ways animals and humans *engage directly* with a threat. Threat signals will stimulate the threat system via, for example, the HPA axis, amygdala, and sympathetic arousal (LeDoux, 2020; Terpou et al., 2019). It is what individuals themselves do that determines the outcome. They may run away or fight or shut down. The middle section indicates that humans (and animals via experience) can learn all kinds of ways of dealing with the threat. Note though, it is still very much that specific individual dealing directly with the threat

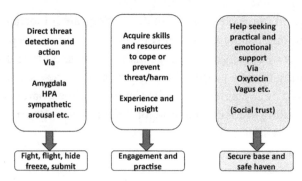

Figure 1.6 Depiction of two threat regulation systems.
Note: © Paul Gilbert

that determines outcome. This is the basis of a lot of psychotherapy, which is to help people learn to try to lower their threat activation thresholds through appropriate exposure to threats, allied with emotion regulation skills and helpful cognitive reframing. The key focus is on ways people directly interact with threats themselves.

However, the attachment system for coping with threat operates in a very different way, with different neurophysiological and physiological processes. This is represented on the right-hand side of Figure 1.6. It highlights that the evolution of attachment meant that, rather than dealing with the threat and needs directly oneself, the child has to wait for, calls to, or turns to and seeks out others for support, help, protection, and soothing. The psychophysiological processes of this system are linked to the parasympathetic system, particularly the vagus nerve (Porges, 2017, 2021), a range of neurocircuits that are sensitive to signals of caring (Kim et al., 2020; Klimecki, 2015; Vrtička et al., 2017), and hormones such as oxytocin and endorphins (Kucerova et al., 2023). Hence, there are two very different threat regulation systems. One is direct engagement with the threat while the other is via activating helpfulness in the environment (from others). In times of emotional turmoil and distress we turn to others we trust who we experience care and empathic understanding from, to ground, settle, and guide us. In addition, we have built cultures where we are fully interdependent and reliant on the skills and wisdom of multiple others to get food into our shops, build our houses, staff our hospitals. The more we trust these services, and the skills and availability of the individuals that supply them, the safer we feel in our communities. We are less fearful of problems because we know there are others we can turn to. The sense of "social safeness" provided by the support of others may constitute an emotion regulation system in its own right (Armstrong et al., 2021; Slavich, 2020).

So, while *safety* is the prevention of harm and personally dealing with threat, *safeness* is this ability to experience oneself as embedded in helpful, supportive relationships, and communities (Gilbert et al., 2009; Kelly et al., 2012). Importantly, these are not new ideas because we have known, for many years, of the ways attachment security (Cassidy & Shaver, 2016), caring, social connectedness (Mikulincer

& Shaver, 2014), and domains of what is called general social support moderate responses to stress and threat. S. E. Taylor (2011) says, "social support is defined as the perception or experience that one is loved and cared for by others, esteemed and valued, and part of a social network of mutual assistance and obligations" (p. 192). Therapists should be familiar with both forms of threat regulation and how clients use both of them appropriately. Therapists should also be aware of the two types of positive emotion that arise from securing resources and how to help clients develop appropriate confidence to pursue them. But in addition, therapists should recognize the positive emotions that are associated with feeling safe, supported, cared about, and embedded in caring relationships and how to engage these processes with empathic, social skills.

In summary, attention can be directed to the very different psychophysiological systems for the regulation of threat and distinguishing between safety and safeness. Looked at in this way, individuals coming to therapy can have two types of difficulty. First, they can be overwhelmed by threat and use avoidant, dissociative, or shutdown defenses (Terpou et al., 2019; Van der Kolk, 2014). But second, if they have come from problematic backgrounds where their ability to trust others and utilize caring as a regulator is compromised, they are at risk of experiencing four other problems. (a) They won't be able to use this "second" evolved threat regulation system and switch attention to helpfulness; hence (b) they will be unable to use the threat-regulation system that recruits the vagus, neurocircuits, oxytocin, and other relevant physiological systems; (c) they will find it difficult to experience positive emotions through feeling loved and connected and, in fact, people getting too close to them might frighten them; and (d) they will find it difficult to deal with issues of shame (as one client said, "one lives one's life in hiding"). CFT therefore targets these four core concerns that can be seen as additional to other established therapeutic ways of helping people.

Competencies

The third fundamental function of the mind relates to "performance" competencies. Competencies are abilities to process information relevant to the enactments of motives and emotions. Competencies support stimulus-assessment, meaning-development, actions, and performance. For example, birds need wings to fly but they also need a brain that can move wings and navigate them in the air. Hence, having a body with wings but also a brain that can move them appropriately are both essential for the competency to fly. However, the reasons and motives they are flying may be for food, to escape a predator, or to find a nest-site. The vigor of their flying will depend on salience of the motive, linked to motivational urgency. If a predator is closing in, or they are very hungry, the behavior will be more vigorous and intense than simply scanning. However, whatever the motive, the competencies and brain systems used to fly are the same. Competencies are crucial to survival and reproduction and cover almost all forms of action, for example having competencies to spot and run from predators, build shelters, or find sexual partners to care for offspring. Being motivated for a life-task or social mentality does not mean that individuals will pursue the motive competently.

What has made us the species we are is the evolution of cognitive competencies for a multi-functional mind enabling complex ways to pursue motives. Part of this is our extraordinary dexterity and insight (Byrne, 2016). For example, we can drive a car which requires paying attention to the road, shifting gears, steering, having a conversation with our passenger, brake appropriately, and sustaining this attention for hours. We can learn very complex memory tasks with fine motor skills, such as how to play Rachmaninoff's piano concerto, or paint a detailed portrait, or solve a mathematical puzzle after years of work (Gilbert, 2009). While the evolution of language played a major role in our capacities for complex thinking, it plays little role in these extraordinary competencies. Not only do multiple talents go into a skill, like playing a piano concerto, there is also the motivation to acquire such skills and the desire to practice over years and to become the best we can at a certain task. People will practice the piano for years simply because they want to be able to play well. Although something of a two-way street, it is possible that such motivation encouraged the evolution of cognitive change. This is because having a skill does not necessarily mean it will be competently utilized, and if it is not utilized, it cannot be a target for evolution.

CFT suggests we can roughly distinguish between three basic forms of recently evolved human cognitive competencies: non-social reasoning, social reasoning, and consciousness of consciousness, but also recognizes it is likely that science may suggest different divisions and subdivisions over time. This does not imply that different degrees of these competencies do not operate in other animals, for example aspects

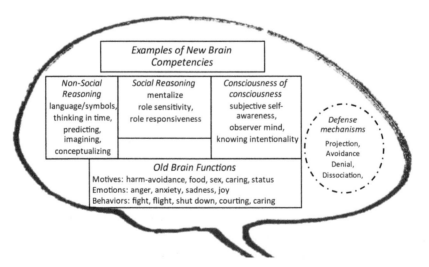

Figure 1.7 Examples of new brain competencies interacting with older functions.
Note: From Gilbert (2022a) © P. Gilbert

of problem solving and empathic competencies are noted in other species. However, in humans they take on much more complex textures. These are given in Figure 1.7.

Non-Social Reasoning

CFT distinguishes between social and non-social motives and also functions. Baron-Cohen (2011) has distinguished between non-social, systematic intelligence (understanding how things work) and social empathic intelligence (understanding how people work). A person may be competent at one but not the other. Non-social reasoning involves types of reasoning and imagining that enable us to understand and gain insight into complex causalities, system relationships, and how things work. Byrne (2016) calls this *insight* and highlights these competencies as central to the evolution of the human mind. We also have a sense of time, with the ability to conceive that what we do now will affect our future (Suddendorf, 2018). The evolution of language also significantly advanced our capacities for systemic reasoning and thinking.

Social Reasoning

When it comes to social reasoning, we need to have competencies that differ from straightforward scientific understanding and logic, emphasizing competencies that are more intuitive and enable insight into the nature of mind and theory of mind. This enables us to understand how and why humans do not follow logic but feel and do things because of their thoughts, motivations, emotions, and so on. Insight into the nature of mind is called mentalizing and has become a fundamental, trainable competency and focus for psychotherapy (Luyten et al., 2020).

Mentalizing enables us to recognize our common humanity: that we all have minds that are pursuing survival and reproductive opportunities and that all humans want to be successful in their motivational pursuits, to be happy, and not suffer motivational failure or experience pain and distress. When we stand back and think about it, we recognize that all of us have just found ourselves born here, with an unfolding mind that we never chose and one that is subject to all kinds of inner conflicts of motives, emotions, beliefs, and so forth. It is this type of awareness that is the ground for self-empathy and empathy for others (Decety & Ickes, 2011; Gilbert, 2000a; Gilbert & Simos, 2022; Luyten et al., 2020).

Unfortunately, we can experience the minds of others through all kinds of lenses that are subject to distortions, projections, delusions, and so forth (Luyten et al., 2020). What is crucial to good psychotherapy, is to try to understand the motivation behind a projection or a delusion—commonly some form of safety-seeking. In other words, they can link into the motivation for protection. Accordingly, CFT (like attachment approaches) focuses on creating a secure base and developing trust that enables people to dissolve their projections, enabling a more empathically accurate, appropriate, and helpful way of relating (Abbass, 2015; Heriot-Maitland, 2022; Luyten et al., 2020).

Consciousness of Consciousness

A third major competency is the ability to be conscious of being conscious, to be aware, self-aware, and to be aware that we are aware. This competency not only underpins self-awareness and reflection, but also mindfulness and the ability to have knowing awareness and knowing intentionality. There is, of course, now a huge literature on the nature of self-consciousness and mindfulness (Austin, 2009; Goleman & Davidson, 2017; Kabat-Zinn, 2015). Importantly, however, mindfulness can have different aims. Kabat-Zinn (1982) first introduced mindfulness into health settings for people with severe pain. This approach was not to help people experience deeper levels of the nature of consciousness, non-duality, and the nature of emptiness, or gain "enlightenment" (Austin, 2009). It was much more practical: to be able to become an observer of the pain, rather than fused and lost into it; to be able to learn to tolerate the pain without fighting with it, being angry about it, or frightened of it. It was this application of mindfulness to health issues that began the explosion of interest in using mindful-attention techniques to help people observe their mind and begin to regulate difficult and painful mental states commonly, but not always, by switching motivation and moving more into a compassionate-holding motivation.

CFT, like other therapies, focuses in on these competencies, helping people become more self-aware of the different patterns of motives, emotions, and thoughts arising in the mind moment-by-moment and how to accept and refocus on the helpful. CFT does not set out to help people experience more complex and poorly understood shifts of mental state, such as emptiness, non-duality, or bliss states (Austin, 2009).

Knowing Intentionality

The evolution of these competencies, particularly those for different levels of awareness, gives rise to new forms of conscious knowing awareness and knowing intentionality. Lions clearly have intentions to hunt and kill prey but probably not knowingly. They cannot reflect on the suffering of their prey or decide to become vegetarians or to go to circuit training to become fitter and better hunters. They are unable to reflect on their behavior, imagine how to hunt better, or consider what they might be doing in a couple of months' time. Nor can they reflect on whether they want to change their behavior now, in order to change the future. Knowing intentionality is a hugely important competency for humans. It enables caring and other motivated behaviors to be voluntary and proactive, rather than reactive.

Chimpanzees show abilities to understand the needs of others and will help others on request, if they can see them. However, they do not show or practice voluntary helping in the way humans do (Yamamoto et al., 2012). They cannot care for each other knowingly, intentionally, and on purpose, providing resources or information that alleviates and prevents suffering, and deliberately practicing skills to improve their caregiving ability. Humans do. The Internet is full of individuals providing information on how to make things from fairy cakes to rockets, how to play musical instruments, or learn a new language. Humans engage in voluntary helping and sharing on an extraordinary scale. Knowing awareness and intentionality are key drivers for all deliberate practice. They are crucial to the pursuit of wisdom and, in the Buddhist traditions, crucial to the ability to experience different dimensions of consciousness and to recognize the illusions of a self (Austin, 2009). In the Buddhist traditions knowingness has a slightly different meaning, which is the knowingness that arises from self-transcendent states and experiences of nonduality.

Knowledge is crucial for knowing awareness. It is our abilities to acquire knowledge and pass it through the generations that have made us the species we are. In CFT, knowing awareness and knowing intentionality are crucially supported by psychoeducation about the nature of the evolved brain. When individuals practice "evolution-informed" mindfulness, they recognize that what can arise in one's conscious awareness may be processes linked to evolved algorithms and motives (the archetypal). These are the basis for experiencing desires, anxieties, angers, joys, and hopes. The *experiencing* of these brain states is made possible because of how DNA has built us. We see that we did not choose these potentials; we do not want to "fuse with them" but we can learn how to work with them in a positive manner and avoid the harmful.

Our cognitive competencies have both helpful and extremely harmful effects. Our cognitive competencies have allowed us to develop farming, medical science, and other technologies that are clearly of benefit to humanity but also to engage in wars and forms of exploitation (slavery) in the most horrific ways. Our methods of farming can involve extraordinary cruelty to animals and become so exploitative that we degrade the land and fish out the seas. Our capacity for self-awareness can become textured by experiences of social relationships such that we can experience ourselves as inferior, useless, and failures, even to the point of wanting to terminate our lives. Our cognitive competencies drive cultures, but culture also feeds back into patterning our motives, emotions, and beliefs in helpful and harmful ways. These are all examples of the importance of learning to use our cognitive competencies textured by compassion concerns.

From Caring to Compassion

While the evolution of caring is at the root of compassion, compassion differs from straightforward caring. The most important difference is the complex

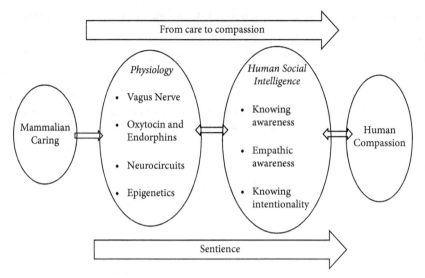

Figure 1.8 From care to compassion.
Note: Adapted from Gilbert (2019). © P. Gilbert

cognitive process that humans bring to the context of caring. This is depicted in Figure 1.8 below.

While many species care for their offspring, we would not call their behavior compassionate. There are five dimensions to compassionate behavior that link to our new (social) brain's cognitive competencies. The first is that compassion has long been focused on the identification of suffering as a conscious and sentient experience. If your garden, prized plants, or car are damaged, you may care for them, but you would not have compassion for them because "you know" they do not have a conscious mind and therefore cannot "suffer" in the way that sentient beings can. Compassion, then, is linked to our understanding of the nature of the sentient experience of suffering.

This leads to a second dimension, knowing the consequences of engaging with suffering and its prevention. Birds will sometimes flutter on the ground to indicate injury to direct predators away from the nest and many mammalian parents will risk themselves defending their offspring against predators; however, it is unclear how much in non-humans this is related to knowing awareness of risk. In contrast, consider firefighters, other rescue services, or staff working on COVID-19 wards and knowing the risk to their lives. This is one of those areas where it is probably unwise to draw sharp distinctions between species but to see how different dispositions evolve (risking self for others) and become more complex with evolution.

The third dimension is that for compassion to be more than automatic caring, we need *empathic awareness* into the causes of suffering, which feeds into empathic awareness of and recognition of what is likely to be helpful. Hence, skills of human empathy and mentalizing (Decety & Ickes, 2011; Luyten et al., 2020) are essential for wise compassion.

A fourth dimension of knowing awareness is linked to how we reason, think things through, and have meta-cognition and mindfully know that we are thinking things through. Knowing awareness is when we become mindfully aware of how our mind is working and what we are wanting to do.

A fifth dimension is that caring behavior evolves with the inhibition of harmful behavior (e.g., from the parent) and with efforts to repair harm if such occurs. Rats will not push a lever for food if it is associated with their cage-mate receiving a mild electric shock, indicating that some forms of causing harm are aversive even to rats and other animals (Sivaselvachandran et al., 2018). Whether or not the rat feels any sense of guilt or remorse or is simply experiencing a sense of threat to seeing their cage-mate harmed, is unknown.

Clearly, humans can be motivated to use their intelligence to hurt others for all kinds of reasons, such as vengeance or power seeking or just for excitement, but there is also evidence that unintended hurting is aversive. Our awareness of our potential to cause harm is clearly linked to our increased cognitive abilities, especially empathic awareness. Human guilt will differ from rat guilt because of our extraordinary capacity for insight and awareness of harm and being the agent of the cause of harm. Hence, empathic guilt is very different from shame (Crook, 1980; Gilbert, 1989, 2019). When we take a caring and compassionate orientation to ourselves and others, we make a commitment to try to live to be helpful, not harmful. This is important because we become more aware of how, out of self-interest, it is easy to be callous and harmful to others (Cameron & Payne, 2012; Gilbert, 2005, 2021). In fact, research has shown that we have a variety of fears, blocks, and resistances to being compassionate to self and others (Gilbert & Mascaro, 2017; Gilbert et al., 2011). These are associated with a range of mental health problems and behavioral difficulties (Kirby et al., 2019).

Behaviors

The fourth function of the evolved mind is direct behavior. For the most part, this involves looking at the specific actions and outputs, recognizing how engaging in psychomotor programs has major impacts on the other three functions of mind. People can process information in all kinds of ways and have all kinds of intentions (e.g., how to eat well and get fit) but that may not translate into behavior change. In addition, behavior change by itself can have profound impacts on how people process information. For example, people gain confidence from doing, not just thinking about doing. One may be very motivated to drive a car or play a piano, or to know a lot about driving or theory of music, but unless one actually drives or plays, one is not going to get good at either nor impact important dimensions of neuroplastic change. Because we are a species that (unlike plants) moves in our environment to both avoid threats and acquire resources, the behavioral outputs of the psychomotor system have very important feedback processes on what and how learning takes place (Gilbert, 2022a).

Approach-Avoidance Conflicts

A central concern for some therapies relates to the management of *internal and external conflict*. In 1947, Liddell noted how Pavlov had found that if you present signals indicating food and no food to animals at the same time, they get confused about what to do, becoming very agitated and disorganized in their behavior. Subsequent studies have found very disorganized behavior when animals and humans are put under incompatible approach-avoidance conflicts (Gilbert, 1984; Mineka & Kihlstrom, 1978). In humans, conflicts and dilemmas can often be about what behavioral option to express, such as whether to stay in a relationship or leave. It is a particular problem for children in neglectful and abusive environments because, under threat, the biological orientation is to approach the parent for support and comfort but their learned defense is avoidance. Hence, they are immediately put into an approach-avoidance conflict which creates disorganization. Although disorganization in attachment has been discussed in various ways (Cassidy & Shaver, 2016), it is helpful to think about it in terms of experimental neurosis and approach-avoidance conflicts, and to talk to clients about it in these terms (Liotti, 2000).

Behavior therapy has highlighted the fact that what we actually do in the world is regulated by multiple processes but ultimately it is action that matters. Motives, emotions, and cognitive processes guide behaviors but it is the behaviors that support survival and reproduction that evolution can work on. It cannot operate by means of a motive or emotion if these have no behavioral effects. No matter how motivated somebody is to secure a particular goal, resource, or value, if the appropriate behavior is not manifest (e.g., the person is too fearful to pursue it) change does not occur. Hence all four functions of mind noted at the beginning of the chapter support adaptive behavior. Generating compassionate behavior, behavior that seeks to alleviate and prevent suffering and harm, is a salient aim of CFT.

Conclusion

This chapter highlighted that integrated approaches to mental health problems in psychotherapy require multifactorial bridging between biological, psychological, and social processes. Contextualized within an evolution-informed approach, the study of biopsychosocial processes enables us to understand why particular interactions are so profoundly important. There are an increasing number of psychotherapies that are pursuing these types of approaches and focusing very much on the psychophysiological domains of psychotherapy (e.g., Cozolino, 2017; Porges & Dana, 2018; Schore, 2019; Siegel, 2019, 2020; Van der Kolk, 2014).

CFT emerged out of an evolutionary-based approach to mental health difficulties, with a particular interest in understanding the complex dynamics of threat-processing and their interaction with motivational systems (Gilbert, 1984, 1989, 1993; see Gilbert, 2020a, 2022a for reviews). This chapter has reviewed some of those dynamics in terms of the interaction between four functions of the mind (motives, emotions, competencies, behaviors), the distinction between motives that are care focused versus competitive focused, and three types of emotion regulation system that arise for the three major life tasks of (a) threat, protection, and defense, (b) resource seeking and acquiring, and (c) rest and digest. The chapter highlighted how and why the evolved motivation of caring, with its evolved psychophysiological architecture, has had such profound effects on the regulation of other motives; the regulation of threat and positive affect; and self-identity, beliefs, and behavioral dispositions.

Compassion is contextual. We need different skills, wisdom, and types of courage to cope with different processes in different contexts. Recognizing the power of compassion, with its psychophysiological regulating properties, also directs our attention to the problems people have when they are not able to access these functions. For example, past abuse, neglect, and other adverse experiences may block our ability to generate compassion. If we lack a secure base or safe haven, these systems may not have matured sufficiently. All people can have fears, blocks, and resistances to compassion, as will be discussed in chapter 10. The central focus of this chapter has been to highlight that there are many potentials within us, which—if they are untextured by compassion—can be and often are very harmful. Until recently compassion has not been regarded as a central process to target therapeutically. Today, with increasing evidence of its psychophysiological integrative effects, compassion is increasingly a foundational therapeutic focus. CFT seeks to target and cultivate the psychophysiological systems that will create helpful changes in the patterning of brain states.

References

Abbass, A. (2015). *Reaching through resistance: Advanced psychotherapy techniques*. Seven Leaves Press.
Abel, J., & Clarke, L. (2020). *The compassion project: A case for hope and human kindness from the town that beat loneliness*. Aster.
Armstrong, III, B. F., Nitschke, J. P., Bilash, U., & Zuroff, D. C. (2021). An affect in its own right: Investigating the relationship of social safeness with positive and negative affect. *Personality and Individual Differences, 168*, Article 109670. https://doi.org/10.1016/j.paid.2019.109670
Ashar, Y. K., Andrews-Hanna, J. R., Halifax, J., Dimidjian, S., & Wager, T. D. (2021). Effects of compassion training on brain responses to suffering others. *Social Cognitive and Affective Neuroscience, 16*(10), 1036–1047. https://doi.org/10.1093/scan/nsab052
Austin, J. H. (2009). *Selfless insight: Zen and the meditative transformation of consciousness*. MIT Press.
Bargh, J. (2017). *Before you know it: The unconscious reasons we do what we do*. Simon and Schuster.
Barkow, J. H. (1989). *Darwin, sex, and status*. Toronto University Press.
Baron-Cohen, S. (2011). *Zero degrees of empathy: A new theory of human cruelty*. Allen Lane.
Basran, J., Pires, C., Matos, M., McEwan, K., & Gilbert, P. (2019). Styles of leadership, fears of compassion, and competing to avoid inferiority. *Frontiers in Psychology, 9*, Article 2460. https://doi.org/10.3389/fpsyg.2018.02460
Baumeister, R. F., Bratslavsky, E., Finkenauer, C., & Vohs, K. D. (2001). Bad is stronger than good. *Review of General Psychology, 5*(4), 323–370. https://doi.org/10.1037/1089-2680.5.4.323

Böckler, A., Tusche, A., & Singer, T. (2016). The structure of human prosociality: Differentiating altruistically motivated, norm motivated, strategically motivated, and self-reported prosocial behavior. *Social Psychological and Personality Science, 7*(6), 530–541. https://doi.org/10.1177/1948550616639650

Boehm, C. (1999). *Hierarchy in the forest: The evolution of egalitarian behavior.* Harvard University Press.

Bornemann, B., Kok, B. E., Böckler, A., & Singer, T. (2016). Helping from the heart: Voluntary upregulation of heart rate variability predicts altruistic behaviour. *Biological Psychiatry, 119,* 54–63. https://doi.org/10.1016/j.biopsycho.2016.07.004

Bowlby, J. (1969). *Attachment and loss, Vol. 1: Attachment.* Basic Books.

Bowlby, J. (1973). *Separation, anxiety and anger: Attachment and loss, Vol. 2.* Basic Books.

Bowlby, J. (1980). *Loss: Sadness and depression: Attachment and loss, Vol. 3.* Hogarth Press.

Brown, S. L., & Brown, R. M. (2015). Connecting prosocial behavior to improved physical health: Contributions from the neurobiology of parenting. *Neuroscience and Biobehavioral Reviews, 55,* 1–17. https://doi.org/10.1016/j.neubiorev.2015.04.004

Buss, D. M. (2019). *Evolutionary psychology: The new science of the mind* (6th ed.). Routledge.

Busso, D. S., McLaughlin, K. A., & Sheridan, M. A. (2017). Dimensions of adversity, physiological reactivity, and externalizing psychopathology in adolescence: Deprivation and threat. *Psychosomatic Medicine, 79*(2), 162. https://doi.org/10.1097/PSY.0000000000000369

Byrne, R. W. (2016). *Evolving insight: How it is we can think about why things happen.* Oxford University Press.

Cacioppo, S., Capitanio, J. P., & Cacioppo, J. T. (2014). Toward a neurology of loneliness. *Psychological Bulletin, 140*(6), 1464–1504. https://doi.org/10.1037/a0037618.

Cameron, C. D., & Payne, B. K. (2012). The cost of callousness: Regulating compassion influences the moral self-concept. *Psychological Science, 23*(3), 225–229. https://doi.org/10.1177/0956797611430334

Camilleri, T., Rockey, S., & Dunbar, R. (2023). *The social brain. The psychology of successful groups.* Cornerstone Press.

Carter, S., Bartal, I. B., & Porges, E. (2017). The roots of compassion: An evolutionary and neurobiological perspective. In E. M. Seppälä, E. Simon-Thomas, S. L. Brown, M. C. Worline, C. D. Cameron, & J. R. Doty (Eds.), *The Oxford handbook of compassion science* (pp. 178–188). Oxford University Press.

Cassidy, J., & Shaver, P. R. (2016). *Handbook of attachment: Theory, research, and clinical applications* (3rd ed.). Guilford Press.

Castonguay, L. G., Eubanks, C. F., Goldfried, M. R., Muran, J. C., & Lutz, W. (2015). Research on psychotherapy integration: Building on the past, looking to the future. *Psychotherapy Research, 25*(3), 365–382. https://doi.org/10.1080/10503307.2015.1014010

Catarino, F., Gilbert, P., McEwan, K., & Baião, R. (2014). Compassion motivations: Distinguishing submissive compassion from genuine compassion and its association with shame, submissive behavior, depression, anxiety, and stress. *Journal of Social and Clinical Psychology, 33*(5), 399–412. https://doi.org/10.1521/jscp.2014.33.5.399

Clarke, M., McEwan, K., Ness, J., Waters, K., Basran, J., & Gilbert, P. (2016). A descriptive study of feelings of arrested escape (entrapment) and arrested anger in people presenting to an emergency department following an episode of self-harm. *Frontiers in Psychiatry, 7,* Article 155. https://doi.org/10.3389/fpsyt.2016.00155

Clegg, K. A., Levine, S. L., Zuroff, D. C., Holding, A. C., Shahar, G., & Koestner, R. (2022). A multilevel perspective on self-determination theory: Predictors and correlates of autonomous and controlled motivation. *Motivation and Emotion, 47,* 229–245. https://doi.org/10.1007/s11031-022-09995-6

Cowan, C. S. M., Callaghan, B. L., Kan, J. M., & Richardson, R. (2016). The lasting impact of early-life adversity on individuals and their descendants: Potential mechanisms and hope for intervention. *Genes, Brain, and Behavior, 15*(1), 155–168. https://doi.org/10.1111/gbb.12263

Cozolino, L. (2017). *The neuroscience of psychotherapy: Healing the social brain* (2nd ed.). W.W. Norton & Company.

Craske, M. G., Meuret, A. E., Ritz, T., Treanor, M., Dour, H., & Rosenfield, D. (2019). Positive affect treatment for depression and anxiety: A randomized clinical trial for a core feature of anhedonia. *Journal of Consulting and Clinical Psychology, 87*(5), 457–471. https://doi.org/10.1037/ccp0000396

Crook, J. H. (1980). *The evolution of human consciousness.* Oxford University Press.
Davey, G. C. (2018). *Psychology.* John Wiley & Sons.
Decety, J., & Ickes, W. (Eds.). (2011). *The social neuroscience of empathy.* MIT Press.
De France, K., Evans, G. W., Brody, G. H., & Doan, S. N. (2022). Cost of resilience: Childhood poverty, mental health, and chronic physiological stress. *Psychoneuroendocrinology, 144,* Article 105872. https://doi.org/10.1016/j.psyneuen.2022.105872
Depue, R. A., & Morrone-Strupinsky, J. V. (2005). A neurobehavioral model of affiliative bonding. *Behavioral and Brain Sciences, 28,* 313–395. https://doi.org/10.1017/S0140525X05000063
Di Bello, M., Ottaviani, C., & Petrocchi, N. (2021). Compassion is not a benzo: Distinctive associations of heart rate variability with its empathic and action components. *Frontiers in Neuroscience, 15,* Article 617443. https://doi.org/10.3389/fnins.2021.617443
Dixon, A. K. (1998). Ethological strategies for defence in animals and humans: Their role in some psychiatric disorders. *British Journal of Medical Psychology, 71*(Pt 4), 417–445. https://doi.org/10.1111/j.2044-8341.1998.tb01001.x
Eisenberg, L. (1977). Development as a unifying concept in psychiatry. *The British Journal of Psychiatry, 131*(3), 225–237. https://doi.org/10.1192/bjp.131.3.225
Ellenberger, H. F. (1970). *The discovery of the unconscious: The history and evolution of dynamic psychiatry, vol. 1.* Basic Books.
Gibbons, C. H. (2019). Basics of autonomic nervous system function. *Handbook of Clinical Neurology, 160,* 407–418. https://doi.org/10.1016/B978-0-444-64032-1.00027-8
Gilbert, P. (1984). *Depression: From psychology to brain state.* Lawrence Erlbaum Associates.
Gilbert, P. (1989). *Human nature and suffering.* Lawrence Erlbaum Associates.
Gilbert, P. (1992). *Depression: The evolution of powerlessness.* Lawrence Erlbaum Associates.
Gilbert, P. (1993). Defence and safety: Their function in social behaviour and psychopathology. *British Journal of Clinical Psychology, 32*(2), 131–153. https://doi.org/10.1111/j.2044-8260.1993.tb01039.x
Gilbert, P. (1995). Biopsychosocial approaches and evolutionary theory as aids to integration in clinical psychology and psychotherapy. *Clinical Psychology and Psychotherapy, 2,* 135–156. https://doi.org/10.1002/cpp.5640020302
Gilbert, P. (2000a). Social mentalities: Internal "social" conflicts and the role of inner warmth and compassion in cognitive therapy. In P. Gilbert & K. G. Bailey (Eds.), *Genes on the couch: Explorations in evolutionary psychotherapy* (pp. 118–150). Psychology Press.
Gilbert, P. (2000b). Varieties of submissive behaviour: Their evolution and role in depression. In L. Sloman & P. Gilbert (Eds.), *Subordination and defeat: An evolutionary approach to mood disorders* (pp. 3–46). Lawrence Erlbaum Associates.
Gilbert, P. (2001). Depression and stress: A biopsychosocial exploration of evolved functions and mechanisms. *Stress: The International Journal of the Biology of Stress, 4*(2), 121–135. https://doi.org/10.3109/10253890109115726
Gilbert, P. (2005). Compassion and cruelty: A biopsychosocial approach. In P. Gilbert (Ed.), *Compassion: Conceptualisations, research, and use in psychotherapy* (pp. 3–74). Routledge.
Gilbert, P. (2009). *The compassionate mind: A new approach to the challenge of life.* Constable & Robinson.
Gilbert, P. (2010). *Compassion focused therapy: The CBT distinctive features series.* Routledge.
Gilbert, P. (2014). The origins and nature of compassion focused therapy. *British Journal of Clinical Psychology, 53*(1), 6–41. https://doi.org/10.1111/bjc.12043
Gilbert, P. (2015a). An evolutionary approach to emotion in mental health with a focus on affiliative emotions. *Emotion Review, 7*(3), 230–237. https://doi.org/10.1177/1754073915576552
Gilbert, P. (2015b). Affiliative and prosocial motives and emotions in mental health. *Dialogues in Clinical Neuroscience, 17*(4), 381–389. https://doi.org/10.31887/DCNS.2015.17.4/pgilbert
Gilbert, P. (2017). *Compassion: Concepts, research, and applications.* Routledge.
Gilbert, P. (2019). Psychotherapy for the 21st century: An integrative, evolutionary, contextual, biopsychosocial approach. *Psychology and Psychotherapy: Theory, Research and Practice, 92*(2), 164–189. https://doi.org/10.1111/papt.12226
Gilbert, P. (2020a). Compassion: From its evolution to a psychotherapy. *Frontiers in Psychology, 11,* Article 586161. https://doi.org/10.3389/fpsyg.2020.586161

Gilbert, P. (2020b). Evolutionary functional analysis: The study of social mentalities, social rank, and caring-compassion. In J. N. Kirby & P. Gilbert (Eds.), *Making an impact on mental health* (pp. 4–42). Routledge.

Gilbert, P. (2021). Creating a compassionate world: Addressing the conflicts between sharing and caring versus controlling and holding evolved strategies. *Frontiers in Psychology, 11*, 582090. https://doi.org/10.3389/fpsyg.2020.582090

Gilbert, P. (2022a). Compassion focused therapy as an evolution informed, biopsychosocial science of the mind: History and challenge. In P. Gilbert & G. Simos (Eds.), *Compassion focused therapy: Clinical practice and applications* (pp. 24–89). Routledge.

Gilbert, P. (2022b). The evolved functions of caring connections as a basis for compassion. In P. Gilbert & G. Simos (Eds.), *Compassion focused therapy: Clinical practice and applications* (pp. 90–121). Routledge.

Gilbert, P. (2022c). Internal shame and self-disconnection from hostile self-criticism to compassionate self-correction and guidance. In P. Gilbert & G. Simos (Eds.), *Compassion focused therapy: Clinical practice and applications* (pp. 164–206). Routledge.

Gilbert, P. (2022d). Shame, social status, and the pain of social disconnection. In P. Gilbert & G. Simos (Eds.), *Compassion focused therapy: Clinical practice and applications* (pp. 122–163). Routledge.

Gilbert, P. (2023). An evolutionary and compassion approach to yearning and grief for what one did not have. In D. Harris & A. H. Y. Ho (Eds.), *Compassion-based approaches to loss and grief* (pp. 18–27). Routledge.

Gilbert, P., & Allan, S. (1998). The role of defeat and entrapment (arrested flight) in depression: An exploration of an evolutionary view. *Psychological Medicine, 28*(3), 584–597. https://doi.org/10.1017/s0033291798006710

Gilbert, P., Allan, S., Brough, S., Melley, S., & Miles, J. (2002). Relationship of anhedonia and anxiety to social rank, defeat and entrapment. *Journal of Affective Disorders, 71*, 141–151.

Gilbert, P., Basran, J. K., Raven, J., Gilbert, H., Petrocchi, N., Cheli, S., Rayner, A., Hayes, A., Lucre, K., Minou, P., Giles, D., Byrne, F., Newton, E., & McEwan, K. (2022). Compassion focused group therapy for people with a diagnosis of bipolar affective disorder: A feasibility study. *Frontiers in Psychology, 13*, 841932. https://doi.org/10.3389/fpsyg.2022.841932

Gilbert, P., Birchwood, M., Gilbert, J., Trower, P., Hay, J., Murray, B., Meaden, A., Olsen, K., & Miles, J. N. V. (2001). An exploration of evolved mental mechanisms for dominant and subordinate behaviour in relation to auditory hallucinations in schizophrenia and critical thoughts in depression. *Psychological Medicine, 31*, 1117–1127. https://doi.org/10.1017/s0033291701004093

Gilbert, P., Boxall, M., Cheung, M., & Irons, C. (2005). The relation of paranoid ideation and social anxiety in a mixed clinical population. *Clinical Psychology and Psychotherapy, 12*(2), 124–133. https://doi.org/10.1002/cpp.438

Gilbert, P., Catarino, F., Duarte, C., Matos, M., Kolts, R., Stubbs, J., Ceresatto, L., Duarte, J., Pinto-Gouveia, J., & Basran, J. (2017). The development of compassionate engagement and action scales for self and others. *Journal of Compassionate Health Care, 4*, Article 4. https://doi.org/10.1186/s40639-017-0033-3

Gilbert, P., & Irons, C. (2005). Focused therapies and compassionate mind training for shame and self-attacking. In P. Gilbert (Ed.), *Compassion: Conceptualisations, research and use in psychotherapy* (pp. 263–325). Routledge.

Gilbert, P., & Mascaro, J. S. (2017). Compassion fears, blocks and resistances: An evolutionary investigation. In E. M. Seppälä, E. Simon-Thomas, S. L. Brown, M. C. Worline, C. D. Cameron, &, J. R. Doty (Eds.), *The Oxford handbook of compassion science* (pp. 399–418). Oxford University Press.

Gilbert, P., McEwan, K., Matos, M., & Rivis, A. (2011). Fears of compassion: Development of three self-report measures. *Psychology and Psychotherapy, 84*(3), 239–255. https://doi.org/10.1348/147608310X526511

Gilbert, P., McEwan, K., Mitra, R., Richter, A., Franks, L., Mills, A., Bellew, R., & Gale, C. (2009). An exploration of different types of positive affect in students and in patients with bipolar disorder. *Clinical Neuropsychiatry, 6*(4), 135–143.

Gilbert, P., & McGuire, M. (1998). Shame, status, and social roles: The psychobiological continuum from monkeys to humans. In P. Gilbert & B. Andrews (Eds.), *Shame: Interpersonal behavior, psychopathology, and culture* (pp. 99–125). Oxford University Press.

Gilbert, P., & Simos, G. (2022). *Compassion focused therapy: Clinical practice and applications*. Routledge.

Goleman, D., & Davidson, R. J. (2017). *Altered traits: Science reveals how meditation changes your mind, brain, and body*. Penguin.

Goodall, J. (1990). *Through a window. Thirty years with the chimpanzees of Gnome*. Penguin.

Heriot-Maitland, C. (2022). Compassion focused therapy for voice hearing and delusions in psychosis. In P. Gilbert & G. Simos (Eds.), *Compassion focused therapy: Clinical practice and applications* (pp. 549–564). Routledge.

Heriot-Maitland, C., McCarthy-Jones, S., Longden, E., & Gilbert, P. (2019). Compassion focused approaches to working with distressing voices. *Frontiers in Psychology, 10*, Article 152. https://doi.org/10.3389/fpsyg.2019.00152

Johnson, S. (2002). *Emergence: The connected lives of ants, brains, cities, and software*. Simon and Schuster.

Jones, D. N., & Figueredo, A. J. (2013). The core of darkness: Uncovering the heart of the Dark Triad. *European Journal of Personality, 27*(6), 521–531. https://doi.org/10.1002/per.1893

Kabat-Zinn, J. (1982). An outpatient program in behavioral medicine for chronic pain patients based on the practice of mindfulness meditation: Theoretical considerations and preliminary results. *General Hospital Psychiatry, 4*(1), 33–47. https://doi.org/10.1016/0163-8343(82)90026-3

Kabat-Zinn, J. (2015). Mindfulness. *Mindfulness, 6*(6), 1481–1483. https://doi.org/10.1007/s12671-015-0456-x

Kelly, A. C., Zuroff, D. C., Leybman, M. J., & Gilbert, P. (2012). Social safeness, received social support, and maladjustment: Testing a tripartite model of affect regulation. *Cognitive Therapy and Research, 36*(6), 815–826. https://doi.org/10.1007/s10608-011-9432-5

Keltner, D., Oatley, K., & Jenkins, J. M. (2018). *Understanding emotions*. Wiley Global Education.

Kessler, S. E. (2020). Why care: Complex evolutionary history of human healthcare networks. *Frontiers in Psychology, 11*, 199. https://doi.org/10.3389/fpsyg.2020.00199

Kim, J. J., Parker, S. L., Doty, J. R., Cunnington, R., Gilbert, P., & Kirby, J. N. (2020). Neurophysiological and behavioural markers of compassion. *Scientific Reports, 10*, Article 6789. https://doi.org/10.1038/s41598-020-63846-3

King's Cultural Community. (n.d.). Compassion for voices: A tale of courage and hope. [Video]. YouTube. https://www.youtube.com/watch?v=VRqI4lxuXAw

Kirby, J. N. (2016). Compassion interventions: The programs, the evidence, and implications for research and practice. *Psychology and Psychotherapy: Theory, Research, and Practice, 90*(3), 432–455. https://doi.org/10.1111/papt.12104

Kirby, J. N., Day, J., & Sagar, V. (2019). The 'flow' of compassion: A meta-analysis of the fears of compassion scales and psychological functioning. *Clinical Psychology Review, 70*, 26–39. https://doi.org/10.1016/j.cpr.2019.03.001

Klimecki, O. M. (2015). The plasticity of social emotions. *Social Neuroscience, 10*(5), 466–473. https://doi.org/10.1080/17470919.2015.1087427

Knox, J. (2003). *Archetype, attachment, analysis: Jungian psychology and the emergent mind*. Psychology Press.

Kucerova, B., Levit-Binnun, N., Gordon, I., & Golland, Y. (2023). From oxytocin to compassion: The saliency of distress. *Biology, 12*(2), 183. https://doi.org/10.3390/biology12020183

Kumsta, R. (2019). The role of epigenetics for understanding mental health difficulties and its implications for psychotherapy research. *Psychology and Psychotherapy: Theory, Research and Practice, 92*(2), 190–207.

LeBouef, T., Yaker, Z., & Whited, L. (2021). Physiology, autonomic nervous system. In *StatPearls [Internet]*. StatPearls Publishing.

LeDoux, J. E. (2020). Thoughtful feelings. *Current Biology, 30*(11), R619–R623. https://doi.org/10.1016/j.cub.2020.04.012

LeDoux, J. E. (2022). As soon as there was life, there was danger: The deep history of survival behaviours and the shallower history of consciousness. *Philosophical Transactions of the Royal Society. Series B, Biological Sciences, 377*(1844), Article 20210292. https://doi.org/10.1098/rstb.2021.0292

Lee, D. A. (2022). Using compassion focused therapy to work with complex PTSD. In P. Gilbert & G. Simos (Eds.), *Compassion focused therapy: Clinical practice and applications* (pp. 565–583). Routledge.

Liotti, G. (2000). Disorganised attachment, models of borderline states, and evolutionary psychotherapy. In P. Gilbert and B. Bailey (Eds.), *Genes on the couch: Explorations in evolutionary psychotherapy* (pp. 232–256). Brunner-Routledge.

Luyten, P., Campbell, C., Allison, E., & Fonagy, P. (2020). The mentalizing approach to psychopathology: State of the art and future directions. *Annual Review of Clinical Psychology, 16,* 297–325. https://doi.org/10.1146/annurev-clinpsy-071919-015355

Martins, M. J., Macedo, A., Carvalho, C. B., Pereira, A. T., & Castilho, P. (2020). Are shame and self-criticism the path to the pervasive effect of social stress reactivity on social functioning in psychosis? *Clinical Psychology and Psychotherapy, 27*(1), 52–60. https://doi.org/10.1002/cpp.2406

Mascaro, J. S., Florian, M. P., Ash, M. J., Palmer, P. K., Frazier, T., Condon, P., & Raison, C. (2020). Ways of knowing compassion: How do we come to know, understand, and measure compassion when we see it? *Frontiers in Psychology, 11,* Article 547241. https://doi.org/10.3389/fpsyg.2020.547241

Mayhew, S., & Gilbert, P. (2008). Compassionate mind training with people who hear malevolent voices: A case series report. *Clinical Psychology and Psychotherapy, 15*(2), 113–138. https://doi.org/10.1002/cpp.566

Mayseless, O. (2016). *The caring motivation: An integrated theory.* Oxford University Press.

McEwan, K., Gilbert, P., & Duarte, J. (2012). An exploration of competitiveness and caring in relation to psychopathology. *British Journal of Clinical Psychology, 51*(1), 19–36. https://doi.org/10.1111/j.2044-8260.2011.02010.x

Mikulincer, M., & Shaver, P. R. (Eds.). (2014). *Mechanisms of social connection: From brain to group.* American Psychological Association. https://doi.org/10.1037/14250-000

Mineka, S., & Kihlstrom, J. F. (1978). Unpredictable and uncontrollable events: A new perspective on experimental neurosis. *Journal of Abnormal Psychology, 87*(2), 256–271. https://doi.org/10.1037/0021-843X.87.2.256

Moore, J. W. (Ed.). (2012). *A neuroscientist's guide to classical conditioning.* Springer Science & Business Media.

Music, G. (2017). *Nurturing natures: Attachment and children's emotional, sociocultural and brain development* (2nd ed.). Routledge.

Music, G. (2022). *Respark: Igniting hope and joy after trauma and depression.* Mind-Nurturing Books.

Nesse, R. M. (2019). *Good reasons for bad feelings: Insights from the frontier of evolutionary psychiatry.* Dutton.

Nguyen, T., Schleihauf, H., Kayhan, E., Matthes, D., Vrtička, P., & Hoehl, S. (2020). The effects of interaction quality on neural synchrony during mother-child problem solving. *Cortex, 124,* 235–249. https://doi.org/10.1016/j.cortex.2019.11.020

O'Donnell, K. J., & Meaney, M. J. (2020). Epigenetics, development, and psychopathology. *Annual Review of Clinical Psychology, 16,* 327–350. https://doi.org/10.1146/annurev-clinpsy-050718-095530

Panksepp, J. (1998). *Affective neuroscience.* Oxford University Press.

Perrez, M., & Reicherts, M. (1992). *Stress, coping, and health: A situation-behavior approach: Theory, methods, and applications.* Hogrefe and Huber.

Petrocchi, N., & Cheli, S. (2019). The social brain and heart rate variability: Implications for psychotherapy. *Psychology and Psychotherapy: Theory, Research, and Practice, 92*(2), 208–223. https://doi.org/10.1111/papt.12224

Petrocchi, N., Di Bello, M., Cheli, S., & Ottaviani, C. (2022). Compassion focused therapy and the body: How physiological underpinnings of prosociality informed clinical practice. In P. Gilbert & G. Simos (Eds.), *Compassion focused therapy: Clinical practice and applications* (pp. 345–359). Routledge.

Petrocchi, N., & Ottaviani, C. (2024). Compassionate bodies, compassionate minds: The second physiological concomitants of compassion focused therapy. In P. Steffen & D. Moss (Eds.), *Integrating psychotherapy and psychophysiology*. Oxford.

Pet Shop Boys. (2009). Numb. [Video]. YouTube. https://www.youtube.com/watch?v=kOyCkjWpz1s

Pilgrim, D. (2002). The biopsychosocial model in Anglo-American psychiatry: Past, present, and future? *Journal of Mental Health, 11*(6), 585–594. https://doi.org/10.1080/09638230020023930

Porges, S. W. (2017). Vagal pathways: Portals to compassion. In E. M. Seppälä, E. Simon-Thomas, S. L. Brown, M. C. Worline, C. D. Cameron, & J. R. Doty (Eds.), *The Oxford handbook of compassion science* (pp. 189–202). Oxford University Press.

Porges, S. W. (2021). Polyvagal theory: A biobehavioral journey to sociality. *Comprehensive Psychoneuroendocrinology, 7*, Article 100069. https://doi.org/10.1016/j.cpnec.2021.100069

Porges, S. W., & Dana, D. (2018). *Clinical applications of the polyvagal theory: The emergence of polyvagal-informed therapies (Norton series on interpersonal neurobiology)*. W. W. Norton & Company.

Pratto, F., Çidam, A., Stewart, A. L., Zeineddine, F. B., Aranda, M., Aiello, A., Chryssochoou, X., Cichocka, A., Cohrs, J. C., Durrheim, K., Eicher, C., Foels, R., Gorska, P., Lee, I.-C., Licata, L., Liu, J. H., Li, L., Meyer, I., Morselli, D., . . . Henkel, K. E. (2013). Social dominance in context and in individuals: Contextual moderation of robust effects of social dominance orientation in 15 languages and 20 countries. *Social Psychological and Personality Science, 4*(5), 587–599. https://doi.org/10.1177/1948550612473663

Riskind, J. H., Sica, C., Caudek, C., Bottesi, G., Disabato, D. J., & Ghisi, M. (2021). Looming cognitive style more consistently predicts anxiety than depressive symptoms: Evidence from a 3-wave yearlong study. *Cognitive Therapy and Research, 45*, 745–758. https://doi.org/10.1007/s10608-020-10189-y

Ryan, R. M., & Deci, E. L. (2000). Intrinsic and extrinsic motivations: Classic definitions and new directions. *Contemporary Educational Psychology, 25*(1), 54–67. https://doi.org/10.1006/ceps.1999.1020.

Ryan, R. M., & Deci, E. L. (2017). *Self-determination theory: Basic psychological needs in motivation, development, and wellness*. Guilford Press.

Schore, A. N. (2019). *Right brain psychotherapy*. Norton.

Schotte, C. K., Van Den Bossche, B., De Doncker, D., Claes, S., & Cosyns, P. (2006). A biopsychosocial model as a guide for psychoeducation and treatment of depression. *Depression and Anxiety, 23*(5), 312–324. https://doi.org/10.1002/da.20177

Seligman, M. E. P. (1975). *Helplessness: On depression, development, and death*. Freeman and Co.

Seppälä, E. M., Simon-Thomas, E., Brown, S. L., Worline, M. C., Cameron, C. D., & Doty, J. R. (Eds.). (2017). *The Oxford handbook of compassion science*. Oxford University Press.

Siddaway, A. P., Taylor, P. J., Wood, A. M., & Schulz, J. (2015). A meta-analysis of perceptions of defeat and entrapment in depression, anxiety problems, posttraumatic stress disorder, and suicidality. *Journal of Affective Disorders, 184*, 149–159. https://doi.org/10.1016/j.jad.2015.05.046

Siegel, D. J. (2019). The mind in psychotherapy: An interpersonal neurobiology framework for understanding and cultivating mental health. *Psychology and Psychotherapy: Theory, Research and Practice, 92*(2), 224–237. https://doi.org/10.1111/papt.12228

Siegel, D. J. (2020). *The developing mind: How relationships in the brain interact to shape who we are* (3rd ed.). Norton.

Sivaselvachandran, S., Acland, E. L., Abdallah, S., & Martin, L. J. (2018). Behavioral and mechanistic insight into rodent empathy. *Neuroscience and Biobehavioral Reviews, 91*, 130–137. https://doi.org/10.1016/j.neubiorev.2016.06.007

Slavich, G. M. (2020). Social safety theory: A biologically based evolutionary perspective on life stress, health, and behavior. *Annual Review of Clinical Psychology, 16*, 265. https://doi.org/10.1146/annurev-clinpsy-032816-045159

Slavich, G. M., Roos, L. G., Mengelkoch, S., Webb, C. A., Shattuck, E. C., Moriarity, D. P., & Alley, J. C. (2023). Social Safety Theory: Conceptual foundation, underlying mechanisms, and future directions. *Health Psychology Review, 17*(1), 5–59. https://doi.org/10.1080/17437199.2023.2171900

Sperry, L. (2008). The biopsychosocial model and chronic illness: Psychotherapeutic implications. *The Journal of Individual Psychology, 64*(3), 369–376.

Spikins, P. (2015). *How compassion made us human: The evolutionary origins of tenderness, trust and morality*. Spear and Sword Books.

Steffen, P. R., Foxx, J., Cattani, K., Alldredge, C., Austin, T., & Burlingame, G. M. (2021). Impact of a 12-week group-based compassion focused therapy intervention on heart rate variability. *Applied Psychophysiology and Biofeedback, 46*, 61–68. https://doi.org/10.1007/s10484-020-09487-8

Stevens, A. (2002). *Archetype revisited: An updated natural history of the self*. Routledge.

Suddendorf, T. (2018). Inside our heads: Two key features created the human mind: Inside our heads. *Scientific American, 319*(3), 42–47. https://doi.org/10.1038/scientificamerican0918-42

Taylor, P. J., Gooding, P., Wood, A. M., & Tarrier, N. (2011). The role of defeat and entrapment in depression, anxiety, and suicide. *Psychological Bulletin, 137*(3), 391–420. https://doi.org/10.1037/a0022935

Taylor, S. E. (2011). Social support: A review. In H. S. Friedman (Ed.), *The Oxford handbook of health psychology* (pp. 189–214). Oxford University Press.

Terpou, B. A., Harricharan, S., McKinnon, M. C., Frewen, P., Jetly, R., & Lanius, R. A. (2019). The effects of trauma on brain and body: A unifying role for the midbrain periaqueductal gray. *Journal of Neuroscience Research, 97*(9), 1110–1140. https://doi.org/10.1002/jnr.24447

Van der Hart, O., Nijenhuis, E. R., & Steele, K. (2006). *The haunted self: Structural dissociation and the treatment of chronic traumatization*. W. W. Norton & Company.

Van der Kolk, B. (2014). *The body keeps the score: Mind, brain and body in the transformation of trauma*. Penguin Publishing Group.

van Kleef, G. A., Oveis, C., van der Löwe, I., LuoKogan, A., Goetz, J., & Keltner, D. (2008). Power, distress, and compassion: Turning a blind eye to the suffering of others. *Psychological Science, 19*(12), 1315–1322. https://doi.org/10.1111/j.1467-9280.2008.02241.x

Vrtička, P., Favre, P., & Singer, T. (2017). Compassion and the brain. In P. Gilbert (Ed.), *Compassion: Concepts, research, and applications* (pp. 135–151). Routledge.

Wilkinson, R. G. (2020). *The impact of inequality: How to make sick societies healthier*. Routledge.

Wilson, E. O. (1999). *Consilience: The unity of knowledge* (Vol. 31). Vintage.

Wu, Y. E., & Hong, W. (2022). Neural basis of prosocial behavior. *Trends in Neurosciences, 45*, 749–762.

Yamamoto, S., Humle, T., & Tanaka, M. (2012). Chimpanzees' flexible targeted helping based on an understanding of conspecifics' goals. *Proceedings of the National Academy of Sciences, 109*(9), 3588–3592. https://doi.org/10.1073/pnas.1108517109

Žvelc, G., & Žvelc, M. (2021). *Integrative psychotherapy: A mindfulness- and compassion-oriented approach*. Routledge.

2
Neuroscientific Principles Underlying Psychotherapy

Rebekka Matheson

Case Study

Alicia, a twenty-six-year-old graduate student, presents to your practice seeking help with depressed mood and persistent worry, both of which have developed and worsened over the past two years. This is her first time seeking psychotherapy; she recently learned about a university perk for a few reimbursed sessions. "The only good thing about this place," she says. You quickly learn that Alicia is beginning her third year of graduate school but is not thriving. She doesn't enjoy her work or find it meaningful, and although she was initially proud to have been accepted to a prestigious university, she worries it will not get her anywhere in the job market. She sounds frustrated and proactively self-deprecating about her chosen field. Maybe she chose the wrong major, she says, or made "stupid" choices about adult life.

This is clearly something she thinks about a lot, and you're interested in learning more. How did she choose her major and career plans? Alicia sighs. She doesn't really know. It was the sort of thing she was "supposed" to do, what her parents expected of her, and now here she was, disappointing them, again. "Again?" you ask. You learn that her parents were both successful professionals, with high expectations for their children's success. Alicia feels like all her aloof and unengaged father saw was her report card and sports stats, and her own self-esteem became dependent on her academic and extracurricular performance. She wasn't a natural athlete, and didn't enjoy her extensive roster of extracurriculars, but she was good at school. Even so, positive feedback from her father was erratic and unpredictable. Just as often, Dad was emotionally abusive, and Alicia felt she had to work harder and harder to try to avoid the abuse and earn approval. You notice that Alicia's mother doesn't factor into the narrative very much, an observation that makes Alicia a little defensive. "I know Mom loves me, but she can't stand up to Dad. She just does and says what Dad wants."

Alicia doesn't report any other reliable social supports in her life—no close friends or confidants at work. She seems embarrassed to admit to a recent messy breakup, and although she's reluctant to talk about it, you wonder if that is the real trigger for the visit, since the worsening of her anxiety and depression seems to have coincided with it. She says she feels devastated and alone and worries nothing will ever change. "I guess this is me. This is adult life," she says. "A loser." She fears she doesn't have the ability to succeed or focus or find a desirable partner. When you try to help her reframe any problems to think about steps she could take to mitigate them, she seems avoidant and unable to engage with problem-solving. "I can't sleep, but then I can't get out of bed. There is literally nothing I feel like doing anymore. Everything sucks."

As you review this chapter, consider: If Alicia is suffering from a clinical depression or anxiety disorder, are these reflected in her brain, or rather just in her "mind?" If they are in the brain, what caused the pathology? Does she have innate or inborn brain differences or risks? Could any of her risk be genetic or from her physical environment? How much is caused by her brain's response to trauma? And is it a normal response to a bad environment, or an errant response that has caused disorder? What implications does this have for psychotherapy?

Introduction: Psychotherapy as a Physical Intervention

Dualism: A Historical Approach

Despite the brain being as much biological tissue as is the liver or kidney, society continues to differentiate between "mental" and "medical" illness both colloquially and in health care and academia. Even for illnesses that are believed to be brain-based, we speak of "psychiatric" versus "neurological" illness, as if psychiatric illness were a disorder of the ether and not of matter. This attitude is a form of *dualism*, or the practice of treating brain and mind as separate entities.

Those seeking to clarify or minimize dualist tensions often define *mind* as the mental processes and the *brain* as the networked cells that execute them, which is useful, but still tends to put the brain in the "black box." For all our cultural struggle with mind–brain dualism, scholars and practitioners focusing on other organ systems don't wrestle with the same issues—no one speaks of "filtration–kidney dualism" or "respiration–lung dualism." Perhaps this is because they have always thought of these systems in terms of *process*. Muscle is not movement; it executes movement and is changed by that movement. Lungs are not breath, and kidneys are not filtration, but they execute those functions and are modified by the context and success of those functions. Pulmonologists and nephrologists move naturally between discussing structural and functional issues in their organ systems, because the pathology is with the *process*. The analogy to brain is straightforward: mind is what the brain *does*, and brain is what the mind modifies through use. Mental health and disorder need not have a tension between mind and brain if we embrace a model of mental process, uniting both.

And yet, dualism persists in the language of behavior and the approach toward understanding it and modifying it in a way that has never existed in other systems. While there may be social practicality to this persistent (and pervasive) dualism, it reflects limits in our neuroscientific understanding of psychiatric illness—and, indeed, behavior!—and in turn creates limitations on how we increase that understanding. Finally, it inhibits the integration of neuroscience into our real-life, in-the-clinic approach.

Our ability to understand the brain's processes and pathologies mechanistically has lagged behind our progress in medicine "below the neck." The reasons are myriad: limitations of the applicability of animal models to behavioral and cognitive research, ethical concerns of experimentation, the inherent complexity of the system, its relative inaccessibility, and the enormous inter- *and* intra-individual variability in cognition and behavior.

Further, some of the most profound risks of—and some of the most powerful interventions for—behavioral pathology appear to be external to biology: a traumatic event occurs in a person's life; a skilled therapist leads a productive discussion. This magnifies the dualist illusion. The symptoms are in the realm of behavior, and the treatment is also in the realm of behavior. It's easy, then, to leave biology as a black box, and as long as that black box stays closed, it's not particularly helpful for the psychotherapist seeking to understand symptoms or to plan treatment.

The reality, of course, is that neurobiology isn't (and never really was) a black box. To the extent it seems unknowable, dark, or vast, it is more like the night sky looking out at a universe than a closed box. Neuroscience is an exploding field, with new methods and techniques for exploration every year. These translate into powerful tools for the psychotherapist. When the brain is understood as an organ that interacts with and processes sensory experience—analogous in part to the way a gastrointestinal tract processes nutrients, or a liver processes toxins—then we don't need to relegate its functions to the ineffable. Instead, we can be empowered by pursuing and articulating the mechanisms by which external experience influences brain tissue for good or for ill, and how changing thoughts and behavior can impact brain function *and* structure.

Introducing Neuroplasticity: The Approach of the Future

A fundamental characteristic of the human brain is *neuroplasticity*—the capacity of brain tissue to change its form and function in response to experience. Although it may take a sophisticated understanding of psychology to understand the roots of disordered behavior and then to successfully alter behavior through therapy, every child knows that *experience changes behavior*. However, the idea that the *brain* physically changes in response to experience is not as intuitive. Study of brain change in response to behavior was a fairly late fruit of the Italian renaissance. In the late 1700s,

Michele Vicenzo Malacarne, an Italian anatomist, described disparity of cerebellar size in trained animals compared to untrained controls (Zanatta et al., 2018). His work, however, did not find widespread traction in medicine, which would not find broad interest in brain tissue for at least a century.

William James introduced the idea of *plasticity of behavior* in his landmark 1890 work *The Principles of Psychology* but did not apply it to brain physiology per se. Santiago Ramón y Cajal was a near contemporary of James, although his work (at the time) would have seemed worlds apart. Ramón y Cajal, a Spanish physician and artist, examined specially prepared brain tissue microscopically and suggested that as a nervous system reaches maturity, its cellular structure changes in a way reflective of the individual's experience and learning (Ramón y Cajal & de Carlos, 2020). Researchers including Jerzy Konorski (1948), a Polish neurophysiologist working in the first half of the twentieth century, began to unite the ideas of psychologists like James and physiologists like Ramón y Cajal. Konorski was one of the first scientists to use the term "neural plasticity," but at the time it was mostly in the framework of development and maturation, rather than an ongoing phenomenon throughout an individual's life.

Plasticity in *adulthood*—as a mechanism of everyday learning and change—was not yet a popular idea. It may seem obvious to us now that neuroplasticity persists into adulthood. The early reluctance to assume continued neuroplasticity, however, proved useful: Patterns and programs that the brain uses to mature and develop are not always the *same* patterns and programs it uses to learn associations and information from later childhood through senescence. Understanding how the mechanisms of change differ through the stages of life is important in clinical practice: Disordered brain mechanisms of change in childhood have different implications for psychopathology than disordered brain mechanisms of change in adulthood.

A modern understanding of the brain, and of neuroplasticity, emphasizes the brain's adaptive and predictive prowess (Steffen et al., 2022). The human brain is powerfully equipped to adapt to its environment. Harkness et al. (2014) have argued that clinical behavioral medicine should incorporate a review of the brain's adaptive systems, specifically those that model reality, detect short-term danger, analyze long-term cost–benefit trade-offs, acquire resources, and protect an individual's agenda. Each of these systems is inherently plastic and ever-changing, and this dynamic, multidimensional neural landscape is where effective psychotherapy functions.

How Can an Understanding of Neuroplasticity Benefit Psychotherapy?

Much of behavioral pathology can be traced to mechanisms of neuroplasticity. Likewise, much of the impact of evidence-based behavioral interventions can also be traced to those same mechanisms of neuroplasticity. In this chapter, we will briefly introduce neuroscientific principles of neuroplasticity that underlie both the etiology of mental illness and its responsiveness to psychotherapy as well as, incidentally, to at least some psychopharmaceuticals. Understanding how brain tissue changes because of experience can help us to better identify our clients' needs and predict how they may respond to different interventional approaches.

Networks, Patterns, and Principles of Neuroplasticity

Broadly defined, neuroplasticity includes any change to the brain no matter how ephemeral: Your sense memory for the previous few words on this page, for example, is stored in a brief, but real, representation in your visual and language systems. More narrowly defined, neuroplasticity refers to reorganization (and sometimes growth) of components of neural networks, from the gross anatomical level (in cases of cortical remapping) to the sub-cellular (modification of synapses, the connections between neurons) (Elimari & Lafargue, 2020).

Neuroplasticity originally found traction in studies of learning and memory, but an increased understanding of these processes has fueled the realization that *any* brain adaptation shares similar mechanisms—from memorizing facts for school to forming a chemical dependence; from developing strong associations with the smell of Grandma's house to becoming hypervigilant to explosive noises after a car crash; from improving on the piano through practice to developing a trigger for panic attacks.

Neuroplasticity in Childhood and Adolescence: A Sculpture, not a Painting

It's tempting to intuit a model of neural development as an additive process, building up neurons and connections as needs arise and as learning occurs. However, it's more instructive to think of early neural development as a subtractive process, chiseling away superfluous connections and honing the contours of useful processes. Fetal neural development is characterized by massive neural proliferation. A newborn infant arrives full of potential, quite literally: they will have upwards of one-hundred billion neurons, each of which can have up to tens of thousands of connections. By the time a child is approximately a year-and-a-half old, they have their full complement of neurons, and every neuron you are using to read this has been your companion since before that time. (Evidence is mixed about neurogenesis, or growth of *new* neurons, in adult humans, but if it occurs, it is likely to be exceptionally limited, and not a major component of neuroplasticity in most parts of the brain).

However, you don't have all the neurons you once had. Visualize how an infant moves: When it moves one small set of muscles, it moves its whole body. The flinch of a finger leads to the flinch of the whole arm, or even, earlier on, the whole torso and contralateral arm. This is not because the infant's motor system does not have enough neurons or enough connections. Rather, it has many motor neurons with thousands of connections across wide muscle groups. It's not particularly useful, though, for the behavior of every neuron to activate so many muscle fibers. Some of those connections are not only superfluous or redundant, but counterproductive to finely controlled, goal-directed movement. Some connections, or *synapses*, will need to be pruned. Cells that end up with no useful synapses will, themselves, need to be culled.

Indeed, each connection is in competition with the others for survival. Each cell in a nervous system is pre-programmed to die, almost as if there is the assumption that a cell's behavior will be counterproductive unless it proves its worth. Programmed cell death is called *apoptosis*. For a neuron to survive, it must receive *trophic factors*— signals which turn off the apoptosis program. These trophic factors are released in active, productive synapses. Cells that have connections that are used purposefully and effectively will receive trophic factors, and apoptosis will be switched off. Cells that are not participating in effective synapses will undergo apoptosis. As you visualize an infant growing and developing gross and fine motor skills, becoming a toddler and then a confident walker, or refining the scrawl of their initial doodles into artwork, what you are visualizing is the enormous but unrefined network of neurons and synapses being pared back to that which is specific, targeted, and useful. The child's motor development is like a sculpture being liberated from marble, not a painting built on a blank canvas.

While it's relatively easy to visualize how this process works for motor skills via neuron–muscle fiber pruning, the same process is happening with neuron–neuron connections all throughout the nervous system. Cognition, emotion, language, and memory can all be visualized metaphorically as the jerky, overly broad movements of an infant being pared into almost infinitesimally specific cognitive programs. The same artist who can draw photo-realistically as an adult once doodled as a toddler; the same adult with refined and sophisticated emotional and cognitive programs had broad, messy cognitive and emotional reactions as a child. This maturation process continues for years, even decades. For example, apoptosis of cells which are not receiving trophic factors continues in the prefrontal lobe through early adulthood. This isn't *disordered* cell death, like that which results from disease or injury, but rather a final sanding of the curves of the sculpture.

Not only do connections become more refined and targeted as a child matures, each connection, or synapse, also becomes more sophisticated and nuanced. At birth, many of a baby's neurons are connected through *electrical synapses*, which operate quickly but bluntly. It is difficult or impossible to modulate these synapses. If one cell is activated, the cells it is electrically coupled to will also be activated. This is useful for tissues like the heart and gut, which need to have all their cells behaving in concert to pump fluid or digestive matter. It's also useful for a developing nervous system trying to establish itself and accomplish a few, broad goals. It's less useful for a system that needs to have almost infinitely nuanced ways to modulate information depending on context and need. Over time, most of a child's surviving neural electrical synapses will be replaced by *chemical synapses,* which have several advantages. They can be fine-tuned in their function according to the precise needs of the moment. They can be turned off when they aren't needed, and emphasized when they are. They can have larger or smaller effects depending on context and timing. And, perhaps most importantly, they are built for continued learning.

Developmental Neuroplasticity and Stress

Understanding the process of maturation of connections and cells in early development as opposed to adulthood, however, has critical implications in psychopathology. Mechanisms of early development underlie the outsized risk of adverse childhood experiences (ACEs). A child who experiences deprivation at home, for example, will strengthen connections between the experience and the context, and readily lose latent connections between concepts that aren't consistently linked, like home and safety. In many ways, this is the learning and development system doing its job. It doesn't mean that there was anything "wrong" with the physiology of the child's brain; rather, the physiology didn't learn that home and safety were linked concepts because in the child's environment they weren't.

If mechanisms of neuroplasticity and learning stayed constant through childhood and adulthood, then simply replacing the child's environment with a safe one should give the brain an opportunity to readily re-learn linked concepts or to un-learn old linkages. Unfortunately, there are two complications to this approach. First, the mechanisms of neuroplasticity change dramatically through childhood and into adulthood. The apoptosis, or pruning, process is nearly complete by adulthood (although some continues in the frontal lobe into the mid- to-late-twenties). Later modifications will have to come through changing the function of the cells that are left. Second, ACEs and environments trigger *stress responses*, which have dramatic effects on neuroplasticity and learning—often, not for the better.

When an individual experiences toxic stress, their body increases production of messengers such as norepinephrine, epinephrine (adrenaline), and cortisol. These messengers have key functions for health; we couldn't survive without them. Not only are they essential to maintaining metabolism and basal functioning at all times, but surges of these messengers provide important power to help remove ourselves from stressful environments. For example, they can help divert blood to muscles of the arms and legs, to run away from a threat, and they can speed up our heart and breathing to supply the oxygen this demands. Of course, these functions are more helpful when faced with a stressor that you can actually run away from—like our ancestors may have faced with saber-toothed tigers. They're less helpful for stressors that can't reasonably be escaped, like an abusive home, poverty, or a stressful job. They also are not as useful for prolonged biological stressors such as chronic pain, illness, or hunger. Nevertheless, as our ancestors did, we still get surges of these messengers when stressed.

Bruce S. McEwen (2017) coined the term *allostatic load* to describe the body's efforts to maintain homeostasis and safety during stress, and *allostatic overload* to describe a system overwhelmed by chronic stress adaptations. Children and adults can both benefit from the presence of stressors and the stress response. Stress that is both time- and magnitude-limited can help children learn and acquire new skills, particularly those that can be useful for high-stakes situations later. However, stress that is too much or lasts too long can disorder learning. Infants and young children who have high cortisol levels also show attenuated electrical activity in their brains during memory formation, and corresponding poorer memory recall. Children with increased cortisol may also have impaired attention and self-regulation, which can exacerbate stressful situations and impair the ability to respond to them functionally and learn from them.

ACEs, then, can lead to lifelong behavioral and psychiatric implications both by leading to maladaptive learned patterns and by stress disordering neuroplasticity itself.

Like all metaphors, the sculpture analogy is limited. The "sculpture" is dynamic and ever-changing throughout adulthood. While the process of apoptosing neurons that do not receive enough trophic factors begins neonatally and lasts through an individual's early adulthood, it ceases to be a major contributor of change later in adulthood. Fortunately, there are other mechanisms of change, which also began in utero but persist throughout adulthood. These are grouped together under the term *Hebbian modification*.

Neuroplasticity of Continued Change: Teamwork Makes the Memory Work

Obviously, and thankfully, learning continues past our early twenties. Aside from synaptic and neural pruning, you've also been *strengthening your useful connections* since you first had synapses. Neuroscientists call this process *Hebbian modification,* and often first learn it with the rhyme "*neurons that fire together wire together/ neurons that fire out of sync lose their link*" (Hebb, 1949; Shatz, 1992). Note that it is not "*strong neurons grow stronger/ weak neurons grow weaker.*" As we will see, neuroplasticity is based on *cooperativity* of multiple cells within a circuit—truly, the goal is to "fire *together.*"

To visualize Hebbian modification, imagine a neuron. Assign that neuron a meaning: When this neuron is active, it means something specific—perhaps a perception, or a component of an emotion or an abstract concept. (Note that this is a simplification, and in truth, it would probably take several or even many neurons to encode this perception or concept. We will reduce it to a single neuron for simplicity.)

Now think of the various types of information this neuron might need in order to be active. For example, perhaps this neuron is active when you are perceiving pancakes. Some elements that might contribute to the recognition of pancakes include certain smells, tastes, visual stimuli, emotional context, or language. Neurons "meaning" these attributes, but not individually meaning "pancake," would all need to communicate with the "pancake" neuron. It wouldn't be useful if the "pancake" neuron were active whenever it got a single input, such as the visual stimulus of a golden-brown circle. Instead, it should be active when there is sufficient input of different types of information. Each of these individual connections will be strengthened *when they work together*—when there is the smell of butter and maple syrup, Saturday mornings, the soft carbohydrate, grandmother visiting. These things together may activate the "pancake" neuron, and when they're all active together and successfully contribute to the recognition of "pancakes," each individual contributory connection with the "pancake" neuron will be strengthened.

An errant connection that does *not* participate in consistent activation of the postsynaptic neuron will instead be actively *weakened*. Perhaps the ketchup your brother put on pancakes once? At first, that connection may be part of the recognition network, but as it continues to be inconsistently present with the rest of the factors, the connection between "ketchup" and "pancake"—and the connections between neurons underlying those concepts—will weaken and disappear.

Pancakes are a benign example, but we can certainly relate this system to more consequential experiences. *Any* elements that coexist in a person's life as consistent sets that lead to consistent outcomes will "wire together." For example, a person experiencing violence at the hands of a domestic partner may come to associate their smell, voice, or body type with pain and abuse. Later, they may have trouble trusting a person with a similar smell, voice, or body type. This is not because they don't consciously recognize that it is a different person but because they have a "wired together" circuit that is activated with the presence of a sensory trigger and which will activate many cognitive components, including a fear response. Another person who has often heard that they are worthless may "wire together" the memory of that voice with any associated perceived failure, no matter how objectively trivial. The cognitive distortions a psychotherapist treats daily often arise from factors that have been "wired together" through bad experience.

The previous example of an abused spouse may be an obvious, if tragic, example. Many of our clients with panic disorders have a story that is harder to understand, but actually follows the same pattern. Panic disorder is not well understood neuromechanistically, but a clearer picture is beginning to emerge. Often, an *initial* "panic attack" does not arise because of any unrecognized or latent fear in the individual. Instead, it may be an idiopathic (or "fluke") discharge of the sympathetic division of the autonomic nervous system, the "fight, flight, or fright" system that is part of the stress response and involves heightened heart rate, blood pressure, and breathing. This initial—and unprovoked—discharge of the sympathetic system is most likely to arise in situations where the individual is alert and attentive—when the sympathetic system was a little active, but not necessarily when they were overtly stressed. Having a sudden *bodily* stress reaction, however, is *cognitively* stressful. This is consistent with the James-Lange model of emotion, which posits that our conscious perception of emotion follows our bodily expression of it. The brain's learning system ascertains that this situation must be highly important to have had such a profound—and scary—response, and the panic response quickly becomes conditioned to follow the environment in which it initially occurred. Now, the individual has associated panic with getting in a car, being on a bridge, or going to their place of worship—not because any of these were initially anything particularly special, but because they were present when a disordered bodily event occurred, and now the brain has "wired them together."

Patients presenting in a medical clinic can often be defensive about an initial panic attack—"I'm *not* scared, I did *not* panic, I think this was a heart attack" or "don't tell me it was all in my head! My head is fine!" Later, they may have trouble articulating *why* a certain trigger is associated with their panic attacks, or they may have retroactively formed a narrative to explain it. Helping them recognize that they may not, in fact, be "scared" of something for its own sake, but rather avoiding *panic itself* by avoiding what has been conditioned to link with said panic, may be empowering—and ultimately more neurobiologically sound than chasing down some latent distaste for cars or churches.

One helpful example is a common chain of events in night-time panic and insomnia. This can be a devastating cycle, with night-time panic leading to insomnia leading to poor daytime functioning, additional stress, and poor health behaviors. The initial domino to fall may be something as non-psychiatric as obstructive sleep apnea—soft tissues collapsing over the airway and interfering with breathing during sleep. A patient may startle awake from an apneic event with increased heart rate, breathing, and blood pressure, and their brain may in turn interpret this not as "my airway was blocked, so my heart had to speed up to get oxygen everywhere it needed to go" and instead as "panic!" The individual may then learn to associate sleep with panic and then fear bedtime itself. The dominos begin to fall. An understanding of the neuroplasticity training their brain to associate one thing with another can help us encourage such a patient to seek treatment for the apnea.

One final point has profound clinical relevance. It is not the *initial strength* of a connection that matters, it is its *cooperativity* with surrounding connections. A stimulus doesn't necessarily need to be a major part of what produces a stress response to become almost indelibly linked with it. Instead, it simply needs to be present with enough other stimuli to, all together, trigger the stress response. A seemingly minor aspect of the stimulus can become strongly linked with stress in one of two ways. First, it may be present with such a powerful trauma that even one occurrence is enough to associate all aspects of the experience with the trauma. Think of a sexual assault victim who associates the color of their assailant's shirt with their trauma. Second, it may be *consistently* present across lesser, but chronic, adverse experiences. Think of a victim of childhood verbal abuse who associates the smell of their parent's cologne with bullying and belittling. In neither case was the stimulus itself "a fault;" the colored shirt did not assault the victim and the cologne did not belittle the child. However, as consistent parts of the trauma experience, they can become strongly linked with the learned, "wired together" memory. They can even become powerful entry points into relived memory, regardless of their initially minor contribution to the trauma.

It is like athletes on the roster of a championship team being awarded the championship regardless of their playing time or their contribution to the final score. They could have scored no points and nevertheless be crowned as champions, with the attendant rings, pennants, or raises. The star of the losing team may have contributed heavily to the score, but if it was not the winning score, they would not get the championship. A strong connection that does not work cooperatively, or in concert with, other connections will over time be weakened. A weak connection that is consistently part of a collaboration will be strengthened.

Understanding that a stimulus becomes a powerful learned trigger due to its consistent presence during trauma, rather than its initial import, is important. It's also important to remember how this works for seemingly positive factors in the patient's life. While something benign, like the color of a shirt, may become part of a conditioned trauma network, so too can something seemingly positive. Think of a rape that occurred in a "good school with good teachers." Attributes of a situation that some people have associated with positive outcomes may be linked to negative outcomes in a traumatized individual. Further, a positive aspect of a person's life may not directly help counteract the effect of forming strongly learned negative responses if they are not occurring consistently during those traumas. Perhaps, for example, a patient has a strong and supportive relationship in their home life. However, when they go to work, they are consistently exposed to trauma. The presence of a positive presence outside of the complex of stimuli associated with the trauma does not necessarily counteract the powerful injury of the trauma, because it was not an aspect of the trauma itself. We should not mistake the presence of a positive factor in a client's life with a free pass out of trauma. Indeed, risk for poor outcomes in many modalities increases with trauma "dose" (Anda et al., 2006).

Neuroplasticity Works Within and Across Networks

How do we synthesize trophic-factor neural development in infancy and childhood with Hebbian neuroplasticity occurring throughout life? Neurons can't "wire together" if they don't "fire together" in the first place, which implies that neurons must develop with some built-in connectivity, independent of experience and use. As neural proliferation occurred in the developing fetus, these billions of cells sent out axons and made connections with broadly targeted areas, forming *pathways* for the senses and motor control and *networks* for perceptual, cognitive, emotional, and behavioral programs. All later development occurs within this inborn architecture. These built-in brain networks connect functional modules in useful ways. For example, visual recognition centers are connected to language centers so that we can identify objects—and these connections are established well before a baby opens his eyes or hears words. In a separate pathway, visual centers are connected to movement and spatial centers so that they can learn to localize and interact with objects.

In fact, networks in general exist to predict likely outcomes based off conceptual inputs. A child learns that if they see a bumpy, mottled green thing with bulging eyes and bent legs, it's likely someone will say the word *frog*. These neurons fire together and wire together. Plastic changes aren't erratic; they follow these predictive brain networks (Friston, 2010). *And since brain networks exist to predict outcomes, errant plastic changes lead to errant predictions.*

Understanding some of these major networks can help us understand and predict the consequences of changes and learning. For example, several behavioral pathologies, including anxiety and depression, appear to involve changes to the *default mode network* (DMN) (Cieri & Esposito, 2019). Disorders characterized by psychosis involve functional changes in *perceptual networks*. Cognitive and negative symptoms of schizophrenia and schizoaffective disorders track with changes to *attentional networks* and *reward networks*. Altered *Theory of Mind* processes are associated with changes in the connections between areas that relate interpretation of language to memory (Bitsch et al., 2019). Obsessive-compulsive disorder (OCD) involves changes to a cognitive and behavioral control network, the *basal nuclei network*. Changes to other areas of this same network can also produce symptoms as varied as Parkinsonism and chemical dependence.

An Interesting Case: The Default Mode Network

Neuroscientists have been studying brain networks since the advent of functional neuroimaging. However, until recently, scientists would focus on what was happening in the brain when a test subject was asked to do something specific (a "task") such as looking at a visual stimulus, listening to auditory cues, answering questions, solving problems, or thinking about something specific. You've probably seen pictorial representations of data like this—the brain "lighting up" when a person is asked to do a task. In reality, all of the brain is working all of the time, and the "lighting up" you see is thought to reflect *differential* or *increased* activity of those areas during the task beyond their normal activity. A person with open eyes will have constant activity in their visual centers, but if presented with a complex system and the instructions to carefully focus on it, there will be *increased* activity of visual areas, and this will be shown in an fMRI summary image as "lighting up."

What the brain is doing when it's not asked to do anything else wasn't considered an interesting question until the twenty-first century. Pioneers of *resting state fMRI* focused on the areas of the brain that seemed to be *more* active when the patient was not asked to do any particular task. This wasn't an intuitive line of inquiry for some scientists, who assumed that "baseline" activity, or mental activity without assignment, should simply show "baseline" brain activity. This didn't turn out to be the case. Instead, there are "task negative" networks, meaning networks that are primarily active in the absence of externally defined tasks, including during periods of wakeful rest and/or attention toward self-oriented and social cognition.

One such "task negative" network is the *DMN*. The DMN is of particular interest to mental health practitioners because changes in the DMN have been implicated in several behavioral pathologies, including anxiety and depression. The activity of the DMN is associated with the subjective state of mind wandering and is suppressed for goal-directed, externally oriented cognition characterized by activation of "task-positive" networks such as dorsal and ventral attention networks (Anticevic et al., 2011). What is the DMN doing if it is suppressed during "tasks?" To understand this, we need to understand the limitations of "task-negative" and "task-positive" terminology, which fails to fully reflect the coordination of these sets of networks. The brain is not a binary toggle switch, interacting with its environments using its attention networks—or not. In reality, DMN functions are never turned off; instead, these functions are carefully enhanced or attenuated depending on need (Raichle, 2015). Rather than use a framework that considers only externally directed cognition as "task," the interplay between DMN and attention networks reflects shifts between internal and externally motivated tasks, both of which are important for survival and both of which are subject to evolutionary pressures (Yeshurun et al., 2021).

In other words, the DMN is one of many networks that cooperate and trade off activity depending on context and the demands of the moment. Even when there are no tasks that demand externally directed cognition, there are internally motivated tasks. Internally motivated tasks may involve processing of signals indicating physical health, planning and prioritizing, reflecting on experience and processing what it means, reflecting on issues of selfhood, and learning predictive patterns associated with emotion and cognition. A disordered DMN may lead to impairment of all these functions. A review of this list of internally motivated tasks should seem familiar to someone who has treated depressed patients, who often have poor health behaviors and lack the motivational cues for adaptive behaviors such as exercise and healthful eating, or who find planning and prioritizing or reflection painful or impossible (Hamilton et al., 2015).

Ultimately, the DMN is a predictive machine. It must (a) process and synthesize context and stimulus; (b) determine the internally directed needs of the situation; (c) plan an approach to meet those needs based on its prediction models; (d) gather data about the outcome of those approaches; (e) learn which approaches work to meet those needs and which don't; and (f) update prediction models to better meet ongoing or emergent needs. Clearly, the DMN must be a highly *plastic* area of the brain in order to learn and improve its predictive models. It is not surprising that it should be particularly susceptible to learned trauma or stress-influenced pathology of neuroplasticity. In turn, the fact that symptoms of stress- and trauma-influenced disorders, such as depression and anxiety, reflect impairment of the DMN makes logical sense. In fact, changes in DMN and attention-network cooperativity or reciprocity are associated with maladaptation, including affect dysregulation and affective disorders (Beucke et al., 2014; Tozzi et al., 2021).

Errant Neuroplasticity Leads to Errant Predictive Networks

The DMN is not the only network involved in prediction. In fact, all brain networks can be characterized as prediction circuits for different circumstances and needs. In aggregate, the brain receives sensory input, analyzes possible courses of action, and predicts the sensory input it is likely to receive for each of these courses of action. These predictions enable the selection of a course of action that is statistically likely to be beneficial in reducing the allostatic load.

The goal of neuroplasticity in these circuits is to minimize prediction errors. If a course of action results in unpredicted outcomes, the brain is built to update its beliefs to make sense of its new observations. Neuroplasticity becomes errant when it fails in minimizing prediction errors. Therefore, neuroplasticity can be errant either because of inherent pathology of neuroplastic processes, perhaps involving the stress response, *or* because it is trying to learn from unhelpful stimuli. Errant pathology from either cause, or a combination of the two, will impair the brain's ability to make effective, adaptive predictions. Impaired predictions lead to worse behavioral outcomes, which may in turn increase risk factors for errant neuroplasticity. This is the cycle of the neurobiology of psychiatric illness.

Monoaminergic Systems and Neuroplasticity

Many effective strategies for the treatment of depression, such as the use of selective serotonin reuptake inhibitors (SSRIs) or exercise, may work through supporting or enhancing neuroplasticity (Gourgouvelis et al., 2017). These treatment approaches likely target a different kind of network—those characterized by unique neurons using particular neurotransmitters, such as dopamine and serotonin. These are often called "diffuse modulatory systems" because a high dopaminergic or serotonergic state modulates activity of a broad—but predictable—array of brain structures. A high serotonergic state or adrenergic state (norepinephrine) would likewise modulate activity of their distinct array of structures and neuron types. An essential characteristic of these monoamine systems is their role in *learning*. Simplistically, dopamine, serotonin, and norepinephrine help the brain to learn to predict and respond to the environment. Dopamine helps the brain learn to predict motivationally relevant information. Serotonin helps the brain learn to usefully interpret consistent and normalized sensory stimuli, and norepinephrine helps the brain to acutely learn from novel stimuli.

Pharmaceutical treatments for disorders as wide-ranging as Parkinson's disease, psychosis, addiction, anxiety, OCD, and depression often focus on enhancing or attenuating the activity of these neurotransmitters. For example, evidence suggests that schizophrenia is associated with hyperactivity of some networks involving dopamine ("dopaminergic") neurons. Antipsychotics act directly to reduce the activity of dopamine. However, it would be reckless to conclude that schizophrenia *is* "too much dopamine." Instead, it is *errant activity of larger networks* that include dopamine neurons. Similarly, characterizing depression as a lack of serotonin isn't neuroscientifically robust. Instead, there are likely to be differences in the neuroplasticity of networks *that include serotonin neurons.* Treating depression as a "lack of serotonin" addresses only *some* of the physiologic consequences of the root problem.

Every network is different, and it is reckless to overapply the pattern of one to the patterns of another. However, it is instructive to examine why depression is better modeled as changes in a network involving serotonin and/or similar monoamine neurotransmitters rather than as a "lack of serotonin." If depression were a "lack of serotonin," then emergently supplying the brain with serotonin should quickly and readily treat its symptoms. The good news is that we have excellent ways to quickly supply the brain with serotonin using SSRIs. This class of medications, which include most first-line antidepressants on the market today, works by keeping serotonin available in synapses for longer. SSRIs do this very quickly and very effectively in most people. Serotonin levels in the synapses rise significantly in the minutes following administration of an SSRI. However, it takes weeks to months to see a clinical benefit to symptoms! (Compare this to administering a substance that has a similar mechanism of action, but for the neurotransmitter dopamine, such as cocaine. It has tremendous and immediate behavioral effects. However, we do not recommend cocaine for any therapeutic use.)

The fact that SSRIs are often effective in spite of a long delay reflects that depression isn't a "lack of serotonin." Rather, it is a difference in the functionality of a network that *uses* serotonin. Increasing the availability of serotonin in the network through time probably modifies its neuroplasticity, or its ability to develop, learn, and change. This underscores what the evidence shows: antidepressants are effective in many people, and psychotherapy is effective in many people. Antidepressants in conjunction with psychotherapy are particularly effective. This may be because SSRIs likely support neuroplasticity of key networks, and psychotherapy helps people to learn more effective and useful patterns of response.

Not all drugs that are effective treatments for depression, anxiety, OCD, and related disorders work through serotonin. Medications that intervene with any monoamine may show clinical efficacy, and many available and effective options work in differing ratios on serotonin, norepinephrine, and dopamine reuptake. Newer treatment options, such as ketamine or hallucinogens, work on monoamines but often in radically different ways, even in ways that seem counterintuitively opposed, than reuptake inhibition. The fact that some patients respond to different ratios of serotonin, dopamine, and norepinephrine effects may reflect a difference in what is leading to their pathology in the first place. At present, the choice of monoaminergic antidepressant or anxiolytic is largely a game of (often prolonged) trial and (often excruciating) error. There is some evidence that response to antidepressants runs in families. In the future, we may be better able to target choice of medication based on genetic and environmental risk and symptomatic presentation. This area may be fertile ground for rapid advancement. Some of the breathtakingly fast improvements in artificial intelligence engineering, for example, have come about by (intentionally or not) mimicking the systems' ability to balance different varieties of learning and prediction (motivational, predictive, stochastic) much like the monoamines do. Perhaps these models will be useful to model pharmaceutical and psychotherapeutic interventions as well.

As a final takeaway about monoaminergic systems, we must try to harvest our own neuroplasticity to unlearn historical misconceptions about monoamines and to update our associations. It is useful to remember that serotonin isn't "happiness." Instead, serotonin, working in networks, facilitates healthy interpretation of an environment. Dopamine, by itself, isn't "reward," but facilitates productive learning of motivational cues. And norepinephrine probably isn't "excitement," but enables learning from novel, fluid environments. A therapy provider can likely identify cases where each of these three, or a combination, is implicated in their client's distress.

Examples of Predictive Networks and Their Susceptibility to Errors in Neuroplasticity
Sensorimotor Systems

Motor (movement) systems are good examples of predictive networks; they analyze a variety of potential motor programs to evaluate which is most likely to achieve a certain goal. For this reason, they are reliant on sensory systems to provide information about context and about the success of the motor program. Successful movement depends on the ability of sensorimotor systems to learn and change because of new sensory input. Individuals who are deaf, but who have intact language centers, motor control centers, and vocal cords, may be impaired in developing natural speech. Individuals with normal motor centers and muscles but damaged proprioception (sensation of limb and joint position and movement) are *ataxic*, meaning they have profound problems with motor coordination. These examples reflect difficulty not with the function and control of muscles themselves, but with sensorimotor prediction and selection of appropriate motor programs. Psychomotor symptoms typical of mood disorders, anxiety disorders, attention disorders, psychotic disorders, and OCD may reflect impairment of sensorimotor systems prediction and neuroplasticity.

Interoceptive Systems

Interoceptive systems are also predictive; they gather information about internal bodily states such as heart rate, blood oxygenation, and gut activity in order to learn and predict which responses (behavioral or neuroendocrine) will help maintain the body within a narrow range of parameters compatible with homeostasis and health. Is eating the best strategy, given the interoceptive information the brain is receiving? Then the brain may prioritize motivated behavior toward food. Is water? Is rest? Interoceptive systems must then learn which strategies were successful, in order to make better predictions (and choices) in the future.

Mood and psychotic disorders are often characterized by disorders in core interoceptive systems, including drive for water, food, and sleep. Consider *psychogenic polydipsia*, characteristic of schizophrenia and characterized by excessive fluid intake unmerited by objective physiological need. Psychogenic polydipsia is poorly understood, but the stakes are high: up to 20 percent of psychiatric inpatients experience it, and the medical complications of the consequent hyponatremia can be devastating (including muscular weakness, confusion, vomiting, tonic-clonic seizure, cerebral edema, coma, cardiac arrest, and death). Individuals with schizophrenia and polydipsia show reduced volume of their insular cortex, a central hub of interoceptive networks. An impaired insular cortex makes it difficult for the brain to properly predict what behavioral programs would treat physiological needs. These deficits may lead to further cognitive symptoms of schizophrenia, such as impaired attention, executive function, and working memory.

Mesocorticolimbic System

The mesocorticolimbic system, often simplistically called the reward system, is predictive. It predicts whether different potential courses of action will result in positive reinforcement or produce an incentive toward continued action. It is highly plastic, as its core functionality is to adapt and learn the value of actions and the stimuli that enable those actions. Addictive substances produce disorder in the mesocorticolimbic system, often by directly interfering with the proper functioning of neurotransmitters and their receptors at different neuroanatomical nodes in the network. Dopamine is a major neurotransmitter within the mesocorticolimbic system. The most potent drugs of dependency radically alter dopamine neurotransmission in the mesocorticolimbic pathway. Chemical dependence is highly comorbid with mood disorders, anxiety disorders, attention disorders, psychotic disorders, and OCD. In fact, mesocorticolimbic system predictivity errors may be a major substrate of OCD (Dichter et al., 2009).

The clinical profiles of medications that intentionally alter mesocorticolimbic function are further evidence of its predictive and learning role. Antipsychotics, which are typically antidopaminergic, treat psychosis with significant efficacy but often worsen cognitive symptoms such as poor working memory. This may reflect an interference with predictive learning of motivational cues.

Interventions in Neuroplasticity

Because psychiatric symptoms reflect neurochemical and neuroanatomical changes in the brain, present developmentally or through neuroplastic modifications, any successful intervention must reflect its own neurochemical and neuroanatomical changes. The ample evidence of efficacy for cognitive behavioral therapy (CBT) is itself evidence that CBT is a *physical* intervention changing functions of mind *because* it changes functions of brain. The field of research bridging the gap between psychotherapy and neurobiological changes is still young and weighted by the inheritance of dualist tensions between "behavioral" research and "neurobiological" research. There's reason for optimism, though, that the fields will continue to come together, and it's no surprise that there is an ever-increasing body of research that shows direct changes to the brain following therapies such as CBT. Experimental evidence for the efficacy of psychotherapy on brain structure and function follows a robust model of why we *expect* to see such changes.

To understand the state of research in neuroanatomical and neurochemical effects of psychotherapy, though, it's important to understand the challenges of this research, and how that affects the sort of work that gets done. First and most obviously, humans aren't lab animals, and we can't subject people to the same biological assays we can use in animal models for medical disease. While animal research has been and still is invaluable for understanding some aspects of psychiatric disease, we can't study the effects of psychotherapy with lab animals. We must live with an unreconcilable trade-off between the impossibility of studying psychotherapy in animal models and the impracticality or unethicality of using extensive biological assays in humans. Secondly, while neuroimaging methods are typically noninvasive and relatively benign, they're expensive as well as time- and effort-intensive. To get meaningful, consistent results, researchers need to collect huge sample sizes and follow up with patients over long time courses. Brain activity changes (often dramatically) from moment to moment for myriad reasons having little or nothing to do with either psychotherapy or psychopharmaceuticals, and these changes can compound over the course of the weeks to months to years needed to understand psychotherapeutic outcomes. Further, important changes in one brain can be lost in the noise of a lot of other, not meaningful, changes, and obscured or lost entirely when averaged with other brains. Looking at a single brain, however, is usually not the answer, because it can do nothing to prove or even suggest causation, nor can it predict changes across a population. Further, being subject to a brain scan can be distressing for anyone, and often even more so for people with psychiatric symptoms such as anxiety. It can also be hard to maintain follow-up on those with psychiatric illnesses.

For these reasons and others, some of the strongest evidence for the efficacy of CBT often comes from either end of the bell curve of our patient populations: those that are relatively healthy and can easily tolerate neuroimaging, are capable of understanding the experimental paradigm, and agree to participate, with little risk of poor outcomes; or those who are extremely ill, have intensive, extensive care, and who have clearer changes on neuroimaging before intervention. Of course, most people who show behavioral evidence of improvement with psychotherapy fall *between* these extremes. This doesn't mean that the findings don't apply to these individuals, just that we must interpret findings with appropriate caution. Many of the mechanisms of illness for the patients we see in our outpatient clinics are similar to mechanisms in sicker individuals, where they are writ large.

Neuroimaging

Neuroimaging offers insight into the cumulative effects of cellular and network changes. Although neuroimaging results are rarely, if ever, reliably *predictive* of psychiatric symptomology (Brooks & Stein, 2015), they make clear that the brain changes along with symptomatic improvement facilitated by psychotherapy (Beauregard, 2014).

It's always been easy for neuroscientists to start their study with fear pathology, and it is among the best understood emotional functions of the brain. Recall that individuals suffering from panic disorder have "wired together" associations between environmental triggers and panic symptoms. When exposed to words associated with their panic trigger, individuals with panic disorder tend to assign those words a negative valence rating and to process them readily in concert with panic symptom words. In other words, their brains are biased toward processing the concepts as negative and panic-inducing. This seems to correlate with activation of the anterior cingulate cortex in the frontal lobe of the brain, an area frequently implicated in mood disorder studies. In research by Yang et al. (2020), individuals with panic disorder had reduced relatedness and negative valence ratings for panic-trigger and panic-symptom words, and they showed less activity in the anterior cingulate cortex, after CBT.

While the anterior cingulate cortex is a likely culprit for errant neuroplasticity in psychiatric disease, it's not the only such area. Individuals suffering from panic disorder with agoraphobia show disordered activity of networks linking the left inferior frontal gyrus with the left hippocampus. Effectively, this likely reflects a heightened linkage between stimulus and *salience* for these individuals. Particularly during times of active panic symptoms, the left inferior frontal gyrus and left hippocampus activity become tightly linked, suggesting runaway feedback from the frontal lobe to the hippocampus—a rut of processing saying "this stimulus is really important!" Individuals with therapist-guided exposure therapy showed increased activation of the hippocampus, but it was decoupled from activity of the left inferior frontal gyrus (Straube et al., 2014). Put behaviorally, the hippocampus could process events without the domineering intervention of the inferior frontal lobe labeling them as hyper-salient. Perhaps you recognize this description from your goals in practice, reframing stimuli to take away their emotional salience and weight. When a psychotherapist successfully decouples a stimulus or environment from a panic response in an individual, they are physically attenuating the linkage in the brain.

Of course, panic disorder with agoraphobia is not the only disorder associated with maladaptive fear processing. Patients experiencing psychosis often show heightened brain responses to threatening stimuli, such as pictures of faces with fearful or angry expressions. Brain networks involved with processing stimuli and predicting negative outcomes in order to produce a fear response include parts of the inferior frontal lobe, insula, thalamus, putamen, and occipital lobe. After patients received CBT for psychosis, focused on processing threats in a less distracting way, these brain responses were attenuated. CBT used the neuroplastic nature of this network to "wire together" elements of stimulus and response that were more productive (Kumari et al., 2011).

Biomarkers and Biofeedback

Of course, it is increasingly clear that while intracranial connectivity is altered in psychiatric disease, how the brain communicates with tissues outside of the cranium may be just as important. While neuroimaging may look through a glass darkly at the physiology of the brain, peripheral biomarkers are more readily accessible. Systems of special interest include the cardiovascular system and the gastrointestinal system. Cardiac biomarkers include blood pressure, heart rate, heart rate variability (HRV), and various molecular biomarkers (C-reactive protein, interleukin 6, and tumor necrosis factor-α, for example). Of these, HRV seems to be the most reliably responsive both to symptomatic status and to psychological treatment (Euteneuer et al., 2022).

Psychopharmaceuticals and Neuroplasticity: A Brief Practical Note

As we have seen, most, if not all, effective antidepressants are likely to work largely through supporting neuroplasticity. Not all clients who can benefit from psychotherapy are good candidates for pharmaceutical intervention. Indeed, psychotherapy alone is a powerful neuroplastic tool. However, for patients who seem to have primary errors of neuroplasticity—who have learned or seem stuck in maladaptive cognitive and behavioral patterns in a way or to an extent beyond what it seems their environment would have taught a healthy mind—antidepressants can be helpful. Indeed, a pharmaceutical that enhances neuroplasticity can have great synergy with psychotherapy. The medication may help the skills and processes learned in psychotherapy to "stick" by facilitating long-term potentiation during treatment.

Conclusion and Re-visitation of the Case Study

Does Alicia suffer from neuropathology? The question seems medical but may ultimately be philosophical. Cognition and behavior sit at the interface between brain and environment, and both brain and environment can disorder cognition and behavior. Brain dysfunction can lead to cognitive or behavioral dysfunction, certainly, but even a healthy brain can produce unhealthy outcomes when it must learn amidst an unhealthy environment. There are several points of process at which disorder can arise. Perhaps Alicia has disordered neuroplasticity that has contributed to mental ruminations and ruts of maladaptive thinking. Or perhaps neurobiologically "healthy" mechanisms have learned unhelpful things from a disordered environment. In reality, it is likely an interplay of both. Fortunately, the therapy provider has powerful tools at their disposal. Psychotherapy, being a neuroplasticity intervention, can help Alicia to unlearn her unhelpful connections and to instead learn helpful and useful cognitive approaches to her environment. Understanding the neurophysiological principles behind psychotherapy goes beyond the academic. It may be helpful for the therapy provider to try to track and parse when their client's patterns of cognition and behavior seem to be learned from a disordered environment and when they arise from disordered perception and interpretation in the first place, or primary problems with learning. Has Alicia learned trauma cues or triggers? Has she had changes in processing of risk and reward cues? Can long-term potentiation help her to learn more useful connections? Perhaps a rudimentary understanding of neuroplasticity can help relieve Alicia of guilt or self-judgment and brighten her sense of her own prognosis. Maybe it can increase comfort levels with the incorporation of a dual pharmaceutical/psychotherapy approach. A more pervasive incorporation of neuroscience into practice can empower client and provider alike.

References

Anda, R. F., Felitti, V. J., Bremner, J. D., Walker, J. D., Whitfield, C., Perry, B. D., Dube, S. R., & Giles, W. H. (2006). The enduring effects of abuse and related adverse experiences in childhood. A convergence of evidence from neurobiology and epidemiology. *European Archives of Psychiatry and Clinical Neuroscience, 256*(3), 174–186. https://doi.org/10.1007/s00406-005-0624-4

Anticevic, A., Repovs, G., Corlett, P. R., & Barch, D. M. (2011). Negative and nonemotional interference with visual working memory in schizophrenia. *Biological Psychiatry, 70*(12), 1159–1168. https://doi.org/10.1016/j.biopsych.2011.07.010

Beauregard, M. (2014). Functional neuroimaging studies of the effects of psychotherapy. *Dialogues in Clinical Neuroscience, 16*(1), 75–81. https://doi.org/10.31887/DCNS.2014.16.1/mbeauregard

Beucke, J. C., Sepulcre, J., Eldaief, M. C., Sebold, M., Kathmann, N., & Kaufmann, C. (2014). Default mode network subsystem alterations in obsessive-compulsive disorder. *The British Journal of Psychiatry: The Journal of Mental Science, 205*(5), 376–382. https://doi.org/10.1192/bjp.bp.113.137380

Bitsch, F., Berger, P., Nagels, A., Falkenberg, I., & Straube, B. (2019). Impaired right temporoparietal junction-hippocampus connectivity in schizophrenia and its relevance for generating representations of other minds. *Schizophrenia Bulletin, 45*(4), 934–945. https://doi.org/10.1093/schbul/sby132

Brooks, S. J., & Stein, D. J. (2015). A systematic review of the neural bases of psychotherapy for anxiety and related disorders. *Dialogues in Clinical Neuroscience, 17*(3), 261–279. https://doi.org/10.31887/DCNS.2015.17.3/sbrooks

Cieri, F., & Esposito, R. (2019). Psychoanalysis and neuroscience: The bridges between mind and brain. *Frontiers in Psychology, 10*, 1790. https://doi.org/10.3389/fpsyg.2019.01983

Dichter, G. S., Felder, J. N., Petty, C., Bizzell, J., Ernst, M., & Smoski, M. J. (2009). The effects of psychotherapy on neural responses to rewards in major depression. *Biological Psychiatry, 66*(9), 886–897. https://doi.org/10.1016/j.biopsych.2009.06.021

Elimari, N., & Lafargue, G. (2020). Network neuroscience and the adapted mind: Rethinking the role of network theories in evolutionary psychology. *Frontiers in Psychology, 11*, 545632. https://doi.org/10.3389/fpsyg.2020.545632

Euteneuer, F., Neuert, M., Salzmann, S., Fischer, S., Ehlert, U., & Rief, W. (2022). Does psychological treatment of major depression reduce cardiac risk biomarkers? An exploratory randomized controlled trial. *Psychological Medicine*, 1–15. Advance online publication. https://doi.org/10.1017/S0033291722000447

Friston, K. (2010). The free-energy principle: A unified brain theory? *Nature Reviews Neuroscience*, 11(2), 127–138. https://doi.org/10.1038/nrn2787

Gourgouvelis, J., Yielder, P., & Murphy, B. (2017). Exercise promotes neuroplasticity in both healthy and depressed brains: An fMRI pilot study. *Neural Plasticity, 2017*, 8305287. https://doi.org/10.1155/2017/8305287

Hamilton, J. P., Farmer, M., Fogelman, P., & Gotlib, I. H. (2015). Depressive rumination, the default-mode network, and the dark matter of clinical neuroscience. *Biological Psychiatry*, 78(4), 224–230. https://doi.org/10.1016/j.biopsych.2015.02.020

Harkness, A. R., Reynolds, S. M., & Lilienfeld, S. O. (2014). A review of systems for psychology and psychiatry: Adaptive systems, personality psychopathology five (PSY-5), and the DSM-5. *Journal of Personality Assessment*, 96(2), 121–139. https://doi.org/10.1080/00223891.2013.823438

Hebb, D. O. (1949). *The organization of behavior: A neuropsychological theory*. Wiley.

James, W. (1890). *The principles of psychology*. Henry Holt and Company.

Konorski, J. (1948). *Conditioned reflexes and neuron organization*. Cambridge University Press.

Kumari, V., Fannon, D., Peters, E. R., Ffytche, D. H., Sumich, A. L., Premkumar, P., Anilkumar, A. P., Andrew, C., Phillips, M. L., Williams, S. C., & Kuipers, E. (2011). Neural changes following cognitive behaviour therapy for psychosis: A longitudinal study. *Brain: A Journal of Neurology*, 134(Pt 8), 2396–2407. https://doi.org/10.1093/brain/awr154

McEwen, B. S. (2017). Neurobiological and systemic effects of chronic stress. *Chronic Stress*, 1, 1–11. https://doi.org/10.1177/2470547017692328

Raichle, M. E. (2015). The brain's default mode network. *Annual Review of Neuroscience*, 38, 433–447. https://doi.org/10.1146/annurev-neuro-071013-014030

Ramón Y Cajal, S., & de Carlos, J. A. (2020). Pedro Ramón y Cajal: The legacy of a neurohistologist, a medical doctor, and a pathologist. *Anatomical Record (Hoboken, N.J. : 2007)*, 303(5), 1189–1202. https://doi.org/10.1002/ar.24137

Shatz, C. J. (1992). The developing brain. *Scientific American*, 267(3), 60–67. https://doi.org/10.1038/scientificamerican0992-60

Steffen, P. R., Hedges, D., & Matheson, R. (2022). The brain is adaptive not triune: How the brain responds to threat, challenge, and change. *Frontiers in Psychiatry*, 13, 802606. https://doi.org/10.3389/fpsyt.2022.802606

Straube, B., Lueken, U., Jansen, A., Konrad, C., Gloster, A. T., Gerlach, A. L., Ströhle, A., Wittmann, A., Pfleiderer, B., Gauggel, S., Wittchen, U., Arolt, V., & Kircher, T. (2014). Neural correlates of procedural variants in cognitive-behavioral therapy: A randomized, controlled multicenter FMRI study. *Psychotherapy and Psychosomatics*, 83(4), 222–233. https://doi.org/10.1159/000359955

Tozzi, L., Zhang, X., Chesnut, M., Holt-Gosselin, B., Ramirez, C. A., & Williams, L. M. (2021). Reduced functional connectivity of default mode network subsystems in depression: Meta-analytic evidence and relationship with trait rumination. *NeuroImage. Clinical*, 30, 102570. https://doi.org/10.1016/j.nicl.2021.102570

Yang, X., Li, Z., & Sun, J. (2020). Effects of cognitive behavioral therapy-based intervention on improving glycaemic, psychological, and physiological outcomes in adult patients with diabetes mellitus: A meta-analysis of randomized controlled trials. *Frontiers in Psychiatry*, 11, 711. https://doi.org/10.3389/fpsyt.2020.00711

Yeshurun, Y., Nguyen, M., & Hasson, U. (2021). The default mode network: Where the idiosyncratic self meets the shared social world. *Nature Reviews Neuroscience*, 22(3), 181–192. https://doi.org/10.1038/s41583-020-00420-w

Zanatta, A., Cherici, C., Bargoni, A., Buzzi, S., Cani, V., Mazzarello, P., & Zampieri, F. (2018). Vincenzo Malacarne (1744-1816) and the first description of the human cerebellum. *Cerebellum (London, England)*, 17(4), 461–464. https://doi.org/10.1007/s12311-018-0932-7

3
Heart Rate Variability in Mental Health and Psychotherapy

Julia Wendt and Julian F. Thayer

In healthy individuals, the heart rate constantly adapts to the current demand depending on their physiological, emotional, and cognitive state. Some of these changes are quite clear to us, for example, an increase in heart rate when we exercise or get scared. Other changes are more subtle and not noticeable for most people, for example, when our heart beats faster on inhalation and then slower again on exhalation. In effect, the interval between heartbeats varies constantly. This temporal variance in the interval between successive heartbeats is referred to as heart rate variability (HRV). Using meta-analyses across a wide range of studies, different research groups showed that poor mental health reliably occurs together with impaired HRV at rest, e.g., in anxiety disorders (Chalmers et al., 2014), posttraumatic stress disorder (Campbell et al., 2019; Ge et al., 2020; Schneider & Schwerdtfeger, 2020), major depressive disorder (Kemp et al., 2010; Koch et al., 2019), borderline personality disorder (Koenig et al., 2016), bipolar disorder (Faurholt-Jepsen et al., 2017), and schizophrenia (Clamor, Lincoln et al., 2016). Based on this extensive empirical evidence, HRV has even been referred to as a transdiagnostic marker of psychopathology (Beauchaine & Thayer, 2015).

While an electrocardiogram (ECG) is the most accurate way to determine HRV, less sophisticated methods such as pulse measurement via a smartwatch also produce quite reliable data (Laborde et al., 2017). This makes HRV an inexpensive, easily accessible, and, as we will show, widely applicable physiological parameter in the field of mental health and psychotherapy. While the relationship between HRV assessed in a resting state and mental health has been reliably shown, the relationship between psychopathology and HRV reactivity, i.e., phasic changes during task processing and/or performance, is far less clear (Beauchaine et al., 2019). Thus, in this chapter, we will focus on the interpretation and application of resting HRV indices in the context of mental health and psychotherapy. For this purpose, we will provide information on the physiological basis of HRV as well as the theoretical underpinnings of its association with mental health and give insight into specific areas of application such as HRV-biofeedback as an adjunct to psychotherapy.

The Physiological Basis of HRV and its Indices

The various indices that can be determined from the collected ECG or pulse data, a sequence of inter-beat intervals, reflect the influence of the two branches of the autonomic nervous system (ANS) on the heart. The sympathetic branch of the ANS, often referred to as the "fight-or-flight" system, activates our body on demand by accelerating the heart rate. The parasympathetic branch, in contrast, is considered the restorative system and decreases the heart rate in times of rest. The parasympathetic effects on the heart, lungs, and various other organs are mediated by the efferent fibers of the vagus nerve. Figure 3.1 shows how sympathetic and parasympathetic dominance affects heart rate and variability between heartbeats. Somewhat counterintuitively, sympathetic influences on the heart are comparatively slow, whereas parasympathetic influences are relatively fast. This speed difference occurs because the two branches use transmitter systems with different signal transmission rates: Once activated, the sympathetic system changes the heart rate on average within four seconds, while the parasympathetic system only needs a fraction of a second. Therefore, the high-frequency (HF) components (0.15–0.40 Hz) in HRV are more likely to be associated with the parasympathetic nervous system, whereas low-frequency (LF) components (0.04–0.15 Hz) can reflect the activity of both ANS-branches.

Those HF- and LF-parameters are determined by decomposing the sequence of inter-beat-intervals into its various frequency components, e.g., using a Fourier transformation. Therefore, these parameters are subsumed under the term frequency-domain parameters, and their power indicates how strongly certain frequencies are represented in the signal. Alternatively, time-domain indices provide different ways to quantify the variability of the intervals between heartbeats in a given time period. The time-domain parameter most commonly used in the mental health field is the root mean square of successive differences between normal heartbeats (RMSSD). HF-HRV and RMSSD are strongly correlated with each other and also

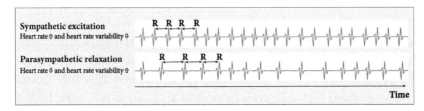

Figure 3.1 Sympathetic excitation and parasympathetic relaxation in a schematic electrocardiogram.

Note: An electrocardiogram (ECG) is used to visualize the different phases of the electrical activity of the heart. The distinct R-wave represents the maximum depolarization of the cardiac muscle (myocardium), during which the myocardial cells' charge becomes more positive. Via electro-mechanical coupling the depolarization triggers a contraction, i.e., the R-wave indicates a heartbeat. The duration between successive R-waves (RR-interval) constantly varies, an observation known as heart rate variability (HRV). Sympathetic activity is associated with higher heart rates and lower HRV, parasympathetic activity is associated with lower heart rates and higher HRV.

with the decrease in mean inter-beat intervals after complete vagal blockade with atropine in a resting condition (Hayano et al., 1991). Thus, both are considered as indices of resting vagally mediated HRV (Laborde et al., 2017). Shaffer and Ginsberg (2017) provide a comprehensive overview of these and other HRV parameters and their analysis methods.

As described above, our heart rate varies with the breathing cycle, an effect called respiratory sinus arrhythmia (RSA). The normal respiratory rate in healthy adults is about nine to twenty-four breaths per minute, i.e., one inspiration every 6.7 to 2.5 seconds, or, expressed in hertz (1/second), has a frequency range of 0.15 to 0.40 Hz. Thus, the RSA corresponds to the HF–HRV parameter during normal respiration. Therefore, depending on the researchers' focus, some parameters, such as RMSSD and HF–HRV, are used as an index of both RSA and vagally mediated HRV. During particularly fast or slow breathing, however, the respiration-related variation in heart rate lies outside of the HF range resulting in a dissociation between RSA and HF–HRV. Therefore and for the sake of clarity, some authors recommend using the term RSA only when referring directly to the changes in heart rate accompanying inhalation and exhalation (Laborde et al., 2017).

Vagally mediated HRV assessed during rest has been associated not only with various mental health conditions in general but also with specific symptoms. A meta-analysis across sixty studies found that perseverative cognitions, i.e., rumination about the past and worries about the future, are associated with lower levels of HRV (Ottaviani et al., 2016). For example, Chalmers et al. (2016) reported that the tendency to worry is associated with robust reductions in resting vagally mediated HRV regardless of whether participants were diagnosed with an anxiety disorder or not. Interestingly, higher resting vagally mediated HRV determined nearly two years before the COVID-19 outbreak even predicted higher feelings of safety and reduced worry during the May 2020 lockdown (Makovac et al., 2021). To better understand this relationship between vagally mediated HRV and perseverative thought processes, Gillie et al. (2014) carried out an experiment during which participants were first instructed to learn a series of word pairs. After successfully learning at least 50 percent of the pairs, participants underwent a phase during which they were instructed to think of the partner word of certain cue words (displayed in green) but to prevent the associated response word from coming to mind for the other half of cue words (displayed in red). In the final phase, the participants' memory was tested for both response word categories, i.e., the ones they were asked to think about in the previous phase as well as the ones they were asked not to think about. Overall, the effort not to think about certain words impaired the recall of those words. However, this suppression was particularly successful in individuals with higher levels of vagally mediated HRV. Gillie and Thayer (2014) and Gillie et al. (2014) interpreted these findings to mean that vagally mediated HRV indicates a person's ability to control unwanted thoughts. More generally speaking, this capacity for inhibitory control allows a person to adaptively respond to changing environmental and internal demands.

The Neurovisceral Integration Model

The neurovisceral integration model (NIM; Thayer & Lane, 2000, 2009) describes how the constant integration of autonomic, attentional, and affective systems enables the necessary adaptation to changing environments and internal states and thereby offers an explanation for the observed relationship between HRV and mental health. To that end, the NIM makes the following assumptions, which are explained in more detail below: (a) The default response to uncertainty is a threat response; (b) Prefrontal cortical (PFC) areas regulate the subcortical brain regions mediating the threat response; (c) An impaired functionality of PFC areas is associated with insufficient subcortical inhibition and results in exuberant threat responses; and (d) HRV is an index of PFC functionality.

Threat as the Default Response to Uncertainty

The NIM assumes that the default response to uncertainty, novelty, and threat is the activating response mediated by the sympathetic nervous system, also known as the fight-and-flight response (Thayer & Lane, 2009). This default threat response shows conceptual proximity to the negativity bias, which describes that negative information is processed with increased priority (Cacioppo & Berntson, 1994). Both, the default threat response and the negativity bias, are explained with an evolutionary perspective, i.e., generally speaking, negative events are more dangerous than positive events are beneficial and negative events tend to unfold more rapidly than positive events (Rozin & Royzman, 2001). This means that to ensure survival, a defensive response must be executed as quickly as possible. Therefore, it makes sense that the defensive response is set up as default and does not have to be initiated in a time-consuming manner if the worst comes to the worst.

Matching its simplicity and face validity, the empirical evidence for the default threat response hypothesis is manifold and will be illustrated here using the example of fear conditioning. According to the theory of classical conditioning, fear acquisition can be described as a new association between a neutral and an unconditioned aversive stimulus that elicits an unconditioned fear response by a joint occurrence of these stimuli (Pavlov, 2010). In human fear conditioning research, the unconditioned aversive stimulus is often an unpleasant electro-tactile stimulus or a sudden loud noise. As a result of the association between the two stimuli, the previously neutral, now conditioned stimulus triggers a conditioned fear response itself. This process explains why, for example, if you have been attacked by a dog (unconditioned stimulus) and understandably panicked (unconditioned response) in the past, the encounter with any dog (conditioned stimulus) can trigger fear (conditioned response). During differential fear acquisition training, one stimulus, the threat cue, is predictive of the aversive stimulus, while another one, the safety cue is not

(Lonsdorf et al., 2017). After training, the two stimuli elicit different responses, one, to the threat cue, resembling a defensive response, the other, to the safety cue, more like an orienting response. However, if you look at the first 250 ms after cue onset, the response to both stimuli resembles a threat response (Weike et al., 2008). In line with the default threat response hypothesis, the authors assume that this observation reflects the rapid activation of the brain regions mediating the threat response, whereas the expression of safety conditioning seems to require more time. But how does the neural mediation of the threat response unfold?

The central brain region mediating the threat response is the amygdala, located subcortically in the medial part of the temporal lobes. Mostly from animal research, we know that the lateral and basolateral nuclei of the amygdala receive not only sensory information from all modalities but also contextual information from the hippocampus and the medial prefrontal cortex (mPFC; Lang et al., 2000). If the integrated information indicates a threat, these nuclei signal the central nucleus of the amygdala (CeA) which in turn projects to different hypothalamic and brain stem areas to initiate the threat response (Lang et al., 2000). The initiated physiological and behavioral responses that follow can be broadly grouped into two classes, either defensive action, i.e., fight or flight, or defensive immobility, also known as freezing. Which response is shown depends primarily on the proximity of the threat and the coping strategies currently available, i.e., the contextual information provided by the hippocampus and PFC (Benarroch, 2012; Fanselow, 2018). Defensive action is initiated when the threat is assessed as manageable, e.g., escapable because the threat is still far away, or possible to overwhelm if the threat does not seem to be stronger than oneself. The fight or flight behavior is then accompanied by a pattern of physiological responses such as hypertension and heart rate acceleration, i.e., a general sympathetic dominance of the ANS (Lang et al., 2000). These physiological changes lead, among other things, to a better blood supply to the muscles and thus to a faster provision of energy, which ultimately increases the probability of survival (Ohman, 1986).

In contrast, defensive immobility, or freezing behavior, is initiated when the threat is assessed as inescapable, e.g., deep visceral pain or a far superior threat (Benarroch, 2012). In this case, the activity of the ANS is characterized by inhibition of the sympathetic and activation of the parasympathetic system resulting in so-called fear bradycardia, i.e., a pronounced slowing of the heart rate. Freezing probably serves on the one hand to avoid detection by the predator, but on the other hand, it is also a state of heightened perceptiveness (Roelofs, 2017). Thus, attentive immobility seems to enable the best possible decision-making even under extreme stress. In addition, the associated slowing down of the blood flow may have the purpose of delaying blood loss in the event of an injury (Alboni et al., 2008). So, all in all, from an evolutionary perspective, it makes sense that our defensive behaviors and the physiological changes that come with them are initiated so quickly, that is, they are built as a default response. In the modern world, however, we are constantly exposed to cues that indicate danger but do not pose a threat to us. For example, when we see violent scenes on television or a lion behind bars at the zoo. So why is it that we do not always react with a full-blown threat response?

Prefrontal Control of Subcortical Activity

The mPFC is part of a network of regions, the *default network*, that is deactivated during task performance but highly active in the resting brain, i.e., when there are no specific demands (Broyd et al., 2009). For example, we were able to show that the processing of a threat signal is associated with a deactivation of the ventromedial PFC (vmPFC), whereas its activity tends to be unchanged during the presentation of the safety signal (Lindner et al., 2015). The mPFC is heavily interconnected with the amygdala and other brain structures involved in the processing of affective information (Broyd et al., 2009). Several mental disorders are associated with alterations in the functional connectivity of the mPFC with subcortical structures, e.g., depression (Northoff, 2016), bipolar disorder (Chepenik et al., 2010), and posttraumatic stress disorder (PTSD; Kunimatsu et al., 2020; Thome et al., 2020). Therefore, we believe that these changes in prefrontal-subcortical interplay lead to a lack of situationally appropriate inhibition of the threat response and, thus, to non-adaptive experience and behavior.

A large body of evidence on the inhibitory influence of the mPFC on the amygdala comes from the study of extinction learning (Milad & Quirk, 2012). During extinction training, a conditioned stimulus as defined above is presented without the aversive, unconditioned stimulus and the conditioned response decreases as a consequence of extinction learning (Lonsdorf et al., 2017). Because the conditioned response can reappear, e.g., in a new context or simply spontaneously, current learning theories assume that new inhibitory associations are learned during extinction that inhibit the old excitatory associations (Bouton, 2004; Myers & Davis, 2006). Studies in animals showed that the vmPFC is particularly necessary for the retrieval of extinction learning (Milad & Quirk, 2012). Translating these findings to human research, Milad et al. (2007) developed a paradigm that allowed them to compare recall of extinguished (now safe) and unextinguished (still threat) stimuli and found that the stronger the activation of the vmPFC, the more an individual was able to inhibit conditioned responding during extinction recall. In other words, PFC functioning seems to be a prerequisite for recognizing safety based on current contextual information.

Impaired Subcortical Inhibition

When inhibition of subcortical structures by the mPFC is chronically impaired, the result is what Brosschot et al. (2017) refer to as "generalized unsafety." In other words, as long as safety signals are perceived, the mPFC inhibits the default threat response. However, this perception of safety signals can be disrupted in several ways. The basic idea of the NIM is that information from different domains is integrated to generate the most appropriate response under the current conditions (Thayer & Lane, 2000, 2009). This explains how, for example, chronic inflammatory processes in the body lead to integrated information indicating unsafety despite safe external circumstances. As a result, chronic inflammatory processes are associated with increased feelings of stress and negative affect (Fournier et al., 2018; Hirten et al., 2021; Pellissier et al., 2014). Affected individuals may then misinterpret these negative feelings because they are not necessarily aware of the inflammatory processes. These misinterpretations may also impact personal relationships and result in less social support for individuals with chronic inflammations (Galvez-Sánchez et al., 2019).

Thus, on the one hand, there may be indications of danger, but we are not aware of them. On the other hand, generalized unsafety may also result from a genuine impairment of inhibition of the subcortical structures that mediate the default threat response. For example, patients with focal, bilateral vmPFC damage show increased amygdala responses to aversive images (Motzkin et al., 2015). Another study shows that patients with generalized anxiety disorder demonstrated reduced vmPFC activation on response to safety signals in a fear conditioning experiment and no differentiation between threat and safety signals (Via et al., 2018). Here, particularly poor threat–safety differentiation was associated with increased worry symptomatology (Via et al., 2018). And yet another study showed that patients suffering from generalized anxiety disorder show altered resting-state functional connectivity between the basolateral amygdala and the vmPFC (Porta-Casteràs et al., 2020). In conclusion, (inappropriate) threat responses in safe environments can occur when the threat information comes from inside the body or when there is impaired functionality of the mPFC and/or its connectivity with subcortical structures mediating the threat response. In the next section, we will elaborate on how this impaired functionality of the brain is reflected in low vagally mediated HRV.

HRV as an Index of PFC Functionality

Evidence for the conclusion that vagally mediated HRV can serve as an index of PFC functionality stems from three areas of research: (a) neuroanatomical research indicating inhibitory efferent pathways from the mPFC to the parasympathetic nervous system (Smith et al., 2017); (b) neuropsychological research demonstrating an association between vagally mediated HRV and performance in executive control tasks (Holzman & Bridgett, 2017; Zahn et al., 2016), and (c) neuroimaging research showing positive correlations between vagally mediated HRV and PFC activity (Thayer et al., 2012).

Central control of cardiac activity occurs through a network of interconnected brain structures, which Benarroch (1993) termed the central autonomic network (CAN). The brain structures involved are distributed across the brain and include the insular cortex, the anterior cingulate gyrus, the amygdala, and the hypothalamus in the forebrain as well as the periaqueductal gray and different nuclei located in the pons and the medulla oblongata in the brainstem (Benarroch, 1993). As outlined in the NIM (Thayer & Lane, 2009), disruption of tonic inhibitory prefrontal control leads to an activation of the CeA. The CeA then activates sympathoexcitatory neurons in the ventrolateral medulla directly as well as indirectly via the inhibition of the nucleus of the solitary tract, which in turn leads to sympathetic activation and a corresponding increase in heart rate. Inhibition of the nucleus of the solitary tract simultaneously leads to reduced activity of parasympathetic neurons in the medulla, i.e., suppression of the parasympathetic nervous system and a corresponding decrease in vagally mediated HRV.

In line with the assumption of tonic prefrontal inhibition of the pathways that regulate cardiac activity, the Wada test results in increased heart rates and reduced vagally mediated HRV (G. L. Ahern et al., 2001). During the Wada or intracarotid sodium amobarbital test, a short-acting barbiturate is injected into one of the internal carotid arteries which supply the brain with blood. As a result, the corresponding hemisphere is deactivated for a few minutes. Increased heart rates and decreased vagally mediated HRV were observed during deactivation of each of the hemispheres, but a little more clearly when the right hemisphere was affected (G. L. Ahern et al., 2001). Other evidence for this inhibitory pathway is provided by Motzkin et al. (2014) who reported that patients with vmPFC damage not only show exaggerated amygdala responses as described above but also reduced resting vagally mediated HRV. Thus, impaired functionality of the PFC and/or altered prefrontal-subcortical connectivity results in both exaggerated threat responses and decreased vagally mediated HRV at rest (Figure 3.2).

In healthy individuals, larger PFC volume and greater thickness are associated with better performance in tests of executive function such as the Wisconsin Card Sorting Test (Yuan & Raz, 2014). And injuries of the vmPFC, in particular, are reliably associated with deficits in decision making and moral reasoning (José et al., 2020). Concurrently, higher resting vagally mediated HRV has been associated with better performance across a wide range of executive function tasks (Forte et al., 2019; Holzman & Bridgett, 2017; Zahn et al., 2016), with the largest effect sizes observed for associations with inhibitory control, i.e., being able to inhibit prepotent impulses to select more appropriate ones (Ottaviani et al., 2019), or attentional control, i.e.,

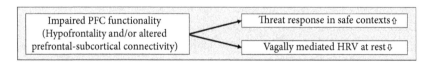

Figure 3.2 Prefrontal functionality, threat responses, and heart rate variability.

Note: Impaired functionality of the prefrontal cortex (PFC) and/or its connectivity with subcortical brain regions is associated with exaggerated threat responses even in safe contexts and lower vagally mediated heart rate variability (HRV) at rest.

being able to direct attention to goal-relevant stimuli and ignore others (Ramírez et al., 2015). Fittingly, aerobic training in the elderly leads to both improvement of performance in executive function tasks and an increase in vagally mediated HRV (Albinet et al., 2010).

Finally, neuroimaging studies show a reliable association between activity in the vmPFC and vagally mediated HRV across tasks (Thayer et al., 2012). In a recent study, Grupe et al. (2020) assessed brain activity during alternating conditions of threat and safety in combat veterans with high and low levels of PTSD symptoms. They found that reduced differentiation of safety and threat conditions was associated with lower vagally mediated HRV at rest and elevated PTSD re-experiencing symptoms. Taken together, these findings support the assumption that vagally mediated HRV can serve as an index of the capacity of the PFC to inhibit subcortical brain regions and, thus, the threat response when it is appropriate because of the current internal and external circumstances.

Beyond Threat: HRV as a Transdiagnostic Marker of Psychopathology

A reduced level of vagally mediated HRV is not only observed in anxiety and stress-related disorders but across a variety of diagnostic groups (Alvares et al., 2016). For example, reduced vagally mediated HRV levels are also found in so-called externalizing disorders such as nicotine and alcohol addicts (Yuksel et al., 2016) and among methamphetamine addicts even in currently abstinent individuals (Henry et al., 2012). Within the psychosis spectrum disorders, both schizophrenia and bipolar disorder are associated with comparably reduced levels of vagally mediated HRV and levels of vagally mediated HRV are predictive of disease severity (Benjamin et al., 2021).

Therefore, Beauchaine and Thayer (2015) hypothesized that vagally mediated HRV indicates a general vulnerability factor, i.e., impaired functionality of the PFC and/or its connectivity with subcortical brain regions, whose co-occurrence with other vulnerability factors such as trait anxiety or trait impulsivity, significantly increases the likelihood of developing a mental disorder. These hypotheses are in line with other, so-called bifactor models of psychopathology (Caspi et al., 2014; Lahey et al., 2012) which assume one latent general factor which reflects variance that is common to all indicators (i.e., disorders) and one or more group factors that reflect additional common variance shared in a subset of indicators (i.e., disorders). In their model, Beauchaine and Thayer (2015) postulate the general vulnerability factor PFC dysfunction as well as the group factors trait anxiety reflecting a vulnerability for internalizing disorders such as anxiety and depression, trait impulsivity reflecting a vulnerability for externalizing disorders such as addiction and conduct disorder,

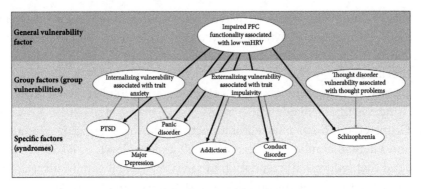

Figure 3.3 General, group, and specific factors in psychopathology.
Note: Based on the high comorbidity observed between mental disorders, bifactor models (see text) that best explain the structure of psychopathological symptoms assessed in longitudinal community studies, and low levels of vagally mediated heart rate variability (vmHRV) observed across diagnostic groups, this model of psychopathology assumes a general vulnerability factor (impaired functionality of the prefrontal cortex and/or its connectivity with subcortical regions indicated by low vmHRV) which interacts with groups factors (vulnerabilities such as trait anxiety and trait impulsivity) to generate specific syndromes (Beauchaine & Thayer, 2015).

and thought problems reflecting a vulnerability for psychotic disorders (Figure 3.3). The authors assume that without this superordinate general vulnerability factor, anxiety and impulsivity would manifest as personality traits rather than as disease factors. Empirical evidence for this assumption comes from studies showing that high vagally mediated HRV can mitigate the effects of other traits on certain functions, behaviors, and experiences. In a recent study, Fantini-Hauwel et al. (2020) were able to show that emotion regulation difficulties were only associated with depressive symptoms when resting vagally mediated HRV was low in a sample of women. That is, high vagally mediated HRV seems to dampen the effect of trait emotion dysregulation on depressive symptoms. Another study demonstrated that vagally mediated HRV modulates the influence of trait anxiety on executive functioning in such a way that participants with low vagally mediated HRV <u>and</u> high trait anxiety show worse attentional control as well as greater risk aversion (Ramírez et al., 2015).

Evidence from different research areas that point to vagally mediated HRV as an indicator of PFC functionality has already been reviewed above. The assumption of PFC functionality as a general vulnerability factor for the development of mental illness is based on several observations. In addition to the abovementioned findings of impaired PFC functionality in anxiety- and stress-related disorders, similar reports exist for depressive disorders, addiction, and schizophrenia. For example, Rock et al. (2014) reviewed studies on executive functions in depressed patients and found moderate deficits independent of their current state (acute or remitted). In another review, cognitive functioning was examined only during the first depressive episode, and here, too, small to large impairments were observed across most cognitive domains (E. Ahern & Semkovska, 2017). While patients showed small improvements in some executive functions after remission of their first depressive episode, impairments in others, e.g., inhibitory control, seem to persist which indicates a phase-independent vulnerability. Furthermore, altered medial prefrontal-brainstem functional connectivity in depressed patients' emotional appraisal seems to be correlated with both HRV and depression severity (Smith et al., 2015).

In addicted individuals, resting functional connectivity between the mPFC and subcortical regions associated with both stress- and reward-processing is reduced (Zhang & Volkow, 2019). The observed altered connectivity seems to be related to both the increased emergence of negative emotions (withdrawal and impaired self-regulation over emotions) and desire for drugs (craving; Zhang & Volkow, 2019), which Clay et al. (2008) refer to as "accelerated 'go' signals and impaired 'stop' signals result[ing] in uncontrolled use despite severe consequences" (para. 1). Furthermore, impaired PFC functionality is not only found in substance use disorders (SUD) but also in other forms of addiction. In their review on neurobiological correlates of internet gaming disorder, Kuss et al. (2018) find that compared to healthy controls, individuals with internet gaming disorder have impaired PFC functioning indicated by reduced gray matter volumes in prefrontal areas as well as indirectly by poorer inhibitory control, working memory, and decision-making capabilities. Further evidence for the relationship between PFC functionality, HRV, and externalizing disorders is the finding that HRV appears to be particularly associated with sustained attention in young adults (Siennicka et al., 2019), an executive function that depends on intact prefrontal-subcortical signaling (Berridge & Spencer, 2016).

The dysconnectivity hypothesis of schizophrenia says that psychotic symptoms are best understood as impaired interactions between brain regions (Friston & Frith, 1995). The authors assume that localized pathophysiology of the PFC (e.g., hypofrontality) may sufficiently explain impaired cognitive functions associated with schizophrenia, that more complex symptoms such as hallucinations or delusions, however, are based on disturbed connectivity between brain regions. Interestingly, when considering the different symptom groups individually, it is mainly the cognitive symptoms of schizophrenia whose severity is related to vagally mediated HRV (Kim et al., 2011). In any case, various authors agree that thought disorders, but also depression, anxiety, autism spectrum disorders, and addiction are based on an impaired functionality of the PFC and its connectivity (Xu et al., 2019). However, impairments of different PFC regions and circuits seem to be associated with different syndromes: Whereas anxiety- and stress-related as well as SUDs appear to be associated with alterations of the vmPFC and its connectivity, depression (Rogers et al., 2004) and schizophrenia (Mwansisya et al., 2017) seem to be associated rather with altered dorsolateral PFC function. Taken together, however, these studies show that impaired PFC functionality is found across diagnostic groups which strengthens the argument for its role as a general vulnerability factor that can be easily assessed using resting vagally mediated HRV as an index.

Application in Research and Practice

Given the described relationship between HRV and mental health, it is not surprising that psychotherapy researchers widely use vagally mediated HRV as an objective index of change in psychotherapy research. In addition, if low resting HRV is determined in patients, specific treatments can be combined with psychotherapy to improve parasympathetic activity. Thus, we highly recommend its use during diagnostics of mental disorders in therapeutic practice. We will explain below how to determine resting HRV. But first, we will review some applications of resting HRV for the prediction of clinical outcome and as an outcome itself in psychotherapy research.

HRV in Psychotherapy Research

Many of the relationships with vagally mediated HRV described above were established using short-term, e.g., five-minute resting HRV measurements. But of course, patients are aware that any assessment taken before and after an intervention is likely meant to test the effect of that intervention. Thus, for intervention studies, the Task Force of The European Society of Cardiology and The North American Society of Pacing and Electrophysiology (1996) has recommended twenty-four-hour measurements to detect stable and expectation-free effects. However, twenty-four-hour measurements necessarily violate the assumption that resting HRV levels are determined under resting conditions. This violation has to be taken into account when dividing the data into interpretable segments. Thus, easier to interpret short-term measurements pre- and post-intervention under comparable conditions, i.e. same time of day and control of confounding variables such as no intense physical training the day before the assessment can be considered an alternative to twenty-four-hour measurements, just with other benefits and pitfalls (Laborde et al., 2017). One has to keep in mind, however, that short-term and twenty-four-hour measurements capture different states and, thus, may yield different results when it comes to outcome assessment in psychotherapy research. In addition, HRV measurements are used both to predict clinical therapy outcomes and as an outcome measure to indicate a positive change in autonomic balance due to psychotherapy.

Soder et al. (2019) compared the effects of standard cognitive behavior therapy (CBT) and a novel treatment to treat co-morbid PTSD and SUD. The standard CBT focused on SUD treatment and included "changing problem thinking, lifestyle balance, increasing nonsubstance activities, enhancing social support, and relapse prevention" (p. 4) but not trauma-related modules. The novel treatment (treatment of integrated post-traumatic stress and substance use; TIPSS) included "psychoeducation regarding PTSD/SUD comorbidity and modules focusing on cognitive-emotional processing of the trauma" (p. 3). They found that higher vagally mediated HRV before treatment predicted a greater reduction of PTSD symptoms following both treatments. In conclusion, patients with lower vagally mediated HRV might be more affected by the general vulnerability factor that goes along with impairments that interfere with the processing of therapeutic content. Or, in other words, the higher regulatory capacity associated with higher vagally mediated HRV may allow patients to process the complex content of therapy more effectively and adjust their behavior accordingly. Very similar conclusions were reached in a recent study by Sigrist et al. (2021), in which they examined the prediction of the clinical outcome when treating patients with adolescent borderline personality disorder with a treatment specifically tailored to risk-taking and self-harm behavior. They found that higher resting vagally mediated HRV before treatment significantly predicted overall clinical improvement during the treatment, irrespective of early life maltreatment and other potentially confounding variables. That is, this study also highlights that low pre-treatment vagally mediated HRV appears to indicate a general vulnerability factor that should be given special attention in psychotherapy.

As mentioned before, one explanation of these findings might be that low levels of vagally mediated HRV may specifically impair the efficacy of treatment methods that rely on the successful activation of inhibitory control. For example, during exposure therapy, we demand a lot of regulative capacity from patients when we ask them to seek out situations and stimuli that trigger fears in them such as going crazy, losing control, or dying. We studied this in a group of patients suffering from panic disorder and agoraphobia who underwent exposure treatment, i.e., over multiple sessions, a therapist guided them to stay in a fear-provoking situation until the fear subsided. Although this treatment was very effective overall (Gloster et al., 2011), we found that patients who had particularly low levels of vagally mediated HRV before treatment were more likely to drop out or to have higher residual symptoms after treatment was completed (Wendt et al., 2018). In this light, it is intriguing that individuals with low vagally mediated HRV also show impairments in extinction learning (Pappens et al., 2014; Wendt et al., 2015, 2019), because extinction learning serves as a laboratory model for exposure-based treatments of anxiety disorders (Craske et al., 2018). As we explained in the section on prefrontal control of subcortical activity, successful extinction learning relies on efficient communication between the vmPFC and the amygdala. Therefore, impaired extinction learning points to impaired PFC functionality and, thus, indicates the presence of this general vulnerability factor.

Other studies focusing on vagally mediated HRV as an outcome of psychotherapy, i.e., investigating whether psychotherapeutic procedures can strengthen the parasympathetic nervous system and establish an autonomic balance, have come to heterogeneous results. For example, one study found an increase in HRV after CBT in patients with panic disorder (Garakani et al., 2009), but another found that HRV remained stable during CBT in a similar group of patients (Mumm et al., 2019). Importantly, the former study included breathing retraining, but the latter did not. Breathing retraining involves slowing the rate of breathing and learning to breathe through the nose. Both techniques stimulate the activity of the parasympathetic nervous system, as we will discuss below. It is therefore quite plausible that CBT has a positive effect on HRV when modules are integrated that directly target a change in the parasympathetic nervous system. In support of this assumption, an effect on HRV was also shown in a study of the impact of a treatment program for alcohol-dependent women that promoted the development of emotion regulation skills and self-care (Buckman et al., 2019), both of which have been associated with increasing HRV before (Mather & Thayer, 2018). In contrast, another recent study found that the decrease in depressive symptoms produced by inpatient treatment of depression was not associated with changes in vagally mediated HRV (Neyer et al., 2021). Importantly, in this study, CBT interventions differed between patients to take into account their individual symptomatology, thus, the patients have not necessarily received a treatment that also addresses the parasympathetic nervous system.

So, in summary, some studies found a change in resting HRV in the course of psychotherapy and that this change was also associated with symptom reduction. However, other studies reported no change in HRV due to psychotherapy. We conclude that some treatments may be suitable to improve specific symptomatology, but not necessarily to improve the general vulnerability factor that can be indexed with vagally mediated HRV. Together with the findings that patients with low levels of vagally mediated HRV may not benefit as much from treatment components that rely on a high capacity of inhibitory control, these results suggest the use of interventions aimed at increasing vagally mediated HRV in advance of these treatment components. We, therefore, recommend determining the vagally mediated HRV level in the diagnostic phase and, in case of established low HRV level, implementing additional treatment methods suitable to increase vagally mediated HRV.

Determining Vagally Mediated HRV Levels

The ECG ensures the most accurate determination of HRV parameters, but this will not be available in most outpatient clinics and psychotherapy practices. Fortunately, especially when determining resting HRV parameters, there is a high agreement between the ECG and affordable measuring devices using breast-belts (Weippert et al., 2010) and even sufficient agreement when estimating HRV from the pulse wave (Schäfer & Vagedes, 2013). Free and easy-to-understand programs are available for processing the data and determining the HRV parameters, e.g., Kubios HRV standard (https://www.kubios.com/hrv-standard/). When measuring HRV at rest, there are a few things to keep in mind to ensure that the HRV values are not subject to the acute influences of sport and diet. In detail, patients should not have done any intensive sports forty-eight hours before the measurement, not have consumed alcohol twenty-four hours before, try to follow a normal sleep routine the night before, and should not have consumed any meals or caffeine-containing drinks two hours before the measurement (Laborde et al., 2017). In addition, short-term physical exertion also has an influence on HRV, so that patients should, for example, better use the elevator if the examination room is on a higher floor. Ideally, multiple measurements should be taken over several sessions so that therapists can arrive at a reliable assessment of HRV levels. Whereas no published cut-off values exist specifically for mental disorders, the first evaluation of vagally mediated HRV as a marker of health risks concludes that for daytime RMSSD, a value of 25 ms and below indicates elevated risk (Jarczok et al., 2019). Accordingly, we recommend offering an intervention aimed at increasing vagally mediated HRV as an adjunct to psychotherapy if the diagnostic workup reliably identified an RMSSD of 25 ms or below.

Interventions Targeting Vagally Mediated HRV

The most investigated methods to increase vagally mediated HRV are exercise interventions, HRV biofeedback, and slow breathing interventions, meditation- and mindfulness-based interventions (MBIs), and supplementation of omega-3 fatty acids. These interventions are usually easy to implement and are therefore suitable as adjuncts to psychotherapy. We discuss HRV biofeedback in more detail in the next section. First, however, we shortly address the remainder of these low-intensity interventions.

Generally, athletes show higher vagally mediated HRV levels than sedentary individuals (Da Silva et al., 2015), and exercise training significantly increases resting vagally mediated HRV (Sandercock et al., 2005). These reliable findings indicate increased parasympathetic activity through exercise. Via this effect on the ANS, but also various other mechanisms, exercise improves different psychopathological symptoms such as anxiety and depression (Mikkelsen et al., 2017). Taking advantage of this effect, sports interventions have long been part of psychiatric care, particularly in inpatient clinics (Taylor et al., 1985). However, limited systematic research, especially on its impact on outpatient treatment and adolescent mental health (R. Carney et al., 2021), prevents more specific recommendations on how to implement sports interventions into the psychotherapeutic process. For example, while initial results on improving the efficacy of exposure-based treatment of PTSD patients are very promising—patients who completed a thirty-minute bout of moderate-intensity treadmill exercise before each exposure session showed a greater improvement of their symptoms than patients undergoing exposure alone (Powers et al., 2015)—those findings are not always replicated (Jacquart et al., 2017). Thus, more research is necessary to find out under which circumstances sport has a positive effect on mental health treatments, for example, whether this is the case in particular for people with initially low vagally mediated HRV.

MBIs affect well-being via various mechanisms, e.g., attention regulation, body awareness, emotion regulation, and a change in the perspective on the self (Hölzel et al., 2011). These self-regulatory mechanisms are in turn related to vagally mediated HRV (Holzman & Bridgett, 2017). Therefore, results showing that MBIs are associated with a decrease in PTSD symptoms and an increase in resting vagally mediated HRV (Kirk et al., 2021) are what we would expect. In contrast, it is surprising that two recent meta-analyses found that MBIs have only small and non-significant effects on increasing resting vagally mediated HRV (Brown et al., 2021; Rådmark et al., 2019). The authors of these meta-analyses attribute their inconclusive findings primarily to the lack of large-scale, rigorously conducted randomized controlled trials testing the effect of MBIs on vagally mediated HRV. Overall, so far, research on the association between MBIs and vagally mediated HRV is insufficient to make clear recommendations.

Omega-3 fatty acids are building blocks of cell membranes and as such are of great importance for a well-functioning metabolism. Specifically, its incorporation in synaptic membranes may influence the autonomic control of the heart and, thus, explain its frequently observed association with HRV (Christensen, 2011). However, the results on using omega-3 fatty acid supplementation in the treatment of depression are inconclusive, e.g., effects on improvement of vagally mediated HRV found by O'Keefe et al. (2006) but not by R. M. Carney et al. (2010). However, sufficient evidence shows the benefit of omega-3 supplementation in treating perinatal depression, child depression, and the elderly. Therefore, the International Society for Nutritional Psychiatry Research recommends using omega-3 fatty acids in depression treatment in these cases (Guu et al., 2019). However, the scope of application of HRV biofeedback seems to be much broader.

Heart Rate Variability Biofeedback

In HRV biofeedback, the ECG or pulse wave is recorded, and the current level of HRV is continuously fed back using visual or acoustic aids. Over several sessions, individuals are guided to modify their breathing to maximize target HRV levels. In commercial systems, a rising balloon or an opening flower then indicates an increase in HRV. Likewise, the instruction may be to follow a cardiotachometer and maximize the amplitudes of your heart rate changes, i.e., the rise and fall in heart rate synchronized with breathing. Different biofeedback training methods differ in whether the instruction is simply to maximize the target parameters or to specifically train a breathing pattern that makes increasing the target parameters more likely. In the second case, the instructions often initially dictate slow breathing of about six breaths per minute. Then the breathing pattern is gradually adjusted to find the individual optimal breathing rate to increase HRV. Furthermore, the instructions are to practice diaphragmatic breathing (also called "abdominal breathing" or "belly breathing") and, optimally, to breathe through the nose. For a more in-depth guide to the HRV biofeedback method, we recommend the published protocol by Lehrer et al. (2013). With the successful application of this breathing technique, synchronization between breathing and changes in heart rate occurs (Figure 3.4). Thus, the technique is called resonance breathing.

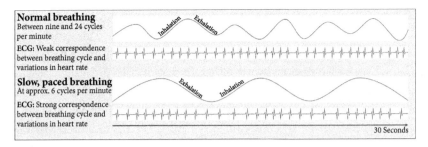

Figure 3.4 Schematic representation of breathing patterns and cardiac activity during normal versus slow, paced breathing.

Note: During normal breathing between nine and twenty-four cycles per minute, there is only a weak correspondence between heart rate and respiration that is not visible to the naked eye. With slow, paced breathing at approximately six cycles per minute, on the other hand, it is visible that the heart beats faster during inhalation, i.e., the distances between the R-waves become shorter, and slower during exhalation, i.e., the distances between the R-waves become longer. Thus, during so-called resonance breathing, we see a clear respiratory sinus arrhythmia (RSA).

Across different populations, be they stressed managers, athletes, pregnant women, or those with mental or physical illnesses, HRV biofeedback has a reliable effect on the reduction of stress and anxiety (Goessl et al., 2017; Lehrer et al., 2020). HRV biofeedback also improves depressive symptoms (Pizzoli et al., 2021), and adding HRV biofeedback to psychotherapy increases HRV and improves the treatment of major depressive disorder (Caldwell & Steffen, 2018). In the latter study, clinically depressed patients either received HRV biofeedback training according to the protocol of Lehrer et al. (2013) in addition to standard psychotherapy consisting of CBT and acceptance and commitment therapy approaches or the standard psychotherapy only. At six-week follow-up, the patients in the HRV biofeedback group experienced a larger decline in their depression levels and this improvement was partially driven by improvements in their HRV levels (Caldwell & Steffen, 2018). Another recent study investigated the stand-alone effect of an HRV biofeedback intervention on individuals with panic disorder in a randomized controlled trial and found an increase in resting vagally mediated HRV and a decrease in panic and agoraphobia symptoms after only four weeks of training (Herhaus et al., 2021). The first results on HRV biofeedback as a treatment for SUDs (Leyro et al., 2019) and psychotic symptoms (Clamor, Koenig et al., 2016) are also very promising. These exemplary findings illustrate the importance of HRV biofeedback in the treatment of mental disorders across diagnostic groups.

How exactly these beneficial effects of HRV biofeedback are achieved is not completely clear and various mechanisms of action are discussed (Lehrer & Gevirtz, 2014). One explanatory approach picks up on the association between PFC hypoactivity/altered prefrontal-subcortical connectivity and low HRV described above (Mather & Thayer, 2018). Slow breathing at approximately six breaths per minute causes high amplitude, low-frequency oscillations in heart rate (Figure 3.4). These high amplitude physiological oscillations may stimulate oscillatory activity in brain areas that are sensitive to interoceptive information such as the insular cortex, the anterior cingulate, and the prefrontal cortex. Nostril breathing in particular also synchronizes oscillations in the amygdala and hippocampus. This synchronization may strengthen the functional connectivity between the regions which all belong to the CAN. These assumptions were put to the test by a recent study, in which researchers measured the prefrontal resting-state connectivity before and after participants received either an eight-week HRV biofeedback intervention or played jump and run games instead (Schumann et al., 2021). When compared to the control group, the functional connectivity of the vmPFC increased to the insula, the amygdala, and lateral prefrontal regions after the HRV biofeedback intervention. Circling back to the assumptions of the NIM (Thayer & Lane, 2000, 2009), this means that HRV biofeedback leads to strengthened connectivity of the very brain regions that are responsible for a situationally appropriate inhibition of the threat response. More generally, strengthened connectivity between these CAN regions may lead to improved regulatory functioning and, thus, improved well-being.

Conclusions and Future Directions

In summary, low vagally mediated HRV is associated with the prevalence of mental disorders across diagnostic groups as well as with abilities mediating mental health such as self-regulation or safety learning. The NIM (Thayer & Lane, 2000, 2009) explains the observed associations with the correspondence of those prefrontal-subcortical inhibitory regulatory circuits that are responsible for both the situationally appropriate inhibition of the threat response and the central control of cardiac activity. Thus, low vagally mediated HRV may serve as an index of impaired functionality of the prefrontal cortex and its connectivity, indicating a general vulnerability to the development of mental disorders. The level of vagally mediated HRV, although relatively stable within an individual, can be increased by various interventions. The best-studied of these interventions as an adjunct to psychotherapy is HRV biofeedback, which effectively reduces symptoms across different mental disorders. Thus, if a patient has been diagnosed with a low level of vagally mediated HRV we recommend using HRV biofeedback as an adjunct to psychotherapy. If HRV biofeedback is not an option for some reason, then the patient and therapist can choose from several interventions for which there is also, albeit weaker, evidence of symptom reduction and an increase in vagally mediated HRV, for example, endurance exercise or yoga.

Further research is needed to understand the mechanisms by which HRV biofeedback and other interventions exert their effects on mental health. In analog to somatic symptoms, researchers should determine the level of vagally mediated HRV, which significantly increases the risk of developing certain symptoms in the mental health domain. And we need to understand which individual characteristics indicate whether and which interventions aimed at increasing vagally mediated HRV also have a positive impact on mental health. For example, a high need for control might be more associated with a response to active interventions such as HRV biofeedback or exercise, whereas a high need to be cared for might be more associated with a positive response to passive interventions such as omega-3 supplementation. However, such assumptions are purely speculative so far. Thus, as in other areas of psychotherapy research, there is still a lot of work to be done in the coming years to establish the basis for an individualized indication. We need to know who benefits from which interventions, targeting vagally mediated HRV, when in the therapeutic process these interventions should be applied, and in combination with which psychotherapeutic measures these interventions are particularly useful.

References

Ahern, E., & Semkovska, M. (2017). Cognitive functioning in the first-episode of major depressive disorder: A systematic review and meta-analysis. *Neuropsychology*, *31*(1), 52–72. https://doi.org/10.1037/NEU0000319

Ahern, G. L., Sollers, J. J., Lane, R. D., Labiner, D. M., Herring, A. M., Weinand, M. E., Hutzler, R., & Thayer, J. F. (2001). Heart rate and heart rate variability changes in the intracarotid sodium amobarbital test. *Epilepsia*, *42*(7), 912–921. https://doi.org/10.1046/J.1528-1157.2001.042007912.X

Albinet, C. T., Boucard, G., Bouquet, C. A., & Audiffren, M. (2010). Increased heart rate variability and executive performance after aerobic training in the elderly. *European Journal of Applied Physiology*, *109*(4), 617–624. https://doi.org/10.1007/S00421-010-1393-Y/TABLES/3

Alboni, P., Alboni, M., & Bertorelle, G. (2008). The origin of vasovagal syncope: To protect the heart or to escape predation? *Clinical Autonomic Research*, *18*(4), 170–178. https://doi.org/10.1007/S10286-008-0479-7

Alvares, G. A., Quintana, D. S., Hickie, I. B., & Guastella, A. J. (2016). Autonomic nervous system dysfunction in psychiatric disorders and the impact of psychotropic medications: A systematic review and meta-analysis. *Journal of Psychiatry & Neuroscience*, *41*(2), 89–104. https://doi.org/10.1503/jpn.140217

Beauchaine, T. P., Bell, Z., Knapton, E., McDonough-Caplan, H., Shader, T., & Zisner, A. (2019). Respiratory sinus arrhythmia reactivity across empirically based structural dimensions of psychopathology: A meta-analysis. *Psychophysiology*, *56*(5), Article e13329. https://doi.org/10.1111/PSYP.13329

Beauchaine, T. P., & Thayer, J. F. (2015). Heart rate variability as a transdiagnostic biomarker of psychopathology. *International Journal of Psychophysiology*, *98*(2), 338–350. https://doi.org/10.1016/j.ijpsycho.2015.08.004

Benarroch, E. E. (1993). The central autonomic network: Functional organization, dysfunction, and perspective. *Mayo Clinic Proceedings*, *68*(10), 988–1001. https://doi.org/10.1016/S0025-6196(12)62272-1

Benarroch, E. E. (2012). Periaqueductal gray: An interface for behavioral control. *Neurology*, *78*(3), 210–217. https://doi.org/10.1212/WNL.0B013E31823FCDEE

Benjamin, B. R., Valstad, M., Elvsåshagen, T., Jönsson, E. G., Moberget, T., Winterton, A., Haram, M., Høegh, M. C., Lagerberg, T. V., Steen, N. E., Larsen, L., Andreassen, O. A., Westlye, L. T., & Quintana, D. S. (2021). Heart rate variability is associated with disease severity in psychosis spectrum disorders. *Progress in Neuro-Psychopharmacology and Biological Psychiatry*, *111*, Article 110108. https://doi.org/10.1016/j.pnpbp.2020.110108

Berridge, C. W., & Spencer, R. C. (2016). Differential cognitive actions of norepinephrine a2 and a1 receptor signaling in the prefrontal cortex. *Brain Research*, *1641*(Pt B), 189–196. https://doi.org/10.1016/J.BRAINRES.2015.11.024

Bouton, M. E. (2004). Context and behavioral processes in extinction. *Learning and Memory*, *11*(5), 485–494. https://doi.org/10.1101/LM.78804

Brosschot, J. F., Verkuil, B., & Thayer, J. F. (2017). Exposed to events that never happen: Generalized unsafety, the default stress response, and prolonged autonomic activity. *Neuroscience and Biobehavioral Reviews, 74*, 287–296. https://doi.org/10.1016/j.neubiorev.2016.07.019

Brown, L., Rando, A. A., Eichel, K., van Dam, N. T., Celano, C. M., Huffman, J. C., & Morris, M. E. (2021). The effects of mindfulness and meditation on vagally mediated heart rate variability: A meta-analysis. *Psychosomatic Medicine, 83*(6), 631–640. https://doi.org/10.1097/PSY.0000000000000900

Broyd, S. J., Demanuele, C., Debener, S., Helps, S. K., James, C. J., & Sonuga-Barke, E. J. S. (2009). Default-mode brain dysfunction in mental disorders: A systematic review. *Neuroscience and Biobehavioral Reviews, 33*(3), 279–296. https://doi.org/10.1016/j.neubiorev.2008.09.002

Buckman, J. F., Vaschillo, B., Vaschillo, E. G., Epstein, E. E., Nguyen-Louie, T. T., Lesnewich, L. M., Eddie, D., & Bates, M. E. (2019). Improvement in women's cardiovascular functioning during cognitive-behavioral therapy for alcohol use disorder. *Psychology of Addictive Behaviors, 33*(8), 659–668. https://doi.org/10.1037/adb0000524

Cacioppo, J. T., & Berntson, G. G. (1994). Relationship between attitudes and evaluative space: A critical review, with emphasis on the separability of positive and negative substrates. *Psychological Bulletin, 115*(3), 401–423. https://doi.org/10.1037/0033-2909.115.3.401

Caldwell, Y. T., & Steffen, P. R. (2018). Adding HRV biofeedback to psychotherapy increases heart rate variability and improves the treatment of major depressive disorder. *International Journal of Psychophysiology, 131*, 96–101. https://doi.org/10.1016/j.ijpsycho.2018.01.001

Campbell, A. A., Wisco, B. E., Silvia, P. J., & Gay, N. G. (2019). Resting respiratory sinus arrhythmia and posttraumatic stress disorder: A meta-analysis. *Biological Psychology, 144*, 125–135. https://doi.org/10.1016/j.biopsycho.2019.02.005

Carney, R., Imran, S., Law, H., Firth, J., & Parker, S. (2021). Physical health interventions on adolescent mental health inpatient units: A systematic review and call to action. *Early Intervention in Psychiatry, 15*(3), 439–448. https://doi.org/10.1111/EIP.12981

Carney, R. M., Freedland, K. E., Stein, P. K., Steinmeyer, B. C., Harris, W. S., Rubin, E. H., Krone, R. J., & Rich, M. W. (2010). Effect of omega-3 fatty acids on heart rate variability in depressed patients with coronary heart disease. *Psychosomatic Medicine, 72*(8), 748–754. https://doi.org/10.1097/PSY.0b013e3181eff148

Caspi, A., Houts, R. M., Belsky, D. W., Goldman-Mellor, S. J., Harrington, H., Israel, S., Meier, M. H., Ramrakha, S., Shalev, I., Poulton, R., & Moffitt, T. E. (2014). The p factor: One general psychopathology factor in the structure of psychiatric disorders? *Clinical Psychological Science, 2*(2), 119–137. https://doi.org/10.1177/2167702613497473

Chalmers, J. A., Heathers, J. A. J., Abbott, M. J., Kemp, A. H., & Quintana, D. S. (2016). Worry is associated with robust reductions in heart rate variability: A transdiagnostic study of anxiety psychopathology. *BMC Psychology, 4*(1), 32. https://doi.org/10.1186/s40359-016-0138-z

Chalmers, J. A., Quintana, D. S., Abbott, M. J.-A., & Kemp, A. H. (2014). Anxiety disorders are associated with reduced heart rate variability: A meta-analysis. *Frontiers in Psychiatry, 5*, 80. https://doi.org/10.3389/fpsyt.2014.00080

Chepenik, L. G., Raffo, M., Hampson, M., Lacadie, C., Wang, F., Jones, M. M., Pittman, B., Skudlarski, P., & Blumberg, H. P. (2010). Functional connectivity between ventral prefrontal cortex and amygdala at low frequency in the resting state in bipolar disorder. *Psychiatry Research, 182*(3), 207–210. https://doi.org/10.1016/J.PSCYCHRESNS.2010.04.002

Christensen, J. H. (2011). Omega-3 polyunsaturated fatty acids and heart rate variability. *Frontiers in Physiology, 2*, 84. https://doi.org/10.3389/fphys.2011.00084

Clamor, A., Koenig, J., Thayer, J. F., & Lincoln, T. M. (2016). A randomized-controlled trial of heart rate variability biofeedback for psychotic symptoms. *Behaviour Research and Therapy, 87*, 207–215. https://doi.org/10.1016/j.brat.2016.10.003

Clamor, A., Lincoln, T. M., Thayer, J. F., & Koenig, J. (2016). Resting vagal activity in schizophrenia: Meta-analysis of heart rate variability as a potential endophenotype. *The British Journal of Psychiatry, 208*(1), 9–16. https://doi.org/10.1192/bjp.bp.114.160762

Clay, S. W., Allen, J., & Parran, T. (2008). A review of addiction. *Postgraduate Medicine, 120*(2), E01–E7. https://doi.10.3810/pgm.2008.07.1802

Craske, M. G., Hermans, D., & Vervliet, B. (2018, March 19). State-of-the-art and future directions for extinction as a translational model for fear and anxiety. *Philosophical Transactions of the Royal Society B, 373*(1742), Article 20170025. https://doi.org/10.1098/rstb.2017.0025

Da Silva, V. P., De Oliveira, N. A., Silveira, H., Mello, R. G. T., & Deslandes, A. C. (2015). Heart rate variability indexes as a marker of chronic adaptation in athletes: A systematic review. *Annals of Noninvasive Electrocardiology, 20*(2), 108–118. https://doi.org/10.1111/anec.12237

Fanselow, M. S. (2018). The role of learning in threat imminence and defensive behaviors. *Current Opinion in Behavioral Sciences, 24*, 44–49. https://doi.org/10.1016/J.COBEHA.2018.03.003

Fantini-Hauwel, C., Batselé, E., Gois, C., & Noel, X. (2020). Emotion regulation difficulties are not always associated with negative outcomes on women: The buffer effect of HRV. *Frontiers in Psychology, 11*, 697. https://doi.org/10.3389/fpsyg.2020.00697

Faurholt-Jepsen, M., Kessing, L. V., & Munkholm, K. (2017). Heart rate variability in bipolar disorder: A systematic review and meta-analysis. *Neuroscience and Biobehavioral Reviews, 73*, 68–80. https://doi.org/10.1016/j.neubiorev.2016.12.007

Forte, G., Favieri, F., & Casagrande, M. (2019). Heart rate variability and cognitive function: A systematic review. *Frontiers in Neuroscience, 13*, Article 710. https://doi.org/10.3389/fnins.2019.00710

Fournier, A., Mondillon, L., Dantzer, C., Gauchez, A.-S., Ducros, V., Mathieu, N., Faure, P., Canini, F., Bonaz, B., & Pellissier, S. (2018). Emotional overactivity in patients with irritable bowel syndrome. *Neurogastroenterology and Motility, 30*(10), Article e13387. https://doi.org/10.1111/nmo.13387

Friston, K. J., & Frith, C. D. (1995). Schizophrenia: A disconnection syndrome? *Clinical Neuroscience (New York, N.Y.), 3*(2), 89–97. https://europepmc.org/article/med/7583624

Galvez-Sánchez, C. M., Duschek, S., & Reyes Del Paso, G. A. (2019). Psychological impact of fibromyalgia: Current perspectives. *Psychology Research and Behavior Management, 12*, 117–127. https://doi.org/10.2147/PRBM.S178240

Garakani, A., Martinez, J. M., Aaronson, C. J., Voustianiouk, A., Kaufmann, H., & Gorman, J. M. (2009). Effect of medication and psychotherapy on heart rate variability in panic disorder. *Depression and Anxiety, 26*(3), 251–258. https://doi.org/10.1002/da.20533

Ge, F., Yuan, M., Li, Y., & Zhang, W. (2020). Posttraumatic stress disorder and alterations in resting heart rate variability: A systematic review and meta-analysis. *Psychiatry Investigation, 17*(1), 9–20. https://doi.org/10.30773/pi.2019.0112

Gillie, B. L., & Thayer, J. F. (2014). Individual differences in resting heart rate variability and cognitive control in posttraumatic stress disorder. *Frontiers in Psychology, 5*, Article 758. https://doi.org/10.3389/fpsyg.2014.00758

Gillie, B. L., Vasey, M. W., & Thayer, J. F. (2014). Heart rate variability predicts control over memory retrieval. *Psychological Science, 25*(2), 458–465. https://doi.org/10.1177/0956797613508789

Gloster, A. T., Wittchen, H. U., Einsle, F., Lang, T., Helbig-Lang, S., Fydrich, T., Fehm, L., Hamm, A. O., Richter, J., Alpers, G. W., Gerlach, A. L., Ströhle, A., Kircher, T., Deckert, J., Zwanzger, P., Höfler, M., & Arolt, V. (2011). Psychological treatment for panic disorder with agoraphobia: A randomized controlled trial to examine the role of therapist-guided exposure in situ in CBT. *Journal of Consulting and Clinical Psychology, 79*(3), 406–420. https://doi.org/10.1037/a0023584

Goessl, V. C., Curtiss, J. E., & Hofmann, S. G. (2017). The effect of heart rate variability biofeedback training on stress and anxiety: A meta-analysis. *Psychological Medicine, 47*(15), 2578–2586. https://doi.org/10.1017/S0033291717001003

Grupe, D. W., Imhoff-Smith, T., Wielgosz, J., Nitschke, J. B., & Davidson, R. J. (2020). A common neural substrate for elevated PTSD symptoms and reduced pulse rate variability in combat-exposed veterans. *Psychophysiology, 57*(1), Article e13352. https://doi.org/10.1111/psyp.13352

Guu, T. W., Mischoulon, D., Sarris, J., Hibbeln, J., McNamara, R. K., Hamazaki, K., Freeman, H. P., Maes, M., Matsuoka, Y. J., Belmaker, R. H., Jacka, F., Pariante, C., Berk, M., Marx, W., & Su, K. P. (2019). International Society for Nutritional Psychiatry Research practice guidelines for omega-3 fatty acids in the treatment of major depressive disorder. *Psychotherapy and Psychosomatics, 88*(5), 263–273. https://doi.org/10.1159/000502652

Hayano, J., Sakakibara, Y., Yamada, A., Yamada, M., Mukai, S., Fujinami, T., Yokoyama, K., Watanabe, Y., & Takata, K. (1991). Accuracy of assessment of cardiac vagal tone by heart rate variability in normal subjects. *The American Journal of Cardiology, 67*(2), 199–204. https://doi.org/10.1016/0002-9149(91)90445-Q

Henry, B. L., Minassian, A., & Perry, W. (2012). Effect of methamphetamine dependence on heart rate variability. *Addiction Biology, 17*(3), 648–658. https://doi.org/10.1111/j.1369-1600.2010.00270.x

Herhaus, B., Siepmann, M., Kahaly, G. J., Conrad, R., & Petrowski, K. (2021). Effect of a biofeedback intervention on heart rate variability in individuals with panic disorder: A randomized controlled trial. *Psychosomatic Medicine, 84*(2), 199–209. https://doi.org/10.1097/PSY.0000000000001031

Hirten, R. P., Danieletto, M., Scheel, R., Shervey, M., Ji, J., Hu, L., Sauk, J., Chang, L., Arnrich, B., Böttinger, M. D., Dudley, J., Keefer, L., & Sands, B. E. (2021). Longitudinal autonomic nervous system measures correlate with stress and ulcerative colitis disease activity and predict flare. *Inflammatory Bowel Diseases, 27*(10), 1576–1584. https://doi.org/10.1093/ibd/izaa323

Hölzel, B. K., Lazar, S. W., Gard, T., Schuman-Olivier, Z., Vago, D. R., & Ott, U. (2011). How does mindfulness meditation work? Proposing mechanisms of action from a conceptual and neural perspective. *Perspectives on Psychological Science, 6*(6), 537–559. https://doi.org/10.1177/1745691611419671

Holzman, J., & Bridgett, D. (2017). Heart rate variability indices as bio-markers of top-down self-regulatory mechanisms: A meta-analytic review. *Neuroscience and Biobehavioral Reviews, 74*(Pt A), 233–255. https://doi.org/10.1016/J.NEUBIOREV.2016.12.032

Jacquart, J., Roquet, R. F., Papini, S., Powers, M. B., Rosenfield, D., Smits, J. A. J., & Monfils, M. H. (2017). Effects of acute exercise on fear extinction in rats and exposure therapy in humans: Null findings from five experiments. *Journal of Anxiety Disorders, 50*, 76–86. https://doi.org/10.1016/J.JANXDIS.2017.05.010

Jarczok, M. N., Koenig, J., Wittling, A., Fischer, J. E., & Thayer, J. F. (2019). First evaluation of an index of low vagally-mediated heart rate variability as a marker of health risks in human adults: Proof of concept. *Journal of Clinical Medicine, 8*(11), 1940. https://doi.org/10.3390/JCM8111940

José, R. G., Samuel, A. S., & Isabel, M. M. (2020). Neuropsychology of executive functions in patients with focal lesion in the prefrontal cortex: A systematic review. *Brain and Cognition, 146*, 105633. https://doi.org/10.1016/J.BANDC.2020.105633

Kemp, A. H., Quintana, D. S., Gray, M. A., Felmingham, K. L., Brown, K., & Gatt, J. M. (2010). Impact of depression and antidepressant treatment on heart rate variability: A review and meta-analysis. *Biological Psychiatry, 67*(11), 1067–1074. https://doi.org/10.1016/j.biopsych.2009.12.012

Kim, J.-H., Ann, J.-H., & Lee, J. (2011). Relationship between heart rate variability and the severity of psychotic symptoms in schizophrenia. *Acta Neuropsychiatrica, 23*(4), 161–166. https://doi.org/10.1111/j.1601-5215.2011.00549.x

Kirk, M. A., Taha, B., McCague, H., Dang, K., Hatzinakos, D., Katz, J., & Ritvo, P. (2021). An online cognitive behavioral therapy, mindfulness meditation, and yoga (CBT-MY) intervention for posttraumatic stress disorder: Psychometric and psychophysiology outcomes. *JMIR Mental Health, 9*(2), e26479. https://doi.org/10.2196/26479

Koch, C., Wilhelm, M., Salzmann, S., Rief, W., & Euteneuer, F. (2019). A meta-analysis of heart rate variability in major depression. *Psychological Medicine, 49*(12), 1948–1957. https://doi.org/10.1017/S0033291719001351

Koenig, J., Kemp, A. H., Feeling, N. R., Thayer, J. F., & Kaess, M. (2016). Resting state vagal tone in borderline personality disorder: A meta-analysis. *Progress in Neuro-Psychopharmacology and Biological Psychiatry, 64*, 18–26. https://doi.org/10.1016/j.pnpbp.2015.07.002

Kunimatsu, A., Yasaka, K., Akai, H., Kunimatsu, N., & Abe, O. (2020). MRI findings in posttraumatic stress disorder. *Journal of Magnetic Resonance Imaging, 52*(2), 380–396. https://doi.org/10.1002/JMRI.26929

Kuss, D. J., Pontes, H. M., & Griffiths, M. D. (2018). Neurobiological correlates in internet gaming disorder: A systematic literature review. *Frontiers in Psychiatry, 9*, 166. https://doi.org/10.3389/FPSYT.2018.00166

Laborde, S., Mosley, E., & Thayer, J. F. (2017). Heart rate variability and cardiac vagal tone in psychophysiological research - Recommendations for experiment planning, data analysis, and data reporting. *Frontiers in Psychology, 8*, 213. https://doi.org/10.3389/fpsyg.2017.00213

Lahey, B. B., Applegate, B., Hakes, J. K., Zald, D. H., Hariri, A. R., & Rathouz, P. J. (2012). Is there a general factor of prevalent psychopathology during adulthood? *Journal of Abnormal Psychology*, *121*(4), 971–977. https://doi.org/10.1037/A0028355

Lang, P. J., Davis, M., & Öhman, A. (2000). Fear and anxiety: Animal models and human cognitive psychophysiology. *Journal of Affective Disorders*, *61*(3), 137–159. https://doi.org/10.1016/S0165-0327(00)00343-8

Lehrer, P. M., & Gevirtz, R. (2014). Heart rate variability biofeedback: How and why does it work? *Frontiers in Psychology*, *5*, 756. https://doi.org/10.3389/fpsyg.2014.00756

Lehrer, P. M., Kaur, K., Sharma, A., Shah, K., Huseby, R., Bhavsar, J., & Zhang, Y. (2020). Heart rate variability biofeedback improves emotional and physical health and performance: A systematic review and meta analysis. *Applied Psychophysiology Biofeedback*, *45*, 109–129. https://doi.org/10.1007/s10484-020-09466-z

Lehrer, P. M., Vaschillo, B., Zucker, T., Graves, J., Katsamanis, M., Aviles, M., & Wamboldt, F. (2013). Protocol for heart rate variability biofeedback training. *Biofeedback*, *41*(3), 98–109. https://doi.org/10.5298/1081-5937-41.3.08

Leyro, T. M., Buckman, J. F., & Bates, M. E. (2019). Theoretical implications and clinical support for heart rate variability biofeedback for substance use disorders. *Current Opinion in Psychology*, *30*, 92–97. https://doi.org/10.1016/j.copsyc.2019.03.008

Lindner, K., Neubert, J., Pfannmöller, J., Lotze, M., Hamm, A. O., & Wendt, J. (2015). Fear-potentiated startle processing in humans: Parallel fMRI and orbicularis EMG assessment during cue conditioning and extinction. *International Journal of Psychophysiology*, *98*(3 Pt 2), 535–545. https://doi.org/10.1016/j.ijpsycho.2015.02.025

Lonsdorf, T. B., Menz, M. M., Andreatta, M., Fullana, M. A., Golkar, A., Haaker, J., Heitland, I., Hermann, A., Kuhn, M., Kruse, O., Drexler, S. M., Meulders, A., Nees, F., Pittig, A., Richter, J., Römer, S., Shiban, Y., Schmitz, A., Straube, B., . . . Merz, C. J. (2017). Don't fear 'fear conditioning': Methodological considerations for the design and analysis of studies on human fear acquisition, extinction, and return of fear. *Neuroscience & Biobehavioral Reviews*, *77*, 247–285. https://doi.org/10.1016/j.neubiorev.2017.02.026

Makovac, E., Carnevali, L., Medina, S., Sgoifo, A., Petrocchi, N., & Ottaviani, C. (2021). Safe in my heart: Resting heart rate variability longitudinally predicts emotion regulation, worry and sense of safeness during COVID-19 lockdown. *Stress: The International Journal on the Biology of Stress*, *25*(1), 9–13. https://doi.org/10.1080/10253890.2021.1999408

Mather, M., & Thayer, J. F. (2018). How heart rate variability affects emotion regulation brain networks. *Current Opinion in Behavioral Sciences*, *19*, 98–104. https://doi.org/10.1016/j.cobeha.2017.12.017

Mikkelsen, K., Stojanovska, L., Polenakovic, M., Bosevski, M., & Apostolopoulos, V. (2017). Exercise and mental health. *Maturitas*, *106*, 48–56. https://doi.org/10.1016/J.MATURITAS.2017.09.003

Milad, M. R., & Quirk, G. J. (2012). Fear extinction as a model for translational neuroscience: Ten years of progress. *Annual Review of Psychology*, *63*, 129–151. https://doi.org/10.1146/annurev.psych.121208.131631

Milad, M. R., Wright, C. I., Orr, S. P., Pitman, R. K., Quirk, G. J., & Rauch, S. L. (2007). Recall of fear extinction in humans activates the ventromedial prefrontal cortex and hippocampus in concert. *Biological Psychiatry*, *62*(5), 446–454. https://doi.org/10.1016/J.BIOPSYCH.2006.10.011

Motzkin, J. C., Philippi, C. L., Wolf, R. C., Baskaya, M. K., & Koenigs, M. (2014). Ventromedial prefrontal cortex lesions alter neural and physiological correlates of anticipation. *The Journal of Neuroscience*, *34*(31), 10430–10437. https://doi.org/10.1523/JNEUROSCI.1446-14.2014

Motzkin, J. C., Philippi, C. L., Wolf, R. C., Baskaya, M. K., & Koenigs, M. (2015). Ventromedial prefrontal cortex is critical for the regulation of amygdala activity in humans. *Biological Psychiatry*, *77*(3), 276–284. https://doi.org/10.1016/J.BIOPSYCH.2014.02.014

Mumm, J. L. M., Pyrkosch, L., Plag, J., Nagel, P., Petzold, M. B., Bischoff, S., Fehm, L., Fydrich, T., & Ströhle, A. (2019). Heart rate variability in patients with agoraphobia with or without panic disorder remains stable during CBT but increases following in-vivo exposure. *Journal of Anxiety Disorders*, *64*, 16–23. https://doi.org/10.1016/j.janxdis.2019.03.001

Mwansisya, T. E., Hu, A., Li, Y., Chen, X., Wu, G., Huang, X., Lv, D., Li, Z., Liu, C., Xue, Z., Feng, J., & Liu, Z. (2017). Task and resting-state fMRI studies in first-episode schizophrenia: A systematic review. *Schizophrenia Research, 189*, 9–18. https://doi.org/10.1016/J.SCHRES.2017.02.026

Myers, K. M., & Davis, M. (2006). Mechanisms of fear extinction. *Molecular Psychiatry, 12*(2), 120–150. https://doi.org/10.1038/sj.mp.4001939

Neyer, S., Witthöft, M., Cropley, M., Pawelzik, M., Lugo, R. G., & Sütterlin, S. (2021). Reduction of depressive symptoms during inpatient treatment is not associated with changes in heart rate variability. *PloS One, 16*(3), Article e0248686. https://doi.org/10.1371/journal.pone.0248686

Northoff, G. (2016). How do resting state changes in depression translate into psychopathological symptoms? From "Spatiotemporal correspondence" to "Spatiotemporal psychopathology." *Current Opinion in Psychiatry, 29*(1), 18–24. https://doi.org/10.1097/YCO.0000000000000222

O'Keefe, J. H., Abuissa, H., Sastre, A., Steinhaus, D. M., & Harris, W. S. (2006). Effects of omega-3 fatty acids on resting heart rate, heart rate recovery after exercise, and heart rate variability in men with healed myocardial infarctions and depressed ejection fractions. *The American Journal of Cardiology, 97*(8), 1127–1130. https://doi.org/10.1016/j.amjcard.2005.11.025

Ohman, A. (1986). Face the beast and fear the face: Animal and social fears as prototypes for evolutionary analyses of emotion. *Psychophysiology, 23*(2), 123–145. https://doi.org/10.1111/J.1469-8986.1986.TB00608.X

Ottaviani, C., Thayer, J. F., Verkuil, B., Lonigro, A., Medea, B., Couyoumdjian, A., & Brosschot, J. F. (2016). Physiological concomitants of perseverative cognition: A systematic review and meta-analysis. *Psychological Bulletin, 142*(3), 231–259. https://doi.org/10.1037/BUL0000036

Ottaviani, C., Zingaretti, P., Petta, A. M., Antonucci, G., Thayer, J. F., & Spitoni, G. F. (2019). Resting heart rate variability predicts inhibitory control above and beyond impulsivity. *Journal of Psychophysiology, 33*(3), 198–206. https://doi.org/10.1027/0269-8803/a000222

Pappens, M., Schroijen, M., Sütterlin, S., Smets, E., Van Den Bergh, O., Thayer, J. F., & Van Diest, I. (2014). Resting heart rate variability predicts safety learning and fear extinction in an interoceptive fear conditioning paradigm. *PLoS One, 9*(9), Article e105054. https://doi.org/10.1371/journal.pone.0105054

Pavlov, I. P. (2010). Conditioned reflexes: An investigation of the physiological activity of the cerebral cortex. *Annals of Neurosciences, 17*(3), 136–141. https://doi.org/10.5214/ans.0972-7531.1017309

Pellissier, S., Dantzer, C., Mondillon, L., Trocme, C., Gauchez, A.-S., Ducros, V., Mathieu, N., Toussaint, B., Fournier, A., Canini, F., & Bonaz, B. (2014). Relationship between vagal tone, cortisol, TNF-alpha, epinephrine and negative affects in Crohn's disease and irritable bowel syndrome. *PloS One, 9*(9), Article e105328. https://doi.org/10.1371/journal.pone.0105328

Pizzoli, S. F. M., Marzorati, C., Gatti, D., Monzani, D., Mazzocco, K., & Pravettoni, G. (2021). A meta-analysis on heart rate variability biofeedback and depressive symptoms. *Scientific Reports, 11*(1), Article 6650. https://doi.org/10.1038/s41598-021-86149-7

Porta-Casteràs, D., Fullana, M. A., Tinoco, D., Martínez-Zalacaín, I., Pujol, J., Palao, D. J., Soriano-Mas, C., Harrison, B. J., Via, E., & Cardoner, N. (2020). Prefrontal-amygdala connectivity in trait anxiety and generalized anxiety disorder: Testing the boundaries between healthy and pathological worries. *Journal of Affective Disorders, 267*, 211–219. https://doi.org/10.1016/J.JAD.2020.02.029

Powers, M. B., Medina, J. L., Burns, S., Kauffman, B. Y., Monfils, M., Asmundson, G. J. G., Diamond, A., McIntyre, C., & Smits, J. A. J. (2015). Exercise augmentation of exposure therapy for PTSD: Rationale and pilot efficacy data. *Cognitive Behaviour Therapy, 44*(4), 314–327. https://doi.org/10.1080/16506073.2015.1012740

Rådmark, L., Sidorchuk, A., Osika, W., & Niemi, M. (2019). A systematic review and meta-analysis of the impact of mindfulness based interventions on heart rate variability and inflammatory markers. *Journal of Clinical Medicine, 8*(10), Article 1638. https://doi.org/10.3390/JCM8101638

Ramírez, E., Ortega, A. R., & Reyes Del Paso, G. A. (2015). Anxiety, attention, and decision making: The moderating role of heart rate variability. *International Journal of Psychophysiology, 98*(3), 490–496. https://doi.org/10.1016/J.IJPSYCHO.2015.10.007

Rock, P. L., Roiser, J. P., Riedel, W. J., & Blackwell, A. D. (2014). Cognitive impairment in depression: A systematic review and meta-analysis. *Psychological Medicine, 44*(10), 2029–2040. https://doi.org/10.1017/S0033291713002535

Roelofs, K. (2017). Freeze for action: Neurobiological mechanisms in animal and human freezing. *Philosophical Transactions of the Royal Society B, 372*(1718), 20160206. https://doi.org/10.1098/RSTB.2016.0206

Rogers, M. A., Kasai, K., Koji, M., Fukuda, R., Iwanami, A., Nakagome, K., Fukuda, M., & Kato, N. (2004). Executive and prefrontal dysfunction in unipolar depression: A review of neuropsychological and imaging evidence. *Neuroscience Research, 50*(1), 1–11. https://doi.org/10.1016/J.NEURES.2004.05.003

Rozin, P., & Royzman, E. B. (2001). Negativity bias, negativity dominance, and contagion. *Personality and Social Psychology Review, 5*(4), 296–320. https://doi.org/10.1207/S15327957PSPR0504_2

Sandercock, G. R. H., Bromley, P. D., & Brodie, D. A. (2005). Effects of exercise on heart rate variability: Inferences from meta-analysis. *Medicine and Science in Sports and Exercise, 37*(3), 433–439. https://doi.org/10.1249/01.MSS.0000155388.39002.9D

Schäfer, A., & Vagedes, J. (2013). How accurate is pulse rate variability as an estimate of heart rate variability? A review on studies comparing photoplethysmographic technology with an electrocardiogram. *International Journal of Cardiology, 166*(1), 15–29. https://doi.org/10.1016/J.IJCARD.2012.03.119

Schneider, M., & Schwerdtfeger, A. (2020). Autonomic dysfunction in posttraumatic stress disorder indexed by heart rate variability: A meta-analysis. *Psychological Medicine, 50*(12), 1937–1948. https://doi.org/10.1017/S003329172000207X

Schumann, A., de la Cruz, F., Köhler, S., Brotte, L., & Bär, K. J. (2021). The influence of heart rate variability biofeedback on cardiac regulation and functional brain connectivity. *Frontiers in Neuroscience, 15*, Article 691988. https://doi.org/10.3389/fnins.2021.691988

Shaffer, F., & Ginsberg, J. P. (2017). An overview of heart rate variability metrics and norms. *Frontiers in Public Health, 5*, 258. https://doi.org/10.3389/fpubh.2017.00258

Siennicka, A., Quintana, D. S., Fedurek, P., Wijata, A., Paleczny, B., Ponikowska, B., & Danel, D. P. (2019). Resting heart rate variability, attention and attention maintenance in young adults. *International Journal of Psychophysiology, 143*, 126–131. https://doi.org/10.1016/j.ijpsycho.2019.06.017

Sigrist, C., Reichl, C., Schmidt, S. J., Brunner, R., Kaess, M., & Koenig, J. (2021). Cardiac autonomic functioning and clinical outcome in adolescent borderline personality disorder over two years. *Progress in Neuro-Psychopharmacology and Biological Psychiatry, 111*, Article 110336. https://doi.org/10.1016/j.pnpbp.2021.110336

Smith, R., Allen, J. J. B., Thayer, J. F., & Lane, R. D. (2015). Altered functional connectivity between medial prefrontal cortex and the inferior brainstem in major depression during appraisal of subjective emotional responses: A preliminary study. *Biological Psychology, 108*, 13–24. https://doi.org/10.1016/j.biopsycho.2015.03.007

Smith, R., Thayer, J. F., Khalsa, S. S., & Lane, R. D. (2017). The hierarchical basis of neurovisceral integration. *Neuroscience and Biobehavioral Reviews, 75*, 274–296. https://doi.org/10.1016/j.neubiorev.2017.02.003

Soder, H. E., Wardle, M. C., Schmitz, J. M., Lane, S. D., Green, C., & Vujanovic, A. A. (2019). Baseline resting heart rate variability predicts post-traumatic stress disorder treatment outcomes in adults with co-occurring substance use disorders and post-traumatic stress. *Psychophysiology, 56*(8), Article e13377. https://doi.org/10.1111/psyp.13377

Task Force of The European Society of Cardiology and The North American Society of Pacing and Electrophysiology. (1996). Heart rate variability. Standards of measurements, physiological interpretation, and clinical use. *European Heart Journal, 17*, 354–381. https://doi.org/10.1161/01.CIR.93.5.1043

Taylor, C. B., Sallis, J. F., & Needle, R. (1985). The relation of physical activity and exercise to mental health. *Public Health Reports, 100*(2), 195–202. https://www.ncbi.nlm.nih.gov/pmc/articles/PMC1424736/

Thayer, J. F., Åhs, F., Fredrikson, M., Sollers, J. J., & Wager, T. D. (2012). A meta-analysis of heart rate variability and neuroimaging studies: Implications for heart rate variability as a marker of stress and health. *Neuroscience and Biobehavioral Reviews, 36*(2), 747–756. https://doi.org/10.1016/J.NEUBIOREV.2011.11.009

Thayer, J. F., & Lane, R. D. (2000). A model of neurovisceral integration in emotion regulation and dysregulation. *Journal of Affective Disorders, 61*(3), 201–216. https://doi.org/10.1016/S0165-0327(00)00338-4

Thayer, J. F., & Lane, R. D. (2009). Claude Bernard and the heart-brain connection: Further elaboration of a model of neurovisceral integration. *Neuroscience and Biobehavioral Reviews, 33*(2), 81–88. https://doi.org/10.1016/j.neubiorev.2008.08.004

Thome, J., Terpou, B. A., McKinnon, M. C., & Lanius, R. A. (2020). The neural correlates of trauma-related autobiographical memory in posttraumatic stress disorder: A meta-analysis. *Depression and Anxiety, 37*(4), 321–345. https://doi.org/10.1002/DA.22977

Via, E., Fullana, M. A., Goldberg, X., Tinoco-González, D., Martínez-Zalacaín, I., Soriano-Mas, C., Davey, C. G., Menchón, J. M., Straube, B., Kircher, T., Pujol, J., Cardoner, N., & Harrison, B. J. (2018). Ventromedial prefrontal cortex activity and pathological worry in generalised anxiety disorder. *The British Journal of Psychiatry, 213*(1), 437–443. https://doi.org/10.1192/BJP.2018.65

Weike, A. I., Schupp, H. T., & Hamm, A. O. (2008). In dubio pro defensio: Initial activation of conditioned fear is not cue specific. *Behavioral Neuroscience, 122*(3), 685–696. https://doi.org/10.1037/0735-7044.122.3.685

Weippert, M., Kumar, M., Kreuzfeld, S., Arndt, D., Rieger, A., & Stoll, R. (2010). Comparison of three mobile devices for measuring R-R intervals and heart rate variability: Polar S810i, Suunto t6, and an ambulatory ECG system. *European Journal of Applied Physiology, 109*(4), 779–786. https://doi.org/10.1007/S00421-010-1415-9/TABLES/4

Wendt, J., Hamm, A. O., Pané-Farré, C. A., Thayer, J. F., Gerlach, A., Gloster, A. T., Lang, T., Helbig-Lang, S., Pauli, P., Fydrich, T., Ströhle, A., Kircher, T., Arolt, V., Deckert, J., Wittchen, H. U., & Richter, J. (2018). Pretreatment cardiac vagal tone predicts dropout from and residual symptoms after exposure therapy in patients with panic disorder and agoraphobia. *Psychotherapy and Psychosomatics, 87*(3), 187–189. https://doi.org/10.1159/000487599

Wendt, J., König, J., Hufenbach, M. C., Koenig, J., Thayer, J. F., & Hamm, A. O. (2019). Vagally mediated heart rate variability and safety learning: Effects of instructions and number of extinction trials. *Psychophysiology, 56*(10), e13404. https://doi.org/10.1111/psyp.13404

Wendt, J., Neubert, J., Koenig, J., Thayer, J. F., & Hamm, A. O. (2015). Resting heart rate variability is associated with inhibition of conditioned fear. *Psychophysiology, 52*(9), 1161–1166. https://doi.org/10.1111/psyp.12456

Xu, P., Chen, A., Li, Y., Xing, X., & Lu, H. (2019). Medial prefrontal cortex in neurological diseases. *Physiological Genomics, 51*(9), 432–442. https://doi.org/10.1152/PHYSIOLGENOMICS.00006.2019

Yuan, P., & Raz, N. (2014). Prefrontal cortex and executive functions in healthy adults: A meta-analysis of structural neuroimaging studies. *Neuroscience & Biobehavioral Reviews, 42*, 180–192. https://doi.org/10.1016/J.NEUBIOREV.2014.02.005

Yuksel, R., Yuksel, R. N., Sengezer, T., & Dane, S. (2016). Autonomic cardiac activity in patients with smoking and alcohol addiction by heart rate variability analysis. *Clinical and Investigative Medicine. Medecine Clinique et Experimentale, 39*(6), Article 27519. https://pubmed.ncbi.nlm.nih.gov/27917809/

Zahn, D., Adams, J., Krohn, J., Wenzel, M., Mann, C., Gomille, L., Jacobi-Scherbening, V., & Kubiak, T. (2016). Heart rate variability and self-control—A meta-analysis. *Biological Psychology, 115*, 9–26. https://doi.org/10.1016/J.BIOPSYCHO.2015.12.007

Zhang, R., & Volkow, N. D. (2019). Brain default-mode network dysfunction in addiction. *NeuroImage, 200*, 313–331. https://doi.org/10.1016/J.NEUROIMAGE.2019.06.036

4
Brain Plasticity and Prediction of Response to Psychotherapy

Sadie J. Zacharek, John D. E. Gabrieli, and Stefan G. Hofmann

Introduction

Psychotherapy for psychiatric disorders has a long history, rising to prominence with the works of Freud and Jung and transforming into modern versions with the work of Aaron Beck and others. Supported by the strong empirical evidence of many well-controlled studies, cognitive and behavioral therapies (CBT) have since become the dominant approach for treating virtually all mental health problems (Hofmann et al., 2012). This psychotherapeutic approach is often contrasted with pharmacological treatments. To the extent that either kind of treatment benefits a patient in regard to changes in thoughts, feelings, and behaviors, however, it must do so through *brain plasticity* that mediates all forms of human psychological change. Advances in neuroimaging methods and technologies over the past three decades have allowed, for the first time, measurement, and visualization of therapeutic brain plasticity for both psychotherapy and pharmacology. Neuroimaging allows for examination of longitudinal changes in brain structure, function, and chemistry that occur in and mediate treatment. Further, associating such brain plasticity with *remission* (no longer meeting criteria for a presenting diagnosis) or *response* (significant reduction of symptoms) identifies the neural mechanisms that may be most important in treatment efficacy. In the last decade, there has also been progress in identifying pre-treatment brain characteristics (*biomarkers*) that are associated with or *predict* post-treatment response. Such biomarkers may allow for scientifically guided treatment selection for individual patients (*personalized* or *precision* medicine), which is needed, as even well-validated psychotherapy and pharmacological treatments vary considerably in how effective they are on behalf of patients (with many treatments being effective for half or less of patients).

Neuroimaging can measure neuroanatomy (structure), neurophysiology (function), and neurochemistry in a variety of ways. Magnetic resonance imaging (MRI) measures brain structure through anatomical MRI (structural volumes, cortical thickness) and diffusion-weighted imaging (DWI) characterizes white-matter tract properties. Brain functions can be measured with relative spatial precision via functional MRI (fMRI) and positron emission tomography (PET). Other functional measures reveal precise temporal time courses of neurophysiology, including electroencephalography (EEG) and evoked response potentials (ERPs). Such functional measures relate regional activations to particular mental processes when a participant performs an experimental task. Both functional and structural measures can also reveal multi-component brain networks (*connectomics*) during task performance or at rest in the absence of a task. Neurochemical methods, such as magnetic resonance spectroscopy (MRS), are used to quantify amounts of biochemicals and metabolites in the brain.

Measuring brain plasticity in response to psychotherapy has potential clinical relevance. For many neuropsychiatric disorders, there have been observed differences in patients' brain structure, function, neurochemistry, and metabolism relative to the brains of healthy control subjects. Following from that, psychotherapy leading to the remission of a patient's symptoms could be expected to *normalize* these pre-treatment brain differences to levels comparable to those of healthy individuals. For treatments where this normalization of aberrant brain structure or activity was robust, measuring in these areas susceptible to therapeutic plasticity could serve as neurobiological markers of treatment progress or success. Alternatively, psychotherapy could induce *compensatory* changes in areas of the patient's brain that did not display pre-treatment differences from healthy individuals. These compensatory changes could shed light on the biological underpinnings of the therapy's mechanism of change. It is also possible that brain plasticity in response to a given treatment could be some combination of normalizing pre-treatment abnormalities and recruiting additional, compensatory brain areas.

Candidate Brain Systems Mediating Psychotherapy

The brain is a highly connected series of multiple interactive networks, and brain plasticity in response to effective psychotherapy likely involves multiple networks that may vary across individuals, treatments, and diagnoses. In general, however, psychotherapy can be viewed as a transformation in relations between thoughts and emotions, and these human capacities have been linked primarily to the prefrontal neocortex (thoughts) and the subcortical limbic system, especially the amygdala (emotions). Prefrontal regions are implicated in cognitive control or regulation (executive functions, inhibition, shifting, flexibility) of both thoughts (Baddeley, 1986) and emotions (e.g., Ochsner et al., 2002). In contrast, the amygdala is implicated in response to emotionally intense experience and appears to play a necessary role in fear learning, the amplification of memory by emotion, and the recognition of fearful facial expressions (Adolphs et al., 1995; Bechara et al., 1995; Cahill et al., 1995).

The ability to cognitively modify how one experiences emotions, known as emotion regulation, is a critical factor in mental health outcomes (e.g., Amstadter, 2008;

Gross & Thompson, 2007; Taylor & Liberzon, 2007). Among the most flexible and effective forms of emotion regulation that have been formally studied is cognitive reappraisal—altering the way in which a stimulus is interpreted to elicit a more positive emotional state. Much research has demonstrated reappraisal's benefits for emotional, social, cognitive, and physiological outcomes for individuals across the lifespan (reviewed in Riepenhausen et al., 2022) and as a result, reappraisal has played a key role in treatments used to remedy internalizing disorders (e.g., J. Yuan et al., 2023).

Neuroimaging studies of reappraisal, in which research participants employ cognitive strategies to reduce negative emotions in response to highly negative scenes, have consistently observed increased fMRI activations in prefrontal cortex (PFC; interpreted as reflecting the generation of the reappraisal) and the anterior cingulate cortex (ACC; interpreted as reflecting the conflict between the positive reappraisal and the negative scene), and decreased amygdala activation (interpreted as reflecting the downregulation of negative feelings) (Buhle et al., 2014; Ochsner et al., 2002). In contrast, reappraisal to enhance negative emotions results in increased amygdala activation (Ochsner et al., 2004).

In this chapter, we focus primarily on one kind of psychotherapy—CBT—and on one major class of psychiatric diagnoses, *anxiety disorders* including generalized anxiety disorder (GAD), social anxiety disorder (SAD), and specific phobia. Anxiety disorders are the most common mental disorders with an estimated lifetime prevalence of 33.7 percent (Kessler et al., 2012). Anxiety disorders result in substantial socioeconomic burdens (Hoffman et al., 2008) and health care costs (Konnopka & König, 2020). They are also frequently co-occurring with one another, with depression, and with substance use disorder (Merikangas & Swanson, 2010).

Broadly, neuroimaging studies of anxiety disorders have often noted a combination of atypically increased activation in the amygdala to negative emotional stimuli and decreased activation in prefrontal regions associated with cognitive control (Etkin & Wager, 2007).

We first review evidence about brain plasticity associated with CBT treatment of anxiety disorders and relate that plasticity to brain differences often found in anxiety disorders. We then review evidence about potential pre-treatment neuroimaging biomarkers that are associated with or predicted of CBT efficacy (e.g., response or non-response) for anxiety disorders.

Brain Plasticity in Response to Psychotherapy

It is no surprise that pharmaceutical interventions can induce biological change in the brain, given that they are physical agents with known biological mechanisms. However, brain plasticity has also been observed in response to purely psychotherapeutic interventions in multiple neuropsychiatric disorders. In some cases, the changes observed following psychological intervention overlap with changes observed in cases of pharmacological intervention, but in other cases the two kinds of treatment show disparate changes, which is perhaps unsurprising given the difference in mechanism. Where pharmaceutical interventions work with a physical mechanism by altering some aspect of biology of the brain to induce change in psychological symptoms, psychotherapies work in an alternate direction with an approach targeting the mind which, in turn, induces a change in the brain.

Multiple instances of brain plasticity have been observed in response to psychotherapy in anxiety disorders in key circuitry related to threat appraisal and fear responses, including the amygdala, insula, ACC, hippocampus, and prefrontal areas. In general, meta-analyses have revealed that across anxiety disorders, successful psychotherapy is associated with decreased functional activation in limbic regions, namely the amygdala, insula, and ACC, which are central to the brain's fear response and display hyperactivation pre-treatment (Schrammen et al., 2022).

Brain Plasticity in the Amygdala

The amygdala is canonically indicated in the fear response and processing of negative emotional stimuli and is often conceptualized as the brain's "alarm system," which is overactive in individuals with anxiety who generate a fear response in the absence of true danger. As such, the amygdala has emerged as a core region of interest in anxiety disorder research (Davis, 1992).

Following CBT, patients with GAD displayed reduced amygdala activation to negative (i.e., fearful and angry) facial expressions (Fonzo et al., 2014). This seems to reflect a normalization of pre-treatment brain differences, because patients with GAD typically exhibit higher amygdala activation while viewing fearful faces (Morris et al., 1996) and lower amygdala activation while viewing happy facial expressions (Fonzo et al., 2014). Heightened amygdala response to threat seems to be present in GAD across development. Pediatric patients displayed higher amygdala activation while viewing negative facial expressions, and there was a positive correlation between amygdala activation and anxiety severity (Monk et al., 2008). Structurally, gray matter volume of the amygdala has consistently been found to be increased in patients with GAD (Etkin et al., 2009), but it remains unclear if these volumetric differences abate with successful psychotherapy.

In SAD, a significant reduction in amygdala volume and hyperactivation was observed following successful CBT, and the reduction in volume correlated with relief of symptoms (Månsson et al., 2016). Of note, this structural reduction in amygdala volume was still present one year after treatment cessation, whereas the functional reduction in amygdala activation observed immediately following treatment did not persist (Månsson et al., 2017). Further, amygdala volume was more reduced in patients who responded to CBT than in patients who did not respond (Månsson et al., 2017). Reductions in amygdala activation were accompanied by reductions in amygdala volume (Månsson et al., 2016), underscoring that changes in function of a brain substructure may be at least partially due to changes in structure. Although reduced amygdala activation did not persist as a long-term functional change, it still seems to represent a normalization of function in this region, as hyperactivation in the amygdala occurs across a range of symptom-provoking paradigms in SAD. Hyperactivation of the amygdala in SAD has been observed during tasks of negative emotional processing (Etkin & Wager, 2007; Phan et al., 2006), public speaking (Tillfors et al., 2001), and critical self-referential comments (Blair et al., 2008). Further, there was a positive correlation between amygdala activation and symptom severity (Phan et al., 2006). Dynamic causal modeling revealed that patients with SAD had reduced attenuation of the amygdala response to emotional faces by the frontal cortex (Sladky et al., 2015), suggesting that the increased activation is at least in part attributed to a failure of prefrontal areas to downregulate the limbic response.

Successful CBT in specific phobia was also associated with reductions in amygdala reactivity (Lipka et al., 2014). The amygdala and bed nucleus of the stria terminalis (BNST) are indicated in the brain's response to a threat stimulus, which can be evolutionarily adaptive when the stimulus presents a true threat. Patients with specific phobia, however, displayed higher activation in the amygdala and BNST and higher functional connectivity between these two regions than did healthy control individuals (Münsterkötter et al., 2015). A PET study also showed that patients with animal phobia had significantly increased cerebral blood flow to the amygdala while viewing photos of the object of their phobia (Wik et al., 1997). This evidence is likely a neural reflection of patients with specific phobia appraising stimuli, in particular the object of their phobia, as disproportionately more threatening—a difference that abates following successful therapy.

Brain Plasticity in the Insula

The insula is an area of the brain centrally involved in emotional awareness, integrating somatic and mental states, and attentional control. Meta-analyses generally indicate hyperactivation of the insula in anxiety disorders, with a few proposed pathology-specific mechanisms (Ipser et al., 2013; Marwood et al., 2018). For instance, the anterior insula has been indicated in subjective evaluation of internal conditions, so hyperactivation might point to greater monitoring of anxious feelings and increased propagation of anxiety symptoms. Given the role of the insula in attentional control and identifying salient stimuli, hyperactivation could also plausibly underlie excessive vigilance that is characteristic of anxiety disorders. A meta-analysis revealed that, across anxiety disorders, the insula is a region subject to decreased activation following psychotherapy (Schrammen et al., 2022).

Prior to treatment, lower activation while viewing happy facial expressions (Fonzo et al., 2014) and higher activation during threat processing (Buff et al., 2016) was observed in the insula of patients with GAD relative to healthy control subjects. The insular response to happy facial expressions was heightened following CBT in patients with GAD (Fonzo et al., 2014). Another study found that successful CBT was associated with a reduction in insular activation during a task of emotional perception, and that the magnitude of reduced insula activation was positively correlated with the magnitude of reduced anxiety symptoms (Gorka et al., 2019). Notably, a similar pattern was observed in patients who had been treated with a selective serotonin reuptake inhibitor (SSRI). The insula not only displays hyperactivation, but also displays altered connectivity to other brain structures in GAD. Notably, patients with GAD displayed stronger connectivity between the insula and amygdala while viewing emotional facial expressions (Fonzo et al., 2014) and during a task of fear conditioning (Greenberg et al., 2013). Hyperconnectivity between these two limbic regions, each with canonical hyperactivation in anxiety disorders, suggests network dysfunction in areas responsible for emotional processing and salient stimuli identification.

Significantly reduced activation in the insula was observed following CBT in patients with SAD (Klumpp et al., 2013). Before CBT treatment, hyperactivation of the insula has been observed during tasks of negative emotional processing in SAD relative to healthy control subjects (Etkin & Wager, 2007; Phan et al., 2006). As patients with SAD improved their ability to appraise social situations as non-threatening during CBT, their previously elevated insular activation was ameliorated.

Patients with specific phobia of spiders had reduced activation of the insula while viewing videos of spiders following successful CBT (Straube et al., 2006). A meta-analysis revealed that treatment with CBT was associated with decreased insular activation across several specific phobia subtypes (Ipser et al., 2013). Similar to the reductions of hyperactivation observed in the amygdala following successful treatment, the insula appears to be another limbic structure that exhibits a normalizing reduction in activation following specific phobia symptom relief. Prior to treatment, patients with a specific phobia of spiders had insula activation that scaled linearly with subjective proximity to images of spiders (Zilverstand et al., 2017) and higher insula activation while viewing videos of spiders (Straube et al., 2006) relative to healthy control participants. Structurally, two studies found increased insular cortical thickness in patients with animal phobia relative to healthy control participants (Rauch et al., 2004; Rosso et al., 2010). Although structure is not directly tied to function, the increased insular thickness observed in phobic patients pre-treatment suggests a structural pathology of this area, warranting further study.

Brain Plasticity in the ACC

In adults with GAD, subgenual ACC (sgACC) activation while viewing angry and fearful facial expressions was reduced following CBT (Fonzo et al., 2014). Adolescents with GAD displayed increased rostral ACC (rACC) activation during a task of implicit threat following successful CBT, comparable to the levels of rACC activation observed in healthy controls, and there was a significant correlation between increased rACC activation and symptom reduction (Burkhouse et al., 2018). This directional difference in ACC activation change could be attributed to the different symptom-provoking paradigms used in each study or could represent a meaningful developmental difference in response to CBT. Prior to treatment, lower ACC activation was observed in adults with GAD while viewing happy facial expressions relative to healthy control subjects (Fonzo et al., 2014), suggesting a blunted response to positive stimuli. Structurally, a causal analysis revealed that the reduction in gray matter volume observed over the course of illness duration in patients with GAD began in the sgACC, which then had downstream effects on the reduction in volume of the prefrontal cortex and insula, amongst other regions (Chen et al., 2020). Importantly, the sgACC and insula displayed bidirectional causality in each other's volume reduction (Chen et al., 2020), once again highlighting the network involvement of the insula in anxiety pathology.

Functionally, SAD patients who underwent group CBT had reduced regional cerebral blood flow to the ACC following treatment, and this reduction was more pronounced in responders relative to non-responders (Furmark et al., 2002). Relative to healthy control subjects, individuals with SAD exhibited elevated ACC reactivity to facial expressions of disgust (Amir et al., 2005). Neurochemically, glutamate, a primary excitatory neurotransmitter in the central nervous system, was elevated in the ACC of patients with SAD relative to healthy controls as measured by MRS (Phan et al., 2005). Excessive glutamatergic signaling is consistent with limbic system hyperactivation that characterizes anxiety disorders. Whole-brain glutamate was reduced following successful pharmaceutical intervention in SAD (Pollack et al., 2008), but to our knowledge no studies have investigated whether psychotherapy has a similar effect. Other noted neurochemical abnormalities in SAD include elevated N-acetylaspartate (NAA), a marker of neuronal integrity, and reduced choline, a marker of membrane integrity, levels in the ACC (Phan et al., 2005). The elevated levels of NAA suggest increases in synaptic connections in this region, perhaps a result of sustained higher activity due to continuous levels of anxiety. Higher levels of glutamate and NAA in the ACC were positively correlated with more severe social anxiety symptoms (Phan et al., 2005).

Reduced activation in the ACC was observed in patients with a specific phobia of spiders following CBT (Lipka et al., 2014; Straube et al., 2006). Prior to treatment, patients with a specific phobia of spiders showed higher ACC activation while viewing images of spiders than healthy control participants, and ACC activation was higher with closer perceived proximity to the depicted spiders (Lipka et al., 2014; Zilverstand et al., 2017). Patients with snake or spider phobia also had higher cerebral blood flow to the ACC when viewing pictures of their feared animal, and this effect was potentiated when the patients were startled with a loud auditory sound (Pissiota et al., 2003). Structurally, patients with two subtypes of specific phobia, dental phobia and snake phobia, both showed increased sgACC volumes relative to healthy control subjects (Hilbert et al., 2015). One study found that patients with animal phobia (the animals which were the object of the participants' phobias were not reported) had significantly greater cortical thickness of the bilateral pregenual ACC relative to that of healthy control subjects (Rauch et al., 2004), whereas another study found that patients with spider phobia had reduced ACC thickness relative to healthy control subjects (Linares et al., 2014). These seemingly discordant results could plausibly be attributed to different brain structural underpinnings if the patient samples had differing objects of their phobias, so further study may be needed to discern the relationship between ACC thickness alterations and specific phobia. Few studies have investigated neurochemistry in specific phobia, perhaps due to the relative infrequency with which most patients encounter the object of their specific phobia. One study found no neurochemical differences in the cingulate gyrus between patients with spider phobia and healthy control subjects (Linares et al., 2014). It remains unclear what neurochemical changes, if any, might accompany remission from specific phobia following psychotherapy, as no studies to our knowledge have investigated this.

Brain Plasticity in Prefrontal Areas

Functional change as a result of psychotherapy is observed in frontal areas, although the direction of change is inconsistent. Some studies find increased activation in frontal regions after treatment, which has been conceptualized as more activity to downregulate limbic regions—essentially a metaphorical brake pedal to counteract the over-sensitive "accelerator" of the limbic system (Davidson, 2002). On the other hand, some studies and meta-analyses find decreased activation in frontal regions, which may represent a proportional decrease in activity levels necessary to regulate frontolimbic circuitry following reductions in limbic areas (e.g., Schrammen et al., 2022).

Patients with GAD showed a reduction in white matter volume in the midbrain and dorsolateral PFC (dlPFC) (Moon & Jeong, 2015). Reduced dlPFC volume correlated with increased duration of illness (Moon & Jeong, 2015) and another study found that gray matter volume of primarily prefrontal regions was causally gradually reduced with increased illness duration (Chen et al., 2020). Presently, there is no evidence to support the ability of psychotherapy to alter these structural differences to comparable levels of healthy controls. Patients with GAD exhibited increased dlPFC NAA and choline levels following successful CBT; of note, the same neurochemical changes were observed in a second cohort of patients who had been treated with sertraline, an SSRI (Mohammadi et al., 2022). These parallel results suggest that increased prefrontal NAA and choline levels may be associated with remission of GAD symptoms regardless of treatment type. At baseline, reduced choline levels were measured in the dlPFC of patients with GAD relative to healthy control subjects (Moon et al., 2015), suggesting a normalizing effect of therapy. Another study found no differences in NAA levels between patients with GAD and healthy control subjects (Strawn et al., 2013), suggesting that increased NAA levels may be a compensatory change associated with successful CBT. At rest, patients with GAD displayed lower connectivity between the PFC and limbic areas, and the magnitude of lower connectivity was associated with the magnitude of higher anxiety symptom severity (W. Li et al., 2016). These findings suggest a weakness in prefrontal regulation of limbic regions that is ameliorated in effective treatment.

Following CBT, activation in the dorsomedial PFC (dmPFC) was reduced in patients with SAD while viewing negative facial expressions (Klumpp et al., 2013). Reappraising negative self-beliefs was associated with increased dmPFC and dlPFC activation following CBT (Goldin et al., 2013). Hyperactivation was also observed in the medial PFC (mPFC) of patients with SAD in response to critical self-referential comments (Blair et al., 2008). Taken together, these studies highlight the modulation of prefrontal areas involved in social cognition and cognitive control to be less sensitive to negative affective stimuli and more engaged in reappraisal after CBT. Further, patients with SAD showed a positive correlation between reduction in bilateral dmPFC volume and reduction in anxiety symptoms (Steiger et al., 2017). Dynamic causal modeling revealed that patients with SAD had reduced attenuation of the amygdala response to emotional faces by the orbitofrontal cortex (OFC) (Sladky et al., 2015), lending support to the model of failure of top-down control in anxiety pathology.

The OFC has been noted as a region crucially involved in restructuring the reinforcement of learned associations (Kringelbach & Rolls, 2004). In one study of patients with specific phobia, successful CBT combined with an exposure to a live spider was followed by increased medial OFC activation while viewing images of spiders immediately after treatment and also at a six-month follow-up, providing a plausible neurobiological mechanism of how successful exposure therapy can disestablish learned phobic associations (Schienle et al., 2007, 2009). As the OFC has been noted to be a region that receives reduced cerebral blood flow in specific phobia while patients view photos of the objects of their animal phobia (Åhs et al., 2009; Fredrikson et al., 1995; Wik et al., 1993), increased OFC activation following combined exposure and CBT points to normalization of this brain aberration in a symptom-provoking context. Activation in another frontal region with reciprocal connections to the OFC, the ventrolateral PFC (vlPFC), was linearly related to perceived proximity to images of spiders in patients with spider phobia, but not healthy control participants, suggesting that this region of the PFC quantitatively represents perceived threat, which is exaggerated in the phobia (Zilverstand et al., 2017). Structurally, patients with dental phobia and snake phobia both showed increased OFC volumes relative to healthy control subjects, and dental phobia patients had increased dmPFC and OFC volumes relative to snake phobia patients (Hilbert et al., 2015). Both phobia subgroups had increased white matter volume in the OFC relative to that of healthy control subjects, and patients with dental phobia had greater white matter volume in the dlPFC relative to patients with snake phobia (Hilbert et al., 2015). Although specific phobia is a single categorical diagnosis, different structural brain morphology seems to underlie each individual subtype, which is perhaps unsurprising given the heterogeneity in the objects of the specific phobias.

Brain Plasticity in Non-Prefrontal Cortical Areas

Instances of brain plasticity associated with CBT have also been noted in cortical regions outside of the PFC. Patients with SAD showed a significant reduction in left inferior parietal cortex thickness following group CBT (Steiger et al., 2017). Given the key role of the inferior parietal cortex in attentional processing, which is a core training facet of CBT, reduction of thickness in this area is a plausible structural reflection of more efficient executive functioning in this domain. Patients with a specific phobia of spiders displayed significantly more activation in the bilateral middle occipital gyrus, bilateral superior parietal lobule, left inferior occipital gyrus, left fusiform gyrus, and right inferior frontal gyrus following CBT (Paquette et al., 2003), highlighting a possibly compensatory widespread recruitment of additional cortical areas associated with amelioration of specific phobia symptoms.

Brain Plasticity in Hippocampal Areas

Patients with specific phobia displayed higher activation in the parahippocampal gyrus relative to healthy control subjects before CBT, and this effect was extinguished after successful treatment (Paquette et al., 2003). As the hippocampus and parahippocampus are centrally involved in contextual fear learning, the normalized reduction of activation in these regions may reflect the learned extinction of the phobia in therapy. During an anxiety-inducing public speaking task, CBT responders with a previous diagnosis of SAD showed reduced regional cerebral blood flow to the hippocampus and parahippocampal cortices, in addition to the amygdala (Furmark et al., 2002), highlighting the dampening of the hippocampal-amygdala alarm system to threat as another mechanistic neurobiological change resulting from CBT.

Future Directions for Studying Brain Plasticity in Response to Psychotherapy

Measuring brain plasticity in response to psychotherapy has the potential to elucidate mechanisms of change induced by the treatment. A few important areas remain to be addressed to provide a more complete understanding of this plasticity. First, some noted brain changes, both pre-treatment differences relative to healthy controls and differences observed following treatment, differ depending on the age of patients. Leveraging large open-source neuroimaging datasets that span development could help to adjudicate this difference and shed light on the variations in neurodevelopmental trajectories associated with the pathogenesis of anxiety disorders (Zacharek et al., 2021). Second, many studies focusing on treatment have taken an approach of collecting a neuroimaging metric before and after patients undergo treatment. However, an unclear understanding of how each modality relates to other modalities (e.g., how structure relates to function) and the heterogeneity of experimental design across studies makes it difficult to draw meaningful conclusions across studies. Studies that integrate multiple neuroimaging metrics and modalities in the same investigation can provide a more complete picture of neuroplasticity. Third, some studies have found converging bases of remission from anxiety in both pharmaceutical and psychotherapy interventions, while other studies have found disparate effects. The inclusion of multiple treatment modalities in studies of anxiety disorders could contribute to knowledge of whether brain plasticity in response to treatment is specific to that therapy or if it is general to recovery from the anxiety disorder being treated. Similarly, studies investigating different psychotherapies could clarify the brain mechanisms underlying each therapeutic approach. A better understanding of the specific way that treatments alter the brain for a given neuropsychiatric disorder has the potential to provide scientific evidence for which therapy a patient would likely benefit from based on their pre-treatment brain.

Brain Imaging Biomarkers to Predict Response to Psychotherapy

About twenty years ago, there was great optimism that insights into psychiatric disorders from neuroimaging and genetics would lead to breakthroughs in understanding the neurobiological bases of those disorders and, in turn, powerful advances in the effective treatment of those disorders. Indeed, there have been considerable advances in understanding the genetic and brain bases of psychiatric disorders, but these advances have yielded little progress in the everyday treatment of patients. Neuroimaging and genetics have not yet generally altered diagnosis, prognosis, or treatment.

Perhaps the most practical problem in the treatment of psychiatric disorders is the high rate of ineffective treatments for both current behavioral and pharmaceutical treatments. Response rates for psychotherapy (significant improvement of symptoms) typically range up to about 50 percent of patients (e.g., Loerinc et al., 2015). There is no scientific basis for a clinician or patient to select among validated alternative treatments in order to identify a treatment more likely to benefit that patient. Failed treatments extend patient suffering and dysfunction, often discourage engagement in a subsequent treatment attempt (Huynh & McIntyre, 2008), and extend the economic costs of a disorder for the patient and the health care system.

It has been hoped that knowledge of a particular patient's characteristics might inform which treatment is most likely to help that patient—a hope termed as *precision* or *personalized* medicine. Such characteristics could include demographic variables (e.g., age, gender, education, socioeconomic status), clinical variables (e.g., disease duration, co-occurring conditions), and, in research settings, patient and clinician rating scales or questionnaires. These measures have the advantage that they are highly scalable in clinical settings. Indeed, many studies report such correlations or associations with treatment efficacy when averaged over a particular group of patients. There is little evidence as yet, however, that these kinds of measures are reasonably reliable for predicting an individual patient's response (although new ones may be developed that are superior in this regard).

It has been hoped that biological measures, or *biomarkers*, taken from brain imaging or genetics might improve *prediction* accuracy. A critical aspect of prediction is that it operates reliably for an individual patient, has a usefully high rate of accuracy for each patient, and generalizes across patients (associations or correlations can reflect somewhat idiosyncratic characteristics of a specific research cohort). Generalization is best achieved by developing a model of prediction on one cohort of patients and then testing that prediction on an independent cohort of patients. In practice, there are as yet few examples of such independent cohorts (probably due to limited resources to support the costs of both treatment and neuroimaging). An intermediate approach is *cross-validation* in which different portions of a data set are used to develop (train) a model and then test the generalizability of that model. In this chapter, the terms *correlations* and *associations* are used to describe relations between pre-treatment biomarkers and post-treatment outcomes in a single group, and *prediction* is used to describe studies that use separable data for model building and model testing that meet the higher standard of generalization.

The degree of necessary individual accuracy for practical value is unclear. On the one hand, any sort of empirical support for treatment selection would represent progress relative to the current absence of scientific support for such selection. On the other hand, a small amount of evidence may be unhelpful, and the value of evidence must be weighed against the cost and practicality of obtaining such evidence. The strength of evidence can be expressed in two ways, as a continuous measure of symptom improvement, which is the most accurate expression, or as a categorical measure of individual accuracy wherein the category is defined as falling below or above a reasonable threshold of treatment efficacy or response. Such category boundaries are inevitably matters of judgment, but they are communicative for the categorical decision of whether to select a particular treatment for a specific patient.

In this field, as so many others currently, artificial intelligence through machine learning (ML) can be a useful tool to identify optimal predictors for treatment efficacy. Such algorithms can process many variables to identify what combination of variables (e.g., demographics, clinical history, additional diagnoses, patient and clinician surveys, neuroimaging, genetics) best predicts treatment efficacy. These variables reflect a range of ease and cost, with measures that can be collected in an office or online being most easily scalable and cost-effective. In this context, neuroimaging measures that are associated with or predictive of treatment response can be viewed in two ways. First, they can offer additional *scientific* insight about brain–behavior relations relevant to treatment, similar to the studies reporting neurochemical, functional, and structural correlates of treatment reviewed earlier in this chapter. Second, if brain measures were to add considerable predictive accuracy relative to in-office or online measures, they could become a practical *clinical* part of personalized/precision treatment selection so that half or more of patients do not have to endure ineffective treatment.

Predictive measures may be more related to brain mechanisms of treatment than they are to brain mechanisms of the etiology or expression of a disorder. Treatment may, for example, involve alternative pathways in the brain that allow an individual to circumvent an anxiety disorder or may instead normalize brain aberrations associated with a disorder. Furthermore, reliable predictors of treatment efficacy may also favor brain measures that are inherently the most reliable.

Predictions Involving Prefrontal Regions

Multiple studies have revealed that variation in fMRI activations in prefrontal regions, including the ACC and mPFC, is predictive of variation in response to psychotherapy in anxiety disorders. A meta-analysis of anxiety-related disorders, including specific phobia, social anxiety disorder, panic disorder/agoraphobia, generalized anxiety disorder, obsessive-compulsive disorder, and posttraumatic stress disorder examined seventeen task-based fMRI studies involving 442 patients (Picó-Pérez et al., 2023). Across tasks and diagnoses, the most consistent predictors of CBT response were activations in a network of regions involved in salience and interoception processing, encompassing fronto-insular (the right inferior frontal gyrus-anterior insular cortex) and fronto-limbic (the dmPFC-dorsal ACC (dACC)) cortices. Another review also noted the predictive value of increased activations in dACC and increased resting state coupling between the ACC and the amygdala (Klumpp & Fitzgerald, 2018). There was considerable variation in the tasks employed to produce the activations, including perception of emotional stimuli (e.g., emotional facial expressions), forms of social rejection, cognitive control, and others. For task-activated studies, it is expected that precise locations of predictive activations may vary as a consequence of the mental processes invoked by specific task demands and contrasts between conditions.

Some studies of patients with SAD have shown particular promise toward prediction of individual outcomes. One fMRI study of forty-eight patients receiving both CBT and medication (the SSRI escitalopram or placebo) found that variation of activation in response to negative facial expressions in the dACC was 81 percent accurate (in a cross-validated analysis) in predicting response versus nonresponse (although the direction of activation was opposite for medication versus placebo) (Frick et al., 2018). Demographic and clinical variables did not predict outcomes. The contrasting directions of prediction for CBT and medication suggests both similarity (in brain location) and difference (in direction of activation) between CBT and medication in regard to mechanism of prediction. The same group reported a study involving internet-delivered CBT plus either medication or placebo and employed ML (Support Vector Machines) and use of a non-emotion cognitive task during fMRI (Frick et al., 2020). Activation in the dACC was 83 percent accurate in predicting responders versus non-responders; demographic, clinical, and genetic information did not predict treatment response.

Multiple other studies with SAD patients report that pre-treatment fMRI activation was associated with treatment efficacy. Greater pre-treatment functional connectivity between the mPFC and pregenual ACC (Klumpp et al., 2013) and also ACC activation during emotion regulation correlated with greater CBT efficacy (Klumpp, Fitzgerald, et al., 2017). Similarly, pre-treatment activation variation in response to fearful faces (in a condition with high demand for cognitive control) in the dACC correlated with CBT efficacy (Klumpp et al., 2016). Pre-treatment activation variation for an emotion reappraisal task in the dlPFC correlated with CBT efficacy (Klumpp, Roberts, et al., 2017); neither demographic nor pre-treatment clinical information was associated with response to CBT. Another study of SAD patients employed brief videos with messages of social rejection and found that greater pre-treatment activation to those videos in the ACC and amygdala was associated with better CBT outcome (Burklund et al., 2017). That study also examined acceptance and commitment therapy (ACT) and found that activation in a different brain region (sensory-focused posterior insula) correlated with better ACT outcome. This finding raises the possibility that neuroimaging might help identify which form of psychotherapy is most likely to be effective for an individual patient. Further, there is evidence that pre-treatment ACC activation may reveal transdiagnostic associations with CBT treatment outcome as such activation was found for both SAD and major depressive disorder (Feurer et al., 2022). Thus, multiple studies have reported that pre-treatment activation in prefrontal brain regions was associated with variation in response to CBT, and that neuroimaging data were more informative than demographic, clinical, and genetic data.

Pre-treatment brain activations have also been associated with CBT efficacy in pediatric studies. In two studies, variation of fMRI activation in response to emotional facial expressions in several prefrontal and anterior cingulate regions (Burkhouse et al., 2018; Kujawa et al., 2016), and ERP responses to angry faces (Bunford et al., 2017) were associated with both CBT and SSRI efficacy.

Several studies have reported associations between pre-treatment fMRI and response to exposure therapy in specific phobias. Variations in fMRI activation in the posterior cingulate cortex related to reward (Papalini et al., 2019) and in ventral mPFC related to fear-conditioning (Lange et al., 2020) were associated with therapeutic efficacy. An intriguing extension of prediction research is to ask whether post-treatment neuroimaging is associated with long-term outcomes after intensive behavioral treatment given high rates of relapse after many treatments. A small study of patients with spider phobia receiving exposure therapy found that pre–post fMRI activation changes in the insula/vlPFC region were associated with phobia severity eight years later (Lange et al., 2016). Although longer-term studies following therapy are relatively rare and uncontrolled, they have ecological value because it is hoped that therapies would have longer-term benefits.

Predictions Involving the Basal Ganglia and Cerebellum

The basal ganglia are implicated in multiple aspects of fear, reward, and learning, and exhibit atypical anatomical volumes (Groenewold et al., 2023) and atypical functional connectivity of the nucleus accumbens (which is especially associated with reward) (Manning et al., 2015) in adult SAD. Anatomical volumetric variation in basal ganglia correlated with treatment response in SAD patients. Greater pre-treatment volume of the left nucleus accumbens was associated with greater treatment response to both CBT and SSRI in both adults and youth with anxiety disorders (Burkhouse et al., 2020). There is also evidence that pre-treatment resting-state fMRI of the cerebellum, a region with extensive interconnectivity with the neocortex, was associated with CBT efficacy (M. Yuan et al., 2017).

Predictions Involving the Amygdala

Greater pre-treatment activation to emotional facial expressions in the amygdala (and insula) has been associated with greater treatment response to both CBT and an SSRI in adults with anxiety and/or depression (Gorka et al., 2019). Greater pre-treatment functional connectivity between the right amygdala and right vlPFC was associated with greater therapeutic response to CBT in SAD patients (Young et al., 2019). Variation in pre-treatment amygdala response to emotional facial expressions was also related to CBT efficacy in pediatric anxiety disorders (McClure et al., 2007).

Predictions Involving Visual Cortex

Although visual cortical areas are not so obviously involved in anxiety as prefrontal and amygdala regions, reviews have noted that activations in visual regions have provided predictive information about treatment efficacy (e.g., Marwood et al., 2018). Such activations may reflect interactions between visual perception and other areas of the brain involved in cognition (e.g., frontal cortex) or emotion (e.g., amygdala). It is possible that the predictive value of a brain region involves not only its local functions but also its network connectivity with other regions as well as the regional strength of fMRI signal.

One study involved thirty-nine patients with SAD who, prior to CBT, viewed angry (versus neutral) faces and negative emotional (versus neutral) scenes during fMRI. Greater pre-treatment activation for angry faces in right occipital regions was associated with better CBT efficacy (there was no relation to the negative scenes, perhaps reflecting the specifically social aspect of SAD) (Doehrmann et al., 2013). In cross-validation analyses, initial symptom severity accounted for 20 percent of the variance in treatment outcome. Adding the neuroimaging activations nearly tripled prediction accuracy to 57 percent of the variance. This finding raises the possibility that neuroimaging and clinical information may be combined to best inform individual treatment selection.

Multimodal Predictions from Neuroimaging, Clinical, and Demographic Information

Prediction models need not be limited to single regional brain measures, but instead can integrate multiple brain measures as well as demographic and clinical measures to optimize prediction accuracy. One fMRI study examined patients with GAD or panic disorder who, before treatment, viewed negative scenes while attempting to regulate emotions or simply view the scenes (Ball et al., 2014, 2018). Rather than focus on a single region, activations were measured in seventy regions, and both activations and demographic/clinical data were analyzed via ML (random forests). Prediction of response for individual patients based on neuroimaging (79 percent accuracy) was higher than those based on clinical or demographic data (69 percent accuracy). Integration of activation with ML (gaussian process classifiers) in multiple brain regions during fear conditioning yielded 73 percent accuracy in individual patient outcomes from CBT treatment of panic disorder with agoraphobia (Hahn et al., 2015).

Another example involved prediction of CBT efficacy in thirty-eight SAD patients (Whitfield-Gabrieli et al., 2016). Analyses include pre-treatment symptom severity, resting-state connectivity of the amygdalae to the whole brain, DWI measure of the right inferior longitudinal fasciculus, and a data-driven multivoxel pattern analysis of whole-brain resting-state connectivity. In combination, and with cross-validation, these measures produced 81 percent accuracy in predicting which patient would respond usefully to CBT (a five-fold improvement above clinical measures alone). Each clinical and brain measure added to the model improved overall predictive accuracy.

EEG Predictions

Although the specific brain bases of EEG and ERP brain signals are uncertain due to spatial imprecision, such measures are lower in cost and more widely deployable than MRI measures. One study combined emotional stimuli and cognitive demands (working memory load) while recording the late positive potential (LPP) in patients with anxiety disorders before treatment with CBT or medicine (an SSRI). Greater LPP before treatment to negative pictures under conditions of low cognitive demand was associated with greater response to the SSRI (but not CBT) (Kinney et al., 2021). The differential associations between the LPP and the two kinds of treatment raise the possibility that biomarkers from neuroimaging may help select among treatment alternatives.

Going Forward with Predictions to Support Precision Selection of Treatments

The above review summarizes considerable progress in identifying biomarkers from neuroimaging that are associated with variation in psychotherapy efficacy for anxiety disorders, particularly SAD, GAD, and specific phobias. There are, however, important challenges to be met in order for this kind of science to support more patients receiving effective treatment. First, other kinds of data, especially demographic and clinical data that are more easily acquired, could guide treatment selection. To date, when analyzed, these kinds of data have had modest associations with treatment efficacy that are insufficient to support selection of a treatment for an individual patient (e.g., Whitfield-Gabrieli et al., 2016, for SAD; and Fonzo et al., 2019, for depression). At present, neuroimaging biomarkers outperform demographic, clinical, and genetic predictors. Second, predictive models may use ML approaches to integrate multiple kinds of neuroimaging, demographic, clinical, and genetic data to optimize prediction accuracy. Third, it will be important to develop predictive models that contrast the likely efficacy of alternative treatment options, e.g., CBT or an SSRI, CBT or ACT, or combined CBT and SSRI. The most important question for a patient and clinician is not whether a particular treatment is more or less likely to be effective, but rather *which* treatment among reasonable alternatives is most likely to be effective. Fourth, to reach clinical relevance, truly predictive studies with independent data sets will be needed to demonstrate the generalizable reliability of a predictor, or combinations of predictors, across patients. In this regard, it will also be important that the patients in such studies include broad representation of the population so that models are applicable across racial, ethnic, and socioeconomic populations (J. Li et al., 2022). All of this will require large-scale, resource-demanding, and multi-disciplinary research studies, but the alternative is to continue without a scientific basis for treatment selection that results in nearly half of patients receiving ineffective treatment instead of the help that they need.

Conclusions

Although neuroimaging has multiple limitations, it has revealed many examples of brain plasticity associated with psychotherapy in regard to neuroanatomy, neurophysiology, and neurochemistry. Further, there is a growing literature documenting the potential of pre-treatment biomarkers derived from neuroimaging to be associated with or predict the high variation in response to psychotherapy. This chapter has been limited in scope to CBT as a form of psychotherapy and to anxiety disorders as a form of neuropsychiatric disorder, but there are many other neuroimaging studies related to other treatments for other disorders, including major depressive disorder. In many ways, the pace of rigorous scientific research is slow relative to the pressing need to improve treatment outcomes for psychiatric disorders, but progress has been substantial in understanding the brain mechanisms of treatment and in thinking about how such progress may translate into better outcomes for patients.

Disclosures

Sadie J. Zacharek receives financial support from the Irene T. Cheng Fellowship in the Department of Brain and Cognitive Sciences and the Janet and Sheldon Razin Fellowship at the McGovern Institute for Brain Research at MIT. John D. E. Gabrieli receives financial support from NIH/NIMH R01MH128377, NIH/NICHD R01R01HD106122, and the Poitras Center for Psychiatric Disorders Research at the McGovern Institute for Brain Research at MIT. Stefan G. Hofmann receives financial support by the Alexander von Humboldt Foundation (as part of the Alexander von Humboldt Professur), the Hessische Ministerium für Wissenschaft und Kunst (as part of the LOEWE Spitzenprofessur), NIH/NIMH R01MH128377, NIH/NIMHU01MH108168, Broderick Foundation/MIT, and the James S. McDonnell Foundation 21st Century Science Initiative in Understanding Human Cognition—Special Initiative. He receives compensation for his work as editor from Springer Nature. He also receives royalties and payments for his work from various publishers.

References

Adolphs, R., Tranel, D., Damasio, H., & Damasio, A. R. (1995). Fear and the human amygdala. *The Journal of Neuroscience*, 15(9), 5879–5891. https://doi.org/10.1523/JNEUROSCI.15-09-05879.1995

Åhs, F., Pissiota, A., Michelgård, Å., Frans, Ö., Furmark, T., Appel, L., & Fredrikson, M. (2009). Disentangling the web of fear: Amygdala reactivity and functional connectivity in spider and snake phobia. *Psychiatry Research: Neuroimaging*, 172(2), 103–108. https://doi.org/10.1016/j.pscychresns.2008.11.004

Amir, N., Klumpp, H., Elias, J., Bedwell, J. S., Yanasak, N., & Miller, L. S. (2005). Increased activation of the anterior cingulate cortex during processing of disgust faces in individuals with social phobia. *Biological Psychiatry*, 57(9), 975–981. https://doi.org/10.1016/j.biopsych.2005.01.044

Amstadter, A. (2008). Emotion regulation and anxiety disorders. *Journal of Anxiety Disorders*, *22*(2), 211–221. https://doi.org/10.1016/j.janxdis.2007.02.004

Baddeley, A. (1986). *Working memory* (pp. xi, 289). Clarendon Press/Oxford University Press.

Ball, T. M., Stein, M. B., Ramsawh, H. J., Campbell-Sills, L., & Paulus, M. P. (2014). Single-subject anxiety treatment outcome prediction using functional neuroimaging. *Neuropsychopharmacology*, *39*(5), Article 5. https://doi.org/10.1038/npp.2013.328

Ball, T. M., Stein, M. B., Ramsawh, H. J., Campbell-Sills, L., & Paulus, M. P. (2018). Erratum: Single-subject anxiety treatment outcome prediction using functional neuroimaging. *Neuropsychopharmacology*, *43*(4), Article 4. https://doi.org/10.1038/npp.2017.272

Bechara, A., Tranel, D., Damasio, H., Adolphs, R., Rockland, C., & Damasio, A. R. (1995). Double dissociation of conditioning and declarative knowledge relative to the amygdala and hippocampus in humans. *Science*, *269*(5227), 1115–1118. https://doi.org/10.1126/science.7652558

Blair, K., Geraci, M., Devido, J., McCaffrey, D., Chen, G., Vythilingam, M., Ng, P., Hollon, N., Jones, M., Blair, R. J. R., & Pine, D. S. (2008). Neural response to self- and other referential praise and criticism in generalized social phobia. *Archives of General Psychiatry*, *65*(10), 1176–1184. https://doi.org/10.1001/archpsyc.65.10.1176

Buff, C., Brinkmann, L., Neumeister, P., Feldker, K., Heitmann, C., Gathmann, B., Andor, T., & Straube, T. (2016). Specifically altered brain responses to threat in generalized anxiety disorder relative to social anxiety disorder and panic disorder. *NeuroImage: Clinical*, *12*, 698–706. https://doi.org/10.1016/j.nicl.2016.09.023

Buhle, J. T., Silvers, J. A., Wager, T. D., Lopez, R., Onyemekwu, C., Kober, H., Weber, J., & Ochsner, K. N. (2014). Cognitive reappraisal of emotion: A meta-analysis of human neuroimaging studies. *Cerebral Cortex*, *24*(11), 2981–2990. https://doi.org/10.1093/cercor/bht154

Bunford, N., Kujawa, A., Fitzgerald, K. D., Swain, J. E., Hanna, G. L., Koschmann, E., Simpson, D., Connolly, S., Monk, C. S., & Phan, K. L. (2017). Neural reactivity to angry faces predicts treatment response in pediatric anxiety. *Journal of Abnormal Child Psychology*, *45*(2), 385–395. https://doi.org/10.1007/s10802-016-0168-2

Burkhouse, K. L., Jimmy, J., Defelice, N., Klumpp, H., Ajilore, O., Hosseini, B., Fitzgerald, K. D., Monk, C. S., & Phan, K. L. (2020). Nucleus accumbens volume as a predictor of anxiety symptom improvement following CBT and SSRI treatment in two independent samples. *Neuropsychopharmacology*, *45*(3), Article 3. https://doi.org/10.1038/s41386-019-0575-5

Burkhouse, K. L., Kujawa, A., Hosseini, B., Klumpp, H., Fitzgerald, K. D., Langenecker, S. A., Monk, C. S., & Phan, K. L. (2018). Anterior cingulate activation to implicit threat before and after treatment for pediatric anxiety disorders. *Progress in Neuro-Psychopharmacology and Biological Psychiatry*, *84*, 250–256. https://doi.org/10.1016/j.pnpbp.2018.03.013

Burklund, L. J., Torre, J. B., Lieberman, M. D., Taylor, S. E., & Craske, M. G. (2017). Neural responses to social threat and predictors of cognitive behavioral therapy and acceptance and commitment therapy in social anxiety disorder. *Psychiatry Research: Neuroimaging*, *261*, 52–64. https://doi.org/10.1016/j.pscychresns.2016.12.012

Cahill, L., Babinsky, R., Markowitsch, H. J., & McGaugh, J. L. (1995). The amygdala and emotional memory. *Nature*, *377*(6547), Article 6547. https://doi.org/10.1038/377295a0

Chen, Y., Cui, Q., Fan, Y.-S., Guo, X., Tang, Q., Sheng, W., Lei, T., Li, D., Lu, F., He, Z., Yang, Y., Hu, S., Deng, J., & Chen, H. (2020). Progressive brain structural alterations assessed via causal analysis in patients with generalized anxiety disorder. *Neuropsychopharmacology*, *45*(10), Article 10. https://doi.org/10.1038/s41386-020-0704-1

Davidson, R. J. (2002). Anxiety and affective style: Role of prefrontal cortex and amygdala. *Biological Psychiatry*, *51*(1), 68–80. https://doi.org/10.1016/S0006-3223(01)01328-2

Davis, M. (1992). The role of the amygdala in fear and anxiety. *Annual Review of Neuroscience*, *15*(1), 353–375. https://doi.org/10.1146/annurev.ne.15.030192.002033

Doehrmann, O., Ghosh, S. S., Polli, F. E., Reynolds, G. O., Horn, F., Keshavan, A., Triantafyllou, C., Saygin, Z. M., Whitfield-Gabrieli, S., Hofmann, S. G., Pollack, M., & Gabrieli, J. D. (2013). Predicting treatment response in social anxiety disorder from functional magnetic resonance imaging. *JAMA Psychiatry*, *70*(1), 87–97. https://doi.org/10.1001/2013.jamapsychiatry.5

Etkin, A., Prater, K. E., Schatzberg, A. F., Menon, V., & Greicius, M. D. (2009). Disrupted amygdalar subregion functional connectivity and evidence of a compensatory network in generalized anxiety disorder. *Archives of General Psychiatry*, *66*(12), 1361–1372. https://doi.org/10.1001/archgenpsychiatry.2009.104

Etkin, A., & Wager, T. D. (2007). Functional neuroimaging of anxiety: A meta-analysis of emotional processing in PTSD, social anxiety disorder, and specific phobia. *American Journal of Psychiatry*, *164*(10), 1476–1488. https://doi.org/10.1176/appi.ajp.2007.07030504

Feurer, C., Jimmy, J., Bhaumik, R., Duffecy, J., Medrano, G. R., Ajilore, O., Shankman, S. A., Langenecker, S. A., Craske, M. G., Phan, K. L., & Klumpp, H. (2022). Anterior cingulate cortex activation during attentional control as a transdiagnostic marker of psychotherapy response: A randomized clinical trial. *Neuropsychopharmacology*, *47*(7), Article 7. https://doi.org/10.1038/s41386-021-01211-2

Fonzo, G. A., Etkin, A., Zhang, Y., Wu, W., Cooper, C., Chin-Fatt, C., Jha, M. K., Trombello, J., Deckersbach, T., Adams, P., McInnis, M., McGrath, P. J., Weissman, M. M., Fava, M., & Trivedi, M. H. (2019). Brain regulation of emotional conflict predicts antidepressant treatment response for depression. *Nature Human Behaviour*, *3*(12), Article 12. https://doi.org/10.1038/s41562-019-0732-1

Fonzo, G. A., Ramsawh, H. J., Flagan, T. M., Sullivan, S. G., Lang, A. J., Simmons, A. N., Paulus, M. P., & Stein, M. B. (2014). Cognitive-behavioral therapy for generalized anxiety disorder is associated with attenuation of limbic activation to threat-related facial emotions. *Journal of Affective Disorders*, *169*, 76–85. https://doi.org/10.1016/j.jad.2014.07.031

Fredrikson, M., Wik, G., Annas, P., Fricson, K., & Stone-Elander, S. (1995). Functional neuroanatomy of visually elicited simple phobic fear: Additional data and theoretical analysis. *Psychophysiology*, *32*(1), 43–48. https://doi.org/10.1111/j.1469-8986.1995.tb03404.x

Frick, A., Engman, J., Alaie, I., Björkstrand, J., Gingnell, M., Larsson, E.-M., Eriksson, E., Wahlstedt, K., Fredrikson, M., & Furmark, T. (2020). Neuroimaging, genetic, clinical, and demographic predictors of treatment response in patients with social anxiety disorder. *Journal of Affective Disorders*, *261*, 230–237. https://doi.org/10.1016/j.jad.2019.10.027

Frick, A., Engman, J., Wahlstedt, K., Gingnell, M., Fredrikson, M., & Furmark, T. (2018). Anterior cingulate cortex activity as a candidate biomarker for treatment selection in social anxiety disorder. *British Journal of Psychiatry Open*, *4*(3), 157–159. https://doi.org/10.1192/bjo.2018.15

Furmark, T., Tillfors, M., Marteinsdottir, I., Fischer, H., Pissiota, A., Långström, B., & Fredrikson, M. (2002). Common changes in cerebral blood flow in patients with social phobia treated with citalopram or cognitive-behavioral therapy. *Archives of General Psychiatry*, *59*(5), 425–433. https://doi.org/10.1001/archpsyc.59.5.425

Goldin, P. R., Ziv, M., Jazaieri, H., Hahn, K., Heimberg, R., & Gross, J. J. (2013). Impact of cognitive behavioral therapy for social anxiety disorder on the neural dynamics of cognitive reappraisal of negative self-beliefs: Randomized clinical trial. *JAMA Psychiatry*, *70*(10), 1048–1056. https://doi.org/10.1001/jamapsychiatry.2013.234

Gorka, S. M., Young, C. B., Klumpp, H., Kennedy, A. E., Francis, J., Ajilore, O., Langenecker, S. A., Shankman, S. A., Craske, M. G., Stein, M. B., & Phan, K. L. (2019). Emotion-based brain mechanisms and predictors for SSRI and CBT treatment of anxiety and depression: A randomized trial. *Neuropsychopharmacology*, *44*(9), Article 9. https://doi.org/10.1038/s41386-019-0407-7

Greenberg, T., Carlson, J. M., Cha, J., Hajcak, G., & Mujica-Parodi, L. R. (2013). Ventromedial prefrontal cortex reactivity is altered in generalized anxiety disorder during fear generalization. *Depression and Anxiety*, *30*(3), 242–250. https://doi.org/10.1002/da.22016

Groenewold, N. A., Bas-Hoogendam, J. M., Amod, A. R., Laansma, M. A., Van Velzen, L. S., Aghajani, M., Hilbert, K., Oh, H., Salas, R., Jackowski, A. P., Pan, P. M., Salum, G. A., Blair, J. R., Blair, K. S., Hirsch, J., Pantazatos, S. P., Schneier, F. R., Talati, A., Roelofs, K., . . . Van Der Wee, N. J. A. (2023). Volume of subcortical brain regions in social anxiety disorder: Mega-analytic results from 37 samples in the ENIGMA-Anxiety Working Group. *Molecular Psychiatry*, *28*(3), 1079–1089. https://doi.org/10.1038/s41380-022-01933-9

Gross, J. J., & Thompson, R. A. (2007). Emotion regulation: Conceptual foundations. In J. J. Gross (Ed.), *Handbook of emotion regulation* (pp. 3–24). The Guilford Press.

Hahn, T., Kircher, T., Straube, B., Wittchen, H.-U., Konrad, C., Ströhle, A., Wittmann, A., Pfleiderer, B., Reif, A., Arolt, V., & Lueken, U. (2015). Predicting treatment response to cognitive behavioral therapy in panic disorder with agoraphobia by integrating local neural information. *JAMA Psychiatry, 72*(1), 68–74. https://doi.org/10.1001/jamapsychiatry.2014.1741

Hilbert, K., Evens, R., Isabel Maslowski, N., Wittchen, H.-U., & Lueken, U. (2015). Neurostructural correlates of two subtypes of specific phobia: A voxel-based morphometry study. *Psychiatry Research: Neuroimaging, 231*(2), 168–175. https://doi.org/10.1016/j.pscychresns.2014.12.003

Hoffman, D. L., Dukes, E. M., & Wittchen, H.-U. (2008). Human and economic burden of generalized anxiety disorder. *Depression and Anxiety, 25*(1), 72–90. https://doi.org/10.1002/da.20257

Hofmann, S. G., Asnaani, A., Vonk, I. J. J., Sawyer, A. T., & Fang, A. (2012). The efficacy of cognitive behavioral therapy: A review of meta-analyses. *Cognitive Therapy and Research, 36*(5), 427–440. https://doi.org/10.1007/s10608-012-9476-1

Huynh, N. N., & McIntyre, R. S. (2008). What are the implications of the STAR*D trial for primary care?: A review and synthesis. *The Primary Care Companion to The Journal of Clinical Psychiatry, 10*(02), 91–96. https://doi.org/10.4088/PCC.v10n0201

Ipser, J. C., Singh, L., & Stein, D. J. (2013). Meta-analysis of functional brain imaging in specific phobia. *Psychiatry and Clinical Neurosciences, 67*(5), 311–322. https://doi.org/10.1111/pcn.12055

Kessler, R. C., Petukhova, M., Sampson, N. A., Zaslavsky, A. M., & Wittchen, H.-U. (2012). Twelve-month and lifetime prevalence and lifetime morbid risk of anxiety and mood disorders in the United States. *International Journal of Methods in Psychiatric Research, 21*(3), 169–184. https://doi.org/10.1002/mpr.1359

Kinney, K. L., Burkhouse, K. L., Chang, F., MacNamara, A., Klumpp, H., & Phan, K. L. (2021). Neural mechanisms and predictors of SSRI and CBT treatment of anxiety: A randomized trial focused on emotion and cognitive processing. *Journal of Anxiety Disorders, 82*, 102449. https://doi.org/10.1016/j.janxdis.2021.102449

Klumpp, H., Fitzgerald, D. A., & Phan, K. L. (2013). Neural predictors and mechanisms of cognitive behavioral therapy on threat processing in social anxiety disorder. *Progress in Neuro-Psychopharmacology & Biological Psychiatry, 45*, 83–91. https://doi.org/10.1016/j.pnpbp.2013.05.004

Klumpp, H., Fitzgerald, D. A., Piejko, K., Roberts, J., Kennedy, A. E., & Phan, K. L. (2016). Prefrontal control and predictors of cognitive behavioral therapy response in social anxiety disorder. *Social Cognitive and Affective Neuroscience, 11*(4), 630–640. https://doi.org/10.1093/scan/nsv146

Klumpp, H., & Fitzgerald, J. M. (2018). Neuroimaging predictors and mechanisms of treatment response in social anxiety disorder: An overview of the amygdala. *Current Psychiatry Reports, 20*(10), 89. https://doi.org/10.1007/s11920-018-0948-1

Klumpp, H., Fitzgerald, J. M., Kinney, K. L., Kennedy, A. E., Shankman, S. A., Langenecker, S. A., & Phan, K. L. (2017). Predicting cognitive behavioral therapy response in social anxiety disorder with anterior cingulate cortex and amygdala during emotion regulation. *NeuroImage: Clinical, 15*, 25–34. https://doi.org/10.1016/j.nicl.2017.04.006

Klumpp, H., Roberts, J., Kennedy, A. E., Shankman, S. A., Langenecker, S. A., Gross, J. J., & Phan, K. L. (2017). Emotion regulation related neural predictors of cognitive behavioral therapy response in social anxiety disorder. *Progress in Neuro-Psychopharmacology and Biological Psychiatry, 75*, 106–112. https://doi.org/10.1016/j.pnpbp.2017.01.010

Konnopka, A., & König, H. (2020). Economic burden of anxiety disorders: A systematic review and meta-analysis. *PharmacoEconomics, 38*(1), 25–37. https://doi.org/10.1007/s40273-019-00849-7

Kringelbach, M. L., & Rolls, E. T. (2004). The functional neuroanatomy of the human orbitofrontal cortex: Evidence from neuroimaging and neuropsychology. *Progress in Neurobiology, 72*(5), 341–372. https://doi.org/10.1016/j.pneurobio.2004.03.006

Kujawa, A., Swain, J. E., Hanna, G. L., Koschmann, E., Simpson, D., Connolly, S., Fitzgerald, K. D., Monk, C. S., & Phan, K. L. (2016). Prefrontal reactivity to social signals of threat as a predictor of treatment response in anxious youth. *Neuropsychopharmacology, 41*(8), Article 8. https://doi.org/10.1038/npp.2015.368

Lange, I., Goossens, L., Leibold, N., Vervliet, B., Sunaert, S., Peeters, R., van Amelsvoort, T., & Schruers, K. (2016). Brain and behavior changes following exposure therapy predict outcome at 8-year follow-up. *Psychotherapy and Psychosomatics, 85*(4), 238–240. https://doi.org/10.1159/000442292

Lange, I., Goossens, L., Michielse, S., Bakker, J., Vervliet, B., Marcelis, M., Wichers, M., van Os, J., van Amelsvoort, T., & Schruers, K. (2020). Neural responses during extinction learning predict exposure therapy outcome in phobia: Results from a randomized-controlled trial. *Neuropsychopharmacology*, 45(3), Article 3. https://doi.org/10.1038/s41386-019-0467-8

Li, J., Bzdok, D., Chen, J., Tam, A., Ooi, L. Q. R., Holmes, A. J., Ge, T., Patil, K. R., Jabbi, M., Eickhoff, S. B., Yeo, B. T. T., & Genon, S. (2022). Cross-ethnicity/race generalization failure of behavioral prediction from resting-state functional connectivity. *Science Advances*, 8(11), eabj1812. https://doi.org/10.1126/sciadv.abj1812

Li, W., Cui, H., Zhu, Z., Kong, L., Guo, Q., Zhu, Y., Hu, Q., Zhang, L., Li, H., Li, Q., Jiang, J., Meyers, J., Li, J., Wang, J., Yang, Z., & Li, C. (2016). Aberrant functional connectivity between the amygdala and the temporal pole in drug-free generalized anxiety disorder. *Frontiers in Human Neuroscience*, 10, 549. https://doi.org/10.3389/fnhum.2016.00549

Linares, I. M. P., Jackowski, A. P., Trzesniak, C. M. F., Arrais, K. C., Chagas, M. H. N., Sato, J. R., Santos, A. C., Hallak, J. E. C., Zuardi, A. W., Nardi, A. E., Coimbra, N. C., & Crippa, J. A. S. (2014). Cortical thinning of the right anterior cingulate cortex in spider phobia: A magnetic resonance imaging and spectroscopy study. *Brain Research*, 1576, 35–42. https://doi.org/10.1016/j.brainres.2014.05.040

Lipka, J., Hoffmann, M., Miltner, W. H. R., & Straube, T. (2014). Effects of cognitive-behavioral therapy on brain responses to subliminal and supraliminal threat and their functional significance in specific phobia. *Biological Psychiatry*, 76(11), 869–877. https://doi.org/10.1016/j.biopsych.2013.11.008

Loerinc, A. G., Meuret, A. E., Twohig, M. P., Rosenfield, D., Bluett, E. J., & Craske, M. G. (2015). Response rates for CBT for anxiety disorders: Need for standardized criteria. *Clinical Psychology Review*, 42, 72–82. https://doi.org/10.1016/j.cpr.2015.08.004

Manning, J., Reynolds, G., Saygin, Z. M., Hofmann, S. G., Pollack, M., Gabrieli, J. D. E., & Whitfield-Gabrieli, S. (2015). Altered resting-state functional connectivity of the frontal-striatal reward system in social anxiety disorder. *PLOS One*, 10(4), e0125286. https://doi.org/10.1371/journal.pone.0125286

Månsson, K. N. T., Salami, A., Carlbring, P., Boraxbekk, C.-J., Andersson, G., & Furmark, T. (2017). Structural but not functional neuroplasticity one year after effective cognitive behaviour therapy for social anxiety disorder. *Behavioural Brain Research*, 318, 45–51. https://doi.org/10.1016/j.bbr.2016.11.018

Månsson, K. N. T., Salami, A., Frick, A., Carlbring, P., Andersson, G., Furmark, T., & Boraxbekk, C.-J. (2016). Neuroplasticity in response to cognitive behavior therapy for social anxiety disorder. *Translational Psychiatry*, 6(2), e727–e727. https://doi.org/10.1038/tp.2015.218

Marwood, L., Wise, T., Perkins, A. M., & Cleare, A. J. (2018). Meta-analyses of the neural mechanisms and predictors of response to psychotherapy in depression and anxiety. *Neuroscience & Biobehavioral Reviews*, 95, 61–72. https://doi.org/10.1016/j.neubiorev.2018.09.022

McClure, E. B., Adler, A., Monk, C. S., Cameron, J., Smith, S., Nelson, E. E., Leibenluft, E., Ernst, M., & Pine, D. S. (2007). FMRI predictors of treatment outcome in pediatric anxiety disorders. *Psychopharmacology*, 191(1), 97–105. https://doi.org/10.1007/s00213-006-0542-9

Merikangas, K. R., & Swanson, S. A. (2010). Comorbidity in anxiety disorders. In M. B. Stein & T. Steckler (Eds.), *Behavioral neurobiology of anxiety and its treatment* (pp. 37–59). Springer. https://doi.org/10.1007/7854_2009_32

Mohammadi, H., Changizi, V., Riyahi Alam, N., Rahiminejad, F., Soleimani, M., & Qardashi, A. (2022). Measurement of post-treatment changes in brain metabolites in patients with generalized anxiety disorder using magnetic resonance spectroscopy. *Journal of Biomedical Physics & Engineering*, 12(1), 51–60. https://doi.org/10.31661/jbpe.v0i0.1224

Monk, C. S., Telzer, E. H., Mogg, K., Bradley, B. P., Mai, X., Louro, H. M. C., Chen, G., McClure-Tone, E. B., Ernst, M., & Pine, D. S. (2008). Amygdala and ventrolateral prefrontal cortex activation to masked angry faces in children and adolescents with generalized anxiety disorder. *Archives of General Psychiatry*, 65(5), 568–576. https://doi.org/10.1001/archpsyc.65.5.568

Moon, C.-M., & Jeong, G.-W. (2015). Alterations in white matter volume and its correlation with clinical characteristics in patients with generalized anxiety disorder. *Neuroradiology*, 57(11), 1127–1134. https://doi.org/10.1007/s00234-015-1572-y

Moon, C.-M., Kang, H.-K., & Jeong, G.-W. (2015). Metabolic change in the right dorsolateral prefrontal cortex and its correlation with symptom severity in patients with generalized anxiety disorder: Proton magnetic resonance spectroscopy at 3 Tesla. *Psychiatry and Clinical Neurosciences*, *69*(7), 422–430. https://doi.org/10.1111/pcn.12279

Morris, J. S., Frith, C. D., Perrett, D. I., Rowland, D., Young, A. W., Calder, A. J., & Dolan, R. J. (1996). A differential neural response in the human amygdala to fearful and happy facial expressions. *Nature*, *383*(6603), Article 6603. https://doi.org/10.1038/383812a0

Münsterkötter, A. L., Notzon, S., Redlich, R., Grotegerd, D., Dohm, K., Arolt, V., Kugel, H., Zwanzger, P., & Dannlowski, U. (2015). Spider or no spider? Neural correlates of sustained and phasic fear in spider phobia. *Depression and Anxiety*, *32*(9), 656–663. https://doi.org/10.1002/da.22382

Ochsner, K. N., Bunge, S. A., Gross, J. J., & Gabrieli, J. D. E. (2002). Rethinking feelings: An fMRI study of the cognitive regulation of emotion. *Journal of Cognitive Neuroscience*, *14*(8), 1215–1229. https://doi.org/10.1162/089892902760807212

Ochsner, K. N., Ray, R. D., Cooper, J. C., Robertson, E. R., Chopra, S., Gabrieli, J. D. E., & Gross, J. J. (2004). For better or for worse: Neural systems supporting the cognitive down- and up-regulation of negative emotion. *NeuroImage*, *23*(2), 483–499. https://doi.org/10.1016/j.neuroimage.2004.06.030

Papalini, S., Lange, I., Bakker, J., Michielse, S., Marcelis, M., Wichers, M., Vervliet, B., van Os, J., Van Amelsvoort, T., Goossens, L., & Schruers, K. (2019). The predictive value of neural reward processing on exposure therapy outcome: Results from a randomized controlled trial. *Progress in Neuro-Psychopharmacology and Biological Psychiatry*, *92*, 339–346. https://doi.org/10.1016/j.pnpbp.2019.02.002

Paquette, V., Lévesque, J., Mensour, B., Leroux, J.-M., Beaudoin, G., Bourgouin, P., & Beauregard, M. (2003). "Change the mind and you change the brain": Effects of cognitive-behavioral therapy on the neural correlates of spider phobia. *NeuroImage*, *18*(2), 401–409. https://doi.org/10.1016/S1053-8119(02)00030-7

Phan, K. L., Fitzgerald, D. A., Cortese, B. M., Seraji-Bozorgzad, N., Tancer, M. E., & Moore, G. J. (2005). Anterior cingulate neurochemistry in social anxiety disorder: 1H-MRS at 4 Tesla. *NeuroReport*, *16*(2), 183–186. https://doi.org/10.1097/00001756-200502080-00024

Phan, K. L., Fitzgerald, D. A., Nathan, P. J., & Tancer, M. E. (2006). Association between amygdala hyperactivity to harsh faces and severity of social anxiety in generalized social phobia. *Biological Psychiatry*, *59*(5), 424–429. https://doi.org/10.1016/j.biopsych.2005.08.012

Picó-Pérez, M., Fullana, M. A., Albajes-Eizagirre, A., Vega, D., Marco-Pallarés, J., Vilar, A., Chamorro, J., Felmingham, K. L., Harrison, B. J., Radua, J., & Soriano-Mas, C. (2023). Neural predictors of cognitive-behavior therapy outcome in anxiety-related disorders: A meta-analysis of task-based fMRI studies. *Psychological Medicine*, *53*(8), 3387–3395. https://doi.org/10.1017/S0033291721005444

Pissiota, A., Frans, Ö., Michelgård, Å., Appel, L., Långström, B., Flaten, M. A., & Fredrikson, M. (2003). Amygdala and anterior cingulate cortex activation during affective startle modulation: A PET study of fear. *The European Journal of Neuroscience*, *18*(5), 1325–1331. https://doi.org/10.1046/j.1460-9568.2003.02855.x

Pollack, M. H., Jensen, J. E., Simon, N. M., Kaufman, R. E., & Renshaw, P. F. (2008). High-field MRS study of GABA, glutamate and glutamine in social anxiety disorder: Response to treatment with levetiracetam. *Progress in Neuro-Psychopharmacology and Biological Psychiatry*, *32*(3), 739–743. https://doi.org/10.1016/j.pnpbp.2007.11.023

Rauch, S. L., Wright, C. I., Martis, B., Busa, E., McMullin, K. G., Shin, L. M., Dale, A. M., & Fischl, B. (2004). A magnetic resonance imaging study of cortical thickness in animal phobia. *Biological Psychiatry*, *55*(9), 946–952. https://doi.org/10.1016/j.biopsych.2003.12.022

Riepenhausen, A., Wackerhagen, C., Reppmann, Z. C., Deter, H.-C., Kalisch, R., Veer, I. M., & Walter, H. (2022). Positive cognitive reappraisal in stress resilience, mental health, and well-being: A comprehensive systematic review. *Emotion Review*, *14*(4), 310–331. https://doi.org/10.1177/17540739221114642

Rosso, I. M., Makris, N., Britton, J. C., Price, L. M., Gold, A. L., Zai, D., Bruyere, J., Deckersbach, T., Killgore, W. D. S., & Rauch, S. L. (2010). Anxiety sensitivity correlates with two indices of right anterior insula structure in specific animal phobia. *Depression and Anxiety*, *27*(12), 1104–1110. https://doi.org/10.1002/da.20765

Schienle, A., Schäfer, A., Hermann, A., Rohrmann, S., & Vaitl, D. (2007). Symptom provocation and reduction in patients suffering from spider phobia. *European Archives of Psychiatry and Clinical Neuroscience, 257*(8), 486–493. https://doi.org/10.1007/s00406-007-0754-y

Schienle, A., Schäfer, A., Stark, R., & Vaitl, D. (2009). Long-term effects of cognitive behavior therapy on brain activation in spider phobia. *Psychiatry Research: Neuroimaging, 172*(2), 99–102. https://doi.org/10.1016/j.pscychresns.2008.11.005

Schrammen, E., Roesmann, K., Rosenbaum, D., Redlich, R., Harenbrock, J., Dannlowski, U., & Leehr, E. J. (2022). Functional neural changes associated with psychotherapy in anxiety disorders – A meta-analysis of longitudinal fMRI studies. *Neuroscience & Biobehavioral Reviews, 142*, 104895. https://doi.org/10.1016/j.neubiorev.2022.104895

Sladky, R., Höflich, A., Küblböck, M., Kraus, C., Baldinger, P., Moser, E., Lanzenberger, R., & Windischberger, C. (2015). Disrupted effective connectivity between the amygdala and orbitofrontal cortex in social anxiety disorder during emotion discrimination revealed by dynamic causal modeling for fMRI. *Cerebral Cortex, 25*(4), 895–903. https://doi.org/10.1093/cercor/bht279

Steiger, V. R., Brühl, A. B., Weidt, S., Delsignore, A., Rufer, M., Jäncke, L., Herwig, U., & Hänggi, J. (2017). Pattern of structural brain changes in social anxiety disorder after cognitive behavioral group therapy: A longitudinal multimodal MRI study. *Molecular Psychiatry, 22*(8), Article 8. https://doi.org/10.1038/mp.2016.217

Straube, T., Glauer, M., Dilger, S., Mentzel, H.-J., & Miltner, W. H. R. (2006). Effects of cognitive-behavioral therapy on brain activation in specific phobia. *NeuroImage, 29*(1), 125–135. https://doi.org/10.1016/j.neuroimage.2005.07.007

Strawn, J. R., Chu, W.-J., Whitsel, R. M., Weber, W. A., Norris, M. M., Adler, C. M., Eliassen, J. C., Phan, K. L., Strakowski, S. M., & DelBello, M. P. (2013). A pilot study of anterior cingulate cortex neurochemistry in adolescents with generalized anxiety disorder. *Neuropsychobiology, 67*(4), 224–229. https://doi.org/10.1159/000347090

Taylor, S. F., & Liberzon, I. (2007). Neural correlates of emotion regulation in psychopathology. *Trends in Cognitive Sciences, 11*(10), 413–418. https://doi.org/10.1016/j.tics.2007.08.006

Tillfors, M., Furmark, T., Marteinsdottir, I., Fischer, H., Pissiota, A., Långström, B., & Fredrikson, M. (2001). Cerebral blood flow in subjects with social phobia during stressful speaking tasks: A PET study. *American Journal of Psychiatry, 158*(8), 1220–1226. https://doi.org/10.1176/appi.ajp.158.8.1220

Whitfield-Gabrieli, S., Ghosh, S. S., Nieto-Castanon, A., Saygin, Z., Doehrmann, O., Chai, X. J., Reynolds, G. O., Hofmann, S. G., Pollack, M. H., & Gabrieli, J. D. E. (2016). Brain connectomics predict response to treatment in social anxiety disorder. *Molecular Psychiatry, 21*(5), Article 5. https://doi.org/10.1038/mp.2015.109

Wik, G., Fredrikson, M., Ericson, K., Eriksson, L., Stone-Elander, S., & Greitz, T. (1993). A functional cerebral response to frightening visual stimulation. *Psychiatry Research: Neuroimaging, 50*(1), 15–24. https://doi.org/10.1016/0925-4927(93)90020-I

Wik, G., Fredrikson, M., & Fischer, H. (1997). Evidence of altered cerebral blood-flow relationships in acute phobia. *International Journal of Neuroscience, 91*(3–4), 253–263. https://doi.org/10.3109/00207459708986381

Young, K. S., LeBeau, R. T., Niles, A. N., Hsu, K. J., Burklund, L. J., Mesri, B., Saxbe, D., Lieberman, M. D., & Craske, M. G. (2019). Neural connectivity during affect labeling predicts treatment response to psychological therapies for social anxiety disorder. *Journal of Affective Disorders, 242*, 105–110. https://doi.org/10.1016/j.jad.2018.08.016

Yuan, J., Zhang, Y., Zhao, Y., Gao, K., Tan, S., & Zhang, D. (2023). The emotion-regulation benefits of implicit reappraisal in clinical depression: Behavioral and electrophysiological evidence. *Neuroscience Bulletin, 39*(6), 973–983. https://doi.org/10.1007/s12264-022-00973-z

Yuan, M., Meng, Y., Zhang, Y., Nie, X., Ren, Z., Zhu, H., Li, Y., Lui, S., Gong, Q., Qiu, C., & Zhang, W. (2017). Cerebellar neural circuits involving executive control network predict response to group cognitive behavior therapy in social anxiety disorder. *The Cerebellum, 16*(3), 673–682. https://doi.org/10.1007/s12311-017-0845-x

Zacharek, S. J., Kribakaran, S., Kitt, E. R., & Gee, D. G. (2021). Leveraging big data to map neurodevelopmental trajectories in pediatric anxiety. *Developmental Cognitive Neuroscience, 50,* 100974. https://doi.org/10.1016/j.dcn.2021.100974

Zilverstand, A., Sorger, B., Kaemingk, A., & Goebel, R. (2017). Quantitative representations of an exaggerated anxiety response in the brain of female spider phobics—A parametric fMRI study. *Human Brain Mapping, 38*(6), 3025–3038. https://doi.org/10.1002/hbm.23571

5
Affect as a Foundation for How We Know and Understand the World

A Framework for Integrating Psychotherapy and Psychophysiology

Travis Anderson and Patrick R. Steffen

Life constantly requires us to cope with many types of situations—positive and negative, helpful and harmful. Affect plays a key psychological and physiological role in this coping process. Affect is generally defined by psychology as the embodied representation of how we evaluate and respond to life's fluctuating situations and demands in ways that are potentially adaptive (Clore & Huntsinger, 2009; Dukes et al., 2021; Duncan & Barrett, 2007; Lang et al., 1990; LeDoux, 2012; Russell, 2003). Russell (2003) defines affect as how we feel at a specific point in time, as determined by our current state of valence (positive or negative attraction) and arousal (high or low level of energy). Lang et al. (1990) similarly define affect as the body's general strategic approach to dealing with life's challenges in terms of valence and arousal. For all these researchers—in various ways and to various degrees—affect colors and conditions how we understand and adapt to the world, how we perceive people and events, and how we make sense of ourselves and our environment. Moods, emotions, feelings, and other forms of affect all help integrate mind and body functioning. Contrary to historical epistemological views that separated thinking and feeling and treated affect as an inessential bodily supplement to mental operations like perception and judgment, philosophers and psychologists today argue with increasing evidence and conviction that mind and body are unified, and that affect is a necessary and potentially adaptive component of cognition.

Why is affect potentially adaptive? The answer seems to lie in why the brain evolved the way it has. To survive, we must constantly cope with external demands (e.g., avoid predators, find food, water, and shelter) while also managing internal needs (e.g., maintain energy and temperature). To help us with those processes our sensory systems continuously monitor our body and the environment, assessing vast quantities of information every second. The conscious mind, however, can only focus on a minute percentage of this information at any given time. And because needs can shift suddenly (e.g., due to an unexpected threat or accident), bodies need the capacity to respond quickly as well as efficiently. Affects are the result. Affects supply immediate and in many cases nonconscious feedback and guidance. And over time they can provide the body with an overall sense of its own condition and environmental circumstances. This panoptic and self-correcting sense of the body's situation at any given moment constitutes our core affect (Barrett, 2017a). In all its various forms, affect is thus the means evolution has provided us to understand and to cope quickly, effectively, and adaptively to our constantly changing environment and needs. Without this capacity, chances of survival and flourishing would be markedly diminished.

The significance and mechanics of affect have attracted widespread attention in recent literature. For instance, in "The Feeling of What Happens: Body and Emotion in the Making of Consciousness," neuroscientist Antonio Damasio (2000) claims affect is central to homeostasis. In "Thinking Fast and Slow," Daniel Kahneman (2011) sees affect as critical to what he calls fast "system 1" processing. In "Strangers to Ourselves: The Adaptive Unconscious," Timothy Wilson (2004) views affect as a necessary element of the adaptive mind. And in "How Emotions are Made: The Secret Life of the Brain," Lisa Feldman Barrett (2017b) argues that a better understanding of affect has the potential to revolutionize psychology and healthcare. These authors (along with many others) assign affect a central role in how we know and respond to the world and ourselves.

Why are advances in our understanding of affect important for psychotherapy and other forms of therapeutic intervention? Apart from simply increasing our overall knowledge of how the mind and body operate, affective responses are not always adaptive. As we grow and mature, we sometimes respond to the world and even to our own bodily states in maladaptive ways. For example, we often try to avoid painful feelings and memories, even though avoidance does not improve our ability to flourish or even cope. In the short term, avoidance can be a satisfying and self-reinforcing remedy for discomfort, but in the long term—or when avoidance becomes our default response to pain or stress—it can prevent us from developing new and more effective response strategies. Additionally, research shows that people who suffer from an excess of negative affect, or who cannot cope effectively with negative feelings, have poorer memories for past life events, which then impairs their ability to learn from experience (Williams et al., 2007) and decreases their autonoetic consciousness—the ability to sense temporal continuity in self-identity (Lemogne et al., 2009). Also, as Banich et al. (2009) note, the tendency to wallow in pain or negatively ruminate on painful experiences interferes with our cognitive ability to effectively distinguish relevant from irrelevant information, which can lead to inflexibility in information processing and attentional bias toward negative thoughts and moods—and in the long run, to increased negativity and even depression. In sum, affect impacts all aspects of mental life for good *or* bad, and should thus be a central concern for psychology in general, but especially for both psychophysiology and psychotherapy.

Most psychotherapies address affect and emotion at some level, and psychophysiology recognizes that affect provides an important framework for organizing perception and response. Nevertheless, theories about affect and the precise functions it serves in cognition and decision-making are diverse and underdeveloped. Moreover, at least two historically problematic questions about mind, brain, body, and their relations still haunt affect theory today. First, there is the longstanding epistemological question of whether mind and brain are identical or different, and relatedly, whether and how mind and body are interconnected. Second, there are the two correlate metaphysical questions of whether the mind is an immaterial substance which perceives and understands the world spiritually, rationally, and objectively, and whether affect is a purely bodily and physical phenomenon which contaminates cognition and contributes nothing essential to understanding. These issues are vestiges of medieval religious dogmas concerning divine creation and the soul, and modern philosophical commitments to a substance (mind–body) dualism. While debates about these questions continue, contemporary theorists working in both neuroscience and philosophy increasingly conceive mind and body as unified, interdependent, and absolutely integral to each other, and research convincingly demonstrates that affect plays a key role in both raw cognition and higher-level reasoning. So, even though psychology has yet to purge itself decisively and completely of substance dualism and the metaphysical presuppositions that nurture it, current thinking has progressed to the point of either tacitly or expressly replacing dualistic models of what Descartes described as an "immaterial mind mysteriously conjoined to a material body," with the conception of a thoroughly "embodied mind" and a holistic view of mind–body functioning.

This chapter briefly reviews some of the complicated history of mind–body philosophy. It then explores recent research and productive connections between philosophy, psychophysiology, and psychotherapy in order to explore possibilities for improving and applying affect theory. We agree with current neuroscience and philosophy that affect is an essentially embodied and potentially adaptive response to the environment and the body's own states. We also agree with the unitary model of mind and body. Building on these agreements we argue, first, that affect, both positive *and* negative, is integral to human perception and understanding, and thus, a critical component in homeostatic well-being. This argument implies that human minds don't primarily perceive and engage the world objectively and rationally, but subjectively and affectively—relative to individual needs and capabilities, bodily states, and social connections—and sometimes, maladaptively. Second, we also argue that affect is not deleterious to, but fundamental to reasoned judgments and contextual agency. Third, we argue that both affective understanding and mental health can be significantly improved through therapeutic intervention informed by better conceptions of affect as such, and of how affect, cognition, and decision-making are related.

Philosophical Theories of Embodiment and Affect

Many conceptions of mind, brain, and body have roots stretching back at least to ancient Greece, but among the most problematic conceptions for modern science and psychology are those that trace directly to Cartesian metaphysics.

Generally speaking, both classical Greek and Stoic philosophers affirmed a close and complicated connection between mind and body. Socrates' reputed teaching that physical pain and pleasure are purely bodily sensations, while rational deliberation is the only sure path to truth, no doubt encouraged subsequent Christian beliefs that the soul and body are independent entities with conflicting natures. Yet, according to Plato's *Phaedrus*, Socrates also taught that passions and at least some emotions are products of a tripartite soul or mind, not just the body—and by extension, have the potential to influence both willful judgment and rational thought (Plato, 2021). In other words, despite what medieval Christian and modernist epistemologies might suggest to the contrary, early Greek philosophy seems to have viewed the human mind in a nuanced way, perhaps even conceiving ideational thought as a form of affective consciousness rather than a purely rational faculty. Such nuanced views were also characteristic of first century C.E. Stoic philosophy, especially the teachings of Epictetus. Stoics admittedly assigned to reason the dominant role in mental functioning, since they agreed with Socrates and Plato that reason must bridle and guide bodily wants, urges, feelings, and emotions if individual choices are to reliably promote happiness, health, and similar beneficial results. But Stoic teachings also implicitly attributed to affect considerable power in the mechanics of cognition (otherwise, they would never have feared that emotions and feelings could sway judgments toward what is merely pleasurable or emotionally satisfying rather than truly salutary, which they manifestly did). Epictetus in particular seems to have believed that to be effective, rational faculties must operate in tandem with bodily affects. In fact, he may have prioritized reason in the pursuit of *eudaimonia* or well-being precisely *because* he so clearly recognized the power of feelings and emotions to influence both thoughts and moods—for better *or* for worse. Nevertheless, these early Greek and Stoic views stand in stark contrast with most subsequent Christian views, for which the body was assumed to have a fallen, carnal nature that can only conflict with the immaterial and ideally spiritual operations of the mind.

The famous metaphysical meditations carried out by the early-modern French philosopher René Descartes (building upon his pre-existing Christian prejudices and bowing to political expediency) convinced him that even though mind and body must be "closely conjoined" in their functions, they are nevertheless two distinct and ontologically independent substances—the former immaterial, and the latter material. This theory occasioned serious and long-lasting problems for modern science and psychology. Endorsing Christianity's identification of the mind with a divinely created, immaterial, and eternal soul, while simultaneously insisting that all physical, temporal bodies must come into being and reproduce, transform, degenerate, and die in naturalistic and purely mechanistic ways, Descartes was forced to conclude that the human mind must be defined as a "rational soul" or "thinking substance," rather than as any organic component of the bodily brain, or as any other physical substance that could operate causally or mechanistically. Correlatively, he also concluded that the mind does not develop physiologically along with the human body but requires a special act of divine creation in each and every case (Descartes, 1985, pp. 134, 141). This set of presumptions and conclusions collectively constituted Descartes' infamous "mind–body dualism," which ultimately entailed an insurmountable problem for philosophy and psychology (recognized almost immediately by Queen Christina Wasa of Sweden, one of Descartes' most astute correspondents and a student of Stoic philosophy): In the absence of any physiological or mechanical connection between the mind and the body, how can bodily perceptions, sensations, and affects causally contribute to mental representations of the physical world, or in turn, be themselves influenced by an immaterial mind and its supposedly spiritual ideas? Even while Cartesian dualism continues to shape modern psychology, this critical question has historically defied all attempts at an answer.

Descartes tried to minimize this problem by dismissing or entirely disregarding the role of bodily processes and sensations in the operations of consciousness and thinking, which predictably occasioned other problems. Curiously, however, he included "feeling" among his list of "thinking" operations—doubting, understanding, affirming, denying, willing, imagining, *and feeling*—an inclusion that implicitly distinguished feelings from overtly physical sensations and emotions, and thereby foreshadowed a parallel distinction between feelings and emotions that modern neuroscientists like Antonio Damasio have also made (see Descartes, 1984, p. 19). Moreover, even though Descartes' mind/body problem lacked a solution, his dualistic ontology encouraged the widely accepted presumption that insofar as mental and material substances are qualitatively and substantially different, only the latter constitutes an "objective reality" that science and psychology can investigate and understand. The ramifications of this presumption for psychology were momentous. Since "material substances" for Descartes did not include the mind, Cartesian-based views of science and reality ended up with neither a method for carrying out psychological investigations nor a coherent conception of the mind's true nature. A related though less obvious consequence was the naïve ideal of a "pure" scientific objectivity that the thinking subject could supposedly achieve in its investigations of the material world. Fortunately, this poorly grounded *epistemological* conception of objectivity has largely been eclipsed in contemporary science by another, more productive Cartesian contribution—a *methodological* conception of objectivity for which discoveries and claims must always be subject to rigorous empirical or experimental verification). As a result of its indefensible mind–body dichotomy, the impact of Cartesian dualism on science is now almost universally characterized as negative, and has been described by Koestler as the "Cartesian Catastrophe" (1964, p. 148)—not only because Descartes assigned the immaterial mind a transcendent status that rendered it immune to physical laws, but because he restricted the mind's operations to conscious thought, conceived non-conscious mental processes as essentially impossible, and judged emotions and passions to be irrational and cognitively unimportant. All of these consequences stunted the progress of psychology despite the fact that less influential philosophers voiced reservations and alternative views almost immediately.

One such philosopher was Descartes' philosophical contemporary Baruch Spinoza, who stridently opposed Cartesian dualism and its manifold problems. Markedly at odds not only with Descartes, but with virtually all philosophical and religious thinking of the time, Spinoza posited a non-dualistic, unified view of mind and body, theorizing that they belong to a single underlying substance (see Bula, 2019, p. 8). Spinoza agreed with the Stoics that cognition and emotion are interconnected and therefore capable of influencing one another—the mind functioning to ensure the survival of the body and to guide the emotions, and the body supporting the mind and providing it with sensory data. Re-examining Spinoza's philosophy in the light of modern neuroscience, Emily Ravven (2003) described his conception of the mind's primary goal as a "consciousness of the body" (p. 258). Ravven observed that for Spinoza, thought is affectively dependent on the body and engaged with the world, not objectively detached and passive. She thinks Spinoza believed the mind to be shaped specifically through environmental and social interactions—which is to say that Spinoza conceived human consciousness as *relationally* constituted (a view which would anticipate aspects of the existential theory of consciousness that Martin Heidegger later developed). Ravven also claimed that for Spinoza affects arise *out of* bodily experience and represent the mental registering of such experience. Building on Spinoza's insights, Ravven herself theorized that the value we attribute to worldly objects and social relations results from our embodied purpose of survival and well-being, which is guided by homeostatic mechanisms seeking regulatory balance of internal needs and external demands.

To what degree Spinoza directly influenced the anti-Cartesian phenomenologist Martin Heidegger is hard to say, but in his 1927 work, *Being and Time,* Heidegger significantly expanded on Spinoza's view, arguing that affect plays a critical role in our understanding of the world, other people, and ourselves (Heidegger, 2010). Heidegger maintained not only that the mind is embodied and affective but drawing on Aristotle's metaphysics of possibility and actuality he also argued that human consciousness is determinately shaped by the exigencies and possibilities of life, predominantly those arising from quotidian, practical existence. Heidegger collectively addressed affects and feelings as "attunements" or "moods," and he understood them as the body's felt physiological and psychological responses both to its own various states and to its environment (2010, Section 29, pp. 134–135). For Heidegger, affects are an essential component of all cognition and interpretation, and moreover, provide the means by which the mind is disclosed and expressed most immediately and transparently *to itself* (2010, Section 31, pp. 141–142). Heidegger delineated three levels of affect-informed cognition—understanding, interpretation, and assertion (2010, Sections 29–33, pp. 130–155). He conceived the first, most fundamental level of understanding as our unreflective engagement with ordinary practical tasks and with other people, and subsequent levels as progressively more determinate and conceptually robust conceptual engagements, with explicit linguistic (propositional) expression in play only at the highest stage (assertive judgment). But he believed affect is integral to all three levels: Meaningful conscious comportment in all its modalities is always a function of perception, cognition, and conceptual thought operating *together with* bodily affects. Dispositional (affect-informed) understanding gives rise to interpretive acts, which in turn can be explicitly conceptualized and expressed as propositions or judgments. Affect "particularizes" all three modalities of understanding and provides them with an individualized bodily "certification," so to speak. Thus, for Heidegger affective states are nothing less than "bodily" forms of understanding.

The German word Heidegger typically uses in describing "mood" or "affect" is *Stimmung*, which literally means "attunement." Heidegger theorizes that affects "attune" us both to the environment and to our own bodily states by "resonating" with them in harmonious or discordant ways. This responsive inter-relatedness is precisely why Heidegger considered every affective attunement a modality of understanding in its most basic form, even before that understanding becomes fully conceptual or precisely articulated by thought, spoken and written words, and judgments; each form of understanding in the conceptual sense is *affectively* attuned to what is *conceptually and linguistically* grasped. Heidegger did not deny that reason and propositional thought contribute in necessary ways to an understanding of ourselves and the world. In fact, science and its mathematical models and postulates are proof that they do. But Heidegger tacitly agreed with Spinoza that conceptual and rational thinking always operate *in conjunction with and in response to* affective experience. What is more, Heidegger also claimed that the reverse is true. To paraphrase Heidegger, a mood (affective attunement) always has its understanding, and understanding always has its mood (2010, Section 31, p. 138).

As noted above, Heidegger further argued that human subjectivity is essentially a *relational* existence, what he termed *Mitsein*, or "Being-in-the-world-with-others." We simultaneously comport ourselves not only toward mental content like memories, fantasies, and ideas, as well as toward worldly things, practical tasks, and the contextual possibilities entailed by them, but toward other human beings and social concerns. In other words, consciousness always directs itself toward some object or content, and is thus by its very nature a conceptual and affective attunement that always affectively resonates with (harmoniously or discordantly) and conceptually understands (rightly or wrongly, and more or less explicitly) people, things, and ideas beyond the seeming immanence of consciousness itself. This "transcendence" might help explain why Descartes was so easily misled into thinking that consciousness must be a "disembodied" activity or substance, and that the mind and body can operate independently of each other. But once we recognize that consciousness by its very nature is always reaching beyond itself in responding to environmental, social, and even bodily stimuli, we can plainly see that it is fundamentally misunderstood when conceived as a disembodied, free-floating "power of awareness and thought"—a Cartesian immaterial "thinking substance" or "rational soul" that could ideally function without the input or encumbrances of physical being. Simply put, an affectively attuned and unified body and mind work *in tandem* to engage and make sense of the environment, other people, and itself, but that work is *essentially* relational. And to say that human perceptions, thoughts, and feelings are constitutively relational simply means that without the capacity to reach beyond itself there would be *no* consciousness *at all*.

One consequence of an *affectively* relational consciousness, according to Heidegger, is that it provides a way to understand ourselves or our environment more immediately (and sometimes, more truthfully) than is possible through empirical observation or detached rational thought—contrary to the claims of Descartes and many other philosophers. Moreover, while conceptual understanding is undeniably important, says Heidegger, it is always and primordially *conditioned by* our affective states. We have already noted that the immediacy of affective responses is adaptively advantageous in some ways, but potentially maladaptive in others: The capacity to respond to our environment without deliberation certainly increases survivability prospects, but it can also occasion the mistakes characteristic of what we call "overly-hasty" judgments and actions. Furthermore, the affective responses produced by painful memories or uncomfortable situations can foster habitual avoidance and denial, which neither improves our ability to cope nor helps us recognize and address the cause of such affects. Heidegger's analysis of moods provides an epistemological ground for explaining such responses. It also highlights and explains the potential for the misunderstandings and flawed judgments that frequently result from affective reactions: Feelings and moods can strongly predispose us toward both positive and negative behavior without us being explicitly aware of that influence, which in turn can lead us to "deceive ourselves" about our personal responsibility for our behavior. And since affective predispositions can be self-perpetuating, they can initiate a cycle of maladaptive behavioral responses. Because this dynamic typically operates outside the scope of our conscious awareness, the excessive or inappropriate behavior resulting from affective mal-attunements and misunderstandings can seem to a "self-deceived" subject both reasonable and beyond one's control. Hence, the dynamic can become very difficult to escape without therapeutic intervention.

Freud's solution to the puzzle of "self-deception" and its maladaptive consequences was to divide the mind or consciousness against itself, positing a subconscious form of desire and decision-making that could operate without the overt knowledge of conscious thought. For manifest reasons, this was an unsatisfactory solution. The Heideggerian remedy to this puzzle avoids the Freudian theory of a fractured and self-opposed consciousness by recasting the "duplicity" in such cases as a discordant tension between our conscious judgments, on the one hand, and on the other hand, the pre-dispositional attunements that are coloring and conditioning judgment without us being consciously aware of their influence. This solution preserves the power of contextual agency to reveal and dispel the "deception"—or intentionally *not* to do so, in cases involving ill intent (what Jean-Paul Sartre called "bad faith")—by demonstrating that a mindful attentiveness to the cognitive role played by affective, dispositional attunements can disclose how they shape our basic perceptions of the environment and thereby influence subsequent decisions with or without our conscious awareness. Heidegger's analyses of moods and dispositions can thus explain "self-deception" without bifurcating the mind or compromising our capacity to make determinative choices: By recognizing that we are always in *some* affective state, and by cultivating a conscious awareness of those states (including what triggers them, whether they are positive or negative, what behavioral modifications can re-shape them, etc.), we can become more cognizant of how our moods, emotions, and feelings (bad *and* good) influence us—which in turn can encourage behavioral changes and habits that circumvent maladaptive affects. Put simply, being mindful of our emotions and moods is as important to adaptive decision-making and self-determination as are the explicit deliberations and judgments we usually identify with conscious choices, but which are always conditioned "behind the scenes" by our affective attunements. Stated in language Damasio might use, mindfully or therapeutically attuning ourselves more transparently and adaptively to the environment and our own bodies can significantly increase our capacity to maintain homeostasis.

Current Scientific Theories on Embodiment and Affect

As these historical notes and examples hopefully demonstrate, the philosophical theories of Spinoza and Heidegger can help us build or improve a framework for better integrating psychotherapy and psychophysiology. At minimum, both perspectives provide ontological precedents for modeling mind, brain, and body as interdependent, not independent, and they anticipate discoveries that human perception is subjectively active and affective not passively objective and purely rational (Damasio, 2003; Heidegger, 2010; Ravven, 2003). These perspectives also fit well with the biopsychosocial model frequently used in psychophysiology, wherein biological, psychological, and social factors are all seen as interdependent and interconnected, and in which all contribute in important ways to health and well-being. But perhaps most importantly, by reconceiving affect as a bodily form of *understanding* ourselves, others, and the world, Spinoza and Heidegger's ideas can help therapists devise more effective ways of making both affective and conceptual understanding more adaptive and healthier.

Current philosophical and empirical research are in agreement that the mind is a function of the affective body, and that consciousness is a product of the human brain and nervous system, with no magic lines dividing mental and physical operations. Generally speaking, the brain is defined by physical elements such as neurons, the mind is conceived in terms of mental functioning, and the central and peripheral nervous systems are considered to be intricately and inseparably connected with each other and with all other parts of the body—with consciousness being the result. In short, although traces of Descartes' substance dualism may still influence some current researchers behind the scenes, bifurcated mind and body theories are being replaced by holistic models in which the brain and the body are thought of as interdependent physiological systems from which an "embodied mind" arises. So too, conceptions of the mind as purely—or even mostly—rational are being replaced by theories in which affect plays an integral and significant role in shaping human consciousness and understanding. We concur with these re-conceptions and argue that therapy can benefit by learning more about them and their implications.

Heavily influenced by Spinoza, the contemporary neuroscientist Antonio Damasio has argued throughout his writings that feeling and thinking are equally important and co-dependent operations of consciousness. He insists that feelings and the emotions on which they are based are indispensable both to cognition and to effective decision-making. Damasio describes feelings as the conscious mind's perception and interpretation of emotions—as the way consciousness "tells the body's story," as it were (Damasio, 2003, pp. 111–112). He defines emotions, in turn, as the body's felt reactions to both outer and inner stimuli—more specifically, as physical manifestations of the body's efforts to maintain homeostasis, the state in which essential physiological functions operate within optimal parameters (Damasio, 2003, pp. 57–64). For Damasio, emotions are homeostatic regulations that begin with the simplest reflexes and metabolic regulations, and end with complex "emotions-proper" like sadness, love, or guilt—and as such they are the foundation of conscious feelings, the mind's attempts to make sense of emotions. Damasio's conclusions regarding moods and affective attunements are thus compatible with Heidegger's, but in studying the physiology of affects Damasio makes important distinctions that Heidegger ignores.

In his somatic marker hypothesis, Damasio argues that emotions consciously and unconsciously influence future decisions by creating biomarkers that can be activated by either physical perceptions or imaginations. Per this hypothesis, Heidegger was right that the brain uses the body and its affects, and does so *prior* to rational thought, as an immediate and physiological metric to understand the world. Emotions are not independent of cognitions but are an essential part of the body and mind's critical interpretive and decision-making processes. But Damasio is specific about how this happens: Emotions are representations and regulations of the complex homeostatic changes that occur in the brain and body as different situations create different demands. Somatic signals emerging from the body's bioregulatory processes indicate emotional reactions to particular response options: For every option represented and contemplated, a somatic signal measures and marks the value of that option. Emotional processes thus guide behavior and decision-making differently than do rational judgments, but they are every bit as essential—and in some situations, perhaps more so. Affective and emotional content is also integrated with rational thought to guide behavior and judgments during subsequent deliberative reasoning.

As we indicated at the outset, researchers in psychophysiology and neuroscience define affect as the embodied representation of how we evaluate and value our situation in ways that are potentially adaptive. Specifically, affect integrates external sensory information with homeostatic and interoceptive information from the body, thereby helping us navigate the world by predicting what will be helpful and harmful. Recent work in psychophysiology and enaction theory has reinforced or revealed further important facts and postulates about affect that should now be noted (Colombetti, 2007; de Haan, 2020).

First, as Spinoza and Heidegger postulated, we are always in some state of affect which provides the mind and body with critical information. Emotions may come and go, but affect is a constant component of conscious experience—which includes not only fluctuating emotions, feelings, and moods, but as Barrett argues, a core affect that arises from the combined awareness of what is occurring internally and externally (Barrett, 2017a), and thus integrates a combination of important external and internal information (Barrett & Bliss-Moreau, 2009). Our current affective state is like an integrated psychophysiological barometer or map of our immediate internal and external condition (Barrett & Bliss-Moreau, 2009). By using affect specifically *as* a barometer or map, we become aware of our current needs and can make more informed, adaptive choices.

Second, affect arises from the activation of neural circuits that evolved to ensure survival (Lang & Bradley, 2010; LeDoux, 2012; Russell, 2003). Rather than having emotional circuits dedicated to this task, as has typically been presumed, current research shows that we have survival circuits that simply use emotions to impact behavior and functioning (Barrett, 2017a; Lang & Bradley, 2010; LeDoux, 2012). For example, there is no "fear circuit" resting quietly until a significant threat or challenge appears. Instead, survival circuits perform that function, signaling the need to avoid what is bad, or emotionally confirming what is good. These circuits evaluate the significance of current and anticipated challenges and based on previous experience help us respond effectively: When one of these circuits is activated, the brain mobilizes resources to enhance survival prospects by synchronizing bodily activities. Survival circuits thus use emotions constantly in all brain functions and behavior to adjust our understanding of internal and external stimuli. Dangerous situations elicit unpleasant affect and beneficial situations elicit pleasant affect, and people usually choose behaviors that increase pleasurable outcomes and decrease unpleasant outcomes.

To be clear, survival circuits seem to have evolved not to *create* feelings but to *use* feelings in performing fight or flight responses and similar survival functions. If this is true, feelings would be the result of distinct evolutionary forces that made it possible for the brain to be aware of its own activities, its own behavioral responses, and the environment in which these brain activities and behaviors occur. In other words, feelings are the means by which we experience need and are motivated to respond efficiently (Barrett, 2017a). Moreover, feelings in humans are greatly influenced by language and how we narrate our experiences and tell stories to ourselves and others about what has happened. Consequently, feelings are also the conscious witnessing and interpretation of our current state, which in turn provides information that is useful for coping with future threats and challenges.

Third, in harmony with Heidegger's claims, scientists increasingly consider affect a form of cognition, not simply a source of raw "felt" data (Duncan & Barrett, 2007). Affect and cognition are two sides of the same coin, with similar functions and goals, and overlapping definitions. Both affect and cognition help us know and understand the world, and they both employ processes by which sensory input is transformed, stored, recovered, and used. Importantly, current research finds there are no brain areas that can be designated specifically as either cognitive or affective. For example, Shackman et al. (2011) and Bush et al. (2002) found that areas previously thought to be either emotion-focused or cognition-focused are in fact interconnected and cannot be meaningfully separated. Specifically, both Shackman et al. and Bush et al. note that brain circuits in the anterior cingulate that were once considered purely "cognitive," and brain circuits once considered purely "emotional," are actually intertwined and inseparably interconnected. They reasonably infer there is no such thing as a purely "cognitive" or a purely "emotional" circuit; rather, cognition and affect are interdependent operations that work together both anatomically and functionally.

Fourth, since affect impacts everything we attend to, and colors all sensory perception, we must conclude it is an intrinsic part of the sensory experience (Duncan & Barrett, 2007). Affect helps direct our attention to sensory information that is most relevant and important, thereby regulating what is processed most fully and brought into memory. Affect also filters, integrates, and organizes perceptual input and modulates sensory processing. When someone feels at risk and becomes hypervigilant, they will focus on the more negative, threatening aspects of their environment, whereas when they are feeling calm, they typically focus on more positive aspects. Because affect influences what sensory information we attend to most closely and how that information is compared, evaluated, and used, decision-making at every level is dependent on affect. We know, for instance, that positive and negative affects direct decision-making by providing "go" and "stop" signals relevant to current behavior (Clore et al., 2018, p. 80). And since decisions by their very nature entail tacit predictions of the future, those choices are not merely informed by *past* affective experience but guided by the expected impact that experience will have on *future* affective states (Van den Bergh, 2021). Correlatively, our degree of affective arousal is determined directly by how much we anticipate being harmed or benefitted by something (Lang & Bradley, 2010).

Predictive processing, a recent theory of cognition, posits that our brains are constantly and proactively predicting changes in the environment, learning patterns from the statistical regularities observed, and correcting for mismatches (prediction errors) between prediction and outcome—all in an effort to minimize prediction errors. This theory understands perception as a form of inference to the best prediction. But according to Van de Cruys (2017), this view requires that cognition and affect be thoroughly intertwined. For Van de Cruys, affective valence (what Heidegger would call attunement) is determined by changes in prediction error patterns. That is, affective valence is a function of prediction error across time, with positive affect resulting from reduced prediction error, negative affect resulting from increased prediction error. In sum, research shows that affect thoroughly informs understanding—guiding both the processing of basic sensory experience, and the application of resulting information to decision-making of all kinds, especially predictive judgments.

Fifth, our scientific understanding of affect is further deepened by enaction theory (or enactivism), a more recent view of the embodied mind that echoes Heideggerian claims about the relational and interpretive structure of affective consciousness. And like the theories reviewed above, it characterizes cognition as thoroughly affective, positing that mind and cognition arise through dynamic interactions between the affective body and its environment. Judgments like appraisal are not just cognitive or prefrontal tasks; rather, the whole body is involved in their performance (Colombetti, 2007; Colombetti & Krueger, 2015).

Enaction theory identifies four key features of the decision-making process and its affective regulation: (1) Decisions and judgments are *embodied*—that is, realized by both our physiology and agency; (2) They are *embedded* (in worldly and social circumstances)—that is, situated within environmental niches that support or constrain them; (3) They are *enacted*—constitutive and reflective of our first-person sense-making and meaning-creating activities; and (4) They are *extended*—reaching beyond the "head" by material and social resources around us (this is also called the 4E Approach; Colombetti et al., 2018). Colombetti et al. explain that these four decision-process traits assure that affect plays a crucial role in integrating the embodied conscious subject with its environment:

> ... processes like believing, remembering, and reasoning depend upon resources beyond the head. The artifacts and cultural institutions we use to support these processes are forms of cognitive "scaffolding:" beyond-the-head structures that, when we interact with them generate ongoing feedback loops that transform our cognitive profile in real-time by opening up new forms of thought and experience. We make and listen to music, adorn walls with artworks, consume drugs, wear specific clothing, and gravitate toward spaces and social groups to evoke and regulate different affective experiences. These practices construct 'affective niches': self-styled environments providing the developmental conditions for affective states to take shape and thrive. (Colombetti et al., 2018, p. 1307)

Colombetti (2007) argues explicitly that this integration includes the *whole* body, not just the brain. And as we have seen with other theories, enactivism recognizes that anatomically there is no discernable dividing line between cognition and affect at any point in the peripheral and central nervous systems; cognitive and emotional processes are all interconnected and interactive throughout both body and brain.

Lastly, current neuroscience decisively opposes the dualistic model of mind–body relations—and in consequence, *tacitly* opposes the possibility of any "objective" form of cognition. As previously mentioned, one historically difficult question that has persistently puzzled philosophers and scientists alike concerns whether we perceive the world in a detached and purely conceptual sense with cognition acting independently of affects, emotions, and individual differences in perception, or subjectively, with each individual's bodily features and affective states contributing in determinate ways to perception and cognition. We have noted that Descartes and his followers defended the former position—claiming that the mind is an immaterial substance capable of operating free from the influence of affect and emotion, and thereby also capable of objectively knowing the real. The emerging sciences of Descartes' age predictably found this claim very attractive, despite objections by thinkers like Spinoza who believed the mind and body constitute a single, unified organism or system which would lack the ontological detachment necessary to pure objectivity. Along with philosophers like Heidegger, current neuroscientists generally support the latter, organic view. In part, this is because their researches demonstrate that the very process of perceiving the world is highly subjective—and always incomplete.

Since we have limited working memory, limited attention, and limited focus, we typically attend to what impacts us most, positively or negatively. And our understanding of the world and ourselves is shaped accordingly. Additionally, the perceptions on which cognition builds are always "objectively deficient," meaning we simply do not have the ability to sense everything in our environment, much less sense it with a high degree of accuracy and reliability. For example, human hearing is not as acute as that of many other animals. Even with the healthiest organs and under the best conditions we only hear a small portion of what we would need to hear in order to form a full and accurate picture of our surroundings. And this is true for all our senses. Thirdly, as we have seen at length, all bodily perceptions are a function of our current affective state. Hence, before we even begin to process and think about sensory information, our own bodily limitations on that information and the affective states that color it prevents us from having a complete or objective understanding of the world. Instead, we always interpret that world incompletely, selectively, and affectively, in response to the bodily conditions, sensory limitations, and fluctuating demands of each individual organism and its situation. Our knowledge is thus unavoidably relative to our perceived needs, limited and particularized sense faculties, and highly variable environmental conditions. Because our bodies are evolutionarily designed for survival, we are programmed to pay close attention to what can most help us or hurt us in the moment, and we either ignore, minimize, or simply are not equipped to perceive the rest. In short, cognition is not only affective, but essentially subjective and biologically restricted in its grasp and representation of the real.

Implications for Integrating Psychotherapy and Psychophysiology and for Optimizing Affect for Healthy Functioning

The consequences for psychotherapy and psychophysiology of mind, brain, and body being anatomically and functionally interdependent, and cognition being essentially affective, subjective, and constitutionally limited are significant. One consequence is that the mix and balance of affective experiences turns out to be surprisingly important, as both positive *and* negative affect play key roles in healthy functioning. And this fact has significant implications for therapy.

Psychophysiologically, both positive and negative affect are critical to health and well-being (Lang & Bradley, 2010; Russell, 2003). This assessment of negative affect runs contrary to prevailing views in positive psychology which devalue negative emotions and advocate eliminating them entirely or reducing them as much as possible. For such views, a purely positive affect is the ideal. But research consistently shows that completely avoiding negative affect does not lead to positive outcomes. Gabriele Oettingen et al. (2013) demonstrated that taking a balanced mental approach to life leads to better outcomes. And evidence across a number of studies shows that fantasizing about exclusively happy outcomes hinders people from realizing their desired goals (see Oettingen & Reininger, 2016, and Oettingen & Schworer, 2013 for reviews). In one study (Oettingen & Mayer, 2002), a group was asked to imagine that their week would be completely happy while another group was asked to write down any and all thoughts about the week that came to mind. The positive fantasy group reported feeling less energized, and they accomplished less than the writing control group. It appears that an exclusive focus on positive thinking fools our minds into perceiving that we have already attained our goals, which decreases our motivation to pursue them. Oettingen et al. (2013) emphasize, however, that going to the other extreme and solely focusing on the negative is not adaptive either. Rather, success requires a balanced, moderate approach that acknowledges both the desired positive outcomes as well as obstacles in the path to achieving those aims.

Likewise, Oishi et al. (2007) found through a series of studies using international samples with thousands of participants that the highest levels of happiness were not always associated with the best outcomes. Interestingly, in addressing the question of whether people can actually be *too* happy, they found that those with moderate levels of happiness (as compared to extremely high or low) were more successful in terms of income and education. They concluded that optimal functioning, particularly with reference to achievement and motivation, occurs at moderate levels of happiness. This perspective is also supported by research from Grant and Schwartz (2011), which also shows that balanced affective outlook leads to better outcomes.

Other research shows similar results. Larsen et al. (2003) proposed that during difficult life experiences, a mix of positive and negative emotions may be optimal for well-being because experiencing positive emotions simultaneously with negative emotions may detoxify the latter, effectively transforming a negative emotional experience into an opportunity for meaning-making and enhanced well-being. Several empirical studies provide support for this hypothesis. Gross and Levenson (1997) found that suppression of emotional reactions led to an increased stress response. Traumatic memories are often disorganized and poorly integrated into personal self-understanding, inhibiting progress in therapy (Christianson, 1992a, 1992b; Foa & Riggs, 1993). Larsen et al. (2003, p. 221) stated that "negative emotions are often aroused for a reason—to interrupt ongoing activity, to counteract a threat, to modify one's actions, or change one's environment." People need to work through negative emotions rather than simply avoiding them or minimizing their importance (Gross, 1998).

Building on these ideas, Hershfield et al. (2013) conducted a ten-year longitudinal study involving participants from a general population sample. Those who reported experiencing mixed emotions had better physical health, and an increase in mixed emotions over time diminished age-related declines in health. In other words, those who experienced both positive and negative emotions had better physical health than those who reported only positive emotions or only negative emotions. Additionally, extended increases in experiences of mixed emotions led to correlative increases in health. Avoidance in the moment may temporarily improve mood but it will not increase adaptability in coping with future stressors. Those who are most able to take the good with the bad are also the most likely to have optimal mental and physical health.

These findings have already been successfully confirmed in therapy. When Adler and Hershfield (2012) studied individuals undergoing psychotherapy, they found that those who reported experiencing a mix of both happy and sad emotions had more positive improvements in psychological well-being over time, with changes in mixed emotional experience preceding improvements in well-being. In their study, each therapy session required participants to complete narratives about thoughts and feelings about the therapy, and these narrative reports were then coded for emotional content. Participants who reported mixed experiences of happiness and sadness displayed the largest improvements in health. This was found even after controlling for passage of time and differences in personality traits, as well as for the independent effects of those happy and sad experiences.

Pennebaker and Francis (1996) and Pennebaker et al. (1988) have people write about their past using an expressive writing paradigm. Instead of taking a broad approach, they ask participants to recount the most negative experience they have had, encouraging them to write about things they have never discussed with anyone previously because of the uncomfortable nature of the experience. By demanding both an awareness and an acceptance of difficult negative emotions, this expressive writing technique requires the very opposite of avoidance. But research finds this approach successful: By thinking deeply about their negative emotions, participants are able to create a meaningful story that allows them to integrate their experiences into their current self-concept (Pennebaker & Francis, 1996). Given the potential traumas that might underlie these negative emotions, it is recommended that this approach be used only within the context of psychotherapy.

Another surprising finding is that avoidance of negative affect reduces one's awareness of the current environment. Research into overly general memories and decreased autobiographical memory specificity provides clues as to why. Autobiographical memory requires a recollection of personally experienced past events. And as Williams et al. (2007, p. 122) noted, autobiographical memory is "central to human functioning, contributing to an individual's sense of self, to their ability to remain oriented in the world and to pursue goals effectively in the light of past problem solving." But people suffering from emotional disorders tend to retrieve overly general memories when attempting to retrieve memories of specific events. In a sample of formerly depressed patients who scored high in rumination, actively ruminating negatively impacted autobiographical memory specificity (Raes et al., 2012). In other words, people learn over time that avoiding specific memories helps reduce the pain associated with self-discrepancy. Remembering only general descriptions can produce less negative affect than recalling specific memories. But while avoiding specific painful memories has the short-term benefit of reducing discomfort, overly general memory and "functional avoidance" reduces problem-solving ability and executive functioning, leading to problems in imagining and predicting future events, as well as delays in recovering from affective disorders. People with reduced autobiographical memory specificity are more likely to have an avoidant coping style and to recall memories from a third person observer view rather than from a first-person perspective (Debeer et al., 2011; Debeer et al., 2012; Hermans et al., 2008; Warne & Rice, 2022). In sum, a coping style that avoids memories associated with negative affect helps reduce uncomfortable thoughts in the moment but leads to long-term difficulties in autobiographical memory and sense of self. Therefore, an avoidant coping style appears to be a key pathway between reduced autobiographical memory specificity and depression.

How Philosophical Models of Affect and the Embodied Mind Might Be Used by Psychotherapy and Psychophysiology

We have seen how Spinoza's perspective on mind and body as one continuous substance has heavily influenced thinkers like Damasio. Psychophysiology does not use Spinoza's ontological language to describe the mind–body connection, or the correlated connection between cognition and affect, but like Spinoza it effectively treats each component in those respective relations as co-extensive and thoroughly integrated. Anything that impacts the one, also impacts the other. Improving physical functioning—for example, using behavioral activation approaches to improve sleep and physical activity—improves mental functioning as well. Improving mental functioning—for example, using cognitive behavioral therapy to address maladaptive thoughts, or using acceptance and commitment therapy to learn to be with whatever thought comes to mind—also improves physical functioning. Therapies specifically attuned to the essential connections between cognition and affect, like the expressive writing approach of Pennebaker, the MEST approach to improve autobiographical memory, cognitive analytic psychotherapy writing exercises, and emotion-focused therapy approaches, have all been found to have beneficial effects on both mental and physical health.

Heidegger's ontological model of human existence has similarly influenced psychology and psychobiology, and still has more to offer. Heidegger was the first philosopher since David Hume to investigate the integral relations between affect and cognition, and the first ever to rigorously do so within an existential conception of the mind as essentially embodied and socially shaped. Heidegger was also the first philosopher to argue that what psychology calls our moods, feelings, and similar affective states are genuine and important forms of understanding, not an insignificant sensuous supplement to previously formed concepts. He realized that what Barrett calls our core affect contributes in important ways both to an efficacious bodily grasp of the environment and to the propositionally structured ideas we commonly use to conceptualize and describe bodily and environmental conditions. And as we have noted, Heidegger also recognized that attending mindfully to our moods and affective states often reveals us to ourselves much more immediately, transparently, and at times, more accurately, than do our mental representations or rational self-reflections. Psychophysiologically speaking, this mindful attention to mood can measurably improve homeostasis and adaptive well-being.

Heidegger's work contains further relevant insights yet to be fully explored by psychology and the human sciences—most notably, the existential role of affect in shaping the world itself as well as self-consciousness. We have noted that for a Heideggerian conception of core affect, affect serves to attune us both to the environment and to our own bodily states by "resonating" with them in either harmonious or discordant ways. But for Heidegger, that affective attunement along with our cognitive perceptions, value judgments, use-relations, and social interactions quite literally "constructs" the meaningful environment in which we exist. In other words, while the lived world is not *solely* a function of our core affect and transient affective understandings, affect nevertheless plays a foundational role in shaping the world. And unlike Kantian philosophy, Heidegger's phenomenology rejects the claim that there is some inaccessible "noumenal" reality of "things in themselves" lurking behind phenomena and our affective understanding of phenomena. (Phenomenology would agree that there is undeniably matter, energy, material organisms, etc., that exist apart from our consciousness of them, but such existents of themselves do not constitute a *meaningful* reality—for there to be *meaning*, conscious minds are a necessary precondition).

Given the impact of affective understanding on reality itself, the world is quite literally a better place for those who are better and more adaptively attuned to it, not only because they live in it differently, but because their outlook and behavior literally changes the world toward which they behave—for themselves *and* for others. Someone's kindness can change not only *their* day, but *my* day. And not just my *perception* of the day, but the *day itself*, for in the last analysis there is no day for me apart from my lived perceptions of it. It would thus follow that some of our most important choices are those that concern how we affectively understand and orient ourselves toward the world, others, and ourselves.

Admittedly, core affect is not directly under our conscious control. Affect can be notoriously capricious or have unaccountable origins. Even moods and emotions we *can* explain, nevertheless stem from situations that were themselves beyond our control or accountability. In Heidegger's terms, we are "thrown" by birth and life's circumstances into a particular existence, and "reborn" as it were into every present situation, the meaning of which is made manifest in our affectively attuned understanding (2010, Section 29, pp. 131–136; Dahlstrom, 2013). This "thrownness" is a ubiquitous characteristic of human life. Moreover, life constantly requires us to make choices whether we want to or not. And because our choices always impact our life to some degree even though they do not fully determine it, we feel responsible for how we act and for the outcomes of our actions even when we should not. Guilt and the traumas of life can overwhelm and depress us. And yet, as behavioral activation therapies have confirmed, even though attempts to "master" our moods and emotions *directly* often end in failure, changing our behavior can *indirectly* alter our moods, and thereby also modify our self-understanding and well-being. Logic and conceptual reasoning of themselves cannot produce either the comprehension or the strength of will necessary to rescue us from debilitating situations by force. However, since an affective attunement to the environment and our own body is a form of understanding by which we grasp our circumstances and potential choices more fundamentally, a self-aware affective attunement can alert us to the *need* to change and help us understand *how* to change. Hence, improvements in both affect and the decisions impacted by affect can be made through strategic and therapy-guided modifications in behavior.

Modifying core affect thus opens significant possibilities for treating maladaptive behavior. To the degree that moods and affective attunements to our circumstances and choices determine how we *perceive* our circumstances, then altering our core affect can increase the effectiveness of our understanding, and thereby, improve the quality of our choices. In a sense, we all know this already. When for example, we stay up later than we know we should, and then we wake up tired and "on the wrong side of the bed," as the saying goes, the resulting affective attunement constructs a negative and misleading understanding of the world. As a result, we might misattribute that affect and respond with anger to a provocation that under other circumstances would provoke only mild annoyance. Since a bad mood can constitute a misleading attunement to our situation and possibilities, that mood of itself can produce false perceptions of the world and our place in it. Choices are inevitably influenced by our core affect and perceptions, so bad moods not only lead to poor choices, but to a false and often debilitating conceptual understanding of those choices—as well as to further maladaptive behavior. Said differently, we can misunderstand and maladaptively employ our contextual agency by accepting responsibility only for the choices we are consciously aware of in the moment, but not for the prior, seemingly unrelated choices that in fact helped produce a harmful affect and its associated misrepresentations.

A philosophically and psychophysiologically integrated view of cognition and affect helps explain such puzzles, as well as how therapies like behavioral activation can modify core affect and its impact on downstream choices by improving physical well-being, such as by improving sleep and physical activity. It also explains how taking time each day to engage in pleasurable activities or hobbies can have significant positive downstream effects by setting core affect to a healthier balance. It confirms that mindfulness, which is often integrated into psychotherapy, can positively adjust core affect by increasing awareness and attunement to the present moment. Writing exercises, focusing on both the negative and the positive, can help integrate life experience and center core affect. And since studies show that mentally healthy people naturally tend toward a mildly positive core affect, while those seeking psychotherapy suffer from chronic negative affect, cognitive behavioral therapy can help moderate chronic negative affect by challenging irrational thoughts. Acceptance and commitment therapy can help moderate core affect by learning to recognize that thoughts are merely information and that our behavior need not be determined by any single thought. Compassion focused therapy can help moderate the social side of core affect by building compassion. The success of all these therapies is accounted for by an integrated view of affect and cognition.

Summary

Affect is a felt cognitive and evaluative attunement to our body and its environment. It is an embodied representation of how we understand and value our current circumstances, informed by past experiences and focused on predicting the best course of action given present context and anticipated results. Due to this predictive function, affect is also a representation of how we remember the past and imagine the future as we make decisions and choices. Mind, brain, and body are thoroughly interconnected and interdependent, and affect is the coordinated integration of possible choices into adaptive action. We are always experiencing some transient affect as well as some form of core affect. Building on the philosophies of Spinoza and Heidegger, we can develop stronger theories of the embodied mind and a more accurate understanding of healthy human functioning by learning more about affect and its cognitive functions. Viewing affect as a foundation for healthy functioning has direct and important implications for integrating psychotherapy and psychophysiology. Focusing on core affect in therapy has numerous downstream effects on mental, emotional, and physical well-being. This approach can easily be integrated into behavioral activation therapy, cognitive behavioral therapy, acceptance and commitment therapy, mindfulness-based therapy, and other approaches.

References

Adler, J. M., & Hershfield, H. E. (2012). Mixed emotional experience is associated with and precedes improvements in psychological well-being. *PLoS One, 7*(4), e35633. https://doi.org/10.1371/journal.pone.0035633

Banich, M. T., Mackiewicz, K. L., Depue, B. E., Whitmer, A. J., Miller, G. A., & Heller, W. (2009). Cognitive control mechanisms, emotion, and memory: A neural perspective with implications for psychopathology. *Neuroscience and Biobehavioral Reviews, 33*(5), 613–630. https://doi.org/10.1016/j.neubiorev.2008.09.010

Barrett, L. F. (2017a). The theory of constructed emotion: An active inference account of interoception and categorization. *Social Cognitive and Affective Neuroscience, 12*(1), 1–23. https://doi.org/10.1093/scan/nsw154

Barrett, L. F. (2017b). *How emotions are made: The secret life of the brain*. Houghton Mifflin Harcourt.

Barrett, L. F., & Bliss-Moreau, E. (2009). Affect as a psychological primitive. *Advances in Experimental Social Psychology, 41*, 167–218. https://doi.org/10.1016/S0065-2601(08)00404-8

Bula, G. (2019). Passions, consciousness, and the Rosetta Stone: Spinoza and embodied, extended, and affective cognition. *Adaptive Behavior, 27*(1), 7–15. https://doi.org/10.1177/1059712318790739

Bush, G., Vogt, B. A., Holmes, J., Dale, A. M., Greve, D., Jenike, M. A., & Rosen, B. R. (2002). Dorsal anterior cingulate cortex: A role in reward-based decision making. *Proceedings of the National Academy of Sciences of the United States of America, 99*(1), 523–528. https://doi.org/10.1073/pnas.012470999

Christianson, S. A. (1992a). Emotional stress and eyewitness memory: A critical review. *Psychological Bulletin, 112*(2), 284–309. https://doi.org/10.1037/0033-2909.112.2.284

Christianson, S. A. (1992b). Remembering emotional events: Potential mechanisms. In S.-Å. Christianson (Ed.), *The handbook of emotion and memory: Research and theory* (pp. 307–340). Lawrence Erlbaum Associates.

Clore, G. L., & Huntsinger, J. R. (2009). How the object of affect guides its impact. *Emotion Review, 1*(1), 39–54. https://doi.org/10.1177/1754073908097185

Clore, G. L., Schiller, A. J., & Shaked, A. (2018). Affect and cognition: Three principles. *Current Opinion in Behavioral Sciences, 19*, 78–82. https://doi.org/10.1016/j.cobeha.2017.11.010

Colombetti, G. (2007). Enactive appraisal. *Phenomenology and the Cognitive Sciences, 6*, 527–546. https://doi.org/10.1007/s11097-007-9077-8

Colombetti, G., & Krueger, J. (2015). Scaffoldings of the affective mind. *Philosophical Psychology, 28*, 1157–1176. http://dx.doi.org/10.1080/09515089.2014.976334

Colombetti, G., Krueger, J., & Roberts, T. (2018). Editorial: Affectivity beyond the skin. *Frontiers in Psychology, 9*, 1307. https://doi.org/10.3389/fpsyg.2018.01307

Dahlstrom, D. O. (2013). Thrownness (Geworfenheit). In D. O. Dahlstrom, *The Heidegger dictionary* (pp. 212–215). Bloomsbury Academic.

Damasio, A. (2000). *The feeling of what happens: Body and emotion in the making of consciousness*. A Harvest Book.

Damasio, A. (2003). *Looking for Spinoza. Joy, sorrow, and the feeling brain*. Harcourt.

Debeer, E., Raes, F., Williams, J. M. G., & Hermans, D. (2011). Context-dependent activation of reduced autobiographical memory specificity as an avoidant coping style. *Emotion, 11*(6), 1500–1506. https://doi.org/10.1037/a0024535

Debeer, E., Raes, F., Claes, S., Vrieze, E., Williams, J. M. G., & Hermans, D. (2012). Relationship between cognitive avoidant coping and changes in overgeneral autobiographical memory retrieval following an acute stressor. *Journal of Behavioral Therapy and Experimental Psychiatry, 43 Suppl 1*, S37–S42. https://doi.org/10.1016/j.jbtep.2011.04.002

de Haan, S. (2020). An enactive approach to psychiatry. *Philosophy, Psychiatry, & Psychology, 27*, 3–25. https://doi.org/10.1353/ppp.2020.0001

Descartes, R. (1984). *The philosophical writing of Descartes, vol. 2* (J. Cottingham, R. Stoothoff, & D. Murdoch, Transl.). Cambridge University Press.

Descartes, R. (1985). *The philosophical writing of Descartes, vol. 1* (J. Cottingham, R. Stoothoff, & D. Murdoch, Transl.). Cambridge University Press.

Dukes, D., Abrams, K., Adolphs, R., Ahmed, M. E., Beatty, A., Berridge, K. C., Broomhall, S., Brosch, T., Campos, J. J., Clay, Z., Clément, F., Cunningham, W. A., Damasio, A., Damasio, H., D'Arms, J., Davidson, J. W., de Gelder, B., Deonna, J., de Sousa, R., Ekman, P., ... Sander, D. (2021). The rise of affectivism. *Nature Human Behavior, 5*(7), 816–820. https://doi.org/10.1038/s41562-021-01130-8

Duncan, S., & Barrett, L. F. (2007). Affect is a form of cognition: A neurobiological analysis. *Cognition and Emotion, 21*(6), 1184–1211. https://doi.org/10.1080/02699930701437931

Foa, E., & Riggs, D. (1993). Post-traumatic stress disorder in rape victims. In J. Oldham, M. B. Riha, & A. Tasman (Eds.), *American psychiatric press review of psychiatry* (vol. 12, pp. 273–303). American Psychiatric Press.

Grant, A. M., & Schwartz, B. (2011). Too much of a good thing: The challenge and opportunity of the inverted U. *Perspectives on Psychological Science, 6*(1), 61–76. https://doi.org/10.1177/1745691610393523

Gross, J. J. (1998). The emerging field of emotion regulation: An integrative review. *Review of General Psychology, 2*(3), 271–299. https://doi.org/10.1037/1089-2680.2.3.271

Gross, J. J., & Levenson, R. W. (1997). Hiding feelings: The acute effects of inhibiting negative and positive emotions. *Journal of Abnormal Psychology, 106*(1), 95–103. https://doi.org/10.1037//0021-843x.106.1.95

Heidegger, M. (2010). *Being and time* (J. Stambaugh, Trans., revised by D. Schmidt). SUNY Press. (Original work published 1927).

Hermans, D., Decker, A., de Peuter, S., Raes, F., Eelen, P., & Williams, J. M. G. (2008). Autobiographical memory specificity and affect regulation: Coping with a negative life event. *Depression and Anxiety, 25*(9), 787–792. https://doi.org/10.1002/da.20326

Hershfield, H. E., Scheibe, S., Sims, T. L., & Carstensen, L. L. (2013). When feeling bad can be good: Mixed emotions benefit physical health across adulthood. *Social Psychological and Personality Science, 4*(1), 54–61. https://doi.org/10.1177/1948550612444616

Kahneman, D. (2011). *Thinking fast and slow*. Farrar, Straus and Giroux.

Koestler, A. (1964). *The act of creation*. Penguin.

Lang, P. J., & Bradley, M. M. (2010). Emotion and the motivational brain. *Biological Psychology, 84*(3), 437–450. https://doi.org/10.1016/j.biopsycho.2009.10.007

Lang, P. J., Bradley, M. M., & Cuthbert, B. N. (1990). Emotion, attention, and the startle reflex. *Psychological Review, 97*(3), 377–395.

Larsen, J. T., Hemenover, S. H., Norris, C. J., & Cacioppo, J. T. (2003). Turning adversity to advantage: On the virtues of the coactivation of positive and negative emotions. In L. G. Aspinwall & U. M. Staudinger (Eds.), *A psychology of human strengths: Fundamental questions and future directions for a positive psychology* (pp. 211–225). American Psychological Association. https://doi.org/10.1037/10566-015

LeDoux, J. (2012). Rethinking the emotional brain. *Neuron, 73*, 653–676. https://doi.org/10.1016/j.neuron.2012.02.004

Lemogne, C., Bergouignan, L., Piolino, P., Jouvent, R., Allilaire, J. F., & Fossati, P. (2009). Cognitive avoidance of intrusive memories and autobiographical memory: Specificity, autonoetic consciousness, and self-perspective. *Memory, 17*(1), 1–7. https://doi.org/10.1080/09658210802438466

Oettingen, G., & Mayer, D. (2002). The motivating function of thinking about the future: Expectations versus fantasies. *Journal of Personality and Social Psychology, 83*, 1198–1212. https://doi.org/10.1037//0022-3514.83.5.1198

Oettingen, G., & Reininger, K. M. (2016). The power of prospection: Mental contrasting and behavior change. *Social and Personality Psychology Compass, 10*, 591–604. https://doi.10.1111/spc3.12271

Oettingen, G., & Schworer, B. (2013). Mind wandering via mental contrasting as a tool for behavior change. *Frontiers in Psychology, 4*, 562. https://doi.org/10.3389/fpsyg.2013.00562

Oettingen, G., Wittchen, M., & Gollwitzer, P. M. (2013). Regulating goal pursuit through mental contrasting with implementation intentions. In E. A. Locke & G. P. Latham (Eds.), *New developments in goal setting and task performance* (pp. 523–548). Routledge/Taylor & Francis Group.

Oishi, S., Diener, E., & Lucas, R. E. (2007). The optimum level of well-being: Can people be too happy? *Perspectives on Psychological Science, 2*(4), 346–360. https://doi.org/10.1111/j.1745-6916.2007.00048.x

Pennebaker, J. W., & Francis, M. E. (1996). Cognitive, emotional, and language processes in disclosure: Physical health and adjustment. *Cognition and Emotion, 10*(6), 601–626. https://doi.org/10.1080/026999396380079

Pennebaker, J. W., Kiecolt-Glaser, J. K., & Glaser, R. (1988). Disclosure of traumas and immune function: Health implications for psychotherapy. *Journal of Consulting and Clinical Psychology, 56*(2), 239–24S. https://doi.org/10.1037//0022-006x.56.2.239

Plato. (2021). *Phaedrus* (B. Jowett, transl). Graphyco Editions.

Raes, F., Schoofs, H., Griffith, J. W., & Hermans, D. (2012). Rumination relates to reduced autobiographical memory specificity in formerly depressed patients following a self-discrepancy challenge: The case of autobiographical memory specificity reactivity. *Journal of Behavioral Therapy and Experimental Psychiatry, 43*(4), 1002–1007. https://doi.org/10.1016/j.jbtep.2012.03.003

Ravven, H. M. (2003). Spinoza's anticipation of contemporary affective neuroscience. *Consciousness and Emotion, 4*(2), 257–290. https://doi.org/10.1075/ce.4.2.07mor

Russell, J. A. (2003). Core affect and the psychological construction of emotion. *Psychological Review, 110*(1), 145–172. https://doi.org/10.1037/0033-295x.110.1.145

Shackman, A. J., Salomons, T. V., Slagter, H. A., Fox, A. S., Winter, J. J., & Davidson, R. J. (2011). The integration of negative affect, pain, and cognitive control in the cingulate cortex. *Nature Reviews Neuroscience, 12*(3), 154–167. https://doi.org/10.1038/nrn2994

Van de Cruys, S. (2017). Affective value in the predictive mind. In T. Metzinger & W. Wiese (Eds.) *Philosophy and predictive processing: 24*. MIND Group. https://doi:10.15502/9783958573253

Van den Bergh, O., Brosschot, J., Critchley, H., Thayer, J. F., & Ottaviani, C. (2021). Better safe than sorry: A common signature of general vulnerability for psychopathology. *Perspectives on Psychological Science, 16*(2), 225–246. https://doi.org/10.1177/1745691620950690

Warne, N., & Rice, F. (2022). Links between depressive symptoms and the observer perspective for autobiographical memories and imagined events: A high familial risk study. *Journal of Cognitive Psychology, 34*(1), 82–97. https://doi.org/10.1080/20445911.2021.1922418

Williams, J. M. G., Barnhofer, T., Crane, C., Hermans, D., Raes, F., Watkins, E., & Dalgleish, T. (2007). Autobiographical memory specificity and emotional disorder. *Psychological Bulletin, 133*(1), 122–148. https://doi.org/10.1037/0033-2909.133.1.122

Wilson, T. (2004). *Strangers to ourselves: Discovering the adaptive unconscious*. The Belknap Press.

SECTION II
ASSESSMENT IN PSYCHOPHYSIOLOGICAL PSYCHOTHERAPY

6

Approaching Psychopathology from a Psychophysiological Perspective

Using Dimensional Diagnostic Approaches as Frameworks to Integrate Psychotherapy and Psychophysiology

Dawson Hedges and Patrick R. Steffen

Introduction

In this chapter, we review strengths and weaknesses of traditional categorical methods of diagnosis in mental health as exemplified by the diagnostic approach taken by the *Diagnostic and Statistical Manual* (*DSM*). We then review two alternative methods of diagnosis, both based on a dimensional approach to diagnosis, focusing first on the Research Domain Criteria (RDoC) (Insel et al., 2010; Vaidyanathan et al., 2020) developed by the U.S. National Institute of Mental Health and second on the Hierarchical Taxonomy of Psychopathology (HiTOP) that instead of a categorical approach to diagnoses emphasize psychopathology as a continuum and include genetic markers and biomarkers where possible (Kotov et al., 2021). Finally, we attempt to situate psychophysiology in the diagnostic approaches of the RDoC and the HiTOP, showing how findings from psychophysiology can be considered as biomarkers that enhance and enrich diagnosis in mental health and have the potential ultimately to improve treatment outcomes.

DSM—Categorical Diagnoses Based on Self-Reported and Behavioral Findings

> *We must accept the fact that our diagnostic classification is the result of historical accretion and accident without any real underlying system or scientific necessity . . . The rules for entry have varied over time and have rarely been very rigorous. Our mental disorders are no more than fallible social constructs.*
> (Allen Frances, cited in Phillips et al., 2012, p. 25)

Psychiatric nosology has a history going back to at least Kraepelin of diagnosing mental illness into discrete categories (Lilienfeld & Treadway, 2016). While categorical approaches to psychiatric diagnosis have been helpful in classifying and understanding causes of psychiatric disease and their treatment, problems associated with a categorial approach to diagnosis have ultimately limited research into the diagnosis and treatment of psychiatric diseases (Conway et al., 2019). The diagnostic approach taken with the *DSM* that has dominated psychiatric diagnosis since its introduction in 1952 relies overwhelmingly on the assumption that psychiatric diagnoses represent discrete, well-defined conditions. In this categorical diagnostic approach, a patient either meets criteria for a disorder or does not meet criteria.

Underlying this categorical approach to psychiatric diagnosis and the notion of discreet diagnostic categories is the additional assumption that each disorder has its own unique pathophysiology (American Psychiatric Association, 2013). This approach, however, does not appear to accurately represent psychopathology. Concerns with categorically based *DSM* diagnoses include categorical overlap, high comorbidity rates, loss of clinically relevant information that occurs with artificial categorization, and poor reliability (Conway et al., 2019; Markon et al., 2011; Meidlinger & Hope, 2017). Additionally, the *DSM* does not provide a theory of normal functioning, other than to say that it is the absence of symptoms. It does not clearly state what healthy functioning looks like.

Evidence suggests that in fact psychiatric disorders are much more etiologically and diagnostically complex than the diagnostic strategy used in the *DSMs* implies (Kozak & Cuthbert, 2016; Meidlinger & Hope, 2017). In contrast to the assumptions underlying the categorically based diagnostic approach underlying the *DSMs*, multiple different pathophysiological pathways and genetic heterogeneity can result in similar disease phenotypes. Conversely, shared genetic vulnerabilities can underlie phenotypically different clinical manifestations (Beauchaine & Thayer, 2015), and findings from brain imaging do not necessarily conform to traditional *DSM* categories (Conway et al., 2019). If the categories of psychopathology as used in a *DSM*-type approach are incorrect and do not represent actual divisions and types of psychopathology, attempts to find biological and genetic markers of psychopathology will not be likely to succeed (Hajcak & Patrick, 2015). Despite findings showing that an enormous number of biological variables are associated with psychiatric and cognitive outcomes, the *DSM* manuals overwhelming rely on behavioral findings to form the bases of categorical diagnoses, even though behavior can be nonspecific (Beauchaine & Thayer, 2015). And despite the *DSM* criteria relying on behavioral findings, clinicians and researchers using the *DSM* often do incorporate a range of information from other sources into their own diagnostic and therapeutic thinking, such as including information from the physical examination, laboratory testing, neuropsychological testing, brain imaging, genetics, and psychophysiology.

However, as Lilienfeld (2020) notes, we do not want to be "guilty of applying high-tech methods to crude diagnostic categories that map poorly onto psychological reality" (p. 111). In addition, accumulating findings indicate that health and well-being cannot be separated into simple mental and physical dichotomies but rather requires a much more integrated approach linking genetic and environmental variables across a broad array of health outcomes that do not separate cleanly into mental and physical categories of disease (Zwir et al., 2021). As such, simple categorically based diagnostic approaches including those used in psychopathology incorporate inadequate information from which to adequately understand, diagnose, and treat human disease including psychopathology.

Despite these limitations, *DSM*-style diagnoses guide most research studies of psychopathology (Insel et al., 2010). Kozak and Cuthbert (2016) note that current neuroscience research findings do not connect well with categorical mental illness diagnoses. They conclude that because categorical diagnoses are inadequately conceptualized, it is impossible for neuroscience research findings to map onto these diagnoses. Therefore, it has not been possible to create an adequate theory of pathophysiology and mental disorder, which has inhibited progress in the understanding and treatment of mental disorders. Two proposed solutions to this difficulty are the RDoC framework, a diagnostic scheme that emphasizes a dimensional approach to assessing mental illness (Kozak & Cuthbert, 2016), and the HiTOP, which is designed to improve research in psychopathology by including empirical, dimensional, and hierarchal approaches (Kotov et al., 2017; Kotov et al., 2021).

Dimensional Approaches to Psychopathology

Research Domain Criteria (RDoC)

The RDoC, developed by the U.S. National Institute of Mental Health, is a particularly influential approach to non-categorical diagnostic assessment (Insel et al., 2010). The aims of the RDoC framework are to provide a surer scientific foundation for psychopathology and diagnosis that can integrate neuroscience with clinical practice. The RDoC approach eschews a categorical approach to diagnosis, instead focusing on empirically supported dimensional criteria to mental disorders (Kozak & Cuthbert, 2016) wherein "psychopathology is viewed as extremes on these dimensional domains" (Craske 2012, p. 253). While not currently meant to replace categorical approaches to diagnosis and treatment (Craske, 2012; Vaidyanathan et al., 2020) and likely not ready for current clinical use, the RDoC is an alternative approach to traditional categorical approaches to diagnosis that provides for inclusion and integration (Cuthbert, 2014) of an array of genetic, biological, psychological, and self-report data into a diagnostic matrix.

The RDoC framework incorporates not only clinical findings but can also include evidence from a range of biological findings. The RDoC takes a systems approach, emphasizing that multiple systems interact in normal functioning. Instead of signs and symptoms, the focus is on psychophysiological systems linked to adaptive and maladaptive functioning. In the RDoC dimensional approach, adaptive functioning occurs in the middle of a given dimension, whereas pathology occurs at the extremes (Craske, 2012; Insel, 2014; Kozak & Cuthbert, 2016; Vaidyanathan et al., 2020). While the RDoC framework is a relatively recent development, the importance of ideas of dimensionality as opposed to categorization have been present in the research literature for much longer, providing a substrate from which the RDoC developed (Beauchaine & Thayer, 2015). Further, psychophysiology has been using dimensional approaches to diagnosis for many years (Hajcak & Patrick, 2015).

Figure 6.1 presents the RDoC framework. The RDoC considers six main domains and their constructs of neuropsychiatric and neurocognitive function: negative valence systems, positive valence systems, cognitive systems, systems for social processes, arousal and modulatory systems, and sensorimotor systems, with each main domain encompassing several subdomains (Vaidyanathan et al., 2020). The domains and constructs are then characterized by associations with known findings from seven different units of analysis: genetic associations, molecular findings, cellular findings, brain circuitry, physiology, behavioral associations, and self-report data. One aim of the RDoC diagnostic approach is to integrate information from across these multiple units of analysis with each domain and construct, thus avoiding a

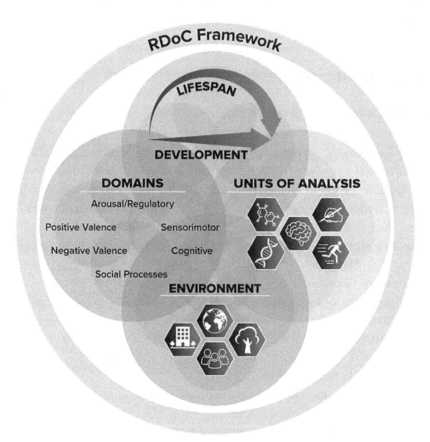

Figure 6.1 The Research Domain Criteria (RDoC) Framework. Reprinted from *About RDoC*, by National Institute of Mental Health, n.d. (https://www.nimh.nih.gov/research/research-funded-by-nimh/rdoc/about-rdoc). In the public domain.

reductionistic approach to understanding and diagnosing mental illness (Cuthbert, 2014). Importantly, the RDoC is a new and developing approach and is currently more of a framework for organizing research than a complete diagnostic system ready for clinical practice (Michelini et al., 2021).

The first two systems of the RDoC framework, negative valence and positive valence, have a long history in psychophysiology. Gray's (1987) motivational theory proposed two key systems of avoidance (behavioral inhibition system) and approach (behavioral approach system) representing dimensional traits that describe how people respond to their environment by avoiding the negative and approaching the positive. Fowles (1980) proposed that Gray's motivational theory could be used to better understand psychopathology from a psychophysiological perspective. The RDoC builds on these concepts. Avoidance, which is tied to negative valence, is an adaptive behavior in general. At the extremes, however, both high and low levels of avoidance and negative valence become pathological (Craske, 2012; Kozak & Cuthbert, 2016). Approach is also an adaptive behavior in general, but it can also become pathological at the extremes, such as in the context of drug use.

The emphasis on adaptive versus maladaptive functioning in the RDoC is a key difference between the RDoC and the *DSM* approaches. In the *DSM* approach, negative emotion is viewed primarily as pathology. In contrast, in the RDoC approach, negative emotion serves an adaptive role, which only becomes maladaptive at the extremes, such as when the emotions become too much and last for too long, or when emotions are suppressed (Kozak & Cuthbert, 2016). Many studies show that the experience of moderate negative emotion is healthy and that the avoidance and suppression of negative emotion is unhealthy (Adler & Hershfield, 2012; Hershfield et al., 2013). For this reason, the RDoC approach can better contribute to diagnosis as it more closely matches reality and better contributes to treatment as the goal is to return negative emotional experience to healthy levels and not to altogether eliminate, avoid, or suppress negative emotions.

In the RDoC approach, the negative valence systems consist of responses to acute threat, potential harm, sustained threat, frustrative nonreward, and loss (Cuthbert & Kozak, 2013; Kozak & Cuthbert, 2016). The main goal is to avoid harm. These systems are organized to engage behaviors that protect against harm by increasing vigilance for current or anticipated threats and increasing readiness to act. Responses can persist when the threat has ended. In the case of frustrative nonreward and loss, effective coping could involve changing how a situation is perceived. In all these situations, the goal is to effectively adapt to negative situations or outcomes.

Positive valence systems consist of approach motivation, initial responsiveness to reward, sustained responsiveness to reward, reward learning, and habit. The main goal is to approach what is beneficial. These systems are organized to predict the probability and benefit of a reward, evaluate effort required, and choose an effective action. Learning over time develops a knowledge base of what is predictive of reward, and habits are developed based on this knowledge to allow effective action to occur without constant attention.

Cognitive systems include attention, perception, working memory, working and declarative memory, language, and cognitive control (Kozak & Cuthbert, 2016; Vaidyanathan et al., 2020). The main goal of this system is awareness and understanding of the world to guide effective adaptation. These systems are organized to sense and perceive the world in ways that are relevant to the individual. This information is integrated with previous knowledge (memory) in order to decide on effective goal-related actions, recognizing limited capacity, focus, and energy. Language plays a critical role in thought and communication, potentially increasing adaptation.

Systems for social processes include affiliation and attachment, social communication, self and other perception, and understanding (Vaidyanathan et al., 2020). The main goal is adaptive relationships and interactions with others. These systems are organized to facilitate social bonding in order to benefit from cooperative action. Human beings are social beings and surviving and thriving is increased through group membership and cohesion.

Arousal/modulatory systems include arousal, circadian rhythms, and sleep/wakefulness. The main goal is effective energy regulation. These systems are organized to maintain homeostatic balance while adaptively interacting with different environments and contexts. Sleep and physical activity also play a significant role in emotional well-being and health in general.

A sixth system, sensorimotor systems, has recently been added to address sensorimotor processing and its impact on overall functioning.

In the RDoC framework, information from the units of analysis level informs the domains level by considering information that can affect domain outcomes. Genetic, molecular, cellular, brain circuitry, and physiologic data are some of the biological data that contribute to domain and construct outcomes, and behavioral and self-report information adds additional data associated with domain and construct outcome. The RDoC framework can readily accommodate new findings into the units of analysis. As new findings develop that are associated with the RDoC domains, they can be incorporated into the RDoC framework, further improving diagnosis and treatment. New brain imaging findings or genetic variants, for example, such as findings showing an association with neuroanatomy or functioning can hone and inform what had been previously known about the RDoC domains, resulting in a flexible diagnostic approach that is responsive to new findings.

A key criticism of the RDoC framework proposed by Insel et al. (2010) is its central focus on brain circuitry dysfunction, as well as the fact that the framework appears to be heavily biological with considerably less attention paid to psychological, social, and cultural factors (Berenbaum, 2013; Lilienfeld, 2014; Whooley, 2014). In this regard, Berenbaum (2013) notes that the RDoC's central focus on brain circuitry dysfunction can limit both how psychopathology is conceptualized as well as potential interventions derived from this view of psychopathology. Further, Lilienfeld (2014) notes there is an overemphasis on biology with five of the seven RDoC units of analysis being biological measures, leaving little room for psychological and social factors. Whooley (2014) critiques the RDoC's inappropriate decontextualization of psychopathology because it does not address social embeddedness, which results from the RDoC's brain-focused conceptualization of dysfunction.

Despite these criticisms, others have argued that the RDoC does in fact include contextualization of the heavy weighting given to biological processes in the RDoC. In Cuthbert's (2014) response to Lilienfeld's and others' critiques of the RDoC, he states that the two-dimensional matrix of domains and units of analysis that people focus on when considering the RDoC diagnostic framework is misleading and has led to confusion. He notes that the RDoC framework is not a two-dimensional matrix but rather a four-dimensional matrix that also includes contextual effects such as environment and neurodevelopmental issues (Cuthbert, 2014). Cuthbert (2014) further notes that while biological data inform the domains and constructs, the domains and constructs are not seen as purely biological constructs because they are also informed by behavioral data. As such, with its inclusion of contextual issues, neurodevelopment, and patient report in addition to biological and genetic factors, the overall framework of the RDoC accommodates the biopsychosocial model of psychopathology. And the RDoC is a new and developing approach undergoing change and development. It is not surprising that changes and additions will occur. In fact, as we argue, the RDoC is designed to readily respond to and incorporate new information that can inform all of its domains.

Hierarchical Taxonomy of Psychopathology (HiTOP)

The HiTOP is a more recent dimensional approach to psychopathology and is currently enjoying more research focus than the RDoC framework (Kotov et al., 2017; Kotov et al., 2021). The HiTOP is designed with the explicit goal of improving research in psychopathology. HiTOP researchers take an empirical, dimensional, and hierarchical approach to diagnosis. The biggest problem with the *DSM* from the HiTOP perspective is that the *DSM* is neither empirically based nor guided by the research literature. The HiTOP approach also addresses other serious problems with the *DSM,* including categorical diagnoses that are unreliable and not supported by existing research, diagnostic heterogeneity leading to individuals with the same diagnosis being very different from each other, problems with diagnostic comorbidity, and arbitrary boundaries between pathology and normality. Further, because no one diagnosis may fit a particular patient, they are often given a diagnosis of other specified/unspecified disorder. Although this is a common diagnosis, it does not provide clear information about patient suffering nor help guide treatment.

In sum, the HiTOP is an empirically derived, hierarchically structured framework of psychopathology that uses a dimensional approach to organize diagnoses into increasingly broad, transdiagnostic criteria (Ruggero et al., 2019). Key goals are improved reliability and validity of diagnoses, enabling diagnoses to be more useful in case conceptualization and identifying treatment targets. HiTOP dimensions are organized hierarchically with components and traits at the bottom, then syndromes, subfactors, spectra, and an overall superspectrum at the top (see Figure 6.2). Statistical analyses guide the grouping of symptoms into coherent dimensional symptom components and traits, which are in turn grouped into broader dimensions

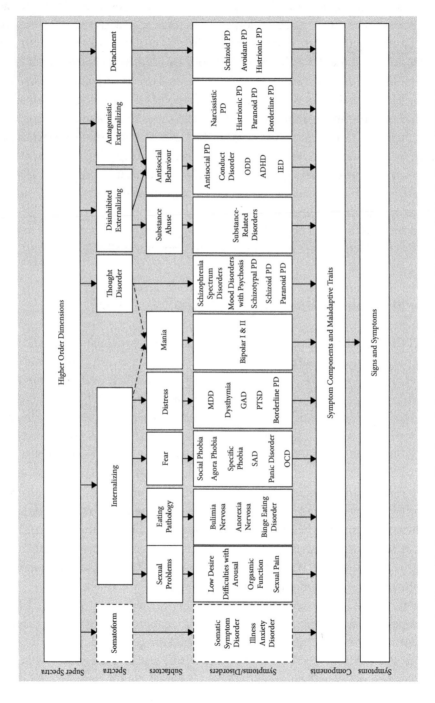

Figure 6.2 The Hierarchical Taxonomy of Psychopathology (HiTOP; Kotov et al., 2017). Available via license: CC BY 3.0

in a hierarchical fashion. Higher level dimensions span diagnostic categories, solving the problem of comorbidity. The components and traits are designed to be coherent dimensions with minimal heterogeneity.

The next step up from components and traits are syndromes or disorders, which are groupings of related components and traits that are strongly related and co-occur. Syndromes most closely relate to *DSM* diagnoses. Syndromes include major disorders such as anxiety and phobias, PTSD, depression, and personality disorders. Above syndromes are subfactors, which reflect clusters of strongly related syndromes, including sexual problems, eating problems, fear, distress, mania, substance abuse, and antisocial behavior.

Above this are spectra, which are broad groups of subfactors that are distinct from one another yet still interrelated. Spectra represent individual difference dimensions, with each spectra representing a range of values or possibilities from low to high. The six spectra are: (1) internalizing, (2) externalizing: disinhibited, (3) externalizing: antagonistic, (4) somatoform, (5) thought disorder, and (6) detachment. The superspectrum is at the highest level of the hierarchy, and reflects overall maladaptation and general psychopathology, often referred to as the "p factor" in the research literature (Caspi et al., 2014).

Thus, the focus and structure of the HiTOP approach is to reduce diagnostic heterogeneity, to account for comorbidity, and to take a dimensional as opposed to a categorical approach to diagnosis affording increased ability to effectively distinguish between health and psychopathology and diagnostic instability. Etiologic factors can affect any level of the diagnostic hierarchy, allowing for the inclusion of multiple different causes and outcomes and enabling determinations of which factors affect which psychopathological outcomes (Conway et al., 2019).

There is clearly overlap between the HiTOP and RDoC approaches (Kotov et al., 2021). Michelini et al. (2021) present an integrated strategy for using HiTOP and RDoC together. They argue that as the RDoC is not yet ready for direct clinical use, the HiTOP approach can provide a clinical assessment while incorporating information about the causes of psychopathology from the RDoC approach. Further, the combination of the RDoC and HiTOP approaches can increase etiological understanding of psychopathology, improve classification of psychopathology, and better inform treatment of psychopathology (Michelini et al., 2021). In this view, dimensional approaches to classification in psychopathology are more powerful than categorical approaches such as *DSM*-type diagnostic schemes in informing etiological understanding due to their ability to include genetic, brain-imaging, and psychophysiological information and by applying both pharmacologic and psychotherapeutic treatment.

Integration of Psychophysiological Biomarkers into Dimensional Diagnostic Approaches

Psychophysiological biomarkers provide significant information about well-being. A number of different biomarkers have been used, including electroencephalography (EEG), heart rate variability (HRV), heart rate, blood pressure, skin conductance, and muscle tension, to identify relationships between physiological functioning and psychopathology. Most of the research in this area has focused on the relationships between psychophysiological functioning and measures of negative affect, such as anxiety, fear, and depression.

Electroencephalography

Electroencephalography (EEG), a recording of the brain's electrophysiological activity, is an electrophysiological method whose results can be readily incorporated into a dimensional diagnostic approach. By measuring changes in electrical potential, EEG identifies an array of different electrical waveforms and their patterns across the brain. Researchers can explore associations between these waveforms and their patterns with cognitive and psychiatric conditions. With event-related potentials, researchers can time lock a short segment of an electroencephalogram tracing to a particular stimulus or cognitive task. After repeated responses to the same stimuli, noise will be averaged out, leaving a tracing showing critical waveforms involved with a particular task or stimulus, waveforms that can then be associated with cognitive functioning or psychopathology. Psychophysiology including EEG and event-related potentials offers a vast amount of data that readily can be incorporated into dimensional models of cognitive dysfunction and mental illness, providing the potential for developing biomarkers of mental illness and cognitive function that can be incorporated into the RDoC, the HiTOP, and other dimensional approaches to the diagnosis of mental illness to better understand, diagnose, and treat mental illness.

Dispositional negativity provides an example of how EEG could be incorporated into a dimensional diagnostic approach. Dispositional negativity is a trait that is associated with a range of psychopathology (Lang et al., 2016; Van den Bergh et al., 2021). While not associated with any one categorical diagnosis, dispositional negativity is a factor that would fit in well with dimensional frameworks such as the RDoC and the HiTOP as it appears to be a general factor for multiple dimensions of psychopathology (Caspi et al., 2014). Further, dispositional negativity could be associated with electroencephalographic abnormalities. While studies looking specifically at associations between dispositional negativity and EEG are lacking, other related constructs such as negative dispositional moods could be associated with electroencephalographic abnormalities, although not all findings agree (Palmiero

& Piccardi, 2017). Nevertheless, dimensional approaches to understanding psychopathology can more effectively incorporate psychophysiological models than traditional categorical diagnoses. This provides a research framework capable of integrating a variety of psychophysiological findings, for example, a correlation found between dispositional negativity and EEG measures.

Heart Rate and Heart Rate Variability

Heart rate is an easily obtainable and frequently measured psychophysiological biomarker. Heart rate change to a stimulus provides a measure of autonomic nervous system activity. Lang et al. (2016) found that changes in heart rate with exposure to imagery varied both between and within *DSM* diagnoses, findings that call into question how well a *DSM*-style approach to classification and diagnosis reflects differences and similarities between anxiety disorders. In contrast, measures of evoked changes in heart rate fit well into classification and diagnostic approaches like the RDoC (Lang et al., 2016; Lang et al., 2017). Inclusion of heart rate change into a unit of analysis in the RDoC can show how heart rate change can vary across an array of anxiety and other clinical presentations, providing an assessment of autonomic nervous system activity in the context of numerous other genetic, molecular, imaging, psychophysiological, and self-report data. In contrast, a traditional *DSM*-based diagnostic approach relying nearly exclusively on patient self-report ignores any but self-report indicators of autonomic nervous system activity.

Among the many physiological findings associated with psychopathology is HRV. Easily assessed, HRV is a measure of how much the heart rate varies from beat to beat over time. Accumulating findings show associations between decreased HRV and a wide variety of different psychopathologies in children, adolescents, and adults, including a variety of associations with different aspects of psychological function such as social competence and ability to sustain attention as well as with autism, attention-deficit disorder, anxiety, depression, schizophrenia, psychopathy (Beauchaine & Thayer, 2015), and bipolar disorder (Hajcak & Patrick, 2015). These associations between reduced HRV and a range of psychopathological conditions suggest that reduced HRV might represent a biomarker of multiple different psychopathological conditions and function as a marker of common physiological dysregulation underlying multiple different types of mental illnesses (Beauchaine & Thayer, 2015). As such, the inclusion of HRV as a variable into the RDoC and the HiTOP would further anchor these diagnostic approaches in relevant pathophysiological variables. As findings regarding the amount of HRV in different domains of the RDoC and the constructs and syndromes of the HiTOP accumulate, the degree of HRV could provide important diagnostic information, show where these domains, constructs, and syndromes differ from each other and where they are similar. In principle, HRV could provide information about underlying pathophysiology, as well as possibly being used to predict which patients might respond to which types of treatment, including both biologically based treatments such as medication, neuromodulatory interventions such as transcranial magnetic stimulation, and psychotherapy.

Skin Conductance and Muscle Tension

Skin conductance, a measure of autonomic activity, is another readily obtainable psychophysiological variable that could be exploited to determine which traits, syndromes, signs, and symptoms are associated with autonomic arousal (Lang et al., 2016; Lang et al., 2017). A categorical approach limits studies of autonomic function to one categorical diagnosis without exploring relationships with autonomic function across a dimension of mental illness (Conway et al., 2019). As a measure of autonomic activity, skin conductance could readily be evaluated across RDoC domains and HiTOP levels to identify associations between domains and levels and autonomic activation, particularly in that both elevated and diminished skin conductance can indicate psychopathology (Toomim & Toomim, 1975), consistent with dimensional approaches to diagnosis. Inclusion of skin conductance into either an RDoC or HiTOP or similar approach could focus diagnostic attention on clinical dimensions, provide an index of severity, and even guide treatment. In addition, more research into the autonomic activity associated with different dimensions of psychopathology could offer theoretical insight into the basic pathophysiology and psychopathology associated with variance along diagnostic dimensions. As such, readily obtainable measures of skin conductance when combined with dimensional approaches to diagnosis could become important markers of psychopathology, aiding both diagnosis and treatment.

As the examples of EEG, HRV, and skin conductance suggest, psychophysiological data have the potential to associate with the different levels of the HiTOP and with the different domains and constructs of the RDoC, as well as with other dimensional diagnostic approaches. Associations of psychophysiological data with different spectra of the HiTOP could identify general psychophysiological markers of psychopathology, whereas associations of psychophysiological data with lower levels of the HiTOP could identify psychophysiological signatures of the signs, symptoms, and components of psychopathology. This same approach also holds for applying psychophysiological data to general domains of the RDoC to identify general psychophysiological factors and to investigate the psychophysiological structure of the RDoC's constructs. Identification of psychophysiological phenotypes of psychopathology using dimensional and hierarchal frameworks of psychopathology capable of incorporating neurobiological data would enable research into investigating the genetic, epigenetic, and environmental contributions to psychopathology based on objective identification of general domains of psychopathology.

In addition to providing for the possibility for new insights into the etiology of psychopathology, inclusions of psychophysiological data into dimensional classification frameworks of psychopathology can offer new ways of integrating psychophysiology and treatment. The different psychophysiological signatures associated with RDoC domains and constructs and with HiTOP spectra, syndromes, signs, symptoms, and components could provide targets for psychotherapeutic modification. For example, a psychophysiological signature of HRV associated with dysphoria could be a target for biofeedback techniques employed in the treatment of a range of HiTOP syndromes including anorexia, obsessive-compulsive disorder, dysthymia, and posttraumatic-stress disorder (Conway et al., 2019).

Case Study

To demonstrate the ideas presented in this chapter, we use a case study first diagnosed in the *DSM* style, followed by diagnoses in RDoC and HiTOP styles to illustrate how psychophysiological data can inform diagnosis in dimensional diagnostic approaches.

A twenty-six-year-old woman presents to an outpatient mental health clinic reporting that she has had a depressed mood for the past two years accompanied by worry and anxiety. She describes several stressors, including problems related to her graduate program and limited income. Both of her parents were high-achieving professionals who had high expectations for their children's academic and professional success. The woman describes her father as being emotionally distant, hard to please, and sometimes even emotionally abusive. She was closer to her mother, who was loving but who also tended to defer to demands made by the father. She additionally describes a somewhat stressful childhood trying to please her father. She was unsuccessful in athletics and often found herself in activities that she did not like while trying to please her parents. She did well academically and found that her self-esteem became increasingly tied to her academic performance and now to her being a graduate student at a prestigious university. However, she reports that graduate school has been stressful for her, and she increasingly wonders whether she is doing it more to obtain approval from her parents rather than doing it for herself. Despite her initial expectations, she is not enjoying graduate school.

While in graduate school, she had a painful breakup with her boyfriend, which left her feeling devastated, alone without any other close friends, and doing worse than she had been before the breakup. She is not particularly close to any of her classmates in school.

She is now doubting her choice to attend graduate school and lacks clarity on what she personally values, as she had always tended to do what her parents thought best and what was in line with cultural values. She reports difficulty sleeping, low energy, poor motivation, anhedonia, and feelings of failure. She worries that nothing will change and that she does not have the ability to truly succeed, both of which have led to ruminations about her self-worth. She struggles to focus while at work. She does not feel like she would be a desirable partner for anyone and worries that she will end up being alone. At the same time, though, she does not do anything specific to address her problems. She tries to avoid thinking about her difficulties but ruminates on her mood and misery. She denies use of drugs and alcohol. Brain-imaging shows bilaterally decreased hippocampal volume, and on testing, the patient is found to have abnormally low HRV.

DSM-V Diagnostic Approach

The patient meets *DSM-V* criteria for severe major depressive disorder, characterized by depressed mood, anhedonia, insomnia, fatigue, feeling worthless, and diminished ability to think, which are causing clinically significant distress and impairment in social and occupational functioning. The episode is not attributable to physiological effects of a substance or to another disorder. She also meets *DSM-V* criteria for generalized anxiety disorder characterized by excessive anxiety and worry, difficulty controlling worry, feeling restless, having difficulty concentrating, and having a sleep disturbance. With these *DSM-V* type diagnoses, the patient would receive psychotherapeutic and pharmacological treatment for major depression and generalized anxiety disorder.

RDoC Diagnostic Approach

In contrast, an RDoC diagnostic approach would emphasize a review of systems (negative valence, etc.) to identify core factors likely involved in the client's functioning (Harkness et al., 2014; Kozak & Cuthbert, 2016; Vaidyanathan et al., 2020).

- *Negative valence systems*: The patient reports chronically high levels of negative affect, with both acute threat and potential threat (anxiety), loss of her boyfriend, and lack of rewards from her graduate program.
- *Positive valence systems*: The patient has chronically low levels of positive affect.
- *Cognitive*: The patient has negative rumination, distraction, and attention, perceptual, and working memory issues.
- *Social Processes*: Patient is socially isolated without close friends or partners. There are potential attachment and social communication issues.
- *Arousal/regulatory*: The patient reports sleep disruption and low energy.

The RDoC approach illustrated here provides a sound framework not only for diagnosis, but also for selecting treatment targets and guiding treatment overall. The brain-imaging and HRV findings could additionally inform the diagnosis. Treatment targets are selected by integrating the RDoC diagnostic information. Interventions that have been empirically demonstrated to address the treatment targets could then be selected and employed.

HiTOP Diagnostic Approach

With the HiTOP approach, the patient's reports would be considered internalizing with high distress, falling into the *DSM-V* categories of generalized anxiety disorder and major depression. Research findings that have shown efficacy for various types of therapeutic interventions for internalizing features could then be used by the therapist. In this case study, the HiTOP approach enables a better conceptualization of the patient and better identification of treatment targets. Because upper HiTOP levels span traditional *DSM* categories, the use of the HiTOP approach in this case would eliminate problems of comorbidity, enable focusing on the patient's actual symptoms, and allow for inclusion of psychosocial and biological data, such as the decreased hippocampal volume bilaterally and abnormal HRV, further guiding conceptualization and treatment. Additional data ranging from self-report to laboratory and brain-imaging findings as they become available could be incorporated into the HiTOP framework, further honing diagnostic conceptualization and guiding treatment.

Conclusion

Dimensional approaches to diagnoses in clinical psychology and psychiatry have the potential to overcome important limitations associated with categorical approaches to diagnosis. Evidence indicates that most mental disorders exist on a continuum that is not easily dichotomized into either not having a disorder or having a disorder. A categorial approach to diagnosis focuses on only the extreme end of a spectrum of symptoms and symptom severity, leaving people on the other end of the spectrum with comparatively mild, but not necessarily benign symptoms, unaccounted for (Rose, 1992), subsyndromal features that might contribute upwards of half of the disability associated with mental disorders (Johnson et al., 2022). In addition, genetic, neuroanatomical, and neurophysiological findings do not necessarily align well with categorial approaches to diagnosis, such as those taken in the *DSM* approach, which has limited progress in understanding the causes of mental disorders and treatment innovation.

The two different dimensional approaches to diagnosis in mental health we review here have the potential to overcome the inherent limitations of traditional categorial approaches to diagnosis in mental health. Both the RDoC and the HiTOP approaches to diagnosis and treatment base diagnosis and treatment on different domains of mental function that can take into account a continuum of function on a particular domain. These approaches also can incorporate genetic, neuroanatomical, brain-circuitry, neuropathological, and psychophysiological data as they become available, further refining diagnosis and enabling ready inclusion of new treatment possibilities.

Numerous findings from psychophysiology including research from EEG, event-related potentials, and HRV that while harder to incorporate into traditional categorical approaches to diagnoses, can be readily incorporated into the dimensional RDoC and HiTOP diagnostic approaches. Psychophysiology has the potential to inform diagnosis and pharmacological and psychotherapeutic treatment of psychopathology when applied to a dimensional diagnostic treatment approach such as the RDoC and HiTOP.

References

Adler, J.M., & Hershfield, H.E. (2012). Mixed emotional experience is associated with and precedes improvements in psychological well-being. *PLoS ONE, 7*(4), e35633. https://doi.org/10.1371/journal.pone.0035633

American Psychiatric Association. (2013). *Diagnostic and statistical manual of mental disorders* (5th ed.). https://doi.org/10.1176/appi.books.9780890425596

Beauchaine, T. P., & Thayer, J. F. (2015). Heart rate variability as a transdiagnostic biomarker of psychopathology. *International Journal of Psychophysiology, 98*(2 Pt 2), 338–350. https://doi.org/10.1016/j.ijpsycho.2015.08.004

Berenbaum, H. (2013). Classification and psychopathology research. *Journal of Abnormal Psychology, 122*(3), 894–901. https://doi.org/10.1037/a0033096

Caspi, A., Houts, R. M., Belsky, D. W., Goldman-Mellor, S. J., Harrington, H., Israel, S., Meier, M. H., Ramrakha, S., Shalev, I., Poulton, R., & Moffitt, T. E. (2014). The p factor: One general psychopathology factor in the structure of psychiatric disorders?. *Clinical Psychological Science: A Journal of the Association for Psychological Science, 2*(2), 119–137. https://doi.org/10.1177/2167702613497473

Conway, C. C., Forbes, M. K., Forbush, K. T., Fried, E. I., Hallquist, M. N., Kotov, R., Mullins-Sweatt, S. N., Shackman, A. J., Skodol, A. E., South, S. C., Sunderland, M., Waszczuk, M. A., Zald, D. H., Afzali, M. H., Bornovalova, M. A., Carragher, N., Docherty, A. R., Jonas, K. G., Krueger, R. F., ... Eaton, N. R. (2019). A hierarchal taxonomy of psychopathology can transform mental health research. *Perspectives on Psychological Science, 14*(3), 419–436. https://doi.org/10.1177/1745691618810696

Craske, M. (2012). The R-DOC initiative: Science and practice. *Depression and Anxiety, 29*(4), 253–256. https://doi.org/10.1002/da.21930

Cuthbert, B. N. (2014). Response to Lilienfeld. *Behavior Research and Therapy, 62*, 140–142. https://doi.org/10.1016/j.brat.2014.08.001

Cuthbert, B.N., & Kozak, M. J. (2013). Constructing constructs for psychopathology: The NIMH research domain criteria. *Journal of Abnormal Psychology, 122*(3), 928–937. https://doi.org/10.1037/a0034028

Fowles, D. C. (1980). The three arousal model: Implications of Gray's two-factor learning theory for heart rate, electrodermal activity, and psychopathy. *Psychophysiology, 17*(2), 87–104. https://doi.org/10.1111/j.1469-8986.1980.tb00117.x

Gray, J. A. (1987). *The psychology of fear and stress*. Cambridge University Press.

Hajcak, G., & Patrick, C. J. (2015). Situating psychological science within the Research Domain Criteria (RDoC) framework. *International Journal of Psychophysiology, 98*(2 Pt 2), 223–226. https://doi.org/10.1016/j.ijpsycho.2015.11.001

Harkness, A. R., Reynolds, S. M., & Lilienfeld, S. O. (2014). A review of systems for psychology and psychiatry: Adaptive systems, personality psychopathology five (PSY-5), and the DMS-5. *Journal of Personality Assessment, 96*, 121–139. https://doi.org/10.1080/00223891.2013.823438

Hershfield, H. E., Scheibe, S., Sims, T. L., & Carstensen, L. L. (2013). When feeling bad can be good: Mixed emotions benefit physical health across adulthood. *Social Psychological and Personality Science, 4*, 54–61. https://doi.org/10.1177/1948550612444616

Insel, T., Cuthbert, B., Garvey, M., Heinssen, R., Pine, D., Quinn, D. S., Sanislow, C., & Wang, P. (2010). Research Domain Criteria (RDoC): Toward a new classification framework for research on mental disorders. *American Journal of Psychiatry, 167*(7), 748–751. https://doi.org/10.1176/appi.ajp.2010.09091379

Insel, T. R. (2014). The NIMH Research Domain Criteria (RDoC) project: Precision medicine for psychiatry. *American Journal of Psychiatry, 171*(4), 395–397. https://doi.org/10.1176/appi.ajp.2014.14020138

Johnson, J. C. S., Byrne, G. J., & Pelecanos, A. M. (2022). The prevalence of subthreshold psychiatric symptoms and associations with alcohol and substance use disorders: From a nationally representative survey of 36,309 adults. *BMC Psychiatry, 22*(1), 270. https://doi.org/10.1186/s12888-022-03834-1

Kotov, R., Krueger, R. F., Watson, D., Achenbach, T. M., Althoff, R. R., Bagby, R. M., Brown, T. A., Carpenter, W. T., Caspi, A., Clark, L. A., Eaton, N. R., Forbes, M. K., Forbush, K. T., Goldberg, D., Hasin, D., Hyman, S. E., Ivanova, M. Y., Lynam, D. R., Markon, K., . . . Zimmerman, M. (2017). The Hierarchical Taxonomy of Psychopathology (HiTOP): A dimensional alternative to traditional nosologies. *Journal of Abnormal Psychology, 126*(4), 454–477. https://doi.org/10.1037/abn0000258

Kotov, R., Krueger, R. F., Watson, D., Cicero, D. C., Conway, C. C., DeYoung, C. G., Eaton, N. R., Forbes, M. K., Hallquist, M. N., Latzman, R. D., Mullins-Sweatt, S. N., Ruggero, C. J., Simms, L. J., Waldman, I. D., Waszczuk, M. A., & Wright, A. G. C. (2021). The Hierarchical Taxonomy of Psychopathology (HiTOP): A quantitative nosology based on consensus of evidence. *Annual Review of Clinical Psychology, 17*, 83–108. https://doi.org/10.1146/annurev-clinpsy-081219-093304

Kozak, M. J., & Cuthbert, B. N. (2016). The NIMH Research Domain Criteria initiative: Background, issues, and pragmatics. *Psychophysiology, 53*, 286–297. https://doi.org/10.1111/psyp.12518

Lang, P. J., McTeague, L. M., & Bradley, M. M. (2016). RDoC, DSM, and the reflex physiology of fear: A biodimensional analysis of the anxiety disorders spectrum. *Psychophysiology, 53*, 336–347. https://doi.org/10.1111/psyp.12462

Lang, P. J., McTeague, L. M., & Bradley, M. M. (2017). The psychophysiology of anxiety and mood disorders: The RDoC challenge. *Zeitschrift für Psychologie, 225*(3), 175–188. https://doi.org/10.1027/2151-2604/a000302

Lilienfeld, S. O. (2014). The Research Domain Criteria (RDoC): An analysis of methodological and conceptual challenges. *Behaviour Research and Therapy, 62*, 129–139. http://dx.doi.org/10.1016/j.brat.2014.07.019

Lilienfeld, S. O. (2020). Three unresolved conceptual issues in personality disorders: Commentary on controversies in the classification and diagnosis of personality disorders. In C. W. Lejuez & K. L. Gratz (Eds.), The Cambridge handbook of personality disorders (pp. 111–114). Cambridge University Press. https://doi.org/10.1017/9781108333931.021

Lilienfeld, S. O., & Treadway, M. T. (2016). Clashing diagnostic approaches: DSM-ICD versus RDoC. *Annual Review of Clinical Psychology, 12*, 435–463. https://doi.org/10.1146/annurev-clinpsy-021815-093122

Markon, K. E., Chmielewski, M., & Miller, C. J. (2011). The reliability and validity of discrete and continuous measures of psychopathology: A quantitative review. *Psychological Bulletin, 137*, 856–879. https://doi.org/10.1037/a0023678

Meidlinger, P. C., & Hope, D. A. (2017). The new transdiagnostic cognitive behavioral treatments: Commentary for clinicians and clinical researchers. *Journal of Anxiety Disorders, 46*, 101–109. https://doi.org/10.1016/j.janxdis.2016.11.002

Michelini, G., Palumbo, I. M., DeYoung, C. G., Latzman, R. O., & Kotov, R. (2021). Linking RDoC and HiTOP: A new interface for advancing psychiatric nosology and neuroscience. *Clinical Psychology Review, 86*, Article 102025. https://doi.org/10.1016/j.cpr.2021.102025

Palmiero, M., & Piccardi, L. (2017). Frontal EEG asymmetry of mood: A mini-review. *Frontiers in Behavioral Neuroscience, 11*, Article 224. https://doi.org/10.3389/fnbeh.2017.00224

Phillips, J., Frances, A., Cerullo, M. A., Chardavoyne, J., Decker, H. S., First, M. B., Ghaemi, N., Greenberg, G., Hinderliter, A. C., Kinghorn, W. A., LoBello, S. G., Martin, E. B., Mishara, A. L., Paris, J., Pierre, J. M., Pies, R. W., Pincus, H. A., Porter, D., Pouncey, C., . . . Zachar, P. (2012). The six most essential questions in psychiatric diagnosis: A pluralogue part 1: Issues of conservatism and pragmatism in psychiatric diagnosis. *Philosophy, Ethics, and Humanities in Medicine, 7*, 1–29. http://doi.org/10.1186/1747-5341-7-3

Rose, G. (1992). *The strategy of preventive medicine*. Oxford University Press.
Ruggero, C. J., Kotov, R., Hopwood, C. J., First, M., Clark, L. A., Skodol, A. E., Mullins-Sweatt, S. N., Patrick, C. J., Bach, B., Cicero, D. C., Docherty, A., Simms, L. J., Bagby, R. M., Krueger, R. F., Callahan, J. L., Chmielewski, M., Conway, C. C., De Clercq, B., Dornbach-Bender, A., . . . Zimmermann, J. (2019). Integrating the Hierarchal Taxonomy of Psychopathology (HiTOP) into clinical practice. *Journal of Consulting and Clinical Psychology, 87*, 1069–1084. https://doi.org/10.1037/ccp0000452
Toomim, M., & Toomim, H. (1975). GSR feedback in psychotherapy: Some clinical observations. *Psychotherapy: Theory, Research and Practice, 12*(1), 33–38.
Vaidyanathan, U., Morris, S., Wagner, A., Sherrill, J., Sommer, D., Garvey, M., Murphy, E., & Cuthbert, B. (2020). The NIMH Research Domain Criteria project: A decade of behavior and brain integration for translational research. In S. C. Hayes & S. G. Hofmann (Eds.), *Beyond the DSM: Toward a process-based alternative for diagnosis and mental health treatment* (pp. 23–45). Context Press/New Harbinger Publications.
Van den Bergh, O., Brosschot, J., Critchley, H., Thayer, J. F., & Ottaviani, C. (2021). Better safe than sorry: A common signature of general vulnerability for psychopathology. *Perspective on Psychological Science, 16*(2), 225–246. https://doi.org/10.1177/1745691620950690
Whooley, O. (2014). Nosological reflections: The failure of *DSM-5*, the emergence of RDoC, and the decontextualization of mental distress. *Society and Mental Health, 4*(2), 92–110. https://doi.org/10.1177/2156869313519114
Zwir, I., Del-Val, C., Arnedo, J., Pulkki-Råback, L., Konte, B., Yang, S. S., Romero-Zaliz, R., Hintsanen, M., Cloninger, K. M., Garcia, D., Svrakic, D. M., Lester, N., Rozsa, S., Mesa, A., Lyytikäinen, L.-P., Giegling, I., Kähönen, M., Martinez, M., Seppälä, I., . . . Cloninger, C. R. (2021). Three genetic-environmental networks for human personality. *Molecular Psychiatry, 26*, 3858–3875. https://doi.org/10.1038/s41380-019-0579-x

7
The Biology of Personality and Stress
Cardiovascular Reactivity as Central to Human Coping

Brian M. Hughes, Siobhán Howard, and Aisling M. Costello

In stress psychology, with its focus on the traits and temperaments that differentiate those who succumb from those who survive, much has been written about the so-called biopsychosocial paradigm. But in reality, most stress psychologists are invested almost exclusively in the psychosocial substrates: the idea that a person might be sick, or get sick, is often the only "bio" concept they have in mind. This is a shortcoming because the direct psychophysiological mechanisms that moderate physical health are intertwined with notions of personality and individual differences. When considering human resilience, it is helpful to consider biological capacities as well as psychological resources. In many senses, the two constructs are one and the same thing—the psychological response to stress is an inherently *biological* phenomenon. Nowhere is this more conspicuous than with regard to the cardiovascular stress response, a real-time indicator of emotional state that places a concomitant load on a vital bodily system (Georgiades, 2007; Jennings et al., 2004; Nazzaro et al., 2002; Treiber et al., 2003). The relevance of affairs of the heart to long-term human well-being is not just metaphorical; our ability to negotiate the vicissitudes of life is a physical as well as mental skill.

A plethora of theories has been developed to deal with the predicament of human stress, each implicating personality differences as potential determinants of well-being. Lazarus and Folkman's (1984) transactional model refines how individual appraisals lead some individuals to suffer stress responses in circumstances where others will survive unscathed. McEwen's (1998) notion of allostatic load describes stress as the wear and tear caused to individuals by the continuous disruptions to the delicate homeostasis of their lives. Greenberg et al.'s (1997) theory of "terror management" highlights self-esteem as a buffer that obviates the existential dread we feel when we become aware of the inevitability of death. Hobfoll's (1989) theory of resource conservation suggests that some people are made more resilient by their ability to replenish lost social capital. Kemeny's (2003) model of integrated specificity attempts to delineate distinctly different outcomes of specific types of stress for various systems of the body, belying notions of a uniform "one-size-fits-all" stress reaction.

These various theoretical frameworks allow us to formulate research questions and to imagine research studies. And they set an agenda for the investigation of different types of risks that, hopefully, will help shed light on those physical processes that link stress to well-being. Key to this, of course, will be the measurement of whatever variables we have in mind. And central to the endeavor will be an understanding of how mental stress, through whatever filters, ends up precipitating material damage to human health in various individual circumstances. In other words, all theoretical models are relevant chiefly insofar as they can plausibly bridge the gap between the emotional and the concrete. Considering *what* stress does to human beings depends not just on understanding *how* stress is experienced by different people, but also on *why* it arises in human life in the first place.

Evolution of Individual Human Stress Responses

One of the central theoretical models of psychological stress refers to the fight-or-flight response as a physical context. This is essentially a paradigm rather than a theory, put forward by Walter Cannon back in the 1930s (Cannon, 1932). Cannon was a medical scientist who worked at Harvard Medical School. He enjoyed many professional privileges, and perhaps his fight-or-flight theory is not necessarily the most brilliant ever formulated, but it certainly has had posterity. It describes the notion that human bodies exhibit an evolved stress response, shaped by the filters of natural selection.

We have many reasons to assume that the contents of today's human gene pool reflect what was left behind by life's survivors. Almost by definition, those survivors were people who were naturally good at "fighting" and "fleeing," avoiding stress, or dealing with stress head-on. The crux of the matter is that the types of stress faced by human beings across evolutionary trajectories have themselves changed over time. Prehistoric stress was surely very different from the stress of the modern world (Slavich, 2020). However, according to the evolutionary perspective, our modern physiological stress *responses* are essentially the same as those elicited by our bodies in prehistoric times, deployed in present-day situations and directed at novel targets (Taborsky et al., 2021).

Non-physiologists will often ask why evolved responses do not themselves "evolve out" of existence over time. Today's modern stressors—after-hours emails, online meeting invites, social media envy, unpaid bills, long commutes, unfulfilling careers, or free-floating angst—are generally not stressful in a way that can easily be "fought" off or "fled" from (Jackson, 2014). In the modern world, humans are not prowled by sabre-toothed tigers or giant alligators. So why does the prehistoric stress response persist? The answer to that question relates to the sheer amount of time involved in the evolution of physical bodies, compared with the relative speed of social and cultural change. Genetic change in human bodies over successive generations is much more incremental and linear than the shifts we see in the circumstances of human environments, which tend to be stark and exponential. We do not always appreciate how recent our own surrounding context actually is.

We often lose sight of the sheer age of our species, and the sheer length of time in which evolution has had to operate. Our species' family tree extends back around seven million years (Tattersall & Schwartz, 2009). For most of that history, our bodies were being shaped by the needs of the environment that we lived in at that time. That environment included many dangers that were threatening to many humans, with the logical result that those of us alive today are the descendants of ancestors who managed to survive the past. Accordingly, the traits we possess today were inherited from predecessors who successfully navigated historic threats long enough to reproduce and bequeath to the gene-pool. The key point is that most of this history was spent in environments where even rudimentary technologies, such as the wheel, had not yet been invented, or where language was not yet spoken. To put things into perspective, if the entire history of human evolution was compressed into a single calendar year, the capacity for human speech would not be observed until 11:58 p.m. on December 31. The invention of writing—the facility to transcribe a thought and record it for even the medium-term—would not take place until *six seconds before midnight* (Hughes, 2016). In short, our contemporary linguistic culture, where most stressors come to our attention linguistically (deadlines, invoices, harassment, existential anxiety, and the like), represents a form of living that has existed for less than 0.00002 percent of human biological history.

The result is that the physiology of the human body, including all of its automatic reactions and reflexes, was shaped by circumstances that are essentially alien to our lived experiences today. This helps to explain why *mental* stressors elicit *physical* reactions. Most of us are familiar with the idea that when we get into scary situations, we experience more than just psychological responses. We also experience physical changes within our bodies. For example, people who participate in extreme sports, such as bungee jumping or skydiving, will describe being embraced by a physical sense of "the jitters" (van Westerloo et al., 2011). Indeed, the entire premise of extreme sports is the very fact that being placed in such situations is *guaranteed* to produce a rush of adrenaline, a physical bodily response. This is true even though the organizers of such activities are legally mandated to institute security measures that more or less guarantee physical safety: not only will the participant not die, most likely they will never even get injured. And yet they will experience physical reactions throughout their bodies, which, of course, is the whole point of the exercise. The essential "thrill" of taking part in these activities results from the body's automatic physiological response to stress, a physical feeling of terror, produced, artificially, by contrivance.

That experience of exhilaration is essentially the fight-or-flight response, in reality a syndrome of multiple responses that includes disparate bodily effects, such as the shunting of blood away from extremities (resulting in cold fingers and toes), the shutting down of the digestive system (leading to loss of appetite), the metabolizing of fats (which can cause stomach upset or indigestion), and several hormonal shifts (including reductions in circulating sex hormones, making it virtually impossible to feel sexually aroused and highly stressed at the same time). In some situations, people will suffer involuntary defecation, urination, regurgitation, or fainting, all of which indicate extreme levels of body shock. These various alterations of physical function help the body to preserve energy that could alternatively be used for fighting or fleeing, as well as helping to lighten the body's physical load to help ensure agility. They will not make a participant better at bungee jumping, but they occur anyway because the participant's brain is primed to respond to stressful situations by precipitating these very reactions (Dhabhar, 2009). It is the human body's "legacy" stress response.

Were we to continue to face modern stressors for as long as we faced predators in the Savannah then our modern stress responses would indeed eventually adapt to reflect modern forms of stress (and who can tell what this eventuality might look like?). In biological terms, natural selection is not finished with us yet. As evolvable organisms, we inevitably *continue* to evolve with every passing generation.

Physiological Stress Reactions as Central to Human Coping

In general terms, all of our body's adaptations reflect a species-level history of reproductive fitness. Many of the things we think of as sickness—such as pain, nausea, or even sickle cell disease—are actually side-effects of processes that, in specific circumstances, serve to protect us. Pain, for example, is like a dashboard alarm system for the body: our pain system provides us with useful information about the things we bump our heads off so that we can better navigate our environments in future (Nesse & Schulkin, 2019). An inability to feel pain would also prevent a person from detecting or reacting to important problem-states *within* the body; they would be unable to realize that their lung was punctured, that their bone was broken, or that they had a serious infection. For this reason, people born with rare diseases featuring congenital insensitivity to pain tend not to live very long. Of course, the problem with pain is that you can have too much of it, and if you are especially hypersensitive to pain, you will have a very uncomfortable life. But within the normal range of human experience, pain is a very important defense mechanism for most people. It is an evolved response that keeps us safe.

Nausea plays a similar role, a physical reaction where your body signals that it needs to purge itself of toxins (Zhong et al., 2021). Feeling nauseous makes you realize that something is wrong, and causes you to stop whatever you are doing. If nausea is sufficiently extreme, you may involuntarily empty your stomach in order to rid yourself of whatever toxins have entered your physiology.

The nature of evolved defense responses is that their protective effects may be dampened if the responses themselves are artificially suppressed. Using medication to suppress nausea may produce illness complications if toxins remain inside, rather than outside, the body. Similarly, painkillers may lead a person to overlook or downplay direct evidence of physical bodily damage.

On balance, our legacy adaptations may be ill-suited to the modern world and elicited inappropriately, or they may be beneficial in unintuitive ways that make it unwise for us to try to suppress them. So our question is ultimately this: *what of the human response to stress?* Is the human stress response an intrusion from our evolutionary past, an ill-fitting defense mechanism that ends up creating more harm than good? Or is it an adaptive multidimensional system that helps to maintain homeostasis and well-being, in ways that are non-obvious but nonetheless critical?

Balance and Adaptation

In psychology, the physiological stress response is frequently discussed in terms of its potential to inflict damage on health and well-being. Stress responses are seen as contributing to both the onset and progression of disease. Many literatures have confirmed that both chronic stress (Steptoe & Kivimäki, 2012) and recurrent stress responsivity (Balanos et al., 2010) contribute to heightened risk of (for example) cardiovascular disease, and that such heightening of risk is not merely coincidental. In short, as well as undermining quality of life in ways that promote unhealthy behaviors (such as poor physical activity, smoking, and over-eating), psychological stress also heightens disease risk by directly causing pathogenic processes to occur within the human body (such as atherosclerosis and hypertension; Spruill, 2010).

At the same time, the physiological stress response can indicate non-obvious benefits for human health. When a person exhibits high blood pressure, it is a sign that their body is doing *something*. However, cardiovascular systems are not discrete entities, and their functions are intertwined with all other systems within the body. Simultaneous to stress-related elevations in blood pressure will be corresponding increases in the arousal of the immune and endocrine systems (Phillips et al., 2009). In this way, cardiovascular responses will correlate with immune responses. While sustained elevations of cardiovascular function (such as seen in tachycardia or hypertension) are seldom conducive to good cardiovascular health, they will usually correlate with pronounced immune responses, which are seldom *bad* for human health. A short, sharp cardiovascular response might place a strain on your heart, but it also logically indicates that your immune system is simultaneously doing good things elsewhere in your body.

In the classic Cannon formulation, prehistoric stress responses represent a futile displacement of physiological effort; a pounding heart during stress, by directing blood to the musculature, might well prepare a person to flee a sabre-toothed tiger, the story goes, but it will be of little use to a modern human who is stuck in rush-hour traffic. However, this formulation is narrow and misleading. It fails to take account of non-obvious benefits that might be appreciated from a wider perspective. A pounding heart during stress helps to confirm that a person is stress-responsive in broad terms; in modern jargon, we can say that they do not have a "blunted" response to stress (Phillips et al., 2013). Among many other benefits, this allows us to confirm that their ability to detect threats in their environment is appropriately functional, and to predict that their immune system is likely to have been engaged.

A central point is that all stressors require some type of response. The problems arise not from hyperreactivity (or hypersensitivity) per se, but from sustained responses that far outlast the immediate physiological needs. A sustained elevation of heart rate and blood pressure is particularly unhealthy because it creates physical demand on the cardiovascular system that leads to material wear-and-tear (Roemmich et al., 2011). In contrast, a short-acting immune response will have many lasting beneficial effects, given the preparatory manner in which cell activation readies an organism to respond to future pathogens. A failure to experience either physiological response would spare the heart and vasculature from physical impact, but would deprive the body of future immune effectiveness. Therefore, the optimal format for a physiological stress response would be to react immediately and subside quickly (Hughes et al., 2018). In other words, a person needs to be able to exhibit a stress response *that habituates promptly over time.*

"Personality" and Stress Responding

An important thing to know about human beings, of course, is that we are animals. We are not unique in nature, except in the most superficial senses of that term. All human bodies are the same as in all other mammals. We are essentially highly evolved tubes; we take food in one end, we expel it through the other end, and we spend our entire existence using hands and other limbs that allow us to perform this process. We repeat the process over and over, and then we die. This is essentially the template of all mammalian forms, and indeed of most non-mammalian forms too. Our stress responses are also part of this cross-species commonality.

Stress responses allow us to adapt to our environments and to respond to threatening circumstances. When we look across species, we can begin to appreciate the interweaving of physiology with psychological experience (Cockrem, 2013). Stress responses have a critical role in absolute survival; all animals require the ability to respond to environmental threats. For example, we know that removing environmental stressors can appreciably alter levels of circulating stress hormones in many species. In one study, even whales were found to exhibit this benefit, when, in 2001, shipping lanes were cleared in the days and weeks following the terrorist attacks on New York (Rolland et al., 2012). During an extended period where the whales were able to explore their swim zones with no ships to negotiate or navigate around, researchers observed massive changes in glucocorticoid measures taken from the animals' faeces. It appears that the more natural habitat, free of ships, was less stressful to them. Likewise, a long tradition of animal behavior research has shown that in many species, different animals will exhibit different temperaments when faced with sudden stress, typically in ways that produce a bimodal distribution; some animals will actively attack or engage with a given stressor, whereas others will seek to passively evade or avoid it. An example is the reaction of young piglets to the so-called back test (Hessing et al., 1993). When placed on their backs, some piglets will attempt to wriggle free, whereas others will remain docile. Notably, the two resulting categories provide important information about future health in these animals. When raised in stressful environments, passive piglets are found to have elevated cortisol, poor weight gain, delayed puberty onset, and relatively shorter life expectancies when compared to active piglets, but when raised in non-stressful environments, the impact of piglet personality on health outcomes disappears (De Jonge et al., 1996).

In humans, many of the relevant phenomena have been studied through the lens of the cardiovascular system. The premise of this research is that various aspects of cardiovascular function—including heart rate and blood pressure—increase in intensity in response to mental stress (Phillips & Hughes, 2011). Not only do these parameters represent useful measures of the physiological stress response, they also are directly involved in the onset and progression of cardiovascular disease (Chida & Steptoe, 2010), the leading cause of premature death in the human population. For any given person, however, the cumulative negative impact of recurrent cardiovascular stress responses will be a function of their individual styles and circumstances (Whittaker et al., 2021).

The impact of these individual differences can be profound. In one study by our group, we examined a dataset emanating from a wider longitudinal study conducted in Germany (Ó Súilleabháin & Hughes, 2018). Specifically, we scrutinized records relating to 400 older adults, with an average age of eighty-five years, all of whom had completed psychological assessments of personality. The longitudinal nature of the dataset was such that by the end of data collection, some nineteen years after commencement, a subset of the adults had died. We found that psychometric measures of neuroticism, part of the Big Five personality model, were predictive of actual mortality in this group: each single standard deviation increase in neuroticism scores was associated with a 14 percent increase in mortality. We observed that lower levels of neuroticism moderated the effects of angiotensin-converting enzyme (ACE) on mortality. ACE is centrally involved in determining human blood pressure, playing a role in the constriction of blood vessels (drugs that *inhibit* ACE are popular pharmaceutical treatments for cardiovascular disease). Beyond the statistical and medical jargon, this type of finding can be seen as profound: how people tick boxes on questionnaires can be shown to predict *whether* they will die during a nineteen-year period, and, to an extent, *how* they will die.

If you just look at blood pressure specifically, most readers will be aware that high blood pressure is bad for human health, as evidenced by the idea of hypertension, where blood pressure increases to a level that warrants pharmaceutical intervention. What is generally less well understood is that that imaginary cut-off between "normal" blood pressure and hypertension is essentially arbitrary (Giles et al., 2009).

Its main use is specifically to identify who should get those blood pressure-lowering drugs and who shouldn't. In reality, the relationship between blood pressure and risk is linear. There is no actual boundary between low (or no) risk and high risk. Every difference in average blood pressure between one person and another represents a corresponding difference in risk of eventual heart disease, even when young healthy people with "normal" blood pressures are compared. When large epidemiological datasets based on millions of cases are examined (e.g., Lewington et al., 2002), we typically see that for middle-aged healthy adults, an increment of 15 mmHg in usual blood pressure equates to a doubling of risk of premature heart disease mortality. In other words, if you compare two forty-year-old adults and find that one of them typically has blood pressure 15 mmHg higher than the other, then that adult will be twice as likely to die from heart disease during the next thirty years. This is especially of interest when we consider that measures of usual daily blood pressure are strongly correlated with psychometric measures of psychosocial variables. When researchers in our group studied a sample of over 200 university staff members, we found that perceived social support was strongly associated with average daily blood pressure (Hughes & Howard, 2009). The range of blood pressures typical of persons reporting low social support was around 15 mmHg higher than for persons reporting high social support. If benchmarked against the available epidemiological data, such a difference in self-reported social support could reasonably be interpreted as reflecting a two-fold differential in long-term mortality risk.

Blood Pressure Stress Reactivity as an Individual Difference Variable

We should note that concepts such as "daily average" or "usual" blood pressure are different to "resting" blood pressure as customarily recorded by your physician (Emdin et al., 2015). Daily average blood pressure will take account of times when an individual is active as well as times when the individual is at rest. The range of blood pressure from low to high across a day is of interest, because it takes account of the person's capacity to deal with daily activities, including stress. If a person finds daily life arduous, they will experience greater elevations in blood pressure. A key point to be aware of is that, even when faced with the same demands, not everybody's blood pressure will be elevated to the same extent; the degree of response of the cardiovascular system to stress varies across individuals.

Not only this, but a person's cardiovascular reactivity to stress is very stable across time. A person who is a high reactor today is very likely to be a high reactor for the rest of their life. A number of studies have confirmed that cardiovascular reactivity in infancy is predictive of blood pressure patterns in later childhood (Lewis et al., 1990), and that such patterns in childhood are predictive of reactivity in adulthood (Hassellund et al., 2010). In addition, higher dispositional stress reactivity in infancy appears to be associated with greater rates of later-childhood illness (Lewis et al.,

1990), consistent with the notion that reactivity itself plays a part in processes underlying health and ill-health. We can combine all of these points with the knowledge that patterns of cardiovascular reactivity can be shown to be associated with personality traits, such as neuroticism (Hughes et al., 2011), which are also known to be stable across time. Together, these findings help to explain how certain personality traits themselves can *predict* illness outcomes, rather than necessarily *cause* them: by reflecting a person's habitual profile of physiological arousability.

Optimal Stress Responding and Personality

As noted above, optimal stress responses need to be substantive, in the same way that all perceptual capacities need to be somewhat responsive to environmental stimuli. A stress response system that fails to react to stress will be counterproductive in the same way as a pain response system that fails to react to pain. The fight-or-flight response is not entirely anachronistic, in that physiological arousal following stress includes elevation of immune function, along with other beneficial outcomes. However, to prevent overload, it is important that stress responses be time-limited rather than sustained. In other words, it is important that stress responses be subject to habituation. In that sense, therefore, the optimal stress response is one that is robust enough to ensure that the appropriate defense mechanisms in the body are engaged, and fluid enough to subside once that outcome has been initiated.

It is only relatively recently that stress psychophysiologists have begun to focus on habituation as a cardinal feature of stress responses. For many decades, the so-called reactivity hypothesis (Obrist, 1981) posited that cardiovascular reactivity was a linear predictor of risk: the higher a person's cardiovascular reactivity to stress, the greater their risk of eventual illness onset. This view began to be challenged when researchers drew attention to a growing number of studies that reported associations between low (or "blunted") reactivity and adverse states, such as depression (Keogh et al., 2021) and obesity (Phillips et al., 2013; see also O'Riordan et al., 2022). The notion of linear risk was also inconsistent with the status of reactivity as an inherent and stable individual difference variable; if fight-or-flight responses are indeed adaptations shaped by natural selection, then we would expect them to be normally distributed, with the most adaptive outcomes associated with the mid-range of the distribution, rather than with one of the extremes (i.e., we would not expect low reactivity to be necessarily more adaptive than high reactivity). Instead, the emerging picture now is that *both* low *and* high cardiovascular reactivity are associated with adverse outcomes (albeit of different types), with mid-range cardiovascular reactivity relatively more likely to be associated with indicators of positive health (Lovallo, 2011). However, even mid-range reactivity involves wear-and-tear on the cardiovascular system and would begin to backfire if it failed to habituate. Therefore, when seeking to account for personality differences in stress resilience, researchers in this field are now focusing more on the capacity of the individual to *habituate* to the stress experience, rather than somehow to be able to withstand the experience of stress by responding as little as possible.

Research Linking Cardiovascular Stress Response Habituation to Personality and Individual Differences

The role of several personality and individual difference variables as predictors of cardiovascular stress-response habituation has been examined across a range of research. These research strands can be classified as encompassing studies of emotional variables, coping styles, and personality traits (Hughes et al., 2018). Research into emotional variables have included studies of trait anxiety, which has been found to be *unrelated* to cardiovascular stress-response adaptation during public speaking stress (Mauss et al., 2003), as well as studies of body-esteem, which has been found to *enhance* the habituation of stress responses among medical trainees (Hughes & Black, 2006). Coping styles research has found both repressive coping style (Howard et al., 2017) and trait resilience (Lü, Wang, & You, 2016) to be of assistance in promoting faster habituation of blood pressure responses to stress. Meanwhile, trait dominance (Lee & Hughes, 2014), trait rumination (Johnson et al., 2012), and trait perfectionism (Albert et al., 2016) have been shown to disrupt such habituation. Global self-esteem, on the other hand, promotes successful habituation to stress (Elfering & Grebner, 2012).

Of the major personality traits, openness (Lü, Wang, & Hughes, 2016; O Súilleabháin et al., 2018) and extraversion (Lü & Wang, 2017; Lü, Xing et al., 2018) have each been found to aid habituation of the cardiovascular stress response. By contrast, neuroticism (Hughes et al., 2011) and hostility (Rodríguez et al., 2018; Tyra et al., 2020) have been found to undermine such habituation. Neuroticism has also been shown to exacerbate the effects of physical fatigue on cardiovascular stress response habituation (Lü, Hughes et al., 2018). Vulnerability to stress, a subcomponent of trait neuroticism, has been identified as especially damaging to habituation (Ó Súilleabháin et al., 2019), and may account for the effects of neuroticism overall. Type D personality, a profile found to be prevalent among patients who have advanced forms of heart disease, has been shown to be especially disruptive of habituation, by causing blood pressure stress responses to *increase* (i.e., sensitize), rather than decrease, over time (Howard & Hughes, 2013).

Cardiovascular Reactivity and Psychotherapy

The fact that cardiovascular stress reactivity is a stable, inherited, and dispositional coping mechanism means that, by and large, it is difficult if not impossible to alter an individual's personal pattern of stress responding. Whether a person is a hyperreactor or a blunter, or whether their response habituates quickly or not, is essentially a *trait* rather than a *behavior*. Ample research evidence confirms that cardiovascular stress reactions are stable over long periods of time, and that any reductions in such reactions that arise from therapeutic intervention are likely to be ephemeral (and so to have no impact on long-term disease risk). As a consequence, the relevance of cardiovascular stress reactivity for therapy relates primarily to the insights gained regarding the nature of individual differences in coping, and to supporting therapists in screening clients (so that their precise needs can be identified) and in tailoring potential therapies.

While the cardiovascular response itself is not easily amenable to change, we can certainly take note of the range of psychological factors that forecast how we respond physiologically to stress, and aim to modify those. All the theoretical models of stress mentioned previously are rooted in some form of psychologic origin. For example, Lazarus and Folkman's (1984) transactional model proposes that psychological appraisal of the stressor is central to how individuals physiologically respond. By describing how an individual might conclude that their resources are no match for the demands of the stressor, such biopsychosocial models explain the body's capacity to physiologically signpost that one is "out of one's depth" (Blascovich, 2013). The way such psychological variables shape the evaluation of stress experiences is key to designing targeted interventions.

Rather than attempting to train clients to exhibit different (cardiovascular) stress *responses*, supporting them to develop skills that help them to manage their overall stress *load* can be beneficial. Multiple such interventions exist, each with varying levels of empirical support. Many principles of psychotherapy have been found to work palliatively subsequent to the stress experience, and therefore to minimize the resulting frequency of stress responses. Social interventions may themselves moderate the overall impact of stress on the body, by determining the extent to which cardiovascular stress responses occur and/or habituate over time. Positive feedback on performance of stressful tasks has been shown to assist the habituation of participants' stress responses (Brown & Creaven, 2017). This echoes prior research showing that participants who rate their own social networks as supportive are more likely to exhibit habituation when engaging in such laboratory tasks (Howard & Hughes, 2012), perhaps suggesting that positive social interactions can have a lasting as well as an immediate effect on stress tolerance.

Psychotherapeutic interventions based on emotional expression have conventionally been described as useful. Early on, Pennebaker and Beall (1986) demonstrated that healthy college students who wrote about traumatic events had stronger immune functioning, visited university health clinics less frequently, and experienced greater subjective well-being compared with control subjects. Similarly, when participants wrote about their emotions in an accepting way, they demonstrated reduced heart rate reactivity during the second experimental session relative to those in an experimentally manipulated rumination condition. This suggests that those in the rumination condition were inhibited from habituating to the second task exposure, instead demonstrating a sensitized response while those in the expressive writing condition demonstrated a decreased response to the second task, thus indicating habituation (Low et al., 2008).

We know that when a person engages in negative mental rumination, and so prolongs the psychological representation of a stressor, that they also prolong the physiological response to that stressor (Brosschot et al., 2006). Mindfulness-based stress reduction interventions may help to reduce the psychological and physiological impact of stress if they can assist people to counteract this ruminative tendency (Daubenmier et al., 2019). Research shows that participants who randomized to meditation interventions show lower levels of inflammatory markers, cortisol, resting heart rate, triglycerides, and blood pressure post-intervention compared to control subjects (Pascoe et al., 2017). Therefore, meditation and related contemplative interventions seem to have at least some predictive utility in this regard.

At a broader level and across longer trajectories, there is also some evidence that psychosocial interventions may have a favorable influence on overall cardiovascular disease progression (Schneiderman et al., 2001). Some randomized controlled trials have found cognitive behavioral therapy interventions to have led to reduced blood pressure in hypertension patients (e.g., Mingming, 2017; Yurong et al., 2012), but other large studies have found no such effect (Li et al., 2021). Research on cognitive reappraisal is certainly mixed, with some studies demonstrating that instructing participants to appraise tasks as less stressful appears to incur a corresponding effect on cardiovascular stress-response habituation (Jamieson et al., 2012), but other studies finding no such effect (Griffin & Howard, 2021).

Social or psychotherapeutic interventions that achieve sustained lowering of blood pressure remain difficult to achieve. Stress-reduction intervention studies often find that participants report feeling better but fail to exhibit corresponding cardiovascular stress profiles to corroborate this subjective improvement (e.g., Horgan et al., 2018, Manigault et al., 2021). We must also consider that any cardiovascular changes following cognitive behavioral therapy may also be the result of changes in behavior (such as improved adherence to medication or physical exercise regimens) rather than the enhancement of physiological stress-response profiles.

Conclusion

What we know for certain is that experiencing stress is central to the human experience. If stress becomes too intense—and more importantly, too persistent—we face threats to our homeostasis. Our futures depend on our ability to adapt to that stress, both psychologically and physiologically. The idea that changing the way we think about stress, and thus altering how stress influences our body's physiologically function, is not new. After many decades of research, the influence of individual differences on physiological responses to stress, and in particular stress-response habituation, reveal interesting avenues for psychotherapeutic intervention. While still not fully explored, social support, emotional expression, mindfulness, meditation, and cognitive behavioral therapy are just some of the interventions to show promise in managing psychological and physiological stress responding—not by interfering with physiological response functions directly, but by moderating overall stress load. Providing people with the psychosocial resources to manage stress exposure is likely to be far more productive than attempting to reprogram their bodies to resist millennia of human evolution.

References

Albert, P., Rice, K. G., & Caffee, L. (2016). Perfectionism affects blood pressure in response to repeated exposure to stress. *Stress and Health*, *32*(2), 157–166. https://doi.org/10.1002/smi.2591

Balanos, G. M., Phillips, A. C., Frenneaux, M. P., McIntyre, D., Lykidis, C., Griffin, H. S., & Carroll, D. (2010). Metabolically exaggerated cardiac reactions to acute psychological stress: The effects of resting blood pressure status and possible underlying mechanisms. *Biological Psychology*, *85*, 104–111.

Blascovich, J. (2013). The biopsychosocial model of challenge and threat: Reflections, theoretical ubiquity, and new directions. In B. Derks, D. Scheepers, & N. Ellemers (Eds.), *Neuroscience of prejudice and intergroup relations* (pp. 229–242). Psychology Press. https://doi.org/10.4324/9780203124635

Brosschot, J. F., Gerin, W., & Thayer, J. F. (2006). The perseverative cognition hypothesis: A review of worry, prolonged stress-related physiological activation, and health. *Journal of Psychosomatic Research*, *60*(2), 113–124. https://doi.org/10.1016/j.jpsychores.2005.06.074

Brown, E. G., & Creaven, A. M. (2017). Performance feedback, self-esteem, and cardiovascular adaptation to recurring stressors. *Anxiety, Stress, and Coping*, *30*(3), 290–303. https://doi.org/10.1080/10615806.2016.1269324

Cannon, W. (1932). *Wisdom of the body*. Norton.

Chida, Y., & Steptoe, A. (2010). Greater cardiovascular responses to laboratory mental stress are associated with poor subsequent cardiovascular risk status: A meta-analysis of prospective evidence. *Hypertension*, *55*(4), 1026–1032. https://doi.org/10.1161/HYPERTENSIONAHA.109.146621

Cockrem, J. F. (2013). Individual variation in glucocorticoid stress responses in animals. *General and Comparative Endocrinology*, *15*, 45–58.

Daubenmier, J., Epel, E. S., Moran, P. J., Thompson, J., Jason, A. E., Acree, M., Goldman, V., Kristeller, J., Hecht, F. M., & Mendes, W. B. (2019). A randomized controlled trial of a mindfulness-based weight loss intervention on cardiovascular reactivity to social-evaluative threat among adults with obesity. *Mindfulness*, *10*, 2583–2595. https://doi.org/10.1007/s12671-019-01232-5

De Jonge, F. H., Bokkers, E. A. M., Schouten, W. G. P., & Helmond, F. A. (1996). Rearing piglets in a poor environment: Developmental aspects of social stress in pigs. *Physiology & Behavior*, *60*(2), 389–396. https://doi.org/10.1016/S0031-9384(96)80009-6

Dhabhar, F. S. (2009). A hassle a day may keep the pathogens away: The fight-or-flight stress response and the augmentation of immune function. *Integrative & Comparative Biology*, *49*, 215–236.

Elfering, A., & Grebner, S. (2012). Getting used to academic public speaking: Global self-esteem predicts habituation in blood pressure response to repeated thesis presentations. *Applied Psychophysiology and Biofeedback*, *37*(2), 109–120. https://doi.org/10.1007/s10484-012-9184-3

Emdin, C. A., Anderson, S. G., Callender, T., Conrad, N., Salimi-Khorshidi, G., Mohseni, H., Woodward, M., & Rahimi, K. (2015). Usual blood pressure, peripheral arterial disease, and vascular risk: Cohort study of 4.2 million adults. *British Medical Journal*, *351*, h4865.

Georgiades, A. (2007). Hyperreactivity (cardiovascular). In G. Fink (Ed.), *Encyclopedia of stress*, 2nd ed. (pp. 372–376). Academic Press.

Giles, T. D., Materson, B. J., Cohn, J. N., & Kostis, J. B. (2009). Definition and classification of hypertension: An update. *Journal of Clinical Hypertension*, *11*, 611–614.

Greenberg, J., Solomon, S., & Pyszczynski, T. (1997). Terror management theory of self-esteem and social behavior: Empirical assessments and conceptual refinements. In M. P. Zanna (Ed.), *Advances in experimental social psychology* (vol. 29, pp. 61–139). Academic Press. https://doi.org/10.1016/S0065-2601(08)60016-7

Griffin, S. M., & Howard, S. (2021). Instructed reappraisal and cardiovascular habituation to recurrent stress. *Psychophysiology, 58*(5), Article e13783. https://doi.org/10.1111/psyp.13783

Hassellund, S. S., Flaa, A., Sandvik, L., Kjeldsen, S. E., & Rostrup, M. (2010). Long-term stability of cardiovascular and catecholamine responses to stress tests: An 18-year follow-up study. *Hypertension, 55*(1), 131–136. https://doi.org/10.1161/HYPERTENSIONAHA.109.143164

Hessing, M. J. C., Hagelsø, A. M., Vanbeek, J. A. M., Wiepkema, P. R., Schouten, W. G. P., & Krukow, R. (1993). Individual behavioral characteristics in pigs. *Applied Animal Behaviour Science, 37*(4), 285–295. https://doi.org/10.1016/0168-1591(93)90118-9

Hobfoll, S. E. (1989). Conservation of resources: A new attempt at conceptualizing stress. *American Psychologist, 44*(3), 513–524. https://doi.org/10.1037//0003-066x.44.3.513

Horgan, K., Howard, S., & Gardiner-Hyland, F. (2018). Pre-service teachers and stress during microteaching: An experimental investigation of the effectiveness of relaxation training with biofeedback on psychological and physiological indices of stress. *Applied Psychophysiology and Biofeedback, 43*(3), 217–225. https://doi.org/10.1007/s10484-018-9401-9

Howard, S., & Hughes, B. M. (2012). Benefit of social support for resilience-building is contingent on social context: Examining cardiovascular adaptation to recurrent stress in women. *Anxiety, Stress, and Coping, 25*(4), 411–423. https://doi.org/10.1080/10615806.2011.640933

Howard, S., & Hughes, B. M. (2013). Type D personality is associated with a sensitized cardiovascular response to recurrent stress in men. *Biological Psychology, 94*(2), 450–455. https://doi.org/10.1016/j.biopsycho.2013.09.001

Howard, S., Myers, L. B., & Hughes, B. M. (2017). Repressive coping and cardiovascular reactivity to novel and recurrent stress. *Anxiety, Stress, and Coping, 30*(5), 562–574. https://doi.org/10.1080/10615806.2016.1274027

Hughes, B. M. (2016). *Rethinking psychology: Good science, bad science, pseudoscience*. Palgrave.

Hughes, B. M., & Black, A. (2006). Body esteem as a moderator of cardiovascular stress responses in anatomy students viewing cadaver dissections. *Journal of Psychosomatic Research, 61*(4), 501–506. https://doi.org/10.1016/j.jpsychores.2006.05.004

Hughes, B. M., & Howard, S. (2009). Social support reduces resting cardiovascular function in women. *Anxiety, Stress, and Coping, 22*(5), 537–548. https://doi.org/10.1080/10615800902814614

Hughes, B. M., Howard, S., James, J. E., & Higgins, N. M. (2011). Individual differences in adaptation of cardiovascular responses to stress. *Biological Psychology, 86*(2), 129–136. https://doi.org/10.1016/j.biopsycho.2010.03.015

Hughes, B. M., Lü, W., & Howard, S. (2018). Cardiovascular stress-response adaptation: Conceptual basis, empirical findings, and implications for disease processes. *International Journal of Psychophysiology, 131*, 4–12. https://doi.org/10.1016/j.ijpsycho.2018.02.003

Jackson, M. (2014). The stress of life: A modern complaint? *Lancet, 383*, 300–301.

Jamieson, J. P., Nock, M. K., & Mendes, W. B. (2012). Mind over matter: Reappraising arousal improves cardiovascular and cognitive responses to stress. *Journal of Experimental Psychology: General, 141*(3), 417–422. https://doi.org/10.1037/a0025719

Jennings, J. R., Kamarck, T. W., Everson-Rose, S. A., Kaplan, G. A., Manuck, S. B., & Salonen, J. T. (2004). Exaggerated blood pressure responses during mental stress are prospectively related to enhanced carotid atherosclerosis in middle-aged Finnish men. *Circulation, 110*, 2198–2203.

Johnson, J. A., Lavoie, K. L., Bacon, S. L., Carlson, L. E., & Campbell, T. S. (2012). The effect of trait rumination on adaptation to repeated stress. *Psychosomatic Medicine, 74*(3), 258–262. https://doi.org/10.1097/PSY.0b013e31824c3ef2

Kemeny, M. E. (2003). The psychobiology of stress. *Current Directions in Psychological Science, 12*(4), 124–129. https://doi.org/10.1111/1467-8721.01246

Keogh, T. M., Howard, S., O'Riordan, A., & Gallagher, S. (2021). Motivational orientation mediates the association between depression and cardiovascular reactivity to acute psychological stress. *Psychophysiology, 58*(2), Article e13732. https://doi.org/10.1111/psyp.13732

Lazarus, R. S., & Folkman, S. (1984). *Stress, appraisal, and coping*. Springer.

Lee, E. M., & Hughes, B. M. (2014). Trait dominance is associated with vascular cardiovascular responses, and attenuated habituation, to social stress. *International Journal of Psychophysiology, 92*(2), 79–84. https://doi.org/10.1016/j.ijpsycho.2014.03.001

Lewington, S., Clarke, R., Qizilbash, N., Peto, R., Collins, R., & Prospective Studies Collaboration. (2002). Age-specific relevance of usual blood pressure to vascular mortality: A meta-analysis of individual data for one million adults in 61 prospective studies. *Lancet, 360*(9349), 1903–1913. https://doi.org/10.1016/s0140-6736(02)11911-8

Lewis, M., Thomas, D. A., & Worobey, J. (1990). Developmental organization, stress, and illness. *Psychological Science, 1*(5), 316–318. https://doi.org/10.1111/j.1467-9280.1990.tb00225.x

Li, Y., Buys, N., Li, Z., Li, L., Song, Q., & Sun, J. (2021). The efficacy of cognitive behavioral therapy-based interventions on patients with hypertension: A systematic review and meta-analysis. *Preventive Medicine Reports, 23*, Article 101477. https://doi.org/10.1016/j.pmedr.2021.101477

Lovallo, W. R. (2011). Do low levels of stress reactivity signal poor states of health? *Biological Psychology, 86*, 121–128. https://doi.org/10.1016/j.biopsycho.2010.01.006

Low, C. A., Stanton, A. L., & Bower, J. E. (2008). Effects of acceptance-oriented versus evaluative emotional processing on heart rate recovery and habituation. *Emotion, 8*(3), 419–424. https://doi.org/10.1037/1528-3542.8.3.419

Lü, W., Hughes, B. M., Howard, S., & James, J. E. (2018). Sleep restriction undermines cardiovascular adaptation during stress, contingent on emotional stability. *Biological Psychology, 132*, 125–132. https://doi.org/10.1016/j.biopsycho.2017.11.013

Lü, W., & Wang, Z. (2017). Physiological adaptation to recurrent social stress of extraversion. *Psychophysiology, 54*(2), 270–278. https://doi.org/10.1111/psyp.12777

Lü, W., Wang, Z., & Hughes, B. M. (2016). The association between openness and physiological responses to recurrent social stress. *International Journal of Psychophysiology, 106*, 135–140. https://doi.org/10.1016/j.ijpsycho.2016.05.004

Lü, W., Wang, Z., & You, X. (2016). Physiological responses to repeated stress in individuals with high and low trait resilience. *Biological Psychology, 120*, 46–52. https://doi.org/10.1016/j.biopsycho.2016.08.005

Lü, W., Xing, W., Hughes, B. M., & Wang, Z. (2018). Extraversion and cardiovascular responses to recurrent social stress: Effect of stress intensity. *International Journal of Psychophysiology, 131*, 144–151. https://doi.org/10.1016/j.ijpsycho.2017.10.008

Manigault, A. W., Shorey, R. C., Decastro, G., Appelmann, H. M., Hamilton, K. R., Scanlin, M. C., France, C. R., & Zoccola, P. (2021). Standardized stress reduction interventions and blood pressure habituation: Secondary results from a randomized control trial. *Health Psychology, 40*(3), 196–206. https://doi.org/10.1037/hea0000954

Mauss, I. B., Wilhelm, F. H., & Gross, J. J. (2003). Autonomic recovery and habituation in social anxiety. *Psychophysiology, 40*(4), 648–653. https://doi.org/10.1111/1469-8986.00066

McEwen, B. S. (1998). Stress, adaptation, and disease: Allostasis and allostatic load. *Annals of the New York Academy of Sciences, 840*, 33–44. https://doi.org/10.1111/j.1749-6632.1998.tb09546.x

Mingming, L. (2017). The influence of psychological intervention on patients with hypertension accompanied by psychological disorder. *Henan Medical Research, 26*, 1531–1532. https://doi.org/10.3969/j.issn.1004-437X.2017.08.129 (Chinese)

Nazzaro, P., Ciancio, L., Vulpis, V., Triggiani, R., Schirosi, G., & Pirrelli, A. (2002). Stress-induced hemodynamic responses are associated with insulin resistance in mild hypertensives. *American Journal of Hypertension, 15*, 865–871.

Nesse, R. M., & Schulkin, J. (2019). An evolutionary medicine perspective on pain and its disorders. *Philosophical Transactions of the Royal Society B, 374*, 20190288.

Obrist, P. (1981). *Cardiovascular psychophysiology: A perspective*. Plenum.

O'Riordan, A., Howard, S., & Gallagher, S. (2022). Blunted cardiovascular reactivity to psychological stress and prospective health: A systematic review. *Health Psychology Review, 17*(1), 121–147. https://doi.org/10.1080/17437199.2022.2068639

Ó Súilleabháin, P. S., Howard, S., & Hughes, B. M. (2018). Openness to experience and adapting to change: Cardiovascular stress habituation to change in acute stress exposure. *Psychophysiology*, 55(5), Article e13023. https://doi.org/10.1111/psyp.13023

Ó Súilleabháin, P. S., & Hughes, B. M. (2018). Neuroticism predicts all-cause mortality over 19 years: The moderating effects on functional status, and the angiotensin-converting enzyme. *Journal of Psychosomatic Research*, 110, 32–37. https://doi.org/10.1016/j.jpsychores.2018.04.013

Ó Súilleabháin, P. S., Hughes, B. M., Oommen, A. M., Joshi, L., & Cunningham, S. (2019). Vulnerability to stress: Personality facet of vulnerability is associated with cardiovascular adaptation to recurring stress. *International Journal of Psychophysiology*, 144, 34–39. https://doi.org/10.1016/j.ijpsycho.2019.06.013

Pascoe, M. C., Thompson, D. R., & Ski, C. F. (2017). Yoga, mindfulness-based stress reduction, and stress-related physiological measures: A meta-analysis. *Psychoneuroendocrinology*, 86, 152–168. https://doi.org/10.1016/j.psyneuen.2017.08.008

Pennebaker, J. W., & Beall, S. K. (1986). Confronting a traumatic event: Toward an understanding of inhibition and disease. *Journal of Abnormal Psychology*, 95(3), 274–281. https://doi.org/10.1037//0021-843x.95.3.274

Phillips, A. C., Carroll, D., Burns, V. E., & Drayson, M. (2009). Cardiovascular activity and the antibody response to vaccination. *Journal of Psychosomatic Research*, 67, 37–43.

Phillips, A. C., Ginty, A. T., & Hughes, B. M. (2013). The other side of the coin: Blunted cardiovascular and cortisol reactivity are associated with negative health outcomes. *International Journal of Psychophysiology*, 90(1), 1–7. https://doi.org/10.1016/j.ijpsycho.2013.02.002

Phillips, A. C., & Hughes, B. M. (2011). Cardiovascular reactivity at a crossroads: Where are we now? *Biological Psychology*, 86, 95–97.

Rodríguez, C. G., Cantero, F. P., & Gómez-Íñiguez, C. (2018). Blood pressure responses of defensive hostile women when facing a real stress task. *Psychology & Health*, 33(8), 978–994. https://doi.org/10.1080/08870446.2018.1449952

Roemmich, J. N., Feda, D. M., Seelbinder, A. M., Lambiase, M. J., Kala, G. K., & Dorn, J. (2011). Stress-inducted cardiovascular reactivity and atherogenesis in adolescents. *Atherosclerosis*, 215, 465–470.

Rolland, R. M., Parks, S. E., Hunt, K. E., Castellote, M., Corkeron, P. J., Nowacek, D. P., Wasser, S. K., & Kraus, S. D. (2012). Evidence that ship noise increases stress in right whales. *Proceedings of the Royal Society B: Biological Sciences*, 279(1737), 2363–2368. https://doi.org/10.1098/rspb.2011.2429

Schneiderman, N., Antoni, M. H., Saab, P. G., & Ironson, G. (2001). Health psychology: Psychosocial and biobehavioral aspects of chronic disease management. *Annual Review of Psychology*, 52, 555–580. https://doi.org/10.1146/annurev.psych.52.1.555

Slavich, G. M. (2020). Social safety theory: A biologically based evolutionary perspective on life stress, health, and behavior. *Annual Review of Clinical Psychology*, 16, 265–295.

Spruill, T. M. (2010). Chronic psychosocial stress and hypertension. *Current Hypertension Reports*, 12, 10–16.

Steptoe, A., & Kivimäki, M. (2012). Stress and cardiovascular disease. *Nature Reviews Cardiology*, 9, 360–370.

Taborsky, B., English, S., Fawcett, T. W., Kuijper, B., Leimar, O., McNamara, J. M., Ruuskanen, S., & Sandi, C. (2021). Towards an evolutionary theory of stress responses. *Trends in Ecology & Evolution*, 36, 39–48.

Tattersall, I., & Schwartz, J. H. (2009). Evolution of the genus *Homo*. *Annual Review of Earth and Planetary Sciences*, 37, 67–92.

Treiber, F. A., Kamarck, T., Schneiderman, N., Sheffield, D., Kapuku, G., & Taylor, T. (2003). Cardiovascular reactivity and development of preclinical and clinical disease states. *Psychosomatic Medicine*, 65, 46–62.

Tyra, A. T., Brindle, R. C., Hughes, B. M., & Ginty, A. T. (2020). Cynical hostility relates to a lack of habituation of the cardiovascular response to repeated acute stress. *Psychophysiology*, 57(12), Article e13681. https://doi.org/10.1111/psyp.13681

van Westerloo, D. J., Choi, G., Löwenberg, E. C., Truijen, J., de Vos, A. F., Endert, E., Meijers, J. C. M., Zhou, L., Pereira, M. P. F. L., Queiroz, K. C. S., Diks, S. H., Levi, M., Peppelenbosch, M. P., & van der Poll, T. (2011). Acute stress elicited by bungee jumping suppresses human innate immunity. *Molecular Medicine, 17,* 180–188.

Whittaker, A. C., Ginty, A., Hughes, B. M., Steptoe, A., & Lovallo, W. R. (2021). Cardiovascular stress reactivity and health: Recent questions and future directions. *Psychosomatic Medicine, 83,* 756–766.

Yurong, S., Mengqi, K., Danhua, Z., Yuanhua, C., & Weide, L. (2012). A study on the effect of psychological intervention for hypertension. *Medical Journal of Chinese People's Health, 24,* 2910–2912.

Zhong, W., Shahbaz, O., Teskey, G., Beever, A., Kachour, N., Venketaraman, V., & Darmani, N. A. (2021). Mechanisms of nausea and vomiting: Current knowledge and recent advances in intracellular emetic signaling systems. *International Journal of Molecular Sciences, 22,* 5797.

8
Using the Research Domain Criteria Framework to Conceptualize and Assess Personality

A Model of Personality for Psychotherapy/Psychophysiology Integration

Patrick R. Steffen and Joseph A. Olsen

Personality encompasses our individual differences in characteristic ways of thinking, feeling, and acting (American Psychological Association, 2023). Twin studies estimate that about 40 to 50 percent of personality traits are heritable with shared family factors having little impact, indicating that non-shared environmental factors and life experiences have a significant impact on personality (McGue & Bouchard, 1998; Nguyen et al., 2021; Plomin, 2011). Personality develops and changes over time as people are impacted by and interact with various life situations and environments, and personality impacts how people respond to life circumstances and cope with stress (McAdams & Pals, 2006; Matthews, 2018; Scollon & Diener, 2006; Segerstrom & Smith, 2019). In this sense, personality emphasizes our individualized ways of adapting to life, characteristic adaptations that we have developed over a lifetime of experiences and learning.

Personality psychology, however, lacks a unifying theory and there are disagreements about methodological approaches to assessment (Dweck, 2017; Larsen & Buss, 2024; Lewis et al., 2020; Matthews, 2018; Mischel & Shoda, 2008). The Research Domain Criteria (RDoC) developed as an alternative to the *Diagnostic and Statistical Manual* (*DSM*) and provides a promising framework to unify personality theory and guide assessment (Kozak & Cuthbert, 2016). The RDoC takes a psychophysiological systems approach focusing on empirically derived fundamental dimensions, emphasizing that multiple systems interact in adaptive and maladaptive functioning. These systems include negative valence systems, positive valence systems, cognitive systems, systems for social processes, arousal/regulatory systems, and sensorimotor systems (Cuthbert, 2022). The RDoC integrates information across research approaches, addressing major factors such as neurobiological, psychological, and behavioral functioning, and emphasizing the impact of developmental and environmental factors over time (Vaidyanathan et al., 2020).

Some researchers (Craske, 2012; Kozak & Cuthbert, 2016) propose that in the RDoC perspective, extremes at either end of a given dimension can be pathological. For example, pathological responses to threat could include either excessive fear or pathological fearlessness (Kozak & Cuthbert, 2016). Similarly, Craske (2012) notes that the negative effects of anxiety can occur at either extreme. One aspect of an RDoC personality model would therefore be to assess personality from a balanced perspective emphasizing adaptive functioning. Rather than examining bipolar contrasts, this proposed RDoC approach emphasizes moderate responding as adaptive, and both excessively low and excessively high responding as maladaptive. An RDoC measure of neuroticism, for example, would place healthy functioning at the middle of the distribution and pathological functioning occurring at either extreme (e.g., too much or too little fear). Several studies have found that excessively low (i.e., over controlled) and excessively high responding (i.e., under controlled) are both related to negative outcomes (Asendorpf & van Aken, 1999; Kogan et al., 2013; Robins et al., 1996; Steffen et al., 2017), suggesting that moderate responses will lead to better outcomes.

Major approaches to personality assessment use a dominance approach, with higher scores typically indicating more of the trait or more positive functioning. Therefore, it has been difficult to assess the impact of moderate responding as proposed by some RDoC researchers. Tay and Ng (2018), in a review of ideal point approaches to self-report measures, argue that the dominance approach used in cognitive assessment is not appropriate for personality assessment. In the ideal point approach, the accurate measure of a trait often occurs at moderate levels instead of at the extremes. Even when a dominance approach is used, curvilinear relationships are found at least half of the time (Carter et al., 2016), and using an ideal point approach usually does a better job of measuring personality traits and their relationships with outcomes (Carter et al., 2016; Grant & Schwartz, 2011; Pierce & Aguinis, 2011). Tay and Ng (2018) emphasize several key distinctions between measuring cognitive and non-cognitive constructs such as personality. Cognitive measurement emphasizes maximal performance and maximum capacity, whereas non-cognitive measures emphasize typical behaviors, habitual characteristics, and maximum accuracy. The non-cognitive approach fits well with an adaptive functioning approach where extreme responses in either direction can be maladaptive, and the adaptive response occurs at moderate levels (typical behaviors and habitual characteristics) or towards the middle of the distribution.

The purpose of this chapter is to explore the RDoC as a framework for unifying personality theory and guiding assessment for psychotherapy/psychophysiology integration. Specifically, this chapter examines taking an ideal point approach to assessment, using an adaptive, balanced functioning conception of personality emphasizing allostatic functioning with moderate responding as the ideal.

Developing a Unified Theory of Personality

Before exploring the RDoC as a framework for developing a unified theory of personality, we want to address three important ideas to provide a broad framework in which to organize the more specific framework of the RDoC. First, balance is an important concept in both psychophysiology and personality. Different lines of research on homeostatically regulated mood and personality provide evidence for set points in mood and neuroticism that are only changed by significant life events or psychotherapy. Second, theories of approach/avoidance and coping are central to adaptation and survival, are particularly important in psychophysiology, and have had a significant impact in personality theories (Carver & Connor-Smith, 2010). Third, although evolution is generally accepted in all approaches to personality, it is not typically addressed in much detail. The RDoC framework is also built on theories that draw from evolutionary perspectives, but evolution is not typically addressed directly. In developing a unified theory of personality for psychotherapy/psychophysiology integration, evolution provides an excellent meta-theory as a broad foundation. After reviewing these three topics we then discuss the RDoC as a specific framework for unifying personality that has the ability to integrate these points.

Homeostatically Regulated Personality and Allostatic Load

Why do we have personalities? From a biological/evolutionary perspective, personality plays a key role in successful adaptation and survival (Buss, 2009; Matthews, 2018). Human beings are built to adapt and survive, and personalities represent various pathways to achieving those goals (Lukaszewski et al., 2020; McAdams & Pals, 2006). People experience different environments and demands, and our personalities result from the interaction between our specific genetic inheritance and the specific environments in which we need to adapt (Buss & Penke, 2015; Carver & Connor-Smith, 2010; McAdams & Pals, 2006). Personality traits represent variability in strategies used to cope with environmental challenges and are linked to evolutionary fitness, having direct consequences for success in adaptation (Buss, 2009; Matthews, 2018). Goldberg (1990) described the Big 5 personality traits of Extraversion, Neuroticism, Conscientiousness, Agreeableness, and Openness to Experience as Power, Affect, Work, Love, and Intellect. These traits are tied to individual differences in adaptive strategies used to cope with environmental challenges (Hogan & Bond, 2009; Matthews, 2018). For example, someone who scores high on conscientiousness uses work as an adaptive strategy for coping with environmental challenges. And conscientiousness is linked directly to healthy lifestyle choices and longevity. In general, personality is tied to functional adaptations made as we adjust to the environments and people we interact with each day. McAdams and Pals'

(2006, p. 204) definition of personality summarizes these concepts: "Personality is an individual's unique variation on the general evolutionary design for human nature, expressed as a developing pattern of dispositional traits, characteristic adaptations, and integrative life stories."

Personality and our characteristic adaptations impact how we balance our internal needs with external demands. In psychophysiology, balance and homeostasis are central concepts. Not long after Cannon theorized homeostasis, personality researchers began considering personality through the lens of homeostasis. Fletcher (1942) stated that psychological functioning, like physiological functioning, seeks equilibrium or homeostatic balance, with psychological adjustments being directly impacted by personality. According to Stagner (1951), homeostasis can function as a unifying concept in personality theory, especially given that personality develops from a biological foundation. Teitelbaum (1956, p. 323) argued that "personality consists of a hierarchy of homeostatic processes of graded degrees of complexity" and that personality homeostasis involves the behavior of the total organism in attaining goals in complex social environments. Personality pathology, on the other hand, is the result of dysregulated homeostasis. Toch and Hastorf (1955, p. 91) argued that " . . . a minimum of stability is required in the experienced world and the experienced self" but that rigidity and intolerance lead to problems.

In the 1970s, Brickman and Campbell (1971) and Brickman et al. (1978) proposed the concept of the "hedonic treadmill." They found that the impact of significant life events, such as winning the lottery or becoming a paraplegic, was not permanent, with mood returning to baseline levels after a relatively short period of time. The impact of both very positive and very negative events do not last, rather people return to their natural baseline mood after a time. From this research arose set point theories of subjective well-being, the concept of homeostatically protected mood, and homeostatic views of personality. Headey and Wearing (1989) proposed a dynamic equilibrium model, in which each person has their typical equilibrium level of subjective well-being (SWB), based on the person's personality traits. Deviations from normal events can change normal levels of SWB, but change is typically temporary, as personality traits return functioning to equilibrium or normal functioning. Similarly, Williams and Thompson (1993) argued for a set-point hypothesis of personality and psychological functioning, with our current status being the interaction between our internal functioning and external experiences. Personality is impacted by physiological functioning, and similar to physiological functioning, personality has a set point with a range of typical functioning that operates around this set point. Each person operates within their own specific range, typically not deviating too far from their personal set point. If the person is pushed beyond the range of their typical functioning, psychopathology may occur. Therapy therefore may include helping the person to broaden their range of functioning and helping them to increase their flexibility in responding to their environments (Bonanno & Burton, 2013; Segerstrom & Smith, 2019).

Researchers have employed the set point hypothesis in studying well-being in general and neuroticism in particular (Diener et al., 2006; Headey, 2010; Ormel et al., 2012; Riese et al., 2014; Scollon & Diener, 2006; Weinberg et al., 2016). Set points can vary considerably across individuals, and these differences are at least partly determined by personality differences. Personality is strongly correlated with well-being; therefore, personality likely predisposes people to experience different levels of well-being. Weinberg et al. (2016) and Diener et al. (2006) note that set points for well-being are moderately heritable and generally stable over time, but that significant life events and stressors can impact set points (see also Headey, 2010). Neuroticism reflects a person's set point for affect, and significant life events can change the set point (Ormel et al., 2012; Riese et al., 2014).

In addition to individual differences in affective set points, people also differ in how much they vary around their set point in response to life events. Intraindividual variability represents affective reactivity to situations over time and is indicative of psychological disequilibrium (Eid & Diener, 1999). It is a stable, individual difference that is related to neuroticism and significantly predicts future negative outcomes. Psychological flexibility, on the other hand, is related to resilience and positive outcomes (Bonanno & Burton, 2013; Hardy & Segerstrom, 2017). Intraindividual variability represents the range of affective responses over time independent of given situations. With psychological flexibility, on the other hand, the variability is dependent on the situation, with the person varying their response to appropriately meet the needs of the situation. Intraindividual variability appears to capture affective lability resulting in negative psychological and physiological adjustment outcomes (Hardy & Segerstrom, 2017). Intraindividual variability and psychological flexibility (or lack thereof) moderate personality traits and their expression, playing a key role in a person's affective set point and response to life stress over time (Bonanno & Burton, 2013; Segerstrom & Smith, 2019). Extremes in total variability are associated with neuroticism, whereas moderate flexibility is associated with positive adaptation.

Intraindividual variability and psychological flexibility likely play key roles in the stress response. A key purpose of the stress response is to help balance internal needs with external demands and unfocused variability leads to imbalance. Stress response research finds that both exaggerated and blunted stress responses are indicative of dysregulated psychophysiological functioning intended to maintain homeostasis, and personality plays a role in psychological and physiological flexibility and regulation (Carroll et al., 2017; Lovallo, 2011; Lovallo, 2013). In terms of neuroticism, those that are more neurotic and have higher negative affect display a blunted stress response and dysregulated homeostatic functioning (Bibbey et al., 2013; Bibbey et al., 2016; Chida & Hamer, 2008). The findings that blunted as well as exaggerated stress responses are maladaptive help to partially explain the inconsistent findings between the psychophysiology of stress and Big 5 measures of personality. This appears to be particularly the case with neuroticism, where the stress response is blunted rather than exaggerated leading to homeostatic dysregulation.

The goal of the stress response is to motivate adaptive approach and avoidance behaviors to optimize coping. Those with neurotic personalities have a more difficult time with adaptive regulation (Lovallo et al., 2012). Neurotic difficulties with regulation can contribute to addictive behaviors through a maladaptive attempt to re-achieve hedonic homeostasis. In this sense, addictive behaviors may represent maladaptive attempts at affective regulation impacted by neurotic personality traits (Koob, 2003; Koob & Kreek, 2007; Koob & Schulkin, 2019). Koob and Shulkin (2019) argue that allostatic dysregulation best describes the addiction process.

Allostasis presents a broader view of homeostatic balance. Allostasis, or stability through change, involves balancing the internal needs of the body with the external demands of changing environments, with the key goal being adaptation (McEwen et al., 2015; Sapolsky, 2015). Whereas homeostasis focuses on balancing specific bodily functions such as body temperature, allostasis refers to the balanced interdependent functioning of all physiological systems to adapt to changing environments. In this approach, personality is part of the brain's efforts to adapt and achieve allostasis, with our characteristic adaptations over time contributing to our personality development, with each person finding unique, personalized ways to balance internal needs with external environments.

Approach/Avoidance and Coping

Approach and avoidance theories of personality are evolutionarily based approaches to understanding human behavior (Corr, 2004). In addition to biological approaches, approach and avoidance theories have been incorporated into social, cognitive, and developmental approaches to personality (Larsen & Buss, 2024). Gray's Reinforcement Sensitivity Theory (RST; Gray & McNaughton, 2000) is arguably the most impactful psychophysiological theory in personality and provides a useful framework for integrating diverse information about personality functioning. Two key neurobiological systems in RST are the behavioral activation system (BAS) and the behavioral inhibition system (BIS). The BAS and the BIS have separate neurobiological pathways resulting in different physiological impacts on functioning. The BAS focuses on reward motivation and approach behavior, is emotionally related to positive affect and impulsivity, and is situated in the mesocorticolimbic dopamine system in the brain (the reward system), which plays a central role in motivation, emotion, and learning. The BIS focuses on aversive motivation and avoidance learning, conflict monitoring, and risk assessment, and is behaviorally expressed as passive avoidance or defensive behavior and is emotionally expressed via anxiety. Physiologically, the BIS is situated in the amygdala and hippocampus (learning and memory). At a basic evolutionary level, approach and avoidance are key behaviors required for survival; for example, we need to approach what is helpful (i.e., food) and avoid what is dangerous (i.e., predators).

RST approaches to personality emphasize the importance of extraversion and neuroticism (Corr, 2009; Corr & Cooper, 2016; Gray, 1994; Gray & McNaughton, 2000; Smilie et al., 2006). The BAS is related to the personality trait of extraversion, with a focus on approach, impulsivity, and positive emotion. The BIS is related to the personality trait of neuroticism, with a focus on avoidance, passivity, and negative emotion. Gray (1994) argued that BAS and BIS functioning correspond to relatively stable individual differences in positive and negative emotion. Additionally, individuals who are more BAS oriented are more sensitive to rewards, and individuals who are more BIS oriented are more sensitive to punishment (Corr, 2004; Corr, 2009). Bijttebier et al. (2009) noted that extreme scores (either high or low) on BAS and BIS functioning are related to adjustment problems and psychopathology. Excessively high BAS functioning is related to externalizing disorders, impulsivity, and conduct disorders. Excessively high BIS functioning is related to anxiety, negative affect, neuroticism, and internalizing disorders. Excessively low BAS functioning is related to increased depression. Excessively low BIS functioning is related to attention-deficit hyperactivity disorder and psychopathy.

Individual differences in approach/avoidance are related to coping and personality (Carver, 2006; Carver & Connor-Smith, 2010). Carver et al. (1989) noted that neurotics often choose ineffective coping strategies, which can lead to greater reactivity to a stressful event. Ferguson (2001) found that personality and coping are correlated, with the trait of neuroticism related to denial and disengagement, and the trait of extroversion related to reappraisal and social support. Gross and John (2003) also found that personality is related to coping and adapting to negative events, with the trait of neuroticism related to less reappraisal, and the trait of extraversion related to more appraisal and less suppression; reappraisers show greater positive emotion and less negative motion and higher well-being, suppressors show greater negative emotion, less positive emotion, and lower well-being.

Evolution as a Meta-Theory for Unifying Personality

Although personality researchers emphasize different aspects of personality (e.g., social, cognitive, biological, etc.), evolution provides a unique meta-theory for all areas of personality (Figueredo et al., 2009; Lewis et al., 2020). Personality theorists, regardless of research focus, typically accept evolution as a general foundational theory. Biological approaches to personality clearly take an evolutionary perspective, and social, cognitive, and developmental approaches also assume evolution plays a role in personality, at least at a general level (Dweck, 2017; Epstein, 2013; Matthews, 2018; Mischel & Shoda, 2008). Bowlby (1980), in his theory of the "environment of evolutionary adaptedness," provides an interesting framework for the impact of evolutionary adaptation over time on personality. In Bowlby's theory, selection pressures molded human adaptation to where we are now in terms of social, cognitive, developmental, and biological functioning, and how this impacts traits and coping styles today (Bowlby, 1980). Human beings are socially situated biological beings with significant cognitive abilities and require an extended developmental period to reach adulthood. All of these factors are interdependent and interact, and all are important in human personality and behavior. Although evolutionary psychology provides a broad foundation for personality theory, it is in the early stage of development (Lewis et al., 2020). The RDoC model provides a specific framework to integrate biological, cognitive, social, and developmental aspects of personality. Accordingly, the RDoC model can be used as a central framework within an evolutionary meta-theory.

The Research Domain Criteria as a Framework to Unify Personality Theory

The RDoC is built upon empirically derived principles and is designed to be in continual development as new knowledge and understanding is gained (Kozak & Cuthbert, 2016; Vaidyanathan et al., 2020). The key domains of the RDoC, the negative valence, positive valence, cognitive, social, arousal, and sensory systems, align with key domains studied in personality psychology, especially the Big 5 factors of neuroticism, extraversion, conscientiousness, agreeableness, and openness to experience. Development and environment are not conceptualized as domains in the RDoC, but they play central roles in how the domains change over time in terms of adaptation and maladaptation. Differing environmental exposures can have a powerful effect on personality development over time, particularly if environments are unsafe or unpredictable (e.g., war, natural disasters), caregivers are abusive (emotional or physical), or there is a lack of resources or opportunities (e.g., poverty). To carefully assess the domains as they are impacted by development and environment over time, the RDoC framework emphasizes using multiple levels of assessment from genes, chemical transmission, and cells, to overall physiology, behavior, and self-perception. Using the RDoC domains and assessment approach provides a unique framework for a unified approach to personality. By assessing across domains and multiple levels of functioning, a more thorough analysis and integration of personality can take place.

Negative and Positive Valence Systems

The first two domains of the RDoC, negative and positive valence systems, are central to allostasis and play key roles in theories of personality, particularly Big 5 approaches. Neuroticism and extroversion, which account for most of the predictive power of Big 5 measures, correspond closely to negative and positive valence systems. These systems have a long research history in psychophysiology and evolutionary psychology, particularly Gray's reinforcement sensitivity theory of activation and inhibition systems describing how people cope and adapt. Before the RDoC was proposed, Fowles (1980) argued for a psychobiological model that incorporated Gray's RST approach of BAS and BIS as a theoretical bridge to connect psychological and biological research. More recently, Caspi et al. (2014) found that neuroticism is a main factor in psychopathology, what they term the "p" factor. The negative valence system in particular aligns well with psychophysiological research where extreme scores in either direction can be maladaptive and moderate scores are typically related to healthier functioning.

The negative valence systems consist of responses to acute and sustained threat, dealing with potential harm and loss, and frustration when not receiving expected rewards (Kozak & Cuthbert, 2016). A key to survival is avoiding harm and injury. The negative valence systems are structured to motivate behaviors to prevent harm by increasing vigilance and readiness to defend when threats are perceived. The end goal is successful adaptation even in difficult environments and situations. The positive valence systems consist of motivated behavior to approach that which is desirable, responding appropriately to rewards, learning what is rewarding, and building habits to maintain successful behaviors over time, reducing the need for cognitive resources.

Cognitive and Social Systems

Cognitive and social factors are key areas studied in personality, and from an evolutionary psychology of personality perspective, our increased cognitive abilities and social connectedness are key results of human evolution. How we think about the world, ourselves, and others plays an important role in personality. And our social relationships play a significant role in shaping and understanding personality. It is interesting to note that in the Big 5 approach, the adjectives that are rated to measure personality are socially derived, they are the words that people use to describe each other. Baumeister and Leary (1995) noted that people need social acceptance and companionship. Interestingly, in an MRI study of social pain and rejection, the same parts of the brain that are activated during physical pain are also activated during social pain (Eisenberg et al., 2003). Our social relationships are so important that our brain sends a very strong signal when our social standing is jeopardized. The personality theorist Robert Hogan argues that the core of personality is "getting along" and "getting ahead," indicating that personality is socially situated and serves social functions (Hogan & Bond, 2009).

In the RDoC framework, cognitive systems consist of attention, perception, working memory, working and declarative memory, language, and cognitive control

(Kozak & Cuthbert, 2016; Vaidyanathan et al., 2020). This system focuses on how we know and understand the world, and how we use that information to make effective decisions and adapt to current circumstances. Goals and decisions are established and acted out based on previous knowledge or memory of similar situations. Language use is contained in this domain, and how we describe each other is central to personality measurement. Systems for social processes consist of attachment, affiliation, perception, and communication. Human beings are social beings and connection to others is critical for survival and adaptation.

Arousal and Sensorimotor Systems

Arousal and sensorimotor function are typically less central in personality assessment, but difficulties in these areas likely will have a significant impact on personality functioning. These systems aid in energy regulation, homeostasis, and allostasis as people are exposed to differing environments. The sensorimotor system is a recent addition to the RDoC domains and may be of more importance in personality pathology.

Issues with Personality Assessed Using a Dominance Approach

The five-factor model of personality (FFM) uses a lexical approach to identify key personality descriptors (Goldberg, 1990). In this approach, trait adjectives people use to describe each other form the key dimensions of personality. The FFM emphasizes factor analysis to derive personality dimensions, arriving at five independent factors accounting for personality. In a sense, the FFM approach to personality is basically a person's reputation (Hogan & Bond, 2009), emphasizing how people know and describe each other using trait adjectives. The Personality Psychopathology-Five (PSY-5), which was derived independently from other FFM models, also resulted in a five-factor solution in measuring personality pathology (Harkness et al., 2012). The five factors, aggressiveness, psychoticism, constraint, negative emotionality, and positive emotionality were developed by having lay people sort personality descriptors. Even though they were developed separately, there is clearly significant overlap between the FFM and PSY-5 in the general factors.

Because these factors are based on descriptions people know and use in everyday language, reliability in assessment is high. There are disagreements, however, regarding validity, beginning with how personality is defined, whether personality is static or dynamic, and the relative importance of context and social factors on personality and expression (Carver & Connor-Smith, 2010; Dweck, 2017; Epstein, 2013; Goldberg, 1990; Hogan & Bond, 2009; Matthews, 2018; Mischel & Shoda, 2008). The disagreement is not whether personality traits exist, but whether they are the whole story. In this sense, the FFM and PSY-5 provide useful information, but are incomplete in describing all aspects of personality. Specifically, although FFM approaches are highly reliable, they often do not predict outcomes that they are hypothesized to predict.

For example, there are many studies examining the relationship between personality traits, life functioning, and health outcomes but the results have been inconsistent, with some studies finding the expected relationships, but many others finding no relationship (Carver & Connor-Smith, 2010; Matthews, 2018; Oveis et al., 2009; Silvia et al., 2014; Sloan et al., 2017; Wang et al., 2013). For example, personality predicts measures of mental health, such as symptoms of depression and anxiety, in some studies but not others.

Similar results are seen in terms of physical health. Heart rate variability (HRV), considered a measure of self-regulatory capacity and adaptation, as well as being a strong predictor of morbidity and mortality, has also seen inconsistent research findings in its relationship with personality traits (Oveis et al., 2009; Sloan et al., 2017). Oveis et al. (2009), in a sample of eighty young adults, found higher baseline HRV related to higher extraversion and agreeableness and lower neuroticism. Wang et al. (2013), studying a sample of ninety-eight young adults, found HRV was related to increased trait positive affect but was not related to trait negative affect. Sloan et al. (2017), examining a community sample of 967 individuals, found no relationships between HRV and the personality measures of extraversion, conscientiousness, agreeableness, and openness to experience; only neuroticism was related to HRV. Similarly, Silvia et al. (2014) using McCrae and Costa's (2007) NEO Five Factor Inventory in a sample of 239 young adults found no relationships between HRV and measures of extraversion, neuroticism, conscientiousness, agreeableness, and openness to experience.

Clearly, these results do not match expectations. Two factors appear to play a role in this. First, because personality is considered stable over time (with many studies treating personality as a static variable), the instructions on self-report measures of personality, such as Big 5 type approaches, ask the respondent how people feel in general and do not take context into account. Given that environmental factors do play an important role in personality functioning, this is not an ideal approach to personality measurement. Second, many studies have found a non-linear relationship between personality and health outcomes, with more moderate responses related to better outcomes.

Measuring and Analyzing Personality

To this point, we have focused primarily on the nature and functions of personality within an RDoC framework. We now turn to the RDoC framework as a way to address some conceptual challenges and some methodological considerations and tools for studying personality.

Dimensional Polarity

A fundamental element of an effective dimensional model like RDoC is the proper specification of the construct continuum for a given dimension, reflecting the varying magnitudes of the theorized attribute of interest. Construct continua can be specified in terms of their polarity, gradation, and coverage. Most constructs can be classified as either unipolar or bipolar. For a unipolar construct, the lower end or pole ideally represents the absence of the construct, while the rest of the continuum represents the increasing extent of the construct's presence. For a bipolar construct, a single continuum jointly represents diametrically opposing concepts positioned at the opposite ends or poles of the continuum. These poles represent the maximum extent of the opposing concepts, such that movement along the continuum toward one pole necessarily represents corresponding movement away from the other pole.

In addition to meaningfully defining the poles of the continuum for unipolar or bipolar constructs, Tay and Jebb (2018) explain that it is also necessary to specify the "nature of the gradation along the continuum" between the poles. Factor analytic or item response theory latent variable models are commonly used to represent locations or distances along the construct continuum in terms of a standardized or another scaled metric. These psychometric models typically make use of self-report item responses, clinician ratings, behavioral observations, or other such indicators to statistically represent the dimension's continuum. Item response theory, in particular, aims to locate individuals and indicators along such a common scale.

Dimensional models of personality and personality disorders (Evans et al., 2020; Monaghan & Bizumic, 2023; Simms et al., 2017; Trull & Widiger, 2013) often address the application of bipolar assessment models, accompanied by further consideration of trait extremity as maladaptive or dysfunctional at both ends of such bipolar continua. Clark et al. (2019, p. 147) concluded that "Taken together, our findings indicate clearly that personality dysfunction and trait extremity are strongly interrelated in existing measures of these constructs." In the context of psychotherapy or other treatment settings, it is common to partition the construct continuum into normal and clinical ranges where the middle part of the continuum represents varying degrees of adaptive functioning, and the extremes reflect maladaptive or dysfunctional trait levels. In the context of prevention activities and programs, Zalta and Shankman (2016) additionally consider demarcating the continuum based on risk thresholds and turning or tipping points that signify suitability for prevention participation, acknowledging that these prevention eligibility thresholds may differ from treatment indication levels.

Adequate measurement of the maladaptive and disordered range of personality traits requires indicator content of sufficient extremity to capture the associated degree of impairment or dysfunction (Dilchert et al., 2014). From the perspective of item response theory, this can be evaluated in terms of the item and test information functions at the upper and lower regions of the trait. Dilchert et al. also discussed how a distributional mismatch between a predictor trait and a criterion measure can result in apparent nonlinear associations.

Nonlinear Relationships to External Criteria

When applying dimensional models, the combination of trait extremity and bipolarity can provide an informative basis for mapping the relation of personality and other non-cognitive traits with impaired or maladaptive functioning (Kozak & Cuthbert, 2016). Northoff and Tumati (2019) described ways that associated neural and mental continua are often nonlinearly related to adaptive functioning such that the normal middle range is linked with optimal or near optimal functioning, while the extremes at either end represent maladaptively deficient or excessive trait levels.

Samuel and Tay (2019) described hypothesized and observed nonmonotonic or curvilinear functional forms of the relationship between personality or other psychosocial traits and separate measures of functioning or impairment as "predictive bipolarity" where both ends of the trait continuum are positively related to maladaptive outcomes. In the standard case of a positively valenced trait, this results in the presence of an inverted U-shaped relation between the trait and an external measure of effective functioning. It is useful here to distinguish between (1) the classic nonmonotonic "too much of a good thing can be a bad thing" inverted U-shaped pattern where the relationship actually reverses direction beyond a certain point, and (2) a more gently curvilinear "after some point it really doesn't make much difference" leveling off pattern.

Many theory-based arguments of evolutionary fitness (Nettle, 2006) and system adaptation (Harkness et al., 2014), along with neural comparisons (Northoff & Tumati, 2019) and clinical accounts, are consistent with the notion of an optimal middle range with counterproductive trait extremes. The testing of maladaptive bipolarity has frequently been addressed from the perspective of predictive bipolarity through the estimation of nonlinear, usually quadratic, regression models. In these models, statistical significance and a meaningful effect size for the quadratic component in a regression that also contains the predictor's linear effect is taken as evidence favoring the "too much of a good thing" hypothesis. However, observation of a significant quadratic effect fails to distinguish between the "leveling off" and "U shaped" patterns, and Simonsohn (2018) has proposed an alternate segmented regression "two lines test" for confirming true inverted U-shaped relationships. Simonsohn's method has been applied along with, and as an alternative to, quadratic regression to assess maladaptive bipolarity in the personality domain, as well as to test U-shaped relationships in other areas such as cognitive ability (e.g., Brown et al., 2021). These expectations stand in contrast to the common "more is better" linear pattern relating evaluatively positive personality traits to improved functioning.

Carter et al. (2018) argued that personality continua in many of the existing measures are often too constricted and thus not optimally sensitive to curvilinearity in the relationships with functioning, and that these continua therefore need to be extended to include greater representation of maladaptivity at both the low and high ends of the continua. They also argue that the traditional sum scoring methods of classical test theory (CTT) fail to properly deal with measurement error and advocate instead the use of item response theory (IRT), and specifically ideal-point IRT models and scoring methods, in personality assessment. We will discuss ideal-point measurement more fully later in the chapter but note here that Carter et al. (2017) and Cao et al. (2018) found that matching the true item response process in the data with the corresponding scoring method produced the most effective detection of curvilinear relationships.

Carter et al. (2016) found that ideal-point modeling detected curvilinear relationships between conscientiousness and job performance more often than traditional dominance IRT modeling, linear factor modeling, or CTT sum scoring methods. However, Nickel et al. (2019) found no evidence of a curvilinear relationship between conscientiousness and various relationship, work, and health outcomes with either dominance or ideal-point IRT models, and Walmsley et al. (2018) found minimal evidence of curvilinearity in the relationship between personality traits (conscientiousness, agreeableness, emotional stability, openness to experience, and extraversion) and job performance. Langwerden et al. (2023) found that of 125 tested quadratic relationships between the five PSY-5-r maladaptive personality traits (aggressiveness, psychoticism, disconstraint, neuroticism, and introversion) and the twenty-five scales of the Patient Description Form (PDF), less than 5 percent were statistically significant and they warned that even these should be interpreted with caution. A recent study by Hobbs et al. (2023) examined hypothesized nonmonotonicity in the relationships of traditional personality dimensions as measured by the International Personality Item Pool NEO (IPIP-NEO) and the Personality Inventory for DSM-5 (PID-5) with quality of life as measured by the World Health Organization Quality of Life-BREF (WHOQOL-BREF) and with functional impairment as measured by the World Health Organization Disability Assessment Schedule (WHODAS). They found that neuroticism, extraversion, conscientiousness, negative affectivity, and detachment were generally monotonically related to quality of life and impairment.

Applying Item Response Theory and Factor Analytic Methods

Suzuki et al. (2015) and van Dijk et al. (2021) applied item response theory methods to the study of personality disorders as maladaptive traits at both extremes of the FFM. Their results provided general support for the hypothesis that personality disorders represented extreme maladaptive variants of general personality traits. Jointly evaluating measures of normative and disordered personality traits, they found substantially overlapping information functions for largely shared dimensions from the

FFM. Still, van Dijk et al. (2021) concluded that truly extreme maladaptive personality traits cannot be fully captured by general FFM measures, requiring additional personality disorder assessment. This echoes the earlier finding of Samuel et al. (2010, p. 19) that "scales assessing personality pathology and general personality traits were shown to lie along common underlying continua, with the two sets of scales generally differing significantly in terms of their respective locations along the latent trait."

The normal and maladaptive ranges of dimensional personality continua are also often studied and evaluated in terms of their factor structure. Widiger and Crego (2019) stated that normal range measures typically include relatively few items to assess maladaptive variants of Five Factor Model (FFM) personality traits, and that "the purportedly normal range measures of the FFM do include a considerable amount of coverage of maladaptive neuroticism, antagonism, introversion, and low conscientiousness" (p. 424). They go on to say that certain of the items in normal range measures "are not appreciably or meaningfully different from the items one would find within a personality disorder measure," and that normal range personality measures have "as much validity for the assessment of personality disorders that emphasize neuroticism, antagonism, introversion and/or low conscientiousness (e.g., borderline, antisocial, schizoid, and narcissistic) as does any direct measure of these personality disorders" (p. 424).

Bagby and Widiger (2018) map a set of FFM personality disorder (FFMPD) facet scales in eight FFMPD inventories to both poles of each of the FFM dimensions, and Crego et al. (2018) compare these measures with those from two alternative personality disorder inventories, the Personality Inventory for the *DSM-5* (PID-5) and the Computerized Adaptive Test-Personality Disorder-Static Form (CAT-PD-SF). Although normal range personality and personality disorder measures have been found to share common underlying dimensions, Widiger and Crego (2019) argue that relationships between normal and abnormal variants of the same trait may be reduced due to "the fact that measures of normality and abnormality will naturally [be] and are typically correlated negatively with one another," and also that relationships between different personality disorders "can be inflated by the presence of a general factor of psychopathology" (p. 425) (for a recent review see Smith et al., 2020). Pettersson et al. (2014) conceptualized such a general factor as reflecting the tendency to endorse items based on their positive or negative valence, akin to social desirability, and found evidence for maladaptive markers at both ends of usual personality trait continua after adjusting for this evaluative factor. Instead of treating such a general factor as an obscuring nuisance, Musek (2007) provides the general factor of personality (GFP) with a substantive interpretation as a general measure of social functioning, conceived as a scientific counterpart of the common-sense concept of "good" versus "difficult" personality.

In addition to a general factor of personality (the GFP) and psychopathology (the *p* factor), there is a related body of research on a general factor of personality disorder (*g*-PD; see Asadi et al., 2022). McCabe et al. (2022; see also Oltmanns et al.,

2018) have examined the relationships among the general factors across these three domains. They find sufficient common variance to suggest that the p factor, g-PD, and GFP "are likely to be assessing largely the same thing rather than three different things." They contend that rather than having specific substantive traits in common, what is shared is that each of these traits "can result in common social, personal, and occupational impairments" (McCabe et al., 2022, p. 150). They also favor a substantive interpretation of these general factors rather than a self-presentation artifactual one: "It is not that persons are attributing to themselves undesirable (or desirable) traits that they do not have; it is that some persons do indeed have many undesirable traits whereas other persons have [instead] many desirable traits" (p. 151).

A different perspective on the relationship between normal range personality and personality disorder was outlined by Morey et al. (2022) who view maladaptive traits as the combination of normal range personality traits plus generalized personality dysfunction. Noting that different maladaptive personality traits are much more strongly intercorrelated than normal range personality traits, they concluded that it is more useful to adopt a general dimension of personality dysfunction that is not trait specific. Maladaptive traits then represent a mixture of ordinary personality traits and overall personality dysfunction. They report incremental validity and mediation findings that they claim run "counter to the assumption that the maladaptive manifestations of personality can be understood solely as extreme extensions of five normal-range personality traits," and further contend that "a significant difference between most normal range and maladaptive trait measures is that the former tend to be bipolar whereas the latter tend to be unipolar" (p. 43).

The Ideal Point Versus Dominance Controversy

Within and beyond the study of personality, the issues of trait dimensionality, polarity, and the form of functional relationships continue to intrigue and challenge researchers. Although the broad contours of these matters have been carefully documented in a general way through the Big 5 and related models, the integration of allostatic considerations into the mapping of the personality domain provides an occasion and opportunity for reengagement and further examination of these topics. We recognize the lively back and forth with respect to the insurgent ideal point and the more traditional tried-and-true dominance-oriented views in the field. It is our intent to explore this sometimes-contested territory rather than to attempt to advance the claims of the enthusiasts or vindicate the stolidity of skeptics. To provide a coherent evidentiary framework for evaluating a variety of these concerns, we offer a specific statistical model, the quadratic factor model, that we think can purchase some leverage on these problems. We recognize that our proposal is incipient and nascent and needs a great deal of further work. Nevertheless, we also believe it to be promising and worthwhile.

In an ideal point measurement process, a person is expected to most strongly endorse statements that are closest to, or are least discrepant from, their preferred position (or ideal point) on the underlying construct continuum. Consequently, they are successively less likely to endorse statements the more distant they are from the person's ideal point. People can therefore disagree from below to the extent that the statement fails to reach their ideal point, or they can disagree from above to the extent that the statement exceeds the ideal point. Statements at intermediate positions along the continuum can elicit nonmonotonic or single-peaked response functions, a pattern often described as displaying an unfolding process. This can be distinguished from a dominance process where item responding instead exhibits a strictly increasing or decreasing (monotonic) pattern through the trait continuum.

In contrast to traditional dominance items with a more readily apparent and unmistakable directional valence, ideal point measurement requires the development of so-called intermediate items with more moderate or nuanced positions along the measured trait continuum (Cao et al., 2015). These are designed to encourage more introspective and attentive responding but are also more difficult to write and require more cognitive effort to answer (Brown & Maydeu-Olivares, 2010). Cao et al. (2015) give a thorough treatment and provide basic guidelines for item writing in ideal point assessment. Ideal point measurement aims to provide better coverage of the construct continuum and more precise estimation of trait levels, especially at the extremes, and Dalal et al. (2010) anticipated that it "will likely revolutionize measurement practice and theory." However, they also alerted researchers that this would require larger samples, longer instruments, new heuristics for writing items, and that they "will need to change the current method of evaluating items" (p. 499).

Most applications of traditional statistical and psychometric methods such as linear factor analysis (LFA) and standard item response theory (IRT) models are based on dominance principles. Dominance-based analyses will typically shunt out intermediate items due to low factor loadings or dimensional ambiguity. Most unfolding or ideal point analysis is currently accomplished with specialized IRT programs such as the General Hyperbolic Cosine Model (GHCM; Andrich, 1996, 2016), and especially, the Generalized Graded Unfolding Model (GGUM; Roberts & Laughlin 1996). GGUM can be readily implemented in freely available software (GGUM2004; Roberts et al., 2006) for Microsoft Windows, and in a more recently developed R package (Tendeiro & Castro-Alvarez, 2019). It can also be accomplished within a widely used IRT R software package for general IRT analysis (mirt; Liu & Chambers, 2018) through specifying the necessary GGUM probability response functions. A number of specialized adaptations and extensions of GGUM and GHCM have been developed by methodologists, especially using Bayesian methods, but these are generally not available or accessible to non-specialist researchers.

The Quadratic Unfolding Model

We focus here on an alternate model, the quadratic unfolding model (Van Schuur & Kiers, 1994; Maraun & Rossi, 2001) whose development, unlike GHCM and GGUM, was not specifically within the IRT framework most commonly used for dichotomous items or for ordered polytomous items having a relatively small number of categories. The quadratic unfolding model is in principle applicable to continuous or quasi-continuous indicators as well as the categorical responses typically addressed with IRT. Data that is ostensibly or approximately continuous can arise in various settings such as magnitude estimation ratings, or slider and visual analogue scales used in computer-based surveys (Menold & Toepoel, 2022). At the same time, we subsequently extend the quadratic unfolding model to the traditional IRT context.

The quadratic factor model (e.g., Maraun & Rossi, 2001; Smits et al., 2016) can be given (see Figure 8.1) as:

$$y_{ij} = v_j + \alpha_j \eta_i^1 + \beta_j \eta_i^2 + \varepsilon_{ij}$$

Here, y_{ij} is the observed response of person i to indicator y_j, v_j is the indicator's intercept, α_j is the indicator's factor *loading* on the model implied *linear latent trait* η_i^1 for person i, β_j is the indicator's factor loading on the squared or *quadratic latent trait* η_i^2, ε_{ij} is an *error* of measurement for person i on indicator y_j, and σ_j^2 is the indicator's residual variance. The model is identified, and the latent trait is scaled by fixing the mean and variance of η_i^1 to 0 and 1, respectively.

In Figure 8.1, squares or rectangles represent observed variables, circles or ovals represent latent variables, and the triangle containing a 1 is used to represent the mean or intercept structure of the data.

We explore here how the quadratic factor model can be used to assess item or indicator unfolding. The loadings of the indicators on the squared or quadratic latent trait depict the extent to which the effects of the latent trait on the indicator are dependent on the level of the latent trait (Molenaar et al., 2010). This can alternatively be conceptualized as a form of conditional or differential indicator functioning such that the strength of the relation between the trait and the indicator is

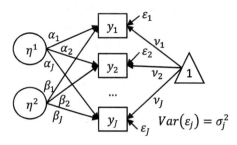

Figure 8.1 The quadratic factor model.

a function of the trait level itself. In this context, indicators exhibiting significant quadratic unfolding can be identified by their relatively large and statistically significant quadratic loading parameters. These parameters represent the departure from the expected linear relationships between the trait and the indicators that is implied by the standard linear (dominance) model. This quadratic unfolding process can be evaluated in terms of statistical tests of the quadratic indicator parameters, either individually or jointly in the form of a multi-parameter Wald test, or by a likelihood ratio model comparison comparing models with and without the quadratic parameters.

We present one, two, and three parameter quadratic unfolding models that can be fit, and their parameters estimated, as special cases of the quadratic factor model. The details of the correspondence between the quadratic unfolding models and the quadratic factor model are given in Table 8.1. The three-parameter quadratic unfolding model has three measurement parameters for each indicator, a discrimination parameter γ_j, a location parameter δ_j, and an offset parameter μ_j, and is equivalent to the unrestricted quadratic factor model in fit and prediction. We show how to transform the three estimated parameters of the quadratic factor model, the factor loading on the linear component α_j, the loading on the squared or quadratic component β_j, and the indicator intercept v_j, into the discrimination, location, and offset parameters of the three-parameter quadratic unfolding model.

Table 8.1 The quadratic factor model and the three parameter quadratic unfolding model

Quadratic factor model	$y_{ij} = v_j + \alpha_j \eta_i^1 + \beta_j \eta_i^2 + \varepsilon_{ij}$		
Three parameter quadratic unfolding model			
Unfolding form	$y_{ij} = \mu_j + \gamma_j(\eta_i^1 - \delta_j)^2 + \varepsilon_{ij}$		
Factor form	$y_{ij} = \mu_j + \gamma_j \delta_j^2 - 2\delta_j \gamma_j \eta_i^1 + \gamma_j \eta_i^2 + \varepsilon_{ij}$		
Parameters:	Factor	Unfolding	
Quadratic	$\beta_j = \gamma_j$	$\gamma_j = \beta_j$	Discrimination
Linear	$\alpha_j = -2\delta_j \gamma_j$	$\delta_j = -\alpha_j / 2\beta_j$	Location
Intercept	$v_j = \mu_j + \gamma_j \delta_j^2$	$\mu_j = v_j - \alpha_j^2 / 4\beta_j$	Offset

The two-parameter quadratic unfolding model, or simple squared unfolding model, has discrimination and location parameters for each indicator, is equivalent in fit and prediction to a particular restricted quadratic factor model, and is nested within the three-parameter unfolding model. The discrimination and location parameters of the two-parameter quadratic unfolding model can be derived from the estimated loadings of the indicators on the linear and quadratic components of the corresponding restricted quadratic factor model. Finally, the one parameter unfolding model is nested within the two-parameter model and is equivalent to a quadratic factor model with necessary further restrictions. Again, the parameters of this restricted quadratic factor model can be transformed into the needed parameters of the one factor quadratic unfolding model.

Latent Nonlinearity

A major point of Van Schuur and Kiers (1994) and Maraun and Rossi (2001) was that traditional dominance-oriented analyses based on linear relationships among the variables will spuriously overestimate the dimensionality of data that actually follows an unfolding process. This "extra factor phenomenon" can thus provide a distorted view of the data's true dimensionality. Data that is really unidimensional will be misrepresented as multidimensional due to misspecification of the model's factor-to-indicator relationships. Extending the argument, restricting analyses to only consider linear factor-to-factor relationships can have similarly misleading results. In addition to addressing possible unfolding at the observed indicator or item level, the quadratic factor model can also be used to address possible nonlinearity at higher levels of the latent structure.

Debates about bipolarity versus bidimensionality of measures such as positive and negative affect or emotion have generally not reached analytic resolution within the dominance tradition. From a different perspective, Kam and Meyer (2022) used a model like the one in Figure 8.2 to assess the structural relationship between items ostensibly designed to measure one pole (the x items) or the other pole (the y items) of a potentially bipolar (versus bidimensional) construct. This is in contradistinction to the usual dominance-based modeling of bidimensionality by omitting η_x^2 and covarying η_x^1 and η_y^1 rather than regressing η_y^1 on η_x^1 and η_x^2, or of modeling bipolarity by either testing whether the correlation η_x^1 and η_y^1 differs from 1.0 or by testing the fit of the bidimensional model against a model with a single factor η affecting both the x and y items. A large and statistically significant effect of η_x^2 on η_y^1 provides evidence akin to item-level unfolding that is clearly relevant to the dimensionality and polarity of the items. This would be especially true if the variance of ζ_y were vanishingly small, indicating the possibility of a single underlying construct.

Note that the quadratic latent component η_x^2 in Figure 8.2 is represented and estimated without direct relations to the x_j items. This is the usual situation for latent quadratic effects models. Recalling our discussion of the centrality of intermediate

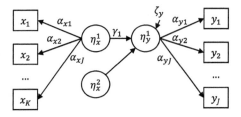

Figure 8.2 Latent nonlinearity.
Note: Latent nonlinearity. The indicator errors and intercepts are omitted to simplify the diagram.

items to ideal point measurement and unfolding models, it would be possible to further elaborate the model in Figure 8.2 to incorporate additional latent components for the intermediate items as well as for positive and negative ones.

Such models, as well as the quadratic unfolding models discussed earlier, come with important potential advantages and disadvantages in terms of statistical modeling. We have already described some important possible advantages and can foresee and imagine various others. At the same time, it is important to recognize the challenges in building and estimating these models, and to anticipate some of the difficulties and impediments facing such a project. One of the first to be encountered is model fit assessment. Because quadratic factor models are no longer situated within readily apparent unconstrained and saturated models (Büchner & Klein, 2020) for the usual mean and covariance structures, many of the usual and alternative fit measures (i.e., CFI, RMSEA, even the usual Chi-Square goodness of fit test) are no longer available. Various likelihood ratio tests and information criteria (AIC, BIC, etc.) measures can be used, but fit assessment remains challenging.

Although other software can fit certain of these models, we have found Mplus (Muthén & Muthén, 2017) to be the most generally capable platform for estimating the models. Mplus can estimate within-model latent variable interactions, and therefore latent quadratic model components. It also provides nonlinear constraints on estimated model parameters, simplifying the imposition of required model restrictions. With maximum likelihood estimation, models having multiple quadratic components can become computationally demanding, but Mplus also supports Bayesian estimation, although we have not explored this fully.

Conclusions

Overall, the RDoC appears to provide a strong framework for personality theory and assessment for use in psychotherapy/psychophysiology integration. Personality psychology lacks a unifying theory. The RDoC dimensions of negative and positive valence systems, cognitive systems, social systems, and arousal and sensory systems, fit well with the major domains addressed in personality psychology, potentially providing a unifying framework within which to organize research findings.

The RDoC approach to assessment involves the concepts of homeostasis and allostasis. Although these concepts are not typically used in personality research, a homeostatic/allostatic approach might better account for personality research findings and provides a bridge to connect psychotherapy and psychophysiology. An ideal point approach to personality assessment (instead of a dominance approach) shows promise in addressing a moderate responding, balanced perspective of personality.

Various methodological considerations affect the application of an RDoC approach to the study and analysis of personality. Examining the dimensionality and mapping the topography of the facets and general factors of personality, personality disorder, and psychopathology can be profitably structured within an RDoC framework. The polarity and gradation of construct continua and research dimensions establish a basis to address the levels and thresholds of maladaptivity of personality dimensions. The expectation of midrange normality with dysfunctionality at the dimensional extremes is consistent with unfolding and ideal point processes in the assessment of personality and other noncognitive attributes. It is also consistent with an expected curvilinear relationship between personality dimensions and external measures of functioning.

We also described and paid particular attention to the sometimes-contested dialectic between dominance and ideal point assessment and analytic methods. Whereas a caricatured dominance traditionalist might expect a person's position on a continuum to be strongly governed by the intensity of a pervading directional imperative, a caricatured ideal point enthusiast might instead expect people to introspectively and exquisitely calibrate their location along the continuum within a relatively narrow latitude of acceptance. Recognizing existing IRT models for addressing these situations, we [re]introduced a quadratic unfolding factor model for ordered categorical items to address possible nonlinearity in the latent structure.

References

American Psychological Association (2023). Personality. https://www.apa.org/topics/personality

Andrich, D. (1996). A hyperbolic cosine latent trait model for unfolding polytomous responses: Reconciling Thurstone and Likert methodologies. *British Journal of Mathematical and Statistical Psychology, 49*, 347–365. https://doi.org/10.1111/j.2044-8317.1996.tb01093.x

Andrich, D. (2016). Hyperbolic cosine model for unfolding responses. In W. J. van der Linden (Ed.), *Handbook of item response theory. Volume one: Models* (pp. 353–367). CRC Press.

Asadi, S., Bagby, R. M., Krueger, R. F., Pollock, B. G., & Quilty, L. C. (2022). Reliability and construct validity of the general factor of personality disorder. *Personality Disorders: Theory, Research, and Treatment, 12*, 662–673. https://doi.org/10.1037/per0000539

Asendorpf, J. B., & van Aken, M. A. G. (1999). Resilient, overcontrolled, and undercontrolled personality prototypes in childhood: Replicability, predictive power, and the trait-type issue. *Journal of Personality and Social Psychology, 77*, 815–832. https://doi.org/10.1037//0022-3514.77.4.815

Bagby, R. M., & Widiger, T. A. (2018). Five Factor Model personality disorder scales: An introduction to a special section on assessment of maladaptive variants of the five factor model. *Psychological Assessment, 30*, 1–9. https://doi.org/10.1037/pas0000523

Baumeister, R. F., & Leary, M. R. (1995). The need to belong: Desire for interpersonal attachments as a fundamental human motivation. *Psychological Bulletin, 117*(3), 497–529. https://doi.org/10.1037/0033-2909.117.3.497

Bibbey, A., Carroll, D., Roseboom, T. J., Phillips, A. C., & de Rooij, S. R. (2013). Personality and physiological reactions to acute psychological stress. *International Journal of Psychophysiology, 90,* 28–36. http://dx.doi.org/10.1016/j.ijpsycho.2012.10.018

Bibbey, A., Ginty, A. T., Brindle, R. C., Phillips, A. C., & Carroll, D. (2016). Blunted cardiac stress reactors exhibit relatively high levels of behavioural impulsivity. *Physiology and Behavior, 159,* 40–44. https://doi.org/10.1016/j.physbeh.2016.03.011

Bijttebier, P., Beck, I., Claes, L., & Vandereycken, W. (2009). Gray's Reinforcement Sensitivity Theory as a framework for research on personality–psychopathology associations. *Clinical Psychology Review, 29,* 421–430. https://doi.org/10.1016/j.cpr.2009.04.002

Bonanno, G. A., & Burton, C. L. (2013). Regulatory flexibility: An individual differences perspective on coping and emotion regulation. *Perspectives on Psychological Science, 8,* 591–612. https://doi.org/10.1177/1745691613504116

Bowlby J. (1980). *Attachment and loss.* Basic Books.

Brickman, P., & Campbell, D. T. (1971). Hedonic relativism and planning the good society. In M. H. Appley (Ed.), *Adaptation-level theory* (pp. 287–305). Academic Press.

Brickman, P., Coates, D., & Janoff-Bulman, R. (1978). Lottery winners and accident victims: Is happiness relative? *Journal of Personality and Social Psychology, 36,* 917–927. https://doi.org/10.1037/0022-3514.36.8.917

Brown, A., & Maydeu-Olivares, A. (2010). Issues that should not be overlooked in the dominance versus ideal point controversy. *Industrial and Organizational Psychology, 3,* 489–493. https://doi.org/10.1111/j.1754-9434.2010.01277.x

Brown, M. I., Wai, J., & Chabris, C. F. (2021). Can you ever be too smart for your own good? Comparing linear and nonlinear effects of cognitive ability on life outcomes. *Perspectives on Psychological Science, 16,* 1337–1359. https://doi.org/10.1177/1745691620964122

Büchner, R. D., & Klein, A. G. (2020). A quasi-likelihood approach to assess model fit in quadratic and interaction SEM. *Multivariate Behavioral Research, 55,* 855–872. https://doi.org/10.1080/00273171.2019.1689349

Buss, D. M. (2009). How can evolutionary psychology successfully explain personality and individual differences? *Perspectives on Psychological Science, 4,* 359–366. https://doi.org/10.1111/j.1745-6924.2009.01138.x

Buss, D. M., & Penke, L. (2015). Evolutionary personality psychology. In M. Mikulincer, P. R. Shaver, M. L. Cooper, & R. J. Larsen (Eds.), *APA handbook of personality and social psychology, Vol. 4. Personality processes and individual differences* (pp. 3–29). American Psychological Association. https://doi.org/10.1037/14343-001

Cao, M., Drasgow, F., & Cho, S. (2015). Developing ideal intermediate personality items for the ideal point model. *Organizational Research Methods, 18*(2), 252–275. https://doi.org/10.1177/1094428114555993

Cao, M., Song, Q. C., & Tay, L. (2018). Detecting curvilinear relationships: A comparison of scoring approaches based on different item response models. *International Journal of Testing, 18*(2), 178–205. https://doi.org/10.1080/15305058.2017.1345913

Carroll, D., Ginty, A. T., Whittaker, A. C., Lovallo, W. R., & de Rooij, S. R. (2017). The behavioural, cognitive, and neural corollaries of blunted cardiovascular and cortisol reactions to acute psychological stress. *Neuroscience and Biobehavioral Reviews, 77,* 74–86. https://doi.org/10.1016/j.neubiorev.2017.02.025

Carter, N. T., Dalal, D. K., Guan, L., LoPilato, A. C., & Withrow, S. A. (2017). Item response theory scoring and the detection of curvilinear relationships. *Psychological Methods, 22,* 191–203. https://doi.org/10.1037/met0000101

Carter, N. T., Guan, L., Maples, J. L., Williamson, R. L., & Miller, J. D. (2016). The downsides of extreme conscientiousness for psychological well-being: The role of obsessive-compulsive tendencies. *Journal of Personality, 84,* 510–522. https://doi.org/10.1111/jopy.12177

Carter, N. T., Miller, J. D., & Widiger, T. A. (2018). Extreme personalities at work and in life. *Current Directions in Psychological Science, 27*, 429–436. https://doi.org/10.1177/0963721418793134

Carver, C. S. (2006). Approach, avoidance, and the self-regulation of affect and action. *Motivation and Emotion, 30*, 105–110. https://doi.org/10.1007/s11031-006-9044-7

Carver, C. S., & Connor-Smith, J. (2010). Personality and coping. *Annual Review of Psychology, 61*, 679–704. https://doi.org/10.1146/annurev.psych.093008.100352

Carver, C. S., Scheier, M. F., & Weintraub, J. K. (1989). Assessing coping strategies: A theoretically based approach. *Journal of Personality and Social Psychology, 56*, 267–283. https://doi.org/10.1037//0022-3514.56.2.267

Caspi, A., Houts, R. M., Belsky, D. W., Goldman-Mellor, S. J., Harrington, H., Israel, S., Meier, M. H., Ramrakha, S., Shalev, I., Poulton, R., & Moffitt, T. E. (2014). The p factor: One general psychopathology factor in the structure of psychiatric disorders? *Clinical Psychological Science, 2*, 119–137. https://doi.org/10.1177/2167702613497473

Chida, Y., & Hamer, M. (2008). Chronic psychosocial factors and acute physiological responses to laboratory-induced stress in healthy populations: A quantitative review of 30 years of investigations. *Psychological Bulletin, 134*, 829–885. https://doi.org/10.1037/a0013342

Clark, L. A., Daly, E. J., Larew, S., Nuzum, H., Kingsbury, T., Shapiro, J. L., Allen, X., & Ro, E. (2019). Personality dysfunction and trait extremity: Conceptually, but not empirically distinct? In D. B. Samuel & D. R. Lynam (Eds.), *Using basic personality research to inform personality pathology* (pp. 122–149). Oxford University Press. https://doi.org/10.1093/med-psych/9780190227074.003.0006

Corr, P. J. (2004). Reinforcement sensitivity theory and personality. *Neuroscience and Biobehavioral Reviews, 28*, 317–332. https://doi.org/10.1016/j.neubiorev.2004.01.005

Corr, P. J. (2009). The reinforcement sensitivity theory of personality. In P. J. Corr & G. Matthews (Eds.), *The Cambridge handbook of personality psychology* (pp. 347–376). Cambridge University Press.

Corr, P. J., & Cooper, A. J. (2016). The reinforcement sensitivity theory of personality questionnaire (RST-PQ): Development and validation. *Psychological Assessment, 28*, 1427–1440. https://doi.org/10.1037/pas0000273

Craske, M. (2012). The R-DOC initiative: Science and practice. *Depression and Anxiety, 29*, 253–256. https://doi.org/10.1002/da.21930

Crego, C., Oltmanns, J. R., & Widiger, T. A. (2018). FFMPD scales: Comparisons with the FFM, PID-5, and CAT-PD-SF. *Psychological Assessment, 30*, 62–73. https://doi.org/10.1037/pas0000495

Cuthbert, B. N. (2022). Research domain criteria (RDoC): Progress and potential. *Current Directions in Psychology Science, 31*, 107–114. https://doi.org/10.1177/09637214211051363

Dalal, D. K., Withrow, S., Gibby, R. E., & Zickar, M. J. (2010). Six questions that practitioners (might) have about ideal point response process items. *Industrial and Organizational Psychology, 3*, 498–501. https://doi.org/10.1111/j.1754-9434.2010.01279.x

Diener, E., Lucas, R. E., & Scollon, C. N. (2006). Beyond the hedonic treadmill: Revising the adaptation theory of well-being. *American Psychologist, 61*, 305–314. https://doi.org/10.1037/0003-066X.61.4.305

Dilchert, S., Ones, D. S., & Krueger, R. F. (2014). Maladaptive personality constructs, measures, and work behaviors. *Industrial and Organizational Psychology, 7*, 98–110. https://doi.org/10.1111/iops.12115

Dweck, C. S. (2017). From needs to goals and representations: Foundations for a unified theory of motivation, personality, and development. *Psychological Review, 146*, 689–719. https://doi.org/10.1037/rev0000082

Eid, M., & Diener, E. (1999). Intraindividual variability in affect: Reliability, validity, and personality correlates. *Journal of Personality and Social Psychology, 76*, 662–676. https://doi.org/10.1037/0022-3514.76.4.662

Eisenberger, N. I., Lieberman, M. D., & Williams, K. D. (2003). Does rejection hurt? An FMRI study of social exclusion. *Science (New York, N.Y.), 302*(5643), 290–292. https://doi.org/10.1126/science.1089134

Epstein, S. (2013). Cognitive-experiential self-theory: An integrative theory of personality. In H. Tennen, J. Suls, & I. B. Weiner (Eds.), *Handbook of psychology: Personality and social psychology* (pp. 93–118). John Wiley & Sons, Inc.

Evans, C. M., Williams, T. F., & Simms, L. J. (2020). Methods and current issues in dimensional assessments of personality pathology. In C. W. Lejuez & K. L. Gratz (Eds.), *The Cambridge handbook of personality disorders* (pp. 329–346). Cambridge University Press. https://doi.org/10.1017/9781108333931.058

Ferguson, E. (2001). Personality and coping traits: A joint factor analysis. *British Journal of Health Psychology, 6*, 311–325. https://doi.org/10.1348/135910701169232

Figueredo, A. J., Gladden, P., Vasquez, G., Wolf, P. S. A., & Jones, D. N. (2009). Evolutionary theories of personality. In P. J. Corr & G. Matthews (Eds.), *The Cambridge handbook of personality psychology* (pp. 265–274). Cambridge University Press.

Fletcher, J. M. (1942). Homeostasis as an explanatory principle in psychology. *Psychological Review, 49*, 80–87. https://doi.org/10.1037/h0058280

Fowles, D. C. (1980). The three arousal model: Implications of Gray's two-factor learning theory for heart rate, electrodermal activity, and psychopathy. *Psychophysiology, 17*(2), 87–104. https://doi.org/10.1111/j.1469-8986.1980.tb00117.x

Goldberg, L. R. (1990). An alternative "description of personality:" The Big-Five factor structure. *Journal of Personality and Social Psychology, 59*, 1216–1229. https://doi.org/10.1037//0022-3514.59.6.1216

Grant, A. M. & Schwartz, B. (2011). Too much of a good thing: The challenge and opportunity of the inverted U. *Perspectives in Psychological Science, 6*, 61–76. https://doi.org/10.1177/1745691610393523

Gray, J. A. (1994). Framework for a taxonomy of psychiatric disorder. In S. H. M. van Goozen, N. E. van de Poll, & J. Sergeant (Eds.), *Emotions: Essays on emotion theory* (pp. 29–59). Lawrence Erlbaum Associates.

Gray, J. A., & McNaughton, N. (2000). *The neuropsychology of anxiety*. Oxford University Press.

Gross, J. J., & John, O. P. (2003). Individual differences in two emotion regulation processes: Implications for affect, relationships, and well-being. *Journal of Personality and Social Psychology, 85*, 348–362. https://doi.org/10.1037/0022-3514.85.2.348

Harkness, A. R., Finn, J. A., McNulty, J. L., & Shields, S. M. (2012). The Personality Psychopathology-Five (PSY-5): Recent constructive replication and assessment literature review. *Psychological Assessment, 24*(2), 432–443. https://doi.org/10.1037/a0025830

Hardy, J., & Segerstrom, S. C. (2017). Intra-individual variability and psychological flexibility: Affect and health in a national US sample. *Journal of Research in Personality, 69*, 13–21. https://doi.org/10.1016/j.jrp.2016.04.002

Harkness, A. R., Reynolds, S. M., & Lilienfeld, S. O. (2014). A review of systems for psychology and psychiatry: Adaptive systems, personality psychopathology five (PSY-5), and the DSM-5. *Journal of Personality Assessment, 96*, 121–139. https://doi.org/10.1080/00223891.2013.823438

Headey, B. (2010). The set point theory of well-being has serious flaws: On the eve of a scientific revolution? *Social Indicators Research, 97*, 7–21. https://doi.org/10.1007/s11205-009-9559-x

Headey, B., & Wearing, A. (1989). Personality, life events, and subjective well-being: Toward a dynamic equilibrium model. *Journal of Personality and Social Psychology, 57*, 731–739. https://doi.org/10.1037/0022-3514.57.4.731

Hobbs, K. A., Mann, F. D., Latzman, R. D., Zimmermann, J., Jaeger, U., Markon, K., & Krueger, R. F. (2023). Pathological personality in relation to multiple domains of quality of life and impairment: Evidence for the specific relevance of the maladaptive poles of major trait domains. *Journal of Psychopathology and Clinical Science, 132*, 135–144. https://doi.org/10.1037/abn0000810

Hogan, R., & Bond, M. H. (2009). Culture and personality. In P. J. Corr & G. Matthews (Eds.), *The Cambridge handbook of personality psychology* (pp. 577–588). Cambridge University Press. https://doi.org/10.1017/CBO9780511596544.036

Kam, C. C. S., & Meyer, J. P. (2022). Testing the nonlinearity assumption underlying the use of reverse-keyed items: A logical response perspective. *Assessment, 30*, 1569–1589. https://doi.org/10.1177/10731911221106775

Kogan, A., Gruber, J., Shallcross, A. J., Ford, B. Q., & Mauss, I. B. (2013). Too much of a good thing? Cardiac vagal tone's nonlinear relationship with well-being. *Emotion, 13*, 599–604. https://doi.org/10.1037/a0032725

Koob, G. F. (2003). Alcoholism: Allostasis and beyond. *Alcoholism, Clinical and Experimental Research, 27*, 232–243. https://doi.org/10.1097/01.ALC.0000057122.36127.C2

Koob, G., & Kreek, M. J. (2007). Stress, dysregulation of drug reward pathways, and the transition to drug dependence. *The American Journal of Psychiatry, 164*, 1149–1159. https://doi.org/10.1176/appi.ajp.2007.05030503

Koob, G. F., & Schulkin, J. (2019). Addiction and stress: An allostatic view. *Neuroscience and Biobehavioral Reviews, 106*, 245–262. https://doi.org/10.1016/j.neubiorev.2018.09.008

Kozak, M. J., & Cuthbert, B. N. (2016). The NIMH Research Domain Criteria initiative: Background, issues, and pragmatics. *Psychophysiology, 53*, 286–297. https://doi.org/10.1111/psyp.12518

Langwerden, R. J., van der Heijden, P. T., Derksen, J. J., & Egger, J. I. (2023). Trait polarity of the Personality Psychopathology 5 (PSY-5-r): A content analysis in relation to the Patient Description Form. *Journal of Psychopathology and Behavioral Assessment, 45*, 496–508. https://doi.org/10.1007/s10862-022-10015-7

Larsen, R. J., & Buss, D. M. (2024). *Personality psychology: Domains of knowledge about human nature.* McGraw Hill.

Lewis, D. M. G., Al-Shawar, L., & Buss, D. M. (2020). Evolutionary personality psychology. In P. J. Corr & G. Matthews (Eds.), *The Cambridge handbook of personality psychology* (pp. 223–234). Cambridge University Press.

Liu, C. W., & Chalmers, R. P. (2018). Fitting item response unfolding models to Likert-scale data using mirt in R. *PLoS One, 13*(5), e0196292. https://doi.org/10.1371/journal.pone.0196292

Lovallo, W. R. (2011). Do low levels of stress reactivity signal poor states of health? *Biological Psychology, 86*, 121–128. https://doi.org/10.1016/j.biopsycho.2010.01.006

Lovallo, W. R. (2013). Early life adversity reduces stress reactivity and enhances impulsive behavior: Implications for health behaviors. *International Journal of Psychophysiology, 90*, 8–16. https://doi.org/10.1016/j.ijpsycho.2012.10.006

Lovallo, W. R., Farag, N. H., Sorocco, K. H., Cohoon, A. J., Vincent, A. S. (2012). Lifetime adversity leads to blunted stress axis reactivity: Studies from the Oklahoma Family Health Patterns Project. *Biological Psychiatry, 71*, 344–349. https://doi.org/10.1016/j.biopsych.2011.10.018

Lukaszewski, A. W., Lewis, D. M. G., Durkee, P. K., Sell, A.N., Sznycer, D., & Buss, D. M. (2020). An adaptationist framework for personality science. *European Journal of Personality, 34*, 1151–1174. https://doi.org/10.1002/per.2292

Maraun, M. D., & Rossi, N. T. (2001). The extra-factor phenomenon revisited: Unidimensional unfolding as quadratic factor analysis. *Applied Psychological Measurement, 25*, 77–87. https://doi.org/10.1177/01466216010251006

Matthews, G. (2018). Cognitive-adaptive trait theory: A shift in perspective in personality. *Journal of Personality, 86*, 69–82. https://doi.org/10.1111/jopy.12319

McAdams, D. P., & Pals, J. L. (2006). A new Big Five: Fundamental principles for an integrative science of personality. *American Psychologist, 61*(3), 204–217. https://doi.org/10.1037/0003-066X.61.3.204

McCabe, G. A., Oltmanns, J. R., & Widiger, T. A. (2022). The general factors of personality disorder, psychopathology, and personality. *Journal of Personality Disorders, 36*, 129–156. https://doi.org/10.1521/pedi_2021_35_530

McCrae, R. R., & Costa, P. T., Jr. (2007). Brief versions of the NEO-PI-3. *Journal of Individual Differences, 28*(3), 116–128. https://doi.org/10.1027/1614-0001.28.3.116

McEwen, B. S., Bowles, N. P., Gray, J. D., Hill, M. N., Hunter, R.G., Karatsoreos, I. N., & Nasca, C. (2015). Mechanisms of stress in the brain. *Nature Neuroscience, 18*, 1353–1363. https://doi.org/10.1038/nn.4086

McGue, M., & Bouchard, T. J. (1998). Genetic and environmental influences on human behavioral differences. *Annual Review of Neuroscience, 21*, 1–24. https://doi.org/10.1146/annurev.neuro.21.1.1

Menold, N., & Toepoel, V. (2022). Do different devices perform equally well with different numbers of scale points and response formats? A test of measurement invariance and reliability. *Sociological Methods & Research*, Online First. https://doi.org/10.1177/00491241221077237.

Mischel, W., & Shoda, Y. (2008). Toward a unified theory of personality: Integrating dispositions and processing dynamics withing the cognitive-affective processing system. In O. P. John, R. W. Robins, & L. A. Pervin (Eds.), *Handbook of personality: Theory and research* (pp. 208–241). The Guilford Press.

Molenaar, D., Dolan, C. V., & Verhelst, N. D. (2010). Testing and modelling non-normality within the one-factor model. *British Journal of Mathematical and Statistical Psychology, 63*, 293–317. https://doi.org/10.1348/000711009X456935

Monaghan, C., & Bizumic, B. (2023). Dimensional models of personality disorders: Challenges and opportunities. *Frontiers in Psychiatry, 14*, Article 1098452. https://doi.org/10.3389/fpsyt.2023.1098452

Morey, L. C., Good, E. W., & Hopwood, C. J. (2022). Global personality dysfunction and the relationship of pathological and normal trait domains in the DSM-5 alternative model for personality disorders. *Journal of Personality, 90*, 34–46. https://doi.org/10.1111/jopy.12560

Musek, J. (2007). A general factor of personality: Evidence for the Big One in the five-factor model. *Journal of Research in Personality, 41*, 1213–1233. https://doi.org/10.1016/j.jrp.2007.02.003

Muthén, L. K., & Muthén, B. (2017). *Mplus user's guide: Statistical analysis with latent variables*. Muthén & Muthén.

Nettle, D. (2006). The evolution of personality variation in humans and other animals. *American Psychologist, 61*, 622–631. https://doi.org/10.1037/0003-066X.61.6.622

Nguyen, P. L. L., Syed, M., & McGue, M. (2021). Behavior genetics and research on personality: Moving beyond traits to examine characteristics adaptations. *Social and Personality Psychology Compass, 15*(8), e12628. https://doi.org/10.1111/spc3.12628

Nickel, L. B., Roberts, B. W., & Chernyshenko, O. S. (2019). No evidence of a curvilinear relation between conscientiousness and relationship, work, and health outcomes. *Journal of Personality and Social Psychology, 116*, 296–312. https://doi.org/10.1037/pspp0000176

Northoff, G., & Tumati, S. (2019). "Average is good, extremes are bad" – Non-linear inverted U-shaped relationship between neural mechanisms and functionality of mental features. *Neuroscience & Biobehavioral Reviews, 104*, 11–25. https://doi.org/10.1016/j.neubiorev.2019.06.030

Oltmanns, J. R., Smith, G. T., Oltmanns, T. F., & Widiger, T. A. (2018). General factors of psychopathology, personality, and personality disorder: Across domain comparisons. *Clinical Psychological Science, 6*, 581–589. https://doi.org/10.1177/2167702617750150

Ormel, J., Riese, H., & Rosmalen, J. G. M. (2012). Interpreting neuroticism scores across the adult life course: Immutable or experience-dependent set points or negative affect? *Clinical Psychology Review, 32*, 71–79. https://doi.org/10.1016/j.cpr.2011.10.004

Oveis, C., Cohen, A. B., Gruber, J., Shiota, M. N., Haidt, J., & Keltner, D. (2009). Resting respiratory sinus arrhythmia is associated with tonic positive emotionality. *Emotion, 9*, 265–270. https://doi.org/10.1037/a0015383

Pettersson, E., Mendle, J., Turkheimer, E., Horn, E. E., Ford, D. C., Simms, L. J., & Clark, L. A. (2014). Do maladaptive behaviors exist at one or both ends of personality traits? *Psychological Assessment, 26*, 433–446. https://doi.org/10.1037/a0035587

Pierce, J. R., & Aguinis, H. (2011). The Too-Much-of-a-Good-Thing effect in management. *Journal of Management, 39*, 313–338. https://doi.org/10.1177/0149206311410060

Plomin, R. (2011). Commentary: Why are children in the same family so different? Non-shared environment three decades later. *International Journal of Epidemiology, 40*, 582–592. https://doi.org/10.1093/ije/dyq144

Riese, H., Snieder, H., Jeronimus, B. F., Korhonen, T., Rose, R. J., Kaprio, J., & Ormel, J. (2014). Timing of stressful life events affects stability and change in neuroticism. *European Journal of Personality, 28*, 193–200. https://doi.org/10.1002/per.1929

Roberts, J. S., Fang, H. R., Cui, W., & Wang, Y. (2006). GGUM2004: A windows-based program to estimate parameters in the generalized graded unfolding model. *Applied Psychological Measurement, 30*, 64–65. https://doi.org/10.1177/0146621605280141

Roberts, J. S., & Laughlin, J. E. (1996). A unidimensional item response model for unfolding responses from a graded disagree-agree response scale. *Applied Psychological Measurement, 20*, 231–255. https://doi.org/10.1177/014662169602000305

Robins, R. W., John, O. P., Caspi, A., Moffitt, T. E., & Stouthamer-Loeber, M. (1996). Resilient, overcontrolled, and undercontrolled boys: Three replicable personality types. *Journal of Personality and Social Psychology, 70*, 157–171. https://doi.org/10.1037//0022-3514.70.1.157

Samuel, D. B., Simms, L. J., Clark, L. A., Livesley, W. J., & Widiger, T. A. (2010). An item response theory integration of normal and abnormal personality scales. *Personality Disorders: Theory, Research, and Treatment, 1*, 5–21. https://doi.org/10.1037/a0018136

Samuel, D. B., & Tay, L. (2019). Aristotle's golden mean and the importance of bipolarity for personality models: A commentary on "Personality traits and maladaptivity: Unipolarity versus bipolarity." *Journal of Personality, 87*, 1097–1102. https://doi.org/10.1111/jopy.12383

Sapolsky, R. M. (2015). Stress and the brain: Individual variability and the inverted-U. *Nature Neuroscience, 18*(10), 1344–1346. https://doi.org/10.1038/nn.4109

Scollon, C. N., & Diener, E. (2006). Love, work, and changes in extraversion and neuroticism over time. *Journal of Personality and Social Psychology, 91*, 1152–1165. https://doi.org/10.1037/0022-3514.91.6.1152

Segerstrom, S. C., & Smith, G. T. (2019). Personality and coping: Individual differences in responses to emotion. *Annual Review of Psychology, 70*, 651–671. https://doi.org/10.1146/annurev-psych-010418102917

Silvia, P. J., Jackson, B. A., & Sopko, R. S. (2014). Does baseline heart rate variability reflect stable positive emotionality? *Personality and Individual Differences, 70*, 183–187. https://doi.org/10.1016/j.paid.2014.07.003

Simms, L. J., Williams, T. F., & Simms, E. N. (2017). Assessment of the five factor model. In T. A. Widiger, (Ed.). *The Oxford handbook of the five factor model* (pp. 353–380). Oxford University Press.

Simonsohn, U. (2018). Two lines: A valid alternative to the invalid testing of U-shaped relationships with quadratic regressions. *Advances in Methods and Practices in Psychological Science, 1*, 538–555. https://doi.org/10.1177/2515245918805755

Sloan, R. P., Schwarz, E., McKinley, P. S., Weinstein, M., Love, G., Ryff, C., Mroczek, D., Choo, T.-H., Lee, S., & Seeman, T. (2017). Vagally-mediated heart rate variability and indices of well-being: Results of a nationally representative study. *Health Psychology, 36*, 73–81. https://doi.org/10.1037/hea0000397

Smilie, L. D., Pickering, A. D., & Jackson, C. J. (2006). The new reinforcement sensitivity theory: Implications for personality measurement. *Personality and Social Psychology Review, 10*, 320–335. https://doi.org/10.1207/s15327957pspr1004_3

Smith, G. T., Atkinson, E. A., Davis, H. A., Riley, E. N., & Oltmanns, J. R. (2020). The general factor of psychopathology. *Annual Review of Clinical Psychology, 16*, 75–98. https://doi.org/10.1146/annurev-clinpsy-071119-115848

Smits, I. A., Timmerman, M. E., & Stegeman, A. (2016). Modelling non-normal data: The relationship between the skew-normal factor model and the quadratic factor model. *British Journal of Mathematical and Statistical Psychology, 69*, 105–121. https://doi.org/10.1111/bmsp.12062

Stagner, R. (1951). Homeostasis as a unifying concept in personality theory. *Psychological Review, 58*, 5–17. https://doi.org/10.1037/h0063598

Steffen, P. R., Elliott, C. H., Lassen, M. K., Olsen, J., & Smith, L. L. (2017). Expanding schema conceptualization and assessment: Towards a richer understanding of adaptive and maladaptive functioning. *Australian Journal of Psychology, 69*, 200–209. https://doi.org/10.1111/ajpy.12141

Suzuki, T., Samuel, D. B., Pahlen, S., & Krueger, R. F. (2015). *DSM-5* alternative personality disorder model traits as maladaptive extreme variants of the five-factor model: An item-response theory analysis. *Journal of Abnormal Psychology, 124*(2), 343–354. https://doi.org/10.1037/abn0000035

Tay, L, & Ng, V. (2018). Ideal point modeling of non-cognitive constructs: Review and recommendations for research. *Frontiers in Psychology, 9*, Article 2423, https://doi.org/10.3389/fpsyg.2018.02423

Tay, L., & Jebb, A. T. (2018). Establishing construct continua in construct validation: The process of continuum specification. *Advances in Methods and Practices in Psychological Science, 1*, 375–388. https://doi.org/10.1177/2515245918775707

Teitelbaum, H. A. (1956). Homeostasis and personality. *A.M.A. Archives of Neurology and Psychiatry, 76*, 317–324. https://doi.org/10.1001/archneurpsyc.1956.02330270089016

Tendeiro, J. N., & Castro-Alvarez, S. (2019). GGUM: An R package for fitting the generalized graded unfolding model. *Applied Psychological Measurement, 43*, 172–173. https://doi.org/10.1177/0146621618772290

Toch, H. H., & Hastorf, A. H. (1955). Homeostasis in psychology. *Psychiatry: Journal for the Study of Interpersonal Processes, 18*, 81–92. https://doi.org/10.1080/00332747.1955.11022996

Trull, T. J., & Widiger, T. A. (2013). Dimensional models of personality: The five-factor model and the DSM-5. *Dialogues in Clinical Neuroscience, 15*, 135–146. https://doi.org/10.31887/DCNS.2013.15.2/ttrull

Vaidyanathan, U., Morris, S., Wagner, A., Sherrill, J., Sommer, D., Garvey, M., Murphy, E., & Cuthbert, B. (2020). The NIMH Research Domain Criteria project: A decade of behavior and brain integration for translational research. In S. C. Hayes & S. G. Hofmann (Eds.), *Beyond the DSM: Toward a process-based alternative for diagnosis and mental health treatment* (pp. 23–45). Context Press/New Harbinger Publications.

van Dijk, I., Krueger, R. F., & Laceulle, O. M. (2021). DSM-5 alternative personality disorder model traits as extreme variants of five-factor model traits in adolescents. *Personality Disorders, 12*(1), 59–69. https://doi.org/10.1037/per0000409

Van Schuur, W. H., & Kiers, H. A. (1994). Why factor analysis often is the incorrect model for analyzing bipolar concepts, and what model to use instead. *Applied Psychological Measurement, 18*, 97–110. https://doi.org/10.1177/014662169401800201

Walmsley, P. T., Sackett, P. R., & Nichols, S. B. (2018). A large sample investigation of the presence of nonlinear personality-job performance relationships. *International Journal of Selection and Assessment, 26*, 145–163. https://doi.org/10.1111/ijsa.12223

Wang, Z., Lü, W., & Qin, R. (2013). Respiratory sinus arrhythmia is associated with trait positive affect and positive emotional expressivity. *Biological Psychology, 93*, 190–196. https://doi.org/10.1016/j.biopsycho.2012.12.006

Weinberg, M. K., Heath, N., & Tomyn, A. J. (2016). Rebound or resignation: Developing a predictive model of return to subjective wellbeing set-point. *Journal of Happiness Studies: An Interdisciplinary Forum on Subjective Well-Being, 17*, 1565–1575. https://doi.org/10.1007/s10902-015-9659-z

Widiger, T. A., & Crego, C. (2019). The bipolarity of normal and abnormal personality structure: Implications for assessment. *Psychological Assessment, 31*, 420–431. https://doi.org/10.1037/pas0000546

Williams, D. F., & Thompson, J. K. (1993). Biology and behavior: A set-point hypothesis of psychological functioning. *Behavior Modification, 17*, 43–57. https://doi.org/10.1177/01454455930171004

Zalta, A. K., & Shankman, S. A. (2016). Conducting psychopathology prevention research in the RDoC era. *Clinical Psychology: Science and Practice, 23*, 94–104. https://doi.org/10.1111/cpsp.12144

SECTION III

IMPLEMENTATION: INTEGRATING PSYCHOPHYSIOLOGICAL INTERVENTIONS INTO PSYCHOTHERAPY

9
Therapist Flexibility

Why a Psychophysiological Component in Psychotherapy is Important

Paul M. Lehrer

People are complicated, and so are their problems. The history of treating emotional problems is long and complicated. For centuries, influenced by the ancient Greeks, emotional problems were thought to be due to various humors in the body, black bile, yellow bile, blood, and phlegm (Hippocrates, 1931). In Biblical times they were sometimes considered to result from moral failures or supernatural or demonic influences (*King James Bible*, 1769/2017, 1 Samuel 16:14, 21, Mark 5:4–5, John 10:20). Today, many people with mental illness are sent to jail, where mental health treatment could have been a viable alternative (Sokolov, 2009). In Chinese traditions of qi gong, tai chi, and acupuncture, emotional problems have been explained as blocked energy systems flowing through the body (Bao, 2020). Treatments have varied accordingly, including bloodletting, consumption of various herbs, purification ceremonies, exorcism, confession, torture, needles, breathing exercises, prayer, and meditation. This chapter is an update and reformulation of a previous paper written on the role of psychophysiological contributions to psychotherapy (Lehrer, 2018).

The various explanations and approaches to treatment often have been influenced by particular symptom patterns. Some symptoms are mostly physical, such as sweating, fatigue, muscle tension, palpitations, gastric upset, and sleeplessness. Others are mostly cognitive: thoughts of danger, interpretations of others' motives, pessimism, grandiosity, peculiar and illogical speech, etc. Still others are manifest in behavior: argumentativeness, violence, avoidance, sluggishness, hyper- or hyposexuality, asociality, etc. Many involve relational difficulties with friends, coworkers, and loved ones. This list just scratches the surface of the varieties of emotional symptoms. To be classified by the *Diagnostic and Statistical Manual of Mental Disorders* (*DSM*) system as a mental illness, any of these manifestations must impair functioning or quality of life.

Throughout history, choice of treatments has been related to the theories underlying causation of problems; and theories have often been influenced by the symptoms. Culture and personal preferences, as well as biases of influential thinkers and writers, also have influenced how people construe emotional symptoms and how they make treatment choices. Indeed, how emotional problems are construed can affect the particular manifestations. For example, emotional disturbance is more often presented as a group of physical symptoms in some Latin American communities (Aragona et al., 2012; Escobar et al., 2006). Depression is more commonly seen in Northern countries, Brazil, Argentina, Chile, and New Zealand and less in Asia, the Caribbean, and in Central and northern South America (Kessler & Bromet, 2013). Some symptoms are culture-bound such as the symptom of *taijin kyofusho* (Essau et al., 2012), an anxiety disorder in Japan related to offending other people from body odor, or *kayak angst* in Greenland related to fear of being in a small ocean-going boat (Gussow, 1963), *koro* in Southeast Asia and Africa, involving a fear that sexual organs are shrinking into the body (Crozier, 2012), or *ataque de nervios* in Caribbean countries, manifesting as somatic symptoms of panic in response to mourning or trauma (Moitra et al., 2018). It is not unreasonable to think that specific treatment components would be particularly helpful for treating each of these conditions. This chapter will cover the various influences on treatment choice and argue that the well-rounded therapist should have expertise in a variety of therapeutic approaches. I will emphasize the psychophysiological approach, since this is the one that currently is often omitted in psychotherapy training and practice.

In Western culture during the past century and a half, treatment choices have been guided, at least to some extent, by scientific theory and findings. However, particularly early on, scientific findings were scarce, and even now there are few effectiveness studies that even approach the Phase III standard of definitiveness required for Food and Drug Administration approval of drugs. Therefore, acceptability of treatments has been based more on case reports by influential clinicians, multiple case studies, and small controlled trials.

Models of Treatment

Late in the nineteenth and early in the twentieth century, a dominant model of emotion was that of the steam engine. Emotional pressure built up, became expressed as symptoms, and had to be neutralized or let out. This was the model proposed by Schultz and Luthe (1966) for the autogenic training method, where hypnotic suggestion caused relaxation that neutralized emotional buildup, while "autogenic discharges" released built-up pressure (Luthe et al., 1963). These discharges were manifest by incidents of pain, anxiety, or tearfulness while relaxing physically and mentally, often followed by reduction in symptoms. Luthe hypothesized that autogenic discharges allowed the body to return to its homeostatic level, while autogenic training taught relaxation skills that could neutralize emotional arousal. Early theories by clinicians such as Freud (1895) and Reich (1973, 1982) postulated that build-up of unreleased sexual energy or anger could produce symptoms, treated by recognition and release of the energy by orgasm, physical activity, medication or by such later discredited methods as "orgone therapy." These approaches were consistent with a theory of emotion proposed by William James (1894), positing that emotions were caused predominantly by physiological events, such that we are happy because we smile, sad because we cry.

Simultaneously with this model, studies of hypnosis and early psychoanalysis were concluding through case observation that ways of interpreting and experiencing emotion, perception, and memory played a role in creation of emotional problems (Freud, 1963). These could be modified by suggestion, memory recall, linking current emotional reactions to past traumatic experiences, and learning to differentiate between reactions appropriate to past experience in childhood and those appropriate to current adult reality. By the mid-twentieth century cognitive therapists, often influenced by both psychoanalysis and the budding empirical emphasis in cognitive and behavioral therapy, began helping people by systematically evaluating and modifying cognitions that produce a persistence of symptoms. We also should note the therapies developed over the centuries influenced by traditional Eastern traditions, including acupuncture, qi gong, and yoga, aimed at allowing circulating life forces to regulate both the body and emotions (Chen, 2021; Kristeller, 2021; Telles et al., 2021).

Toward the mid-twentieth century, family systems and relational therapy procedures developed from roots in both psychoanalytic therapy and social systems theory and research (Bowen, 1985; Greenberg & Mitchell, 1983; Minuchin & Fishman, 1981; Sullivan, 1964). These therapies have focused on relationships with important others, such as parents, coworkers, lovers, children, etc., and how these are shaped by childhood trauma and social interaction norms. The effects of childhood experience of trauma and emotional conflict are known to imprint strongly on emotional development, and often are expressed in psychopathology and relational problems in later life (Macedo et al., 2019; Steine et al., 2017). Therapies addressing this process focus on understanding the relationship between early emotional conditioning and current emotional state and neutralizing imprinted emotional feelings and behaviors by discussing and reliving them in the context of a relationship with a nurturing psychotherapist, and/or by altering current interaction norms among family members by which patterns of interaction reinforce psychopathology.

Following World War II, a new movement developed, primarily among psychologists. Having had training in scientific study of human behavior and ways to modify it, many had been drafted into military service, but found themselves unable to use their training to help people with emotional problems. Behavior therapy then developed as a method grounded in this research (Franks, 1965). Although at the beginning much behavior therapy was based on theories of conditioning and learning (Salter, 1949; Wolpe, 1958), it rapidly encompassed all areas of human behavior. Years later, a "second wave" of behavior therapy developed from psychoanalytically trained psychiatrists and psychologists who reframed the psychoanalytic cognitive elements to behavioral terms, treating cognitions as modifiable behaviors (A. T. Beck, 1991; Ellis, 1994). More recently a "third wave" of behavior therapy has emerged: "acceptance and commitment therapy." It emphasizes overcoming barriers to identifying and following personal values, achieving personal goals, and a cognitive orientation of mindfulness and acceptance of symptoms (Hayes et al., 2016).

Emergence of Psychophysiology and Psychophysiological Contributions to Psychotherapy

In the 1950s the field of psychophysiology developed, primarily stemming from a seminal paper by Razran (1958), reviewing the more recent contributions from Pavlov's followers in Russia. This work was not known in the West, and, since Pavlov's laboratory operated under the auspices of the military, much of it had been kept secret. This work greatly interested researchers with interests in psychosomatics in the West, where work on psychosomatics had mostly focused on psychoanalytic approaches (e.g., Alexander & French, 1948).

The clinical research of Reich and his followers also focused on psychophysiology (Heller, 2012; Sharaf, 1983), but Reich's advocacy of the discredited "orgone" treatment (Roeckelein, 2006) and the perhaps unsubstantiated stories of his Communist political proclivities (Bennett, 2014) both relegated his contributions to the sidelines. He also proposed paying psychoanalytic attention to various body sensations and reactions, which led to some early experiments in psychophysiology and "vegetotherapy" (Reich, 1970) and developed into the "body therapy" movement (Totten, 2003), wherein people develop greater awareness of body sensations, often through touch and stimulation, while exploring their emotional reactions.

At the same time, some work on hypnosis was directed at psychophysiological problems (Lassner, 1967; Sachs, 1982). One of the most influential of hypnotic methods was Johannes Schultz's method of autogenic training, developed early in the twentieth century, whereby people used self-suggestions to affect various body systems. The method is widely used in psychosomatic medicine in parts of Europe and Asia and is increasingly used by psychophysiologically oriented psychotherapists in the United States (Linden, 2021), although Schultz's later collaboration in some Nazi atrocities in the 1930s and 1940s has marred his credibility (Brunner et al., 2008). This method focuses on mental control of physiological problems.

In the early to mid-1900s, in the United States, Edmund Jacobson began publishing prolifically on the contribution of muscular tension to various psychological and physical problems, and introduced his method of progressive relaxation (Jacobson, 1938). Much of his work focused on physical disorders, although he did publish a volume on control of anxiety (Jacobson, 1964). Nevertheless, he was always considered an outsider in the medical and mental health community, and besides a few students and devotees, his work developed little currency until the early prominent behavior therapist Joseph Wolpe (1958) incorporated the method into his technique of systematic desensitization, whereby people overcome phobias by relaxing their muscles and, while relaxed, imagining a set of scenes arranged in a hierarchy from least to most threatening, thereby "deconditioning" anxiety. Interest then mushroomed in the method, but the technique itself morphed away from Jacobson's rigorous attention to eliminating small amounts of muscle tension, down to the level of underlying muscle tone. Later versions of the method relied heavily on suggestion, and involved large-scale muscle tension, which could make people less sensitive to low-level muscle tone and therefore not teach how to eliminate it.

Jacobson vehemently disagreed with the use of suggestion, under the assumption that this may lead people to *think* that they were relaxing even when they were not. In collaboration with engineers from Bell Laboratories, Jacobson (1940) developed the "integrating neurovoltmeter," capable of detecting muscle tension from surface electrodes to a sensitivity of less than a single microvolt, and he sometimes used this instrument to monitor the progress of his patients, where the aim of treatment was to reduce tension to the lowest levels that could be recorded. Spinoffs from this device developed into the widely used technology of surface electromyography, now applied most often as an adjunct to physical therapy and the treatment of musculoskeletal pain. Modern applications of the progressive relaxation technique often do not train to this criterion (Lehrer et al., 1986). The rationale for Jacobson's work was bolstered by research of the physiologist Ernst Gellhorn, who performed animal research using curare, a drug long used in poison darts by native South American civilizations, which blocks transmission at the neuromuscular junction and causes complete paralysis. Gellhorn found that curarization led to a state of somnolence and low physiological arousal in animals and concluded that muscle tension had profound effects on both the autonomic nervous system and cortical arousal (Gellhorn, 1958; Gellhorn & Loofbourrow, 1963).

The 1960s saw the emergence of the biofeedback field, in simultaneous programmatic investigation by Neal Miller at Yale (Dienstfrey, 1991) and by David Shapiro at Harvard (Lehrer, Ottaviani, et al., 2020). At the time, the "two-factor" theory was dominant in psychological thinking, positing that physiological events were modifiable only through methods of Pavlovian "classical" or "respondent" conditioning (Mowrer, 1953). According to this theory, vegetative activity associated with emotions such as anxiety could be conditioned only through respondent conditioning, although body sensations associated with these sensations could set the condition for thoughts and behaviors that could be brought under voluntary control. It was not thought possible that autonomic activity could be directly controlled voluntarily. However, later work on autonomic biofeedback elegantly proved the opposite. In the course of programmatic research, Shapiro and his colleagues found that skin conductance, heart rate, and finger temperature could indeed be brought under operant control, and that this could be done directly without mediation from other voluntary activity, such as by changes in breathing or muscle tension (Lehrer, Ottaviani, et al., 2020). The most dramatic of these demonstrations was a study in his laboratory by the brave young psychiatrist, Lee Birk, who volunteered to have himself curarized, and demonstrated that he was able to control his skin conductance without the use of his skeletal muscles, under conditions where even his respiration was controlled mechanically (Birk et al., 1966). A rash of similar demonstrations of electrodermal operant conditioning appeared at approximately the same time (Ascough & Sipprelle, 1968; Defran et al., 1969; Helmer & Furedy, 1968; Kimmel & Kimmel, 1968; May & Johnson, 1969; Schwartz & Johnson, 1969; Stern & Kaplan, 1967). Some earlier demonstrations of biofeedback effects on the autonomic nervous system had been done by Simonov and colleagues in the Soviet Union (Simonov et al., 1964a, 1964b), but were largely unknown in the outside world, and a few early studies of control of subliminal or "involuntary" muscle activity had been done in the United States (Brogden, 1961; Fleming & Grant, 1966; Hefferline & Keenan, 1963). Joe Kamiya and colleagues performed early studies on voluntary control of electroencephalogram rhythms (Kamiya, 2011; Nowlis & Kamiya, 1970; Spilker et al., 1969). Several other independent demonstrations of voluntary autonomic control also began appearing at about the same time (Ascough & Sipprelle, 1968; Engel & Melmon, 1968). In a precursor to later work on heart rate variability biofeedback (HRVB), Brener and Hothersall (1966) found that people could voluntarily lower heart rate in the presence of a brief visual stimulus.

Symptom-Treatment Specificity

In the same time period, Peter Lang (1968) performed a seminal experiment demonstrating that psychophysiological, behavioral, and cognitive aspects of anxiety could be decoupled. He asked people afraid of snakes to enter a long room at the end of which was a cage with a harmless snake. Participants were instructed to approach the cage, pick it up, and play with it. Lang found little relationship among self-report of anxiety, closeness with which people were willing to approach the snake, and physiological responses. He developed this work into a psychotherapeutic approach emphasizing separate treatment components for each of the three anxiety components: cognitive, behavioral, and physiological. Later Lazarus (1981) pointed out that emotional problems often have many dimensions and argued that each dimension may require a unique form of targeted treatment. His categories were summarized in the acronym "BASIC ID": behavior, affect, sensation, imagery, cognition, interpersonal, and drugs (physiological). He called this approach "multi modal therapy," an approach that greatly influenced the writing of this paper.

If the approach of Lang and Lazarus is correct, then specific interventions should have specific effects on individual dimensions of problems. For phobias, then, a psychophysiological intervention may have a greater effect on physiological arousal when confronting a phobic stimulus, while a cognitive intervention such as cognitive restructuring may have greater effects on evaluating the threat that the object presents and de-catastrophizing it, and a behavioral intervention such as exposure may allow the person to do things that they previously avoided. Success of the therapy, then would depend partially on how it is measured—by physical symptoms, self-report measures of phobic anxiety, or avoidance behavior. This would be similar for depression. A psychophysiological intervention such as HRVB or relaxation therapy may be expected to target fatigue and the gnawing feelings of sadness, while a cognitive intervention such as cognitive restructuring, self-understanding through psychodynamic therapy, or mindfulness training may target self-deprecation and promote self-acceptance, and a behavioral intervention may target the vicious cycle of anhedonia whereby the depressed person stops engaging in meaningful and enjoyable activity because the prospect of doing these things does not seem appealing. Presumably relationship problems may be most effectively targeted through relational and system therapies and emotional reactions conditioned early in life may be most effectively treated by therapies directed at extinguishing these connections. Then, although there may be some spillover from one dimension to another, this approach would hypothesize that a therapy including many dimensions would have more profound effects across the board than an approach focusing on only one, and that an individual with primary symptoms in only one of the dimensions would do best with a treatment focusing specifically on that one.

We could expand Lang's argument to include some methods emphasized in relational and systems therapies. Because many, if not most, people with problems requiring mental health care have some problems relating to important people in their lives, and because childhood traumas can influence these problems and cause greater emotional reactivity in adulthood, therapy skills that address these issues could be more widely important than is often described in behavior therapy textbooks. These may include observations of how current behavior and emotional reactions toward others, including the therapist, may mimic those learned in early life. Awareness of this connection and desensitization to eliciting conditions through a nurturing and trusting relationship with the therapist can help to mitigate the problem. Patterns of marital interaction, marital problems, and mate preferences in adulthood can be influenced by parents' personality traits in the person's childhood (Tambs, 1991). Various characteristics of parents' behavior can have long-term effects, including parental psychopathology (Auty et al., 2021; van Dijk et al., 2021), how parents behaved and interacted with the client and with each other, occurrence of domestic violence (Carroll, 1980), and parental substance addiction (Schuckit et al., 1994). Adult interpersonal adjustment also can be affected by other forms of childhood trauma (Wang & Chen, 2016). Such factors are addressed in therapies that focus on childhood experiences, and how emotions generated in childhood can persist into adulthood, often interfering with important relationships. Similarly, family therapy methods focus on increasing awareness of interaction norms that foster dysfunctional feelings and behavior and help to alter the rules by which family members behave toward each other, while mindful of the intergenerational nature of these norms (Carroll, 1980).

Another factor that may contribute to treatment effectiveness is compatibility of a particular treatment with an individual's interests, personality, capacity, and beliefs. People will engage more in a treatment that is consistent with these. If an individual does not practice relaxation, cognitive restructuring exercises, or exposure, then it will not work. A person low on hypnotic susceptibility will not practice or respond well to methods emphasizing suggestion (Lehrer & Woolfolk, 2021). A person who thinks more about muscular activity, such as an athlete or dancer, may more easily learn and gravitate more to methods involving control of muscles. A particular religious or spiritual orientation may bias a person toward or against particular treatment components, such as hypnotic suggestion, meditation, cognitive challenges, etc. Some cultural or ethnic groups may find a stigma related to accepting a mental health intervention but find psychophysiological interventions more acceptable because they can be considered physical rather than mental (DeBarros, 2021). Alternatively, people who are aware of experiencing emotions in a particular modality, such as aggressive behavior, self-punitive cognitions, or somatic symptoms may benefit from greater awareness of other modalities affecting them, if they can understand their relevance, since all modalities may contribute to a particular problem. Similarly, people seeking self-understanding as a way to manage their problems might best take to an insight-focused therapy. However, forcing a patient too strenuously into a particular mold of treatment is most probably fruitless, since methods and skills that the person finds disagreeable may not be practiced, used, or taken seriously. Methods that are not used will not work. A dramatic illustration of this may be in response to hypnotic methods. People with low scores on measures of hypnotic susceptibility tend to dislike and respond poorly to hypnotic interventions and may not think them useful (Barabasz & Perez, 2007; Spiegel et al., 2015). Patients with somatization disorders will often reject talk therapies, thinking that they invalidate the conviction that they are physically sick. Some psychophysiologically oriented therapists call biofeedback therapy a "Trojan horse" to induce somatization disorder patients to talk about feelings and engage in other forms of therapy (Wickramasekera, 1988). When the somatic symptoms are measured and taken seriously it becomes possible to draw connections between body feelings and emotion-laden thoughts and situations.

Thus, flexibility on the part of the therapist and acquiring skills in a variety of therapeutic approaches should be the goal for training of competent therapists. Furthermore, most clinical conditions are multidimensional, so different procedures may affect specific aspects of each condition. The *DSM* and *International Classification of Disease* systems for defining mental illnesses include psychophysiological, behavioral, cognitive, and relational symptoms for many disorders. Thus, the various approaches to treatment may all have some beneficial effects, as they target particular dimensions of each person's problem. Additionally, some "spillover" effect is bound to happen that may reinforce each therapist's view that their specialization is the best treatment for everything. Control over psychophysiology may give people courage to expose themselves to feared situations, while improved social skills and relationships may lessen psychophysiological stress symptoms and improve behavioral functioning, etc. However, the strongest effects for each symptom may be with a symptom-specific treatment modality, and with a treatment that is compatible with the individual's personality and beliefs.

A good example of a condition where a multicomponent treatment (including a psychophysiological component) is particularly useful is borderline personality. As described by Linehan, in her rationale for treating it with the multicomponent treatment of dialectical behavior therapy (DBT), this condition often occurs among people who have been sexually abused as children, often by a relative or family friend. Where parents deny that anything bad has happened, they fail to validate the child's feelings of hurt, anger, anxiety, and violation, so the child never learns to correctly label their own feelings. This confusion can persist into adulthood, where, when negative feelings are aroused by interpersonal conflict or rejection, the feelings become intolerable because they have not been correctly labeled, so the person may overreact, become self-destructive and even suicidal, and create havoc with important relationships. DBT has many components, including learning to accurately identify feelings without exaggeration, learning to manage interpersonal conflict more skillfully and appropriately, and learning to manage bad feelings so they do not reach intolerable levels. The last of these is the realm of the psychophysiological component in therapy. Relaxation training is a standard component in DBT (Wenzel, 2013), with uncontrolled data suggesting that HRVB could also be an effective component (Nance, 2015).

The necessity of flexibility in psychotherapeutic technique is, of course not a new idea. A movement of psychotherapy integration has spurred creation of a society dedicated to this principle, the Society for the Exploration of Psychotherapy Integration. A recent chapter on the topic (Gold & Stricker, 2020) includes some of the material covered here, but omits coverage of the most prominent psychophysiological treatment approaches and mentions only eye movement desensitization and reprocessing (EMDR). The current chapter fills that gap.

The Relevance of Psychophysiological Interventions in Multidimensional Therapy

Despite not being a major component in contemporary training or practice of psychotherapy, research has clearly demonstrated large effects of biofeedback, autogenic, and relaxation approaches, particularly for physiological components of patients' problems, as will be reviewed below. However, even where effectiveness is equal but not greater than that of various verbal or behavioral therapies, they can play an important role in a therapist's skill set, particularly for people whose main complaints are physical.

Equivalence or near equivalence in effectiveness to other effective psychotherapeutic methods has been demonstrated for stress management (Dolbier & Rush, 2012; Haney, 2004; McGuigan, 1994; Pawlow et al., 2003; Pifarré et al., 2015), anxiety (Hayes-Skelton et al., 2013; Rice, 2009), panic (J. G. Beck et al., 1994), depression (Kahn et al., 1990; Vazquez et al., 2012), sleep problems (Gustafson, 1992; Means et al., 2000; Nicassio et al., 1982), headache (Nestoriuc et al., 2008), Raynaud's disease

(Karavidas et al., 2006), and high blood pressure (Amigo et al., 2002; Blanchard et al., 1996; Cullins et al., 2013; de Matos Chicayban & Novaes Malagris, 2014; Yucha et al., 2005). In a meta-analysis of heart rate variability studies for all conditions, Lehrer, Kaur et al. (2020) found no differences between HRVB and other effective psychotherapeutic methods, indicating that all of them, used alone, may be equally effective.

Adding a psychophysiological component to other modalities sometimes does increase treatment effects. Yung and Keltner (1996) found muscle relaxation to be more effective than a cognitive relaxation strategy for reducing blood pressure. Also, psychophysiological treatments often are incorporated in both behavioral and psychodynamic therapies, with overlapping and complementary results (Fiskum, 2019; Fox et al., 2021; Gennaro et al., 2019; Michael et al., 2020). Adding biofeedback as a component to various other psychotherapies has been found to improve outcome (Caldwell & Steffen, 2018; Wheeler, 2018). Murphy (2009) found that adding HRVB to cognitive behavior therapy (CBT) had a greater effect in reducing symptoms of generalized anxiety disorder along with autonomic concomitants of generalized anxiety than adding progressive muscle relaxation.

Sometimes psychophysiological interventions can target specific components of a psychological disorder more effectively than other approaches, which also may have their specific effects. Cohen and Fried (2007) found relaxation training and CBT to have equivalent effects in reducing general distress among women with breast cancer, but relaxation had greater effects on fatigue and sleep problems whereas CBT had greater effects in reducing external health locus of control (the extent to which an individual thinks that health issues cannot be controlled by them, but are mainly under the influence of outside forces), suggesting that patients felt better able to control their disease. In this study, a psychophysiological approach thus had greater effects on the physiological symptoms of the disease, while CBT had a greater effect on cognitive orientation toward it.

Consistent with our argument for flexibility in treatment, there is evidence that using psychophysiological approaches as a monotherapy also may not be the most effective way to practice psychotherapy. Consistent with the multidimensional theory, and depending on outcome measures used, psychophysiological therapies have sometimes been found to be inferior to other therapies for specific symptoms of problems that may have non-physiological dimensions. Hinton et al. (2011) found that culturally adapted CBT has greater effects on female Latina patients with treatment-resistant posttraumatic stress disorder than a psychophysiological monotherapy, although, notably, in this study, the CBT treatment included major elements of psychophysiological procedures. Thorsell et al. (2011) found greater pain reduction effects on quality of life for acceptance and commitment therapy than for applied relaxation therapy for chronic pain (but not depression or anxiety). Various quality of life measures are more cognitive than psychophysiological, and therefore would appear to be more specifically targeted by acceptance and commitment therapy than by applied relaxation. Perception of pain intensity also has cognitive and emotional components, and, although psychophysiological therapies can target particular sources of pain, such as muscular, vascular, or gastrointestinal mechanisms, they do not target pain afferents per se, and pain tolerance involves alterations in how one thinks about pain sensations and reacts to them, hence, perhaps, its greater sensitivity to cognitive intervention. In a study with more surprising results, Clark et al. (1994) found greater effects for cognitive therapy than for applied relaxation therapy in treating panic disorder. However, although panic symptoms are largely physiological, the outcome measures in this study were largely cognitive: general anxiety, fear of body sensations, etc., and did not directly assess physiological panic symptoms. Greist et al. (2002) and Kyrios et al. (2018) found greater effects for CBT than for relaxation therapy for obsessive compulsive symptoms. This is consistent with other studies finding poor effects for relaxation in treating obsessive compulsive symptoms (Montero-Marin et al., 2018), which tend to be exclusively cognitive (obsessions) or behavioral (compulsions).

Some Examples of Psychophysiological Interventions and Mechanisms of Action

Muscle Relaxation

As described above, intensive muscle relaxation teaches people to reduce muscle tension to levels below ordinary resting muscle tone (Jacobson, 1938). Because muscles are closely connected to the sympathetic nervous system, muscle relaxation tends to decrease sympathetic arousal and reactivity (Lehrer, 1978). Indeed, in Jacobson's research on the role of muscular activity in human emotion and function, he found that states of anxiety and stress are systematically associated with increased muscle tension (Jacobson, 1967). Emotion is usually recognizable in facial expression, which necessarily involves muscles of the face (Wolf et al., 2005). It is perhaps by relaxing these muscles, along with general decreases in sympathetic arousal, that progressive relaxation has profound anxiolytic effects.

Control of Blood Flow

Early biofeedback research found that people can learn to control blood flow to the hands (Surwit et al., 1976). Blood vessels in these areas are constricted by alpha sympathetic arousal, and thus are systematically affected by stress, causing cold hands and feet. Biofeedback is easily given through the thermistor on an indoor–outdoor thermometer, particularly if output is given in 1/10th degree Fahrenheit. This method is particularly useful for people with Raynaud's symptoms (Freedman, 1987), where blood flow to the hands decreases to the point where the fingers may become blue from lack of oxygen. Although Raynaud's symptoms usually are produced by exposure to cold air, they also can be induced by stress. However autonomic processes affecting finger temperature are complex. While alpha sympathetic activity can decrease blood flow to the fingers (and cool them) through vasoconstriction, beta sympathetic activity can warm the hands through greater cardiac output. Stress can increase both sympathetic processes, so stress-induced Raynaud's symptoms are probably due to vasoconstriction (alpha sympathetic). Relaxation can decrease both sympathetic processes. Freedman et al. (1988) found that finger temperature biofeedback produces greater hand warming effects than autogenic training, which tends to act as a relaxation method. Relaxation causes heart rate to decrease, therefore decreasing beta sympathetic arousal, which cools the hands, while also decreasing alpha sympathetic activity, which warms the hands. Biofeedback increases heart rate while warming the hands more than autogenic training, by both increasing beta sympathetic arousal, which warms the hands, and decreasing alpha sympathetic arousal, which also warms the hands. Thus, most Raynaud's disease patients might benefit more from finger temperature biofeedback than from autogenic training, although it is possible that people with a greater stress contribution to Raynaud's symptoms might possibly benefit more from a relaxation method, which would specifically target that component.

Control of Breathing

Dysfunctional breathing patterns can contribute to a variety of functional physical and psychological symptoms. Most prominent are symptoms of hyperventilation, often referred to as a "hyperventilation syndrome" (Folgering, 1999; Fried, 1989). Various stimuli can increase respiratory drive, including altitude, air pollution, exercise, asthma exacerbation, and emotional stress. When respiratory volume exceeds metabolic need, an imbalance can occur between oxygen and carbon dioxide in the blood. If this exceeds a particular point, usually a level of less than 25 mmHg in partial pressure of carbon dioxide in the blood, the alkalinity of the blood causes hemoglobin's affinity to oxygen to increase, to a level where insufficient oxygen is released to the tissues. Simultaneously, blood vessels constrict, adding to this effect. The tissues, therefore, react in the same way as they would in response to asphyxia, causing various mental, autonomic, and muscular symptoms. These include clouded thought, tremor and muscle pain, palpitations, tingling, breathlessness, and symptoms of oxygen deprivation from various other body organs. Several methods have been proposed to counter hyperventilation. Breath-by-breath biofeedback from a capnometer has been used (Meuret & Ritz, 2021), as well as biofeedback of respiratory rate to slow respiration (Schein et al., 2001).

Additionally, dysfunctional breathing often includes overinvolvement of muscles in the chest and shoulders. These can lead to muscle pain, sometimes postural distortion, and increased sympathetic arousal from generally increased muscle tension. Courtney has described patterns of "dysfunctional breathing," including thoracic-dominant breathing involving heavy use of accessory muscles in respiration, with consequent hyperventilation and sensations of dyspnea (Courtney et al., 2008, 2011).

Several methods of teaching relaxed breathing, primarily diaphragmatic, have been tried and tested, producing reduction in a broad array of symptoms. These include the autogenic training method, which includes the self-suggestion, "It breathes me," or "My breathing is automatic." van Dixhoorn (2021) has described a method of "whole body breathing" to treat dysfunctional breathing patterns, whereby respiratory effects throughout the body are targeted using a "hands on" method for assessment and feedback, with training in muscle awareness, body posture, and sensitivity to respiratory sensations. This method has found particularly widespread use in the Netherlands and Australia in recent years. Leyro et al. (2021) recently published a meta-analysis of respiratory retraining therapies for treating anxiety and found moderate to large effects. They additionally reported that studies employing biofeedback methods had stronger effects than studies not using this technology, perhaps due to stronger training effects in modifying respiratory behavior.

Heart Rate Variability Biofeedback

HRVB uses biofeedback equipment to teach people to breathe at a rate that stimulates an important reflex that controls both autonomic and emotional activity, while also stimulating brain centers that improve muscular coordination and performance. The method teaches people to synchronize two important reflexes affecting heart rate: respiratory sinus arrhythmia (RSA) and the baroreflex (Lehrer & Gevirtz, 2014). RSA is a systematic respiratory-linked oscillation in heart rate, such that it increases during inhalation and decreases during exhalation. The reflex is controlled by the vagus nerve, the parasympathetic nerve whose activity lowers heart rate and keeps it below the rate of the intrinsic cardiac pacemaker. The baroreflex helps control blood pressure fluctuations from sensors in the aorta and carotid artery, such that, when blood pressure rises, heart rate falls, and when blood pressure falls, heart rate rises. This produces an oscillation in heart rate that, on average, approximates eleven seconds for each oscillation (Vaschillo et al., 2006). If a person breathes at the same rate as the baroreflex, inhaling just as blood pressure falls and exhaling just as it rises, then RSA and the baroreflex combine, producing a much larger heart rate oscillation at the baroreflex frequency. This effect is magnified severalfold by resonance effects in the baroreflex system (Vaschillo et al., 2002, 2006). The resulting very large oscillations in heart rate then exercise the baroreflex, magnify its effects, and make it stronger (Lehrer et al., 2003). However, these effects are not limited to effects on respiration and blood pressure control. Neural control of the baroreflex produces rhythms that project throughout the brain, particularly to pathways involved in modulation of emotion (Mather & Thayer, 2018). Anxiety and mood disorders, as defined by *DSM*-5, include a variety of physiological symptoms. These symptoms are particularly targeted by HRVB (Lehrer, Kaur, et al., 2020), with medium to large effect sizes for effects on anger anxiety, and depression, as well as athletic performance, and various somatic problems affected by autonomic nervous system activity.

Cross-Modality Spill-Over Effects

The argument above specifically related to physiological components in various psychological disorders. However, improvement in any component in a disorder usually leads to general improvement. Perhaps for this reason, in our meta-analysis of HRVB effects (Lehrer, Kaur et al., 2020) we found no differences in effects between HRVB and other effective treatments across all disorders that have been studied, although there are instances where cognitive interventions (e.g., cognitive therapy, psychotherapy) have produced greater cognitive effects, behavioral interventions (e.g., exposure, behavior activation, assertion training) more behavioral effects, and psychophysiological interventions (e.g., biofeedback, muscle relaxation) more physiological effects. Some methods, e.g., mindfulness meditation, include both specific cognitive components (e.g., acceptance, focus of attention) and physiological components (e.g., attention to breathing and other physical sensations). Our own experience in teaching a variety of stress management techniques to college students finds that people vary with respect to the relative usefulness of various cognitive and psychophysiological interventions (Lehrer & Woolfolk, 2021). Although this may partially reflect the types of symptoms that people have, it also includes personal and cultural predilections. Students who were relatively more hypnotically susceptible found hypnosis or autogenic training to be more useful. People who are less hypnotically susceptible, who are more empirically oriented, or who have a greater interest in physical processes (e.g., athletes, dancers, musicians) tended to prefer HRVB or muscle relaxation, and people who had a personal or cultural interest in meditation and mental focus tended to prefer meditation methods. People with a more cognitive bent tended to prefer cognitive therapy. Although therapy preference is not always a strong predictor of outcome (Adamson et al., 2005), people in general do tend to take some methods more seriously than others and tend to practice them more. Thus, it behooves psychotherapists to gain expertise in a variety of treatment methods.

Conclusion

Flexibility and skill in various treatment modalities are important elements in successful psychotherapy and should be part of any psychotherapist's skill set. However, flexibility is diminished if psychophysiological skills are absent. Most disorders treated by psychotherapy include symptoms with a psychophysiological as well as behavioral and cognitive components, and therapy specifically directed at these symptoms are expected to have greater effects on them. Also, some patients prefer a psychophysiological approach and, in our clinical experience, will take it more seriously and practice it more. Psychophysiological interventions are easy to administer and are effective, particularly for physiological components in various emotional problems. Psychotherapy training programs would foster more effective therapists if training in psychophysiological methods were part of the curriculum.

Acknowledgments

The author is indebted to Wendy Lubin and Stanley Messer for their thoughtful comments on previous versions of this paper.

References

Adamson, S. J., Sellman, J. D., & Dore, G. M. (2005). Therapy preference and treatment outcome in clients with mild to moderate alcohol dependence. *Drug and Alcohol Review*, *24*(3), 209–216. https://doi.org/10.1080/09595230500167502

Alexander, F., & French, T. M. (1948). *Studies in psychosomatic medicine*. Ronald Press.

Amigo, I., Fernandez, A., Gonzalez, A., & Herrera, J. (2002). Muscle relaxation and continuous ambulatory blood pressure in mild hypertension. *Psicothema*, *14*(1), 47–52. https://www.psicothema.com/pdf/685.pdf

Aragona, M., Rovetta, E., Pucci, D., Spoto, J., & Villa, A. M. (2012). Somatization in a primary care service for immigrants. *Ethnicity and Health*, *17*(5), 477–491. https://doi.org/10.1080/13557858.2012.661406

Ascough, J. C., & Sipprelle, C. N. (1968). Operant verbal conditioning of autonomic responses. *Behaviour Research and Therapy*, *6*, 363–370. https://doi.org/10.1016/0005-7967(68)90069-7

Auty, K. M., Farrington, D. P., & Coid, J. W. (2021). Intergenerational transmission of personality disorder severity and the role of psychosocial risk factors. *Criminal Behaviour and Mental Health*, *32*(1), 5–20. https://doi.org/10.1002/cbm.2225

Bao, G. C. (2020). The idealist and pragmatist view of qi in tai chi and qigong: A narrative commentary and review. *The Journal of Integrative Medicine*, *18*(5), 363–368. https://doi.org/10.1016/j.joim.2020.06.004

Barabasz, A., & Perez, N. (2007). Salient findings: Hypnotizability as core construct and the clinical utility of hypnosis. *International Journal of Clinical and Experimental Hypnosis*, *55*(3), 372–379. https://doi.org/10.1080/00207140701339793

Beck, A. T. (1991). Cognitive therapy: A 30-year retrospective. *American Psychologist*, *46*(4), 368–375. https://doi.org/10.1037//0003-066x.46.4.368

Beck, J. G., Stanley, M. A., Baldwin, L. E., Deagle, E. A., & Averill, P. M. (1994). Comparison of cognitive therapy and relaxation training for panic disorder. *Journal of Consulting and Clinical Psychology*, *62*(4), 818–826. https://doi.org/10.1037/0022-006X.62.4.818

Bennett, P. W. (2014). Wilhelm Reich, the FBI and the Norwegian Communist Party: The consequences of an unsubstantiated rumor. *Psychoanalysis and History*, *16*(1), 95–114. https://doi.org/10.3366/pah.2014.0141

Birk, L., Crider, A., Shapiro, D., & Tursky, B. (1966). Operant electrodermal conditioning under partial curarization. *Journal of Comparative and Physiological Psychology*, *62*(1), 165–166. https://doi.org/10.1037/h0023475

Blanchard, E. B., Eisele, G., Vollmer, A., Payne, A., Gordon, M., Cornish, P., & Gilmore, L. (1996). Controlled evaluation of thermal biofeedback in treatment of elevated blood pressure in unmedicated mild hypertension. *Biofeedback and Self-Regulation, 21*(2), 167–190. https://doi.org/10.1007/BF02284694

Bowen, M. (1985). *Family therapy in clinical practice*. Jason Aronson.

Brener, J., & Hothersall, D. (1966). Heart rate control under conditions of augmented sensory feedback. *Psychophysiology, 3*(1), 23–28. https://doi.org/10.1111/j.1469-8986.1966.tb02675.x

Brogden, W. J. (1961). Conditioning and "voluntary" control. *Psychological Reports, 8*(2), 351–352. https://doi.org/10.2466/pr0.1961.8.2.351

Brunner, J., Schrempf, M., & Steger, F. (2008). Johannes Heinrich Schultz and National Socialism. *Israeli Journal of Psychiatry and Relational Science, 45*(4), 257–262. https://doctorsonly.co.il/wp-content/uploads/2011/12/2008_4_5.pdf

Caldwell, Y. T., & Steffen, P. R. (2018). Adding HRV biofeedback to psychotherapy increases heart rate variability and improves the treatment of major depressive disorder. *International Journal of Psychophysiology, 131*, 96–101. https://doi.org/10.1016/j.ijpsycho.2018.01.001

Carroll, J. C. (1980). The intergenerational transmission of family violence: The long-term effects of aggressive behavior. *Advances in Family Psychiatry, 2*, 171–181.

Chen, K. W. (2021). Qigong therapy for stress management. In P. M. Lehrer & R. L. Woolfolk (Eds.), *Principles and practice of stress management* (4th ed., pp. 428–448). Guilford Press.

Clark, D. M., Salkovskis, P. M., Hackmann, A., Middleton, H., Anastasiades, P., & Gelder, M. (1994). A comparison of cognitive therapy, applied relaxation and imipramine in the treatment of panic disorder. *The British Journal of Psychiatry, 164*(6), 759–769. https://doi.org/10.1192/bjp.164.6.759

Cohen, M., & Fried, G. (2007). Comparing relaxation training and cognitive-behavioral group therapy for women with breast cancer. *Research on Social Work Practice, 17*(3), 313–323. https://doi.org/10.1177/1049731506293741

Courtney, R., Greenwood, K. M., & Cohen, M. (2011). Relationships between measures of dysfunctional breathing in a population with concerns about their breathing. *Journal of Bodywork & Movement Therapies, 15*(1), 24–34. https://doi.org/10.1016/j.jbmt.2010.06.004

Courtney, R., van Dixhoorn, J., & Cohen, M. (2008). Evaluation of breathing pattern: Comparison of a manual assessment of respiratory motion (marm) and respiratory induction plethysmography. *Applied Psychophysiology & Biofeedback, 33*, 91–100. https://doi.org/10.1007/s10484-008-9052-3

Crozier, I. (2012). Making up koro: Multiplicity, psychiatry, culture, and penis-shrinking anxieties. *Journal of the History of Medicine & Allied Sciences, 67*(1), 36–70. https://doi.org/10.1093/jhmas/jrr008

Cullins, S. W., Gevirtz, R. N., Poeltler, D. M., Cousins, L. M., Harpin, R., & Muench, F. (2013). An exploratory analysis of the utility of adding cardiorespiratory biofeedback in the standard care of pregnancy-induced hypertension. *Applied Psychophysiology and Biofeedback, 38*(3), 161–170. https://doi.org/10.1007/s10484-013-9219-4

DeBarros, A. M. V. (2021). Examining psychotherapeutic treatment approach preference in a Hispanic population. *ProQuest Dissertations Publishing*, 28353607.

Defran, R. H., Badia, P., & Lewis, P. (1969). Stimulus control over operant galvanic skin responses. *Psychophysiology, 6*(1), 101–106. https://doi.org/10.1111/j.1469-8986.1969.tb02888.x

de Matos Chicayban, L., & Novaes Malagris, L. E. (2014). Breathing and relaxation training for patients with hypertension and stress. *Estudios de Psicologia, 31*(1), 115–126. https://doi.org/10.1590/0103-166x2014000100012

Dienstfrey, H. (1991). Neal Miller, the dumb autonomic nervous system, and biofeedback. *Advances, 7*(4), 33–44.

Dolbier, C. L., & Rush, T. E. (2012). Efficacy of abbreviated progressive muscle relaxation in a high-stress college sample. *International Journal of Stress Management, 19*(1), 48–68. https://doi.org/10.1037/a0027326

Ellis, A. (1994). *Reason and emotion in psychotherapy* (2nd ed.). Birch Lane Press.

Engel, T., & Melmon, L. (1968). Operant conditioning of heart rate in patients with cardiac arrhythmias. *Conditional Reflex, 3*(2), 130.

Escobar, J. I., Interian, A., Diaz-Martinez, A., & Gara, M. (2006). Idiopathic physical symptoms: A common manifestation of psychiatric disorders in primary care. *CNS Spectrums, 11*(3), 201–210. https://doi.org/10.1017/s1092852900014371

Essau, C. A., Sasagawa, S., Ishikawa, S., Okajima, I., O'Callaghan, J., & Bray, D. (2012). A Japanese form of social anxiety (taijin kyofusho): Frequency and correlates in two generations of the same family. *International Journal of Social Psychiatry, 58*(6), 635–642. https://doi.org/10.1177/0020764011421099

Fiskum, C. (2019). Psychotherapy beyond all the words: Dyadic expansion, vagal regulation, and biofeedback in psychotherapy. *Journal of Psychotherapy Integration, 29*(4), 412–425. https://doi.org/10.1037/int0000174

Fleming, R. A., & Grant, D. A. (1966). A comparison of rate and contingency of classical and instrumental reinforcement upon the acquisition and extinction of the human eyelid CR. *Journal of Experimental Psychology, 72*(4), 488–491. https://doi.org/10.1037/h0023771

Folgering, H. (1999). The pathophysiology of hyperventilation syndrome. *Monaldi Archives for Chest Disease, 54*(4), 365–72.

Fox, S. T., Ghelfi, E. A., & Goates-Jones, M. K. (2021). Common factors in biofeedback administered by psychotherapists. *Applied Psychophysiology and Biofeedback, 46,* 151–159. https://doi.org/10.1007/s10484-021-09504-4

Franks, C. M. (1965). Behavior therapy, psychology and the psychiatrist: Contributions, evaluation and overview. *American Journal of Orthopsychiatry, 35*(1), 145–151. https://doi.org/10.1111/j.1939-0025.1965.tb02278.x

Freedman, R. R. (1987). Long-term effectiveness of behavioral treatments for Raynaud's disease. *Behavior Therapy, 18*(4), 387–399. https://doi.org/10.1016/S0005-7894%2887%2980006-0

Freedman, R. R., Morris, M., Norton, D. A., Masselink, D., Sabharwal, S. C., & Mayes, M. (1988). Physiological mechanism of digital vasoconstriction training. *Biofeedback & Self-Regulation, 13,* 299–305. https://doi.org/10.1007/BF00999086

Freud, S. (1895). On the grounds for detaching a particular syndrome from neurasthenia under the description "anxiety neurosis." *Neurologisches Zentralblatt, 14*(2), 50–66.

Freud, S. (1963). *Therapy and technique.* Crowell-Collier.

Fried, R. (1989). The hyperventilation syndrome. *Biofeedback & Self-Regulation, 14*(3), 259–261. https://doi.org/10.1007/BF01000098

Gellhorn, E. (1958). The influence of curare on hypothalamic excitability and the electroencephalogram. *Electroencephalography and Clinical Neurophysiology, 10*(4), 697–703. https://doi.org/10.1016/0013-4694(58)90071-3

Gellhorn, E., & Loofbourrow, G. N. (1963). *Emotions and emotional disorders: A neurophysiological study.* Hoeber Medical Division, Harper and Row.

Gennaro, A., Kleinbub, J. R., Mannarini, S., Salvatore, S., & Palmieri, A. (2019). Training in psychotherapy: A call for embodied and psychophysiological approaches. *Research in Psychotherapy: Psychopathology, Process and Outcome, 22*(3), 333–343. https://doi.org/10.4081/ripppo.2019.395

Gold, J., & Stricker, G. (2020). Integrative approaches to psychotherapy. In S. B. Messer and N. J. Kaslow (Eds.), *Essential psychotherapies: Theory and practice* (4th ed., pp. 443–480). Guilford Press.

Greenberg, J. R., & Mitchell, S. A. (1983). *Object relations in psychoanalytic theory.* Harvard University Press.

Greist, J. H., Marks, I. M., Baer, L., Kobak, K. A., Wenzel, K. W., Hirsch, M. J., Mantle, J. M., & Clary, C. M. (2002). Behavior therapy for obsessive-compulsive disorder guided by a computer or by a clinician compared with relaxation as a control. *The Journal of Clinical Psychiatry, 63*(2), 138–145. https://doi.org/10.4088/JCP.v63n0209

Gussow, Z. (1963). A preliminary report of kayak-angst among the Eskimo of West Greenland: A study in sensory deprivation. *International Journal of Social Psychiatry, 9*(1), 18–26. https://doi.org/10.1177/002076406300900103

Gustafson, R. (1992). Treating insomnia with a self-administered muscle relaxation training program: A follow-up. *Psychological Reports, 70*(1), 124–126. https://doi.org/10.2466/pr0.1992.70.1.124

Haney, C. J. (2004). Stress-management interventions for female athletes: Relaxation and cognitive restructuring. *International Journal of Sport Psychology, 35*(2), 109–118.

Hayes, S. C., Strosahl, K. D., & Wilson, K. G. (2016). *Acceptance and commitment therapy: The process and practice of mindful change* (2nd ed.). Guilford Press.

Hayes-Skelton, S. A., Roemer, L., & Orsillo, S. M. (2013). A randomized clinical trial comparing an acceptance-based behavior therapy to applied relaxation for generalized anxiety disorder. *Journal of Consulting and Clinical Psychology, 81*(5), 761–773. https://doi.org/10.1037/a0032871

Hefferline, R. F., & Keenan, B. (1963). Amplitude-induction gradient of a small-scale (covert) operant. *Journal of the Experimental Analysis of Behavior, 6*(3), 307–315. https://doi.org/10.1901/jeab.1963.6-307

Heller, M. C. (2012). *Body psychotherapy: History, concepts, and methods.* W. W. Norton.

Helmer, J. E., & Furedy, J. J. (1968). Operant conditioning of GSR amplitude. *Journal of Experimental Psychology, 78*(3, Pt.1), 463–467. https://doi.org/10.1037/h0026472

Hinton, D. E., Hofmann, S. G., Rivera, E., Otto, M. W., & Pollack, M. H. (2011). Culturally adapted CBT (CA-CBT) for Latino women with treatment-resistant PTSD: A pilot study comparing CA-CBT to applied muscle relaxation. *Behaviour Research and Therapy, 49*(4), 275–280. https://doi.org/10.1016/j.brat.2011.01.005

Hippocrates. (1931). *Hippocrates, volume IV: Nature of man. (Loeb Classical Library, No. 150).* Harvard University Press. (Original work c. 500 BCE).

Jacobson, E. (1938). *Progressive relaxation.* University of Chicago Press.

Jacobson, E. (1940). An integrating voltmeter for the study of nerve and muscle potentials. *Review of Scientific Instruments, 11*(12), 415–418. https://doi.org/10.1063/1.1751599

Jacobson, E. (1964). *Anxiety and tension control: A physiologic approach.* J. P. Lippincott Company.

Jacobson, E. (1967). *Biology of emotions.* Charles C. Thomas.

James, W. (1894). Discussion: The physical basis of emotion. *Psychological Review, 1*(5), 516–529. https://doi.org/10.1037/h0065078

Kahn, J. S., Kehle, T. J., Jenson, W. R., & Clark, E. (1990). Comparison of cognitive-behavioral, relaxation, and self-modeling interventions for depression among middle-school students. *School Psychology Review, 19*(2), 196–211. https://doi.org/10.1080/02796015.1990.12085457

Kamiya, J. (2011). The first communications about operant conditioning of the EEG. *Journal of Neurotherapy, 15*(1), 65–73. https://doi.org/10.1080/10874208.2011.545764

Karavidas, M. K., Tsai, P.-S., Yucha, C., McGrady, A., & Lehrer, P. M. (2006). Thermal biofeedback for primary Raynaud's phenomenon: A review of the literature. *Applied Psychophysiology and Biofeedback, 31*(3), 203–216. https://doi.org/10.1007/s10484-006-9018-2

Kessler, R. C., & Bromet, E. J. (2013). The epidemiology of depression across cultures. *Annual Review of Public Health, 34,* 119–138. https://doi.org/10.1146/annurev-publhealth-031912-114409

Kimmel, E., & Kimmel, H. D. (1968). Instrumental conditioning of the GSR: Serendipitous escape and punishment training. *Journal of Experimental Psychology, 77*(1), 48–51. https://doi.org/10.1037/h0025767

King James Bible. (2017). King James Bible Online. https://www.kingjamesbibleonline.org/ (Original work published 1769)

Kristeller, J. L. (2021). Mindfulness meditation for stress manatement. In P. M. Lehrer & R. L. Woolfolk (Eds.), *Principles and practice of stress management* (4th ed., pp. 412–449). Guilford Press.

Kyrios, M., Ahern, C., Fassnacht, D. B., Nedeljkovic, M., Moulding, R., & Meyer, D. (2018). Therapist-assisted Internet-based cognitive behavioral therapy versus progressive relaxation in obsessive-compulsive disorder: Randomized controlled trial. *Journal of Medical Internet Research, 20*(8), Article e242, https://doi.org/10.2196/jmir.9566

Lang, P. J. (1968). Fear reduction and fear behavior: Problems in treating a construct. In J. M. Shlien (Ed.), *Research in psychotherapy* (pp. 90–102). American Psychological Association. https://doi.org/10.1037/10546-004

Lassner, L. (Ed.). (1967). *Hypnosis and psychosomatic medicine.* Springer.

Lazarus, A. A. (1981). *The practice of multimodal therapy* (1st ed.). McGraw Hill.

Lehrer, P. M. (1978). Psychophysiological effects of progressive relaxation in anxiety neurotic patients and of progressive relaxation and alpha feedback in non-patients. *Journal of Consulting and Clinical Psychology, 46*(3), 389–404. https://doi.org/10.1037//0022-006x.46.3.389

Lehrer, P. M. (2018). Heart rate variability biofeedback and other psychophysiological procedures as important elements in psychotherapy. *International Journal of Psychophysiology, 131,* 89–95. https://doi.org/10.1016/j.ijpsycho.2017.09.012

Lehrer, P. M., & Gevirtz, R. (2014). Heart rate variability biofeedback: How and why does it work? *Frontiers in Psychology, 21*(5), Article 756. https://doi.org/10.3389/fpsyg.2014.00756

Lehrer, P. M., Kaur, K., Sharma, A., Shah, K., Huseby, R., Bhavsar, J., & Zhang, Y. (2020). Heart rate variability biofeedback improves emotional and physical health and performance: A systematic review and meta analysis. *Applied Psychophysiology and Biofeedback, 45*(3), 100–129. https://doi.org/10.1007/s10484-020-09466-z

Lehrer, P. M., Ottaviani, C., & Jamner, L. (2020). In memoriam: David Shapiro (1924–2020). *Psychophysiology, 57*(11), Article e13677. https://doi.org/10.1111/psyp.13677

Lehrer, P. M., Vaschillo, E., Vaschillo, B., Lu, S.-E., Eckberg, D. L., Edelberg, R., Shih, W. J., Lin, Y., Kuusela, T. A., Tahvanainen, K. U. O., & Hamer, R. M. (2003). Heart rate variability biofeedback increases baroreflex gain and peak expiratory flow. *Psychosomatic Medicine, 65*(5), 796–805. https://doi.org/10.1097/01.PSY.0000089200.81962.19

Lehrer, P. M., & Woolfolk, R. L. (2021). Wearing the clinical hat. In P. M. Lehrer & R. L. Woolfolk (Eds.), *Principles and practice of stress management* (4th ed., pp. 649–656). Guilford Press.

Lehrer, P. M., Woolfolk, R. L., & Goldman, N. (1986). Progressive relaxation then and now: Does change always mean progress? In R. Davidson, G. Schwartz, & D. Shapiro (Eds.), *Consciousness and self-regulation. Vol 4.* (pp. 183–216). Plenum.

Leyro, T. M., Versella, M. V., Yang, M.-J., Brinkman, H. R., Hoyt, D. L., & Lehrer, P. (2021). Respiratory therapy for the treatment of anxiety: Meta-analytic review and regression. *Clinical Psychology Review, 84*, Article 101980. https://doi.org/10.1016/j.cpr.2021.101980

Linden, W. (2021). The autogenic training method of J. H. Schultz. In P. M. Lehrer & R. L. Woolfolk (Eds.), *Principles and practice of stress management* (4th ed., pp. 527–552). Guilford Press.

Luthe, W., Jus, A., & Geissmann, P. (1963). Autogenic state and autogenic shift: Psychophysiologic and neurophysiologic aspects. *Acta Psychotherapeutica, 11*(1), 1–13. https://doi.org/10.1159/000285660

Macedo, B. B. D., von Werne Baes, C., Menezes, I. C., & Juruena, M. F. (2019). Child abuse and neglect as risk factors for comorbidity between depression and chronic pain in adulthood. *Journal of Nervous and Mental Disease, 207*(7), 538–545. https://doi.org/10.1097/NMD.0000000000001031

Mather, M., & Thayer, J. (2018). How heart rate variability affects emotion regulation brain networks. *Current Opinion in Behavioral Sciences, 19*, 98–104. https://doi.org/10.1016/j.cobeha.2017.12.017

May, J. R., & Johnson, H. J. (1969). Positive reinforcement and suppression of spontaneous GSR activity. *Journal of Experimental Psychology, 80*(1), 193–195. https://doi.org/10.1037/h0027124

McGuigan, F. J. (1994). Stress management through progressive relaxation. *International Journal of Stress Management, 1*(2), 205–214. https://doi.org/10.1007/BF01857612

Means, M. K., Lichstein, K. L., Epperson, M. T., & Johnson, C. T. (2000). Relaxation therapy for insomnia: Nighttime and day time effects. *Behaviour Research and Therapy, 38*(7), 665–678. https://doi.org/10.1016/S0005-7967(99)00091-1

Meuret, A. E., & Ritz, T. (2021). Capnometry-assisted respiration training: Principles and findings. In P. M. Lehrer & R. L. Woolfolk (Eds.), *Principles and practice of stress management* (4th ed., pp. 303–326). Guilford Press.

Michael, T., Schanz, C. G., Mattheus, H. K., Issler, T. T., Frommberger, U., Kollner, V., & Equit, M. (2020). Adjuvant interventions in adult patients receiving trauma-focused psychotherapy: Which evidence exists? *Trauma & Gewalt, 14*(2), 112–121. https://doi.org/10.21706/tg-14-2-112

Minuchin, S., & Fishman, H. C. (1981). *Family therapy techniques*. Harvard University Press.

Moitra, E., Duarte-Velez, Y., Lewis-Fernandez, R., Weisberg, R. B., & Keller, M. B. (2018). Examination of ataque de nervios and ataque de nervios like events in a diverse sample of adults with anxiety disorders. *Depression & Anxiety, 35*(12), 1190–1197. https://doi.org/10.1002/da.22853

Montero-Marin, J., Garcia-Campayo, J., Lopez-Montoyo, A., Zabaleta-del-Olmo, E., & Cuijpers, P. (2018). Is cognitive-behavioural therapy more effective than relaxation therapy in the treatment of anxiety disorders? A meta-analysis. *Psychological Medicine, 48*(9), 1427–1436. https://doi.org/10.1017/S0033291717003099

Mowrer, O. H. (1953). Neurosis, psychotherapy, and two-factor learning theory. In O. H. Mowrer (Ed.), *Psychotherapy: Theory and research* (pp. 140–149). Ronald Press Company. https://doi.org/10.1037/10572-006

Murphy, J. A. W. (2009). Comparison of relaxation techniques for group cognitive behavioral therapy for generalized anxiety disorder. *ProQuest Dissertations Publishing*, 2251245.

Nance, J. A. (2015). An exploration of heart rate variability biofeedback as an ancillary treatment for patients diagnosed with borderline personality disorder, an initial feasibility study. *ProQuest Dissertations Publishing*, 3619861.

Nestoriuc, Y., Martin, A., Rief, W., & Andrasik, F. (2008). Biofeedback treatment for headache disorders: A comprehensive efficacy review. *Applied Psychophysiology and Biofeedback*, *33*(3), 125–140. https://doi.org/10.1007/s10484-008-9060-3

Nicassio, P. M., Boylan, M. B., & McCabe, T. G. (1982). Progressive relaxation, EMG biofeedback and biofeedback placebo in the treatment of sleep-onset insomnia. *British Journal of Medical Psychology*, *55*(2), 159–166. https://doi.org/10.1111/j.2044-8341.1982.tb01494.x

Nowlis, D. P., & Kamiya, J. (1970). The control of electroencephalographic alpha rhythms through auditory feedback and the associated mental activity. *Psychophysiology*, *6*(4), 476–484. https://doi.org/10.1111/j.1469-8986.1970.tb01756.x

Pawlow, L., O'Neil, P., & Malcolm, R. (2003). Night eating syndrome: Effects of brief relaxation training on stress, mood, hunger, and eating patterns. *International Journal of Obesity*, *27*(8), 970–978. https://doi.org/10.1038/sj.ijo.0802320

Pifarré, P., Simó, M., Gispert, J., Plaza, P., Fernandez, A., & Pujol, J. (2015). Diazepam and Jacobson's progressive relaxation show similar attenuating short-term effects on stress-related brain glucose consumption. *European Psychiatry*, *30*(2), 187–192. https://doi.org/10.1016/j.eurpsy.2014.03.002

Razran, G. (1958). Soviet psychology and psychophysiology. *Science*, *128*(3333), 1187–1194. https://doi.org/10.1126/science.128.3333.1187

Reich, W. (1970). Psychic contact and vegetative current. In W. Reich (Ed.), *Character analysis* (3rd ed., pp. 285–354). Farrar, Straus, and Giroux.

Reich, W. (1973). *The function of the orgasm: Sex-economic problems of biological energy*. Farrar, Straus, and Giroux.

Reich, W. (1982). *The bioelectrical investigation of sexuality and anxiety* (M. Faber, Trans.) Farrar, Straus, and Giroux.

Rice, C. L. (2009). Reducing anxiety in middle school and high school students: A comparison of cognitive-behavioral therapy and relaxation training approaches (Publication number 3315629). Doctoral dissertation. The University of Arizona. ProQuest Dissertations Publishing.

Roeckelein, J. E. (2006). Reich's orgone/orgonomy theory. In J. E. Roeckelein (Ed.), *Elsevier's dictionary of psychological theories*. Elsevier.

Sachs, B. C. (1982). Hypnosis in psychiatry and psychosomatic medicine. *Psychosomatics*, *23*(5), 523–525. https://doi.org/10.1016/S0033-3182(82)73384-5

Salter, A. (1949). *Conditioned reflex therapy*. Creative Age Press.

Schein, M., Gavish, B., Herz, M., Rosner-Kahana, D., Naveh, P., Knishkowy, B., Zlotnikov, E., Ben-Zvi, N., & Melmed, R. N. (2001). Treating hypertension with a device that slows and regularizes breathing: A randomized, double-blind controlled study. *Journal of Human Hypertension*, *15*(4), 271–278. https://doi.org/10.1038/sj.jhh.1001148

Schuckit, M. A., Tipp, J. E., & Kelner, E. (1994). Are daughters of alcoholics more likely to marry alcoholics? *The American Journal of Drug and Alcohol Abuse*, *20*(2), 237–245. https://doi.org/10.3109/00952999409106784

Schultz, J., & Luthe, W. (1966). *Autogenic therapy, v 1-6*. Grune and Stratton.

Schwartz, G. E., & Johnson, H. J. (1969). Affective visual stimuli as operant reinforcers of the GSR. *Journal of Experimental Psychology*, *80*(1), 28–32. https://doi.org/10.1037/h0027126

Sharaf, M. (1983). *Fury on earth*. St. Martin's Press.

Simonov, P. V., Valueva, M. N., & Ershov, P. M. (1964a). Voluntary control of the galvanic skin response. *Voprosy Psychologii*, *6*, 45–50.

Simonov, P. V., Valueva, M. N., & Ershov, P. M. (1964b). Voluntary and involuntary emotional reactions in man. *Zhurnal Vysshei Nervnoi Deyatel'nosti*, *14*(2), 204–210.

Sokolov, H. (2009). Review of mental health courts: Decriminalizing the mentally ill. *Journal of the American Academy of Psychiatry and the Law*, *37*(1), 133–134.

Spiegel, D., Maruffi, B., Frischholz, E. J., & Spiegel, H. (2015). Hypnotic responsivity and the treatment of flying phobia. *American Journal of Clinical Hypnosis, 57*(2), 156–164. https://doi.org/10.1080/00029157.2015.967086

Spilker, B., Kamiya, J., Callaway, E., & Yeager, C. L. (1969). Visual evoked responses in subjects trained to control alpha rhythms. *Psychophysiology, 5*(6), 683–695. https://doi.org/10.1111/j.1469-8986.1969.tb02871.x

Steine, I. M., Winje, D., Krystal, J. H., Bjorvatn, B., Milde, A. M., Grønli, J., Nordhus, I. H., & Palleson, S. (2017). Cumulative childhood maltreatment and its dose-response relation with adult symptomatology: Findings in a sample of adult survivors of sexual abuse. *Child Abuse & Neglect, 65*, 99–111. https://doi.org/10.1016/j.chiabu.2017.01.008

Stern, R. M., & Kaplan, B. E. (1967). Galvanic skin response: Voluntary control and externalization. *Journal of Psychosomatic Research, 10*(4), 349–353. https://doi.org/10.1016/0022-3999%2867%2990071-2

Sullivan, H. S. (1964). *The fusion of psychiatry and social science*. Norton.

Surwit, R. S., Shapiro, D., & Feld, J. L. (1976). Digital temperature autoregulation and associated cardiovascular changes. *Psychophysiology, 13*(3), 242–248. https://doi.org/10.1111/j.1469-8986.1976.tb00106.x

Tambs, K. (1991). Transmission of symptoms of anxiety and depression in nuclear families. *Journal of Affective Disorders, 21*(2), 117–126. https://doi.org/10.1016/0165-0327%2891%2990058-Z

Telles, S., Kala, N., Gupta, R. K., & Balkrishna, A. (2021). Yoga for stress management: History, research, and practical details. In P. M. Lehrer & R. L. Woolfolk (Eds.), *Principles and practice of stress management* (4th ed., pp. 472–486). Guilford Press.

Thorsell, J., Finnes, A., Dahl, J., Lundgren, T., Gybrant, M., Gordh, T., & Buhrman, M. (2011). A comparative study of 2 manual-based self-help interventions, acceptance and commitment therapy and applied relaxation, for persons with chronic pain. *The Clinical Journal of Pain, 27*(8), 716–723. https://doi.org/10.1097/AJP.0b013e318219a933

Totten, N. (2003). *Body psychotherapy: An introduction*. McGraw-Hill Education.

van Dijk, M. T., Murphy, E., Posner, J. E., Talati, A., & Weissman, M. M. (2021). Association of multigenerational family history of depression with lifetime depressive and other psychiatric disorders in children: Results from the Adolescent Brain Cognitive Development (ABCD) study. *JAMA Psychiatry, 78*(7), 778–787. https://doi.org/10.1001/jamapsychiatry.2021.0350

van Dixhoorn, J. (2021). Whole body breathing. In P. M. Lehrer & R. L. Woolfolk (Eds.), *Principles and practice of stress management* (4th ed., pp. 327–374). Guilford Press.

Vaschillo, E., Lehrer, P., Rishe, N., & Konstantinov, M. (2002). Heart rate variability biofeedback as a method for assessing baroreflex function: A preliminary study of resonance in the cardiovascular system. *Applied Psychophysiology and Biofeedback, 27*(1), 1–27. https://doi.org/10.1023/a:1014587304314

Vaschillo, E., Vaschillo, B., & Lehrer, P. (2006). Characteristics of resonance in heart rate variability stimulated by biofeedback. *Applied Psychophysiology and Biofeedback, 31*(2), 129–142. https://doi.org/10.1007/s10484-006-9009-3

Vazquez, F. L., Torres, A., Blanco, V., Diaz, O., Otero, P., & Hermida, E. (2012). Comparison of relaxation training with a cognitive-behavioural intervention for indicated prevention of depression in university students: A randomized controlled trial. *Journal of Psychiatric Research, 46*(11), 1456–1463. https://doi.org/10.1016/j.jpsychires.2012.08.007

Wang, J., & Chen, B. B. (2016). The influence of childhood stress and mortality threat on mating standards. *Acta Psychologica Sinica, 48*(7), 857–866. https://doi.org/10.3724/SP.J.1041.2016.00857

Wenzel, A. (2013). Affective coping skills. In A. Wenzel (Ed.), *Strategic decision making in cognitive behavioral therapy* (pp. 187–202). American Psychological Association. https://doi.org/10.1037/14188-010

Wheeler, L. F. (2018). *Stress and psychotherapy outcome: Implementation of a heart rate variability biofeedback intervention to improve psychotherapy outcome* (Publication number 10606620). Doctoral dissertation. Brigham Young University. ProQuest Dissertations Publishing.

Wickramasekera, I. (1988). *Clinical behavioral medicine: Some concepts and procedures*. Springer.

Wolf, K., Mass, R., Ingenbleek, T., Kiefer, F., Naber, D., & Wiedemann, K. (2005). The facial pattern of disgust, appetence, excited joy and relaxed joy: An improved facial EMG study. *Scandinavian Journal of Psychology, 46*(5), 403–409. https://doi.org/10.1111/j.1467-9450.2005.00471.x

Wolpe, J. (1958). *Psychotherapy by reciprocal inhibition.* Stanford University Press.

Yucha, C. B.,Tsai, P.-S., Calderon, K. S., & Tian, L. (2005). Biofeedback-assisted relaxation training for essential hypertension: Who is most likely to benefit? *Journal of Cardiovascular Nursing, 20*(3), 198–205. https://doi.org/10.1097/00005082-200505000-00012

Yung, P. M., & Keltner, A. A. (1996). A controlled comparison on the effect of muscle and cognitive relaxation procedures on blood pressure: Implications for the behavioural treatment of borderline hypertensives. *Behaviour Research and Therapy, 34*(10), 821–826. https://doi.org/10.1016/0005-7967%2896%2900062-9

10
Compassion as an Integrative and Integrating Therapeutic Process

Paul Gilbert

Historical Reflection on Psychotherapy

The development of methods and practices to help people with mental health problems, difficult states of mind and life circumstances is thousands of years old (Ellenberger, 1970; Zilboorg & Henry, 1941). Many are rooted in ancient cultural community rituals, the use of hallucinogens and herbs, contemplative and philosophical traditions, spiritual guidance, connecting with higher consciousness, and basic advice. Most of these practices were not designed to be used alone but in relationship to a guru or mentor who guided you through the experiences and facilitated different experiences of connectedness (Gilbert & Gilbert, 2011). In essence these processes of change were mostly contextualized within a caring, guiding relationship. Formal psychotherapy as a "science and profession" is more recent but follows the same process by which one individual, who has a particular skill or experience, guides another individual into exploring, understanding, and cultivating their minds. Compassion-focused therapy (CFT) highlights this distinction too, with particular focus on the properties of the CFT therapeutic process including the therapeutic relationship, which distinguishes CFT from compassionate mind training (H. Gilbert, 2022; Gilbert & Simos, 2022). CFT is one of an increasing number of therapies that are incorporating compassion as a therapeutic process (Kirby, 2016). Crucial for this book is the recognition that the therapeutic relationship itself has multiple psychophysiological effects (Cozolino, 2017; Geller, 2018; Schore, 2019).

A major cultural development occurred in the post-Darwinian era as we came to terms with the fact that we are evolved beings like other lifeforms, and the implications that had on how we understood the nature of the mind. The early psychodynamic theorists were deeply embedded in these fresh evolutionary concepts, seeing them as a source of understanding for the mind and mental health difficulties (Ellenberger, 1970; Ritvo & Haynal, 1994). Hence, therapists of the immediate post-Darwinian 1880s era, like Freud, Jung, and Adler, were oriented to focus on identifying evolved mechanisms underpinning mental states (Ellenberger, 1970). Problems arose on two fronts. First were therapeutic techniques such as free association and interpretation used to try to identify non-conscious processing. Second were techniques to produce change with the awareness that "bringing into consciousness new insights or avoided emotions and memories and offering interpretations" may not be sufficient for change. Indeed Freud, Jung, and Adler had many disputes about the nature of the mind and hence the value of interpretation. Jung's concept of archetypes was very different from Freud's concept of diverted drives. Moreover, Freud also realized that clients needed to act on their new insights and used forms of exposure interventions with some clients (Yalom, 1980).

By the 1950s, focus had shifted away from unconscious processes and links to physiology and through the ego analytical approaches of Bibring (1894–1959) and Horney (1885–1952), on to clients' needs, attitudes, values, and beliefs. These approaches, along with the emergence of Rogerian person-centered therapy, dropped all concerns with physiological processes. As L. Eisenberg (1986) noted, with psychiatry becoming more and more organic, centered on synapses and drug development, and psychotherapists less and less interested in physiology, we entered the period of "mindless versus brainless science" (p. 497).

The subsequent two decades saw the emergence of Beck, Ellis, and Kelly, who moved away from concerns with unconscious processes in favor of helping people identify what they could consciously monitor and change. They promoted what became known as the cognitive revolution and approach. Their focus was almost entirely on recently evolved human cognitive competencies for reasoning and attitude-formation, in the regulation of motivation, emotion, and behavior. However, Beck always argued that cognitive processes interacted with evolved mechanisms (Beck et al., 1985). The first third of the book on the cognitive approach to anxiety addresses evolved mechanisms of defense. The activation of an evolved defensive response was also central to a landmark behavioral therapy book by Isaac Marks (1987). Beck (2008) also sought to link cognitive processes to neurophysiology, seeking to open the way to understand how cognitive change could produce physiological change and vice versa.

Nonetheless, although many of the newer therapies recognize the importance of understanding mental phenomena in relation to their evolved functions, cognitive behavioral therapy (CBT) emerged in the age of non-physiological computers and computer language, such as "information processing." Information processing became a way to talk and think about how minds reach decisions. But identifying cognition with information processing is problematic. Clearly, computers, DNA, and organic cells are information processing systems, but they do not have cognitions or beliefs. The failure to define cognition separately from information processing and highlight that organic (brains) and non-organic systems (computers) process information quite differently, led to disputes between emotion-focused and cognitive therapists. Zajonc (1980) argued that emotions can be directly, physiologically triggered and do not require cognitive processes to precede them. The cognitive theorist, Richard Lazarus (1981), suggested that these processes were often fused and could not be separated. Zajonc (1984) countered that by saying, "to satisfy this concept of emotion, Lazarus has broadened the definition of cognitive appraisal to include even the most primitive forms of sensory excitation, thus obliterating all distinction between cognition, sensation, and perception" (p. 117).

The issue of whether or not, or the degree to which, cognitive processes are involved in automatic direct physiological reactions remains a complex research area. Many researchers now highlight the complex, multi-level conscious and nonconscious dimensions of processing (Bargh, 2017), and emphasize that these cannot be easily located in either emotion or cognition (LeDoux, 2022). Van der Kolk's (2014) focus on how the "body keeps the score" and Porges' (2011, 2021) concept of neuroception (as an automatic monitoring of threat and safeness) follow on from these debates. They also influence how classical conditioning is construed.

Cognitive therapists highlighted that we are often irrational, suffering from a range of *biases* in attention, attributions of causality, predictions, and perceived implications (sometimes called cognitive distortions). Today, we recognize that some biases are not only generated by acquired beliefs and social contexts but evolved dispositions (Gilbert, 1998). For example, our negativity bias is a form of evolved "better safe than sorry" attending. For example, many animals are highly attuned to threat and will take flight from feeding areas at the slightest sound or movement that could indicate a threat. Losing access to a meal is much less costly than losing one's life! Better safe than sorry is a brain heuristic that can lead to overestimating threat and then, with our new cognitive competencies, becoming locked into loops of threat-focused rumination (Baumeister et al., 2001; Gilbert, 1998; Nesse, 2019; Watkins & Roberts, 2020). Brosschot et al. (2016) point out that "better safe and sorry" is the default mode making animals highly sensitive to threat until they learn safety, that is, learn that certain stimuli are not "harmful" (see also Gilbert, 1993). CFT adds that sensitivity to threat can be shifted not only by learning that stimuli are not harmful or how to cope with them if they are, but also by learning that help is available by turning to, and being helped by, others. This new learning stimulates the vagus and various neurocircuits that evolved along with caring circuits that support specific functions of threat arousal regulation (see Chapter 1, Figure 1.6).

Cognitive therapists highlight the importance of learned, core beliefs that can drive focus. It may be religious or political beliefs that lead us to construe others in a particular way, such as threats or opportunities and thereby to war, but that is only possible because our brain states have the potential to be tuned for tribal violence. A brain state that is oriented to war is one that will also turn off empathy toward others who are going to be harmed by our actions. The war-oriented individual can become callous and may even experience positive affect associated with harming others, called *Schadenfreude* in German. Chimpanzees go to war and will kill chimpanzees from other groups, but they go to war because of interacting strategies, not beliefs. Species like bonobos, which have a very different form of social structure and use sex as a soothing social-bonding process, have never been known to go to war. Had we evolved from that line, we would have been a very different species with a very different and probably far less tragic history. Hence, be it tribal violence, social anxiety, paranoia, or some depressions, each of these factors relates to how we see "the other" as a threat and how we can become locked into threat processing (Watkins & Roberts, 2020). CFT seeks to help people shift from threat processing into empathic-compassion processing (see below) with a different physiological profile.

Psychotherapy and Physiology

Key debates in psychotherapy include topics such as conscious versus nonconscious, emotion versus cognition, acquired belief versus innate disposition, and the focus of this book, psychophysiology and psychotherapy. Central to these debates is the question of whether clinical change requires specific forms of physiological change and, if so, the insight into which physiological changes can help to direct psychotherapy. For example, if we know that some individuals have problems with the autonomic nervous system, particularly the vagus nerve (Petrocchi et al., 2022; Porges, 2021), or neurocircuits underpinning compassion (Kim et al., 2020; Novak et al., 2022; Singer & Engert, 2019) and empathy (Decety & Ickes, 2011; Singer & Engert, 2019), then a range of interventions such as breathing exercises, postures, exposure, imagery, behavior practices, empathy, and compassion facilitation can be aimed at generating and monitoring appropriate psychophysiological change. There are now many studies exploring the physiological impact of compassion training in various forms (Ashar et al., 2021; Weng et al., 2013, 2018). Singer and Engert (2019) compared mindfulness, empathy, and compassion training and found that these trainings have overlapping, but also different, specific neurophysiological impacts suggesting that therapies need to be tailored for specific competencies.

However, for some clients there may be no one-to-one relationships between "mind training" and physiological change. For example, Freud recognized that some clients are fearful or resistant to various motives, emotions, and memories; they engage in experiential avoidance (Hayes, 2019) including avoidance of mindfulness and compassion (Kirby et al., 2019). This may be because compassion work stimulates unprocessed care-linked trauma requiring grief work for the traumas and losses of the past (Gilbert & Simos, 2022). Part of this can be grieving for the unlived life, yearning for a parent who would have provided love, care, joy, and protection (Gilbert, 2023; Knox, 2003). These are important concerns because different trainings such as mindfulness, empathy, and compassion have different psychophysiological effects (Singer & Engert, 2019). Steffen et al. (2021) found that if people did not improve in their heart rate variability with CFT then they were less likely to develop their ability to use compassion to help themselves or achieve change. Given that CFT is rooted in brain state theory (Gilbert, 1984, 1989), three salient questions emerge: (a) to what degree can we work out which physiological mechanisms underpin which mental health difficulties for which individuals, (b) what interventions best target them, and (c) what are the fears, blocks, and resistances to change in these individuals, which can be biological, psychological, and social?

CFT also incorporates a classical conditioning view of emotion regulation where the physiological processes of compassion and caring can act as counters to the physiological processes of threat (see Chapter 1, Figure 1.6). For many years the physiological effects of relaxation training were regarded as the standard counter-conditioning process for the desensitization of anxiety and other mental health conditions, with evidence of effectiveness particularly when combined with other interventions such as exposure and cognitive reappraisal (Barlow et al., 2007). CFT also suggests a different physiological profile from that of relaxation, rooted in the compassion and caring system, which links to creating experiences of safeness (see Chapter 1, Figure 1.6; Gilbert, 1989, 1993, 2007a,b, 2020; Porges & Dana, 2018; Slavich, 2020). The physiological processes that are generated through compassion can help with other threat-based conditioned emotions too. For example, Ferster (1973) noted that threatening and punishing children for being angry can trigger anxiety to internal cues to their own anger, meaning that as they begin to experience anger they switch to anxiety and thus never properly process anger (see Gilbert, 1992, 2007a, 2007b, for discussion). They are handicapped when it comes to conflicts and assertiveness and are prone to be submissive and appeasing or show poor regulation of anxiety or rage (see Gilbert & Irons, 2005, for a review). In such a scenario, learning to recognize and tolerate anger and transform it into helpful assertiveness may be required. Taking a compassion-focused approach can facilitate individuals to experience the physiological arousal of anger but also the regulating processes of the compassion (e.g., vagal nervous activation and the hormone oxytocin's effects) system. In other words, compassion does not seek to get rid of anger but creates the courage and psychophysiological contexts to be able to process, tolerate, and transform it. Creating compassion-based brain states can provide inner psychophysiological contexts for processing many difficult emotions and memories (Gilbert & Simos, 2022).

One therapeutic practice to help bring the threat and compassion psychophysiological processes together can involve clients moving between anger (or other emotions) and compassion mental states, using a two-chair intervention or other means, for exploring the impact of taking a compassion orientation toward one's anger (Bell et al., 2020; Gilbert, 2022a). We can, for example, explore how a compassionate orientation to anger can support acceptance, seeing the vulnerability or hurt that might sit behind anger, and how to generate wise courageous assertiveness. These techniques are similar to acting techniques. We can change our brain states by deliberately, like actors, creating and entering into different characters, exploring thoughts, feelings, and behavioral impulses that make up "versions of self" (Gilbert, 2022a). We can then deliberately shift from a troublesome state and switch into a compassion state and back again.

Another technique to bring the psychophysiological effects of compassion to an exposure program is via imagining a compassionate interaction during exposure to threat (Gilbert & Irons, 2004). Brown et al. (2020) explored the impact of developing and relating to an internal, self-generated compassionate image for people with paranoid beliefs. They used virtual reality to simulate entering a lift and tube train whilst participants envisioned being accompanied by their imagined compassionate coach. This CFT was highly effective. They say:

> The aim is to harness the experience of being nurtured and eventually internalize it, so that a new and distinctive memory is created that can be easily accessed. A compassionate coach can have any identity, but must embody all the qualities of compassion, including strength, warmth, wisdom, and kindness, and should encourage the individual to be kind toward them-self. (Brown et al., 2020, p. 2)

CFT suggests that these processes are also very dependent on the psychophysiological infrastructures that evolved to support them and, hence, can be targets for therapy.

Social Minds

When using a biopsychosocial approach, the psychophysiological mechanisms that can be targets for therapeutic intervention need to be integrated with the social processes. Our brains are constantly co-regulated through social relationships of threat, safeness, and sharing-cooperating (Siegel, 2020; Slavich, 2020). Chapter 1 outlined how evolution created specialized, social mentalities that process different types of social information, allowing for the formation of different types of social role-relationships such as caring, cooperation, competing, and sexuality. Hence different social relationships will impact on the psychophysiology of the brain, particularly, threat, reward, and safeness systems, differently. The challenge of processing these different social roles was a crucial driver for the evolution of human intelligence and ways of thinking about the world and social relationships (Camilleri et al., 2023).

Because human brains are so attuned to interpersonal relationships, the social relationships we are embedded within choreograph what we think and believe about ourselves in relationship to the world. Hence ways of thinking and believing are partly co-created in the social dynamics of relating through the different social mentalities. Siegel (2019, 2020) argued that we need to see our minds as engaged in *information flow between minds*; we are socially embedded in the flow of information, indicating what and how we should think and act. This information flow has major physiological effects too, including epigenetic ones (Slavich, 2020).

Cultural discourse involves creating and regulating people's basic beliefs because they are powerful regulators of motives, emotions, and social (conformist) behaviors. Heath et al. (2001) explored how legends and traditions (including religious beliefs) arise in cultures and become adopted and exchanged in the minds of a group. They pointed out that to adopt a belief system, like a belief in witchcraft, God, *or the power of compassion*, the focus must be on something that is relevant to a person and is transpersonal (affects others). The belief system usually contains messages about types of threat and how to deal with them. The belief system must (a) fit with the ecological needs of the group (e.g., developing beliefs in Gods of the sea is relevant to sea farers but not landlocked people), (b) guide social behaviors and informs rituals, (c) be emotionally textured, and (d) provide a sense of group coherence and belonging.

One function of co-constructed, socially shared, and reinforced belief systems is that they articulate (and sometimes create) fears and threats, offering ways of dealing with threats. Whether we are focused on individual beliefs, group threat-defensive beliefs and behaviors, witchcraft, diseases, or ethnic cleansing, beliefs can take the form of "myths" that orchestrate the defensive/protective behaviors of detect, protect, avoid, subjugate, persecute, and eradicate (Heath et al., 2001). Sometimes these are played out in rituals (e.g., sacrifice) or mob violence. Eidelson and Eidelson (2003) labeled certain beliefs "dangerous" because they accentuate threat focus and reasons to be exploitative and aggressive to others. They are socially reinforced in groups sharing these beliefs. People develop beliefs and styles of thinking that fit and reflect their social worlds, enabling them to disengage, dissociate from, or turn off care-focused mentalities that attend to others' welfare (Zimbardo, 2007, 2015).

Socially constructed core beliefs then can be regulators of our basic, evolved motive processes and the physiological systems that underpin them. These include our vulnerability to threats and regulation of threat processes; what foods are and are not acceptable; how and why we seek status (Anderson et al., 2015); who and for what people are stigmatized (Pinel & Bosson, 2013) and the degree to which groups feel entitled to exploit others for their own benefit (Ho et al., 2012) or be morally caring of others (Dalai Lama, 1995); how and with whom we have sex (Diogo, 2019); what our body shapes should be; and our experiences of body shame (Mills et al., 2022). Just a few hundred years ago, we believed it was acceptable to treat human beings as slaves, put children to work in mines, treat women as inferior to men and beat them for noncompliance (Gilbert, 2019b). Still today, some believe it is acceptable for a religion to ban the use of contraceptives or prohibit homosexuality, threatening people with hell, killing them for noncompliance, and stoning women for adultery. Humans have sacrificed their own children, bound the feet of their daughters sentencing them to a life of pain, and mutilated their genitals—all regulated through socially supported harmful beliefs. Today we live in a world of climate change deniers and those that believe the wealthy have no responsibility to help those that are less fortunate.

As psychotherapists, we must contribute to the understanding of how these beliefs emerge and how to prevent and stop them. This includes beliefs that it is acceptable to spend vast critical human resources on armaments and use them to invade other countries, suppress opposition, and murder, maim, and brutalize tribal and political opponents. Harmful beliefs are a problem not just in the clinic but for all humanity. The challenge is how to create socially supported beliefs that will foster compassion motivation, with the recognition that intention without wisdom can lead to non-compassionate outcomes. Given that so many mental health problems are the result of harmful beliefs arising in harmful cultures, these have to be addressed if we are to make any impact on prevention and assist the vast numbers of people who suffer with mental health problems.

Beliefs also impact the intensity of the motivation maintaining them and the sense of behavioral urgency, as well as the complex feelings and emotions that they express and suppress. Although social sanction, stigma, and shame can change some behaviors, they do not necessarily change people's underlying motives or beliefs. This is why it is fundamental to distinguish shame and guilt as emerging from, and operating within, different social mentalities that have different physiological regulators. Guilt helps us understand and empathically connect with the harm that we do, whereas shame is primarily focused on self-judgment and social presentation and may block "caring" empathic awareness to the harm we cause (see Gilbert, 2022b, pp. 122–163).

The Evolution of Caring Behavior and its Therapeutic Implications

Chapter 1 presented compassion as a derivative of the evolution of caring motivation. As such it has the algorithm of having: (a) feature detectors to pay attention to and engage with signals of distress and suffering which triggers, (b) action responses to try to alleviate and prevent it. Di Bello et al. (2021) showed that when people first engage with suffering, they can have an increase in sadness and a reduction in heart rate variability. However, when they switch to thinking about how to be helpful there is a reduction in sadness and an increase in heart rate variability. Hence the motive to, and the chosen means to be helpful play a crucial role in which brain systems are stimulated when addressing suffering (Kim et al., 2020; Singer & Engert, 2019). Given this, CFT notes that people can pursue cognitive and behavioral change for all kinds of reasons but stimulating compassion motivation creates psychophysiological contexts for that change. For example, pursuing justice out of a desire for vengeance is different from the desire to create a compassionate and caring society. Trying to lose weight because one is angry and ashamed of one's size is different from trying to lose weight because it is important for health, well-being, and a sense of personal control. Positive compassion orientation elicits a supportive, friendly, and encouraging focus.

As outlined in Chapter 1 (see Figure 1.6), the evolution of the attachment processes led to a range of psychophysiological processes that came to regulate threat sensitivity, threat responding, resource-seeking behavior (confidence), and rest and digest modes (feeling safe). Threat operates through the amygdala and sympathetic nervous system, and it is what the individual does and thinks about the threat that determines the outcome. The attachment system introduced a completely new set of psychophysiological systems that, when activated, soothe and balance threat responding (Cassidy & Shaver, 2016; Gilbert, 1989, 2020; Mayseless, 2016; Porges, 2021). As outlined in Chapter 1, it is not just what the individual does but what those around that individual do to support and help them that is crucial. Indeed, most humans in caring relationships will turn to others for emotional support and comfort when they are stressed. Those providing support and caring will be stimulating the vagus-oxytocin-immune regulating systems, which can have profound effects on threat physiological systems (Porges & Dana, 2018; Slavich, 2020). For people who have been traumatized and/or suffer mental health problems, this second threat regulation system for social safeness is less available (Gilbert, 1989, 1993, 2020). CFT therefore targets the care motivational system so that these physiological regulating systems can become available. A key issue concerns the core functions and processes of the caring system (Mayseless, 2016).

CFT has always been significantly informed by attachment theory and attachment therapists (Bowlby, 1969, 1973, 1980; Cassidy & Shaver, 2016; Holmes & Slade, 2017; Mikulincer et al., 2013; Music, 2019, 2022; Shaver et al., 2017; for history see Gilbert, 1984, 1989, 1993, 2020, and Gilbert & Simos, 2022). Bowlby (1969, 1973) outlined three psychological functions of the attachment relationship: (a) to provide a secure base, (b) to develop a safe haven, and (c) to sustain close contact between mother and infant, with continuous awareness of each other's accessibility (this function is called proximity maintenance). CFT has sought to explore and integrate three functions of a secure base and two functions of a safe haven (these are not exclusive) (Gilbert & Simos, 2022). These functions play a very important role in the therapeutic relationship and the therapeutic process in CFT (Carvalho & Matos, 2021; H. Gilbert, 2022).

Secure base functions include (a) encouraging engagement and learning in the world, (b) supporting validation and the ability to understand and regulate one's own mind, while also learning social rules, and (c) providing a source of interpersonal warmth, joy, and positive rewards in relationships through play, shared positive affect (affection, positive mirroring) such that children develop social trust and a positive orientation to others. Since these are all ways to help others (e.g., children) become equipped to navigate the challenges of life, address their needs, and prevent causing harm to self and others, they are essential parts of a compassion-focused orientation. Regarding safe haven, clients can have difficulties in emotion regulation, partly because they are not able to use the attachment-evolved emotion regulation systems (see Chapter 1, Figure 1.6).

Matos et al. (2013, 2015) and Steindl, Matos et al. (2018) have shown that memories of a lack of social safeness and warmth are associated with problems of depression, shame, and self-criticism. Therefore, the functions of a secure base and safe haven conveyed through experiences of safeness, social trust, and therapeutic warmth, can be crucial for therapy (H. Gilbert, 2022; Seewald & Rief, 2022). These provide the context (internalized caring other) to begin to experience the psychophysiological processes of caregiving and care receiving, which provide the platform

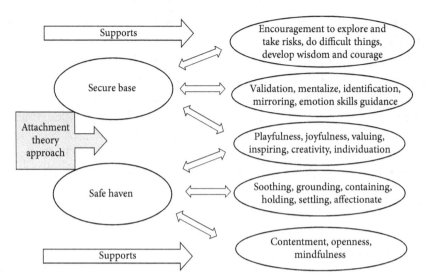

Figure 10.1 Some typical functions associated with secure base and safe haven.
Note: Adapted from Gilbert (2022b). © Paul Gilbert

to help clients to begin to develop new ways of experiencing themselves and thereby create sources of emotion regulation and prosocial behavior to self and others.

Figure 10.1 offers a brief guide into the different therapeutic aspects of a secure base and safe haven. For example, in addition to providing interpersonal textures such as therapeutic warmth and empathy, therapists are a source of information (psychoeducation), which carries the framework to engage with difficult situations. Therapists provide a source of validation, mentalization, and emotion regulation skills. Therapists are also concerned with generating positive affect, sources of joy, "openness to the new," and a sense of personal creativity and coping (Craske et al., 2019). Friendly verbal and non-verbal communication, which can have powerful impacts on brain systems such as the amygdala and autonomic nervous system, can be crucial for creating the context for a sense of safeness, enabling the integration of new learning. Therapists can also guide clients in their personal use of "safe haven" techniques that target breathing, posture, use of imagery, and other mechanisms.

Courage and Wisdom at the Core of Compassion

In many ways the processes of a secure base and safe haven support the courage and wisdom necessary to engage compassionately with suffering and take helpful actions.

Courage

Being sensitive to and able to detect sources of suffering and being motivated to do something about them are central to compassion but not sufficient. In the detection of distress or suffering, we are immediately stimulating our threat system processes, because we are approaching suffering, and the first movement is always stressful and stimulates the threat system. We may become emotionally distressed and overwhelmed by our sympathetic reactions of anger, anxiety, and sadness and consequently withdraw (N. Eisenberg & Eggum, 2009; N. Eisenberg et al., 2015). Clearly, we and our clients will have to manage our own and their fear and distress to work with suffering and threat (Di Bello et al., 2021). In a way, these moments demand courage, that is, the individual *knowingly and purposefully engages in risk to pursue the helpful whilst remaining able to tolerate the aversive experiences in doing so.* Not only did the pursuit of vaccines for COVID-19 require dedicated scientists, but many volunteered to test a vaccine without knowing whether it would work or whether they would get the virus and if so could become seriously ill. That is an extraordinary example of courageous compassion in the search for wisdom for the benefit of others. People who engage in risky behavior but are unaware of the risks would not be regarded as courageous.

Courage is clearly different from impulsive behavior and recklessness. For example, jumping into a fast-flowing river to save somebody if I cannot swim myself is reckless and could end up getting us both killed. At times, psychotherapists can be triggered into impulsive rescuing behavior that is not helpful. Courage may involve altruistic sacrifice when we recognize that we have to give up some of our resources and privileges to help those less fortunate than ourselves (Ricard, 2015). Indeed, Zimbardo (2015) has highlighted the issue of what he calls heroic compassion.

When we treat *ourselves* with compassion, we need the same psychology, which is the preparedness to engage with aspects of our lives or minds that are causing our suffering. Rachman (1990) highlighted the fact that engaging in psychotherapy and self-change are courageous acts and involve building courage. In psychotherapy, client and therapist must be open to discover things in themselves that they may not like (shame), and expose themselves to processes that frighten them, ranging from phobias to trauma memories. Courage may be needed when they (and we) have to change our lives, such as leaving a toxic marriage or job, or beginning a course of frightening treatment for cancer. Courage is required when we must engage in life changes that cause significant grief, such as the death of somebody we love. Again, there are no simple processes underpinning courage. Some people can show immense physical courage but struggle with emotional courage and with tolerating painful mental states, such as deep grief or vulnerability. In a group of veterans in therapy, one of them noted, "I had the courage to die but not to cry." Some people can appear to show immense emotional courage, for example coping with grief, but they are actually in a process of emotional defense, and it may be years later that the inhibited grief process begins to emerge.

Wisdom

There have been many definitions of wisdom but, generally in CFT, wisdom relates to the acquisition and use of knowledge to gain and apply an experience to an intention. It is one of the processes that would be very difficult to pin down with physiological systems. Wisdom is also the recognition that we do not have the wisdom we need to achieve the ends we wish. Although we can commit ourselves to acquiring the knowledge and experience, we need that pursuit to be wise as well. Repeatedly practicing poor techniques will not help us. Wisdom can apply to any skilful task, such as how to be a good footballer or coach, chef, or brain surgeon, how to treat one's unruly children, and how to work with one's own mind. Wisdom can come from "wise" and trusted others, persistent practice, and determination. We can acquire wisdom about the external world and how to interact with it. This depends upon drawing on the accumulated knowledge of humans and the science that is available to us. We can also acquire wisdom about our own internal worlds (minds and bodies), how and why they work the way they do, and how we can work with them to bring out the helpful and not the harmful.

Mental wisdom depends on both. When it comes to understanding the nature and causes of our distress, CFT highlights that wisdom requires us to understand what it is to be human, to understand our origins, and to recognize how our brains and bodies have been built by DNA. Wisdom requires us to accept that our brains and bodies are capable of generating mental states that many of us would not want. Our bodies and brains have been built for us, not by us. Much of what we are capable of is not our fault and not our own doing. This is an important aspect of wisdom that enables us to become mindfully aware of the contents of our mind and then make wise and compassionate choices on how to act with and on what arises. We learn not to fight with our minds any more than a sailor fights with the sea. Rather, we learn how to navigate safely.

Our distressing and harmful states of mind may well have had adaptive functions over millions of years, in some contexts but now, with our human new brain competencies and potentially harmful social cultures, the same states of mind can become sources of great distress and harm (Gilbert, 1989, 2019b, 2021; Nesse, 2019). We discuss with clients that no one practices having panic attacks, no one seeks out training to have suicidal depressions. In CFT, psychoeducation requires discussing with the client the nature of the evolved brain and highlighting how our brains are actually very tricky because of how they have evolved. Understanding this supports a compassionate, non-blaming framework enabling people to stand back and become observers of the workings of a nature-built "unchosen" mind, sculpted by the social circumstances of our lives. This offers insight into the fact that we are a set of complex, interacting, and at times conflicting brain circuits serving motives and emotions. Our sense of an individual "self" is a way of bringing some coherence to these complex processes but, in itself, this sense of self is an illusion (Hood, 2011). Being open to these propositions and allowing them to resonate within oneself is an example of pursuing courageous wisdom.

The Flows of Compassion

All psychological processes have interpersonal flow. For example, we can be angry, anxious, or friendly to others, they to us, and we to ourselves. The sending and receiving of information relating to different emotions and motives is crucial to social, motive, and relation formation (called social mentalities; Gilbert, 1989, 2019a; Chapter 1, this volume). Hence, we can be compassionate to others, they to us, and we to ourselves. Although the focus will differ, the competencies are fairly similar (Gilbert, 2009; Gilbert et al., 2017). For example, the compassion I have for you will be linked to my capacity for empathic engagement; the experience you have of my compassion to you will be linked to how (empathically) receptive you are to my caring for you. It will depend upon how you read my motivations and whether you see them as genuine or not. The compassion I have for myself will also depend on my empathic insights into my own mind of memories, feelings, desires, and needs, their origins and regulations, and an understanding of what will help me. These flows are also interdependent, in the sense that the more compassionate care we experienced in early life, the more compassionate we tend to be to ourselves and others (Gilbert & Simos, 2022). There is now good evidence that being compassionate to others, being open and receptive to the compassion from others, and being self-compassionate all have very powerful physiological effects (for reviews, see Kim et al., 2020; Seppälä et al., 2017; Singer & Engert, 2019; Weng et al., 2018). There is also good evidence that the compassion we received in childhood and our attachment security lays the foundations for being compassionate to self and others later in life (Shaver et al., 2017).

Fears, Blocks, and Resistances

Despite the many benefits of compassion, some people can be resistant to and fearful of compassion (Gilbert et al., 2011, 2022b; Gilbert & Mascaro, 2017; Kirby et al., 2019; Matos et al., 2017) and of the therapist (Steindl et al., 2021). Indeed, much of CFT involves working through fears, blocks, and resistances to facilitate and gradually enable clients to access the psychophysiological benefits of utilizing compassion motivation systems (Steindl et al., 2022).

In regard to the flows of compassion, one dimension that can impact on people's preparedness to be compassionate to others is that caring and compassion are expensive to dispense, and therefore we have built-in, evolved tendencies to favor some individuals over others. We are more likely to be compassionate to those we are genetically linked to, those we are in (friendly) relation with, and those we identify to be like us with the same values, in contrast to those we perceive as genetically different, strangers, and those we do not like or who we see as enemies. For this reason, we cannot rely simply on automatic, emotional dimensions of empathy for compassion. Rather, we must use our new brain competencies to bridge beyond the limitations evolution has built into our care and compassion (Gilbert, 2019a; Kirby, 2022; Loewenstein & Small, 2007). It is one of the human tragedies that we have insight into what would prevent suffering in many parts of the world (for example to alleviate poverty or provide clean water), but we do not take the actions needed. Today, the poor international sharing of vaccines is one such example.

The flows of compassion are important for another reason, which is that compassionate concern, courage, and wisdom often flow from others. One of the functions of a secure base is to provide and encourage the child to explore the world, take risks, and learn. The giving of courage through a relationship, enabling us to face things that are difficult, is a major process of compassion and CFT (Mikulincer et al., 2013). An over-focus on self-compassion risks undervaluing the importance others have to us and for us. This is why helping clients build relational skills is so important (Luyten et al., 2020). In regard to self-compassion, one of the most courageous and wise compassionate actions is, at appropriate times, to turn to others for help and not try to cope alone. Others can be sources of resources and wisdom. There is a large literature on the benefits of the emotional and practical support of others in helping us cope with the ups and downs of life (Taylor, 2011). Being able to experience "receiving" and gratitude and appreciation has strong links to mental health and well-being (Wood et al., 2010). While the processes affecting gratitude are complex (Forster et al., 2022), an inability to experience gratitude can become a therapeutic issue.

Counter to an ability to turn to others with gratitude, some individuals can experience what Bowlby (1980) called compulsive self-reliance. These people tend to be fearful or resistant to the help of others. This resistance is sometimes shame based, sometimes mistrust based, and sometimes linked with avoidant-attachment issues. Compulsive self-reliance can be acquired in many ways, such as from parents who were critical of or rejecting of a child's needs for help, making it essentially a shame issue. A different form of this involves a fear of being a burden to others and an accompanying sense of guilt. Another problem with the inability to accept or acknowledge help can be that some individuals loath showing gratitude and appreciation when they do receive help.

An inability to show appreciation to those who have been helpful can arise from narcissism and can cause serious difficulties in relationships (Solom et al., 2017). As bosses, narcissistic persons are experienced as miserly with praise and rarely show appreciation of the people who work for them. Another variant on the inability to feel gratitude has been identified in object relations theory and is related to envy (Fonagy, 2018). There are different dynamics here (Gilbert, 1992). One form is related to the recognition that one's needs can only be met by "another" who may or may not give the care one needs. In response to this lack of control and painful "dependency," the individual seeks to control the person that they need, sometimes aggressively. This has been offered as one explanation for why men seek to aggressively control women, because they cannot cope with being dependent and vulnerable to rejection or being "not wanted/chosen." It is precisely because the choice of giving or not is in the hands of the giver, and that this giving is not cost free to the giver, that gratitude arises. It has been noted that in some cultures the killing of animals was accompanied with gratitude and the spirit of the animal was thanked. In Western society and from traditions that go back to Adam and Eve and to capitalism, animals are regarded simply as objects to be used regardless of the suffering we cause. We live in a society that constantly undermines and minimizes the importance of gratitude. This dynamic results in an objectification of the other, seeing the other as an object existing for the satisfaction of the self, an object stripped of all "feeling;" this dynamic can drive envious control and anger.

Inhibition to the flows of compassion can have many sources. One is linked to shame. The individuals are ashamed to admit what it is they need help with, for fear it might elicit social sanction and contempt. Resistance can rise because people misunderstand the concept of compassion. They link compassion to softness and weakness and value competitiveness and being strong over compassion (McEwan & Minou, 2022). This is important because some of the definitions of compassion on the Internet are unhelpful. Therefore, CFT gives clear examples of compassion indicating its courage and wisdom and explains why compassion is not to be confused with western concepts such as love. The understanding of compassion as flow, therefore, indicates multiple complexities in the reciprocal dynamics of compassion, which are often essential subtleties in the therapeutic journey. Hence, there are considerable complexities to the physiological "mind-to-mind" interplays that operate in these compassion-based interactions.

Last but not least are the fears, blocks, and resistances to self-compassion and self-care, which are directly related to mental health problems (Gilbert et al., 2011; Kirby et al., 2019). Fears of compassion to the self can be linked to a sense of not deserving, being overwhelmed, and/or feeling weak and unhelpful. There is considerable evidence that difficulties in being self-compassionate arise from how others (especially but not only in childhood) have treated the self compassionately or not (see Gilbert, 2022c, for a review). Matos et al. (2017) found that shame-based trauma memories were positively correlated with fears of being compassionate to the self, while memories of warmth and safeness negatively correlated with fears of compassion. There is considerable evidence that shame-based self-criticism, acquired from relationships with others, underpins many forms of mental health problems and is a major inhibitor of the ability to use compassion and hence the care-based psychophysiological mechanisms for self-regulation (see Gilbert, 2022c, for a review).

Compassion Is a Multifaceted Process

For CFT, compassion is a complex, multifaceted, multi-textured motivational process that is rooted in evolved caring systems, but more complex, cognitive processes are necessary to experience and engage compassion (see Chapter 1, Figure 1.8). Second, it is important to see that, as a motive, compassion has a stimulus-response algorithm of "if A, then do B" that involves: [A] a stimulus-sensitivity, that triggers [B] an appropriate action. In earlier versions of this model, these two processes were labeled differently (attributes and skills in Gilbert, 2009; and then first and second psychology in Gilbert, 2017), but it is preferable to use the standard behavioral language of a stimulus-response algorithm. Different competencies are needed for these two different aspects of the algorithm (Di Bello et al., 2021; Gilbert, 2009, 2020). Hence, we can distinguish the psychophysiological competencies that help us to be stimulus-sensitive to "distress and need," move toward, engage, tolerate sympathetic distress, and empathically understand suffering, rather than be overwhelmed, turn away, dissociate, or deny it. Second, once engaging with suffering (which can be stressful), we can explore the courage and wisdom necessary for appropriate action, and act. Poulin (2017) pointed out that people may be aware of suffering, know what would help, and even be motivated to help, but still do not act. These are not uncommon problems. For example, we may know that we would become healthier if we ate better and less and exercised more. We may be motivated (want) to be healthy and yet do not translate that motivation into actual behaviors. Indeed, behavior change, particularly if it involves "habits of practice," has its own regulators beyond simple motivation and good intentions. Because care-compassion is rooted in a basic stimulus-response algorithm, these different aspects should be simply labeled what they are: engagement and action. "The Compassion Engagement and Action Scales" were developed to measure the subcomponents and processes supporting engagement and action (Gilbert et al., 2017).

Identifying the Subcomponents

An overview of the subcomponents regarding engagement and action is given in Figure 10.2. CFT has suggested six competencies for helping us engage with suffering and the causes of suffering (inner circle), and six to respond—to try to alleviate suffering and set about prevention (outer circle). These were not designed to be exhaustive but serve as heuristics and therapeutic guides. When set against

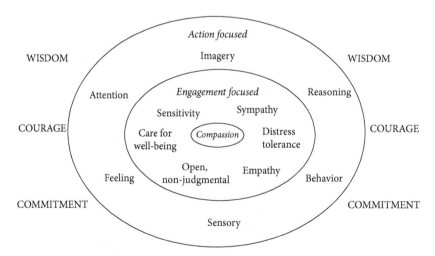

Figure 10.2 Domains for the therapeutic process.

Note: Adapted from Gilbert (2009) with permission from Little Brown. © Paul Gilbert the framework of our evolved tricky brain and the processes of self-awareness and self-regulation, these competencies give rise to the wisdom and courage to address suffering and commit to doing so, and to live to be (mindfully) helpful, not harmful. The six competencies supporting engagement and the six competencies supporting responding and action can be directed toward ourselves or others; we can also experience others directing them toward ourselves. Figure 10.2 is, therefore, relevant for the three flows of compassion. Hence, there are three different scales that measure compassion action and engagement: one for self-compassion, one for compassion toward others, and one for compassion from others.

Six Competencies for Engagement

The twelve competencies discussed below are considered as guides rather than set in stone. They constantly interact and support and build each other. The emphasis is on helping clinicians distinguish between (a) the processes that are necessary for individuals to be able to move toward and engage, and (b) those that are focused on what is helpful, because they depend on each other. Although compassion itself is a motive, the first competency explores the motive to consider and understand compassion as a way to engage with one's own mind and the minds of others.

Motives to Cultivate Compassion

The first stage of therapeutic engagement is to cultivate the desire to (compassionately) care for one's own well-being and that of others. Motivational interviewing has many recommendations that follow on from counselling micro skills (Miller & Rollnick, 2012; Steindl, Kirby et al., 2018). It includes the importance of developing a supportive and collaborative therapeutic relationship, agreeing on goals and shared purpose, exploring reasons for change and any ambivalence, and focusing on change talk and the "hows" of change. These frameworks are important for CFT in ensuring that people understand what compassion means in CFT, as it is easily confused with kindness, softness, weakness, indulgence, or letting oneself off the hook (McEwan & Minou, 2022). Clients can be invited to think about how they would respond if a good friend was frightened to go to a hospital and was distressed. The therapist guides the client to see that they would be sensitive to their friend's distress *and* would be thinking about how to help them. They might consider going with them because having support when we're frightened helps us and encourages us. From here the therapist is able to highlight the importance of sensitivity allied with empathic action. The therapist can explore how the client can apply those processes (empathic sensitivity to distress plus empathic action) to themselves, including how open they would be to the help of others and what resistances or ambivalence they might have. The therapist highlights the importance of courage and wisdom, thus avoiding confusions about the "weakness" or "softness" of compassion.

While people with psychopathic difficulties can lack caring motivation, it may be possible to stimulate caring (Ribeiro da Silva et al., 2021). Although we have feature detectors that alert us to signals of distress and threat, for various reasons we may deny, minimize, justify, dissociate, or turn away from them. Apart from misunderstanding the nature of compassion as a therapy process (McEwan & Minou, 2022; Steindl et al., 2021), there are many reasons for the fears, blocks, and resistances to compassion: (a) compassion may trigger distress that overwhelms people with personal distress (N. Eisenberg & Eggum, 2009); (b) compassion may stimulate unprocessed grief or anger from early attachment experiences that are coded in the care system; (c) people may be ashamed of the source of their distress (e.g., sexual abuse, substance abuse) and not wish to reveal or engage with it; or (d) people may feel they don't deserve compassion, particularly if they misunderstand it. People may see helping as too costly, that is, one has to give up too much to help others (Kirby et al., 2019). Another obstacle is that signals of distress and suffering may be positively experienced, as in vengeance or even (horror) entertainment. Therefore, clarity around the algorithm and definition of compassion, with the use of specific examples, can be essential (see Gilbert & Simos, 2022, pp. 243–247).

Attention Sensitivity (Awareness)

Once clients begin to engage with their difficulties, CFT, like many therapies, helps clients to become more attentive to the triggers and the nature of their distress and to monitor what is going on in their minds. As a general process, this can link to forms of mindfulness (Gilbert & Choden, 2013). There is considerable work now on the nature of attentional bias, particularly to threat, for individuals with mental health difficulties. Individuals with anxiety and depression show an elevated sensitivity to threat, whereas those who are impulsive or psychopathic show deficient threat sensitivity (MacLeod et al., 2019). Psychodynamic approaches help people become more aware and sensitive to mental contents that may be outside of consciousness (Ellenberger, 1970). Cognitive therapy targets consciously available selective attentional and reasoning biases directly, by guiding clients to pay attention to the flow of their automatic thoughts and beliefs (Beck et al., 1979). Embodied therapies guide clients to pay attention to changes in their body, and behavior therapies guide clients to attend to their behaviors and their consequences. In addition, CFT invites clients to think about some of the (often thwarted) motives that may underpin their distress. A client may come to recognize that "I was really upset when I didn't get the job *because* I so wanted the job and had pinned my hopes for the future on it." In CFT, helping people understand the "because" aspects of one's distress is important. Developing sensitivity to the nature and form of suffering prepares the client to pay attention, notice, and engage with indicators of suffering and their causes. Again, fears, blocks, and resistances can begin to emerge at this point of expanding attention sensitivity and awareness.

Sympathy

As we become more attentive and attuned to the experience of suffering, we will be "moved" by it. The way we are moved, our personal reaction, is called a sympathetic reaction. There has been some confusion that sympathy is not helpful, but there is now considerable research showing that sympathy is an important personal reaction to the experiences of our own and other sentient minds (N. Eisenberg et al., 2015). For example, imagine a friend who just received a diagnosis of cancer. We could experience multi-faceted, sympathetic personal distress reactions such as feelings of anger, anxiety, sadness, and hope for them. We might notice reactions such as wanting to immediately reach out to them or close down. Sympathy reactions (our distress at our own and others' distress) can give rise to personal distress, which can result in wanting to push away, deny, and cut off from suffering (N. Eisenberg & Eggum, 2009). CFT fosters the ability to experience the multiple textures of distress of our sympathetic reactions, such as anger, anxiety, sadness, disgust, etc., and still engage with the courage and wisdom that is essential for compassion. Crucially then, CFT helps people to build a compassionate mind that will enable engagement with the personal distress of sympathetic reactions and reduce avoidance. Sympathy can be linked to positive emotions, as in the concept of sympathetic joy in the Buddhist traditions where the good that falls to other people brings us joy (rather than envy).

Distress Tolerance

Distress tolerance, in contrast to avoidance, is central to many therapies. Our new brain competencies enable us to have a new type of "knowing awareness" (see Chapter 1). For example, we can know we grow old, lose functions, get sick and injured, and will die; we can recognize the suffering entailed. Having a mind with this type of self-awareness greatly adds to our potential for tolerating distress. Distress tolerance will, therefore, need to engage both with direct raw experiences of the emotion of suffering and with the distress that arises from cognitive knowing awareness of the implications of our difficulties. Many therapies have various procedures for helping people develop distress tolerance, ranging from gradual exposure, to processes of reappraisal, to developing new meaning about the nature of suffering.

For clients who are concerned about engaging to develop distress tolerance, motivational interviewing (as above) can again be very useful in helping to build clarity about how and why developing tolerance would be helpful. Clients who believe that "engaging to build tolerance" will be unhelpful or overwhelming can be guided in small steps to explore distress tolerance using compassion grounding that may be challenging but not overwhelming. If clients get overwhelmed, they may distrust the therapist. Common examples of distress tolerance include tolerating anxiety when treating phobias, panic, or agoraphobia. These need to be wisely experienced in a gradient.

CFT suggests that recruiting the care-motivational system with its physiological infrastructures (the vagus and oxytocin), which evolved in part to regulate the threat system, will make the process of distress tolerance easier—reducing the chances of dropping out of therapy. Additionally, this process helps build transformative frameworks for the integration of the experience. Tolerance must be understood to be more than just "grin and bear it," but rather a wise way to facilitate one's body to process and work with the distress one is seeking to tolerate.

Empathy

Empathy is a crucial component of all caring relationships including therapeutic relationships, as well as the ability to mindfully understand oneself. It matures and unfolds in a series of stages (Hoffman, 1990). Its early forms are simply resonance where, for example, one baby in a nursery cries, so others start crying. Watching a sad film, we feel sad along with the characters and plot, and this can happen despite the fact that we know it is all acted. Stimulus characteristics are so strong as to override that awareness. However, if the acting is poor, you may not get that empathy-connection or impact, highlighting the automaticity and stimulus specificity of some forms of empathy. Gradually, empathy develops with our cognitive competencies (such as theory of mind; Frith & Frith, 2005), self–other differentiation, and forms of mentalizing (Luyten et al., 2020). These are competencies that people with autism spectrum problems can struggle with (Baron-Cohen, 2011).

The empathic process is commonly linked to emotion contagion or resonance and second to a more cognitive, effortful, imaginal process called perspective taking (Decety & Ickes, 2011). Emotional resonance is when we directly experience (to some degree) the feelings and desires of another mind. Empathy must be distinguished from processes such as projection, overidentification, sympathy, self–other fusion, and other interpersonal processes (Decety & Ickes, 2011; N. Eisenberg et al., 2015; Hoffman, 1990; Luyten et al., 2020; Nickerson, 1999). Empathy for others' distress must be identified as arising in the other and not the self. If we feel sad listening to a sad story, we are experiencing their sadness rather than our own. Krol and Bartz (2021) reviewed and explored how this relates to what is called "self-concept clarity" (SCC) that supports self–other differentiation. Low SCC is associated with personal distress and withdrawal in the face of others' distress whereas higher SCC is associated with engagement and helping behavior. This is clearly important for therapists as well as clients.

If people can tolerate what arises when they empathically engage with suffering, they become able to develop deeper empathic insights into the nature, forms, and causes of suffering, and what will be helpful. Perspective-taking involves an effortful, deliberate process of working out what might be happening in the mind of another and what might be helpful. SCC is important here too because there is a difference between imagining what we would feel in the other person's situation compared to stepping into their shoes and imagining what they are feeling, wanting, or experiencing, what might have got them there, and what would be helpful for *them*. There are some experiences that we know we can only empathize with via careful listening and "feeling into," such as for example, a man empathizing with a woman's experience of pregnancy and having a baby. Many clinicians have acknowledged that they didn't emotionally understand depression until they had a serious episode themselves, indicating that personal experience affects our texturing perspective taking.

To help perspective taking, I would sometimes sit in the client's chair, just before they arrived and imagine being them and receiving therapy from me, to try to enable empathic connectedness. However, these are only aides to empathy because misunderstandings can be easily introduced. Group therapy seeks to create conditions in which individuals can become more interested in both giving and receiving empathic engagement. In addition, people can find being compassionately empathic to things they are ashamed about difficult because the natural tendency is to push away and condemn rather than to understand and engage. Hence, helping people develop empathic sensitivity to complex depressions, trauma, shame, or for criminal acts can be difficult but important. Compassion is not about letting oneself "off the hook" but rather involves courageously and wisely engaging the causes of one's behavior. The study of the neuroscience of empathy has accelerated (Decety & Ickes, 2011; Singer & Engert, 2019). We know that our brain circuits for empathy light up dramatically when we identify suffering in somebody we associate with but light up much less in somebody on an opposing team or in somebody we do not like (Hein et al., 2010). Currently, there have been no studies looking into what happens to empathic circuits in the brain as therapists interact with clients they like or perhaps do not like so much, but these are processes that affect outcomes (Vivino, 2009).

How a therapist uses empathy (e.g., reflective, predictive, connective) is also crucial. For example, therapists can be empathic in recognizing emotions that clients are unable to process (e.g., a client who is locked into sadness may not be able to process rage). Some trauma clients describe trauma but without emotion. Helping them to connect emotion to the trauma memory is important and may require repeated empathic reflections with a particular pacing and voice tone. For example, a client relates often being hit and sent to their room. The therapist reflects that that was a very lonely and frightening experience for them. The client dismisses it as something they "just had to get on with." The therapist empathically notes this is a problem in processing emotion in that memory and when opportunities arise returns to it with a gentle soft voice tone again reflecting the fear and loneliness. Over the weeks the client begins to respond with more emotion and gradually becomes in touch with that loneliness that might also be associated with anger and grieving. However, this process may require repeated empathic engagement, with particular voice tones and a slowing down in speech, to enable the client to experience the empathy from the therapist. The way therapists use empathy in terms of voice tones, pacing, silences, reflections, and anticipations is a part of complex therapeutic skills.

Nonjudgment

Nonjudgment is related to tolerance and acceptance together. Indeed, acceptance is difficult without tolerance. As we develop empathic wisdom into the nature of our minds, we do not fight or criticize ourselves for what arises and what we are experiencing but develop the courage to accept it. Acceptance does not mean resignation and doing nothing. The more engaged with suffering we are, the more we will want to alleviate and prevent it. For example, a client might notice self-criticism arising but crucially not argue with it and not become critical of being critical. Rather, the issue is to notice, accept, and switch attention, becoming aware of the fear of rejection that may be driving self-criticism and comprehending what is likely to be helpful. An example of this is creating an inner compassionate dialogue (Gilbert & Simos, 2022).

Six Competencies for Action

As we develop the ability to engage with and make sense of suffering, we need courage and wisdom for what to actually do about the suffering. This can range from forms of acceptance to radical action. Switching into the response function of the compassion algorithm requires changes in attention, thinking, actions-behaviors, and the emotions-feelings elicited by thinking about and taking action. Preparing and developing the competencies for actions also involves guided practices. Importantly, we may be able and motivated to take action but still not act (Poulin, 2017). Many of us may have experienced this when wanting to get fit and lose weight. We know how to exercise or how to design a healthful diet, but we do not actually do it. Behavior change can be difficult to initiate and maintain (Heino et al., 2021). The six competencies outlined here are only possible steps toward behavior change and finding ways for people to practice and maintain them is part of the therapeutic challenge. Motivational interviewing can be extremely valuable to help people with behavior change (Hettema et al., 2005) and cultivating compassion (Steindl, Kirby et al., 2018).

Short-term changes in behavior are relatively easy to achieve with motivated individuals but can be difficult to sustain. In a systematic review, Kwasnicka et al. (2016) identified the range of processes that contribute to sustaining and maintaining behavior change. These include trusting one's ability to change, knowledge of how to change, enjoying the benefits from change, changing with others or gaining social support for change, and opportunities to regularly be monitored for change.

Attention

Clients are guided to explore the nature of attention by, for example, moving attention around the body. This enables us to recognize that *what* we pay attention to becomes clearer, larger, and more focused in the mind, but also that we lose awareness of *that* to which we are not paying attention. Sometimes it is most important to note what our moods or negative biases have pushed out of attention; that is, we can draw attention to what is not in mind, rather than just what is in mind. Clients therefore recognize that attention is like a zoom lens that can be moved about, and this movement transforms our awareness.

There is a large literature on the value of learning mindfulness and becoming attentive and aware of the nature of one's mind in psychotherapy (Michalak et al., 2019). CFT focuses on how to use our attention awareness and mindfulness to switch our attention to the helpful. Maintaining attention on just the sympathetic and empathic engagement with suffering, and its causes, can lead to feeling overwhelmed and resuming avoidance (Gilbert et al., 2017). While it is important that clients feel empathically listened to, which is the beginning of a healing process, attention also needs to focus on "what is likely to be helpful." This involves learning what to bring to mind. For example, Craske et al. (2019) have developed behavior therapies for depression that invite people to remember, focus, and pay attention to past experiences of positive events and successes. The basic question then is: what would be useful for people to bring into mind to help with this event, moment, or mental state? CFT guides people to the importance of attention and attention switching and invites the client to practice this re-directing of attention in the therapy session.

Imagery

Guided imagery is well-used in many therapies, spiritual traditions, and development contexts (e.g., sport). Although some people can struggle with imagery, suffering what is called aphantasia (Zeman et al., 2016), imagery is used in many ways for many different functions and is an essential component in cognitive behavior and other therapies (Saulsman et al., 2019). Exploring people's imagery can be crucial in uncovering how they engage with suffering, and the kinds of images that might trigger memories that could make some situations feel overwhelming. Learning to switch attention to what is helpful can involve bringing into mind compassionate imagery in those contexts.

For change processes, we can use imagery to run scenarios in one's mind about certain actions and ways of thinking and explore how helpful they are likely to be. This is related to if-then thinking: "if I was to do X, then maybe Y would happen, but if I was to do K, then maybe J would happen." We have the ability to imagine the future, a future that may be a few minutes, weeks, months, or years away. In this way, we can anticipate that something might be difficult now, but will later have helpful payoffs. If we cannot imagine "what might be helpful" and "imagine doing or becoming that," then change may become difficult. Clients may be able to imagine many helpful things but then feel they cannot do them. Here, imagery might be directed to breaking things down step-by-step and making each step possible. Hence, therapists might say things like "let's imagine this . . ." or "suppose you were to imagine that . . ."

Imagery also has specific physiological effects (e.g., sexual imagery). Hence, CFT also uses imagery specifically to stimulate the care social mentality and thereby trigger its psychophysiological subcomponents, as a way to reorganize the mind. Clients are guided to engage in compassionate imagery, where they may imagine themselves at their compassionate best and focus on those qualities of compassion (Gilbert & Simos, 2022). It is often better to focus on very precise behavior that the client can practice each day. For example, invite the client to choose a top compassionate competency such as patience or friendliness and then to see how they can practice that one competency each day. Another way of using imagery is to image oneself in different ways (e.g., as a coping self, a courageous self, a wise self). These practices have been used in studies to enhance performance, such as in sport, artistic performance, and in therapy, to good effect (see Gilbert & Basran, 2018, for a review). The therapist checks on how imagery impacts the body: "When you imagine that, what do you notice in your body? What does your 'face' want to say/express?"

Clients can be invited to practice compassionate relating imagery, where they imagine interacting with another compassionate mind that is completely accepting and compassionate toward them. It is important to advise clients that they may not see any clear pictures; they may have just a sense of their compassion image and maybe a sense of the sorts of voice tones in which they dialogue with the other. Also, they can try to feel themselves into the intention, into their compassion image, into its basic motive. They may focus on different sensory qualities, such as voice tone, a general sense of "presence," a sense of warmth and physical closeness, or a sense of protection, without any clear visual representation of a compassionate other. They may explore the impact that imagining receiving compassion has on their body and mental state. Crucially, the therapist constantly explores the fears, blocks, and resistances that arise during these guided-discovery journeys (see H. Gilbert, 2022).

Reasoning

We can use our new brain competencies to problem solve; reasoning and imagining are intimately linked. For example, we used our new brain reasoning competencies to develop vaccines for COVID-19. But we can also use our reasoning to explore how we are thinking/appraising within ourselves, coming to conclusions and decisions about ourselves as social agents able to pursue goals and needs (or not). Rooted in the Greek Stoic traditions, cognitive therapies highlight the importance of helping people pay attention to *what* they think about and to *the way* they pay attention and are thinking. CBT uses Socratic dialogues as a key process for guided discovery. People can explore the origins of their beliefs, reflect on their helpfulness or unhelpfulness today, and consider what changes would be useful. CFT utilizes many basic CBT techniques. However, once again, CFT suggests that these processes can be very different according to the motivational state. People who are in high threat or competitive states of mind tend to reason and reflect differently from those who are in compassion states of mind. Hence, deliberately generating a compassionate state of mind will have an impact on these cognitive behavioral interventions (Gilbert & Basran, 2018). Clients practice various exercises where they can explore how an angry mind reasons, how an anxious mind reasons, how a hopeful mind reasons, and how a compassionate mind reasons. This offers them the insight that reasoning is textured by these other processes, not just by logic. Therefore, the deliberate intention to create compassionate mind states will impact on how we reason, and how we reason will impact on compassionate mind states.

Reasoning is supported by knowledge. Part of CFT reasoning is integrating insight into the nature of the tricky brain and recognizing just how many of our difficult brain states are being generated by processes and algorithms we never chose. To be compassionate to ourselves and others requires basic knowledge of our minds, hence the importance of psychoeducation in CFT.

Behavior

Behavior therapies highlight the importance of engaging in actions as ways to learn, internalize processes, change behavior, and build helpful habits. It does not matter how much we know about a car; if we don't drive, we will never get any good at driving. Changing behaviors has powerful impacts on changing physiology. There is a huge literature on the importance of behavioral interventions such as direct exposure and practicing different skills that are enacted in everyday scenarios. CFT draws heavily from that scientific literature on the importance of turning intentions into actual behaviors, and highlighting the need for clients to develop the courage and wisdom to pursue behavior change and maintain it (Poulin, 2017). Hence, it is important that therapists agree on a set of "doable" behavioral practices. In the early stages, behavioral practices may need to be practiced in the therapy session. The client can explore fears, blocks, and resistances in that moment. Like many therapies, CFT encourages clients to conduct their own behavioral experiments, becoming innovators for their own change process. New insights and ideas can be translated by the therapist into "how would you bring that into your life? What would you actually do?" One of the crucial processes is to try to turn behavior change into habits and routines (Kwasnicka et al., 2016).

Sensory

Although CFT labels this competency as a sensory dimension, it involves more than just the physical senses but also sensing into our bodies. It links to a large body of literature on embodiment processes of psychotherapy. These processes are very important for engaging with suffering but are also key to how we switch to helpful action. There are many aspects to this domain, such as understanding the role of our diet, body inflammation, and the value of exercise. CFT uses the phrase "helping/cultivating the body to support the mind." There are a number of sensory and body-based practices that have specific physiological effects. Common ones include the use of posture and movement, breathing, and grounding. There are now a number of ways to directly help clients improve heart rate variability (Matos, Duarte, Duarte et al., 2017, 2022), which in itself has impacts on well-being and social behavior (Bornemann et al., 2016). These different ways of cultivating psychophysiological systems, such as the vagus nerve and neurocircuits, can help people feel grounded and stabilized in the body. It is important that clients understand that grounding is (mostly) not intended to try and avoid or soothe away difficult emotions, but to make them more tolerable and to discover how to work with them in helpful ways. For example, if an individual is stressed, the therapist brings attention to what is happening in the body and may guide them to ground themselves by feeling into their posture, maybe holding their shoulders, attending to the feeling of feet flat on the floor, slowing the breath, and seeking to settle the body as best they can before considering what would be helpful action. How we use the body to support us with difficult emotions depends on the emotion because, for example, in the case of anger, physical activity such as going for a fast walk or running up and down stairs will often be more helpful than trying to use soothing rhythmic breathing. Hence, again it is about how to use the body wisely and knowingly.

Feeling

When we work to alleviate suffering, we will encounter feelings in taking action. There is increasing interest in the fact that emotions might be behavioral action potentials, different from the kinds of feelings humans have. This is because, for humans, these basic emotional and behavioral action systems are modified considerably with our new brain, especially, but not only, with the frontal cortex giving rise to very subtle textures (LeDoux, 2020). Leaving that to one side for now, different actions will stimulate different emotions and feelings. For example, a firefighter heading into a burning house will have to tolerate anxiety. The firefighter only feels anxious because of the action they are going to take to prevent suffering. In fighting injustice, we may have to work with anger, but if counselling a dying patient, we have to tolerate their own and our sympathetic sadness and other feelings. Hence, compassion is not an emotion or feeling state, it is a motive. The feelings we have will depend very much on the type of suffering and the path to alleviation.

In many situations, clients may not want to take helpful action because of the feelings it stirs up. The obvious and simple case is anxiety exposure. For example, the person with agoraphobia does not want to have to experience anxiety when they go out. Crucially then, how we deal with the fears arising from taking action is very important. Holding the feelings that arise when taking action in a compassionate mindset makes them more tolerable and thereby more workable. CFT makes clear distinctions between the feelings that arise from engaging with their suffering, those arising when trying to take actions, help and heal their suffering in contrast to trying to avoid and therefore perpetuate suffering in the long term. This leads to the understanding that the healing of suffering can sometimes take us into difficult brain states; we descend into pain and suffering and do not try to ascend (as avoidance) out of it. We come back to the idea that compassion is about the courage and wisdom to engage with suffering, take wise action, and recognize that both engagement and action have different textures of thinking, feeling, and behavior.

Overview of the Twelve Competencies Model

The twelve competencies model is designed to offer useful therapeutic heuristics based on the distinction between engagement and response aspects for compassion, requiring different processes. However, these should not be treated mechanistically. All the competencies co-regulate each other. For example, imagine losing any one of them and the impact that would have on the others. Consider the impact if individuals could not develop distress tolerance, empathy, wise reasoning, or the courage they need to engage in behavior change. Or consider therapeutic skills like empathy; there are multiple dimensions to the skilful use of empathy. In addition, there are multiple interventions that support different elements of the twelve competencies. For example, the therapeutic relationship and creating a secure base, guided discovery, functional analysis, the use of chair work, acting, letter writing, mindfulness, guided exposure, and other practices. It is crucial to recognize that, today, psychotherapy interventions are multi-textured, multi-focused, and can be derived from many different schools of therapy. CFT integrates many well-developed, evidence-based interventions for specific kinds of functions, such as empathy and distress tolerance, but contextualizes them through the psychophysiological processes made available in the care-social mentality. This is because the psychophysiological patterns of that system have such profound effects on the regulation of emotion and threat, and on the abilities for mature confidence.

Conclusion

This chapter presented CFT as an integrative and integrating therapy. The chapter looked at the different dimensions of integration including cross-disciplinary, biopsychosocial dimensions, and cross-therapy approaches. Crucial to CFT is the concept of compassion as an algorithm. This encompasses six competencies linked to the ability to engage and make sense of distress and suffering, and six competencies that direct attention, thinking, and behavior toward taking action and being helpful to others. The integration of these twelve competencies facilitates the development of a compassionate mind that is open and flexible. Finally, the chapter highlighted basic domains that many therapies focus on, but in different ways. The six basic domains are mind awareness, differentiation, tolerance, integration, transformation, and adaptation. In general, CFT focuses on helping people to develop a compassionate self-identity and live as individuals who try to be helpful not harmful. To do this, individuals pursue training both body and mind for compassion. Compassionate mind training therefore supports and sustains compassionate self-identity.

References

Anderson, C., Hildreth, J. A. D., & Howland, L. (2015). Is the desire for status a fundamental human motive? A review of the empirical literature. *Psychological Bulletin, 141*(3), 574–601. https://doi.org/10.1037/a0038781

Ashar, Y. K., Andrews-Hanna, J. R., Halifax, J., Dimidjian, S., & Wager, T. D. (2021). Effects of compassion training on brain responses to suffering others. *Social Cognitive and Affective Neuroscience, 16*(10), 1036–1047. https://doi.org/10.1093/scan/nsab052

Bargh, J. (2017). *Before you know it: The unconscious reasons we do what we do*. Simon and Schuster.

Barlow, D. H., Allen, L. B., & Basden, S. L. (2007). Psychological treatments for panic disorders, phobias, and generalized anxiety disorder. In P. E. Nathan & J. M. Gorman (Eds.), *A guide to treatments that work* (pp. 351–394). Oxford University Press.

Baron-Cohen, S. (2011). *Zero degrees of empathy: A new theory of human cruelty*. Penguin.

Baumeister, R. F., Bratslavsky, E., Finkenauer, C., & Vohs, K. D. (2001). Bad is stronger than good. *Review of General Psychology*, 5(4), 323–370. https://doi.org/10.1037//1089-2680.5.4.323

Beck, A. T. (2008). The evolution of the cognitive model of depression and its neurobiological correlates. *American Journal of Psychiatry*, 165(8), 969–977. https://doi.org/10.1176/appi.ajp.2008.08050721

Beck, A. T., Emery, G., & Greenberg, R. (1985). *Anxiety disorders and phobias: A cognitive perspective*. Basic Books.

Beck, A. T., Rush, A. J., Shaw, B. F., & Emery, G. (1979). *Cognitive therapy of depression*. Wiley.

Bell, T., Montague, J., Elander, J., & Gilbert, P. (2020). "A definite feel-it moment:" Embodiment, externalisation, and emotion during chair-work in compassion-focused therapy. *Counselling and Psychotherapy Research*, 20(1), 143–153. https://doi.org/10.1002/capr.12248

Bornemann, B., Kok, B. E., Boeckler, A., & Singer, T. (2016). Helping from the heart: Voluntary upregulation of heart rate variability predicts altruistic behavior. *Biological Psychology*, 119, 54–63. https://doi.org/10.1016/j.biopsycho.2016.07.004

Bowlby, J. (1969). *Attachment and loss (Vol. 1)*. Random House.

Bowlby, J. (1973). *Separation, anxiety and anger: Attachment and loss (Vol. 2)*. Hogarth Press.

Bowlby, J. (1980). *Loss: Sadness and depression: Attachment and loss (Vol. 3)*. Hogarth Press.

Brosschot, J. F., Verkuil, B., & Thayer, J. F. (2016). The default response to uncertainty and the importance of perceived safety in anxiety and stress: An evolution-theoretical perspective. *Journal of Anxiety Disorders*, 41, 22–34. https://doi.org/10.1016/j.janxdis.2016.04.012

Brown, P., Waite, F., Rovira, A., Nickless, A., & Freeman, D. (2020). Virtual reality clinical-experimental tests of compassion treatment techniques to reduce paranoia. *Scientific Reports*, 10(1), 1–9. https://doi.org/10.1038/s41598-020-64957-7

Camilleri, T., Rockey, S., & Dunbar, R. (2023). *The social brain. The psychology of successful groups*. Cornerstone Press.

Carvalho, H. M., & Matos, P. M. (2021). Psychotherapist as a secure base figure: Validation of the Secure Base Questionnaire (SBQ). *Professional Psychology: Research and Practice*, 52(4), 396. https://doi.org/10.1037/pro0000366

Cassidy, J., & Shaver, P. R. (2016). *Handbook of attachment: Theory, research, and clinical applications* (3rd ed.). Guilford.

Cozolino, L. (2017). *The neuroscience of psychotherapy: Healing the social brain* (2nd ed.). W.W. Norton & Company.

Craske, M. G., Meuret, A. E., Ritz, T., Treanor, M., Dour, H., & Rosenfield, D. (2019). Positive affect treatment for depression and anxiety: A randomized clinical trial for a core feature of anhedonia. *Journal of Consulting and Clinical Psychology*, 87(5), 457–471. https://doi.org/10.1037/ccp0000396

Dalai Lama. (1995). *The power of compassion*. Harper Collins.

Decety, J., & Ickes, W. (Eds.). (2011). *The social neuroscience of empathy*. MIT Press.

Di Bello, M., Ottaviani, C., & Petrocchi, N. (2021). Compassion is not a benzo: Distinctive associations of heart rate variability with its empathic and action components. *Frontiers in Neuroscience*, 15, Article 617443. https://doi.org/10.3389/fnins.2021.617443

Diogo, R. (2019). Sex at dusk, sex at dawn, selfish genes: How old-dated evolutionary ideas are used to defend fallacious misogynistic views on sex evolution. *Journal of Social Sciences and Humanities*, 5(4), 350–367. http://www.aiscience.org/journal/jssh

Eidelson, R. Y., & Eidelson, J. I. (2003). Dangerous ideas. Five beliefs that propel groups towards conflicts. *American Psychologist*, 58, 182–192. https://doi.org/10.1037/0003-066x.58.3.182

Eisenberg, L. (1986). Mindlessness and brainlessness in psychiatry. *The British Journal of Psychiatry*, 148(5), 497–508. https://doi.org/10.1192/bjp.148.5.497

Eisenberg, N., & Eggum, N. D. (2009). Empathic responding: Sympathy and personal distress. In J. Decety, & W. Ickes (Eds.), *The social neuroscience of empathy* (pp. 71–83). MIT Press.

Eisenberg, N., VanSchyndel, S. K., & Hofer, C. (2015). The association of maternal socialization in childhood and adolescence with adult offsprings' sympathy/caring. *Developmental Psychology*, *51*(1), 7–16. https://doi.org/10.1037/a0038137

Ellenberger, H. F. (1970). *The discovery of the unconscious: The history and evolution of dynamic psychiatry*. Basic Books.

Ferster, C. B. (1973). A functional analysis of depression. *American Psychologist*, *28*(10), 857–870. https://doi.org/10.1037/h0035605

Fonagy, P. (2018). Being envious of envy and gratitude. In A. Lemma & P. Roth (Eds.), *Envy and gratitude revisited* (pp. 201–210). Routledge.

Forster, D. E., Pedersen, E. J., McCullough, M. E., & Lieberman, D. (2022). Evaluating benefits, costs, and social value as predictors of gratitude. *Psychological Science*, *33*(4), 538–549. https://doi.org/10.1177/09567976211031215

Freud, S. (1895). *A project for a scientific psychology* (Standard Edition of the Complete Psychological Works of Sigmund Freud, vol. 1, pp. 283–397). Hogarth.

Frith, C., & Frith, U. (2005). Theory of mind. *Current Biology*, *15*(17), R644–R645. https://doi.org/10.1016/j.cub.2005.08.041

Geller, S. M. (2018). Therapeutic presence and polyvagal theory: Principles and practices for cultivating effective therapeutic relationships. In S. W Porges & D. Dana (Eds.), *Clinical applications of the polyvagal theory: The emergence of polyvagal-informed therapies* (pp. 106–126). Norton.

Gilbert, H. (2022). The therapeutic relationship in compassion focused therapy. In P. Gilbert & G. Simos (Eds.), *Compassion focused therapy: Clinical practice and applications* (pp. 385–400). Routledge.

Gilbert, P. (1984). *Depression: From psychology to brain state*. Lawrence Erlbaum Associates.

Gilbert, P. (1989). *Human nature and suffering*. Lawrence Erlbaum Associates.

Gilbert, P. (1992). *Depression: The evolution of powerlessness*. Lawrence Erlbaum Associates.

Gilbert, P. (1993). Defence and safety: Their function in social behaviour and psychopathology. *British Journal of Clinical Psychology*, *32*, 131–153. https://doi.org/10.1111/j.2044-8260.1993.tb01039.x

Gilbert, P. (1998). The evolved basis and adaptive functions of cognitive distortions. *British Journal of Medical Psychology*, *71*(Pt 4), 447–463. https://doi.org/10.1111/j.2044-8341.1998.tb01002.x

Gilbert, P. (2007a). *Psychotherapy and counselling for depression* (3rd ed.). Sage.

Gilbert, P. (2007b). Evolved minds and compassion in the therapeutic relationship. In P. Gilbert & R. Leahy (Eds.), *The therapeutic relationship in the cognitive behavioural psychotherapies* (pp. 106–142). Routledge.

Gilbert, P. (2009). *The compassionate mind: A new approach to the challenge of life*. Constable and Robinson.

Gilbert, P. (2017). Compassion as a social mentality. In P. Gilbert (Ed)., *Compassion: Concepts, research, and applications* (pp. 31–168). Routledge.

Gilbert, P. (2019a). Psychotherapy for the 21st century: An integrative, evolutionary, contextual, biopsychosocial approach. *Psychology and Psychotherapy: Theory, Research and Practice*, *92*, 164–189. https://doi.org/10.1111/papt.12226

Gilbert, P. (2019b). *Living like crazy* (2nd ed.). Compassionate Wellbeing.

Gilbert, P. (2020). Compassion: From its evolution to a psychotherapy. *Frontiers in Psychology*, *11*, Article 586161. https://doi.10.3389/fpsyg.2020.586161

Gilbert, P. (2021). Creating a compassionate world: Addressing the conflicts between sharing and caring versus controlling and holding evolved strategies. *Frontiers in Psychology*, *11*, Article 582090. https://doi.org/10.3389/fpsyg.2020.582090

Gilbert, P. (2022a). Meeting the challenges of a multi mind and the role of grieving. In P. Gilbert & G. Simos (Eds). *Compassion focused therapy: Clinical practice and applications* (pp. 313–344). Routledge.

Gilbert, P. (2022b). Shame, social status, and the pain of social disconnection. In P. Gilbert & G. Simos (Eds.), *Compassion focused therapy: Clinical practice and applications* (pp. 122–163). Routledge.

Gilbert, P. (2022c). Internal shame and self-disconnection. From hostile self-criticism to compassionate self-correction and guidance. In P. Gilbert & G. Simos (Eds.), *Compassion focused therapy: Clinical practice and applications* (pp. 163–206). Routledge.

Gilbert, P. (2023). An evolutionary and compassion approach to yearning and grief for what one did not have. In D. Harris & A. H. Y. Ho (Eds.), *Compassion-based approaches in loss and grief* (pp. 18–27). Routledge.

Gilbert, P., & Basran, J. (2018). Imagining one's compassionate self and coping with life difficulties. *EC Psychology and Psychiatry, 7*(12), 971–978. https://www.researchgate.net/publication/330662450_Imagining_One's_Compassionate_Self_and_Coping_with_Life_Difficulties

Gilbert, P., Basran, J., Minou, L., Rayner, A., Hayes, A., Lucre, K., McEwan, F., Byrne, F., & Newton, L. (2022). Compassion focused group therapy for people with a diagnosis of bipolar affective disorder: A feasibility study. *Frontiers in Psychology, 13*, Article 841932. https://doi.org/10.3389/fpsyg.2022.841932

Gilbert, P., Catarino, F., Duarte, C., Matos, M., Kolts, R., Stubbs, J., Ceresatto, L., Duarte, J., Pinto-Gouveia, J., & Basran, J. (2017). The development of compassionate engagement and action scales for self and others. *Journal of Compassionate Health Care, 4*(1), 1–24. https://doi.org/10.1186/s40639-017-0033-3

Gilbert, P., & Choden. (2013). *Mindful compassion.* Constable Robinson.

Gilbert, P., & Gilbert, H. (2011). Spiritual healing in the context of the human need for safeness, connectedness, and warmth: A biopsychosocial approach. In F. Watts (Ed.), *Spiritual healing: Scientific and religious perspectives* (pp. 112–127). Cambridge University Press.

Gilbert, P., & Irons, C. (2004). A pilot exploration of the use of compassionate images in a group of self-critical people. *Memory, 12*, 507–516. https://doi.org/10.1080/09658210444000115

Gilbert, P., & Irons, C. (2005). Focused therapies and compassionate mind training for shame and self-attacking. In P. Gilbert (Ed.), *Compassion: Conceptualisations, research, and use in psychotherapy* (pp. 263–325). Routledge.

Gilbert, P., & Mascaro, J. (2017). Compassion, fears, blocks and resistances: An evolutionary investigation. In E. M. Seppälä, E. Simon-Thomas, S. L. Brown, M. C. Worline, C. D. Cameron, & J. R. Dory (Eds.), *The Oxford handbook of compassion science* (pp. 399–420). Oxford University Press.

Gilbert, P., McEwan, K., Matos, M., & Rivis, A. (2011). Fears of compassion: Development of three self-report measures. *Psychology and Psychotherapy, 84*, 239–255. https://doi.org/10.1348/147608310X526511

Gilbert, P., & Simos, G. (Eds.). (2022). *Compassion focused therapy: Clinical practice and applications.* Routledge.

Hayes, S. (2019). *A liberated mind: The essential guide to ACT.* Random House

Heath, C., Bell, C., & Sternberg, E. (2001). Emotional selection in memes: The case of urban legends. *Journal of Personality and Social Psychology, 81*(6), 1028–1041. https://doi.org/10.1037/0022-3514.81.6.1028

Hein, G., Silani, G., Preuschoff, K., Batson, C. D., & Singer, T. (2010). Neural responses to ingroup and outgroup members' suffering predict individual differences in costly helping. *Neuron, 68*(1), 149–160. https://doi.org/10.1016/j.neuron.2010.09.003

Heino, M. T., Knittle, K., Noone, C., Hasselman, F., & Hankonen, N. (2021). Studying behaviour change mechanisms under complexity. *Behavioral Sciences, 11*(5), Article 77. https://doi.org/10.3390/bs11050077

Hettema, J., Steele, J., & Miller, W. R. (2005). Motivational interviewing. *Annual Review of Clinical Psychology, 1*(1), 91–111. https://doi.org/10.1146/annurev.clinpsy.1.102803.143833

Ho, A. K., Sidanius, J., Pratto, F., Levin, S., Thomsen, L., Kteily, N., & Sheehy-Skeffington, J. (2012). Social dominance orientation: Revisiting the structure and function of a variable predicting social and political attitudes. *Personality and Social Psychology Bulletin, 38*, 583–606. https://doi.org/10.1177/0146167211432765

Hoffman, M. L. (1990). Empathy and justice motivation. *Motivation and emotion, 14*(2), 151–172. https://doi.org/10.1007/BF00991641

Holmes, J., & Slade, A. (2017). *Attachment in therapeutic practice.* Sage.

Hood, B. (2011). *The self illusion: Why there is no 'you' inside your head.* Constable.

Kim, J. J., Cunnington, R., & Kirby, J. N. (2020). The neurophysiological basis of compassion: An fMRI meta-analysis of compassion and its related neural processes. *Neuroscience and Biobehavioral Reviews, 108*, 112–123. https://doi.org/10.1016/j.neubiorev.2019.10.023

Kirby, J. N. (2016). Compassion interventions: The programs, the evidence, and implications for research and practice. *Psychology and Psychotherapy: Theory, Research, and Practice*, 90(3), 432–455. https://doi.org/10.1111/papt.12104

Kirby, J. N. (2022). *Choose compassion*. University of Queensland Press.

Kirby, J. N., Day, J., & Sagar, V. (2019). The 'flow' of compassion: A meta-analysis of the fears of compassion scales and psychological functioning. *Clinical Psychology Review*, 70, 26–39. https://doi.org/10.1016/j.cpr.2019.03.001

Knox, J. (2003). *Archetype, attachment, analysis: Jungian psychology and the emergent mind*. Psychology Press.

Krol, S. A., & Bartz, J. A. (2021). The self and empathy: Lacking a clear and stable sense of self undermines empathy and helping behavior. *Emotion*, 22(7), 1554–1571. https://doi.org/10.1037/emo0000943

Kwasnicka, D., Dombrowski, S. U., White, M., & Sniehotta, F. (2016). Theoretical explanations for maintenance of behaviour change: A systematic review of behaviour theories. *Health Psychology Review*, 10(3), 277–296. https://doi.org/10.1080/17437199.2016.1151372

Lazarus, R. S. (1981). A cognitivist's reply to Zajonc on emotion and cognition. *American Psychologist*, 36(2), 222–223. https://doi.org/10.1037/0003-066X.36.2.222

LeDoux, J. E. (2020). Thoughtful feelings. *Current Biology*, 30(11), R619–R623. https://doi.org/10.1016/j.cub.2020.04.012

LeDoux, J. E. (2022). As soon as there was life, there was danger: The deep history of survival behaviours and the shallower history of consciousness. *Philosophical Transactions of the Royal Society of London. Series B, Biological sciences*, 377(1844), 20210292. https://doi.org/10.1098/rstb.2021.0292

Loewenstein, G., & Small, D. A. (2007). The scarecrow and the tin man: The vicissitudes of human sympathy and caring. *Review of General Psychology*, 11, 112–126. https://doi.org/10.1037/1089-2680.11.2.112

Luyten, P., Campbell, C., Allison, E., & Fonagy, P. (2020). The mentalizing approach to psychopathology: State of the art and future directions. *Annual Review of Clinical Psychology*, 16, 297–325. https://doi.org/10.1146/annurev-clinpsy-071919-015355

MacLeod, C., Grafton, B., & Notebaert, L. (2019). Anxiety-linked attentional bias: Is it reliable? *Annual Review of Clinical Psychology*, 15, 529–554. https://doi.org/10.1146/annurev-clinpsy-050718-095505

Marks, I. M. (1987). *Fears, phobias, and rituals: Panic, anxiety, and their disorders*. Oxford University Press.

Matos, M., Duarte, C., Duarte, J., Pinto-Gouveia, J., Petrocchi, N., Basran, J., & Gilbert, P. (2017). Psychological and physiological effects of compassionate mind training: A pilot randomised controlled study. *Mindfulness*, 8(6), 1699–1712. https://doi.org/10.1007/s12671-017-0745-7

Matos, M., Duarte, C., Duarte, J., Pinto-Gouveia, J., Petrocchi, N., & Gilbert, P. (2022). Cultivating the compassionate self: An exploration of the mechanisms of change in compassionate mind training. *Mindfulness*, 13, 66–79. https://doi.org/10.1007/s12671-021-01717-2

Matos, M., Duarte, C., & Pinto-Gouveia, J. (2015). Constructing a self protected against shame: The importance of warmth and safeness memories and feelings on the association between shame memories and depression. *International Journal of Psychology and Psychological Therapy*, 15(3), 317–335. https://www.ijpsy.com/volumen15/num3/419.html

Matos, M., Duarte, J., & Pinto-Gouveia, J. (2017). The origins of fears of compassion: Shame and lack of safeness memories, fears of compassion and psychopathology. *Journal of Psychology*, 151(8), 804–819. https://doi.org/10.1080/00223980.2017.1393380

Matos, M., Pinto-Gouveia, J., & Duarte, C. (2013). Internalizing early memories of shame and lack of safeness and warmth: The mediating role of shame on depression. *Behavioural and Cognitive Psychotherapy*, 41(4), 479–493. https://doi.org/10.1017/S1352465812001099

Mayseless, O. (2016). *The caring motivation: An integrated theory*. Oxford University Press. https://doi.org/10.1093/acprof:oso/9780199913619.001.0001

McEwan, K., & Minou, L. (2022). Defining compassion: A Delphi study of compassion therapists' experiences when introducing patients to the term 'compassion'. *Psychology and Psychotherapy: Theory, Research and Practice*, 96(1), 16–24. https://doi.org/10.1111/papt.12423

Michalak, J., Crane, C., Germer, C. K., Gold, E., Heidenreich, T., Mander, J., Meibert, P., & Segal, Z. V. (2019). Principles for a responsible integration of mindfulness in individual therapy. *Mindfulness*, *10*(5), 799–811. https://doi.org/10.1007/s12671-019-01142-6

Mikulincer, M., Shaver, P. R., & Berant, E. (2013). An attachment perspective on therapeutic processes and outcomes. *Journal of Personality*, *81*(6), 606–616. https://doi.org/10.1111/j.1467-6494.2012.00806.x

Miller, W. R., & Rollnick, S. (2012). *Motivational interviewing: Helping people change*. Guilford Press.

Mills, J., Minister, C., & Samson, L. (2022). Enriching sociocultural perspectives on the effects of idealized body norms: Integrating shame, positive body image, and self-compassion. *Frontiers in Psychology*, *13*, Article 983534. https://doi.org/10.3389/fpsyg.2022.983534

Music, G. (2019). *Nurturing children. From trauma to growth using attachment theory, psychoanalysis, and neurobiology*. Routledge.

Music, G. (2022). *Respark: Igniting hope and joy after trauma and depression*. Mind-Nurturing Books.

Nesse, R. M. (2019). *Good reasons for bad feelings: Insights from the frontier of evolutionary psychiatry*. Dutton.

Nickerson, R. S. (1999). How we know—and sometimes misjudge—what others know: Inputting one's own knowledge to others. *Psychological Bulletin*, *125*, 737–759. https://doi.org/10.1037/0033-2909.125.6.737

Northoff, G. (2012). Psychoanalysis and the brain–why did Freud abandon neuroscience?. *Frontiers in Psychology*, *3*, 71.

Novak, L., Malinakova, K., Mikoska, P., van Dijk, J. P., & Tavel, P. (2022). Neural correlates of compassion—An integrative systematic review. *International Journal of Psychophysiology*, *172*, 46–59. https://doi.org/10.1016/j.ijpsycho.2021.12.004

Petrocchi, P., Di Bello, M., Cheli, S., & Ottaviani, C. (2022). Compassion focused therapy and the body: How physiological underpinnings of prosociality inform clinical practice. In P. Gilbert & G. Simos (Eds.), *Compassion focused therapy: Clinical practice and applications* (pp. 345–359). Routledge.

Pinel, E. C., & Bosson, J. K. (2013). Turning our attention to stigma: An objective self-awareness analysis of stigma and its consequences. *Basic and Applied Social Psychology*, *35*(1), 55–63.

Porges, S. W. (2011). *The polyvagal theory: Neurophysiological foundations of emotions, attachment, communication, and self-regulation* (Norton Series on Interpersonal Neurobiology). W.W. Norton & Company.

Porges, S. W. (2021). Polyvagal theory: A biobehavioral journey to sociality. *Comprehensive Psychoneuroendocrinology*, *7*, Article 100069. https://doi.org/10.1016/j.cpnec.2021.100069

Porges, S. W., & Dana, D. (Eds.). (2018). *Clinical applications of the polyvagal theory: The emergence of polyvagal-informed therapies*. Norton

Poulin, M. J. (2017). To help or not to help: Goal commitment and the goodness of compassion. In E. M. Seppälä, E. Simon-Thomas, S. L. Brown, M. C. Worline, L. Cameron, & J. R. Doty (Eds.), *The Oxford handbook of compassion science* (pp. 355–367). Oxford University Press.

Rachman, S. J. (1990). *Fear and courage*. W. H. Freeman & Co. Ltd.

Ribeiro da Silva, D., Rijo, D., Brazão, N., Paulo, M., Miguel, R., Castilho, P., Vagos, P., Gilbert, P., & Salekin, R. T. (2021). The efficacy of the PSYCHOPATHY.COMP program in reducing psychopathic traits: A controlled trial with male detained youth. *Journal of Consulting and Clinical Psychology*, *89*(6), 499–513. https://doi.org/10.1037/ccp0000659

Ricard, M. (2015). *Altruism: The power of compassion to change yourself and the world*. Atlantic Books.

Ritvo, L. B., & Haynal, A. E. (1994). Darwin's influence on Freud: A tale of two sciences. *History and Philosophy of the Life Sciences*, *16*(1), 155.

Saulsman, L. M., Ji, J. L., & McEvoy, P. M. (2019). The essential role of mental imagery in cognitive behaviour therapy: What is old is new again. *Australian Psychologist*, *54*(4), 237–244. https://doi.org/10.1111/ap.12406

Schore, A. N. (1997). A century after Freud's project: Is a rapprochement between psychoanalysis and neurobiology at hand?. *Journal of the American Psychoanalytic Association*, *45*(3), 807–840.

Schore, A. N. (2019). *The development of the unconscious mind*. Norton.

Seewald, A., & Rief, W. (2022). How to change negative outcome expectations in psychotherapy? The role of the therapist's warmth and competence. *Clinical Psychological Science, 11*(1), 149–163. https://doi.org/10.1177/2167702622109433

Seppälä, E. M., Simon-Thomas, E., Brown, S. L., Worline, M. C., Cameron, C. D., &, Doty, J. R. (Eds.). (2017). *The Oxford handbook of compassion science.* Oxford University Press.

Shaver, P. R., Mikulincer, M., Sahdra, B. K., & Gross, J. T. (2017). Attachment security as a foundation for kindness toward self and others. In K. W. Brown & M. R. Leary (Eds.), *The Oxford handbook of hypo-egoic phenomena* (pp. 223–242). Oxford University Press.

Siegel, D. J. (2019). The mind in psychotherapy: An interpersonal neurobiology framework for understanding and cultivating mental health. *Psychology and Psychotherapy: Theory, Research and Practice, 92*(2), 224–237. https://doi.org/10.1111/papt.12228

Siegel, D. J. (2020). *The developing mind: How relationships in the brain interact to shape who we are* (3rd ed.). Norton.

Singer, T., & Engert, V. (2019). It matters what you practice: Differential training effects on subjective experience, behavior, brain and body in the ReSource Project. *Current Opinion in Psychology, 28,* 151–158. https://doi.org/10.1016/j.copsyc.2018.12.005

Slavich, G. M. (2020). Social safety theory: A biologically based evolutionary perspective on life stress, health, and behavior. *Annual Review of Clinical Psychology, 16,* 265–295.

Solom, R., Watkins, P. C., McCurrach, D., & Scheibe, D. (2017). Thieves of thankfulness: Traits that inhibit gratitude. *The Journal of Positive Psychology, 12*(2), 120–129.

Steffen, P. R., Foxx, J., Cattani, K., Alldredge, C., Austin, T., & Burlingame, G. M. (2021). Impact of a 12-week group-based compassion focused therapy intervention on heart rate variability. *Applied Psychophysiology and Biofeedback, 46*(1), 61–68. https://doi.org/10.1007/s10484-020-09487-8

Steindl, S. R., Bell, T., Dixon, A., & Kirby, J. N. (2022). Therapist perspectives on working with fears, blocks, and resistances to compassion in compassion focused therapy. *Counselling and Psychotherapy Research, 23*(3), 850–863. https://doi.org/10.1002/capr.12530

Steindl, S. R., Kirby, J. N., & Tellegan, C. (2018). Motivational interviewing in compassion-based interventions: Theory and practical applications. *Clinical Psychologist, 22*(3), 265–279. https://doi.org/10.1111/cp.12146

Steindl, S. R., Matos, M., & Creed, A. K. (2018). Early shame and safeness memories, and later depressive symptoms and safe affect: The mediating role of self-compassion. *Current Psychology, 40*(2), 761–771. https://doi.org/10.1007/s12144-018-9990-8

Steindl, S. R., Tellegen, C. L., Filus, A., Seppälä, E., Doty, J. R., & Kirby, J. N. (2021). The Compassion Motivation and Action Scales: A self-report measure of compassionate and self-compassionate behaviours. *Australian Psychologist, 56*(2), 93–110. https://doi.org/10.1080/00050067.2021.1893110

Tagliazucchi, E., Llobenes, L., & Gumily, N. (2022). Psychedelics, connectedness, and compassion. In P. Gilbert & G. Simos (Eds.), *Compassion focused therapy: Clinical practice and applications* (pp. 360–371). Routledge.

Taylor, S. E. (2011). Social support: A review. In H. S. Friedman (Ed.), *The Oxford handbook of health psychology* (pp. 189–214). Oxford University Press.

Van der Kolk, B. (2014). *The body keeps the score: Brain, mind, and body in the healing of trauma.* Penguin

Vivino, B. L., Thompson, B. J., Hill, C. E., & Ladany, N. (2009). Compassion in psychotherapy: The perspective of therapists nominated as compassionate. *Psychotherapy Research, 19*(2), 157–171. https://doi.org/10.1080/10503300802430681

Watkins, E. R., & Roberts, H. (2020). Reflecting on rumination: Consequences, causes, mechanisms and treatment of rumination. *Behaviour Research and Therapy, 127,* Article 103573. https://doi.org/10.1016/j.brat.2020.103573

Weng, H. Y., Fox, A. S., Shackman, A. J., Stodola, D. E., Caldwell, J. Z., Olson, M. C., Rogers, G. M., & Davidson, R. J. (2013). Compassion training alters altruism and neural responses to suffering. *Psychological Science, 24*(7), 1171–1180. https://doi.org/10.1177/0956797612469537

Weng, H. Y., Lapate, R. C., Stodola, D. E., Rogers, G. M., & Davidson, R. J. (2018). Visual attention to suffering after compassion training is associated with decreased amygdala responses. *Frontiers in Psychology, 9,* Article 771. https://doi.org/10.3389/fpsyg.2018.00771

Wood, A. M., Froh, J. J., & Geraghty, A. W. (2010). Gratitude and well-being: A review and theoretical integration. *Clinical Psychology Review, 30*(7), 890–905. https://doi.org/10.1016/j.cpr.2010.03.005

Yalom, I. D. (1980). *Existential psychotherapy*. Basic Books.

Zajonc, R. B. (1980). Feeling and thinking: Preferences need no inferences. *American Psychologist, 35*(2), 151–175. https://doi.org/10.1037/0003-066X.35.2.151

Zajonc, R. B. (1984). On the primacy of affect. *American Psychologist, 39*(2), 117–123. https://doi.org/10.1037/0003-066X.39.2.117

Zeman, A., Dewar, M., & Della Sala, S. (2016). Reflections on aphantasia. *Cortex, 74*, 336–337. https://doi.org/10.1016/j.cortex.2015.08.015

Zilboorg, G., & Henry, G. W. (1941). *A history of medical psychology*. Norton.

Zimbardo, P. (2007). *The Lucifer effect: Understanding how good people turn evil*. Rider.

Zimbardo, P. (2015). Transforming society by teaching everyday people the characteristics of a modern hero. *The Futurist, 49*(1), 24–25.

11

An Interpersonal Perspective on the Physiological Stress Response

Implications for Therapeutic Interventions in Coronary Heart Disease

Timothy W. Smith and Jenny M. Cundiff

The physiological effects of psychological stress play a role in many major health problems (O'Connor et al., 2021). As a result, stress reduction is a cornerstone of many interventions in health psychology and behavioral medicine. Stress management is useful in high-risk groups, such as patients with coronary heart disease (CHD) (Levine et al., 2021). Most stress management interventions have a decidedly *intra*-personal emphasis, focused on dampening physiological responses directly through relaxation, meditation, or biofeedback techniques, or using cognitive-behavioral interventions to alter cognitive factors (e.g., appraisals, catastrophizing, worry, rumination) that heighten stress responses. As an alternative or complement to this traditional approach, this chapter presents an interpersonal perspective on physiological stress responses and discusses its implications for therapeutic interventions.

We review this interpersonal perspective on psychosocial risk and protective factors for CHD (Smith & Cundiff, 2011; Smith et al., 2014), and discuss its implications for stress-reduction interventions in this population (Levine et al., 2021). However, this perspective is applicable to other diseases and disorders in which stress predicts the development or course of the condition, and for which there are plausible underlying psychophysiological mechanisms. These other conditions include—but are not limited to—various cancers (Antoni et al., 2023), Type 2 diabetes (Kelly & Ismail, 2015), and other forms of cardiovascular disease such as stroke (Booth et al., 2015) and hypertension (M. Liu et al., 2017).

We begin with an overview of the role of stress and related psychosocial factors in the development and course of CHD and related psychosocial interventions in CHD. We then provide an introduction to current interpersonal theory and research (Hopwood et al., 2021; Pincus & Ansell, 2013; Wright et al., 2023), and use this framework to describe interpersonal influences on physiological stress responses (Smith et al., 2003). We conclude with a discussion of the implications of this interpersonal perspective for augmenting the more conventional intra-personal approaches to stress management. At its core, an interpersonally enhanced approach to stress management focuses on modifying recurring patterns of interpersonal situations that confer risk or resilience through their effects on physiological responses.

The Development and Course of Coronary Heart Disease: Psychosocial Factors, Physiological Mechanisms, and Interventions

Clinically apparent CHD (i.e., angina pectoris, myocardial infarction, sudden coronary death) is the result of a decades-long process comprising the initiation and progression of atherosclerosis in the coronary arteries, or coronary artery disease (CAD). Beginning as early as childhood or adolescence, the build-up of fat and inflammatory material within the walls of these arteries grows asymptomatically. In later stages of the disease these lesions or their complications (e.g., plaque rupture with thrombus) limit blood flow to the heart muscle itself, producing myocardial ischemia and clinically apparent CHD when myocardial demands for oxygen exceed a supply limited by narrowed or occluded arteries (Libby et al., 2011). Atherosclerosis is typically a systemic condition occurring at multiple sites; in the carotid arteries that bring blood to the brain it results in ischemic (i.e., occlusive) stroke.

Beyond the effects of traditional risk factors (e.g., smoking, hypertension, elevated blood lipids and glucose, excessive dietary intake of fat and calories, physical inactivity), several psychosocial characteristics predict the presence, severity, and progression of CAD, as well as CHD events (i.e., acute coronary syndrome, myocardial infarction, sudden coronary death) and prognosis among patients with established disease (e.g., re-infarction, re-hospitalization, CHD death) (Kivimaki & Steptoe, 2018). These characteristics include aspects of the broader social environment such as low socio-economic status (SES) (De Mestral & Stringhini, 2017) and chronic job stress (Sara et al., 2018; Taouk et al., 2020). Black Americans suffer higher rates and worse outcomes of CHD (Leigh et al., 2016), and these disparities are attributable to social causes—various forms of racism—rather than inherent biological or genetic differences associated with skin color (Bryant et al., 2022; Haeny et al., 2021; Lewis et al., 2015).

Qualities of personal relationships, such as social support (Barth et al., 2010) and marriage and similar intimate relationships (Dupre et al., 2015; Dupre & Nelson, 2016; Manfredini et al., 2017), have robust associations with the onset and course of CHD. Other interpersonal patterns such as social isolation or loneliness (Paul et al., 2021; Valtorta et al., 2016) and conflict and strain in intimate relationships (Joseph et al., 2014; Lund et al., 2014; Wang et al., 2007) confer CHD risk, as does disruption (i.e., separation, divorce) in these relationships (Smith et al., 2011a; Dupre & Nelson, 2016).

Several personality characteristics and forms of emotional distress are associated with increased CHD risk, including depression (Gan et al., 2014; Meijer et al., 2013), anxiety (Celano et al., 2015; Emdin et al., 2016), posttraumatic stress disorder (Edmondson et al., 2013), perceived stress and negative affectivity (Dahlen et al., 2022; Richardson et al., 2012), the combination of negative affect and social inhibition labeled the distress-prone or Type D personality (Lodder et al., 2023), and a group of inter-related traits involving anger, hostility, and antagonism (Chida & Steptoe, 2009; Dahlen et al., 2022; Mostofsky et al., 2014). The personality trait of dominance, assessed via self-reports, informant ratings, or interview-based ratings, is also associated with increased risk of CAD and CHD (Houston et al., 1992; Siegman et al., 2000; Smith et al., 2008). Other personality characteristics and individual differences are associated with reduced CHD risk, such as positive affectivity, optimism, conscientiousness, and some forms of spirituality and religiousness (Boehm, 2021; Dahlen et al., 2022; Jokela et al., 2014; Masters & Hooker, 2013).

Most of these psychosocial risk and protective factors are associated with behavioral risk factors (e.g., smoking, inactivity), which likely contribute to their associations with CAD and CHD. However, models of the mechanisms linking social environments, personal relationships, and emotional adjustment and personality to CHD also describe more direct physiological pathways involving the experience and consequences of psychological stress (O'Connor et al., 2021).

Cardiovascular reactivity (CVR) is a central example of these psychophysiological mechanisms, where metabolically excessive increases in heart rate, blood pressure, and their related determinants (e.g., cardiac sympathetic activation, parasympathetic withdrawal, cardiac output, peripheral vascular resistance) in response to psychological stressors are hypothesized to promote atherosclerosis and eventually the emergence of clinical manifestations of CHD later in the disease process (Carroll et al., 2017; Turner et al., 2020). Heightened cortisol responses to stress also contribute to CAD/CHD (e.g., Iob & Steptoe, 2019), at least in part through effects on systemic inflammatory processes linked to the disease process (Floranelli et al., 2018). Stress can also play an important role among individuals with pre-existing CHD (Kivimaki & Steptoe, 2018). For example, myocardial ischemia evoked by psychological stressors predicts subsequent coronary events in this population (Vaccarino et al., 2021; Wei et al., 2014).

This general model of excessive physiological stress responses as linking psychosocial factors with health outcomes has been clarified and expanded. For example, characteristically blunted responses to mental stressors predict increased risk of some adverse health outcomes, while exaggerated reactivity predicts cardiovascular disease (CVD) (e.g., Carroll et al., 2017; O'Riordan et al., 2023; Turner et al., 2020). Other models suggest that CVR characterized by heightened sympathetic nervous system activity and increased peripheral vascular resistance represents an unhealthy physiological response pattern associated with the experience of psychological threat, whereas the combination of sympathetic activation and increased cardiac output reflects a more adaptive response indicative of experiencing potential stressors as challenges (Howard, 2023; Seery, 2011). Other recent models have suggested that the failure of adaptation of physiological responses to repeated exposure to stressors, rather than the magnitude of initial reactivity during single exposures, is unhealthy and confers CVD risk (Hughes et al., 2018).

The traditional focus of psychophysiological theory and research on stress and CHD has emphasized responses produced by the sympathetic nervous system (SNS) (e.g., cardiovascular reactivity) and the hypothalamic-pituitary-adrenal (HPA) axis (e.g., cortisol levels and reactivity) (Kivimaki & Steptoe, 2018). Recent approaches have broadened this focus to include parasympathetic processes that reduce risk, usually measured through vagally mediated heart rate variability (vmHRV) (Thayer & Lane, 2007). Higher tonic or resting levels of vmHRV are associated with reduced CHD risk and mortality (Hillebrand et al., 2013; Jarczok et al., 2022), and are also associated with a wide variety of adaptive psychosocial characteristics (Smith, Deits-Lebehn, et al., 2020). Brosschot et al. (2017) have suggested that the parasympathetic nervous system (PNS) exerts tonic inhibition over pre-potent SNS responses, permitting rapid physiological mobilization when this parasympathetic inhibition is withdrawn in response to feelings of uncertainty, perceptions of reduced safety, or actual threat. Thus, both resting and reactive vmHRV are potentially important mechanisms in CHD risk (Thayer & Lane, 2007).

As an individual responds to multiple stressors over time, the total aggregate or burden of stress responses across physiological systems is captured in McEwen's (1998) concept of *allostatic load*. Theoretically, the magnitude of this aggregate physiological burden influences the development of CAD and its progression to clinically apparent CHD (Kivimaki & Steptoe, 2018). Allostatic load can be seen as comprising four distinct stress processes, specifically exposure, reactivity, recovery, and restoration (Williams et al., 2011), depicted in Figure 11.1.

The degree of stress exposure is a key influence on overall physiological burden, and reflects the frequency, duration, and magnitude or severity of events experienced as stressful, depicted by the number, width, and height, respectively, of bars indicating stressor occurrence in Figure 11.1. As illustrated, more frequent, prolonged, and severe stressors result in greater overall physiological activation. However, for any given stressor, individuals differ in the magnitude of physiological reactivity, as well as the rate and extent to which they recover physiologically after the stressor (Panaite et al., 2015). Greater reactivity and slower or more limited recovery contribute to overall physiological burden, also depicted in Figure 11.1.

Finally, individuals experience varying degrees of physiological restoration, such as the nighttime dipping in blood pressure below waking levels (Gavriilaki et al., 2020). Given that stress is associated with poor sleep and insomnia symptoms (Gardani et al., 2022), limitations in physiologic restoration such as less nocturnal blood pressure dipping accompanying low quantity or quality of sleep (e.g., Loredo et al., 2004) could also contribute to overall burden (Christensen et al., 2022). Thus, the composite of these four stress processes, reflected in the relative area under the

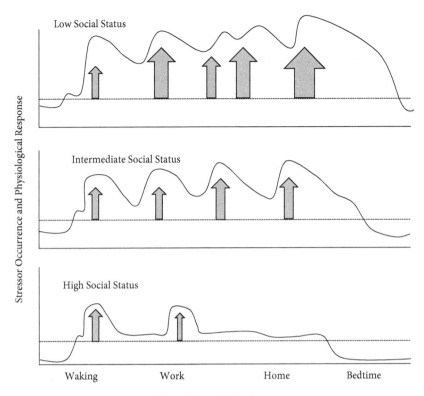

Figure 11.1 Four stress processes within allostatic load.

Note: The contribution of four stress processes (exposure, reactivity, recovery, and restoration) to overall physiological stress responses across the day for individuals experiencing high (top panel, low SES), intermediate (middle panel), and low (bottom panel, high SES) stress environments. Bars represent stressors, with height and width representing the magnitude and duration, respectively. Continuous lines represent physiological stress responses varying across the day, with total physiological burden (i.e., allostatic load) depicted as area under the curve for individuals experiencing the three levels of stress.

three curves depicted in Figure 11.1, contribute to the risk of CAD/CHD associated with low, intermediate, and high-risk contexts.

Stress management interventions intended to improve heart health typically attempt to reduce perceived stress and negative emotions that often accompany CHD (Levine et al., 2021), but they can also reduce the overall magnitude of allostatic load, as a possible avenue for improving prognosis. Relaxation, meditation, and biofeedback techniques can reduce overall physiological burden by limiting reactivity and facilitating recovery. They may have additional benefits in enhancing restoration to the extent that they improve sleep quality (T. Chen et al., 2020; Scott et al., 2021). These approaches are often combined with cognitive-behavioral interventions that can reduce the frequency, magnitude, and duration of stress exposure through modification of stress-engendering appraisals and other maladaptive psychological factors, such as worry and rumination, that can otherwise evoke, exacerbate, and prolong physiological activation.

In an early meta-analysis of intervention trials, Linden et al. (1996) found that psychosocial interventions for patients with coronary artery disease improved emotional adjustment, reduced several biologic risk factors (e.g., blood pressure, cholesterol), reduced CHD recurrence, and improved survival. Later reviews of an expanded literature indicated that the benefits for medical outcomes (e.g., survival) were significant only among male patients (Linden et al., 2007). However, a subsequent randomized trial evaluating an intervention designed and implemented with a specific focus on women with CHD also produced significant effects on survival (Orth-Gomér et al., 2009). Further trials of psychosocial interventions with a major focus on stress management have produced beneficial effects for psychosocial and medical outcomes (e.g., Blumenthal et al., 2016). However, recent meta-analytic reviews suggest that the effects are more robust for psychosocial than medical outcomes (Richards et al., 2018; Shi & Lan, 2021; Zhang et al., 2021). It is possible that additional consideration of *interpersonal*, as opposed to *intrapersonal*, contributions to physiological burden could produce further health benefits from interventions with CHD patients.

Contemporary Integrative Interpersonal Theory

When applied to the role of stress in CHD, the interpersonal tradition in personality and clinical psychology (Horowitz & Strack, 2011; Pincus & Ansell, 2013) identifies interpersonal situations as key sources of physiological stress responses s (Smith & Cundiff, 2011; Smith et al., 2003). In current interpersonal theory (Pincus & Ansell, 2013; Wright et al., 2023), recurring patterns of these situations are the primary manifestation of personality and emotional (mal)adjustment. These patterns also comprise the extent and quality of personal relationships. Interpersonal situations involve both in-person interactions between individuals during daily life, as well as internal mental representations or rehearsals of such interactions (e.g., recalled, imagined, or anticipated interactions). In-person interactions with family members, other close social network members, and co-workers are particularly relevant, given their frequency and importance. Internal representations include calling to mind warm and supportive relationships or savoring pleasant past or future interactions, as well as imagining possible negative social contexts (e.g., worry about an up-coming job interview) or mentally replaying a previous argument, conflict, or episode of perceived mistreatment.

These real and imagined interpersonal situations, as well as related behaviors and motives, can be described with the two broad dimensions of *agency* (i.e., dominance, control, independence, achievement, and high status versus deference, subordination, and low status) and *communion* (i.e., warmth, connection, and inclusion versus hostility, isolation, ostracism, and rejection). Bakan (1966) described these dimensions as fundamental modalities of human existence; agency refers to striving for mastery over the environment, competence, achievement, status and power, whereas communion refers to the desire for connection, closeness, and cooperation with others.

These two dimensions appear in several conceptual frameworks across social, personality, clinical psychology, and other fields (Wiggins & Trapnell, 1996). For example, status (e.g., respect) and non-romantic love (e.g., inclusion, connection, appreciation) are the two primary commodities granted or withheld in social exchanges (Foa & Foa, 2012). Several models suggest that as group-living primates, humans face the key adaptive challenges of "getting along" or maintaining adequate cooperative ties and group inclusion, as well as "getting ahead" or achieving and maintaining adequate social standing or status relative to others in the group (Anderson et al., 2015; Baumeister & Leary, 1995; Hogan, 1983; Kenrick et al., 2010). Agency and communion are also primary dimensions of social cognition (e.g., appraisals and evaluations of the self, other individuals, and groups) (Abele et al., 2021) and personal narratives or life stories (McAdams et al., 1996). The essential nature of these concerns is evident in the fact that connection with others and relative social status are distinct influences on self-esteem (Leary et al., 2001), and that both the level and stability of perceived status and inclusion predict self-esteem (Benson & Giacomin, 2020; Mahadevan et al., 2023).

The independent dimensions of agency and communion form the interpersonal circumplex (IPC) (Kiesler, 1983), although the IPC dimensions are typically labeled *control* and *affiliation*. Specific social behaviors, related personality styles, broad social motives, more focused and transient social goals, and impressions of others

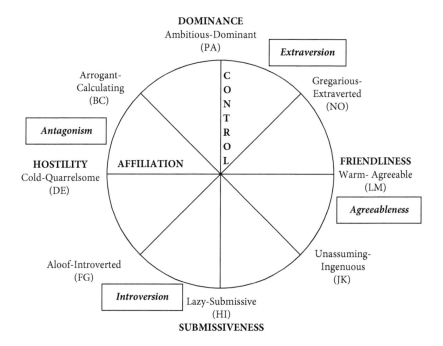

Figure 11.2 The interpersonal circumplex.
Note: The interpersonal circumplex comprises the main dimensions of affiliation and control and describes blends of these dimensions (e.g., warm-dominance versus hostile-submissiveness). The locations of the five-factor model of personality traits of extraversion and agreeableness are also indicated.

can be organized as blends of these two dimensions, as depicted in Figure 11.2. Importantly, individual difference characteristics, aspects of personal relationships, and broader social-environmental contexts, psychosocial risk and protective factors for CHD can be conceptually and empirically located in the IPC (Smith et al., 2010; Wiggins & Broughton, 1991).

For example, symptoms of depression and anxiety are associated with a hostile-submissive interpersonal style, as measured by IPC-based instruments, and measures of trait anger and hostility are associated with hostile and hostile-dominant styles (Smith et al., 2010). In contrast, optimism (Smith et al., 2010) and other positive individual characteristics such as several aspects of religiousness and spirituality are associated with a warm-dominant style (Jordan et al., 2014). Individuals reporting high levels of social support have a warm interpersonal style (Gallo & Smith, 1999), and reports of support from spouses and high marital quality are associated with IPC-based ratings of spouses as warm. In contrast, reports of marital conflict are associated with ratings of spouses as hostile and dominant (Smith et al., 2010). Low SES is also associated with the perception of others encountered during daily interactions as more hostile and dominant (Gallo et al., 2006). Thus, in general, risk factors for CVD are associated with a general pattern of hostile interpersonal behavior and experiences, whereas protective factors are associated with warmth. Yet, there is potentially important variation along the dominance versus deference or submissiveness axis of the IPC within both the risk and protective characteristic categories.

An additional tenet of the interpersonal perspective increases the importance of these IPC correlates. According to the complementarity principle (Kiesler, 1983; Sadler et al., 2011) expressions of warmth invite or evoke warmth in return from interaction partners; expressions of hostility invite or evoke hostile responses. Further, control or dominance invites deference or submission, and expressions of deference or submissiveness invite dominance from others. A large body of evidence supports these predictions, especially for complementarity of affiliation (Sadler et al., 2011). Although expressions of dominance are often met with deference, they sometimes evoke dominant responses from interaction partners, especially when dominance is combined with hostility (Cundiff et al., 2016; Smith & Baron, 2016). This latter pattern likely reflects disagreement about partners' relative levels of status or position, as in instances of contested control.

Once the interpersonal style associated with a given personality characteristic or type of emotional distress is established in IPC-based analyses, the complementarity principle provides theory-based predictions about social correlates that are relevant to CVD risk. At the most general level, characteristics associated with a warm interpersonal style should also be associated with friendly and supportive interactions and relationships. Characteristics associated with a hostile interpersonal style would be associated with social isolation, less support, greater conflict, and more interaction episodes and relationships involving quarrelsomeness (Kiesler, 1983).

Consistent with the complementarity principle, all well-established individual-level CHD risk and protective factors have robust associations with the presence and quality of social relationships, both generally and in central personal relationships such as marriage and similar intimate relationships. These associations of individual and relational risk and protective factors include depression (Beach, 2014; Proulx et al., 2007), anxiety (Malouff et al., 2010; Pankiewicz et al., 2012), PTSD (Caska et al., 2014; Lambert et al., 2012), and anger and hostility (K. Baron et al., 2007; Smith et al., 1990), where these characteristics are associated with higher conflict and lower warmth and support in important relationships. In contrast, optimism (Assad et al., 2007; Smith et al., 2013) and conscientiousness (Malouff et al., 2010; Roberts et al., 2007) are associated with greater warmth and support and lower conflict, strain, and disruption in important relationships. These robust associations point to processes that may contribute to the development and course of CHD. That is, rather than distinct classes of influences on CHD, individual characteristics (i.e., emotional adjustment, personality) and aspects of social relationships that predict CHD may be overlapping markers of recurring interpersonal situations and experiences that influence disease (Gallo & Smith, 1999; Smith et al., 2022).

The various forms of complementarity, as well as non-complementary sequences such as contested dominance, can be seen as recurring interaction patterns. In interpersonal theory, the specific elements of these patterns are articulated in the *transactional cycle*, depicted in Figure 11.3. Using an example of an actual, rather than internally represented, interaction between two individuals, the cycle begins—albeit somewhat arbitrarily in the case of longer-standing interactions and relationships—with the internal or covert experience of one of the two people. This individual's goals, appraisals, affect, strategies, expectations, and other internal processes promote related forms of expressive behavior, varying along the dimensions of the IPC. Warm goals and expectations prompt expressions of affiliation, whereas hostile goals and expectations prompt cold or quarrelsome behavior. The first person's expressive behavior, in turn, constrains the second person's internal or covert experiences. The first person's expression of warm approach is likely to evoke pleasant affect in the second person, and activate affiliative appraisals and goals, increasing the likelihood of the reciprocated warmth that is a hallmark of affiliative complementarity. In contrast, if the first actor harbors negative expectations, attributes ambiguous social behavior as reflecting others' hostile intent, is experiencing irritation or anger, and has defensive of aggressive goals, their hostile expressive behavior is likely to evoke cold or even hostile responses from the interaction partner and an ongoing sequence of negative reciprocity, the other hallmark of (non)affiliative complementarity.

The *context* of transactional cycles is an important consideration, as some contexts facilitate recurring warm transactions that are sources of protection from CHD, whereas other contexts promote transactions that confer risk, such as reciprocated hostility or unwelcome expressions of dominance and deference. For example, low household SES often makes warm interactions with intimate partners and other

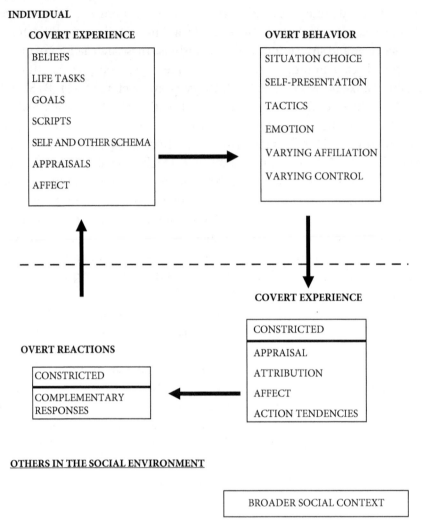

Figure 11.3 The transactional cycle.

Note: In the transactional cycle, actors' covert or internal processes guide their expressive behavior, which in turn influences the internal processes of others in the social environment. The influenced or restricted internal experiences of interaction partners influence their expressive behaviors, in ways that tend to reinforce the initial actors' expectations.

family members less likely and hostile interactions more likely, given the chronic stresses associated with lower levels of income and other resources (e.g., Neppl et al., 2016). The CHD risk factor of job stress not only directly involves strained interactions at work, but also promotes "spillover" of work stress to reduce warmth and increase conflict at home (Repetti et al., 2009). Thus, broader contextual factors related to CHD can promote transactional patterns that have parallel associations with risk or resilience.

Interpersonal Influences on Physiological Stress Responses

In the interpersonal perspective, experiences that threaten status and connection with others are potent sources of stress. This is consistent with models of social-evaluative threat that identify "situations that provide the potential for a loss of social esteem, social status, or social acceptance" (Dickerson et al., 2004, p. 1195) as key sources of physiological stress responses that impact physical health. The threat of even temporary loss of these key social resources can evoke physiological stress responses directly. These threats also increase individuals' self-involvement, the perceived importance of successful performance, and effortful engagement in the task(s) at hand, further increasing physiological stress responses (Gendolla et al., 2019; Seery, 2011).

The Trier Social Stress Test (TSST; Kirschbaum et al., 1993), where participants perform cognitive and social tasks in front of raters, is the most widely used method of inducing social-evaluative threat in psychophysiological research. Studies with necessary experimental controls demonstrate that evaluative threat in the TSST and similar stressors evokes large responses (Bosch et al., 2009; Cundiff et al., 2016; Smith et al., 1997), with robust effects on HPA axis activity (i.e., cortisol reactivity), sympathetically mediated cardiac responses (e.g., SBP, pre-ejection period, cardiac output), vascular responses (e.g., DBP, peripheral resistance), and parasympathetic withdrawal (Allen et al., 2014). Further, momentary changes in social-evaluative threat predict changes in ambulatory blood pressure, suggesting that the results of laboratory-based research generalize to "real-world" settings (e.g., Smith, Birmingham, & Uchino, 2012).

However, in the vast majority of these studies it is not clear if threats of loss of social connection and inclusion (e.g., rejection) or loss of status and respect (e.g., performance failure) are the primary influences on these stress responses. The standard TSST instructions emphasize task performance, an evaluative focus more relevant to agentic than communal concerns. Specific manipulation of such achievement-related threats clearly evokes physiological stress responses (Bosch et al., 2009; Cundiff et al., 2016). However, social acceptance threats (e.g., ostracism, rejection) also evoke heightened reactivity (e.g., Blackhart et al., 2007; Ford & Collins, 2010; Stroud et al., 2009). In studies with independent manipulations of both themes of social evaluation, threats focused on social inclusion and status have independent and additive effects on cardiovascular and cortisol reactivity (Jordan & Smith, 2023; Smith & Jordan, 2015). Hence, interpersonal situations that threaten either of the two broad and central motives in the interpersonal perspective (Locke, 2015) can evoke potentially deleterious physiological responses. Of course, some particularly stressful interpersonal situations activate both themes, where individuals are simultaneously concerned about being demeaned and rejected.

The IPC is also a useful framework for organizing research on psychophysiological effects of exposure to others' social behavior and effects of the individual's own expressive social behavior, as well as psychophysiological correlates of individual and social risk and protective characteristics (Smith et al., 2003). Turning first to the affiliation axis, a large body of research demonstrates that exposure to hostile behavior (e.g., harassment, conflict, criticism) displayed by interaction partners evokes robust physiological stress responses across multiple cardiovascular and neuroendocrine responses (e.g., Gallo et al., 2000; Lobbestael et al., 2008; see Smith et al., 2003, for a review), as well as decreases in parasympathetic activity (Deits-Lebehn et al., 2023; Shahrestani et al., 2015). In laboratory-based assessments and ambulatory monitoring during daily life, anger is associated with increased blood pressure, as is the suppression of anger (Schum et al., 2003; Thayer et al., 2020).

In contrast, exposure to warmth from others, such as the provision of social support, can reduce physiological stress responses (Uchino, 2006). Although laboratory-based studies do not find that positive social interactions evoke increases in parasympathetic activity (i.e., vmHRV) (Deits-Lebehn et al., 2023; Shahrestani et al., 2015), some ambulatory research does suggest that positive interactions in real life evoke increased vmHRV (H. Liu et al., 2022). Further, exercises that involve self-compassion evoke an increase in vmHRV (Kirschner et al., 2019). Mental activation of supportive ties can also attenuate physiological stress responses (Smith et al., 2004).

In laboratory studies, personality traits associated with low levels of the IPC dimension of affiliation (e.g., hostility, anger) are often associated with heightened physiological reactivity and delayed recovery in response to relevant stressors, such as conflict or harassment (e.g., Neumann et al., 2004; see Smith et al., 2003, for a review), and trait affiliation is inversely related to ambulatory blood pressure during daily activities (e.g., C. E. Baron et al., 2016).

For the IPC control axis, efforts to exert influence or control (i.e., dominance) over others evoke heightened cardiovascular responses, especially if those efforts are important and difficult. Exposure to dominant behavior expressed by others also evokes heightened stress responses (Cundiff et al., 2016; see Newton, 2009, and Smith, Cundiff, & Uchino, 2012, for reviews). Trait dominance is also generally associated with heightened physiological responses to relevant stressors (e.g., competition), although in some circumstances submissive or deferential individuals display greater reactivity (Smith, Cundiff, & Uchino, 2012). Outside the laboratory, trait dominance is positively associated with ambulatory blood pressure (C. E. Baron et al., 2016).

Relative social status also influences the physiological stress responses of interaction partners. Higher status individuals display smaller responses, whereas lower status persons display heightened reactivity (Cundiff et al., 2016; Smith, Cundiff, & Uchino, 2012). However, the stability of interaction partners' relative status is an important moderating factor. Lower status persons display patterns indicative of threat (i.e., increased vascular resistance) in stable status hierarchies or relationships, but display response patterns indicative of challenge (i.e., increased cardiac output) in unstable status situations. For high status individuals, instability in status hierarchies or relationships is associated with CVR patterns indicative of threat (Scheepers & Knight, 2020). Thus, having a secure sense of higher status is associated with an adaptive pattern of physiological response, whereas consistent low status or threatened high status evoke maladaptive response patterns. As a personality trait, hostile dominance may be associated with both heightened reactivity to relevant stressors (e.g., conflict or contested status) and increased exposure to such threats if this expressive behavior evokes contested dominance rather than deference from interaction partners. Via transactional processes described previously, such interaction sequences would render the relative social status of hostile-dominant persons unstable. Thus, the combined effects of greater reactivity and greater exposure may produce high levels of allostatic load that contribute to the unhealthy effects of hostile-dominance.

In the context of close personal relationships, such as married couples and other intimate relationships, affiliation and control have similar physiological correlates. Conflict (i.e., low affiliation) evokes heightened reactivity (Nealey-Moore et al., 2007; see Robles et al., 2014, for a review), as do efforts to exert control (P. C. Brown & Smith, 1992; Smith, Baron, et al., 2020). In romantic dyads, couples comprised of two partners high in power display patterns of physiological reactivity indicative of increased threat responses (Gresham et al., 2023). Individuals high in restrictiveness, a form of dominance in close relationships, display heightened physiological challenge responses, whereas their partners display threat (Tudder et al., 2020).

As noted previously, the increased rates of CHD among Black Americans likely involve exposure to racism, among other factors. In everyday experiences, exposure to racism evokes biological correlates of stress and negative emotion (Ong et al., 2018). From the interpersonal perspective, these exposures can be seen as including exposure to greater hostility and unwelcome control from others, as well as lower relative social status and decreased warmth in many social contexts. Exposure to racism also promotes anger suppression and resentful deference in response to provocations (Thayer et al., 2020), chronic feelings of unsafety (Brosschot et al., 2017), and worry and rumination over past, present, and future mistreatment (Ottaviani et al., 2016), all of which contribute to unhealthy physiological activation.

This application of the interpersonal perspective to physiological stress responses that contribute to CHD suggests a specific conceptualization of risk and resilience. Well-established psychosocial risk and protective factors are associated with recurring interpersonal situations and reciprocally determined patterns of interpersonal transaction that influence physiological stress responses. Specifically, physiological stress responses are heightened in interpersonal situations involving (a) exposure to others' expressions of hostility, exclusion, and unwelcome control, and/or (b) one's own expressions of hostility and efforts to exert influence or control over others. In contrast, physiological stress responses are minimized by (a) exposure to others' expressions of warmth and inclusion, and/or (b) one's own expressions of warmth and inclusion (Smith et al., 2010). These interpersonal situations confer risk or protection to the extent that they threaten or enhance individuals' perceived social status and/or connection with others. Further, these patterns of stress responses are maintained through reciprocal influences between individuals' expressive behavior and the (re)actions of others, such that both unhealthy and protective interaction patterns and their physiological effects are maintained over time.

Implications for Intervention

In planning interventions for patients with CHD or those at risk due to the presence of other cardiometabolic risk factors (Mottillo et al., 2010), exercise-based cardiac rehabilitation (Dibben et al., 2023; Ostman et al., 2017), adherence to medication regimens (Du et al., 2017) and smoking cessation (Wu et al., 2022) are clear priorities. However, as noted previously, psychosocial interventions including stress management are useful additions in overall patient management (Levine et al., 2021). In addition to efforts to reduce unhealthy physiological activation through relaxation, meditation, and biofeedback, or through modification of stress-engendering cognitive-behavioral processes, an interpersonally enhanced approach to stress management targets elements of transactional cycles as opportunities for intervention. Specifically, existing approaches for reducing exposure to maladaptive interpersonal situations (e.g., others' expressions of hostility and unwelcome control), reducing unhealthy expressive behavior, and cultivating warmth and social connection could be useful additions to current interventions.

Intervention Goals and Methods Related to Affiliation and Control

The intervention implications for interpersonal situations and experiences falling along the affiliation axis of the IPC are clear. Therapeutic goals include reducing individuals' own expressions of hostility and reducing their exposure and reactivity to expressions of hostility by others. Given the strong complementarity in hostility during social interaction, these goals are two sides of the same coin. The large literature on modifying anger and aggressive behavior is directly relevant and includes a focus on cultivating relaxation and self-calming skills, as well as increasing awareness of thoughts that promote anger and aggression and restructuring these maladaptive cognitions (Lee & DiGiuseppe, 2018).

For some individuals, the mental rehearsal of past mistreatment by others (e.g., rumination, brooding) is a key correlate of their anger and hostility (Wilkowski & Robinson, 2010), depression and anxiety (Rickerby et al., 2022), and PTSD symptoms among trauma-exposed individuals (Moulds et al., 2020). Unchecked, these internal representations of past interpersonal events can be important sources of recurring physiological stress responses (Ottaviani et al., 2016). In addition to CBT techniques addressing these recurring cognitions directly, forgiveness interventions may be useful in not only increasing forgiveness toward offending parties, but in reducing negative affective characteristics related to CHD and promoting increased well-being (Akhtar & Barlow, 2018; Wade et al., 2014), and potentially improving physical health (Rasmussen et al., 2019).

The affiliation axis of the IPC suggests an additional goal of increasing exposure to warmth from others and overall social connection, as well as increasing the individual's own expressions of warmth and inclusion toward others. Again, given the strong complementarity of warmth during social interaction, these two goals are closely related. There is preliminary evidence that loving kindness meditation and other contemplative interventions facilitate these prosocial behaviors and experiences and related elements of positive transactional cycles, and can reduce negativity in interpersonal relationships, although variable results and methodological limitations preclude more definitive conclusions (Kreplin et al., 2018; Uchino et al., 2016; Zhou et al., 2022). Further, some evidence suggests that CBT and social skill interventions can reduce loneliness and social isolation (Hill et al., 2021; Kall et al., 2020).

The implications for the control axis of the IPC are less obvious. Certainly, reduced exposure and reactivity to unwelcome dominance expressed by others would attenuate overall physiological burden. Further, reducing expressions of excessive or unnecessary dominance, especially in its hostile form, is an important goal, given that attempts to exert control over others reliably evoke heightened physiological reactivity (Smith, Cundiff, & Uchino, 2012) and may evoke contested dominance from others, further exacerbating physiological burden associated with the IPC control axis. However, therapeutic goals for modifications in the individual's expressive behaviors are not straightforward, given that expressions of both excessive dominance *and* expressions of resentful deference (e.g., suppressed anger) promote unhealthy physiological activity.

Further, through complementarity and transactional processes, expression of unfriendly deference and submissiveness—a style associated with several psychosocial risk factors for CHD (Smith et al., 2010)—invites or evokes hostile-dominance from others, which as noted previously also contributes to heightened physiological stress responses. Thus, alternatives to expression of both dominance and submissiveness are needed.

A refinement of interpersonal theory suggests a viable solution. Unlike the traditional IPC, in the Structural Analysis of Social Behavior (SASB) model (Benjamin, 1974; Benjamin et al., 2006) dominance and submissiveness are not conceptualized as opposite ends of a single dimension. Rather, they are on separate interpersonal surfaces distinguished by a focus on others in social interaction versus a focus on the self, as presented in Figure 11.4. On the focus on other or *transitive* surface (Figure 11.4, top panel), actions are done to, for, or about another person (e.g., "She watches and controls him"). On the focus on self or *intransitive* surface (Figure 11.4, middle panel), actions are done to, for, or about the self in relation to the other person (e.g., "He defers to her"). On both of these circumplex surfaces, social behavior is defined by the two dimensions of affiliation (i.e., warmth versus hostility) and autonomy (i.e., separation versus enmeshment).

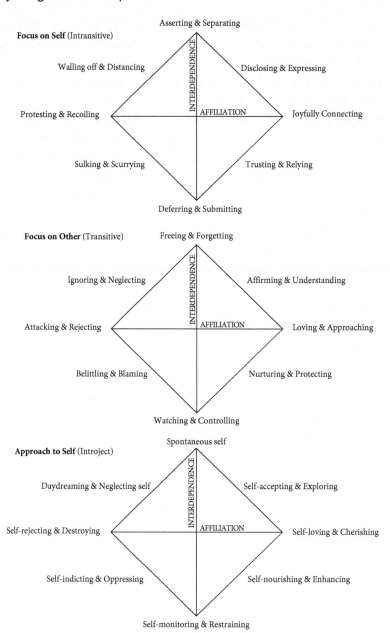

Figure 11.4 The structural analysis of social behavior.
Note: Benjamin's organization of interpersonal (focus on self, focus on other) and intrapersonal (introject) behavior. Quadrant and axis labels from Benjamin (1987).

Expression of dominance or control toward others is an enmeshed or *interconnected* transitive action, and its opposite is not submitting or deferring but instead granting autonomy or *separation* to others (i.e., "freeing and forgetting"). Expressions of submissiveness or deference are on the second (i.e., intransitive: focus on self) SASB surface, and their opposite is not the expression of dominance toward others but rather the assertion of one's own independence or *autonomy*, such as straightforward expressions of feelings, experiences, preferences, and beliefs.

In the SASB model, complementary behaviors describing common interaction sequences involve the two behaviors located in similar places on these two surfaces. For example, warm-autonomous interactions involve one person's (transitive) behavior that communicates affirmation and understanding toward the other, while the other's (intransitive) behavior involves disclosing and expressing personal feelings or experiences. In contrast, hostile enmeshment involves one person's (transitive) behavior of belittling and blaming (e.g., criticizing) an interaction partner who, in turn, expresses the (intransitive) behavior of resentful or defensive deference and compliance (i.e., "sulking and scurrying"). It is important to note that psychosocial risk factors for CHD involve various SASB interaction patterns on the hostile side of these two surfaces, whereas protective factors (i.e., social support, optimism) involve interaction patterns on the warm side. Further, cultivating patterns of comfortable assertion of one's own autonomy and, whenever appropriate, granting autonomy to others provides alternatives to enmeshed deference and dominance, respectively, and their potentially unhealthy physiological correlates.

Mindfulness-Based Stress Reduction (MBSR) (Kabat-Zinn, 1990) is a well-developed intervention with documented benefits, including reduced stress and improved social functioning (de Vibe et al., 2017). Importantly, the approach includes elements that promote warm autonomy. Both dispositional and cultivated mindfulness are associated with warmth (e.g., Deits-Lebehn et al., 2022), as well as granting autonomy to others (e.g., acknowledging and accepting their experiences and independence) and acting in an autonomous manner (e.g., expressing, acknowledging, and accepting one's own experience and independence). This SASB-based account of contemplative states and practices as involving autonomy has been described in meditative traditions that are similar to mindfulness (Sweet & Johnson, 1990), and the general interpersonal stance of warm autonomy is a major element of mindfulness-based interventions for adult relationships (Carson et al., 2004) and parenting (Parent & DiMarzio, 2021).

Dispositional and cultivated mindfulness are associated with reduced psychological and physiological responses to social stress (Britton et al., 2012; K. W. Brown et al., 2012; Creswell et al., 2014; Johnson et al., 2019). Emerging evidence suggest that mindfulness-based and related contemplative interventions are also useful in reducing psychosocial and physiological risk factors among adults with CVD (Heppner et al., 2008; Nijjar et al., 2019; Scott-Sheldon et al., 2020). For example, MBSR is effective in reducing blood pressure among hypertensives (Conversano et al., 2021; Geiger et al., 2023). Given the elevated risk for CHD among Black Americans, it is important to note that evidence suggests that Transcendental Meditation can improve medical outcomes in this patient population (Schneider et al., 2012). Mindfulness-based approaches are certainly useful in cultivating relaxation techniques that reduce physiological reactivity and facilitate recovery, even among people with symptoms of emotional dysregulation associated with borderline personality disorder (Yeh & Lin, 2022).

Importantly, mindfulness techniques also cultivate a sense of detachment and perspective (i.e., autonomy) during potentially stressful circumstances, which may be particularly useful in disrupting otherwise automatic patterns of negative complementarity, such as reciprocated hostility and competitive struggles for control or status. Thus, autonomy provides a valuable alternative to various forms of hostile-enmeshment associated with psychosocial risk. Individuals can refuse to "bite the hook" (Powell, 1996) when interaction partners issue an implicit invitation to conflict or offense. Neutral or even warm assertion of one's preferences and opinions is a useful, autonomous alternative to hostile deference, criticism or dominance in such situations.

The SASB model of interpersonal behavior includes a third surface that describes internal self-directed behavior, using the same two dimensions of affiliation and autonomy (see Figure 11.4, bottom panel). In a variety of psychosocial risk factors for CHD, individuals engage in hostile-enmeshment with themselves, specifically in their self-directed internal dialogues that involve self-criticism or self-blame. In contrast, protective factors often involve warm self-directed internal responses, such as self-acceptance, self-forgiveness, and self-compassion. This additional interpersonal focus in the SASB model may be particularly relevant in addressing the negative internal processes associated with worry and rumination that would otherwise be a source of more frequent, internally activated physiological stress responses (i.e., covert stressor exposures), as well as increased magnitude of the related reactivity and delayed recovery following these self-induced episodes of stress (Ottaviani et al., 2016). Traditional CBT techniques address maladaptive self-beliefs and self-criticism, and third wave approaches such as mindfulness and loving kindness meditation also promote adaptive disengagement and self-directed warmth (Reilly & Stuyvenberg, 2022). Compassion Focused Therapy (Gilbert, 2014) has an explicit focus on enhancing both self- and other-directed compassion, and a growing body of controlled trials documents its effectiveness in increasing self- and other-directed compassion, reducing self-criticism and improving adjustment (Millard et al., 2023).

Many individuals have difficulty effectively asserting their own autonomy and granting it to others, especially during interpersonal conflicts. The skills-based intervention of assertiveness training (e.g., Alberti & Emmons, 2017) is directly relevant to an interpersonally enhanced stress management in this regard. Although neglected in recent years, assertiveness training remains highly relevant in the treatment of problematic interpersonal functioning (Speed et al., 2018). It is useful for internalizing disorders and relationship problems and can be used to treat anger and aggressiveness by cultivating adaptive alternative skills for conflictual situations. Improved assertiveness and related social skills reduce occasions of hostile-enmeshment, by providing a lower-stress alternative to both resentful deference (i.e., hostile submission) and aggressive or controlling behavior (i.e., hostile dominance). That is, assertiveness provides an autonomous alternative to both the dominant and submissive forms of enmeshment. Over time, new skills in assertiveness can also decrease the perceived difficulty of previously daunting interpersonal interactions, with potential for reduced physiological effects of task difficulty.

Interpersonal Assessment for Stress Management and Psychotherapy

In evaluating the presence, severity, and type of maladaptive interpersonal functioning that could be usefully addressed in stress management and related psychotherapy for CHD risk, a variety of well-validated assessment measures are available (Locke, 2011). Perhaps most relevant, IPC-based inventories of interpersonal problems can provide specific descriptions of these patterns (Boudreaux et al., 2018). For example, some individuals may report difficulties establishing warm relationships with others, whereas others may report excessive dominance and control in their behavior toward others.

Interpersonal problems are associated with most forms of chronic stress and emotional distress but are particularly apparent in personality disorders (Wilson et al., 2017). Personality disorders and related symptoms, in turn, are associated with increased risk for CVD (Barber et al., 2020; Tiosano et al., 2022). Thus, although generally appropriate across a wide range of cases, an interpersonally enhanced approach to stress management or psychotherapy may be particularly useful for patients with long-standing and more severe interpersonal difficulties.

Conclusions and Future Directions

Consideration of these issues suggests the outlines of an interpersonally enhanced approach to therapeutic interventions in CHD. In addition to relaxation, biofeedback, or meditative/contemplative interventions as core intervention components to reduce physiological reactivity and facilitate recovery directly, CBT techniques are also undoubtedly helpful, especially those that address the interpretation of and response to on-going internal and external interpersonal sources of stress. Such elements within transactional cycles have been described for anger and aggressive behavior (Smith, Glazer, et al., 2004; Smith & Traupman, 2012; Wilkowski & Robinson, 2010), depression (Hames et al., 2013; Kupferberg & Hasler, 2023), anxiety (Whisman & Beach, 2010), loneliness (Cacioppo et al., 2015), and other CHD risk factors, and represent useful intervention targets. Approaches such as MBSR and other "third wave" cognitive-behavioral therapies have an added advantage by promoting detachment and affiliative connection rather than enmeshment and engagement in reciprocating patterns of hostility, struggles for control, or resentful deference and bitterness. Assertiveness training, interventions for loneliness and social isolation, and interventions that promote forgiveness and compassion toward the self and others also address key elements in the transactional processes related to risk and resilience.

It is possible that in many cases basic relaxation skills and CBT elements of stress management will provide adequate reductions in overall allostatic load or physiologic burden. Further, some evidence suggests that interpersonal problems do change with CBT and other forms of psychotherapy, even in interventions lacking an interpersonal focus (McFarquhar et al., 2018). However, more pronounced interpersonal problems at the beginning of therapy predict less positive response to CBT for depression and anxiety (Gomez Penedo & Fluckiger, 2023), suggesting that an interpersonal focus can be useful in many cases. For people whose recurring problematic interpersonal processes are primarily evident in intimate relationships, well-established relationship therapies may be useful in reducing CHD risk (Smith & Baucom, 2017).

Our perspective is largely based on a unidirectional view of the causal association of interpersonal processes and physiological activity, in which the former drives the latter. However, bidirectional processes are possible as well. For example, heart rate variability (HRV) biofeedback increases PNS activity. Resting levels of vmHRV are associated with a variety of adaptive emotional and social functioning, as parasympathetic capacity facilitates prosocial and self-regulatory capabilities (Di Bello et al., 2020; Smith, Deits-Lebehn, et al., 2020). HRV biofeedback is useful in the management of chronic disease, including cardiovascular conditions (Fournie et al., 2021). It is also useful in reducing a variety of forms of emotional distress that predict the development and course of CHD, including anger (Lehrer et al., 2020). For example, increased HRV achieved through biofeedback can reduce anger in response to provocation (Francis et al., 2016). Hence, in addition to reduced physiological stress responses resulting from psychosocial interventions, it is possible that some physiological interventions can reduce psychosocial risks, including those related to interpersonal functioning.

For all interventions in the prevention and management of CHD, it is important to consider socio-economic and racial health disparities. As noted previously, low SES is associated with increased incidence of CHD and worse prognosis among CHD patients. These effects likely involve psychosocial mechanisms (E. Chen & Miller, 2013), including the interpersonal processes reviewed here. Further, like low SES, racism experienced by Black Americans and other minority groups is evident in pervasive features of social contexts that promote recurring stressful experiences (e.g., Zestcott et al., 2022). Hence, to be optimally useful, an interpersonally enhanced approach to stress management for CHD must be tailored to the unique health-relevant social contexts individuals face.

References

Abele, A. E., Ellemers, N., Fiske, S. T., Koch, A., & Yzerbyt, V. (2021). Navigating the social world: Toward an integrated framework for evaluating self, individuals, and groups. *Psychological Review, 128*, 290–314. https://doi.org/10.1037/rev0000262

Akhtar, S., & Barlow, J. (2018). Forgiveness therapy for the promotion of mental well-being: A systematic review and meta-analysis. *Trauma, Violence, & Abuse, 19*, 107–122. https://doi.org/10.1177/1524838016637079

Alberti, R., & Emmons, M. (2017). *Your perfect right: Assertiveness and equality in your life and relationships* (10th ed.). Impact Publishers.

Allen, A. P., Kennedy, P. J., Cryan, J. F., Dinan, T. G., & Clarke, G. (2014). Biological and psychological markers of stress in humans: Focus on the Trier Social Stress Test. *Neuroscience and Biobehavioral Reviews, 38*, 94–124. https://doi.org/10.1016/j.neubiorev.2013.11.005

Anderson, C., Hildreth, J. A. D., & Howland, L. (2015). Is the desire for status a fundamental human motive? A review of the empirical literature. *Psychological Bulletin, 141*, 574–601. https://doi.org/10.1037/a0038781

Antoni, M. H., Moreno, P. I., & Penedo, F. J. (2023). Stress management interventions to facilitate psychological and physiological adaptation and optimal health outcomes in cancer patients and survivors. *Annual Review of Psychology, 74*, 423–455. https://doi.org/10.1146/annurev-psych-030122-124119

Assad, K. K., Donnellan, M. B., & Conger, R. D. (2007). Optimism: An enduring resource for romantic relationships. *Journal of Personality and Social Psychology, 93*, 285–297. https://doi.org/10.1037/0022-3514.93.2.285

Bakan, D. (1966). *The duality of human existence: An essay on psychology and religion*. Rand McNally.

Barber, T. A., Ringwald, W. R., Wright, A. G. C., & Manuck, S. B. (2020). Borderline personality disorder traits associate with midlife cardiometabolic risk. *Personality Disorders: Theory, Research, and Treatment, 11*, 151–156. https://doi.org/10.1037/per0000373

Baron, C. E., Smith, T. W., Uchino, B. N., Baucom, B. R., & Birmingham, W. C. (2016). Getting along and getting ahead: Affiliation and dominance predict ambulatory blood pressure. *Health Psychology, 35*, 253–261. https://doi.org/10.1037/hea0000290

Baron, K., Smith, T. W., Butner, J., Nealey-Moore, J., Hawkins, M., & Uchino, B. (2007). Hostility, anger, and marital adjustment: Concurrent and prospective associations with psychosocial vulnerability. *Journal of Behavioral Medicine, 30*, 1–10. https://doi.org/10.1007/s10865-006-9086-z

Barth, J., Schneider, S., & von Kanel, R. (2010). Lack of social support in the etiology and the prognosis of coronary heart disease: A systematic review and meta-analysis. *Psychosomatic Medicine, 72*, 229–238. https://doi.org/10.1097/PSY.0b013e3181d01611

Baumeister, R. F., & Leary, M. R. (1995). The need to belong: Desire for interpersonal attachments as a fundamental human motivation. *Psychological Bulletin, 117*(3), 497–529. https://doi.org/10.1037/0033-2909.117.3.497

Beach, S. R. H. (2014). The couple and family discord model of depression: Updates and future directions. In C. R. Agnew & S. C. South (Eds.), *Interpersonal relationships and health: Social and clinical psychological mechanisms* (pp. 113–155). Oxford University Press.

Benjamin, L. S. (1974). Structural analysis of social behavior. *Psychological Review, 81*, 392–425. https://doi.org/10.1037/h0037024

Benjamin, L. S. (1987). Use of the SASB dimensional model to develop treatment plans for personality disorders: I. Narcissism. *Journal of Personality Disorders, 1*(1), 43–70. https://doi.org/10.1521/pedi.1987.1.1.43

Benjamin, L. S., Rothweiler, J. C., & Critchfield, K. L. (2006). The use of structural analysis of social behavior (SASB) as an assessment tool. *Annual Review of Clinical Psychology, 2*, 83–109. https://doi.org/10.1146/annurev.clinpsy.2.022305.095337

Benson, A. J., & Giacomin, M. (2020). How self-esteem and narcissism differentially relate to high and (un)stable feelings of status and inclusion. *Journal of Personality, 88*, 1177–1195. https://doi.org/10.1111/jopy.12565

Blackhart, G., Eckel, L., & Tice, D. (2007). Salivary cortisol in response to acute social rejection and acceptance by peers. *Biological Psychology, 75*, 267–276. https://doi.org/10.1016/j.biopsycho.2007.03.005

Blumenthal, J. A., Sherwood, A., Smith, P., Watkins, L., Mabe, S., Kraus, W., Ingle, K., Miller, P., & Hinderliter, A. (2016). Enhancing cardiac rehabilitation with stress management training: A randomized, clinical efficacy trial. *Circulation, 133*, 1341–1350. https://doi.org/10.1161/CIRCULATIONAHA.115.018926

Boehm, J. K. (2021). Positive psychological well-being and cardiovascular disease: Exploring mechanistic and developmental pathways. *Social and Personality Psychology Compass, 15*, e12599. https://doi.org/10.1111/spc3.12599

Booth, J., Connelly, L., Lawrence, M., Chalmers, C., Joice, S., Becker, C., & Dougall, N. (2015). Evidence of perceived psychosocial stress as a risk factor for stroke in adults: A meta-analysis. *BMC Neurology, 15*, 23. https://doi.org/10.1186/s12883-015-0456-4

Bosch, J. A., de Geus, E. J., Carroll, D., Goedhart, A. D., Anane, L. A., van Zanten, J. J., Helmerhorst, E. J., & Edwards, K. M. (2009). A general enhancement of autonomic and cortisol responses during social evaluative threat. *Psychosomatic Medicine, 71*, 877–885. https://doi.org/10.1097/PSY.0b013e3181baef05

Boudreaux, M. J., Ozer, D. J., Oltmanns, T. F., & Wright, A. G. C. (2018). Development and validation of the circumplex scale of interpersonal problems. *Psychological Assessment, 30*, 594–609. https://doi.org/10.1037/pas0000505

Britton, W. B., Shahar, B., Szepsenwol, O., & Jacobs, W. J. (2012). Mindfulness-based cognitive therapy improves emotional reactivity to social stress: Results from a randomized controlled trial. *Behavior Therapy, 43*, 365–380. https://doi.org/10.1016/j.beth.2011.08.006

Brosschot, J. F., Verkuil, B., & Thayer, J. F. (2017). Exposed to events that never happen: Generalized unsafety, the default stress response, and prolonged autonomic activity. *Neuroscience and Biobehavioral Reviews, 74*, 287–296. https://doi.org/10.1016/j.neubiorev.2016.07.019

Brown, K. W., Weinstein, N., & Creswell, J. D. (2012). Trait mindfulness modulates neuroendocrine and affective responses to social evaluative threat. *Psychoneuroendocrinology, 37*, 2037–2041. https://doi.org/10.1016/j.psyneuen.2012.04.003

Brown, P. C., & Smith, T. W. (1992). Social influence, marriage, and the heart: Cardiovascular consequences of interpersonal control in husbands and wives. *Health Psychology, 11*, 88–96. https://doi.org/10.1037/0278-6133.11.2.88

Bryant, B. E., Jordan, A., & Clark, U. S. (2022). Race as a social construct in psychiatry research and practice. *JAMA Psychiatry, 79*, 93–94. https://doi.org/10.101/jamapsychiatry.2021.2877

Cacioppo, S., Grippo, A., London, S., Goosssens, L., & Cacioppo, J. T. (2015). Loneliness: Clinical import and interventions. *Perspectives in Psychological Science, 10*, 238–249. https://doi.org/10.1177/1745691615570616

Carroll, D., Ginty, A. T., Whittaker, A. C., Lovallo, W. R., & de Rooij, S. R. (2017). The behavioral, cognitive, and neural corollaries of blunted cardiovascular and cortisol reactions to acute psychological stress. *Neuroscience and Biobehavioral Reviews, 77*, 74–86. https://doi.org/10.1016/j.neubiorev.2017.02.025

Carson, J. W., Carson, K. M., Gil, K. M., & Baucom, D. H. (2004). Mindfulness-based relationship enhancement. *Behavior Therapy, 35*, 471–494. https://doi.org/10.1016/S0005-7894(04)80028-5

Caska, C. M., Smith, T. W., Renshaw, K. D., Allen, S. N., Uchino, B. N., Birmingham, W., & Carlisle, M. (2014). Posttraumatic stress disorder and responses to couple conflict: Implications for cardiovascular risk. *Health Psychology, 33*(11), 1273–1280. https://doi.org/10.1037/hea0000133

Celano, C., Millstein, R., Bedoya, C., Healey, B., Roest, A., & Huffman, J. (2015). Association between anxiety and mortality in patients with coronary artery disease: A meta-analysis. *American Heart Journal, 170*, 1105–1115. https://doi.org/10.1016/j.ahj.2015.09.013

Chen, E., & Miller, G. (2013). Socioeconomic status and health: Mediating and moderating factors. *Annual Review of Clinical Psychology, 9*, 723–749. https://doi.org/10.1146/annurev-clinpsy-050212-185634

Chen, T., Chang, S., Hsieh, H., Huang, C., Chuang, J., & Wang, H. (2020). Effects of mindfulness-based stress reduction on sleep quality and mental health for insomnia patients: A meta-analysis. *Journal of Psychosomatic Research, 135*, 110144. https://doi.org/10.1016/j.psychores.2020.110144

Chida, Y., & Steptoe, A. (2009). The association of anger and hostility with future coronary heart disease: A meta-analytic review of prospective evidence. *Journal of the American College of Cardiology, 53*, 774–778. https://doi.org/10.1016/j.jacc.2008.11.044

Christensen, D. S., Zachariae, R., Amidi, A., & Wu, L. M. (2022). Sleep and allostatic load: A systematic review and meta-analysis. *Sleep Medicine Review, 64*, 101650. https://doi.org/10.1016/j.smrv.2022.101650

Conversano, C., Orru, G., Pozza, A., Miccoli, M., Ciacchini, R., Marchi, L., & Gemignani, A. (2021). Is mindfulness-based stress reduction effective for people with hypertension? A systematic review and meta-analysis of 30 years of evidence. *International Journal of Environmental Research in Public Health, 18*, 2882. https://doi.org/10.3390/ijerph18062882

Creswell, J. D., Pacilio, L. E., Lindsay, E. K., & Brown, K. W. (2014). Brief mindfulness meditation training alters psychological and neuroendocrine responses to social evaluative stress. *Psychoneuroendocrinology, 44*, 1–12. https://doi.org/10.1016/j.psyneuen.2014.02.007

Cundiff, J. M., Smith, T. W., Baron, C. E., & Uchino, B. N. (2016). Hierarchy and health: Physiological effects of interpersonal experiences associated with socioeconomic position. *Health Psychology, 35*, 356–365. https://doi.org/10.1037/hea0000227

Dahlen, A. D., Miguet, M., Schioth, H., & Rukh, G. (2022). The influence of personality on the risk of myocardial infarction in the UK Biobank cohort. *Scientific Reports, 12*, 6706. https://doi.org/10.1038/s41598-022-10573-6

Deits-Lebehn, C., Smith, T. W., Grove, J. L., Williams, P. G., & Uchino, B. N. (2022). Interpersonal style contributes to the association of dispositional mindfulness with social functioning. *Mindfulness, 13*, 373–384. https://doi.org/10.1007/s12671-021-01798z

Deits-Lebehn, C., Smith, T. W., Williams, P. G., & Uchino, B. N. (2023). Heart rate variability during social interaction: Effects of valence and emotion regulation. *International Journal of Psychophysiology, 190*, 20–29. https://doi.org/10.1016/j.ijpsycho.2023.06.004

de Vibe, M., Bjordal, A., Fattah, S., Dyrdal, G., Halland, E., & Tanner-Smith, E. (2017). Mindfulness-based stress reduction (MBSR) for improving health, quality of life and social functioning in adults: A systematic review and meta-analysis. *Campbell Systematic Reviews, 11*. https://doi.org/10.4073/csr.2017.11

De Mestral, C., & Stringhini, S. (2017). Socioeconomic status and cardiovascular disease. *Current Cardiology Reports, 19*, 115. https://doi.org/10.1007/s11886-017-0917-z

Dibben, G. O., Faulkner, J., Oldridge, N., Rees, K., Thompson, D. R., Zwisler, A., & Taylor, R. S. (2023). Exercise-based cardiac rehabilitation for coronary heart disease: A meta-analysis. *European Heart Journal, 44*, 452–469. https://doi.org/10.1093/eurheartj/ehac747

Di Bello, M., Carnevali, L., Petrocchi, N., Thayer, J. F., Gilbert, P., & Ottaviani, C. (2020). The compassionate vagus: A meta-analysis on the connection between compassion and heart rate variability. *Neuroscience and Biobehavioral Reviews, 116*, 21–30. https://doi.org/10.1016/j.neubiorev.2020.06.016

Dickerson, S. S., Gruenwald, T. L., & Kemeny, M. E. (2004). When the social self is threatened: Shame, physiology, and health. *Journal of Personality, 72*, 1191–1216. https://doi.org/10.1111/j.1467-6494.2004.00295.x

Du, L., Cheng, Z., Zhang, Y., Li, Y., & Mei, D. (2017). The impact of medication adherence on clinical outcomes of coronary artery disease: A meta-analysis. *European Journal of Preventive Cardiology, 24*, 962–970. https://doi.org/10.1177/2047487317695628

Dupre, M. E., George, L. K., Liu, G., & Peterson, E. D. (2015). Association between divorce and risks for acute myocardial infarction. *Circulation: Cardiovascular Quality and Outcomes*. https://doi.org/10.1161/CIRCOUTCOMES.114.001291

Dupre, M. E., & Nelson, A. (2016). Marital history and survival after a heart attack. *Social Science and Medicine, 170*, 114–123. https://doi.org/10.1016/j.socscimed.2016.10.013

Edmondson, D., Kronish, I., Shaffer, J., Falzon, L., & Burg, M. (2013). Posttraumatic stress disorder and risk for coronary heart disease: A meta-analytic review. *American Heart Journal, 166*, 806–814. https://doi.org/10.1016/j.ahj.2013.07.031

Emdin, C. A., Odutayo, A., Wong, C., Tran, J., Hsiao, A., & Hunn, B. (2016). Meta-analysis of anxiety as a risk factor for cardiovascular disease. *American Journal of Cardiology, 118*, 511–519. https://doi.org/10.1016/j.amjcard.2016.05.041

Floranelli, M., Bottaccioli, A., Bottaccioli, F., Bianchi, M., Rovesti, M., & Roccia, M. G. (2018). Stress and inflammation in coronary artery disease: A review psychoneuroendocrineimmunology-based. *Frontiers in Immunology, 9*, Art no. 2031. https://doi.org/10.3389/fimmu.2018.02031

Foa, E. B., & Foa, U. G. (2012). Resource theory of social exchange. In K. Tornblom & A. Kazemi (Eds.), *Handbook of social resource theory: Theoretical extensions, empirical insights, and social applications* (pp. 15–32). Springer.

Ford, M. B., & Collins, N. L. (2010). Self-esteem moderates neuroendocrine and psychological responses to interpersonal rejection. *Journal of Personality and Social Psychology, 98*, 405–419. https://doi.org/10.1037/a0017345

Fournie, C., Chouchou, F., Dalleau, G., Caderby, T., Cabrera, Q., & Verkindt, C. (2021). Heart rate variability biofeedback in chronic disease management: A systematic review. *Complementary Therapies in Medicine, 60*, 102750. https://doi.org/10.1016/j.ctim.2021.102750

Francis, H. M., Penglis, K. M., & McDonald, S. (2016). Manipulation of heart rate variability can modify response to anger-inducing stimuli. *Social Neuroscience, 11*, 545–552. https://doi.org/10.1080/17470919.2015.1115777

Gallo, L. C., & Smith, T. W. (1999). Patterns of hostility and social support: Conceptualizing psychosocial risk factors as characteristics of the person *and* the environment. *Journal of Research in Personality, 33*, 281–310. https://doi.org/10.1006/jrpe.1999.2250

Gallo, L. C., Smith, T. W., & Kircher, J. C. (2000). Cardiovascular and electrodermal responses to support and provocation: Interpersonal methods in the study of psychophysiological reactivity. *Psychophysiology, 37*, 289–301. https://doi.org/10.1017/S0048577200982222

Gallo, L. C., Smith, T. W., & Cox, C. M. (2006). Socioeconomic status, psychosocial processes, and perceived health: An interpersonal perspective. *Annals of Behavioral Medicine, 31*, 109–119. https://doi.org/10.1207/s15324796abm3102_2

Gan, Y., Gong, Y., Tong, X., Sun, H., Cong, Y., Dong, X., Wang, Y., Xu, X., Yin, X., Deng, J., Li, L., Cao, S., & Lu, Z. (2014). Depression and the risk of coronary heart disease: A meta-analysis of prospective cohort studies. *BMC Psychiatry, 14*, 371. https://doi.org/10.1186/s12888-014-0371-z

Gardani, M., Bradford, D., Russell, K., Allan, S., Beattie, L., Ellis, J., & Akram, U. (2022). A systematic review and meta-analysis of poor sleep, insomnia symptoms and stress in undergraduate students. *Sleep Medicine Reviews, 61*, 101565. https://doi.org/10.1016/j.smrv.2021.101565

Gavriilaki, M., Anyfanti, P., Nikolaidou, B., Lazaridis, A., Gavriilaki, E., Douma, S., & Gkaliagkousi, E. (2020). Nighttime dipping status and risk of cardiovascular events in patients with untreated hypertension: A systematic review and meta-analysis. *Journal of Clinical Hypertension, 22*, 1951–1959. https://doi.org/10.1111/jch.14039

Geiger, C., Cramer, H., Dobos, G., & Kohl-Heckl, W. K. (2023). A systematic review and meta-analysis of mindfulness-based stress reduction for arterial hypertension. *Journal of Human Hypertension, 37*, 161–169. https://doi.org/10.1038/s41371-022-00764-z

Gendolla, G. H. E., Wright, R. A., & Richter, M. (2019). Advancing issues in motivational intensity research: Updated insights from the cardiovascular system. In R. M. Ryan (Ed.), *The Oxford handbook of human motivation* (2nd ed., pp. 373–392). Oxford University Press.

Gilbert, P. (2014). The origins and nature of compassion focused therapy. *British Journal of Clinical Psychology, 53*, 6–41. https://doi.org/10.1111/bjc.12043

Gomez Penedo, J. M., & Fluckiger, C. (2023). Interpersonal problems as a predictor of outcome in psychotherapy for depressive and anxiety disorders: A multi-level meta-analysis. *Journal of Consulting and Clinical Psychology*. Advance on-line publication. https://doi.org/10.1037/ccp0000828

Gresham, A. M., Peters, B. J., Tudder, A., & Simpson, J. A. (2023). Sense of power and markers of challenge and threat during extra-dyadic problem discussions with romantic partners. *Psychophysiology*, e14379. https://doi.org/10.1111/psyp.14379

Haeny, A. M., Holmes, S. C., & Williams, M. (2021). The need for shared nomenclature on racism and related terminology in psychology. *Perspectives on Psychological Science, 16*, 886–892. https://doi.org/10.1177/17456916211000760

Hames, J. L., Hagan, C. R., & Joiner, T. E. (2013). Interpersonal processes in depression. *Annual Review of Clinical Psychology, 9*, 355–377. https://doi.org/10.1146/annurev-clinpsy-050212-185553

Heppner, W. L., Kernis, M. H., Lakey, C. E., Campbell, W. K., Goldman, B. M., Davis, P. J., & Cascio, E. V. (2008). Mindfulness as a means of reducing aggressive behavior: Dispositional and situational evidence. *Aggressive Behavior, 34*, 486–496. https://doi.org/10.1002/ab.20258

Hill, N., Kall, A., Shafran, R., Sutcliffe, S., Manzotti, G., & Langan, D. (2021). The effectiveness of psychological interventions for loneliness: A systematic review and meta-analysis. *Clinical Psychology Review, 88*, 102066. https://doi.org/10.1016/j.cpr.2021.102066.

Hillebrand, S., Gast, K., de Mutsert, R., Swenne, C., Jukema, J. W., Middeldorp, S., Rosendaal, F., & Dekkers, O. (2013). Heart rate variability and first cardiovascular event in populations without known cardiovascular disease: Meta-analysis and dose-response meta-regression. *Europace, 15*, 742–749. https://doi.org/10.1093/europace/eus341.

Hogan, R. (1983). A socioanalytic theory of personality. In M. M. Page (Ed.), *Nebraska symposium on motivation: Personality—Current theory and research* (pp. 55–90). University of Nebraska Press.

Hopwood, C. J., Pincus, A. L., & Wright, A. G. C. (2021). Six assumptions of contemporary integrative interpersonal theory of personality and psychopathology. *Current Opinion in Psychology, 41*, 65–70. https://doi.org/10.1016/j.copsyc.2021.03.007

Horowitz, L. M., & Strack, S. (Eds). (2011). *Handbook of interpersonal psychology: Theory, research, assessment and therapeutic interventions*. Wiley.

Houston, B. K., Chesney, M. A., Black, G. W., Cates, D. S., & Hecker, M. L. (1992). Behavioral clusters and coronary heart disease risk. *Psychosomatic Medicine, 54*, 447–461. https://doi.org/10.1097/00006842-199207000-00007

Howard, S. (2023). Old ideas, new directions: Re-examining the predictive utility of the hemodynamic profile of the stress response in health populations. *Health Psychology Review, 17*, 104–120. https://doi.org/10.1080/17437199.2022.2067210

Hughes, B. M., Lu, W., & Howard, S. (2018). Cardiovascular stress-response adaptation: Conceptual basis, empirical findings, and implications for disease processes. *International Journal of Psychophysiology, 131*, 4–12. https://doi.org/10.1016/j.ijpsycho.2018.02.003

Iob, E., & Steptoe, A. (2019). Cardiovascular disease and hair cortisol: A novel biomarker of chronic stress. *Current Cardiology Reports, 21*, 116. https://doi.org/10.1007/s11886-019-1208-7

Jarczok, M. N., Weimer, K., Braun, C., Williams, D. P., Thayer, J. F., Gündel, H. O., & Balint, E. M. (2022). Heart rate variability in the prediction of mortality: A systematic review and meta-analysis of healthy and patient populations. *Neuroscience and Biobehavioral Reviews, 143*, 104907. https://doi.org/10.1016/j.neubiorev.2022.104907

Johnson, K. T., Merritt, M. M., Zawadski, M. J., Di Paolo, M., & Ayazi, M. (2019). Cardiovascular and affective responses to speech and anger: Proactive benefits of a single brief session of mindfulness meditation. *Journal of Applied Behavioral Research, 24*, e12167. https://doi.org/10.1111/jabr.12167

Jokela, M., Pulkki-Rabak, L., Elovainio, M., & Kivimaki, M. (2014). Personality traits as risk factors for stroke and coronary heart disease mortality: Pooled analysis of three cohort studies. *Journal of Behavioral Medicine, 37*, 881–889. https://doi.org/10.1007/s10865-013-9548-z

Jordan, K. D., Masters, K. S., Hooker, S. A., Ruiz, J. M., & Smith, T. W. (2014). An interpersonal approach to religiousness and spirituality: Implications for health and well-being. *Journal of Personality, 82*, 418–431. https://doi.org/10.1111/jopy.12072

Jordan, K. D., & Smith, T. W. (2023). Adaptation to social-evaluative threat: Effects of repeated acceptance and status stressors on cardiovascular reactivity. *International Journal of Psychophysiology, 183*, 61–70. https://doi.org/10.1016/j.ijpsycho.2022.11.008

Joseph, N. T., Kamarck, T. W., Muldoon, M. F., & Manuck, S. B. (2014). Daily marital interaction quality and carotid artery intima-medial thickness in healthy middle-aged adults. *Psychosomatic Medicine, 76*, 347–354. https://doi.org/10.1097/PSY0000000000000071

Kabat-Zinn, J. (1990). *Full catastrophe living: Using the wisdom of your body and mind to face stress, pain, and illness*. Bantam.

Kall, A., Shafran, R., Lindegaard, T., Bennett, S., Cooper, Z., Coughtrey, A., & Andersson, G. (2020). A common elements approach to the development of a modular cognitive behavioral theory for chronic loneliness. *Journal of Consulting and Clinical Psychology, 88*, 269–282. https://doi.org/10.1037/ccp0000454

Kelly, S., & Ismail, M. (2015). Stress and type 2 diabetes: A review of how stress contributes to the development of type 2 diabetes. *Annual Review of Public Health, 36*, 441–462. https://doi.org/10.1146/annurev-publhealth-031914-122921

Kenrick, D. T., Griskevicious, V., Neuberg, S. L., & Shaller, M. (2010). Renovating the pyramid of needs: Contemporary extensions built on ancient foundations. *Perspectives in Psychological Science, 5*, 292–314. https://doi.org/10.1177/1745691610369469

Kiesler, D. J. (1983). The 1982 Interpersonal Circle: A taxonomy for complementarity in human transactions. *Psychological Review, 90*, 185–214. https://doi.org/10.103/0033-295X.90.3.185

Kirschbaum, C., Pirke, K. M., & Hellhammer, D. H. (1993). The "Trier Social Stress Test": A tool for investigating psychobiological responses in a laboratory setting. *Neuropsychobiology, 28*(1–2), 76–81. https://doi.org/10.1159/000119004

Kirschner, H., Kuyken, W., Wright, K., Roberts, H., Brejcha, C., & Karl, A. (2019). Soothing your heart and feeling connected: A new experimental paradigm to study the benefits of self-compassion. *Clinical Psychological Science, 7*, 545–565. https://doi.org/10.1177/2167702618812438

Kivimaki, M., & Steptoe, A. (2018). Effects of stress on the development and progression of cardiovascular disease. *Nature Reviews Cardiology, 15*, 215–229. https://doi.org/10.1038/nrcardo.2017.189

Kreplin, U., Farias, M., & Brazil, I. A. (2018). The limited prosocial effects of meditation: A systematic review and meta-analysis. *Scientific Reports, 8*, 2403 (2018). https://doi.org/10.1038/s41598-018-20299-z

Kupferberg, A., & Hasler, G. (2023). The social cost of depression: Investigating the impact of impaired social emotion regulation, social cognition, and interpersonal behavior on social functioning. *Journal of Affective Disorders Reports, 14*, 100631. https://doi.org/10.1016/j.jadr.2023.100631

Lambert, J. E., Engh, R., Hasbun, A., & Holzer, J. (2012). Impact of posttraumatic stress disorder on the relationship quality and psychological distress of intimate partners: A meta-analytic review. *Journal of Family Psychology, 26*(5), 729–737. https://doi.org/10.1037/a0029341

Leary, M. R., Cottrell, C. A., & Phillips, M. (2001). Deconfounding the effects of dominance and social acceptance on self-esteem. *Journal of Personality and Social Psychology, 81*, 898–909. https://doi.org/10.1037/0022-3514.81.5.898

Lee, A. H., & DiGiuseppe, R. (2018). Anger and aggression treatments: A review of meta-analyses. *Current Opinion in Psychology, 19*, 65–74. https://doi.org/10.1016/j.copsyc.2017.04.004

Lehrer, P., Kaur, K., Sharma, A., Shah, K., Huseby, R., Bhavsar, J., & Zhang, Y. (2020). Heart rate variability biofeedback improves emotional and physical health and performance: A systematic review and meta-analysis. *Applied Psychophysiology and Biofeedback, 45*, 109–129. Ethnic minorities and coronary heart disease: An update and future directions. https://doi.org/10.1007/s10484-020-09466-z

Leigh, J. A., Alvarez, M., & Rodriguez, C. J. (2016). Ethnic minorities and coronary heart disease: An update and future directions. *Current Atherosclerosis Reports, 18* (2), 9. https://doi.org/10.1007/s11883-016-0559-4

Levine, G. N., Cohen, B. E., Commodore-Mensah, Y., Fleury, J., Huffman, J. C., Khalid, U., Labarthe, D. R., Lavretsky, H., Michos, E. D., Spatz, E. S., & Kubzansky, L. D. (2021). Psychological health, well-being, and the mind-heart-body connection: A scientific statement from the American Heart Association. *Circulation, 143*, e763-e783. https://doi.org/10.1161/CIR.0000000000000947

Lewis, T. T., Cogburn, C., & Williams, D. (2015). Self-reported experiences of discrimination and health: Scientific advances, ongoing controversies, and emerging issues. *Annual Review of Clinical Psychology, 11*, 407–440. https://doi.org/10.1146/annurev-clinpsy-032814-112728

Libby, P., Ridker, P. M., & Hansson, G. K. (2011). Progress and challenges in translating the biology of atherosclerosis. *Nature, 473*, 317–325. https://doi.org/10.1038/nature10146

Linden, W., Phillips, M. J., & Leclerc, J. (2007). Psychological treatment of cardiac patients: A meta-analysis. *European Heart Journal, 28*, 2972–2984. https://doi.org/10.1093/eurheartj/ehm504

Linden, W., Stossel, C., & Maurice, J. (1996). Psychosocial interventions for patients with coronary artery disease: A meta-analysis. *Archives of Internal Medicine, 156*, 745–752. https://doi.org/10.1001/archinte.1996.00440070065008

Liu, H., Chen, B., Wang, Y., Zhao, X., & Hu, J. (2022). Social affiliation moderates the link between depressive symptoms and heart rate variability in healthy middle-aged and older individuals: An intensive ecologic momentary assessment study. *Psychophysiology, 59*, e13958. https://doi.org/10.1111/psyp.13958

Liu, M., Li, N., Li, W., & Khan, H. (2017). Association between psychosocial stress and hypertension: A systematic review and meta-analysis. *Neurological Research, 39*, 573–580. https://doi.org/10.1080/01616412.2017.1317904

Lobbestael, J., Arntz, A., & Wiers, R. (2008). How to push someone's buttons: A comparison of four anger-induction methods. *Cognition and Emotion, 22*, 353–373. https://doi.org/10.1080/02699930701438285

Locke, K. D. (2011). Circumplex measures of interpersonal constructs. In L. M. Horowitz & S. Strack (Eds.), *Handbook of interpersonal psychology: Theory, research, assessment and therapeutic interventions* (pp. 313–324). Wiley. https://doi.org/10.1002/9781118001868.ch19

Locke, K. D. (2015). Agentic and communal social motives. *Social and Personality Science Compass, 9*, 525–538. https://doi.org/10.1111/spc3.12201

Lodder, P., Wicherts, J. M., Antens, M., Albus, C., Bessonov, I. S., Condén, E., Dulfer, K., Gostoli, S., Grande, G., Hedberg, P., Herrmann-Lingen, C., Jaarsma, T., Koo, M., Lin, P., Lin, T. K., Meyer, T., Pushkarev, G., Rafanelli, C., Raykh, O. I., ... Kupper, N. (2023). Type D personality as a risk factor for adverse outcome in patients with cardiovascular disease: An individual patient-data meta-analysis. *Psychosomatic Medicine, 85*, 188–202. https://doi.org/10.1097/PSY.0000000000001164

Loredo, J. S., Nelesen, R., Ancoli-Israel, S., & Dimsdale, J. E. (2004). Sleep quality and blood pressure dipping in normal adults. *Sleep, 27*, 1097–1103. https://doi.org/10.1093/sleep/27.6.1097

Lund, R., Rod, N., Thielen, K., Nilsson, C., & Christensen, U. (2014). Negative aspects of social relations and 10-year incident ischaemic heart disease hospitalization among middle-aged Danes. *European Journal of Preventive Cardiology, 21*, 1249–1256. https://doi.org/10.1177/2047487313486041

Mahadevan, N., Gregg, A., & Sedikides, C. (2023). Daily fluctuations in social status, self-esteem, and clinically relevant emotions: Testing hierometer theory and social rank theory at a within-person level. *Journal of Personality, 91*, 519–536. https://doi.org/10.1111/jopy.12752.

Malouff, J. M., Thorsteinsson, E. B., Schutte, N. S., Bhullar, N., & Rooke, S. E. (2010). The five-factor model of personality and relationship satisfaction of intimate partners: A meta-analysis. *Journal of Research in Personality, 44*, 124–127. https://doi.org/10.1016/j.jrp.2009.09.004

Manfredini, R., De Giorgi, A., Tiseo, R., Boari, B., Cappadona, R., Salmi, R., Gallerani, M., Signani, F., Manfredini, F., Mikhailidis, D. P., & Fabbian, F. (2017). Marital status, cardiovascular diseases, and cardiovascular risk factors: A review of the evidence. *Journal of Women's Health, 26*(6), 624–632. https://doi.org/10.1089/jwh.2016.6103

Masters, K. S., & Hooker, S. A. (2013). Religiousness/Spirituality, cardiovascular disease, and cancer: Cultural integration for health research and intervention. *Journal of Consulting and Clinical Psychology, 81*, 206–216. https://doi.org/10.1037/a0030813

McAdams, D. P., Hoffman, B. J., Mansfield, E. D., & Day, R. (1996). Themes of agency and communion in significant autobiographical scenes. *Journal of Personality, 64*, 339–377. https://doi.org/10.1111/j.1467-6494.1996.tb00514.x

McEwen, B. S. (1998). Stress, adaptation, and disease. Allostatsis and allostatic load. *Annals of the New York Academy of Science, 840*, 33–44. https://doi.org/10.1111/j.1749-6632.tb09546.x

McFarquhar, T., Luyten, P., & Fongay, P. (2018). Changes in interpersonal problems in the psychotherapeutic treatment of depression as measured by the Inventory of Interpersonal problems: A systematic review and meta-analysis. *Journal of Affective Disorders, 226*, 108–123. https://doi.org/10.1016/j.jad.2017.09.036

Meijer, A., Conradi, H. J., Bos, E. H., Anselmino, M., Carney, R. M., Denollet, J., Doyle, F., Freedland, K. E., Grace, S. L., Hosseini, S. H., Lane, D. A., Pilote, L., Parakh, K., Rafanelli, C., Sato, H., Steeds, R. P., Welin, C., & de Jonge, P. (2013). Adjusted prognostic association of depression following myocardial infarction with mortality and cardiovascular events: Individual patient data meta-analysis. *British Journal of Psychiatry, 203*, 90–102. https://doi.org/10.1192/bjp.bp.112.111195

Millard, L. A., Wan, M. W., Smith, D. M., & Wittkowski, A. (2023). The effectiveness of compassion focused therapy with clinical populations: A systematic review and meta-analysis. *Journal of Affective Disorders, 326*, 168–192. https://doi.org/10.1016/j.jad.2023.01.010

Mostofsky, E., Penner, E. A., & Mittleman, M. A. (2014). Outbursts of anger as a trigger of acute cardiovascular events: A systematic review and meta-analysis. *European Heart Journal, 35*, 1404–1410. https://doi.org/10.1093/eurheartj/ehu033

Mottillo, S., Filion, K. B., Genest, J., Joseph, L., Pilote, L., Poirier, P., Rinfret, S., Schiffrin, E. L., & Eisenberg, M. J. (2010). The metabolic syndrome and cardiovascular risk: A systematic review and meta-analysis. *Journal of the American College of Cardiology, 56*(14), 1113–1132. https://doi.org/10.1016/j.jacc.2010.05.034

Moulds, M. L., Bisby, M., Wild, J., & Bryant, R. (2020). Rumination in posttraumatic stress disorder: A systematic review. *Clinical Psychology Review, 82*, 101910. https://doi.org/10.1016/j.cpr.2020.101910

Nealey-Moore, J. B., Smith, T. W., Uchino, B. N., Hawkins, M. W., & Olson-Cerny, C. (2007). Cardiovascular reactivity during positive and negative marital interactions. *Journal of Behavioral Medicine, 30*, 505–519. https://doi.org/10.1007/s10865-0079124-5

Neppl, T., Senia, J., & Donellen, M. B. (2016). Effects of economic hardship: Testing the family stress model over time. *Journal of Family Psychology, 30*, 12–21. https://doi.org/10.1037/fam0000168

Neumann, S. A., Waldstein, S. R., Sollers, III, J. J., Thayer, J. F., & Sorkin, J. D. (2004). Hostility and distraction have differential influences on vardiovascular reacovery from anger in women. *Health Psychology, 23*, 631–640. https://doi.org/10.1037/0278-6133.23.6.631

Newton, T. L. (2009). Cardiovascular functioning, personality, and the social world: The domain of hierarchical power. *Neuroscience and Biobehavioral Reviews, 33*, 145–159. https://doi.org/10.1016/j.neubiorev.2008.07.005

Nijjar, P. S., Connett, J. E., Lindquist, R., Brown, R., Burt, M., Pergolski, A., Wolfe, A., Balaji, P., Chandiramani, N., Yu, X., Kreitzer, M. J., & Everson-Rose, S. A. (2019). Randomized trial of mindfulness-based stress reduction in cardiac patients eligible for cardiac rehabilitation. *Scientific Reports, 9*(1), 18415. https://doi.org/10.1038/s41598-019-54932-2

O'Connor, D. B., Thayer, J. F., & Vedhara, K. (2021). Stress and health: A review of psychobiological processes. *Annual Review of Psychology, 72*, 663–688. https://doi.org/10.1146/annurev-psych-062520-122331

Ong, A. D., Deshpande, S., & Williams, D. R. (2018). Biological consequences of unfair treatment: A theoretical and empirical review. In J. M. Causadias, E. H., Telzer, & N. A. Gonzalez (Eds.), *The handbook of culture and biology* (pp. 279–315). John Wiley & Sons.

O'Riordan, A., Howard, S., & Gallagher, S. (2023). Blunted cardiovascular reactivity to psychological stress and prospective health: A systematic review. *Health Psychology Review, 17*, 121–147. https://doi.org/10.1080/17437199.2022.2068639

Orth-Gomér, K., Schneiderman, N., Wang, H. X., Walldin, C., Blom, M., & Jernberg, T. (2009). Stress reduction prolongs life in women with coronary disease: The Stockholm Women's Intervention Trial for Coronary Heart Disease (SWITCHD). *Circulation. Cardiovascular Quality and Outcomes, 2*, 25–32. https://doi.org/10.1161/CIRCOUTCOMES.108.812859

Ostman, C., Smart, N. A., Morcos, D., Duller, A., Ridley, W., & Jewis, D. (2017). The effect of exercise training on clinical outcomes in patients with metabolic syndrome: A systematic review and meta-analysis. *Cardiovascular Diabetology, 16*, 110. https://doi.org/10.1186/s12933-017-0590-y

Ottaviani, C., Thayer, J. F., Verkuil, B., Lonigro, A., Medea, B., Couyoumdjian, A., & Brosschot, J. F. (2016). Physiological concomitants of perseverative cognition: A systematic review and meta-analysis. *Psychological Bulletin, 142*, 231–259. https://doi.org/10.1037/bul0000036

Panaite, V., Salomon, K., Jin, A., & Rottenberg, J. (2015). Cardiovascular recovery from psychological and physiological challenge and risk for adverse cardiovascular outcomes and all-cause mortality. *Psychosomatic Medicine, 77*, 215–226. https://doi.org/10.1097/PSY.0000000000000171

Pankiewicz, P., Majkowicz, M., & Krzykowski, G. (2012). Anxiety disorders in intimate partners and the quality of their relationship. *Journal of Affective Disorders, 140*, 176–180. https://doi.org/10.1016/j.jad.2012.02.005

Parent, J., & DiMarzio, K. (2021). Advancing mindful parenting research: An introduction. *Mindfulness, 12*, 261–265. https://doi.org/10.1007/s12671-020-01572-7

Paul, E., Bu, F., & Fancourt, D. (2021). Loneliness and risk for cardiovascular disease: Mechanisms and future directions. *Current Cardiology Reports, 23*, 68. https://doi.org/10.1007/s11886-021-01495-2

Pincus, A. L., & Ansell, E. B. (2013). Interpersonal theory of personality. In T. Millon & M. J. Lerner (Eds.), *Handbook of psychology (Vol. 5): Personality and social psychology* (2nd ed., pp. 141–159). John Wiley.

Powell, L. H. (1996). The hook: A metaphor for gaining control of emotional reactivity. In R. Allan & S. Scheidt (Eds.), *Heart and mind: The practice of cardiac psychology* (pp. 313–327). American Psychological Association. https://doi.org/10.1037/10210-011.

Proulx, C., Helms, H., & Buehler, C. (2007). Marital quality and personal well-being: A meta-analysis. *Journal of Marriage and Family, 69*, 576–593. https://doi.org/10.1111/j.1741-3737.2007.00393.x

Rasmussen, K. R., Stackhouse, M., Boon, S., Comstock, K., & Ross, R. (2019). Meta-analytic connections between forgiveness and health: The moderating effects of forgiveness-related distinctions. *Psychology and Health, 34*, 515–534. https://doi.org/10.1080/08870446.2018.1545906

Reilly, E. B., & Stuyvenberg, C. L. (2022). A meta-analysis of loving-kindness meditations on self-compassion. *Mindfulness, 14*(10), 2299–2310. https://doi.org/10.1007/s12671-022-01972-x

Repetti, R., Wang, S., & Saxbe, D. (2009). Bringing it all back home: How outside stressors shape families' everyday lives. *Current Directions in Psychological Science, 18*, 106–111. https://doi.org/10.1111/j.1467-8721.2009.01618.x

Richards, S. H., Anderson, L., Jenkinson, C., Whalley, B., Rees, K., Davies, P., Bennett, P., Liu, Z., West, R., Thompson, D. R., & Taylor, R. (2018). Psychological interventions for coronary heart disease: Cochrane systematic review and meta-analysis. *European Journal of Preventive Cardiology, 25*(3), 247–259. https://doi.org/10.1177/2047487317739978

Richardson, S., Shaffer, J., Falzon, L., Krupka, D., Davidson, K., & Edmondson, D. (2012). Meta-analysis of perceived stress and its association with incident coronary heart disease. *American Journal of Cardiology, 110*, 1711–1716. https://doi.org/10.1016/j.amjcard.2012.08.004

Rickerby, N., Krug, I., Fuller-Tyszkiewicz, M., Forte, E., Davenport, R., Chayadi, E., & Kiropoulos, L. (2022). Rumination across depression, anxiety, and eating disorders in adults: A meta-analytic review. *Clinical Psychology: Science and Practice,* Advance Online Publication. https://doi.org/10.1037/cps0000110

Roberts, B. W., Kuncel, N. R., Shiner, R., Caspi, A., & Goldberg, L. R. (2007). The power of personality: The comparative validity of personality traits, socioeconomic status, and cognitive ability for predicting important life outcomes. *Perspectives in Psychological Science, 2*, 313–345. https://doi.org/10.1111/j.1745-6916.2007.00047.x

Robles, T. F., Slatcher, R. B., Trombello, J. M., & McGinn, M. M. (2014). Marital quality and health: A meta-analytic review. *Psychological Bulletin, 140*, 140–187. https://doi.org/10.1037/a0031859

Sadler, P., Ethier, N., & Woody, E. (2011). Interpersonal complementarity. In L. M. Horowitz & S. Strack (Eds.), *Handbook of interpersonal psychology: Theory, research, assessment and therapeutic interventions* (pp. 123–142). Wiley.

Sara, J. D., Prasad, M., Eleid, M. F., Zhang, M., Widmer, J., & Lerman, A. (2018). Association between work-related stress and coronary heart disease: A review of prospective studies through the job strain, effort-reward balance, and organizational justice models. *Journal of the American Heart Association, 7*, e008073. https://doi.org/10.1161/JAHA.117.008073

Scheepers, D., & Knight, E. L. (2020). Neuroendocrine and cardiovascular responses to shifting status. *Current Opinion in Psychology, 33*, 115–119. https://doi.org/10.1016/j.copsyc.2019.07.035

Schneider, R. H., Grim, C. E., Rainforth, M., Kotchen, T., Nidich, S., Gaylord-King, C., Salerno, J. W., Kotchen, J. M., & Alexander, C. N. (2012). Stress reduction in the secondary prevention of cardiovascular disease: Randomized, controlled trial of Transcendental Meditation and health education in Blacks. *Circulation Cardiovascular Quality and Outcomes, 5*, 750–758. https://doi.org/10.1161/CIRCOUTCOMES.112.967406

Schum, J. L., Jorgensen, R. S., Verhaeghen, P., Sauro, M., & Thibodeau, R. (2003). Trait anger, anger expression, and ambulatory blood pressure: A meta-analytic review. *Journal of Behavioral Medicine, 26*, 395–415. https://doi.org/10.1023/A:1025767900757

Scott, A. J., Webb, T. L., Martyn-St James, M., Rowse, G., & Weich, S. (2021). Improving sleep quality leads to better mental health: A meta-analysis of randomized controlled trials. *Sleep Medicine Reviews, 60*, 101556. https://doi.org/10.1016/j.smrv.2021.101556

Scott-Sheldon, L. A. J., Gathright, E. C., Donahue, M. L., Balletto, B., Feulner, M. M., DeCosta, J., Cruess, D. G., Wing, R. R., Carey, M. P., & Salmoirago-Blothcher, E. (2020). Mindfulness-based interventions for adults with cardiovascular disease: A systematic review and meta-analysis. *Annals of Behavioral Medicine, 54*, 67–73. https://doi.org/10.1093/abm/kaz020

Seery, M. D. (2011). Challenge or threat? Cardiovascular indexes of resilience and vulnerability to potential stress in humans. *Neuroscience and Biobehavioral Reviews, 35*, 1603–1610. https://doi.org/10.1016/j.neubiorev.2011.03.003

Shahrestani, S., Steward, E. M., Quintana, D. S., Hickie, I. A., & Guastella, A. J. (2015). Heart rate variability during adolescent and adult social interactions: A meta-analysis. *Biological Psychology, 105*, 43–50. http://dx.doi.org/10.1016/j.biopsycho.2014.12.012

Shi, Y., & Lan, J. (2021). Effect of stress management training in cardiac rehabilitation among coronary heart disease: A systematic review and meta-analysis. *Reviews in Cardiovascular Medicine, 22*, 1491–1501. https://doi.org/10.31083/j.rcm2204153

Siegman, A. W., Kubzansky, L. D., Kawachi, I., Boyle, S., Vokonas, P. S., & Sparrow, D. (2000). A prospective study of dominance and coronary heart disease in the normative aging study. *American Journal of Cardiology, 86*, 145–149. https://doi.org/10.1016/s0002-9149(00)00850-x

Smith, T. W., & Baron, C. E. (2016). Marital discord in the later years. In J. Bookwala (Ed.), *Couple relationships in the middle and later years: Their nature, complexity, and role in health and illness* (pp. 37–56). American Psychological Association. https://doi.org/10.1037/15897-003

Smith, T. W., Baron, C. E., Deits-Lebehn, C., Uchino, B. N., & Berg, C. A. (2020). Is it me or you? Marital conflict behavior and blood pressure reactivity. *Journal of Family Psychology, 34*, 503–508. https://doi.org/10.1037/fam0000624

Smith, T. W., Baron, C. E., & Grove, J. (2014). Personality, emotional adjustment, and cardiovascular risk: Marriage as a mechanism. *Journal of Personality, 82*, 502–514. https://doi.org/10.1111/jopy.12074

Smith, T. W., & Baucom, B. R. W. (2017). Intimate relationships, individual adjustment, and coronary heart disease: Implications of overlapping associations in psychosocial risk. *American Psychologist, 72*, 578–589. https://doi.org/10.1037/amp0000123

Smith, T. W., Birmingham, W., & Uchino, B. N. (2012). Evaluative threat and ambulatory blood pressure: Cardiovascular effects of social stress in daily experience. *Health Psychology, 31*, 763–766. https://doi.org/10.1037/a0026947

Smith, T. W., & Cundiff, J. M. (2011). An interpersonal perspective on risk for coronary heart disease. In L. M. Horowitz & S. Strack (Eds.), *Handbook of interpersonal psychology: Theory, research, assessment, and therapeutic interventions* (pp. 471–489). John Wiley & Sons.

Smith, T. W., Cundiff, J. M., & Baucom, B. R. (2022). Aggregation of psychosocial risk factors: Models and methods. In S. R. Waldstein, W. J. Kop, E. C. Suarez, W. R. Lovallo, & L. I. Katzel (Eds.), *Handbook of cardiovascular behavioral medicine* (pp. 675–700). Springer Nature.

Smith, T. W., Cundiff, J. M., & Uchino, B. N. (2012). Interpersonal motives and cardiovascular response: Mechanisms linking dominance and social status with cardiovascular disease. In R. A. Wright & G. H. E. Gendolla (Eds.), *How motivation affects cardiovascular response: Mechanisms and applications* (pp. 287–305). American Psychological Association.

Smith, T. W., Deits-Lebehn, C., Williams, P. G., Baucom, B. R. W., & Uchino, B. N. (2020). Toward a social psychophysiology of vagally mediated heart rate variability: Concepts and methods in self-regulation, emotion, and interpersonal processes. *Social and Personality Psychology Compass, 14*, e12516. https://doi.org/10.1111/spc3.12516

Smith, T. W., Gallo, L. C., & Ruiz, J. M. (2003). Toward a social psychophysiology of cardiovascular reactivity: Interpersonal concepts and methods in the study of stress, coronary disease. In J. Suls & K. Wallston (Eds.), *Social psychological foundations of health and illness* (pp. 335–366). Blackwell Publishers.

Smith, T. W., Glazer, K., Ruiz, J. M., & Gallo, L. (2004). Hostility, anger, aggressiveness, and coronary heart disease: An interpersonal perspective on personality, emotion, and health. *Journal of Personality, 72*(6), 1217–1270. https://doi.org/10.1111/j.1467-6494.2004.00296.x

Smith, T. W., & Jordan, K. D. (2015). Interpersonal motives and social-evaluative threat: Effects of acceptance and status stressors on cardiovascular reactivity and salivary cortisol response. *Psychophysiology, 52*, 269–276. https://doi.org/10.1111/psyp.12318

Smith, T. W., Nealey, J. B., Kircher, J. C., & Limon, J. P. (1997). Social determinants of cardiovascular reactivity: Effects of incentive to exert influence and evaluative threat. *Psychophysiology, 34*, 65–73. https://doi.org/10.1111/j.1469-8986.1997.tb02417.x

Smith, T. W., Ruiz, J. M., Cundiff, J. M., Baron, K. G., & Nealey-Moore, J. B. (2013). Optimism and pessimism in social context: An interpersonal perspective on resilience and risk. *Journal of Research in Personality, 47*, 553–562. https://doi.org/10.1016/j.jrp.2013.04.006

Smith, T. W., Ruiz, J. M., & Uchino, B. N. (2004). Mental activation of supportive ties, hostility, and cardiovascular reactivity to laboratory stress in young men and women. *Health Psychology, 23*, 476–485. https://doi.org/10.1037/0278-6133.23.5.476

Smith, T. W., Sanders, J. D., & Alexander, J. F. (1990). What does the Cook and Medley Hostility scale measure? Affect, behavior, and attributions in the marital context. *Journal of Personality and Social Psychology, 58*, 699–708. https://doi.org/10.1037/0022-3514.58.4.699.

Smith, T. W., & Traupman, E. K. (2012). Anger, hostility, and aggressiveness in coronary heart disease: Clinical applications of an interpersonal perspective. In R. Allan & J. Fisher (Eds.), *Heart and mind: The practice of cardiac psychology* (2nd ed., pp. 197–217). American Psychological Association.

Smith, T. W., Traupman, E. K., Uchino, B. N., & Berg, C. A. (2010). Interpersonal circumplex descriptions of psychosocial risk factors for physical illness: Application to hostility, neuroticism, and marital adjustment. *Journal of Personality, 78*, 1011–1036. https://doi.org/10.1111/j.1467-6494.2010.00641.x

Smith, T. W., Uchino, B. N., Berg, C. A., Florsheim, P., Pearce, G., Hawkins, M., Henry, N. J., Beveridge, R. M., Skinner, M. A., Hopkins, P. N., & Yoon, H.-C. (2008). Associations of self-reports versus spouse ratings of negative affectivity, dominance, and affiliation with coronary artery disease: Where should we look and who should we ask when studying personality and health? *Health Psychology, 27*(6), 676–684. https://doi.org/10.1037/0278-6133.27.6.676

Smith, T. W., Uchino, B. N., Bosch, J. A., & Kent, R. G. (2014). Trait hostility is associated with systemic inflammation in married couples: An actor-partner analysis. *Biological Psychology, 102*, 51–53. https://doi.org/10.1016/j.biopsycho.2014.07.005

Smith, T. W., Uchino, B. N., Florsheim, P., Berg, C. A., Butner, J., Hawkins, M., Henry, N. J., Beveridge, R. M., Pearce, G., Hopkins, P. N., & Yoon, H.-C. (2011a). Affiliation and control during marital disagreement, history of divorce, and asymptomatic coronary artery calcification in older couples. *Psychosomatic Medicine, 73*(4), 350–357. https://doi.org/10.1097/PSY.0b013e31821188ca

Speed, B. C., Goldstein, B. L., & Goldfried, M. R. (2018). Assertiveness training: A forgotten evidence-based treatment. *Clinical Psychology: Science and Practice, 25*, 1–20. https://doi.org/10.1111/cpsp.12216

Stroud, L., Foster, E., Papadonatos, G., Handwerger, K., Granger, D., Kivlighan, K., & Niaura, R. (2009). Stress response and the adolescent transition: Performance versus peer rejection stressors. *Development and Psychopathology, 21*, 47–68. https://doi.org/10.1017/S0954579409000042

Sweet, M. J., & Johnson, C. G. (1990). Enhancing empathy: The interpersonal implications of a Buddhist meditation technique. *Psychotherapy, 27*, 19–29. https://doi.org/10.1037/0033-3204.27.1.19

Taouk, Y., Spittal, M. J., LaMontagne, A., & Milner, A. J. (2020). Psychosocial work stressors and risk of all-cause and coronary heart disease mortality: A systematic review and meta-analysis. *Scandinavian Journal of Work, Environment and Health, 46*, 19–31. https://doi.org/10.5271/sjweh.3854

Thayer, J. F., Carevali, L., Sgoifo, A., & Williams, D. P. (2020). Angry in America: Psychophysiological responses to unfair treatment. *Annals of Behavioral Medicine, 54*, 924–931. https://doi.org/10.1093/abm/kaaa094

Thayer, J. F., & Lane, R. D. (2007). The role of vagal function in the risk for cardiovascular disease and mortality. *Biological Psychology, 74*, 224–242. https://doi.org/10.1016/j.biopsycho.2005.11.013

Tiosano, S., Laur, L., Tirosh, A., Furer, A., Afek, A., Fink, N., Derazne, E., Tzur, D., Fruchter, E., Ben-Yehuda, A., Bader, T., Amital, H., Szklo, M., Weiser, M., & Twig, G. (2022). Personality disorders and cause-specific mortality: A nationwide study of 2 million adolescents. *Psychological Medicine, 52*, 1746–1754. https://doi.org/10.1017/S0033291720003530

Tudder, A., Gresham, A. M., Peters, B., Reis, H. T., & Jamieson, J. P. (2020). The effects of dispositional restrictiveness on phsyiological markers of challenge and threat during a hypothetical transitional period in romantic relationships. *Psychophysiology, 57*, e13624 https://doi.org/10.1111/psyp.13624

Turner, A. I., Smyth, N., Hall, S. J., Torres, S. J., Hussein, M., Jayasinghe, S., Ball, K., & Clow, A. (2020). Psychological stress reactivity and future health and disease outcomes: A systematic review of prospective evidence. *Psychoneuroendocrinology*,114, Article 104599. https://doi.org/10.1016/j.psyneuen.2020.104599

Uchino, B. N. (2006). Social support and health: A review of physiological processes potentially underlying links to disease outcomes. *Journal of Behavioral Medicine, 29*, 377–387. https://doi.org/10.1007/s10865-006-9056-5

Uchino, B. N., Bowen, K., Kent de Grey, R. G., Smith, T. W., Baucom, B. R., Light, K. C., & Ray, S. (2016). Loving kindness meditation improves relationship negativity and psychological well-being: A pilot study. *Psychology, 7*, 6–11. https://doi.org/10.4236/psych.2016.71002

Vaccarino, V., Almuwaqqat, Z., Kim, J. H., Hammadah, M., Shah, A., Alkhoder, A., Lima, B. B., Pearce, B., Ward, L., Kutner, M., Hu, Y., Lewis, T. T., Garcia, E. V., Nye, J., Sheps, D. S., Raggi, P., . . . Quyyumi, A. A. (2021). Association of mental stress-induced myocardial ischemia with cardiovascular events in patients with coronary heart disease. *JAMA, 326*(18), 1818–1828. https://doi.org/10.1001/jama.2021.17649

Valtorta, N. K., Kanaan, M., Gilbody, S., Ronzi, S., & Hanraty, B. (2016). Loneliness and social isolation as risk factors for coronary heart disease and stroke: Systematic review and meta-analysis of longitudinal observation studies. *Heart, 102*, 1009–1016. https://doi.org/10.1136/heartjnl-2015-308790

Wade, N. G., Hoyt, W. T., Kidwell, J. E. M., & Worthington, E. L., Jr. (2014). Efficacy of psychotherapeutic interventions to promote forgiveness: A meta-analysis. *Journal of Consulting and Clinical Psychology, 82*, 154–170. https://doi.org/10.1037/a0035268

Wang, H., Leineweber, C., Kirkeeide, R., Svane, B., Schenck-Gustafsson, K., Theorell, T., & Orth-Gomer, K. (2007). Psychosocial stress and atherosclerosis: Family and work stress accelerate progression of coronary artery disease in women. *Journal of Internal Medicine, 261*, 245–254. https://doi.org/10.1111/j.1365-2796.2006.01759.x

Wei, J., Rooks, C., Ramadan, R., Shah, A., Bremmer, J. D., Quyyumi, A., Kutner, M., & Vaccarino, V. (2014). Meta-analysis of mental stress-induced myocardial ischemia and subsequent cardiac events in patients with coronary artery disease. *American Journal of Cardiology, 114*, 187–192. https://doi.org/10.1016/j.amjcard.2014.04.022

Whisman, M. A., & Beach, S. R. H. (2010). Models for understanding interpersonal processes and relationships in anxiety disorders. In J. G. Beck (Ed.), *Interpersonal processes in the anxiety disorders: Implications for understanding psychopathology and treatment* (pp. 9–35). American Psychological Association.

Wiggins, J. S., & Broughton, R. (1991). A geometric taxonomy of personality scales. *European Journal of Personality, 5*(5), 343–365. https://doi.org/10.1002/per.2410050503

Wiggins, J. S., & Trapnell, P. D. (1996). A dyadic-interactional perspective on the five-factor model. In J. S. Wiggins (Ed.), *The five-factor model of personality: Theoretical perspectives* (pp. 88–162). Guilford Press.

Wilkowski, B. M., & Robinson, M. D. (2010). The anatomy of anger: An integrative cognitive model of trait anger and reactive aggression. *Journal of Personality, 78*, 9–38. https://doi.org/10.1111/j.1467-6494.2009.00607.x

Williams, P. G., Smith, T. W., Gunn, H., & Uchino, B. N. (2011). Personality and stress: Individual differences in exposure, reactivity, recovery, and restoration. In R. J. Contrada and A. Baum (Eds.), *The handbook of stress science: Biology, psychology, and health* (pp. 231–245). Springer.

Wilson, S., Stroud, C., & Durbin, C. E. (2017). Interpersonal dysfunction in personality disorders: A meta-analytic review. *Psychological Bulletin, 143*, 677–734. https://doi.org/10.1037/bul0000101

Wright, A. G. C., Pincus, A. L., & Hopwood, C. J. (2023). Contemporary integrative interpersonal theory: Integrating structure, dynamics, temporal scale, and levels of analysis. *Journal of Psychopathology and Clinical Science, 132*, 263–276. https://doi.org/10.1037/abn0000741

Wu, A., Lindson, N., Hartmann-Boyce, J., Wahedi, A., Hajizadeh, A., Theodoulou, A., Thomas, E. T., Lee, C., & Aveyard, P. (2022). Smoking cessation for secondary prevention of cardiovascular disease. *Cochrane Database of Systematic Reviews*. https://doi.org/10.1002/14651858.CD014936.pub2

Yeh, Z., & Lin, C. (2022). Mindfulness-based stress reduction intervention and emotional recovery in borderline personality features: Evidence from psychophysiological assessment. *Mindfulness, 13*, 881–896. https://doi.org/10.1007/s12671-022-01829-3

Zestcott, C. A., Ruiz, J. M., Tietje, K. R., & Stone, J. (2022). The relationship between racial prejudice and cardiovascular disease mortality risk at the state and county level. *Annals of Behavioral Medicine, 56*, 959–968. https://doi.org/10.1093/abm/kaab103

Zhang, Y., Liang, Y., Huang, H., & Xu, Y. (2021). Systematic review and meta-analysis of psychological interventions on patients with coronary heart disease. *Annals of Palliative Medicine, 10*, 8848–8857. https://doi.org/10.21037/apm-21-1623

Zhou, J., Lang, Y., Wang, Z., Gao, C., Lv, J., Zheng, Y., Gu, X., Yan, L., Chen, Y., Zhang, X., Zhao, X., Luo, W., Chen, Y., Jiang, Y., Li, R., & Zeng, X. (2022). A meta-analysis and systematic review of the effect of loving-kindness and compassion meditations on negative interpersonal attitudes. *Current Psychology, 42*, 27813–27827. https://doi.org/10.1007/s12144-022-03866-6

12
As I Lay Dreaming

A Case Study in Psychophysiological Psychotherapy

Donald Moss

Introducing Jacob

At seventy-five, Jacob first called to request help from a psychologist. He described his presenting problem as a sleep disorder, but it wasn't one ever listed in *The Diagnostic and Statistical Manual of Mental Disorders, Fifth Edition* (*DSM-V*) (American Psychiatric Association, 2013). Jacob appeared for his first appointment with his wife of forty-six years, Agnes. When Jacob again stated he wished help with a sleep disorder, Agnes interrupted to claim she was fed up with his "ladies." Jacob explained his recurrent dream encounters involved several different women with whom he also engaged in audible dialogue. Recently, during sleep, he even demanded that Agnes "go on and leave us alone." Each time Agnes awakened him, he denied recalling the encounters. Most distressing, she felt his erection against her during his dreams, even though he had been impotent with her for over a decade.

Family and Marital History

Jacob was the second son of now deceased parents. His mother died of breast cancer in her early 70s and his father died "of a broken heart." He grieved deeply for his wife and died of a heart attack on her birthday two years later. Jacob explained his father's death and said, "We Meredith men feel deeply, we don't let go easily..."

Jacob served in the Marine Corps during the Korean War, trained as a medical corpsman, and briefly saw combat service. He married Lois during his first year in the Marines. After eighteen months they divorced due to her impulsive spending and their long service-related separations. The decision to divorce was mutual, but Jacob continued to phone Lois for several years and periodically awakened in the night crying and dreaming of her.

After discharge from the Marines, he became an ambulance driver and an emergency medical technician. He met and married Agnes in 1964; the marriage produced two daughters and one son, all now raising children of their own.

In the early 1980s, the marriage grew tense and conflictual. He desired more sexual contact and time together; she wanted more time with her girlfriends and "more space." In 1985, she filed for divorce and moved into an apartment. During the separation, she pursued a relationship with her married boss, Raymond, and became pregnant. When Raymond refused to leave his marriage, she underwent an abortion. Subsequently, since the divorce was never finalized, Agnes returned to the marital home two years to the day after she had left. She later admitted to Jacob that an initial flirtation with her boss evolved into an affair. They'd seen each other intermittently for several years, thus her demand for more "space."

Jacob struggled to forgive Agnes, and ruminated on her affair, her pregnancy, and the abortion. He berated her for aborting the baby, insisting she should have known he would have wanted to raise the baby. They slept apart most nights for almost a decade. Jacob began experiencing impotence at the time they reconnected and attempted to resume a sexual relationship.

In 2000, Jacob retired from his long-time ambulance and emergency room job and began working part-time for a local golf course. He experienced an elevated mood with retirement, enjoyed his time at the golf course, and took Agnes on frequent getaway weekends. Looking back, Agnes reported this was one of the best times in their marriage, although she blamed herself for his impotence and felt guilty that her affair may have caused his sexual problems.

In 2000, Jacob became one of his physician's first patients to receive Viagra. He wanted to recover his sexual relationship with Agnes. Over the next ten years, Jacob attempted several new medications and medical treatments for impotence, with no apparent effect. Also, in the early 2000s, Jacob began his nocturnal oneiric relationships with a string of fantasy sexual partners.

Jacob's Dreams

Jacob remembered the first, or at least one early nocturnal sexual encounter. In it, he opened the bedroom closet to discover a young, nude girl gazing at him. He asked her what she was doing, but she didn't speak. She looked like Lois, a former employee at the golf course, but was younger, with larger breasts. In the dream, he retrieved some clothing, told her to dress, and "get the hell out of here." He found the dream upsetting yet couldn't understand it.

After his dream of the girl in the closet, he frequently spoke aloud in the night, and Agnes realized he was visualizing sexual encounters. Initially, most of Jacob's dream encounters were with his ex-wife Lois and his "golf dream girl," also Lois, to whom he'd been attracted. Each time, Agnes shook him awake, and each time, he claimed to recall nothing. She repeated his lengthy sexual dialogues and his calling out the name "Lois." He initially questioned whether she was delusional. Over time, he retained glimpses of his encounters with the Lois figures. Later, he remembered snippets of dreams with his son's girlfriend and two other women whose names seemed familiar from teen years. Once each of these women appeared in his dreams, they visited him regularly. Sometimes, one dream-woman faded into another while he sexually engaged with them.

Jacob insisted to Agnes that he had never flirted with the golf course Lois nor seen her outside work. He admitted, however, that he enjoyed watching her drive a golf cart around the rough terrain of the course, which caused her breasts to bounce against her knit blouse. He also admitted driving past her house in the winter months when the golf course was closed, wondering what she was wearing, what she was doing. He denied any contact with his ex-wife Lois, since the divorce in the 1950s. Agnes reminded him that he had once confessed calling the ex-wife for several years after the divorce. She also reminded him that Lois had called the house one evening, fifty years after the divorce, asked for Jacob, but then hung up without speaking to him.

Agnes was alternately tearful and enraged, suspecting him of an actual affair, past or present. She also felt a deep sense of rejection that he failed to become aroused with her yet responded with an erection night after night with his dream partners. She attempted on several occasions to have intercourse with him while he was dreaming, but he told her to "leave us alone." She moved out of the bedroom. He invited her back, insisting she accept his night-time encounters, since he could not stop them.

Psychophysiological Psychotherapy

Jacob's psychotherapist invited him to undergo a trial of psychophysiological psychotherapy (Lehrer, 2018; Moss, 2005, 2008, 2020a). Psychophysiological psychotherapy is based in part on the recognition that cultivating physiologically relaxed states facilitates psychotherapy. Freud began his psychoanalytic practice initially with hypnosis, and after he abandoned hypnosis, continued to invite the patient to recline on a couch. The early psychoanalyst Sandor Ferenczi (1953) advised the use of relaxation exercises to overcome inhibitions to free association. Commencing a psychotherapy session with a brief relaxation exercise often increases the patient's awareness and expression of emotion and eases those inhibitions that impede therapeutic awareness (Moss & Lehrer, 1998).

Emotions are not purely "in the mind." Gross and Levenson (1993), for example, defined emotions as "biologically based reactions that organize an individual's responses to important events" (p. 970). The experience of emotions is from the outset psychophysiological (Cacioppo et al., 2000). Human beings experience emergent emotions in the body often before they recognize the specific emotions. The relationship between physiological reactivity and emotions is a subject of extensive laboratory research (Pace-Schott et al., 2019). Willman et al. (2012) reported that the presence of greater trait anxiety increased the physiological reactivity in stressful situations. Research has also shown that different situations also moderate or augment connections among personality, emotion, and physiological response (Stemmler & Wacker, 2010).

Further, the suppression of emotion utilizes both psychological and physiological mechanisms (Gross & Levenson, 1993). When human beings experience an emotional state as threatening or distressing, they utilize their bodies to block emerging thoughts, feelings, and impulses. Gross and Levenson emphasized sympathetic nervous activation in the suppression of emotion. Reich and Anna Freud identified patterns of bracing and tension in the musculature supporting the defensive operations of the mind. The repetitive and chronic suppression of emotions and impulses creates an "armoring" in the musculature, as described by Wilhelm Reich (1942, 1945). Anna Freud (1980) observed that bodily postures, such as rigidity, are in fact defensive processes which have become independent of the original situation in which they arose, and become permanent features of character, which she called "character armor," following Reich's term (p. 225).

Research since Reich and Anna Freud has continued to document a connection between muscular activation and the emotions. Cacioppo et al. (1986) conducted laboratory studies of facial muscle activity and its relationship to emotional reactivity. They concluded that "gradients of EMG [electromyographic] activity over the muscles of facial expression can provide objective and continuous probes of affective processes that are too subtle or fleeting to evoke expressions observable under normal conditions of social interaction" (p. 260). Hovanitz et al. (2002) identified a strong correlation between the magnitude of muscle tension and depression, and a similar correlation between muscle tension and anxiety. The psychotherapy provided to Jacob utilized electronic monitoring to identify physiological correlates of emotions not within his conscious awareness (Moss, 2020a).

Jacob's Therapy

Jacob's therapist explained to him that his mind and body were working hard to express and resolve a number of important emotional and relationship problems. Yet, Jacob repeatedly declared no conscious awareness of the dreams and expressed confusion about what they meant. Jacob's therapist suggested that cultivating a relaxed state in his therapy sessions, and cultivating deeply relaxed states at bedtime, might facilitate an emerging awareness of the messages his dreams were conveying. Each therapy session commenced with three minutes in which the therapist guided Jacob in meditation, paced breathing, or progressive muscle relaxation, with instructions to practice these self-calming skills each day and at bedtime.

Further, monitoring his physiology during therapy sessions would provide Jacob and his therapist with a window into what his body might be telling him. Cognitively, individuals can deny many emotions and desires, yet the body will disclose undeniable physical reactions when the subject is discussed (Wickramasekera, 1998). Increases in skin conductance and heart rate, changes in rate and manner of breathing, and increases in muscle tension may all be a warning of such unrecognized emotional distress or conflict.

Training in Mindful Breathing and Meditation

Initially, Jacob's therapist applied several physiological sensors, including heart rate (HR), respiration (RESP), skin conductance (SCL), and muscle activity (SEMG). Then, he trained Jacob to create a state of mind–body relaxation by focusing his awareness entirely on the process of his breathing. These are the words initially used to guide Jacob:

> I like to start my sessions with each patient with a moment of meditation. This reduces my stress and yours and enables me to more fully listen to you and understand you and may help you to better express your problems to me. Will you please join me in three minutes of gentle, relaxed breathing? I encourage you to get comfortable in your chair, set aside any stress or baggage of the day. If it is comfortable for you to do so, allow your eyes to close. Now, begin to notice your body and any areas of tension. Release the tension and notice how your musculature begins to relax. And now notice your breathing, be aware of the slow gentle process of inhaling, bringing air into your body, and then notice the process of exhaling. You may notice a slight rise in tension as you inhale, and then a release of tension as you exhale. And now simply be aware of this inward quiet and enjoy this moment of respite from your day. (Moss, 2020b, p. 22)

Jacob enjoyed the process of slow breathing, and initially fell asleep in his therapist's office as he was guided into the mindful breathing. After being awakened, he resumed slow gentle breathing. He talked about his lingering emotional pain over Agnes's affair and abortion. He emphasized that he loves children, and felt he had a right to be consulted. Agnes repeatedly reminded Jacob they had been separated. Since he was not the father, he had no place in the decision. But Jacob insisted that because he was her lawful husband, she should not have aborted without consulting him.

When asked about his current feelings toward his wife, Jacob emphasized that he loves her, and she is a "good Christian woman." However, as he made these statements, his respiration became erratic and a spectral display of his heart rate variability began to show a peak in the "very low frequency" area, typically indicating parasympathetic withdrawal and emotional activation. When asked what might be causing this physiological response, Jacob remarked that maybe he still resents her more than he likes to admit. Jacob complained that the physiological monitors were "showing no mercy" in revealing his emotions.

Over the course of several sessions, Jacob recalled past relationships, including the women he could identify in his dreams. He spoke most fondly of his ex-wife, Lois. He regretted the end of that relationship and blamed himself as much as Lois. She spent impulsively, but they were both young with a great deal to learn. He expressed regret he had not sought outside help with their financial problems and regretted that he volunteered for one long Navy cruise after their arguing had escalated. He showed strong physiological activation to his memories of Lois, and he acknowledged a lingering physical attraction to her, more so than to Agnes. "I shouldn't feel this way," he commented, "but I really want her, not Agnes." Jacob quickly added: "That's just my feelings, I am married to Agnes."

The therapist suggested to Jacob that his dreams might be expressing a great deal about the realities of his heart, and he grew angry with the therapist. He insisted that since he is a grown man, he should be able to decide to forgive his wife. His feelings should conform. His point of view was that although he felt drawn to Lois, and even to his golf course co-worker Lois, he knew he did not have a real relationship with either woman, so they should not be disrupting his marriage. Further, he was angry with Agnes because during his waking hours he treated her well. He resented that she should be so distraught over the "nonsense" of his dreams.

Breakthrough: Early Sexual Experience

During his fifth session of psychophysiological psychotherapy, Jacob reported a change in his dreaming. He awakened himself and his wife two consecutive nights screaming, "No, bring me Loie." As he reported these incidents, his SCL, HR, and RESP rate accelerated dramatically, and his HRV shifted with a strong elevation in the "very low frequency" range, all indicating emotional activation.

The therapist inquired "who is Loie?" Jacob responded sharply, "No, she isn't part of this." The therapist asked again, "who is Loie?" He responded sharply again, "It can't be her, not her." The therapist instructed Jacob to watch his physiology on the computer display and be aware of relaxing and quieting his mind. His physiology slowly quieted. Again, the therapist asked, "Who is Loie?" Jacob's physiology again accelerated. The therapist waited and Jacob began to cry, gently at first, and then sobbed.

Finally, Jacob began to speak about the years he was in junior high school. He had been assigned a math tutor to help him with algebra. He liked math but struggled to convert story problems into a formula. The tutor's name was Lois, but she asked students to call her Loie. Jacob was thirteen and he believed the tutor was about twenty-one.

Jacob was entranced from their first math session, and he eagerly welcomed her invitation for extra sessions at her apartment after school and Saturdays. Loie welcomed him with cookies and tutoring sessions by her fireplace. Jacob tried to hug Loie as he left after their first Saturday session, but she pushed him away, commenting that "Mr. Jones (the school principal) wouldn't like that." The second time he tried to hug her, however, she responded by hugging and kissing him. She began to offer some cuddle time if he would make progress on algebra. She repeatedly cautioned him, "now, we better be careful" and "don't you go talking about this." The cuddling became more sexual but never included intercourse. Jacob spent his eighth-grade year pre-occupied with Loie and algebra, pleading for more weekend tutoring sessions. He was heartbroken when Loie moved away that May, thus ending their contact. Jacob wrote to her several times the summer after eighth grade, but never had further contact.

Jacob again cried as he described Loie's departure. He commented that he knew their contact was a mistake, against the law, and should not have happened, but he saw her as "owning his heart." The therapist used the word "abuse," and Jacob became angry and defensive about his "true love with Loie." His physiology accelerated again during the discussion of the word abuse, and then his physiology again calmed following the conversation.

The therapist instructed Jacob to write a letter each day that week to Loie, saying "goodbye," and describing what their relationship meant to him. Jacob found that the tone of the emotional expression changed over the week. His first three letters were full of longing before a thread of anger entered the letters as he berated Loie for letting him think she loved him, and then leaving. His dreams and sleep talking also increased in intensity in parallel as the anger entered his letters. His wife informed him that one night he screamed out, "Loie, leave me alone."

Behavioral Desensitization with Physiological Monitoring

In the following therapy session, Jacob read to the therapist passages of his letters to Loie, and watched his physiology react to the content. His physiological reactivity was intense for SCL, HR, and RESP rate, and moderate for SEMG. Repeatedly, he was instructed to relax his physiology, in a form of systematic desensitization. Systematic desensitization is a therapeutic strategy introduced by Joseph Wolpe (1958). In the systematic desensitization model, the therapist helps the patient construct a hierarchy of situations that trigger anxiety or negative emotion, organized from the least to the most distressing. Then, the therapist guides patients to calm themselves using muscle relaxation or meditation. As the patients expose themselves to progressively more distressing stimuli while working to maintain and recover a relaxed state, the power of the situations to upset is greatly reduced or de-sensitized. In systematic desensitization, the therapist may ask the patient to visualize the troubling situation in imagery or face the situation in vivo (in real life). McLeod (2015) described the systematic desensitization procedure in more detail and its use with anxiety disorders.

By the close of the session, Jacob was able to re-read several letters, with decreased physiological and emotional reactivity thanks to the systematic desensitization.

Next, Jacob's therapist suggested to him that the later Lois figures in his life were perhaps somewhat important for who they were individually, but also might be "stand-ins" for the original Loie. The therapist suggested that it was no accident he was repeatedly attracted to women named Lois, after his early experience with Loie. Jacob seemed puzzled but remained quiet while his HR and RESP rate increased. Then as his physiology relaxed, Jacob expressed feeling calmer and more accepting of the original Loie's importance. He now reported a dream he had "forgotten" to mention. The night before his session, he again encountered the nude girl in his closet, but this time she was Loie. In the dream, he covered her up and yelled for her to go away. He awakened screaming, "Now Loie, you go away."

The therapist instructed Jacob to write private letters, daily, for a week, to his past Lois figures, the first wife and the golf course co-worker, expressing his attraction and sexual desire, and any other lingering sadness or other emotions. The therapist also suggested he write a letter saying "goodbye." Jacob readily agreed to say goodbye to the Lois figures. Once again, the emotional tone of the letters shifted over the week. The first three days, the letters to his first wife Lois were full of yearning and regret, but then he found himself almost empty of feeling, with little to say. His message to both women became short and factual by the end of the week. His final message to the golf course co-worker included an instruction, "You keep your bouncy self out of my dreams. I am sick of it." He recalled little of his dreaming that week and there were no spoken outbursts in the night.

In the next therapy session, the therapist repeated the systematic desensitization process. Jacob read the letters, observed his physiology, and relaxed deeply after each letter. The physiological activation was moderate to these letters, and as the session progressed, Jacob was able to relax his physiology more quickly and fully after each letter. The physiological reactivity included moderate increases in SCL, HR, and RESP rate, with minimal changes in SEMG.

The therapist instructed Jacob to write brief letters to Loie or one of the Lois figures each day for the next week, and to force himself to write at least a half page, regardless of how little he felt. Jacob described writing bland letters to each of the women, with less and less feeling. He could not recall any dreaming except some dreams of a beach he and Agnes had visited the previous year. Jacob showed very little physiological reaction as he read the bland letters. This diminution in the physiological signals indicated that the behavioral desensitization was succeeding in decreasing his emotional reactivity to the past relationships.

The therapist then shifted the session focus to memories of his separation from Agnes, her affair, and her abortion. His physiology became more reactive, and again the therapist guided Jacob to visualize the distressing events, watch his physiology react, and then self-calm and watch his physiology recover a relaxed state.

Couples Focus and Behavioral Prescriptions

Jacob's therapist instructed him to make several plans with his wife for the coming months, to visit places he and Agnes had enjoyed. He also referred them for marriage counseling, to work on their communication and achieve mutual forgiveness. He scheduled Jacob for a series of individual follow-up sessions initially every three weeks and instructed him to continue to write one letter per week each to Loie and the two Lois figures. Jacob also committed to practice relaxation briefly each day, including paced breathing and progressive muscle relaxation.

Finally, the therapist invited Jacob's wife to join him in the session. He then provided the following instruction:

> For the success of Jacob's therapy and for the benefit of your future sexual relationship, I ask you to accept the following instructions. If you possibly can, please try your very hardest not to engage in intercourse for at least ninety days. You may hug, cuddle, or even enjoy touching one another, but for these first 90 days, it is of the utmost importance that you try to avoid frequent sexual intercourse.

This instruction was strategically constructed as a therapeutic paradox. First, the instruction suggests not only that sexual intercourse will resume, but that it will be a challenge to avoid sex for ninety days. Second, it suggests that they will desire lower-level affection and that is acceptable. Finally, the choice of the words "... try your very hardest" suggests that they will probably fail in trying and may have sex.

Three weeks later, Agnes called the therapist and pleaded with him to please continue therapy with Jacob. The couple had been unable to hold off and had resumed frequent sexual intercourse. She apologized profusely, asking the therapist to accept that it was not possible for them to wait, given the intensity of their desire, and begged that he please continue to counsel Jacob.

Jacob continued in individual psychophysiological psychotherapy every four to six weeks for six months. He reported occasional recurrences of nocturnal visits, but the three Lois figures did not appear again. The therapist guided Jacob in a repeated process of writing letters to his son's former girlfriend and the two teen era girls who had reappeared in the recent nocturnal dream visits. Each time, writing goodbye letters brought a stirring of emotions, then a waning of emotion, and a cessation of the dreams. Therapy sessions were used for systematic desensitization to the letters, using physiological monitoring and alternating between reading the letters and engaging in self-calming, until the letters to that female figure could no longer produce physiological reactivity.

Jacob and Agnes continued in intermittent marital therapy, with a positive improvement in communication and more joy in shared travel. Jacob reached a point of regretful acceptance for the abortion, and Agnes reluctantly acknowledged her regret over the abortion. Their physical relationship grew more comfortable. Jacob became content with Agnes awakening him when he exhibited a spontaneous erection, and they enjoyed both sexual play and some intercourse those nights.

Conclusions: Patient Perspectives on Psychophysiological Psychotherapy

Jacob's perspective on his psychophysiological psychotherapy was that the computer display of his physiological/emotional reactions was the most important factor in his recovery. He felt he could not argue with physiology. If his body showed a strong emotional reactivity, he was able to stay with that signal and connect with its significance. The letters and the systematic desensitization were also helpful to him. When the computer display showed less and less reaction to the letters, he felt relief that he was done with another part of the problem.

Jacob also credited his "magic meditations" with helping him resolve his dreams. He was instructed that once he began to quiet his mind effectively at bedtime, he would begin to remember more from his dreams, which happened. He also appreciated that when Agnes said something upsetting, he could listen mindfully, breathe gently, and accept what she was saying. As he became less contentious, her temperament also smoothed, and he found himself enjoying her more. In his final session, he again apologized that he had not been able to avoid sex for ninety days. The therapist accepted the apology and praised Jacob and Agnes for finding their own pathways to healing their sexuality.

This case narrative illustrates some basic principles of psychophysiological psychotherapy. (1) Relaxation practices can enhance the patient's openness to emotional experiencing in psychotherapy. (2) Monitoring physiological processes can assist the patient in identifying and understanding emotions relevant for the patient's original complaint. (3) Physiological monitoring can assist a therapeutic desensitization process, reducing the patient's reactivity to once painful memories.

Further, chapters in the present volume by Petrocchi and Ottaviani (2024) and Wendt and Thayer (2024) have highlighted the enhancement of therapeutic processes when heart rate variability (HRV) is higher, whether by long-term spontaneous vagal activity or through HRV training. The mindful breathing practices described in the present chapter facilitate breathing at approximately six breaths per minute. This is an approximation to the resonance frequency described by Lehrer (2018), which induces increased HRV (Lehrer, 2018; Lehrer et al., 2016). Thus, mindful slow breathing also impacts on neural structures, including the parasympathetic nervous system, the prefrontal cortex, and limbic structures, in a fashion supportive of psychotherapeutic change.

References

American Psychiatric Association. (2013). *Diagnostic and statistical manual of mental disorders* (5th ed.). https://doi.org/10.1176/appi.books.9780890425596

Cacioppo, J. T., Berntson, G. G., Larsen, J. T., Poehlmann, K. M., & Ito, T. A. (2000). The psychophysiology of emotion. In M. Lewis, & J. M. Haviland (Eds.), *Handbook of emotions* (pp. 173–191). Guilford.

Cacioppo, J. T., Petty, R. E., Losch, M. E., & Kim, H. S. (1986). Electromyographic activity over facial muscle regions can differentiate the valence and intensity of affective reactions. *Journal of Personality and Social Psychology*, *50*(2), 260–268. https://doi:10.1037//0022-3514.50.2.260

Ferenczi, S. (1953). Contraindications to the "active" psycho-analytical therapy in psycho-analysis. In S. Ferenczi (Ed.), *Further contributions to the theory and technique of psychoanalysis* (pp. 198–217). Basic Books.

Freud, A. (1980). *Die Schriften von Anna Freud* (vol. 1). [*The papers of Anna Freud, vol. 1*]. Kindler Verlag.

Gross, J. J., & Levenson, R. W. (1993). Emotional suppression: Physiology, self-report, and expressive behavior. *Journal of Personality and Social Psychology*, *64*(6), 970–986.

Hovanitz, C. A., Filippedes, M., Lindsay, D., & Scheff, J. (2002). Muscle tension and physiologic hyperarousal, performance, and state affectivity: Assessing the independence of effects in frequent headache and depression. *Applied Psychophysiology and Biofeedback*, *27*(1), 29–44. https://doi.org/10.1023/a:1014524521152

Lehrer, P. M. (2018). Heart rate variability biofeedback and other psychophysiological procedures as important elements in psychotherapy. *International Journal of Psychophysiology*, *131*, 89–95. https://doi.org/10.1016/j.ijpsycho.2017.09.012

Lehrer, P. M., Vaschillo, B., Zucker, T., Graves, J., Katsamanis, M., Velez, M. A., & Wamboldt, F. (2016). Protocol for heart rate variability training. In D. Moss & F. Shaffer (Eds.), *Foundations of heart rate variability biofeedback* (pp. 9–19). Association for Applied Psychophysiology and Biofeedback.

McLeod, S. A. (2015). *Systematic desensitization as a counter conditioning process*. Simply Psychology. www.simplypsychology.org/Systematic-Desensitisation.html

Moss, D. (2005). Psychophysiological psychotherapy: The use of biofeedback, biological monitoring, and stress management principles in psychotherapy. *Psychophysiology Today: The Magazine for Mind-Body Medicine*, *2*(1), 14–18.

Moss, D. (2008). *15 Grundsätze für die Anwendung von Biofeedback in einer psychosomatische Psychotherapie* [15 principles for the application of biofeedback in a psychosomatic psychotherapy]. In I. Pirker-Binder (Ed.), *Biofeedback in der Praxis, Band II. Erwachsene*. [*Biofeedback in practice, vol. 2. Adults*] (pp. 108–114). Springer Medizin.

Moss, D. (2020a). Physiological monitoring to enhance clinical hypnosis and psychotherapy. *International Journal of Clinical and Experimental Hypnosis*, *68*(4), 466–474. https://doi.org/10.1080/00207144.2020.1790992

Moss, D. (2020b). The role of mindfulness approaches in integrative medicine. In I. Khazan & D. Moss (Eds.), *Mindfulness, acceptance, and compassion in biofeedback practice* (pp. 19–25). Association for Applied Psychophysiology and Biofeedback.

Moss, D., & Lehrer, P. M. (1998). Body work in psychotherapy before biofeedback. *Biofeedback*, *26*(1), 4–7, 31.

Pace-Schott, E. F., Amole, M. C., Aue, T., Balconi, M., Bylsma, L. M., Critchley, H., Demaree, H. A., Friedman, B. H., Gooding, A. E. K., Gosseries, O., Jovanovic, T., Kirby, L. A. J., Kozlowska, K., Laureys, S., Lowe, L., Magee, K., Marin, M.-F., Merner, A. R., Robinson, J. L., . . . Elzakker, M. B. (2019). Physiological feelings. *Neuroscience and Biobehavioral Reviews*, *103*, 267–304. https://doi.org/10.1016/j.neubiorev.2019.05.002

Petrocchi, N., & Ottaviani, C. (2024). Compassionate bodies, compassionate minds: Psychophysiological concomitants of compassion-focused therapy. In P. Steffen & D. Moss (Eds.), *Integrating psychotherapy and psychophysiology*. Oxford University Press.

Reich, W. (1942). *The function of the orgasm*. Orgone Institute Press.

Reich, W. (1945). *Character analysis*. Orgone Institute Press.

Stemmler, G., & Wacker, J. (2010). Personality, emotion, and individual differences in physiological responses. *Biological Psychology, 84*(3), 541–551. https://doi.org/10.1016/j.biopsycho.2009.09.012

Wendt, J., & Thayer, J. F. (2024). Heart rate variability in mental health and psychotherapy. In P. Steffen & D. Moss (Eds.), *Integrating psychotherapy and psychophysiology*. Oxford University Press.

Wickramasekera, I. (1998). Secrets kept from the body but not the body or behavior: The unsolved problems of identifying and treating somatization and psychophysiological disease. *Advances in Mind-Body Medicine, 14*(2), 81–98.

Willman, M., Langlet, C., Hainaut, J.-P., & Bolmont, B. (2012). The time course of autonomic parameters and muscle tension during recovery following a moderate cognitive stressor: Dependency on trait anxiety level. *International Journal of Psychophysiology, 84*(1), 51–58. https://doi.org/10.1016/j.ijpsycho.2012.01.009

Wolpe, J. (1958). *Psychotherapy by reciprocal inhibition*. Stanford University Press. http://garfield.library.upenn.edu/classics1980/A1980JV28300001.pdf

13

The Most Beautiful Man

The Integration of Hypnosis and Biofeedback

Donald Moss

The present article[1] presents a case narrative involving a thirty-six-year-old woman who initially presented with post-partum depression and eventually manifested features of dissociative identity disorder. The treatment combines breath training, physiological monitoring, heart rate variability (HRV) biofeedback training, and self-hypnosis skills, in combination with psychotherapy and clinical hypnosis.

Introducing Marguerite

Marguerite was referred by her primary care physician for post-partum depression, following the birth of her first child, a daughter named Adeline. Marguerite was a music teacher in the local high school, and a newcomer to the community. She was born in France, the first child of an American naval officer, Richard, stationed in the Mediterranean, and a French American mother, Angelique. She attended French schools for her elementary and middle school years, and after her parents divorced attended a private girl's high school in Washington, DC. Her mother opened a restaurant in Dupont Circle, and Marguerite and her only sibling, a younger sister Renee, worked in the restaurant when school activities permitted. Marguerite also studied piano, practiced for many hours, and played keyboard in a girlfriend's all girl jazz group.

Marguerite experienced good physical and mental health except for a period of drug and alcohol use in her high school years, which her mother attributed to the stress of the parental divorce. Marguerite was interviewed by her physician initially with her mother who had arranged for the referral and appointment, and later separately. Once she was interviewed alone, Marguerite explained that the divorce was difficult for both she and her sister. They were accustomed

---

[1] This chapter is adapted with permission from a previous publication: Moss, D. (2019). The most beautiful man: An integration of hypnosis and biofeedback for depression and dissociation. *American Journal of Clinical Hypnosis*, 62(4), 322–334. https://doi.org/10.1080/00029157.2018.1517082

to the father being gone for a month or two when he was at sea, but he disappeared for a year after the divorce. Worse, however, their mother was a binge alcoholic and Marguerite and Renee never knew when she would awaken them in the night, scream and throw things, and blame the girls for the father's departure. Marguerite remembered that she began to drink her mother's alcohol after these midnight episodes, and then began to drink and smoke marijuana with her girlfriends from the band. Her problems escalated until her father arranged for her to enter a teen alcohol and drug abuse unit, with two months of follow-up counseling. Thereafter, the girls spent their summers with the father who by then was retired in Annapolis. This seemed to moderate both Marguerite's emotional turbulence and the mother's outbursts; Marguerite felt more herself and was better able to focus on her music and school.

After high school, Marguerite attended college in northern Virginia, became certified as a secondary school teacher and music teacher, and began teaching in a high school in Arlington. She met and married another teacher, a Midwestern-born man, and after some visits to his hometown, they decided to move to the Midwest and raise children there.

Marguerite and her husband David were excited at her pregnancy. Their life seemed well established and they both felt ready to welcome a baby. The pregnancy seemed to go well, although she did experience some episodes of depressive mood and anxiety. Marguerite shopped with enthusiasm for infant clothing and accessories and engaged with David in designing the nursery furnishings and decor. She cried with happiness when the obstetrician announced that they could expect a daughter, and she suggested the name of her favorite teacher in France, Adeline, as the baby's name. David was present for the birthing, and the labor and delivery was long but without difficulty. Both parents were exhausted by the birth process but alternately giddy and tearful at showing Adeline to family.

The initial indication of difficulty came on the first day that Marguerite and Adeline were home alone, while David left for groceries. Marguerite was bathing Adeline, sponging her off, and began to shake and sob. She experienced images of her own body and Adeline's somehow confusedly merging. When David returned from the supermarket, he found Marguerite nervously pacing and sobbing in the hall outside the nursery, muttering incoherently. David called his mother and asked her to come assist with the infant care and help Marguerite with her adjustments to the new baby. He held Marguerite and soothed her, but she continued to shake and cry throughout much of the day.

In the following days, Marguerite participated in caring for Adeline, but routine care seemed to trigger more outbursts of tearfulness and shaking. She often seemed to clutch Adeline tightly, without any apparent reason. When neither Marguerite's mother nor the mother-in-law could calm her and everyday encouragement had no effect, her mother arranged for a primary care appointment.

Referral for Behavioral Health Care

Nearly two weeks passed between the birth and the first primary care appointment, and the physician found her to be still tearful and anxious. She diagnosed a major depressive disorder with postpartum onset and prescribed a selective serotonin reuptake inhibitor for depression and anxiety. The primary care office referred Marguerite to a local psychologist for evaluation and treatment of postpartum depression. The physician also called after the initial referral and requested to speak directly to the assigned psychologist. She conveyed a concern about the possibility of postpartum psychosis because Marguerite had seemed out of touch and had poor eye contact. Marguerite was not as communicative as she had been in past primary care visits. Marguerite also reported images of her body and Adeline's body somehow merging. She also talked to herself disjointedly during the interview, in a way that the physician could not understand.

Assessment

Marguerite completed an intake packet prior to her first session, that included a Beck Depression Inventory-II (BDI-II) and a Beck Anxiety Inventory (BAI). She obtained a score of 34 on the BDI-II, indicating severe depression, and a score of 30 on the BAI, indicating severe anxiety.

In her first session, Marguerite's psychologist emphasized welcoming Marguerite, seated her in a comfortable chair by a fireplace, and invited her to explain what she saw as her most pressing problems and what hopes she had for changing her life and herself through treatment. Marguerite explained that she didn't understand her current problems but was sure they were connected to the years following her parents' divorce. She felt confused and not herself and was afraid she would not be a good mother for her daughter Adeline. She most wanted to recover her enthusiasm for mothering and care for her daughter, as she had imagined, without breaking down.

Next, her psychologist invited her to begin narrating her life history and any medical history. He also encouraged her to stop at any time and to express any requests that might help her to feel safe and comfortable with the process. He encouraged her to take her time in telling her story, and to stop wherever she needed, to breathe slowly and become comfortable again before proceeding.

Marguerite spoke fluidly at first, describing at length her happy childhood years with her father, mother, and sister in the south of France. She described her school years, her enthusiasm for learning and for music, and her love for one teacher especially, her piano and voice teacher, Adeline. She paused more frequently and seemed distracted and even confused in describing her parents' divorce, and her speech became somewhat fragmented. She expressed fatigue and asked if she could stop the history taking and resume in her next session.

Physiological Monitoring

At the close of her first session, her psychologist explained that he would like to monitor Marguerite's physiology during the future therapy sessions, explaining that our bodies know where the important memories are, where the key emotions are, and changes in her physiology would assist the psychologist make Marguerite's treatment more successful. Marguerite commented that "then there will be no secrets here, you know." The psychologist asked Marguerite whether she was ready for this level of openness, and she became very still and said, "it is time." Marguerite also agreed to a ninety-minute time frame for her second session, so there would be time for her psychologist to set up and explain the physiological monitoring before they began their therapeutic dialogue.

Homework: Mindful Breathing and Emotional Journaling

Her psychologist also engaged Marguerite in two kinds of homework for the days between sessions, throughout her treatment. First, he provided Marguerite with instructions for a *mindful breathing* exercise:

> Please follow these instructions and enjoy five to ten minutes of gentle relaxed breathing once or twice a day, or more, whenever you have time. I encourage you to get comfortable in your chair and set aside any stress or baggage of the day. If it is comfortable for you to do so, allow your eyes to close. Now, notice your body and any areas of tension. Release the tension and notice how your musculature begins to relax. And now, simply notice your breathing. Be mindfully aware of the slow gentle process of inhaling, bringing air into your body, and then notice the process of exhaling. It is usually best to breathe in gently through your nostrils, and then breathe out slowly and gently through pursed lips. That is, form a little circle with your lips, and feel your breath as it leaves your mouth, through this little circle. It may also be helpful for you to place one hand on your abdomen, to feel the gentle expansion and contraction of your abdomen as you breathe. You may experience a slight rise in tension as you inhale, and then a release of tensions as you exhale. And now, simply be aware of this inward quiet and enjoy this moment of respite from your day. At times, emotions or memories may surface during your breathing exercise. If they do, accept them as a gift for your therapy, jot them down on a piece of paper, and resume your breathing.

Second, Marguerite's therapist encouraged her to undertake daily emotional journaling. Here too, he gave her detailed instructions:

> I would like you to dedicate a relatively short time period (fifteen to twenty minutes) each day to writing. Use that time to write about your deepest and most intense emotions, especially emotions about painful and traumatic times in your life. You may find feelings

and memories emerging that are important for your current problems, or you may not. Regardless of what emerges, it will prove to be important in your full recovery. Allow yourself to express yourself freely, without concern about handwriting, grammar, or literary concerns. If it becomes too painful to continue writing, please be aware of accepting that emotional pain, and do your mindful breathing exercise. If your breathing calms you enough that you can resume your writing, then do so. Remind yourself that this writing is for you—for you alone. No one else will ever read it unless you decide to share it. Once you have reached the fifteen- or twenty-minute point, please, please, please close the journal, place it in a drawer, and go on about your day. If you wish me to read anything you have written, bring the journal with you and I will read it together with you.

Finally, he gave her a copy of a workbook published by James Pennebaker, *Expressive Writing, Words that Heal* (Pennebaker & Evans, 2014). Pennebaker's research has shown salutogenic effects from expressing one's emotions in a journal, with documented therapeutic effects including improved mood, reduced anxiety and fearfulness, enhanced immune function, reduced blood pressure, and many other positive effects (Klapow et al., 2001; Pennebaker, 1997).

Physiological Monitoring

The combination of physiological monitoring and psychotherapy is called psychophysiological psychotherapy (Caldwell & Steffen, 2018; Lehrer, 2018; Moss, 2005, 2008, 2020). The patient's physiology is monitored and displayed on a computer monitor and shows both therapist and patient when affective reactions occur during the therapeutic dialogue. For example, in the presence of strong emotion, breathing alters with hyperventilation or breath holding, heart rate (HR) accelerates, and the dominant HRV shifts into the "very low frequency" range. Muscle tension also increases, with muscular bracing against emotion, and the electrodermal signal increases dramatically.

At her second session, the psychologist initially asked Marguerite for her permission to apply physiological sensors and monitor what was happening in her body. He explained each sensor, as he applied it, including surface electromyography sensors on her shoulders, a thermometer on her non-dominant middle finger, a photoplethysmograph for HR on her non-dominant thumb, electrodermal sensors on her non-dominant index and ring finger, electroencephalographic (EEG) sensors (an active sensor at the vertex and two reference sensors on the ears), and a respirometer band around her abdomen (see Table 13.1). He observed and explained to Marguerite her physiological baseline on the computer, noting elevated HR, rapid breathing, and an elevation of EEG amplitude in the high Beta range (23–38 Hz). He discussed each element of the physiological signals displayed on the computer screen, explaining that the high HR, rapid breathing, and EEG elevation all were

Table 13.1 Biofeedback modalities utilized

Modality	Acronym	Activity Measured	Measurement Unit
Surface Electromyograph	SEMG	muscle action potentials	microvolts (μV)
Thermometer	TEMP	peripheral blood flow	degrees F or C
Photoplethysmograph	PPG, HR, HRV	peripheral blood flow, heart rate, heart rate variability	arbitrary units
Electrodermograph	EDR, GSR, SCL	eccrine sweat gland activity, electrical conductance/ resistance in skin	microsiemens (μS)
Electroencephalograph	EEG	cortical postsynaptic potentials	microvolts (μV)
Respirometer	RESP	abdominal/chest expansion	arbitrary units

indicative of significant anxiety. Marguerite acknowledged that she felt extreme anxiety about the memories she might share this day.

Next, he invited Marguerite to do the mindful breathing exercise together with him. As she slowed her breathing, he highlighted the changes on the computer display, indicating that her breathing was slowing to a rate of about seven breaths per minute, her HR was now slower, and the EEG high Beta range had moderated. She was surprised she could affect this level of change in five minutes, as she was still aware that today's conversation was going to be painful. He encouraged her to use her breathing at any time she wished during their discussion, to make the process less distressing.

Marguerite's Story

Marguerite's psychologist invited her to begin where she had stopped the previous session, with the divorce, the move to Washington DC, and her high school years. Marguerite began several times to describe her early teen experiences, and several times lapsed into a tearful silence. Each time she tried to begin again with another event. Finally, Marguerite seemed to freeze, and her physiological signals on the display elevated dramatically. Marguerite's psychologist asked her what was happening, and she spoke haltingly and said: "it's her, it's . . . she . . . she . . . no it's . . . no . . . Renee doesn't know."

He again asked her what was happening with her, and she spoke again. "It's Armand, you have to know, Armand." He asked who Armand was, and she spoke very quietly, "The most beautiful man . . . the most beautiful man I have ever touched." Armand was a young man of about thirty, who began to appear in the family's restaurant regularly in Marguerite's second year working in the restaurant. He was elegantly dressed, tall and slender, and French, with delicate, beautiful, almost feminine features. Both Marguerite and Renee were fascinated with Armand, who greeted them at each visit with embraces and kisses to both cheeks. Quickly, however, the girls' mother Angelique staked her claim to Armand, and began to lunch with him regularly, and then to disappear with him for several days on end.

Shortly after Marguerite's fifteenth birthday, in October, a routine began to develop, in which Armand dropped in on evenings when Marguerite was alone in the family apartment near the restaurant. He was there, he said, to meet Angelique, yet Angelique and Renee were still away closing the restaurant. Often, Marguerite was practicing her piano exercises, and each time Armand joined her at the keyboard and played a third hand on the keyboard with her, forming harmonies and occasionally interjecting dissonant chords, frequently brushing her hands as they played. She was drawn to him by his beauty and his musical sensitivity and began to embrace him sensually as he left the apartment with Angelique. Marguerite's mother seemed unconcerned, but told Marguerite to "knock it off, this one is mine."

As weeks passed, Armand began to come earlier and earlier, and their brushing hands progressed to embracing, and the embracing progressed to undressing, and the undressing proceeded to making love. Marguerite felt the happiest she had been since her parents' divorce and Armand began to speak to her of their escaping to his family home near Nice.

On a Thursday evening in December, Armand and Marguerite were in her bed, exhausted and gently cuddling, when the bedroom door flew open. Angelique stood frozen in the doorway, and then commenced to scream at Marguerite, "You bitch, you whore, you Jezebel, get out, get out, get out, he's mine." Angelique was carrying a dripping umbrella that she began to swing at Marguerite, battering her from head to toe. Marguerite clutched for Armand who rolled away, climbed out of the bed, grabbed his clothing, and escaped the room. Angelique continued to bash at Marguerite, increasingly shrill, "You took him, you bitch, you sneak, I hate you." Marguerite was cut and bruised all over her body, and felt too much pain to move, but her mother pulled her out of the bed, pushed her toward the door, until Marguerite grabbed her clothing and half walked, half crawled out of the apartment.

Armand was gone and Marguerite never saw him again. Marguerite stayed with a friend for several days, and then began spending time at home while her mother worked. Renee pleaded to know what had happened, but Marguerite never told her. Marguerite began to drink her mother's liquor and began to smoke marijuana with her jazz band friend. She began to spend nights at home, with her door locked, but several times her mother broke the lock and entered the room drunk, screaming at Marguerite and throwing objects at her, blaming her for her husband's leaving and Armand's absence. The screaming was not new, the midnight scenes had happened intermittently since the divorce, but everything was now more intense.

Marguerite's physiology had been "screaming pain" on the computer display as she related the painful events ending her time with Armand. After she described her mother's midnight visits, she became quiet, and her physiology calmed as well. Her psychologist asked her if that was enough for the day, and she agreed that it was. He encouraged her to end the session by breathing slowly and mindfully with him. He also encouraged her to continue her journaling and her breath exercises at home.

Hypnotically Assisted Psychotherapy

At the next session, Marguerite's therapist asked her what hurt the most about the incidents when she was fifteen. Marguerite was not sure. The entire memory hurt, the entire period was a blur from that ugly evening to the following autumn, after her sixteenth birthday, when her father re-entered her life and personally escorted her to a teen addictions treatment center.

Marguerite explained that as an adult and a teacher she knew that what Armand did was wrong, especially pursuing mother and underage daughter at the same time, but she also could not stop grieving for him and yearning for him. She felt injured, not by their sexual encounter, but by his leaving her in the middle of her mother's violence. She had called him repeatedly afterward and sent letters for six months and heard nothing. She felt that Armand's departure and her mother's rages at her were equal in the pain they evoked. She also felt that her special closeness with her sister Renee was wounded by this traumatic period. Renee sensed that Marguerite had never "come clean" about what happened, and it felt as her though there was always a kind of obstacle between them in the two decades since.

Hypnotic Age Regression

Marguerite's psychologist offered her a series of options, and she embraced them all. She would continue her mindful breathing practices, spend some time at the beginning of each session, practicing her breathing and learning some self-hypnosis exercises, while watching the effects on her physiology. She committed to continuing her journaling, which that week had evolved into letters written to her sister, mother, and father. Her psychologist agreed to use hypnosis to assist her in re-visiting the critical events of her fifteenth year, first at a distance and then "close up."

Marguerite's psychologist began inducing hypnosis, using a variety of induction and deepening techniques, including an eye roll, a calm scene, a descending staircase image, and counting down into a deeper trance state. She responded well to hypnosis, going easily into a trance state. He invited her to visit moments of happiness in her years in France, and then moments of joy in the Dupont Circle apartment and in her high school. She found herself smiling and laughing lightly, picturing several memories with her sister Renee. Then he invited her to walk down P Street, past the apartment, looking up at the apartment window as Marguerite and Armand played at the piano. When she became anxious, he invited her to slow her breathing, and walk toward Logan Circle, away from the apartment.

For three sessions, Marguerite's therapist guided her in hypnotically induced age regressions, touching on experiences around and in the traumatic evening. She peered into the bedroom where she lay in Armand's arms, observed her mother climbing the stairs on the night she arrived home early, and observed Armand walking hurriedly away from the apartment building. Finally, Marguerite felt ready to witness her mother's fury in the bedroom. In her mind's eye, she watched her mother walking down the hall, watched her swinging the bedroom door open, and listened to her shrill voice screaming her anger at Marguerite. For one or two minutes, she experienced herself in the bed with her mother swinging the umbrella and Armand pulling away and sliding off the bed. Then Marguerite returned to the present and used her breathing to quiet her emotions. "Enough," she muttered, and opened her eyes into the present.

Respiratory and Heart Rate Variability Biofeedback

Marguerite's therapist agreed with stopping the age regression at this juncture but offered another activity to soothe her emotional state. She was already "wired" for physiological monitoring during the psychotherapy sessions, so her psychologist brought the monitor cart closer, and shifted the display to a breath training screen. He asked her to breathe with a breath pacer on the screen, at six breaths per minute, and to simply become mindfully aware of the process of her breathing. Marguerite had been practicing mindful diaphragmatic breathing for several weeks, and she found it easy and comfortable to breathe with the pacer. She felt reassured when her psychologist showed her the calming of her physiology.

Marguerite's therapist began the next session with five minutes of breathing, and this time the psychologist used a biofeedback breath and HR screen to guide her. Marguerite practiced making smooth wave-like curves of breathing and HR across the screen. This process of simultaneously training smooth slow breathing and large, smooth, parallel oscillations in heart rate is the core of HRV biofeedback training, eliciting significant effects on the autonomic nervous system. Smooth, paced breathing elicits parallel changes in HR, with a gentle rise in HR during the inhale and a gentle drop in HR with the exhale. At the same time, the amplitude of the HR oscillations increases (Moss & Shaffer, 2016).

After the brief biofeedback exercise, Marguerite handed her therapist her journal with pages marked for his inspection. She had experienced a recurrent dream of herself holding a dead infant. She shook as she showed the passages in her journal and pleaded for reassurance that she would not harm her baby. Marguerite denied any urges to harm her infant and denied any hurtful or even rough actions toward Adeline.

Marguerite's psychologist conducted a series of age regressions in the next two sessions, using images from her recurrent dream to prompt and search for any historic roots of the dream. In the second session, she began to shake and described a visual image of a white tiled room and blood, and eventually a bloody baby. She came back to the present sobbing and shaking. At first Marguerite thought this was an image of herself harming Adeline and then she got images of herself in her favorite blue jumper from high school and a nurse wearing scrubs.

This scene was alien for her, unrecognizable. Marguerite had always remembered Armand, although at times she could not remember the night her mother found them together. She had no recollections of a baby or a hospital visit.

Marguerite's psychotherapist invited her to stay into a second hour and utilized further age regressive procedures. Additional images and memories slowly but painfully emerged. She experienced shame, suspecting an abortion, and then finally she pieced together memories of a spontaneous miscarriage. During a night of drinking, Marguerite had begun to hemorrhage, and then miscarried Armand's baby in an emergency room.

Marguerite was initially relieved that the bloody baby in her dream was not Adeline, but grief-stricken that she had lost a baby, and especially Armand's baby. She blamed herself, thinking that her drinking and drug use had killed the baby. Then her face contorted, and she remembered her mother's battering her the night she found her with Armand. She hated her mother for the violence, which may have killed the baby.

Marguerite's psychologist emphasized self-soothing after this session. He taught her self-hypnosis exercises, using techniques he had already used with her in therapy: an eye roll with a long soothing breath, a calm scene, and a descending staircase image. Marguerite agreed to alternate self-hypnosis with mindful breathing as self-calming strategies. He also encouraged her to schedule twice weekly sessions for the next month or two, and to feel free to share anything in her journaling in the session. He suggested to her that her journal and her dreams might show her a path for healing.

Marguerite reported in at her next session, that she experienced breakthrough episodes of shaking, sobbing, with a flood of new memories. Most important to her was a memory of a nurse washing off the miscarried infant and showing her that it was a girl. This image overlapped in her mind with the image that had begun the present time of distress in her life. She was washing her infant Adeline, and looking at her naked female body, when she first began to shake and sob at home. She had a further image of her father in the hospital emergency room. He was a part of that evening. She understood now that her bathing of Adeline had triggered a resurgence of dissociated memories of the teen era traumatic events, including her romance with an adult, the scene with her mother and Armand, and the miscarriage.

After this session, Marguerite wrote another letter to Armand in her journal and a letter to her father. She phoned her therapist and asked if she could bring her father to the next session, since he was a witness to the hospitalization, and could help her to place her disjointed memories into context.

Resolution

In the following weeks, Adeline continued her hypnotically assisted psychotherapy. She journaled almost daily and utilized self-hypnosis and breathing exercises for self-calming. She reported increasing comfort with all aspects of her daughter Adeline's care. She shared the painful memories with her husband, David, who was shaken by the incidents but provided her with unwavering support. She also disclosed the entire sequence of events to her sister Renee, who had suspected that Armand was somehow at the heart of their estrangement. It was a relief to both sisters to recover their openness and comfort with one another.

Marguerite's psychologist conducted several sessions with Marguerite and her father and several separate sessions with she and her mother. The father acknowledged the accuracy of her memories, which were now more complete and more continuous. She had been out with her friend after a jazz band practice, drinking and using marijuana, and noticed that she was hemorrhaging. She called her father who drove in from Annapolis and met her at the hospital. She miscarried a female baby. She stayed with her father for a month after the miscarriage, but never discussed the event again with him. He never brought it up, thinking this was better for her emotional well-being. Her drinking and drug use escalated after the miscarriage, and he then intervened. One afternoon she passed out in her car at an intersection, and the police called him. He physically carried her into an addictions treatment center and remained by her side through the entire detoxification process. He experienced a deep patience with her addictive behaviors, more than he had ever felt for her mother's drinking, because he understood the pain she felt with the miscarriage and the divorce. As far as he knew, she never discussed the miscarriage in her addictions setting, yet she made steady progress in the months following, avoiding drug and alcohol use and re-dedicating herself to her music and her education.

In the sessions with Marguerite, Angelique initially grew stone cold and non-communicative when Marguerite accused her of killing Armand's baby. She defended herself, saying that she was just a concerned mother, not wanting her daughter to be exploited by an adult. She seemed to deny the extent of her violence in the scene with Armand, then slowly admitted the hurtfulness of her drunken midnight rages. Angelique never knew about the pregnancy or the miscarriage and cried with Marguerite after learning of the miscarriage. During that moment of tearfulness, Angelique said something that stopped Marguerite mid-sentence. Angelique said, "you know we both wanted Armand because Richard was gone." Marguerite stared at her mother, and then they both began to clutch each other and sob more deeply. Richard, Marguerite's father, was their first beautiful man, and he had left them both. This recognition brought them together emotionally, in a loss they still shared two decades later.

Marguerite asked for one more session with her father. Marguerite thanked her father for coming to her at her lowest point, in the night of the miscarriage, and for his steady presence ever since. But she asked him how he could so completely abandon her in the divorce. Richard now cried too and held her and said only "I am so sorry, Grite. I was so lost, I was. I am sorry."

Dissociative Identity Disorder

Marguerite received further evaluation by her therapist's colleague who specialized in treating women with sexual abuse histories and dissociative features. Marguerite identified episodes of dissociation throughout the years since her miscarriage. She recalled denying pregnancy in several medical evaluations over the years, without any subjective recognition of dissonance or falsehood. She reported intermittent episodes of lost time, not recalling periods of time and discovering objects among her personal things that she could not recall acquiring. She was unable to recall any previous history of sexual or physical abuse and believed that Armand was her first sexual partner. The traumatic memories of her childhood seemed to center entirely on the divorce, the father's absence, the mother's nocturnal rages at Marguerite, the night Marguerite was caught with Armand, and the miscarriage.

Marguerite benefitted from eighteen months of psychotherapy augmented by her affective journaling, breathing exercises, and self-hypnosis. At the final session, she completed the BDI-II and a BAI. She obtained a score of 12 on the BDI-II, indicating minimal depression, and a score of 11, indicating mild to moderate anxiety. She described herself as living fully again, more fully than at any time since her pregnancy. Looking back, she suspected she was "getting ready to have my breakdown" throughout her pregnancy. She suffered several depressive episodes and anxious times, which she attributed to being pregnant. Marguerite reported in annually for five years after her treatment ended, at her psychologist's request. She gave birth to a second daughter two years later and reported better physical and emotional health throughout that pregnancy and after the birth. There was no further sign of "lost time" or dissociative breaks in consciousness.

This case narrative illustrates the integration of hypnosis, physiological monitoring, affective journaling, biofeedback training, and self-hypnosis as components to augment the effectiveness of dynamic psychophysiological psychotherapy. The author has also published two volumes with a co-author on integrative mind-body-spirit approaches to treating both mental health and medical disorders (McGrady & Moss, 2013, 2018). Those volumes advocate for a combination of self-care practices, lifestyle modifications, complementary therapies, and mainstream medical and mental health interventions.

References

Caldwell, Y. T., & Steffen, P. R. (2018). Adding HRV biofeedback to psychotherapy increases heart rate variability and improves the treatment of major depressive disorder. *International Journal of Psychophysiology*, *131*, 96–101. https://doi.10.1016/j.ijpsycho.2018.01.001

Klapow, J. C., Schmidt, S. M., Taylor, L. A., Roller, P., Li, Q., Calhoun, J. W., Wallander J., & Pennebaker, J. (2001). Symptom management in older primary care patients: Feasibility of an experimental, written self-disclosure protocol. *Annals of Internal Medicine*, *134*(9 Pt 2), 905–911. https://doi.10.7326/0003-4819-134-9_Part_2-200105011-00015

Lehrer, P. M. (2018). Heart rate variability biofeedback and other psychophysiological procedures as important elements in psychotherapy. *International Journal of Psychophysiology*, *131*, 89–95. https://doi.10.1016/j.ijpsycho.2017.09.012

McGrady, A., & Moss, D. (2013). *Pathways to illness, pathways to health*. Springer.

McGrady, A., & Moss, D. (2018). *Integrative pathways: Navigating chronic illness with a mind-body-spirit approach*. Springer.

Moss, D. (2005). Psychophysiological psychotherapy: The use of biofeedback, biological monitoring, and stress management principles in psychotherapy. *Psychophysiology Today: The Magazine for Mind-Body Medicine*, *2*(1), 14–18.

Moss, D. (2008). 15 Grundsätze für die Anwendung von Biofeedback in einer psychosomatische Psychotherapie (15 principles for the application of biofeedback in a psychosomatic psychotherapy). In I. Pirker-Binder (Ed.), *Biofeedback in der Praxis, Band II. Erwachsene* (Biofeedback in practice: vol. 2. Adults) (pp. 108–114). Springer Medizin.

Moss, D. (2019). The most beautiful man: An integration of hypnosis and biofeedback for depression and dissociation. *American Journal of Clinical Hypnosis*, *62*(4), 322–334. https://doi.org/10.1080/00029157.2018.1517082

Moss, D. (2020). Physiological monitoring to enhance clinical hypnosis and psychotherapy. *International Journal of Clinical and Experimental Hypnosis*, *68*(4), 466–474. https://doi.org/10.1080/00207144.2020.1790992

Moss, D., & Shaffer, F. (Eds.). (2016). *Foundations of heart rate variability*. Association for Applied Psychophysiology and Biofeedback.

Pennebaker, J. (1997). *Opening up: The healing power of expressing emotions* (revised edition). Guilford.

Pennebaker, J., & Evans, J. (2014). *Expressive writing: Words that heal*. Idyll Arbor.

14

Integrating Heart Rate Variability Biofeedback into Acceptance and Commitment Therapy (ACT)

Richard N. Gevirtz

Acceptance and commitment therapy (ACT) is one of the most popular "third wave" therapies. Originally called Comprehensive Distancing, ACT was created by Steve Hayes and his colleagues at the University of Nevada-Reno (Hayes et al., 2012) in 1982 as an attempt to combine elements of cognitive behavioral therapy (CBT), covert conditioning, linguistic analysis, and eastern mindfulness elements. It is based on ideas called *functional contextualism* and *relational frame theory* and was heavily influenced by the limitations and strengths of B. F. Skinner's radical behaviorism. Along with CBT, it is now considered one of the primary empirically based therapies and is taught in almost all accredited clinical psychology programs. In scores of head-to-head studies with CBT, ACT has been found to be either comparable or superior. For example, in a recent meta-analysis, Samaan et al. (2021) concluded that "results support previous research findings showing that both ACT and CBT lead to significant improvements in symptom distress and life satisfaction" (p. 382).

In this chapter, I present the advantages of using heart rate variability biofeedback (HRVB) in conjunction with ACT for a variety of physical, stress-related, and psychological disorders. In my experience as a therapist, supervisor, and researcher, ACT is a better fit with HRVB than CBT or other therapeutic approaches. This chapter will examine how HRVB can be creatively integrated into ACT.

Heart Rate Variability Biofeedback Basics

HRVB has been extensively described (Gevirtz et al., 2016a, 2016b; Lehrer et al., 2000). A special issue of *Applied Psychophysiology and Biofeedback*, describes the historical antecedents of this form of biofeedback (Gevirtz, 2022). Briefly, the client is connected to sensors for beat-to-beat heart rate (HR), respiration, skin conductance, and finger temperature and paced through a series of breath rates in an attempt to find "resonance frequency," the frequency where blood pressure rhythms are in resonance with the slow respiratory frequency. At this point, large peak to valley heart rate waves are produced during each breath cycle. Home practice establishes a powerful tool to affect autonomic shift or a shift in unconscious perception of safety (called "neuroception" in polyvagal theory; Porges, 2007). Subsequent sessions continue to utilize these skills as described below. The basic protocol, however, is the foundation for each process.

Numerous reviews have shown that this procedure has a plethora of positive effects, physically, psychologically, and cognitively (Gevirtz, 2013; Goessl et al., 2017; Lehrer & Gevirtz, 2014; Lehrer et al., 2020). Furthermore, very recent studies have shown the profound effect that daily practice of this protocol has on central nervous system structures (Bachman et al., 2022; Gevirtz, 2017; Mather & Thayer, 2018; Nashiro et al., 2021; Schumann et al., 2021). These studies have shown that regular practice of the protocol can have profound effects on brain centers thought to be involved in processes such as anxiety, depression, and rumination.

Integrative Autonomic Process Theories

Two complementary theoretical perspectives are relevant here: Porges' (2007, 2011) polyvagal theory, and Thayer and Lane's (2009) neurovisceral integration theory. Porges (2001) has postulated that there are three global evolutionary phases:

- The first phase of immobilization, governed by the: "primitive unmyelinated visceral vagus that fosters digestion and responds to threat by depressing metabolic activity" (p. 123).
- The second phase of fight or flight, governed by the: "sympathetic nervous system that is capable of increasing metabolic output and inhibiting the visceral vagus to foster mobilization for 'fight or flight'" (p. 123).
- "The third phase, unique to mammals, is characterized by a myelinated vagus system that can rapidly regulate cardiac output to foster engagement and disengagement with the environment" (p. 123). In phase three, the myelinated vagus is linked to the cranial nerves and facial muscles.

The most recently evolved component of the vagus nerve—the myelinated vagus—acts as a "surveillance" system for the body signaling information through the nucleus tractus solitarius to higher brain using afferent vagal fibers. Through an unconscious process that Porges (2007) called "neuroception" or perception of safety, the organism will only be able to function socially or have optimal physiological adaptations when outside or internally generated threat is minimal, allowing the more recently evolved neural structures to self-regulate. The concept of dissolution (coined by the neurologist John Hughlings Jackson) proposes that with increasing threat, the organism devolves to older, more primitive states (York & Steinberg, 2011).

The tenth cranial nerve, the vagus, is the primary two-way (efferent and afferent) pathway for this physiological regulation. It can be accessed through beat-to-beat HR measurement, analyzed as heart rate variability (HRV). Thayer and Lane (2009) have convincingly shown that HRV metrics are sensitive indicators of an extensive range of brain functions (e.g., amygdala to pre-frontal networks, locus coeruleus, insula, etc.). Thus, the impact of interpersonal interactions such as talk therapies have been shown to be partially dependent on physiological states that can be affected or modified by the autonomic nervous system.

Acceptance and Commitment Therapy

Harris (2008) describes six core principles of ACT:

1. Defusion: Relating to your thoughts in a new way, so they have much less impact and influence over you.
2. Expansion: Making room for unpleasant feelings and sensations instead of pushing them away.
3. Connection: Connecting fully with whatever is happening right here, right now.
4. The observing self: The powerful aspect of the mind, which has been largely ignored by western psychology until now.
5. Values: Clarifying your values is essential for making life meaningful.
6. Committed action: A rich and meaningful life is created through taking action. But not just any action. It happens through effective action, guided and motivated by your values.

We have found Harris' (2006, 2008, 2019) approach to ACT to work well with clients aged eight to eighty. It integrates the core principles of ACT in an accessible manner and is easy for the client to comprehend.

Core Principle 1. Cognitive Defusion: Learning Methods to Reduce the Tendency to Reify Thoughts, Images, Emotions, and Memories

Hayes and Strosahl (2005) define fusion as the "human tendency to interact with events on the basis of their verbally ascribed functions rather than their direct functions, while being oblivious to the ongoing relational framing that establishes these functions. *The event and ones thinking about it become so fused as to be inseparable* [emphasis added] and that creates the impression that verbal construal is not present at all" (p. 25).

A key element to ACT is the concept of cognitive defusion or its opposite cognitive fusion. Modern neuroscience has helped us understand that the "triune" brain, despite being capable of self-observation, often fuses emotions, thoughts, or beliefs stemming from limbic structures (especially the amygdala), so that the client identifies with them or cannot unhook from them. In CBT, these cognitions are usually thought of as "dysfunctional" and capable of conscious challenge. In ACT, it is believed that the phenomenon is largely automatic and that struggling against them is counterproductive. During periods of cognitive fusion, the organism feels incapable of unhooking or separating from negative thought processes. This can be a beneficial process that allows humans to be engaged in a novel or movie by attaching emotions to narratives or events. However, the process can be negative when negative thoughts become "stuck." Examples might be:

- "I am feeling hopeless, so I will never be happy."
- Someone is criticized and then feels that "nothing they do will ever be successful."
- Critical parenting may be interpreted in such a way that any negative evaluation will trigger a fusion state of hopelessness, shame, guilt, or self-loathing.

Proposed Neurophysiology. From a neurophysiological perspective, fusion produces an autonomic state characterized by vagal withdrawal, the domination of more primitive structures, the shutting down of inhibitory processes in the pre-frontal cortex, and potentially a more active sympathetic (fight/flight/fright) response. A parallel concept to fusion is rumination or prolonged worry states. Several studies have found that rumination has a characteristic autonomic phenotype (Brosschot et al., 2007). As stated by Ottaviani et al. (2009),

> Rumination has been previously described as characterized by prepotent perseverative cognitive and behavioral programs that have the effect of taking the prefrontal cortex temporarily "off-line." As the prefrontal cortex normally exerts tonic inhibitory control on sympatho-excitatory neural circuits, the consequence of ruminative thoughts is a disinhibition of these circuits, thus parasympathetic withdrawal (i.e., low HRV) and relative sympathetic dominance... (p. 272).

A prolonged period of this ruminative state would have negative consequences physiologically (gastrointestinal dysregulation, increased pain, poor regulation of many systems), and psychologically (poor impulse control, emotional memory, anxiety, depression) (Carnevali et al., 2018).

Interventions. In ACT, defusion skills are developed to allow the client to be able to begin to separate automatic thoughts, emotions, or beliefs from reality. The ACT literature is filled with metaphors and exercises to promote defusion (Harris, 2019; Stoddard & Afari, 2014). Defusion exercises can be categorized into five types: language conventions, metaphors, exercises that change language parameters, exercises that promote distancing from private events, and exercises aiming to undermine verbal rules and narratives (Blackledge, 2018). But as Ruiz et al. (2023) stated "it is worth noting that the therapist should establish an adequate context before

> **Box 14.1 Defusion Techniques Suggested by Harris (2019) and Others**
>
> Leaves on a stream (or on a moving black strip)
> Repetition—e.g., Lemon, lemon, lemon
> I'm having the thought that...
> I notice that I'm having the thought that...
> Recite thoughts in ultra-slow motion, a silly voice, or sing them aloud
> Hear thoughts sung to the tune of *Happy Birthday* or other tunes
> See thoughts on a screen change font, case, color (with or without a bouncing Karaoke ball)
> Two radios metaphor
> Thank your mind
> Naming the story

introducing some defusion exercises because they might seem rather odd to clients and make them feel invalidated" (p. 5). In this context, it is imperative to develop an atmosphere of safety where vagal influences can be active.

Heart Rate Variability Biofeedback Integration. HRVB can be used in this phase of ACT to facilitate defusion skills. For example, we often prompt the client to restate an I/me statement such as "I am such a loser" to "I am having the thought that I am a loser." The premise is that the restatement begins to create some ability to get "unhooked" from that automatic thought. We have found that using the HRVB protocol together with ACT exercises such as those presented in Box 14.1.1 can increase the ability to sustain the defusion.

For example, for a client who goes into a tailspin with any mistake, the combination of the HRVB breathing and shifting the language to "I notice that I am having a thought that I am a total loser" seems to facilitate defusion and this results in a shortened period of vagal withdrawal. The weekly homework typical of the ACT process is then a combination of the cognitive skills engendered by the metaphors and language changes and gains in autonomic flexibility accomplished through home practice of HRVB.

Core Principle 2. Acceptance: Allowing Unwanted Private Experiences (Thoughts, Feelings, and Urges) to Come and Go Without Struggling With Them

Acceptance is a crucial component of ACT, especially in the early stages of the therapy. Unlike CBT, in ACT unwanted thoughts, feelings, and urges are presented as automatic, inevitable, and very difficult to get rid of. In fact, it is the struggle with these mental constructs that is seen as the problem. Harris (2019) wisely avoids the term acceptance but uses phrases like:

- allow it to be there (simply because it already is)
- give it permission to be where it already is
- let go of struggling with it
- stop fighting with it
- make peace with it
- make room for it
- soften up around it
- let it be
- breathe into it
- stop wasting your energy on pushing it away (p. 12).

Proposed Neurophysiology. As was the case for fusion, lack of acceptance and the resulting struggle is seen as one of the core problems for human beings. What was functional in our evolutionary past, is now one of the main causes of human suffering and psychopathology. Using physiological monitoring, it is easy to show the client that the struggle produces vagal withdrawal and sympathetic activation and that the inability to use acceptance produces bad outcomes.

Heart Rate Variability Biofeedback Integration. HRVB is a very useful add-on in the development of acceptance skills. Clients identify an area of difficulty that involves lack of acceptance. They are then instructed to use HRV rescue breathing to try and tolerate the discomfort the emotion brings. I use the word "courage" to characterize the willingness to just let go of the struggle and tolerate the emotion. The tale from Homer's *The Odyssey* where Odysseus has his crew tie him to the mast so that he can experience the torment of the Sirens without crashing the ship onto the rocks is useful. The client is instructed to fully experience the unwanted emotion, to breathe at resonance frequency, and observe the discomfort, its time course, and valence. A good example comes from the treatment of a client with obsessive compulsive disorder (OCD), with prominent compulsions to engage in "checking."

> Joyce was unable to leave the house without at least twenty checks of water, gas, lights, the stove, an iron, etc. We used exposure and restraint as usual but emphasized the acceptance component. Joyce began reducing her checking behavior weekly. When we got to about sixteen checks before leaving, she was instructed to leave the house and call me from her car. I asked her to rate the unwanted urge to go back and check on a 1–100 SUDS scale. She reported a 65. We then did some slow rescue breathing together and I had her observe her urge ("I am having an urge to check again") and rate the struggle with it. She began to get much better at being willing to be with the urge and let the breathing surround it so that it began to drift away. This softened the difficulty of living with the terrible urges and allowed her to reduce "experiential avoidance" and the negative consequences of this avoidance on her quality of life (Harris, 2019).

Core Principle 3. Contact With the Present Moment: Awareness of the Here and Now, Experienced With Openness, Interest, and Receptiveness (e.g., Mindfulness)

Mindfulness has been a key element of many third-wave therapies and popular movements. Brought to western awareness by Jon Kabat-Zinn (2003), mindfulness concepts, long espoused in Eastern cultures, have become a staple of many modern therapy training programs. Kabat-Zinn (1994) described mindfulness as "paying attention in a particular way, on purpose, in the present moment, and nonjudgmentally" (p. 4). Mindful acceptance is a central theme of ACT and sustains effective contact with this time and place.

Proposed Neurophysiology. The popularity of mindfulness practices has led to preliminary studies on how the brain is affected by mindfulness practice. Strawn et al. (2016) concluded that mindfulness practices produce "increased activation of brain structures that subserve interoception and the processing of internal stimuli—functions that are ostensibly improved by this treatment" (p. 372). Several electroencephalogram studies found that "mindfulness is associated with increased alpha and theta power in both healthy individuals and in patient groups. This co-presence of elevated alpha and theta may signify a state of relaxed alertness which is conducive to mental health" (Lomas et al., 2015, p. 401). These summaries overlap with the HRVB literature showing effects on brain functions that may be involved with the skills needed in ACT.

Heart Rate Variability Biofeedback Integration. Higher HRV is also associated with *self-regulation and skills necessary to manage thoughts, emotions, and goals.* HRV theoretically overlaps with neurobiological mechanisms associated with mindfulness training, particularly those located in neural regions involved in self-regulation. Due to this association, HRV has become an increasingly utilized biomarker in mindfulness-based intervention research (Christodoulou et al., 2020).

Prinsloo et al. (2013) found that even a single session of HRVB increased many aspects of mindfulness compared to controls. More research is needed, but it appears that HRVB can help improve mindfulness skills. Mindfulness is an important tool in ACT and many therapies in and of itself. In ACT, it is additionally important in that it potentiates many of the other ACT core principles (acceptance, defusion, etc.). HRVB is a useful tool to improve mindfulness skills.

Core Principle 4. The Observing Self: Accessing a Transcendent Sense of Self, a Continuity of Consciousness Which Is Unchanging

ACT advocates cultivating a transcendent sense of self, a consistent perspective from which to observe and accept all changing experiences. This experience is often called the observing self. This sense of self is a process, not a thing: it involves an awareness of awareness itself—"pure awareness." This principle is similar to mindfulness, but with a slightly different emphasis. Harris (2008, p. 158) has provided the following guidance:

> Observe as if you are a friendly scientist encountering a new phenomenon. As a friendly scientist, you are not trying to interfere with or destroy it. You are simply studying it; observing it with curiosity; trying to find out as much about it as you can. (This is a particularly useful metaphor for observing unpleasant sensations).

Proposed Neurophysiology. A great deal of recent brain research has identified networks connecting the limbic structures to pre-frontal structures thought to allow self-reflection. As cited earlier, HRVB appears to strengthen the ability of the pre-frontal cortex to engage in self-reflection. In recent studies, Mather and Thayer (2018) and Nashiro et al. (2021) have shown that HRV can be a sensitive index of the central autonomic network's ability to regulate affective networks. Mather and Thayer (2018) concluded, "the findings we outlined in this paper suggest that HR oscillations can enhance emotion by entraining brain rhythms in ways that enhance regulatory brain networks" (p. 6).

Heart Rate Variability Biofeedback Integration. Here we presume that regular practice of HRVB promotes the capacity for the individual to be self-observant and to achieve some level of transcendence. This should aid in all of the other core skills in ACT (Nashiro et al., 2021; Schumann et al., 2021).

Core Principle 5. Values: Discovering What Is Most Important to Oneself

Values are our heart's deepest desires for the way we want to interact with and relate to the world, other people, and ourselves (Harris, 2008). Values play an important role in ACT. All of the other skills are made salient based on values. Learning defusion and acceptance skills are crucial so that the client can move toward the values they identify. Values usually fall within categories such as family relations, marriage/couples/intimate relations, parenting, friendships/social life, career/employment, education/personal growth and development, recreation/fun/leisure, spirituality, citizenship/environment/community life, and health/physical well-being.

Proposed Neurophysiology. Little work has been done on the neurophysiology of values. As brain scanning techniques progress, we should be able to understand how values are processed.

Heart Rate Variability Biofeedback Integration. HRVB plays a very minor role in this area. However, having the client learn to shift his or her physiology or sense of neuroception, can facilitate the values clarification process. I usually introduce the values exercises after a ten-minute HRVB session where the peaks and valleys in the HR line graph display produce warmer dryer hands.

Core Principle 6. Committed Action

Ultimately, the goal of ACT therapy is to enable the client to move forward in life towards his or her true values. To do this, all of the skills listed above are useful. However, the final test of effectiveness will be whether the client actually engages in committed actions that are not self-defeating, avoidant, or accompanied by chronic struggle.

Proposed Neurophysiology. Valued action depends on one's ability to deal with urges, cravings, hedonic activities, etc. Earlier we cited research showing the impact of HRVB on central nervous system structures (Mather & Thayer, 2018; Nashiro et al., 2021). Two recent fMRI studies have found that HRVB affects inhibitory pathways involved in affect regulation. Schumann et al. (2021) assigned thirty-two participants to an HRVB training or a game playing control condition. Results indicated "that increased heart rate variability induced by HRV-biofeedback is accompanied by changes in functional brain connectivity during resting state" (p. 1). Similarly, Nashiro et al. (2021) randomized 104 participants to an HRVB condition or to a clever sham condition. The HRVB group showed dramatic increases in the right amygdala to pre-frontal cortex network, often thought of as involved in regulating inhibitory affect. Consider also the research showing the effect of HRVB on reducing cravings (Eddie et al., 2014, 2018; Kim, 2014). This research suggests that HRVB is useful in overcoming cravings and urges and acting more in accordance with values and aspirations.

Heart Rate Variability Biofeedback Integration. In the execution of defusion and acceptance to move in valued directions, overcoming urges and cravings can be a critical skill. Once the HRVB skills are well established, the weekly homework often centers on obstacles to committed action. This very often involves dealing with all sorts of dysphoria, with cravings, with "gut" desires, and with fixation on feeling better. The ACT intervention stresses trying to evaluate immediate and distal consequences and building up a repertoire of techniques, self-talk, or other devices to stay on the valued path. As with the OCD client introduced above, HRVB rescue breathing is quite useful. Clients often report success using the slow diaphragmatic breathing in the face of an addictive substance, a desired food, or an impulsive thought, or desires to escape feeling bad. In addition, studies that have shown that

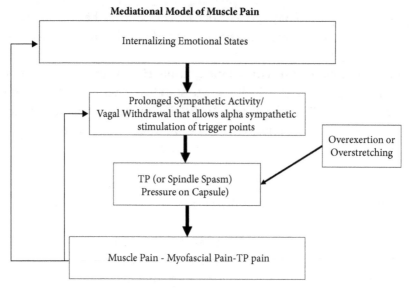

Figure 14.1 Mediational model for chronic muscle pain.

inhibitory networks are strengthened by daily practice of HRVB add another tool to helping maintain committed action (Nashiro et al., 2021; Schumann et al., 2021).

Case Example

To illustrate the integration of HRVB and ACT, I present a case that is pretty typical of the referrals that I receive. Most clients are referred to me for stress-related physical symptoms, in this case chronic shoulder and arm pain. Judith, a forty-one-year-old married mother of two, was referred by a chiropractor for shoulder and arm pain that did not fully resolve with chiropractic interventions (including myofascial release). After each session, Judith experienced temporary relief, but upon return to work, the pain and stiffness returned. She presented as a people pleaser with no notable psychopathology. She reported that her marriage was good, her kids were "great," and she was therefore puzzled by the referral. We started with my usual psychoeducational material for myofascial pain, a YouTube video, a pain drawing, and slides that explain the model we use for these disorders (Gevirtz, 2006). We then started the HRVB protocol. In this version of the protocol, along with daily practice and short rescue breathing exercises, she was instructed to use her resonance frequency breathing (in her case 6.5/minute) before, during, and after the myofascial release work the chiropractor was using. Over the course of the next three weeks, Judith mastered the HRVB, practiced daily, and experienced much longer pain relief periods after release.

However, she reported pain that usually built after a day of work but was better on the weekends. We had already been working with the mediational model for chronic muscle pain (see Figure 14.1), so this allowed an opening to explore the possible stressors without any implications of "mental illness." With this in mind, we began to explore her work environment. Judith was a medical receptionist. She worked for a large medical clinic and was responsible for all of the intake paperwork. She worked with four other women in a noisy setting with cubicles. She and all of her co-workers agreed that they were understaffed since patients often had a forty-five-minute to one-hour wait. Judith was clearly an ethical, conscientious person and so "felt bad and guilty" for the long waits. After some discussion, it turned out that three of the other co-workers were taking "long" smoking breaks, exacerbating the wait times. This, she admitted, made her angry and stressed because she could not change the situation without "ratting out" her coworkers (the supervisor was ineffective). So, based on the mediational model I was able to begin to introduce ACT concepts and exercises. She was able to recognize the concept of fusion fairly quickly. Her husband and friends, in an effort to help, always urged her to just stop fretting about the patients' wait time. Afterall, none of this was her fault. I was able to convince her that her brain was automatically going to be upset with the situation, and that efforts to stop that or struggle with it were fruitless. We worked over a few sessions on her seeing that the struggle with her fused feelings could *actually* be the problem, not the feelings themselves. We watched the YouTube video *The Unwanted Party Guest*, and I gave her a Chinese finger puzzle to remind her that the harder you try to escape, the more stuck you get. In the meantime, we had been working with mindfulness and self-observer skills so that she was getting pretty proficient with exercises like "Leaves on a Stream."

To be able to move forward in a valued direction, we agreed that she could learn to shorten the "attacks" created by the situation and this would affect her pain and allow her to be the mother, wife, friend, and employee that she wanted to be. For the next two sessions, we monitored the number of "attacks," how long they lasted, and how well she was able to move on. While hooked up to biofeedback equipment, I would present the image of the co-workers standing outside, smoking, cynically ignoring the patients. We watched the HR rise and flatten, skin conductance rise, and peripheral temperature dip. Then using her HRVB and ACT skills, we watched her return to a large, smooth HR sine wave, with temperature rising, and skin conductance dropping. At this point, her pain decreased from an 8 to a 2 out of 10 at the end of the workday. In a three-month follow-up, she reported only occasional pain or stiffness that she could handle with a release from her husband and "breathing."

Conclusion

Adding ACT to HRVB or HRVB to ACT can produce synergistic effects that potentiate both. In our clinic we have found that the transition from HRVB (which we almost always begin with) is much smoother than starting out with talk therapies. This has sometimes been called the "trojan horse" strategy in that it gets clients feeling safe and destigmatizes their symptoms. Then suggesting ACT principles is seen as a logical next step. In our experience, ACT is an easier sell than CBT. Expecting clients to challenge and change dysfunctional cognitions is always challenging, whereas the principles outlined above in ACT take some of the pressure off of the client. For problems that involve exposure (post-traumatic stress disorder, phobias, OCD), the HRVB offers a safety net that we find greatly reduces dropout rates. Overall, combining HRVB and ACT offers a myriad of advantages for the clinician and client.

References

Bachman, S. L., Cole, S., Yoo, H. J., Nashiro, K., Min, J., Mercer, N., Nassieri, P., Thayer, J., Lehrer, P., & Mather, M. (2022). Daily heart rate variability biofeedback training decreases locus coeruleus MRI contrast in younger adults. *International Journal of Psychophysiology: Official Journal of the International Organization of Psychophysiology*, *193*, 112241. https://doi.org/10.1016/j.ijpsycho.2023.08.014

Blackledge, J. (2018). Cognitive defusion. In S. C. Hayes & S. G. Hofmann (Eds.), *Process-based CBT: The science and core clinical competencies of cognitive behavioral therapy* (pp. 351–362). New Harbinger Publications, Inc.

Brosschot, J. F., Van Dijk, E., & Thayer, J. F. (2007). Daily worry is related to low heart rate variability during waking and the subsequent nocturnal sleep period. *International Journal of Psychophysiology*, *63*(1), 39–47. https://doi.org/10.1016/j.ijpsycho.2006.07.016

Carnevali, L., Thayer, J. F., Brosschot, J. F., & Ottaviani, C. (2018). Heart rate variability mediates the link between rumination and depressive symptoms: A longitudinal study. *International Journal of Psychophysiology*, *131*, 131–138. https://doi.org/10.1016/j.ijpsycho.2017.11.002

Christodoulou, G., Salami, N., & Black, D. S. (2020). The utility of heart rate variability in mindfulness research. *Mindfulness*, *11*, 554–570. https://doi.org/10.1007/s12671-019-01296-3

Eddie, D., Conway, F. N., Alayan, N., Buckman, J., & Bates, M. E. (2018). Assessing heart rate variability biofeedback as an adjunct to college recovery housing programs. *Journal of Substance Abuse Treatment*, *92*, 70–76. https://doi.org/10.1016/j.jsat.2018.06.014

Eddie, D., Kim, C., Lehrer, P., Deneke, E., & Bates, M. E. (2014). A pilot study of brief heart rate variability biofeedback to reduce craving in young adult men receiving inpatient treatment for substance use disorders. *Applied Psychophysiology and Biofeedback*, *39*, 181–192. https://doi.org/10.1007/s10484-014-9251-z

Gevirtz, R. N. (2006). The muscle spindle trigger point model of chronic pain. *Biofeedback*, *34*(2), 53–56.

Gevirtz, R. N. (2013). The promise of heart rate variability biofeedback: Evidence-based applications. *Biofeedback*, *41*(3), 110–120. https://doi.org/10.5298/1081-5937-41.3.01

Gevirtz, R. N. (2017). The central autonomic network in trauma etiology and treatment. In S. N. Gold (Ed.), *APA handbook of trauma psychology: Trauma practice* (pp. 213–226). American Psychological Association. https://doi.org/10.1037/0000020-000

Gevirtz, R. N. (2022). From GSR to heart rate variability: A long and winding (actually, wiggly) road. *Applied Psychophysiology and Biofeedback*, *47*(4), 299–303. https://doi.org/10.1007/s10484-022-09540-8

Gevirtz, R. N., Lehrer, P., & Schwartz, M. S. (2016a). Cardio-respiratory biofeedback. In M. S. Schwartz & F. Andrasik (Eds.), *Biofeedback: A practitioner's guide* (4th ed., pp. 196–213). Guilford Press.

Gevirtz, R. N., Lehrer, P., & Schwartz, M. S. (2016b). Cardio/respiratory measurement and assessment in applied psychophysiology. In M. S. Schwarts & F. Andrasik (Eds.), *Biofeedback: A practitioner's guide* (4th ed., pp. 85–97). Guilford Press.

Goessl, V. C., Curtiss, J. E., & Hofmann, S. G. (2017). The effect of heart rate variability biofeedback training on stress and anxiety: A meta-analysis. *Psychological Medicine*, *47*(15), 2578–2586. https://doi.org/10.1017/S0033291717001003

Harris, R. (2006). Embracing your demons: An overview of acceptance and commitment therapy. *Psychotherapy in Australia, 12*(4), 2–8.

Harris, R. (2008). *The happiness trap: How to stop struggling, start living: A guide to ACT*. Trumpeter.

Harris, R. (2019). *ACT made simple: An easy-to-read primer on acceptance and commitment therapy* (2nd ed.). New Harbinger Publications.

Hayes, S. C., & Strosahl, K. D. (2005). *A practical guide to acceptance and commitment therapy*. Springer. https://doi.org/10.1007/978-0-387-23369-7

Hayes, S. C., Strosahl, K. D., & Wilson, K. G. (2012). *Acceptance and commitment therapy: The process and practice of mindful change* (2nd ed.). Guilford Press.

Kabat-Zinn, J. (1994). *Wherever you go, there you are: Mindfulness meditation in everyday life*. Hyperion.

Kabat-Zinn, J. (2003). Mindfulness-based stress reduction (MBSR). *Constructivism in the Human Sciences, 8*(2), 73–107.

Kim, H. (2014). Heart rate variability (HRV) biofeedback training with young adult male patients in treatment for addiction [Doctoral dissertation, Rutgers The State University of New Jersey]. ProQuest Dissertations and Theses Global. https://doi.org/10.7282/T3MC8XGZ

Lehrer, P. M., & Gevirtz, R. (2014). Heart rate variability biofeedback: How and why does it work? *Frontiers in Psychology, 5*, Article 756. https://doi.org/10.3389/fpsyg.2014.00756

Lehrer, P. M., Kaur, K., Sharma, A., Shah, K., Huseby, R., Bhavsar, J., Sgobba, P., & Zhang, Y. (2020). Heart rate variability biofeedback improves emotional and physical health and performance: A systematic review and meta-analysis. *Applied Psychophysiology and Biofeedback, 45*, 109–129. https://doi.org/10.1007/s10484-020-09466-z

Lehrer, P. M., Vaschillo, E., & Vaschillo, B. (2000). Resonant frequency biofeedback training to increase cardiac variability: Rationale and manual for training. *Applied Psychophysiology and Biofeedback, 25*(3), 177–191. https://doi.org/10.1023/A:1009554825745

Lomas, T., Ivtzan, I., & Fu, C. H. Y. (2015). A systematic review of the neurophysiology of mindfulness on EEG oscillations. *Neuroscience and Biobehavioral Reviews, 57*, 401–410. https://doi.org/10.1016/j.neubiorev.2015.09.018

Mather, M., & Thayer, J. F. (2018). How heart rate variability affects emotion regulation brain networks. *Current Opinion in Behavioral Sciences, 19*, 98–104. https://doi.org/10.1016/j.cobeha.2017.12.017

Nashiro, K., Min, J., Yoo, H. J., Cho, C., Bachman, S. L., Dutt, S., Thayer, J., Lehrer, P., Feng, T., Mercer, N., Nassieri, P., Wang, D., Chang, C., Marmarelis, V. Z., Narayanan, S., Nation, D. A., & Mather, M. (2021). Enhancing the brain's emotion regulation capacity with a randomised trial of a 5-week heart rate variability biofeedback intervention. *medRxiv*. https://doi.org/10.1101/2021.09.28.21264206

Ottaviani, C., Shapiro, D., Davydov, D. M., Goldstein, I. B., & Mills, P. J. (2009). The autonomic phenotype of rumination. *International Journal of Psychophysiology, 72*(3), 267–275. https://doi.org/10.1016/j.ijpsycho.2008.12.014

Porges, S. W. (2001). The polyvagal theory: Phylogenetic substrates of a social nervous system. *International Journal of Psychophysiology, 42*(2), 123–146. https://doi.org/10.1016/s0167-8760(01)00162-3

Porges, S. W. (2007). The polyvagal perspective. *Biological Psychology, 74*(2), 116–143. https://doi.org/10.1016/j.biopsycho.2006.06.009

Porges, S. W. (2011). *The polyvagal theory: Neurophysiological foundations of emotions, attachment, communication, and self-regulation*. W. W. Norton & Company.

Prinsloo, G. E., Derman, W. E., Lambert, M. I., & Rauch, H. G. (2013). The effect of a single episode of short duration heart rate variability biofeedback on measures of anxiety and relaxation states. *International Journal of Stress Management, 20*(4), 391–411. https://doi.org/10.1037/a0034777

Ruiz, F. J., Gil-Luciano, B., & Segura-Vargas, M. A. (2023). Cognitive defusion. In M. P. Twohig, M. E. Levin, & J. M. Petersen (Eds.), *Oxford handbook of acceptance and commitment therapy* (pp. 206–229). Oxford University Press.

Samaan, M., Diefenbacher, A., Schade, C., Dambacher, C., Pontow, I. M., Pakenham, K., & Fydrich, T. (2021). A clinical effectiveness trial comparing ACT and CBT for inpatients with depressive and mixed mental disorders. *Psychotherapy Research, 31*(3), 355–368. https://doi.org/10.1080/10503307.2020.1802080

Schumann, A., de la Cruz, F., Köhler, S., Brotte, L., & Bär, K. J. (2021). The influence of heart rate variability biofeedback on cardiac regulation and functional brain connectivity. *Frontiers in Neuroscience, 15*, Article 691988. https://doi.org/10.3389/fnins.2021.691988

Stoddard, J. A., & Afari, N. (2014). *The big book of ACT metaphors: A practitioner's guide to experiential exercises and metaphors in acceptance and commitment therapy*. New Harbinger Publications.

Strawn, J. R., Cotton, S., Luberto, C. M., Patino, L. R., Stahl, L. A., Weber, W. A., Eliassen, J. C., Sears, R., & DelBello, M. P. (2016). Neural function before and after mindfulness-based cognitive therapy in anxious adolescents at risk for developing bipolar disorder. *Journal of Child and Adolescent Psychopharmacology, 26*(4), 372–379. https://doi.org/10.1089/cap.2015.0054

Thayer, J. F., & Lane, R. D. (2009). Claude Bernard and the heart–brain connection: Further elaboration of a model of neurovisceral integration. *Neuroscience & Biobehavioral Reviews, 33*(2), 81–88. https://doi.org/10.1016/j.neubiorev.2008.08.004

York, III, G. K., & Steinberg, D. A. (2011). Hughlings Jackson's neurological ideas. *Brain, 134*(Pt 10), 3106–3113. https://doi.org/10.1093/brain/awr219

15
Breathing, Heart Rate Variability, and Their Application in Psychotherapy

Inna Khazan

Breathing practice has become ubiquitous in the areas of emotion regulation, coping with difficult emotional states such as anxiety, anger, and depression, reducing pain, as well as basic stress management. One of the most frequent suggestions we all hear when feeling distressed is to take a deep breath. Not surprisingly, most therapists teach some kind of breathing practice to their clients, most of which are intended to ameliorate distress and suffering. Breath-related practices such as yoga are aimed at improving emotional regulation and reducing stress. Breath-focused meditation practice is frequently recommended as a way of improving physical and emotional health. Research supports this common knowledge, with several studies demonstrating that breathing interventions are effective in stress management (Hopper et al., 2019), reducing symptoms of anxiety, depression, and pain (Jerath et al., 2015; Kuvačić et al., 2018; Gerbarg et al., 2015), calming anger (Fennell et al., 2016), as well as an overall improvement in well-being (Zaccaro et al., 2018).

At the same time, breath-related discomfort also plays a significant role in numerous psychophysiological conditions, such as generalized anxiety, panic disorder, specific phobias, chronic pain, posttraumatic stress disorder, and many others. Research shows that clients that come into therapy with dysregulated breathing are much more likely to drop out of treatment early (Tolin et al., 2017) and are less likely to benefit from psychotherapy (Davies & Craske, 2014). Such research points to the importance of addressing underlying respiratory dysregulation prior to therapy for most optimal outcomes.

Moreover, the breath can be used as a way to stimulate a powerful self-regulatory mechanism innate to every human—our heart rate variability (HRV). HRV refers to the moment-to-moment changes in the time intervals between heartbeats. As we'll discuss later in this chapter, HRV is an important indicator of our ability to adapt to change, respond to stress in healthy ways, and be resilient in the face of challenges (Perna et al., 2020). HRV measurement is a valid and widely used index of other treatment effectiveness and outcomes (Ferreira-Garcia et al., 2021), while HRV biofeedback training has been shown be an efficacious intervention for numerous psychophysiological disorders (Lehrer et al., 2020).

At this point, the science is clear—the breath is a vital part of improving our clients' health and well-being. However, it is crucial that the breathing practice we teach our clients promotes healthy respiratory physiology, rather than exacerbating or triggering breathing dysregulation. Because respiratory physiology and its effects on other physiological functioning change from moment to moment with each breath, the breath practice our clients engage in can be extremely beneficial or can cause further harm. It is therefore important for therapists to fully understand the basic principles of respiratory physiology, learn ways to identify unhealthy breathing patterns, and teach healthy breathing as part of therapy.

The aim of this chapter is two-fold: First, to review the physiological foundations of respiration and the physiological effects of breathing practices, with the goal of providing an understanding necessary for teaching healthy breathing. Second, to discuss a way of using breath to produce long-term improvements in our ability to self-regulate, adapt to change, and be resilient in the face of challenges.

Teaching Healthy Breathing in Psychotherapy

Respiratory Physiology

We as therapists need to have a basic understanding of respiratory physiology to teach healthy breathing to our clients, as well as to guide them in a helpful response to emotional or physiological distress. Let's start with dispelling two common misconceptions about breathing that often lead to breath-related discomfort and may exacerbate rather than alleviate emotional or physical distress.

First, most of our clients believe that for them to feel calmer, be more relaxed, have less pain, and be better at managing stress, they need more oxygen. Out of that belief comes the common suggestion of "just take a deep breath" in response to many challenges. Because our clients believe that we need to get more oxygen to feel better, and that deep breath typically involves a very large inhalation for the purpose of getting more oxygen into their lungs. The second common misconception is the belief that carbon dioxide is toxic and needs to be expelled at all costs, with the idea of cleansing our bodies of the toxin. As a result, clients will often exhale quickly and forcefully after taking that deep breath. Both of these beliefs are erroneous and lead to an exacerbation of the problem rather than its solution.

To better understand the fallacy of these two beliefs, let's discuss the physiology of oxygen delivery in the human body. When we breathe in, oxygen-rich air enters the lungs, where it diffuses into our blood stream, and binds to hemoglobin. Hemoglobin is an iron-rich protein in the red blood cells that carries oxygen and other gases throughout the body, releasing them as needed. Hemoglobin relies on information supplied by our pH level to determine the amount of oxygen needed to maintain proper physiological function.

pH stands for the "Power of Hydrogen" and refers to the acid-base balance in our bodies. In other words, pH describes the level of acidity and alkalinity in our bloodstream and other fluids in the body. A pH of 7.0 (such as in distilled water) is considered to be neutral. pH lower than 7 is acidic, and pH higher than 7 is alkaline. We need to maintain a pH of 7.35–7.45 (slightly alkaline) for our bodies to function properly.

The pH level in our bodies is determined by only two elements—carbon dioxide and bicarbonates. Bicarbonates, which are alkaline, are regulated by the kidneys, which typically take at least eight hours (and possibly longer) to do anything about a dysregulated pH level. Carbon dioxide, on the other hand, is regulated by moment-to-moment breathing and takes only moments to change pH levels. Carbon dioxide is acidic, dissolved in the blood as carbonic acid.

Our bodies produce carbon dioxide as a result of metabolism. As the cells in our organs and tissues receive oxygen from the blood stream and use it for energy, they produce water and carbon dioxide, which they return back to the blood steam for reallocation. As we become more active, our metabolism increases and the body produces more carbon dioxide, releasing it into the blood steam. Because carbon dioxide is acidic, the pH level decreases, signaling hemoglobin that the body needs more oxygen. In response, hemoglobin releases more oxygen to the organs and tissues with higher metabolic needs. When, on the other hand, our activity and, therefore, metabolism, slow down, the body produces less carbon dioxide, and pH level rises (becomes more alkaline). As a result, hemoglobin releases less oxygen because the body needs less oxygen as it becomes less active. This process was first described by the Danish physiologist Christian Bohr and is therefore known as the Bohr effect (West, 2019).

In addition to oxygen, hemoglobin also carries nitric oxide, a gas, which in the human body acts as a neurotransmitter that regulates dilation and constriction of the blood vessels. Nitric oxide (NO) is not to be confused with NO_2, a very different gas known as laughing gas that is used for sedation. Nitric oxide is released at the same time as oxygen when activity levels rise and pH decreases (becomes more acidic). Release of NO produces dilation of the blood vessels, allowing delivery of greater amounts of oxygen and glucose to organs and tissues with greater metabolic needs. In the same way, as activity and metabolism decrease, hemoglobin releases less nitric oxide, resulting in constriction of the blood vessels.

This is the normal relationship between activity and delivery of oxygen. See Figure 15.1 for a summary.

This relationship can easily get disrupted with unhelpful breathing patterns, such as efforts to get more oxygen when none is actually needed. Demand for oxygen changes solely with a change in activity level. We need more oxygen when we become more active (i.e., going for a run) and we need less oxygen when we become less active (i.e., going to sleep). Breathing in extra oxygen without a change in activity will not prompt the body to make use of that oxygen. Once an oxygen molecule binds to the hemoglobin, it takes up one of the available spaces. Once all the spaces

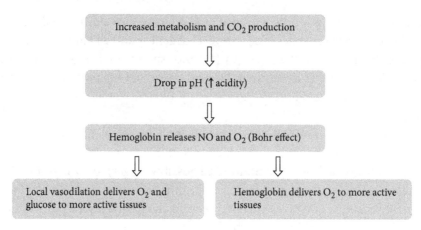

Figure 15.1 Normal respiratory physiology.

are taken, more cannot be created. New oxygen molecules can bind to hemoglobin only once the previous molecule has been released from its place. In other words, hemoglobin cannot be more than 100 percent saturated. Any extra oxygen that we breathe in gets expelled during exhalation. At a resting state, with healthy lungs and healthy heart, at or close to sea level, the air we breathe in contains about 21 percent oxygen, and the air we breathe out contains about 16 percent oxygen. We retain only about a quarter of the oxygen we take in. We do not need any more oxygen at rest, nor are we able to use it (Dunn et al., 2016)!

We do not require more oxygen when feeling stressed or anxious. However, many people believe that they need that deep breath in order to get more oxygen to manage stress and reduce anxiety. So, in an attempt to get more oxygen, people take a very big breath in. They then exhale the same large volume of air quickly, either because they don't really care about the exhalation, or, perhaps, in an attempt to rid their bodies of the erroneously maligned carbon dioxide. As a result, they exhale too much carbon dioxide, the level of carbon dioxide in the blood decreases, and pH becomes overly alkaline (pH increases). This change mimics the kind of decrease in acidity as might happen when someone goes to sleep and their metabolism decreases. However, remember that metabolism does not actually change in this situation. Hemoglobin receives an incorrect signal that metabolism has decreased and interprets that as a corresponding decrease in oxygen demand. Hemoglobin now releases less oxygen and less nitric oxide, decreasing the availability of oxygen and glucose to organs and tissues. Since the metabolism did not actually decrease, and the demand for oxygen did not actually change, the person is now not receiving sufficient oxygen. So, ironically, in an effort to get more oxygen to feel better, the person ends up being oxygen deprived.

Another frequent reason for a similar mismatch between the body's metabolic needs and the rate and depth of the breath is the onset of the stress response, also known as the fight or flight response. The fight or flight response evolved to prepare

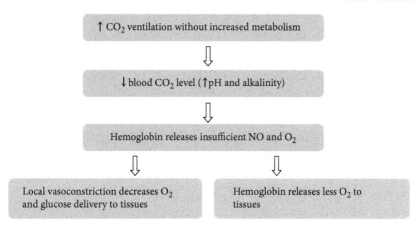

Figure 15.2 Overbreathing physiology.

our ancestors to get out of physical danger as quickly as possible. When the fight or flight response is triggered, the body prepares for quick and intense physical action, with a corresponding increase in metabolism and demand for oxygen. A faster, deeper breathing rate is one of the first changes that happen as the body prepares for action. However, today, the stress response is not triggered by tigers coming to eat us, but often by anxious thoughts, worries about upcoming events, or regrets of the past. While the body prepares for an increased activity level, none actually takes place. We might be sitting at the desk worrying about an upcoming meeting with the boss or an unpleasant conversation we have to have with a partner, none of which produce an actual increase in metabolism. However, the brain does not communicate this information to the body, and the body continues taking larger, faster breaths in, without a need for more oxygen, breathing out too much carbon dioxide and depriving the body and the brain of oxygen as a result. See Figure 15.2 for a summary.

This behavioral mismatch of the rate and depth of the breath resulting in breathing out too much carbon dioxide is called overbreathing. The physiological state created by overbreathing is called hypocapnia, or lack of carbon dioxide. Hypocapnia leads to a myriad of unpleasant symptoms listed below:

- lightheadedness or dizziness
- rapid heartbeat
- shortness of breath
- chest pain or tightness
- tingling or numbness in hands, fingers, or feet
- gastrointestinal distress
- nausea
- feeling of unreality
- fuzzy mind
- difficulty concentrating, thinking straight, and remembering things
- sweating or shivering

- muscle tension
- blurry vision
- dry mouth

If you look at this list carefully, you might notice a striking similarity to symptoms of a panic attack. In fact, symptoms of a panic attack and overbreathing are identical, because every panic attack necessarily involves overbreathing and the physiological cascade described previously. A smaller subset of symptoms is likely to accompany less intense anxious states.

In addition to disruptions in the delivery of oxygen, overbreathing also disrupts your electrolyte balance, creating another set of unpleasant experiences. Electrolytes are substances which contain compound molecules, such as salts, that can be dissociated into free ions which carry an electric charge. For example, table salt (NaCl) can be dissolved into sodium (Na^+) and chloride (Cl^-) ions. Electrolytes are used by cells in your body (muscles, heart, nerves) to communicate with other cells, and are therefore extremely important for proper physiological functioning. When our pH balance gets disrupted by overbreathing, electrolyte balance gets disrupted as well. For example, in your muscles, calcium (Ca^{+2}) ions migrate into the muscle cells instead of staying in the fluid surrounding the cell. In the skeletal muscles (such as in your arms and legs) this results in muscle spasms, weakness, and fatigue. In the smooth muscle of the blood vessels, this may result in vasoconstriction and precipitate a rise in blood pressure or trigger a Raynaud's attack. In the smooth muscle of the respiratory tract, this may result in bronchoconstriction, and trigger an asthma attack. Finally, in the smooth muscle of the gastrointestinal tract, this may result in symptoms such as nausea and motility changes (Laffey & Kavanagh, 2002).

Overbreathing and the resulting physiological changes can not only produce discomfort, but also trigger or exacerbate various psychophysiological disorders, such as anxiety episodes, panic attacks, asthma attacks, gastrointestinal distress, and flare up of pain or headache.

Breathing can be both the culprit of these unpleasant events and, when taught properly, can be a way to alleviate the symptoms. In the next section, we discuss how to teach healthy breathing to our clients, minimizing the chances of overbreathing.

Teaching Healthy Breathing

Teaching healthy breathing skills depends as much on the specific skill as on the client's understanding of the reasoning behind teaching that skill. It is important to explain to clients the reasons for why traditional deep breathing is not a skill of choice and how the breathing that you might teach them is different. The simplest explanation might go something like this:

At or close to sea level, with healthy lungs and healthy heart, you have plenty of oxygen. You do not need any more unless your activity level increases. You do, however, need to conserve your carbon dioxide for the oxygen to get to where it needs to go. The breathing skills I am going to teach you will help you conserve carbon dioxide and help your body to use the oxygen most efficiently.

Of course, you can add more physiological details if the client is interested.

The next step is to teach a specific breathing skill that promotes healthy respiratory physiology, minimizing the chances of overbreathing—mindful low and slow breathing. Following are the mindful low and slow breathing practice steps:

1. This practice is easiest to start while lying down or reclining. This position allows the diaphragm, the muscle that controls breathing, to move most easily.
2. Begin with shifting your breath from your chest to the abdomen. Allow your abdominal muscles to expand as you breathe in and contract when you breathe out. It may help to imagine a balloon in the belly. With each breath in, gently inflate the balloon. With each breath out, gently let the air out of the balloon. While a new practice will always require a conscious decision to make a change, and therefore some cognitive effort may be required, there should not be a physical effort with the breath. In other words, don't pull the air in, don't push the air out. Just allow the air to come in and go out of the lungs.
3. Take a normal size breath in, through the nose, as if smelling a flower. There is no need for a deep or large breath. Just a comfortable, normal sized inhalation.
4. Exhale slowly and fully, until the lungs feel comfortably empty. Allow the exhalation to be slightly longer than the inhalation (about 40 percent of your breath for the inhalation, and about 60 percent of your breath for the exhalation). Breathe out through the nose or through pursed lips, as if blowing out a candle. Pursed lips exhalation is particularly helpful if it is difficult to slow down exhalation through the nose. Make sure to *never* breathe out through a widely open mouth—that is an excellent way to overbreathe.
5. Practice low and slow breathing for about five minutes, just noticing the sensations of your breath coming in through your nose and out through your nose or pursed lips.
6. Remember that breathing practice may not always feel relaxing. If you find yourself worried about not feeling relaxed, or struggling to relax during breathing practice, let go of the intention to relax and bring your focus to the process of breathing itself.

Many clients have trouble extending their exhalations initially. If that happens, ask your client to breathe out through pursed lips, as if blowing out a candle. If it is still difficult to extend the exhalation, ask the client to slow down the start of exhalation, since that is when most people blow out the most air, and then don't have enough air left to extend the exhalation.

Once the client is comfortably breathing low and slow in your office, encourage them to continue this practice on their own, starting with five minutes a day and increasing from there. Low and slow breathing practice can also be folded into HRV training, discussed in the next section.

Breathing, Heart Rate Variability, and Psychotherapy

In addition to promoting healthy respiratory physiology, integrating breathing skills in psychotherapy will help train the nervous system's ability to regulate itself through stimulating HRV. HRV is a strong indicator of the flexibility and resilience of our nervous system. Tracking HRV can help in assessing progress in therapy as well as estimating the client's overall health and well-being (Jarczok et al., 2019; Perna et al., 2020; McCraty & Shaffer, 2015; Taralov et al., 2015). This chapter will discuss how to train HRV through biofeedback using breathing skills. This will help improve self-regulation and alleviate symptoms of psychophysiological disorders, such as anxiety, depression, trauma, and chronic pain. Let's dig more into HRV next.

HRV is the change in time interval that passes from one heartbeat to the next. If you were to take your pulse on your wrist or on your neck, you would feel a steady beat. If you were to count the number of beats for a minute, you would probably count somewhere between sixty and eighty of them. That is your heart rate. But the time that passes from one beat to the next is changing all the time. Sometimes, the heartbeats come closer together, the interval from one beat to the next is shorter, meaning that the heart rate is speeding up. Then, the heartbeats come further apart, the interval from one beat to the next gets longer, and the heart rate is slowing down. These accelerations and decelerations of the heartbeat are HRV. The greater your HRV, the healthier and more resilient you are (Mulcahy et al., 2019).

Let me be clear, I am not talking about the increase in your heart rate when you are going for a run or a decrease in the heart rate when you go to sleep. I am talking about beat-to-beat changes in the instantaneous heart rate that happen all the time. In fact, your average heart rate may remain the same, but your HRV may be higher or lower. For example, your average heart rate may be sixty beats per minute, but your instantaneous heart rate may vary from fifty-eight to sixty-two for each breath cycle, for a HR change of four beats per minute, or your instantaneous heart rate may vary from fifty to seventy for each breath cycle for a HR change of twenty beats per minute.

Research over the last six decades has consistently shown the importance of HRV for our cardiovascular health (Fang et al., 2020), overall physical health (Fournié et al., 2021), mental health (Lehrer et al., 2020), ability to manage stress (H. G. Kim et al., 2018), and perform at our best (Granero-Gallegos et al., 2020; Lehrer et al., 2020; Holzman & Bridgett, 2017). The data from the Framingham Heart Study (Tsuji et al., 1996) showed that HRV is a better predictor of cardiovascular health than blood pressure, resting heart rate, and cholesterol levels. Research shows that people suffering from psychophysiological disorders such as anxiety (Cheng et al., 2022), depression (Koch et al., 2019), posttraumatic stress disorder (Ge at al., 2020; Schneider & Schwerdtfeger, 2020), chronic pain (Tracy et al., 2016), gastrointestinal disorders (K. N. Kim et al., 2020; Sadowski et al., 2021), high blood pressure (Sharma et al., 2021), headaches (Koenig et al., 2016), diabetes (Benichou et al., 2018), and other conditions, not only show low HRV at baseline, but also that HRV training with biofeedback helps improve symptoms of these disorders (e.g., Goessl et al., 2017; Fernández-Álvarez et al., 2022; Fournié et al., 2021; Lehrer et al., 2020; Pagaduan et al., 2021; Pizzoli et al., 2021; Tinello et al., 2021).

Given that the great majority of clients seeking psychotherapy present with one or more of these conditions (Druss et al., 2007), adding HRV to the psychotherapy process may help increase the success of therapy and provide an objective data-driven way of assessing progress and effectiveness of interventions.

Studies such as those by Caldwell and Steffen (2018) and Economides et al. (2020) demonstrate the increased effectiveness of psychotherapy with the addition of HRV biofeedback. Moreover, HRV has long been recognized as a valid measurement of the autonomic nervous system (ANS) functioning (Blase et al., 2021) and is used to assess the effectiveness of other interventions. For example, a review study by Christodoulou et al. (2020) determined HRV to be an objective biomarker to quantify the effects of mindfulness-based interventions (MBIs). This study examined the effectiveness of a MBI and fluoxetine in treating generalized anxiety disorder. Results revealed that pre-treatment HRV measurement could be used to identify a subgroup of patients for whom MBI was less effective than fluoxetine.

HRV also plays a significant role in administering compassion- and self-compassion-based interventions. Brain imaging studies show that higher HRV is associated with greater connectivity between the ventromedial prefrontal cortex and areas of the brain also strongly connected with experience of compassion, such as the insula, anterior cingulate cortex, middle cingulate cortex, and the amygdala (e.g., Mulcahy et al., 2019; Schumann et al., 2021). Similarly, studies show that higher baseline HRV is strongly associated with high self-reported trait and state compassion (Di Bello et al., 2020; Svendsen et al., 2016).

These studies support the utility of using HRV in psychotherapy both as an assessment tool and an intervention in itself. In the next few sections, we'll discuss ways of measuring HRV, using those measurements for tracking progress and evaluating the effectiveness of interventions, and doing HRV biofeedback with breathing.

Measuring Heart Rate Variability

With recent technological advances, there are now numerous ways to measure HRV. However, each method yields different results which cannot be compared to one another. Because of this, it is important to understand the different kinds of HRV measurements to interpret HRV readings correctly. Given the great number of methods, I will only review those that you are most likely to come across and use with your clients. For a more comprehensive review of HRV measurements, please see an excellent paper by Shaffer and Ginsberg (2017).

Among these methods, there are two main ways to measure HRV: time domain and frequency domain measurements. First, time domain measurements refer to those that graph instantaneous heart rate (derived from the intervals between heartbeats) over time.

- HR Max-Min measures the difference between the highest and lowest heart rate for each breath cycle, yielding results in beats per minute (see Figure 15.3). This measurement is most useful clinically to show clients the cyclical accelerations and decelerations of the heart.
- Standard deviation of the normal to normal internal (SDNN) refers to the standard deviation of the beat-to-beat time intervals, telling us how spread out or variable these times are. SDNN is a general measure of all ANS functioning and all inputs into HRV. This measurement has well-established short-term norms and can be used as a way to track progress. It is commonly used in research.
- Root mean square of successive differences (RMSSD) tells us how different each inter-beat interval is from the adjacent intervals. While RMSSD is a general measure of ANS function, it skews more towards measuring the vagal tone, or the strength of the parasympathetic nervous system (PNS) in our ability to self-regulate. RMSSD is more resistant to artifact than other measures of HRV, has well-established short-term norms, and is also commonly used in research.

Frequency domain measures separate the total heart rate signal into component frequencies and tell us about the contribution of the different components of the ANS to HRV. This is done through an algorithm called Fast Fourier Transform (FFT), which breaks the heart rate signal into component frequencies. This works similarly to a prism and white light. White light is composed of seven different color

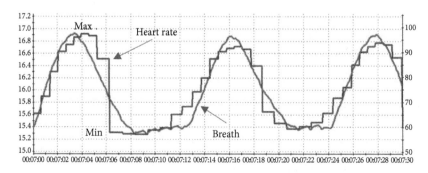

Figure 15.3 HR Max-Min.

frequencies, mixed up together. Looking at white light through a prism separates the individual color frequencies enabling us to see a rainbow. FFT does the same to the heart rate signal, allowing us to see signal frequencies generated by various components of the ANS.

- High frequency (HF) signal is generated by the PNS, telling us about the strength of one's vagal nerve. Because the spectral domain signals are not normally distributed, it is best to take the natural log of the total power of HF signal to take advantage of existing population norms. Given the significance of the PNS in HRV and self-regulation, it is the HF power that we seek to increase over time with HRV training.
- Very low frequency signal is generated by the sympathetic nervous system. However, in short recordings (<5 minutes), signal in that frequency may be more indicative of vagal withdrawal—the vagal nerve taking its foot off the brake, allowing sympathetic activation to increase.
- Low frequency (LF) signal is generated by the baroreflex (the mechanism responsible for regulating our blood pressure) and the PNS. We used to believe that LF power was indicative of sympathetic activation; however, more recent research demonstrates that there is no sympathetic contribution to the LF signal (Hayano & Yuda, 2019; Reyes del Paso et al., 2013). LF signal range is one where the main contributors to HRV (baroreflex and respiratory sinus arrhythmia [RSA]) are maximized. It is therefore at LF that we train HRV, which with time and practice, translates into an increase in HF power, strengthening the PNS, increasing both HRV and our ability to self-regulate.

Typical values (norms) have been established for several HRV measurements. See Table 15.1 for a summary of the most common measurements. HRV varies by age and gender (Voss et al., 2015), which are not accounted for in this table due to the complexity. The purpose of this table is to give you an idea of the typical numbers

Table 15.1 Heart rate variability norms

HRV Measure	Meaning	Typical Range
RMSSD	Overall autonomic nervous system flexibility	35–100ms
SDNN	Autonomic nervous system general, but more reflective of vagal activity	30–100ms
lnHF	Strength of the vagal tone (parasympathetic nervous system)	4.5–7.5ms^2

Note: All norms decrease with age. Higher end of the scale is typical for younger people, lower end of the scale for older people.

you might be looking for at an easy glance. For a comprehensive and detailed list of age- and gender-adjusted norms, please see Voss et al. (2015).

When doing HRV training, it is important to establish a baseline and keep track of progress. The best way to establish a baseline is through taking daily three-minute morning readings for five to seven days. A one- or two-day baseline is problematic because on any one day, HRV can be influenced by things like a poor night's sleep, having too much to drink the night before, or having an unusual stressor (Cvejic et al., 2018; Ralevski et al., 2019). A baseline reading averaged over several days will help to drown out those outliers and create a more accurate picture. Daily readings are best taken first thing in the morning, before stressors of the day start accumulating and affecting one's HRV. These daily readings can be taken with a client's personal HRV reader and app (see Table 15.4 at the end of the chapter for a list of currently available options).

I strongly recommend that the client continue to take daily readings for the duration of their HRV training and beyond, as that is the most reliable way to keep track of progress and to catch signs of increasing unresolved stress, as is described in the last section of the chapter ("Heart Rate Variability in Psychotherapy").

Once the client has been trained in slow breathing, it is extremely important to make sure that the client does not use their slow breathing skills during daily measurements, since slowing down of the breath will temporarily increase HRV and provide an inaccurate picture of the client's internal state and overall changes. Remind the client to breathe normally, and, if that proves difficult, distract themselves with reading/listening/watching something neutral during the three-minute measurement in order not to go into slow breathing.

Heart Rate Variability Training

While we do not possess much direct conscious control over our heart rate, we can consciously regulate our breath. We use the breath as the basic tool for HRV training. The breath stimulates changes in heart rate—as you breathe in, the heart rate goes up, and as you breathe out the heart rate goes down. For each person, there exists an optimal breathing rate that produces maximal oscillations of the heart rate. This breathing rate is called resonance frequency breathing. The concept of resonance is not specific to HRV training, or to the cardiovascular system. It is a physics term that refers to the property of an oscillating system in which stimulation at specific frequencies produces large increases in oscillation amplitudes. Your cardiovascular system is one such oscillating system. Breathing at resonance frequency (RF) causes the highest amplitudes of heart rate oscillations—as you breathe in, the heart rate goes up as much as possible, and as you breathe out the heart rate goes down as much as possible.

The easiest way to think about it is by comparing this system to pushing a child on a swing. There are lots of different ways to push that swing. You could push it infrequently and with a lot of force. The swing would go up high, but not smoothly, and it would gradually decrease its oscillations. The child in this scenario would not be pleased! You could also push the swing with short, frequent bursts. The swing would go up a bit and come down right away, never going up high. Again, the child would not be pleased. Another approach is to find a regular rhythm of pushing the swing that allows the swing to go up as much as possible and come down as much as possible with each push. In this scenario, when you find that optimal rate of pushing the swing, you maximize the child's delight. The breath stimulates the heart rate in the same way as the person pushing the swing. When we find our RF breathing rate, each inhalation produces maximum acceleration of the heart rate, and each exhalation produces maximal deceleration. For most people, RF breathing rate is between four and seven breaths per minute (Shaffer & Meehan, 2020). Resonance frequency breathing is a powerful tool to increase HRV, increase resilience, improve physical health, improve mental health, and enhance everyday performance (Steffen et al., 2017).

To determine your client's resonance frequency breathing rate, you will need a sensor that measures HRV connected to an app or software that has a breathing pacer and ability to display HRV measurements. See Table 15.4 at the end of the chapter for suggestions of HRV apps and devices.

The steps below outline the process of determining one's RF breathing rate.

1. Teach low and slow breathing, as described earlier in this chapter. Start with teaching the breathing skill without pacing or monitoring, then teach the client to follow a breath pacer at six breaths per minute (bpm), to make sure they are comfortable doing so. This is a crucial step before determining RF breathing rate. If the client is not comfortable breathing slowly and is unable to comfortably follow the pacer, the RF assessment may be inaccurate.
2. Pace the client's breathing for two minutes at each of the following breathing rates (1.5 minutes can be okay if pressed for time): 7 bpm, 6.5 bpm, 6 bpm, 5.5 bpm, 5 bpm, 4.5 bpm, and 4 bpm. Set the breathing pacer to 40 percent inhalation, 60 percent exhalation to minimize chances of overbreathing during the assessment and subsequent HRV training.

Refer to Table 15.2 for suggested inhalation and exhalation duration for each breathing rate. I include duration with and without a pause after the inhalation and exhalation. Including a pause is discretionary, only for the client's comfort if they wish.

3. RF is determined by three HRV measurements: LF power, HR max-min, and synchrony between heart rate and breathing, in this order of importance. The only way to determine the synchrony between heart rate and breath is if you have a respirometer (breathing belt) in addition to the HRV monitor. If one is not available, you can omit the third measurement from consideration. Some

Table 15.2 Inhalation and exhalation duration for resonance frequency assessment, with and without pauses

Breathing rate (Breaths per minute)	Inhalation (seconds) Without pause	Inhalation (seconds) With 0.5 second pause after inhalation	Exhalation (seconds) Without pause	Exhalation (seconds) With 0.5 second pause after exhalation
7	3.4	2.9	5.2	4.7
6.5	3.7	3.2	5.5	5
6	4	3.5	6	5.5
5.5	4.4	3.9	6.5	6
5	4.8	4.3	7.2	6.7
4.5	5.3	4.8	8	7.5
4.0	6	5.5	9	8.5

HRV apps do not display HR max-min but do show RMSSD. In this case, you may use RMSSD in place of HR max-min. If HR max-min is available, it is a better determinant of RF. LF power is the most important determinant and should not be omitted. The breathing rate with highest measurements is the RF. You may use Table 15.3 as a template to fill in data for RF assessment if your app/software does not provide one.

If one breathing rate produces the highest LF and HR max-min, together with good heart rate to breath synchrony, you have the RF breathing rate. Unfortunately, it is often not quite so straightforward, and you may need to pick a breathing rate

Table 15.3 Template for assessing resonance frequency breathing rate

Breathing Rate	Low Frequency Total Power	HR Max-Min	Synchronicity of Heart Rate and Breath (If software does not provide a number, "eyeball" it and rate on scale 1–5)
7 bpm			
6.5 bpm			
6 bpm			
5.5 bpm			
5 bpm			
4.5 bpm			
4 bpm			

based on its meeting the most characteristics. The highest LF peak is the most important characteristic of RF breathing. Highest HR max-min is the second most important. RSA is a useful "tiebreaker" if needed. If one breathing rate produces the best LF peak, but one of the "adjacent" breathing rates produces the most consistently high HR max-min, it is safe to conclude that RF is somewhere between those two breathing rates and to train the client to breathe somewhere between those two rates. Most people will not be able to consistently breathe at a specific rate with 100 percent accuracy without a pacer, so giving them a small range can be quite helpful.

Once you determine the client's RF breathing rate, the client should begin practicing breathing at that rate. They may use a pacer to assist them, although I encourage clients to also learn to breathe at RF pace without an external pacer in case one is not available when they need it.

HRV practice using RF breathing seems to be most effective at twenty minutes a day. However, given how difficult it is to establish new habits and find time for new things, encourage your clients to start slowly—start with five minutes of HRV training each day for a week, then move to ten minutes a day for the second week, fifteen minutes a day for the third week, and then settle at twenty minutes a day after the fourth week.

Clients often wonder whether they should be breathing at RF all the time. This is not necessary and often not even possible, as this breathing rate is quite slow. Daily practice for twenty minutes a day will train the nervous system to improve its ability to regulate itself, over time, improving resilience and ability to respond to challenges in healthier ways. This training is like a strength workout—as long as you get to the gym on a regular basis, you will be able to make progress and maintain gains without having to carry your dumbbells around with you at all times. With time, your muscle strength will increase, and if a friend asks you to help them move a couch, you will be able to do so much more easily than prior to beginning your workouts. Similarly, as you long as you do your HRV training at RF for twenty minutes a day most days of the week, after about five to six weeks, your ability to handle stress will improve, and when faced with a challenge you'll find it easier to respond in a more thoughtful and helpful way. So, while it is not necessary to breathe at RF outside of the daily practice times, the skill is available to you when needed to remind the body to self-regulate.

Using Heart Rate Variability in Psychotherapy

In addition to using HRV to improve resilience, adaptability, and response to challenges, HRV can also be used to assess clients' readiness for certain interventions and evaluate the effectiveness of various non-HRV-specific interventions.

Heart Rate Variability as a Sign of Building Distress or Health Issue

When the client continues taking daily HRV readings, it is easier to keep track of trends and note sustained dips in HRV, which may signal an arising or increasing issue that needs to be addressed. A one- or two-day dip in HRV may not signal a serious issue. However, a multiple-day dip or a downward trend over a week warrants a conversation with the client as to what might be going on in their life. Possible triggers may be poor sleep, a physical illness, unresolved social/relationship stress, substance abuse relapse, overtraining (for athletes), a flair up in pain or trauma symptoms, etc. (Fatisson et al., 2016). Downward-trending HRV provides an opportunity to check in with the client before they may be fully aware of an issue or may prompt them to talk about something they have been avoiding or suppressing.

Heart Rate Variability to Assess Readiness for Therapeutic Interventions

Many therapeutic interventions bring up difficult feelings and may require some resilience and coping skills on the part of the client. For example, exposure to feared stimuli, exposure and response prevention, and interoceptive exposure by definition come with anxiety, which may sometimes feel intense.[1] Having an understanding of the client's internal state on the day of the intervention may help the therapist to decide on the intensity of the intervention, the amount of support the client may need, or even whether to postpone the intervention to another day. Low HRV on the morning of the proposed intervention may mean that extra care should be taken during that day's session, with possible modification needed. If on the other hand, the HRV reading is higher than typical that morning, it may mean that the client is ready for a bit of an extra challenge.

For example, mindfulness and self-compassion-based interventions may not appear to be particularly difficult on the surface, but nonetheless require a certain degree of self-regulation and resilience. These interventions require the client to face difficult thoughts and feelings. Poor self-regulation makes this difficult and clients may feel overwhelmed or simply unwilling to take part in these practices. In such

---

[1] Each of these exposure strategies is used in psychotherapy to desensitize triggers for anxiety. *Exposure to feared stimuli* refers to the strategy of inviting the patient to systematically confront and maintain contact with an anxiety trigger, with the goal of reducing the fearful reaction to the trigger. *Exposure and response prevention* refers to the therapeutic strategy of asking the patient to face a stimulus that frequently triggers anxiety, and deliberately not engage in one's usual avoidant response. For example, a patient with obsessive compulsive disorder might be asked to touch a doorknob and deliberately not engage in compulsive hand washing, to desensitize their anxious response to the doorknob stimulus. *Interoceptive exposure* refers to the therapeutic strategy of inviting the patient to induce internal somatic symptoms (such as rapid heartbeat) associated with threat, and deliberately maintain contact with the sensation, to desensitize associated anxiety.

situations, it may be helpful to do a few weeks of HRV training prior to re-engaging in mindfulness and self-compassion-based interventions.

Heart Rate Variability to Evaluate Effectiveness of Therapeutic Interventions

Taking daily HRV readings helps evaluate effectiveness of any intervention, not just HRV-specific training, and adds objective data in addition to the client's subjective experience. For example, tracking HRV throughout an eight-week mindful self-compassion course gives the therapist and the client an opportunity to evaluate the effectiveness of the intervention. Tracking HRV over a longer-term psychotherapy will, of course, have quite a few ups and downs, but an overall trajectory will give the therapist a way to evaluate effectiveness of the therapy, while shorter-term changes will provide warning of increasing distress or improvement.

The power of HRV tracking and training lies in its effectiveness and versatility. Using the same basic method of HRV training outlined in this chapter, therapists can work with multiple disorders. When clients present with comorbid disorders, HRV training may offer a unified way of working with all of them. HRV tracking and training can be seamlessly integrated into standard psychotherapy treatment, further improving psychotherapy outcomes (Caldwell & Steffen, 2018; Economides et al., 2020). Together with a focus on optimal respiratory physiology, this chapter proposed a practical guide to using breathing training either as a stand-alone

Table 15.4 Heart rate variability devices for personal and professional use

Name	Professional or personal use	Type of sensor
Optimal HRV	Both	Arm band, photoplethysmograph
Thought Technology, Infiniti or Procomp 5	Professional	Comprehensive system with finger pulse and EKG sensor
eVu TPS by Thought Technology	Both	Finger sensor, photoplethysmograph
Alive by Somatic vision	Both	Finger sensor, photoplethysmograph
Nexus 10 by Mind Media	Professional	Comprehensive system with finger pulse and EKG sensor
EmWave by Heartmath	Both	Finger or ear sensor, photoplethysmograph
Polar Strap	Personal	EKG sensor that can be connected to multiple apps
Elite HRV	Personal	Finger sensor, photoplethysmograph
Mindfield	Both	Chest strap, EKG

intervention or as part of other approaches to psychotherapy, with the hope of equipping psychotherapists with a new powerful skill to improve their clients' lives.

References

Benichou, T., Pereira, B., Mermillod, M., Tauveron, I., Pfabigan, D., Maqdasy, S., & Dutheil, F. (2018). Heart rate variability in type 2 diabetes mellitus: A systematic review and meta–analysis. *PLoS One, 13*(4), e0195166. https://doi.org/10.1371/journal.pone.0195166

Blase, K., Vermetten, E., Lehrer, P., & Gevirtz, R. (2021). Neurophysiological approach by self-control of your stress-related autonomic nervous system with depression, stress and anxiety patients. *International Journal of Environmental Research and Public Health, 18*(7), 3329. https://doi.org/10.3390/ijerph18073329

Caldwell, Y. T., & Steffen, P. R. (2018). Adding HRV biofeedback to psychotherapy increases heart rate variability and improves the treatment of major depressive disorder. *International Journal of Psychophysiology, 131*, 96–101. https://doi.org/10.1016/j.ijpsycho.2018.01.001

Cheng, Y. C., Su, M. I., Liu, C. W., Huang, Y. C., & Huang, W. L. (2022). Heart rate variability in patients with anxiety disorders: A systematic review and meta-analysis. *Psychiatry and Clinical Neurosciences, 76*(7), 292–302. https://doi.org/10.1111/pcn.13356

Christodoulou, G., Salami, N., & Black, D. S. (2020). The utility of heart rate variability in mindfulness research. *Mindfulness, 11*, 554–570. https://doi.org/10.1007/s12671-019-01296-3

Cvejic, E., Huang, S., & Vollmer-Conna, U. (2018). Can you snooze your way to an 'A'? Exploring the complex relationship between sleep, autonomic activity, wellbeing and performance in medical students. *Australian and New Zealand Journal of Psychiatry, 52*(1), 39–46. https://doi.org/10.1177/000486741771

Davies, C. D., & Craske, M. G. (2014). Low baseline pCO2 predicts poorer outcome from behavioral treatment: Evidence from a mixed anxiety disorders sample. *Psychiatry Research, 219*(2), 311–315. https://doi.org/10.1016/j.psychres.2014.06.003.

Di Bello, M., Carnevali, L., Petrocchi, N., Thayer, J. F., Gilbert, P., & Ottaviani, C. (2020). The compassionate vagus: A meta-analysis on the connection between compassion and heart rate variability. *Neuroscience & Biobehavioral Reviews, 116*, 21–30. https://doi.org/10.1016/j.neubiorev.2020.06.016

Druss, B. G., Wang, P. S., Sampson, N. A., Olfson, M., Pincus, H. A., Wells, K. B., & Kessler, R. C. (2007). Understanding mental health treatment in persons without mental diagnoses: Results from the National Comorbidity Survey Replication. *Archives of General Psychiatry, 64*(10), 1196–1203. https://doi.org/10.1001/archpsyc.64.10.1196

Dunn, J. O., Mythen, M. G., & Grocott, M. P. (2016). Physiology of oxygen transport. *BJA Education, 16*(10), 341–348. https://doi.org/10.1093/bjaed/mkw012

Economides, M., Lehrer, P., Ranta, K., Nazander, A., Hilgert, O., Raevuori, A., Gevirtz, R., Khazan, I., & Forman-Hoffman, V. L. (2020). Feasibility and efficacy of the addition of heart rate variability biofeedback to a remote digital health intervention for depression. *Applied Psychophysiology and Biofeedback, 45*(2), 75–86. https://doi.org/10.1007/s10484-020-09458-z

Fang, S. C., Wu, Y. L., & Tsai, P. S. (2020). Heart rate variability and risk of all-cause death and cardiovascular events in patients with cardiovascular disease: A meta-analysis of cohort studies. *Biological Research for Nursing, 22*(1), 45–56. https://doi.org/10.1177/1099800419877442

Fatisson, J., Oswald, V., & Lalonde, F. (2016). Influence diagram of physiological and environmental factors affecting heart rate variability: An extended literature overview. *Heart International, 11*(1), e32–e40. https://doi.org/10.5301/heartint.5000232

Fennell, A. B., Benau, E. M., & Atchley, R. A. (2016). A single session of meditation reduces physiological indices of anger in both experienced and novice meditators. *Consciousness and Cognition, 40*, 54–66. https://doi.org/10.1016/j.concog.2015.12.010

Fernández-Álvarez, J., Grassi, M., Colombo, D., Botella, C., Cipresso, P., Perna, G., & Riva, G. (2022). Efficacy of bio- and neurofeedback for depression: A meta-analysis. *Psychological Medicine, 52*(2), 201–216. https://doi.org/10.1017/S0033291721004396

Ferreira-Garcia, R., de Abreu Costa, M., Goncalves, F. G., de Nonohay, R. G., Nardi, A. E., da Rocha Freire, R. C., & Manfro, G. G. (2021). Heart rate variability: A biomarker of selective response to mindfulness-based treatment versus fluoxetine in generalized anxiety disorder. *Journal of Affective Disorders*, *295*, 1087–1092. https://doi.org/10.1016/j.jad.2021.08.121

Fournié, C., Chouchou, F., Dalleau, G., Caderby, T., Cabrera, Q., & Verkindt, C. (2021). Heart rate variability biofeedback in chronic disease management: A systematic review. *Complementary Therapies in Medicine*, *60*, 102750. https://doi.org/10.1016/j.ctim.2021.102750

Ge, F., Yuan, M., Li, Y., & Zhang, W. (2020). Posttraumatic stress disorder and alterations in resting heart rate variability: A systematic review and meta-analysis. *Psychiatry Investigation*, *17*(1), 9. https://doi.org/10.30773/pi.2019.0112

Gerbarg, P. L., Jacob, V. E., Stevens, L., Bosworth, B. P., Chabouni, F., DeFilippis, E. M., Warren, R., Trivellas, M., Patel, P. V., Webb, C. D., Harbus, M. D., Christos, P. J., Brown, R. P., & Scherl, E. J. (2015). The effect of breathing, movement, and meditation on psychological and physical symptoms and inflammatory biomarkers in inflammatory bowel disease: A randomized controlled trial. *Inflammatory Bowel Diseases*, *21*(12), 2886–2896. https://doi.org/10.1097/MIB.0000000000000568

Goessl, V. C., Curtiss, J. E., & Hofmann, S. G. (2017). The effect of heart rate variability biofeedback training on stress and anxiety: A meta-analysis. *Psychological Medicine*, *47*(15), 2578–2586. https://doi.org/10.1017/S0033291717001003

Granero-Gallegos, A., González-Quílez, A., Plews, D., & Carrasco-Poyatos, M. (2020). HRV-based training for improving VO2max in endurance athletes. A systematic review with meta-analysis. *International Journal of Environmental Research and Public Health*, *17*(21), 7999. https://doi.org/10.3390/ijerph17217999

Hayano, J., & Yuda, E. (2019). Pitfalls of assessment of autonomic function by heart rate variability. *Journal of Physiological Anthropology*, *38*(1), 1–8. https://doi.org/10.1186/s40101-019-0193-2

Holzman, J. B., & Bridgett, D. J. (2017). Heart rate variability indices as bio-markers of top-down self-regulatory mechanisms: A meta-analytic review. *Neuroscience & Biobehavioral Reviews*, *74*, 233–255. https://doi.org/10.1016/j.neubiorev.2016.12.032

Hopper, S. I., Murray, S. L., Ferrara, L. R., & Singleton, J. K. (2019). Effectiveness of diaphragmatic breathing for reducing physiological and psychological stress in adults: A quantitative systematic review. *JBI Database of Systematic Reviews and Implementation Reports*, *17*(9), 1855–1876. https://doi.org/10.11124/JBISRIR-2017-003848

Jarczok, M. N., Koenig, J., Wittling, A., Fischer, J. E., & Thayer, J. F. (2019). First evaluation of an index of low vagally-mediated heart rate variability as a marker of health risks in human adults: Proof of concept. *Journal of Clinical Medicine*, *8*(11), 1940. https://doi.org/10.3390/jcm8111940

Jerath, R., Crawford, M. W., Barnes, V. A., & Harden, K. (2015). Self-regulation of breathing as a primary treatment for anxiety. *Applied Psychophysiology and Biofeedback*, *40*(2), 107–115. https://doi.org/10.1007/s10484-015-9279-8

Kim, H. G., Cheon, E. J., Bai, D. S., Lee, Y. H., & Koo, B. H. (2018). Stress and heart rate variability: A meta-analysis and review of the literature. *Psychiatry Investigation*, *15*(3), 235–245. https://doi.org/10.30773/pi.2017.08.17

Kim, K. N., Yao, Y., & Ju, S. Y. (2020). Heart rate variability and inflammatory bowel disease in humans: A systematic review and meta-analysis. *Medicine*, *99*(48), e23430. https://doi.org/10.1097/MD.0000000000023430

Koch, C., Wilhelm, M., Salzmann, S., Rief, W., & Euteneuer, F. (2019). A meta-analysis of heart rate variability in major depression. *Psychological Medicine*, *49*(12), 1948–1957. https://doi.org/10.1017/S0033291719001351

Koenig, J., Williams, D. P., Kemp, A. H., & Thayer, J. F. (2016). Vagally mediated heart rate variability in headache patients—A systematic review and meta-analysis. *Cephalalgia*, *36*(3), 265–278. https://doi.org/10.1177/0333102415583989

Kuvačić, G., Fratini, P., Padulo, J., Antonio, D. I., & De Giorgio, A. (2018). Effectiveness of yoga and educational intervention on disability, anxiety, depression, and pain in people with CLBP: A randomized controlled trial. *Complementary Therapies in Clinical Practice*, *31*, 262–267. https://doi.org/10.1016/j.ctcp.2018.03.008

Laffey, J. G., & Kavanagh, B. P. (2002). Hypocapnia. *New England Journal of Medicine, 347*(1), 43–53. https://doi.org/10.1056/NEJMra012457

Lehrer, P., Kaur, K., Sharma, A., Shah, K., Huseby, R., Bhavsar, J., & Zhang, Y. (2020). Heart rate variability biofeedback improves emotional and physical health and performance: A systematic review and meta-analysis. *Applied Psychophysiology and Biofeedback, 45,* 109–129. https://doi.org/10.1007/s10484-021-09526-y

McCraty, R., & Shaffer, F. (2015). Heart rate variability: New perspectives on physiological mechanisms, assessment of self-regulatory capacity, and health risk. *Global Advances in Health and Medicine, 4*(1), 46–61. https://doi.org/10.7453/gahmj.2014.073

Mulcahy, J. S., Larsson, D. E., Garfinkel, S. N., & Critchley, H. D. (2019). Heart rate variability as a biomarker in health and affective disorders: A perspective on neuroimaging studies. *Neuroimage, 202,* 116072. https://doi.org/10.1016/j.neuroimage.2019.116072

Pagaduan, J. C., Chen, Y. S., Fell, J. W., & Wu, S. S. X. (2021). A preliminary systematic review and meta-analysis on the effects of heart rate variability biofeedback on heart rate variability and respiration of athletes. *Journal of Complementary and Integrative Medicine, 19*(4), 817–826. https://doi.org/10.1515/jcim-2020-0528

Perna, G., Riva, A., Defillo, A., Sangiorgio, E., Nobile, M., & Caldirola, D. (2020). Heart rate variability: Can it serve as a marker of mental health resilience? Special Section on "Translational and Neuroscience Studies in Affective Disorders," Section Editor, Maria Nobile MD, PhD. *Journal of Affective Disorders, 263,* 754–761. https://doi.org/10.1016/j.jad.2019.10.017

Pizzoli, S. F., Marzorati, C., Gatti, D., Monzani, D., Mazzocco, K., & Pravettoni, G. (2021). A meta-analysis on heart rate variability biofeedback and depressive symptoms. *Scientific Reports, 11*(1), 6650. https://doi.org/10.1038/s41598-021-86149-7

Ralevski, E., Petrakis, I., & Altemus, M. (2019). Heart rate variability in alcohol use: A review. *Pharmacology Biochemistry and Behavior, 176,* 83–92. https://doi.org/10.1016/j.pbb.2018.12.003

Reyes del Paso, G. A., Langewitz, W., Mulder, L. J., van Roon, A., & Duschek, S. (2013). The utility of low frequency heart rate variability as an index of sympathetic cardiac tone: A review with emphasis on a reanalysis of previous studies. *Psychophysiology, 50*(5), 477–487. https://doi.org/10.1111/psyp.12027

Sadowski, A., Dunlap, C., Lacombe, A., & Hanes, D. (2021). Alterations in heart rate variability associated with irritable bowel syndrome or inflammatory bowel disease: A systematic review and meta-analysis. *Clinical and Translational Gastroenterology, 12*(1), e00275. https://doi.org/10.14309/ctg.0000000000000275

Schneider, M., & Schwerdtfeger, A. (2020). Autonomic dysfunction in posttraumatic stress disorder indexed by heart rate variability: A meta-analysis. *Psychological Medicine, 50*(12), 1937–1948. https://doi.org/10.1017/S003329172000207X

Schumann, A., de la Cruz, F., Köhler, S., Brotte, L., & Bär, K. J. (2021). The influence of heart rate variability biofeedback on cardiac regulation and functional brain connectivity. *Frontiers in Neuroscience, 15,* 691988. https://doi.org/10.3389/fnins.2021.691988

Shaffer, F., & Ginsberg, J. P. (2017). An overview of heart rate variability metrics and norms. *Frontiers in Public Health, 5,* Article 258. https://doi.org/10.3389/fpubh.2017.00258

Shaffer, F., & Meehan, Z. M. (2020). A practical guide to resonance frequency assessment for heart rate variability biofeedback. *Frontiers in Neuroscience, 14,* 570400. https://doi.org/10.3389/fnins.2020.570400

Sharma, M., Rajput, J. S., Tan, R. S., & Acharya, U. R. (2021). Automated detection of hypertension using physiological signals: A review. *International Journal of Environmental Research and Public Health, 18*(11), 5838. https://doi.org/10.3390/ijerph18115838

Steffen, P. R., Austin, T., DeBarros, A., & Brown, T. (2017). The impact of resonance frequency breathing on measures of heart rate variability, blood pressure, and mood. *Frontiers in Public Health, 5,* 222. https://doi.org/10.3389/fpubh.2017.00222

Svendsen, J. L., Osnes, B., Binder, P. E., Dundas, I., Visted, E., Nordby, H., Schanche, E., & Sørensen, L. (2016). Trait self-compassion reflects emotional flexibility through an association with high vagally mediated heart rate variability. *Mindfulness, 7,* 1103–1113. https://doi.org/10.1007/s12671-016-0549-1

Taralov, Z. Z., Terziyski, K. V., & Kostianev, S. S. (2015). Heart rate variability as a method for assessment of the autonomic nervous system and the adaptations to different physiological and pathological conditions. *Folia Medica*, *57*(3/4), 173. https://doi.org/10.1515/folmed-2015-0036

Tinello, D., Kliegel, M., & Zuber, S. (2021). Does heart rate variability biofeedback enhance executive functions across the lifespan? A systematic review. *Journal of Cognitive Enhancement*, *6*(1), 126–142. https://doi.org/10.1007/s41465-021-00218-3

Tolin, D. F., Billingsley, A. L., Hallion, L. S., & Diefenbach, G. J. (2017). Low pre-treatment end-tidal CO2 predicts dropout from cognitive-behavioral therapy for anxiety and related disorders. *Behaviour Research and Therapy*, *90*, 32–40. https://doi.org/10.1016/j.brat.2016.12.005

Tracy, L. M., Ioannou, L., Baker, K. S., Gibson, S. J., Georgiou-Karistianis, N., & Giummarra, M. J. (2016). Meta-analytic evidence for decreased heart rate variability in chronic pain implicating parasympathetic nervous system dysregulation. *Pain*, *157*(1), 7–29. https://doi.org/10.1097/j.pain.0000000000000360

Tsuji, H., Larson, M. G., Venditti, F. J., Jr., Manders, E. S., Evans, J. C., Feldman, C. L., & Levy, D. (1996). Impact of reduced heart rate variability on risk for cardiac events. The Framingham Heart Study. *Circulation*, *94*(11), 2850–2855. https://doi.org/10.1161/01.cir.94.11.2850

Voss, A., Schroeder, R., Heitmann, A., Peters, A., & Perz, S. (2015). Short-term heart rate variability—Influence of gender and age in healthy subjects. *PLoS One*, *10*(3), e0118308. https://doi.org/10.1371/journal.pone.0118308

West, J. B. (2019). Three classical papers in respiratory physiology by Christian Bohr (1855–1911) whose work is frequently cited but seldom read. *American Journal of Physiology-Lung Cellular and Molecular Physiology*, *316*(4), L585–L588. https://doi.org/10.1152/ajplung.00527.2018

Zaccaro, A., Piarulli, A., Laurino, M., Garbella, E., Menicucci, D., Neri, B., & Gemignani, A. (2018). How breath-control can change your life: A systematic review on psycho-physiological correlates of slow breathing. *Frontiers in Human Neuroscience*, *12*, 353. https://doi.org/10.3389/fnhum.2018.00353

16
Compassionate Bodies, Compassionate Minds

Psychophysiological Concomitants of Compassion-Focused Therapy

Nicola Petrocchi and Cristina Ottaviani

Over the past decades, researchers in the social, behavioral, and cognitive sciences have increasingly used concepts derived from the evolutionary approach to formulate and test new hypotheses in the field of human psychology (Nesse, 2005). Indeed, evolutionary psychology constitutes the answer to what Charles Darwin (1859) had postulated in his *On the Origin of Species* when he stated, "In the distant future I see fields open for much more important research. Psychology will be based on new foundations, those of the necessary acquisition of every mental faculty and ability by virtue of gradual adaptations to the environment" (p. 488). It is precisely in light of this evolutionary perspective that we understand the meaning and usefulness of the compassion-focused interventions that are increasingly being proposed to treat different psychological disorders.

In this chapter, in line with the bio-psycho-social approach of compassion-focused therapy (CFT), we will conceptualize compassion as a purely human motivational system evolved from the caregiving motivation that we share with other mammals (Gilbert, 2017). Framing compassion in the context of the affiliative motivations that characterize mammals, and in particular our species, will help us understand the psychophysiological changes that compassion generates in our organism, and how these can be voluntarily induced and used to promote therapeutic change. We will focus specifically on the impact that compassionate motivation has on the parasympathetic nervous system. In fact, the effective modulation of this branch of the autonomic nervous system has been shown to be crucial in therapeutic settings, not only because of its bi-directional relationship with cognitive and behavioral variables that are usually the target of clinical interventions (such as, for example, meta-cognitive and emotional regulation skills), but also because of its link to our need for "social safeness" (Brosschot et al., 2018; Gilbert, 1993; Petrocchi & Cheli, 2019).

The Evolution of Social Motivations

Humans evolved in the mammalian phylogenetic lineage as a highly social species. Although most species exhibit social behaviors, such as competition for resources, mating, and caring for offspring, the human brain is unusually eusocial, capable of providing care for extended periods, caring for the dying and infirm, and entertaining complex cooperative dynamics. These adaptations have been characterized by major changes in the brain. Compared with the first humanoids two million years ago, our "brain capacity" today has been greatly enhanced, with the frontal cortex playing a particularly important role (DeSilva et al., 2021). These changes provide the physiological substrate for a wide range of complex skills, including language, symbolic thinking, self-awareness, and empathy. What induced these massive changes in our brains? According to the social brain hypothesis, human intelligence and its neural substrate evolved to facilitate survival in a specific context characterized by increasingly large and complex social groups (Dunbar, 2016). In particular, a number of motivational systems have evolved because they helped to meet the challenges of survival and genetic replication in competitive environments (Gilbert, 1989, 2015).

An evolutionary adaptation that characterizes mammals, and humans in particular, is "affiliative" sociality, and in particular, the dyad consisting of two complementary motivational tendencies: caregiving (the provision of care) and the search for care, help, and support, characteristic of the attachment system (Gilbert, 1989; Mayseless, 2016). Caregiving and attachment motivations are defining characteristics of human nature (Panksepp, 1998). Indeed, "unlike reptiles and other phylogenetically older vertebrates, for mammals birth is not a transition to independence, but an extension of the period of dependence that begins in utero" (Porges & Furman, 2010, p. 3). Even when humans become more physically and emotionally independent of caregiving figures, they create dyads with other figures (partners, friends, therapists, etc.), with whom they initiate patterns of interaction, "dances" of psychophysiological co-regulation, referred to as social mentalities—caregiving, attachment, competition, sexuality, cooperation, and, in humans, compassion (Gilbert, 1989, 2015).

Human "Hyper-Affiliation" and the Vagus Nerve

The evolution of the motivation toward care and "hyper-affiliation" typical of human beings has been marked by changes in the neural apparatus of the autonomic nervous system (Porges, 2007). According to Porges' (2007) polyvagal theory, one of the main physiological changes related to the human affiliative capacity has been the evolution of a branch of the parasympathetic system, the myelinated vagus nerve. The myelinated vagus inhibits threat-defense behaviors (e.g., fight/flight) mediated by sympathetic system activation and hypothalamic-pituitary-adrenal axis activity.

This inhibition promotes a physiological state of calming that facilitates social affiliation, caring, and sharing. The myelinated section of the vagus nerve would thus have evolved with the parents' aptitude to slow down their physiology, notice and respond to the infants' needs, and, reciprocally, with the infants' predisposition to be calmed by their parents' caring behaviors (Depue & Morrone-Strupinsky, 2005).

This dynamic of mutual regulation of the two branches of the autonomic nervous system generates a variable pattern of acceleration and slowing down of cardiac activity. The consequence is that the time between one heartbeat and the next is never the same but varies according to the patterns of acceleration and deceleration. A measure of the degree of variation in the times between consecutive heartbeats is called heart rate variability (HRV), resulting from the described dynamic interplay between the fast-acting parasympathetic nervous system and the relatively slower sympathetic nervous system. Since the vagus nerve carries 80 percent of the fibers of the parasympathetic nervous system, vagally mediated HRV can be considered an indirect index of vagal modulation on the heart (Kuo et al., 2005). Without the inhibitory influence of the vagus nerve (referred to as the *vagal brake*; Porges, 2007), the heart would generate an intrinsic heart rate of about 120 beats per minute through impulses produced by the sinoatrial node, its natural pacemaker (Jose & Collison, 1970; Opthof, 2000).

The interplay between the parasympathetic and the sympathetic nervous systems is also linked to the different ways of dealing with threat and stress (Gilbert, 1989, 1993, 2022; Porges, 2007). Under conditions of perceived threat, vagal restraint is lost, which leads to an increase in heart rate and a decrease in HRV. In the absence of threats, a condition defined as *safety*, the vagus nerve activity acts as a brake that slows heart rate and inhibits cognitive and behavioral processes related to threat processing (Gilbert, 1993, 2022; Petrocchi & Cheli, 2019). The vagal activity under safe conditions also increases HRV. Safety is linked to successful avoidance of threatening stimuli (Gilbert, 2022), to the availability of helpful others, a condition defined as *interpersonal safeness*, or to a helpful inner dialogue, a condition defined as *intrapersonal safeness*. Conditions of safety and safeness are characterized by different but interacting physiological processes, which have vagal activity as a central hub system. The vagus nerve innervates most of the organs of our body, such as the lungs, the digestive system, but also the vocal apparatus and the facial muscles charged with the expression of emotions, thus contributing, on the one hand, to the mobilization of the fight-or-flight response and, on the other hand, to affiliative behaviors (Porges, 2007).

Not surprisingly, then, higher HRV (i.e., greater variability in time intervals between consecutive heart beats) is associated with greater emotion regulation (Mather & J. F. Thayer, 2018), metacognitive awareness and mind-reading ability (Meessen et al., 2018), empathy and lower levels of alexithymia (Lischke et al., 2018), and higher performance on several cognitive tasks involving attention, working memory, and inhibitory control (Hansen et al., 2009; Ottaviani et al., 2018). It becomes clear that HRV is associated with a number of psychological and behavioral variables that are usually the target of psychotherapeutic interventions. Thus, practices that impact HRV (for example, compassion-focused practices; Gilbert, 2010) should not be perceived, by the patient and therapist, as mere means to relax, but rather as interventions on variables that we usually seek to modify in therapy through purely dialogic, verbal modalities.

The Neurovisceral Integration Model and Compassion

To explain the complex interrelationship between HRV, behavior, emotions, and motivation, J. F. Thayer and Lane (2000, 2009) described the neurovisceral integration model—a set of neural structures (including the anterior cingulate, insula, ventromedial prefrontal cortex, amygdala, and hypothalamus) through which the brain regulates visceromotor, neuroendocrine, and behavioral responses that are fundamental to goal-oriented behavior and adaptability to the environment. According to the authors, this regulation is achieved primarily through inhibitory processes. For example, in safe contexts, the amygdala is inhibited by the ventromedial prefrontal cortex (Delgado et al., 2008). Under conditions of reduced safeness and/or threat, the latter would loosen its inhibitory capacity allowing amygdala activation and fight-or-flight response in the face of threat, with corresponding reductions in HRV (Makovac et al., 2016). Vagally mediated HRV is more than just an index of healthy heart function; rather it is an indirect measure of the efficiency of inhibitory prefrontal processes, as confirmed by a recent meta-analysis (J. F. Thayer et al., 2012).

As anticipated in the previous section, when the organism does not perceive safeness, the prefrontal inhibitory capacity decreases, and the activity of subcortical structures such as the amygdala increases, causing the default response to threat to remain active (a condition characterized by lower HRV; Brosschot et al., 2017; Coan & Sbarra, 2015). This occurs in social environments dominated by loneliness, denial of separation, or power and subordination dynamics. The evolved human mind is also capable of creating internal relationships with ourselves that generate a sense of "intrapersonal unsafeness" (Longe et al., 2010). For example, we may feel sympathetic, indifferent, or hostile toward ourselves, generating such a sense of unsafeness. Being exposed to mistreatment, criticism, and invalidation of our emotions is associated with reduced HRV whether the criticism comes from our interpersonal relationships or our intrapersonal relationships, where we ourselves mistreat, criticize, or invalidate what we are experiencing (Dale et al., 2018; Petrocchi, Ottaviani, et al., 2017). In CFT, we consider it crucial that patients understand the effect that safeness, or its absence, can generate at the psychophysiological level, and recognize how it allows them to feel less guilty about seemingly incomprehensible reactions they experience (e.g., a depressive relapse). The following case narrative illustrates the psychophysiological and emotional impact of experiencing unsafeness.

Case Narrative: Frank Frank had always suffered from depressive episodes, which he had tried to cope with through cognitive behavioral therapy since he was thirteen years old, a time when he was bullied. In the later years of his life, although he was doing better, he experienced recurring moments of black mood. Frank could not explain these episodes and automatically attributed them to the violent bullying he experienced in his childhood. Accordingly, he thought he should work in therapy primarily for the purpose of reducing the memories and moderating the outcomes of those traumatic events.

In his current CFT therapy, tracing the circumstances around the onset of the last depressive episode, Frank came to understand the role that the loss of social safeness, and not so much the presence of threats, played in his relapses. He had decided to leave the school where he worked, and where he had gotten along particularly well: he had been welcomed there by friendly and not overly competitive colleagues, and he had also made particularly deep friendships. However, he had decided to move to Chicago for a higher paying job. It was his choice, nothing threatened him, so why was he feeling depressed again?

Using the behavioral chain through the lens of CFT, it emerged that the precise moment he began to feel the onset of a dark mood—a deep sense of fatigue and loss of motivation—was when he said goodbye to his friends in the teacher's lounge and handed back his locker key. It was the loss of that social network (interpersonal safeness) and the immediate sense of loneliness, not so much the memories or the threat of bullying, that activated the threat response in the form of freezing, with demotivation, lethargy, and behavioral inhibition.

In addition, Frank, not knowing the role that loss of safeness plays in regulating our psychophysiology, criticized himself harshly for his own incomprehensible depressive reaction, invalidated his own malaise, creating a condition of reduced intrapersonal safeness. This further impaired the vagal brake and the inhibitory capacity of the prefrontal cortex, with resulting increased negative emotions and depressive condition. Imaginatively recreating the feeling of safeness through CFT visualization techniques induced in him an immediate sense of lightening, warmth in his hands, feet and stomach, and a sense of increased motivation and drive to action. He understood the impact that—at a physiological level—the presence or absence of safeness had on him, and the role it had played in his many depressive relapses. This motivated him to actively try to recreate nurturing social relationships in his everyday life, and to develop more compassion toward himself as a way to regulate his mood.

When we activate a specific affiliative motivational attitude toward self and others, such as compassion, it fosters a greater sense of perceived social safeness, and thus greater emotion regulation and inhibition of the threat response (Gilbert, 2014; Hermanto & Zuroff, 2016; Petrocchi & Couyoumdjian, 2016). This is the fundamental rationale for compassion-focused practices.

The Regulatory Power of Compassion

Where does the regulatory power of compassionate motivation come from? As anticipated, compassion is regarded as a motivational system in its own right, which evolved from the caring motivation that predisposes us to identify and respond to the needs of offspring. The caring motivation that we have in common with mammals would have extended, in the evolution of the human species, to the well-being of all living creatures and the self (Gilbert, 1989; Mayseless, 2016; Wang, 2005). This aspect is captured in the definition of compassion as having "a sensitivity to suffering in oneself and others, combined with a commitment to alleviate and prevent it" (Gilbert, 2014, p. 19). Human beings are on one hand able to observe and respond to a type of suffering that manifests itself in the present moment (e.g., someone falls and breaks a leg right in front of me and I feel the urge to help that person; my child cries and I immediately feed him); on the other hand, because of our evolved higher cognitive faculties, we are also able to contemplate a type of suffering that does not manifest in front of our eyes, but is connected with the inherently tragic and vulnerable nature of human beings (and experience a wish for help, or a wish for well-being).

We experience suffering and longing for help in seeing a child in poverty looking at us, barefoot, dirty and half-naked, from his bed of rags. We experience pain at the sight of a young boy in a coma, or when we meet the now dull and empty gaze of our elderly parent with Alzheimer's. In all these cases, no one is crying or asking us for help. No obvious stimulus of suffering is triggering our mammalian caregiving social mentality. Yet, we are able to contemplate and resonate with the suffering and/or injustice of that condition; we are touched by a quality of suffering that is less situational, as much as existential. The intention to contemplate this level of suffering that pertains to human nature ("a sensitivity to suffering in oneself and in others"), and to allow the natural desire to alleviate it that comes with it ("a commitment to alleviate and prevent it") is the evolved social mentality of compassion.

Having evolved from the caregiving system, compassion shares with it the same vagally mediated underlying physiology (e.g., Colonnello et al., 2017, for a review). Unlike mammalian caregiving, however, which implies a one-way directionality of care from the caregiver to the receiver, compassion can be manifested in three basic orientations: the compassion we give to others, the compassion we give to ourselves, and the compassion we derive from others (Gilbert, 2010, 2014).

Compassion and Heart Rate Variability

Experimental research has shown that activation of the motivational state of compassion for others and ourselves produces an increase in HRV (Di Bello et al., 2020). For example, as early as in children, a video projection of others' suffering has been found to generate a vagally mediated deceleration of heart rate (and increase in HRV), which facilitates and predisposes subsequent helping behavior (Eisenberg et al., 1989). Importantly, an increase in HRV in adults is specifically related to the emotional state of safeness and compassion, but not to positive emotions in general (Stellar et al., 2015). In this regard, an experimental study using noninvasive transcranial direct current stimulation (a technique that can modulate cortical excitability of the underlying brain areas) at the level of the insular cortex, reported a correlation between increased HRV and increased positive emotions related to calmness and soothing and not, for example, joy (Petrocchi, Piccirillo et al., 2017).

It is important to note that the element of sensitivity to suffering and care seems to be particularly related to increased HRV. For example, a very similar prosocial motivation, cooperation, is not always related to an increase in vagal tone (Sariñana-González et al., 2019). In fact, cooperating with someone does not necessarily imply sensitivity to the other's suffering and a desire to alleviate it, nor does it imply affiliation, benevolence, or interest in his or her well-being. In support of the inextricable, bidirectional link between HRV and prosocial orientation, Bornemann et al. (2016) have shown that participants who were asked to voluntarily increase HRV via the use of the biofeedback technique also reported significant increases in altruistic prosocial behaviors (e.g., helping behaviors, charitable giving, generosity, interpersonal trust), but not in non-altruistic forms of prosociality (i.e., based on norm adherence or self-focused motivations).

It is possible to observe a kind of virtuous circle in which emotional regulation (and the related feeling of safeness) and compassionate motivation reinforce each other through a feedback loop. If I am physiologically equipped with higher basal (i.e., tonic) HRV, and thus I am better able to regulate my emotions and feel safe (Lischke et al., 2019; Wendt et al., 2015), I am also more equipped and predisposed to open up to stimuli of suffering in myself and others, to resonate with them (Lischke et al., 2018, 2019), and to embark on the often difficult process of trying to alleviate that suffering (Stellar et al., 2015). However, choosing to activate compassion toward self and others will itself produce a further increase in our emotional regulation, thanks to the impact that this affiliative social motive has on our physiology but also to the sense of safeness that this motivational state generates. Thus, a virtuous upward spiral emerges, which has already been described in the literature with respect to the relationship between kindness-based practices and vagal tone (Kok et al., 2013).

This is the reason why in CFT it is crucial from the very beginning to help the patient to develop both a compassionate intention and a calming physiology since, as we have seen, these two elements reinforce each other (Gilbert, 2010). The cultivation of compassionate motivation begins with experiential psychoeducation that helps the person become familiar with the chaotic, often conflicting, but mostly unchosen nature of one's brain ("it's not our fault if we have a tricky brain"), and the inevitable nature of human pain. As mammals endowed with conscious awareness, however, we can choose how we want to confront that pain, and with what motivational set-up. We find that we can tap into the calming power of certain processes in our bodies that are under our control (e.g., breathing, posture, etc.) and access affiliative motivations, whose psychophysiological mechanisms are devised to regulate the activation of the threat system. We then initially help people discover how to activate their parasympathetic system and benefit from its capacity for psychophysiological regulation, through practices involving the body, such as "six breath per minute" breathing training or compassion-focused soothing rhythm breathing (Steffen, Bartlett et al., 2021). Other body-based practices (training of a certain body posture, tone of voice, facial expressions; see Petrocchi et al., 2022) precede and, subsequently, inform and sustain practices designed to activate compassionate motivation (visualizations and experiential techniques in which all three streams of compassion are activated; for a more detailed description of compassionate mind training, see Gilbert, 2010).

Physiological Effect of Training a Compassionate Mind

A recent randomized controlled trial showed that compassionate mind training (CMT) is able to increase participants' HRV, as well as to reduce shame, self-criticism, depression, and stress (Matos et al., 2017). The impact of compassion-focused practices on HRV has also been found in nonclinical populations, such as teachers in public settings who experienced an increase in this physiological measure after three months of CMT (Matos et al., 2022). Other studies have also shown that CMT is able to increase the HRV in clinically at-risk individuals (Kim et al., 2020).

In general, individual practices designed to increase compassionate orientation toward ourselves and others have been found to increase HRV. Petrocchi, Ottaviani et al. (2017) reported a significant increase in HRV in a group of individuals who were asked to speak compassionately to themselves in the mirror after an experimental induction of self-criticism. Notably, such increase was greater in the group exposed to the mirror than in participants who were simply asked to formulate the same compassionate sentences aloud (without using the mirror), suggesting that the affiliative intention (self-compassion) enhanced by the mirror, and not just the content of the sentences, generated the observed physiological change. In agreement with these observations, a meta-analysis found a significant positive association of medium size between compassion (both toward ourselves and others) and HRV (Hedges' g = .54; Di Bello et al., 2020). The authors of the meta-analysis pointed out that the effect of compassion practices on HRV appears to be comparable in size to that of physical exercise-based interventions (Cohen's d = .46; Sandercock et al., 2005), and of larger size than that of mindfulness-based interventions (considering the different HRV indices; Hedges' g = .02 for root mean square successive difference; Hedges' g = -.55 for standard deviation normal to normal; Hedges' g = -.21 for high-frequency HRV; Rådmark et al., 2019).

This is not surprising, if we consider that mindfulness skills, regardless of the affiliative context in which they were created, can be used in the service of different motivations, including, for example, that of achieving better performance and improving operational readiness in warfare (Blacker et al., 2018). The setting in which mindfulness was cultivated was the Sangha, i.e., the community of lay and non-secular practitioners of Buddhist teachings, which is animated by a strong spirit of affiliation and collaboration.

Indeed, explicitly enhancing compassionate motivation during mindfulness practices could also prevent some of the adverse effects of mindfulness training that some studies have found. For example, Aizik-Reebs et al. (2021) monitored eighty-two participants in a twenty-one-day mindfulness course daily, before and after the training, finding that 87 percent of the participants exhibited various states of anxiety during the training, and also that 25 percent reported adverse consequences even after the end of the training. The authors suggested that these adverse effects were mainly related to the actual increase in awareness of the internal states that the training itself generated, an observation also made in other similar studies (Goldberg et al., 2022). Thus, it seems useful to foster in patients not only a greater, nonjudgmental awareness of the present moment and a heightened consciousness of their inner states, but also a greater ability to meet this awareness with a compassionate motivation, enabling them to regulate their own physiology and alleviate the self-criticism, sense of shame, and loneliness that the contact with pain often generates in all of us.

Compassion Is Not a Benzodiazepine

To provide an exhaustive and complete picture of the examined topic, it has to be highlighted that a recent study suggested that it is simplistic to broadly link compassion with higher HRV (Di Bello et al., 2021). Compassion should not be confused with reassuring positive emotions because it does not simply produce the suppression of the threat response (and, in this sense, it is not a benzodiazepine). In order to engage in actions that alleviate our own or others' suffering, we must first have the ability to connect and resonate with pain, first experiencing a condition of empathic sensitivity. Di Bello et al. (2021) recently found that asking nonclinical volunteers to empathize with a compassionate scenario (a boy who notices the suffering of several individuals and takes actions to alleviate the suffering) initially induces an increased sensitivity to emotional pain, which is naturally associated with a reduction in HRV, and subsequently an increase in HRV when the protagonist engages in actions aimed at alleviating the suffering of others (Di Bello et al., 2021). In contrast, when participants were asked to simply empathize with the suffering (empathic resonance condition), without enacting alleviation-motivated actions, only a reduction in HRV was observed.

This seems to be the fundamental difference between compassion and empathic resonance, as also confirmed by neuroscientific studies that have shown the activation of different neural patterns in response to empathy (*I learn to empathize with your emotional state and feel your pain*) and compassion (*I tune in to your pain, contemplate the human, unchosen vulnerability that produces it in you as it potentially does in me, and generate a sincere wish for its alleviation*) training (Klimecki et al., 2014). Indeed, a twelve-week CFT intervention not only produced an increase in HRV, but also a general increase in HRV responsiveness to self-critical writing and self-compassion tasks (Steffen, Foxx et al., 2021). Such increase in physiological responsiveness suggests that compassion practices do not represent an avoidance strategy (attempting to generate a sense of safety resulting from the removal of unpleasant emotions), but a means of increasing safeness, which correlates with an increased ability to cope with, rather than avoid, difficult emotions in psychotherapy.

This observation is supported by experimental studies on the role and mechanisms of self-compassion in pain perception. Luo et al. (2020) reported that a short period of compassionate self-talk resulted in higher HRV during a pain induction protocol, which was associated with lower pain ratings. The authors suggested that decreased experimental pain was not caused by a dissociation from the pain but by increased bodily control over pain-related arousal, as indicated by higher HRV. This concept is crucial because it further helps to understand the different mechanisms behind the effectiveness of two connected and apparently similar trainings, mindfulness-based and compassion-based training. In a study by Desbordes et al. (2012), healthy adults with no prior meditation experience took part in eight weeks of either mindfulness-based, compassion-based, or active control interventions, and underwent an fMRI assessment during which they were presented with images having positive, negative, and neutral emotional valences. The authors found a longitudinal decrease in right amygdala activation in the mindful group in response to positive images, and in response to images of all valences overall, suggesting that the benefits of this training might be primarily linked to an increased ability to defuse and be less triggered by emotional stimuli. On the other hand, in the compassion group, a trend towards increased right amygdala response to negative images was found, which was significantly correlated with a decrease in depression score (Desbordes et al., 2012). The compassion training increased participants' ability to connect and resonate with pain. Moreover, it was exactly this increased capacity to open up to and resonate with painful stimuli with courage as well as helping intention that correlated with the psychological benefits (i.e., reduced depression) of the training (Desbordes et al., 2012).

Cultivating Compassionate Intention to Enhance Other Therapeutic Approaches

HRV levels reflect an organism's ability to self-regulate and respond flexibly to changing and challenging environments, one being precisely the therapeutic path. Starting and continuing psychotherapy, which usually demands patients to expose themselves to the feared emotions and situations, requires self-regulation abilities.

Patients with a lower resting vagal tone (i.e., low tonic HRV) at the beginning of treatment, and thus with a lower capacity for self-regulation, may have more pronounced difficulties in entering and/or staying in psychotherapy (F. Thayer, 2018). In fact, a significant association between pre-treatment vagal tone, and treatment dropout and residual symptoms after exposure therapy has been reported in a sample of 228 patients treated for panic disorder and agoraphobia (Wendt et al., 2018). Importantly, in this study, patients with residual symptoms or those who dropped out of treatment were characterized by lower pre-treatment HRV levels than the group undergoing full recovery, despite the fact that the two groups did not differ in symptom severity at the beginning of treatment. Similarly, baseline (tonic) HRV predicted psychotherapy outcomes in disorders such as social anxiety and depression, even when treated with antidepressant medications (F. Thayer, 2018; Petrocchi & Cheli, 2019). Indeed, given the strong influence of HRV on psychological functioning and flexibility, lower pre-treatment levels of HRV could compromise the effectiveness of some therapeutic procedures. Not surprisingly, HRV is considered a primary outcome in research exploring the effectiveness of compassion-focused interventions (Kirby & Gilbert, 2017). Because of this, assessment of tonic HRV levels before treatment should ideally become a common practice in clinical settings.

A reduced tonic vagal tone may also indicate the need for compassion-focused work aimed at regulating parasympathetic system modulation (e.g., using calming breath or approaching one's self-criticism with compassion) as a booster of other techniques employed in therapy. Indeed, this is precisely the origin of the term CFT rather than compassion therapy. Far from trying to become yet another psychotherapeutic approach and toolbox of techniques available "on the market," at the heart of CFT is the intent to make therapists aware of the impact that inter- and intra-personal motivation, activated moment by moment in the patient, regardless of whatever practice or therapeutic intervention is being implemented, has on the effectiveness of the intervention itself.

Any technique used in therapy, whether cognitive-behavioral or based on meditative approaches, can be short-circuited by a patient's excessive self-criticism (thus, by an attitude that keeps HRV chronically low). Indeed, an invalidating, self-critical attitude has been shown to "impermeabilize" the patient with respect to all procedures the therapist will employ, including the formation of a good therapeutic alliance (Blatt et al., 2010). For this reason, it has been suggested that techniques focused on increasing compassion toward oneself and others should be considered as a specific training that not only can be paired with any form of psychotherapy, but whose principles can inform the practices that the therapist already implements, making them "compassion-focused" and thus facilitating the sympatho-vagal balance that the compassionate attitude seems to produce. Due to the particular impact they have on our physiology, compassion-focused practices can also be an effective booster to HRV biofeedback interventions that rely on a specific modulation of respiratory rhythm that has an immediate impact on HRV (Lehrer & Gevirtz, 2014). Although further experimental studies are needed, Ehrenreich (2020) suggests that adding an affiliative motivational element to standard biofeedback procedures may increase the effectiveness of such interventions.

Compassion in Dyadic Exchanges

Mindfulness, that is the ability to return to the present in a nonjudgmental way (Kabat-Zinn, 2013), has long been recognized as one of the most powerful ingredients for facilitating a dyadic exchange, both when it occurs between members of a romantic couple (Winter et al., 2021) and when it occurs within the therapist–patient relationship (Germer et al., 2016). The empathy and compassion shown by members of the interaction seem to play a role in the effectiveness of these dyadic exchanges, precisely due to the regulating effect that these affiliative attitudes have on our physiology. Indeed, we now know that the type of relationship the therapist has with him/herself (critical and disqualifying, or compassionate and encouraging), influences moment by moment the relationship with the patient, and the type of relationship the patient has with him/herself (inner dialogue) (Gale et al., 2017). When therapists are able to experience compassion toward themselves during a difficult interaction (a stall in the therapeutic process, or a strong dysregulation in the patient), they will be better able to regulate their own physiology: this will offer the patient not only a more solid "container" for the difficult contents, but also an implicit model of self-regulation that they will progressively incorporate (Gilbert, 2007).

Indeed, it is well known that when people engage in positive social interactions, they not only tend to synchronize their gestures, vocal tone, posture, rhythm of speech, and length of pauses (Hatfield, 1994), but also other important aspects of their physiology, such as heart rate (e.g., Ogolsky et al., 2022). For example, it has been shown that during face-to-face interactions, mother and child unconsciously adapt their heart rhythms, resulting in a biological synchronization that can predict the capacity for self-control exhibited by the child at later moments in their development (Feldman et al., 2011). These episodes of micro-synchronization play an important role in the development of the child's emotional security and, in particular, in the ability to reduce emotional distress, even when caregivers are physically absent (Feldman, 2015). The link between interpersonal physiological synchronization during compassionate interactions and emotion regulation remains crucial in adulthood and is one of the possible explanations for the effectiveness that therapeutic alliance has shown in promoting the desired change across different therapeutic approaches.

Given that our minds have evolved to co-regulate each other (Dunbar, 2016), a therapeutic relationship characterized by compassionate interactions is a basic active therapeutic agent that helps the patient acquire greater emotion regulation. For example, Kiema et al. (2014) examined the change in HRV of ten clients during a counseling session and found a significant association with the level of compassionate support skills exhibited by the counselors. A counselor who is particularly skilled at showing compassion increases the client's parasympathetic activity, reducing his/her distress levels, without inducing emotional numbing. In fact, the same study also showed that clients were better able to contact and express their emotions during sessions characterized by both higher levels of compassionate support skills in the therapist and increased changes in HRV (Kiema et al., 2014). The compassionate attitude in the therapist, and the one promoted in the patient through specific practices, could facilitate the difficult process of self-awareness and self-disclosure that characterizes the most effective therapeutic sessions.

At the heart of compassion is indeed an awareness of the shared experience of suffering of all humanity; in a compassionate approach, the patient is constantly reminded that it is not "his or her fault" if the brain generates such painful content and processes, and that at that same moment many other human beings are dealing with the same pain. The "depersonalization" of pain that compassion promotes ("this is not only my pain, but it is potentially the pain of all human creatures on earth") is what makes compassion a powerful antidote against the shame and loneliness that we often experience in states of suffering, and which tend to exacerbate emotional pain and render it chronic (Matos et al., 2017).

The following case narrative illustrates the therapeutic process of re-engaging with a blocked self-compassion, and the emotional benefit to the individual of doing so.

Case Narrative: Julia Julia, with bipolar disorder and two major depressive episodes that had led to her hospitalization, was terrified of making compassionate contact with her sad part. She didn't want to experience or assist that part of herself; she didn't want to go "back there" anymore. She hated the bedridden version of herself, paralyzed by emptiness and despair. That part disgusted her, and she preferred to reach out as much as possible and entrench herself in her hyper-active Julia. Yet, she knew that scotomizing[1] that sad part of herself had in the past been one of the central ingredients of her depressive relapses. How could she manage to approach that part again without feeling overwhelmed?

It helped her during one session to imagine, at the therapist's suggestion, that slowly approaching the sad part of herself would help not only her but so many others—all the people who were in a therapist's office, terrified of "opening that door." She was not alone in that process, and she could imagine that she was connected by an invisible thread to all those who, at the very same moment, were struggling to do the same. She could feel their presence, their fear, their desire to get better, and she could send wishes to all of them, including herself and the therapist, that they could have the courage and compassion they needed to take that step. This thought calmed her, made her feel stronger, and less alone in that shared vulnerability. She was now able to open up to the many unheard messages the sad part of herself had for her.

---

[1] To *scotomize* is to mentally block an unwanted perception, analogous to a visual scotoma or blind spot.

The regulating effect of this ingredient of compassion (common humanity) appears to be related to an increase in HRV, as suggested by the previously mentioned study on the repetition of compassionate sentences in front of the mirror by Petrocchi, Ottaviani, et al. (2017). In fact, the increase in HRV in those who repeated compassionate phrases in the mirror was partially explained by an increase in "common humanity" that looking at the reflection of one's own face seemed to have facilitated.

Conclusion

This chapter explored the main elements that constitute the physiological concomitants and consequences of compassion, described as a motivational system resulting from the evolution of the caring system. It described the effect that activation of compassionate motivation, both toward self and others, has on our parasympathetic nervous system, promoting emotional regulation and feelings of intra- and inter-personal safeness. In fact, safeness, in mammals and particularly in humans, is strongly related to prosocial motivations, such as compassion, and to the inhibitory function of the prefrontal cortex. To conclude, if mindfulness promotes nonjudgmental contact with the present moment, compassion supports and encourages us to meet as well as welcome with courage and care whatever manifests pain and vulnerability in that present moment.

References

Aizik-Reebs, A., Shoham, A., & Bernstein, A. (2021). First, do no harm: An intensive experience sampling study of adverse effects to mindfulness training. *Behaviour Research and Therapy, 145*, Article 103941. https://doi.org/10.1016/j.brat.2021.103941

Blacker, K. J., Hamilton, J., Roush, G., Pettijohn, K. A., & Biggs, A. T. (2018). Cognitive training for military application: A review of the literature and practical guide. *Journal of Cognitive Enhancement, 3*(1), 30–51. https://doi.org/10.1007/s41465-018-0076-1

Blatt, S., Zuroff, D., Hawley, L., & Auerbach, J. (2010). Predictors of sustained therapeutic change. *Psychotherapy Research, 20*(1), 37–54. https://doi.org/10.1080/10503300903121080

Bornemann, B., Kok, B. E., Böckler, A., & Singer, T. (2016). Helping from the heart: Voluntary upregulation of heart rate variability predicts altruistic behavior. *Biological Psychology, 119*, 54–63. https://doi.org/10.1016/j.biopsycho.2016.07.004

Brosschot, J. F., Verkuil, B., & Thayer, J. F. (2017). Exposed to events that never happen: Generalized unsafety, the default stress response, and prolonged autonomic activity. *Neuroscience and Biobehavioral Reviews, 74*(Pt B), 287–296. https://doi.org/10.1016/j.neubiorev.2016.07.019

Brosschot, J. F., Verkuil, B., & Thayer, J. F. (2018). Generalized Unsafety Theory of Stress: Unsafe environments and conditions, and the default stress response. *International Journal of Environmental Research and Public Health, 15*(3), Article 464. https://doi.org/10.3390/ijerph15030464

Coan, J. A., & Sbarra, D. A. (2015). Social Baseline Theory: The social regulation of risk and effort. *Current Opinion in Psychology, 1*, 87–91. https://doi.org/10.1016/j.copsyc.2014.12.021

Colonnello, V., Petrocchi, N., Farinelli, M., & Ottaviani, C. (2017). Positive social interactions in a lifespan perspective with a focus on opioidergic and oxytocinergic systems: Implications for neuroprotection. *Current Neuropharmacology, 15*(4), 543–561. https://doi.org/10.2174/1570159X14666160816120209

Dale, L. P., Shaikh, S. K., Fasciano, L. C., Watorek, V. D., Heilman, K. J., & Porges, S. W. (2018). College females with maltreatment histories have atypical autonomic regulation and poor psychological wellbeing. *Psychological Trauma: Theory, Research, Practice, and Policy, 10*(4), 427–434. https://doi.org/10.1037/tra0000342

Darwin, C. (1859). *On the origin of species by means of natural selection, or, The preservation of favoured races in the struggle for life*. John Murray.

Delgado, M. R., Nearing, K. I., Ledoux, J. E., & Phelps, E. A. (2008). Neural circuitry underlying the regulation of conditioned fear and its relation to extinction. *Neuron, 59*(5), 829–838. https://doi.org/10.1016/j.neuron.2008.06.029

Depue, R. A., & Morrone-Strupinsky, J. V. (2005). A neurobehavioral model of affiliative bonding: Implications for conceptualizing a human trait of affiliation. *Behavioral and Brain Sciences, 28*(3), 313–395. https://doi.org/10.1017/s0140525x05000063

Desbordes, G., Negi, L. T., Pace, T. W. W., Wallace, B. A., Raison, C. L., & Schwartz, E. L. (2012). Effects of mindful-attention and compassion meditation training on amygdala response to emotional stimuli in an ordinary, non-meditative state. *Frontiers in Human Neuroscience, 6*, Article 292. https://doi.org/10.3389/fnhum.2012.00292

DeSilva, J. M., Traniello, J. F. A., Claxton, A. G., & Fannin, L. D. (2021). When and why did human brains decrease in size? A new change-point analysis and insights from brain evolution in ants. *Frontiers in Ecology and Evolution, 9*, Article 742639. https://doi.org/10.3389/fevo.2021.742639

Di Bello, M., Carnevali, L., Petrocchi, N., Thayer, J. F., Gilbert, P., & Ottaviani, C. (2020). The compassionate vagus: A meta-analysis on the connection between compassion and heart rate variability. *Neuroscience and Biobehavioral Reviews, 116*, 21–30. https://doi.org/10.1016/j.neubiorev.2020.06.00016

Di Bello, M., Ottaviani, C., & Petrocchi, N. (2021). Compassion is not a benzo: Distinctive associations of heart rate variability with its empathic and action components. *Frontiers in Neuroscience, 15*, Article 617443. https://doi.org/10.3389/fnins.2021.617443

Dunbar, R. I. (2016). The social brain hypothesis and human evolution. *Oxford Research Encyclopedia of Psychology*. https://doi.org/10.1093/acrefore/9780190236557.013.44

Ehrenreich, Y. (2020). A happy heart comes first: Heart-based compassion training. *Biofeedback, 48*(4), 73–80. https://doi.org/10.5298/1081-5937-48.4.3

Eisenberg, N., Fabes, R. A., Miller, P. A., Fultz, J., & Al, E. (1989). Relation of sympathy and personal distress to prosocial behavior: A multimethod study. *Journal of Personality and Social Psychology, 57*(1), 55–66. https://doi.org/10.1037//0022-3514.57.1.55

Feldman, R. (2015). Mutual influences between child emotion regulation and parent–child reciprocity support development across the first 10 years of life: Implications for developmental psychopathology. *Development and Psychopathology, 27*(4pt1), 1007–1023. https://doi.org/10.1017/s0954579415000656

Feldman, R., Magori-Cohen, R., Galili, G., Singer, M., & Louzoun, Y. (2011). Mother and infant coordinate heart rhythms through episodes of interaction synchrony. *Infant Behavior and Development, 34*(4), 569–577. https://doi.org/10.1016/j.infbeh.2011.06.008

Gale, C., Schröder, T., & Gilbert, P. (2017). "Do you practice what you preach?" A qualitative exploration of therapists' personal practice of compassion focused therapy. *Clinical Psychology & Psychotherapy, 24*(1), 171–185. https://doi-org.jerome.stjohns.edu/10.1002/cpp.1993

Germer, C. K., Siegel, R. D., & Fulton, P. R. (2016). *Mindfulness and psychotherapy* (2nd ed.). Guilford Press.

Gilbert, P. (1989). *Human nature and suffering*. Lawrence Erlbaum Associates.

Gilbert, P. (1993). Defence and safety: Their function in social behaviour and psychopathology. *British Journal of Clinical Psychology, 32*(2), 131–153. https://doi.org/10.1111/j.2044-8260.1993.tb01039.x

Gilbert, P. (2007). Evolved minds and compassion in the therapeutic relationship. In P. Gilbert & R. L. Leahy (Eds.), *The therapeutic relationship in the cognitive behavioral psychotherapies* (pp. 106–142). Routledge/Taylor & Francis Group.

Gilbert, P. (2010). *Compassion focused therapy: Distinctive features*. Routledge/Taylor & Francis Group.

Gilbert, P. (2014). The origins and nature of compassion focused therapy. *British Journal of Clinical Psychology, 53*(1), 6–41. https://doi.org/10.1111/bjc.12043

Gilbert, P. (2015). The evolution and social dynamics of compassion. *Social and Personality Psychology Compass, 9*(6), 239–254. https://doi.org/10.1111/spc3.12176

Gilbert, P. (2017). Compassion as a social mentality: An evolutionary approach. In P. Gilbert (Ed.), *Compassion: Concepts, research and applications* (pp. 31–68). Routledge.

Gilbert, P. (2022). The evolved functions of caring connections as a basis for compassion. In P. Gilbert & G. Simos (Eds.), *Compassion focused therapy: Clinical practice and applications* (pp. 31–68). Routledge.

Goldberg, S. B., Lam, S. U., Britton, W. B., & Davidson, R. J. (2022). Prevalence of meditation-related adverse effects in a population-based sample in the United States. *Psychotherapy Research: Journal of the Society for Psychotherapy Research, 32*(3), 291–305. https://doi.org/10.1080/10503307.2021.1933646

Hansen, A., Johnsen, B., & Thayer, J. F. (2009). Relationship between heart rate variability and cognitive function during threat of shock. *Anxiety, Stress, and Coping, 22*(1), 77–89. https://doi.org/10.1080/10615800802272510

Hatfield, E. (1994). *Emotional contagion*. Cambridge University Press.

Hermanto, N., & Zuroff, D. (2016). The social mentality theory of self-compassion and self-reassurance: The interactive effect of care-seeking and caregiving. *The Journal of Social Psychology, 156*(5), 523–535. https://doi.org/10.1080/00224545.2015.1135779

Jose, A. D., & Collison, D. (1970). The normal range and determinants of the intrinsic heart rate in man. *Cardiovascular Research, 4*(2), 160–167. https://doi.org/10.1093/cvr/4.2.160

Kabat-Zinn, J. (2013). *Full catastrophe living: Using the wisdom of your body and mind to face stress, pain, and illness*. Bantam Dell.

Kiema, H., Rantanen, A., Laukka, S., Siipo, A., & Soini, H. (2014). The connection between skilled counseling and client's heart rate variability. *Procedia - Social and Behavioral Sciences, 159*, 802–807. https://doi.org/10.1016/j.sbspro.2014.12.452

Kim, J. J., Parker, S. L., Doty, J. R., Cunnington, R., Gilbert, P., & Kirby, J. N. (2020). Neurophysiological and behavioural markers of compassion. *Scientific Reports, 10*(1), Article 6789. https://doi.org/10.1038/s41598-020-63846-3

Kirby, J., & Gilbert, P. (2017). The emergence of the compassion focused therapies. In P. Gilbert (Ed.), *Compassion: Concepts, research, and applications* (pp. 258–285). Routledge.

Klimecki, O. M., Leiberg, S., Ricard, M., & Singer, T. (2014). Differential pattern of functional brain plasticity after compassion and empathy training. *Social Cognitive and Affective Neuroscience, 9*(6), 873–879. https://doi.org/10.1093/scan/nst060

Kok, B. E., Coffey, K. A., Cohn, M. A., Catalino, L. I., Vacharkulksemsuk, T., Algoe, S. B., Brantley, M., & Fredrickson, B. L. (2013). How positive emotions build physical health: Perceived positive social connections account for the upward spiral between positive emotions and vagal tone. *Psychological Science, 24*(7), 1123–1132. https://doi.org/10.1177/0956797612470827

Kuo, T. B. J., Lai, C. J., Huang, Y.-T., & Yang, C. C. H. (2005). Regression analysis between heart rate variability and baroreflex-related vagus nerve activity in rats. *Journal of Cardiovascular Electrophysiology, 16*(8), 864–869. https://doi.org/10.1111/j.1540-8167.2005.40656.x

Lehrer, P. M., & Gevirtz, R. (2014). Heart rate variability biofeedback: How and why does it work? *Frontiers in Psychology, 5*, Article 756. https://doi.org/10.3389/fpsyg.2014.00756

Lischke, A., Pahnke, R., Mau-Moeller, A., Behrens, M., Grabe, H., Freyberger, H., Hamm, A. O., & Weippert, M. (2018). Inter-individual differences in heart rate variability are associated with inter-individual differences in empathy and alexithymia. *Frontiers in Psychology, 9*, Article 229. https://doi.org/10.3389/fpsyg.2018.00229

Lischke, A., Weippert, M., Mau-Moeller, A., Päschke, S., Jacksteit, R., Hamm, A. O., & Pahnke, R. (2019). Sex-specific associations between inter-individual differences in heart rate variability and inter-individual differences in emotion regulation. *Frontiers in Neuroscience, 12*, Article 1040. https://doi.org/10.3389/fnins.2018.01040

Longe, O., Maratos, F. A., Gilbert, P., Evans, G., Volker, F., Rockliff, H., & Rippon, G. (2010). Having a word with yourself: Neural correlates of self-criticism and self-reassurance. *NeuroImage, 49*(2), 1849–1856. https://doi.org/10.1016/j.neuroimage.2009.09.019

Luo, X., Liu, J., & Che, X. (2020). Investigating the influence and a potential mechanism of self-compassion on experimental pain: Evidence from a compassionate self-talk protocol and heart rate variability. *The Journal of Pain, 21*(7–8), 790–797. https://doi.org/10.1016/j.jpain.2019.11.006

Makovac, E., Watson, D. R., Meeten, F., Garfinkel, S. N., Cercignani, M., Critchley, H. D., & Ottaviani, C. (2016). Amygdala functional connectivity as a longitudinal biomarker of symptom changes in generalized anxiety. *Social Cognitive and Affective Neuroscience, 11*(11), 1719–1728. https://doi.org/10.1093/scan/nsw091

Mather, M., & Thayer, J. F. (2018). How heart rate variability affects emotion regulation brain networks. *Current Opinion in Behavioral Sciences, 19*, 98–104. https://doi.org/10.1016/j.cobeha.2017.12.017

Matos, M., Albuquerque, I., Galhardo, A., Cunha, M., Pedroso Lima, M., Palmeira, L., Petrocchi, N., McEwan, K., Maratos, F. A., & Gilbert, P. (2022). Nurturing compassion in schools: A randomized controlled trial of the effectiveness of a Compassionate Mind Training program for teachers. *PLoS One, 17*(3), Article e0263480. https://doi.org/10.1371/journal.pone.0263480

Matos, M., Duarte, J., & Pinto-Gouveia, J. (2017). The origins of fears of compassion: Shame and lack of safeness memories, fears of compassion and psychopathology. *Journal of Psychology, 151*(8), 804–819. https://doi.org/10.1080/00223980.2017.1393380

Mayseless, O. (2016). *The caring motivation: An integrated theory*. Oxford University Press.

Meessen, J., Sütterlin, S., Gauggel, S., & Forkmann, T. (2018). Learning by heart—The relationship between resting vagal tone and metacognitive judgments: A pilot study. *Cognitive Processing, 19*, 557–561. https://doi.org/10.1007/s10339-018-0865-6

Nesse, R. M. (2005). Natural selection and the regulation of defenses. *Evolution and Human Behavior, 26*(1), 88–105. https://doi.org/10.1016/j.evolhumbehav.2004.08.002

Ogolsky, B. G., Mejia, S. T., Chronopoulou, A., Dobson, K., Maniotes, C. R., Rice, T. M., Hu, Y., Theisen, J. C., & Carvalho Manhães Leite, C. (2022). Spatial proximity as a behavioral marker of relationship dynamics in older adult couples. *Journal of Social and Personal Relationships, 39*(10), 3116–3132. https://doi.org/10.1177/02654075211050073

Opthof, T. (2000). The normal range and determinants of the intrinsic heart rate in man. *Cardiovascular Research, 45*(1), 177–184. https://doi.org/10.1016/S0008-6363(99)00322-3

Ottaviani, C., Zingaretti, P., Petta, A. M., Antonucci, G., Thayer, J. F., & Spitoni, G. F. (2018). Resting heart rate variability predicts inhibitory control above and beyond impulsivity. *Journal of Psychophysiology, 33*(3), 198–206. https://doi.org/10.1027/0269-8803/a000222

Panksepp, J. (1998). *Affective neuroscience: The foundations of human and animal emotions*. Oxford University Press.

Petrocchi, N., & Cheli, S. (2019). The social brain and heart rate variability: Implications for psychotherapy. *Psychology and Psychotherapy: Theory, Research, and Practice, 92*(2), 208–223. https://doi.org/10.1111/papt.12224

Petrocchi, N., Cheli, S., Di Bello, M., & Ottaviani, C. (2022). Compassion focused therapy and the body: How physiological underpinnings of prosociality inform clinical practice. In P. Gilbert and G. Simos (Eds.), *Compassion focused therapy: Clinical practice and applications* (pp. 345–359). Routledge.

Petrocchi, N., & Couyoumdjian, A. (2016). The impact of gratitude on depression and anxiety: The mediating role of criticizing, attacking, and reassuring the self. *Self and Identity, 15*(2), 191–205. https://doi.org/10.1080/15298868.2015.1095794

Petrocchi, N., Ottaviani, C., & Couyoumdjian, A. (2017). Compassion at the mirror: Exposure to a mirror increases the efficacy of a self-compassion manipulation in enhancing soothing positive affect and heart rate variability. *The Journal of Positive Psychology, 12*(6), 525–536. https://doi.org/10.1080/17439760.2016.1209544

Petrocchi, N., Piccirillo, G., Fiorucci, C., Moscucci, F., Di Iorio, C., Mastropietri, F., Parrotta, I., Pascucci, M., Magrì, D., & Ottaviani, C. (2017). Transcranial direct current stimulation enhances soothing positive affect and vagal tone. *Neuropsychologia, 96*, 256–261. https://doi.org/10.1016/j.neuropsychologia.2017.01.028

Porges, S. W. (2007). The polyvagal perspective. *Biological Psychology, 74*(2), 116–143. https://doi.org/10.1016/j.biopsycho.2006.06.009

Porges, S. W., & Furman, S. A. (2010). The early development of the autonomic nervous system provides a neural platform for social behaviour: A polyvagal perspective. *Infant and Child Development*, *20*(1), 106–118. https://doi.org/10.1002/icd.688

Rådmark, L., Sidorchuk, A., Osika, W., & Niemi, M. (2019). A systematic review and meta-analysis of the impact of mindfulness-based interventions on heart rate variability and inflammatory markers. *Journal of Clinical Medicine*, *8*(10), Article 1638. https://doi.org/10.3390/jcm8101638

Sandercock, G. R., Bromley, P. D., & Brodie, D. A. (2005). Effects of exercise on heart rate variability: Inferences from meta-analysis. *Medicine and Science in Sports and Exercise*, *37*(3), 433–439. https://doi.10.1249/01.mss.0000155388.39002.9d

Sariñana-González, P., Romero-Martínez, Á., & Moya-Albiol, L. (2019). Cooperation between strangers in face-to-face dyads produces more cardiovascular activation than competition or working alone. *Journal of Psychophysiology*, *33*(2), 1–11. https://doi.org/10.1027/0269-8803/a000210

Steffen, P. R., Foxx, J., Cattani, K., Alldredge, C., Austin, T., & Burlingame, G. M. (2021). Impact of a 12-week group-based compassion focused therapy intervention on heart rate variability. *Applied Psychophysiology and Biofeedback*, *46*(1), 61–68. https://doi.org/10.1007/s10484-020-09487-8

Steffen, P. R., Bartlett, D., Channell, R. M., Jackman, K., Cressman, M., Bills, J., & Pescatello, M. (2021). Integrating breathing techniques into psychotherapy to improve HRV: Which approach is best? *Frontiers in Psychology*, *12*, Article 624254. https://doi.org/10.3389/fpsyg.2021.624254

Stellar, J. E., Cohen, A., Oveis, C., & Keltner, D. (2015). Affective and physiological responses to the suffering of others: Compassion and vagal activity. *Journal of Personality and Social Psychology*, *108*(4), 572–585. https://doi.org/10.1037/pspi0000010

Thayer, F. (2018). Heart rate variability predicts therapy outcome in anxiety disorders. *International Journal of Psychophysiology*, *131*(Supplement), S45. https://doi.org/10.1016/j.ijpsycho.2018.07.137

Thayer, J. F., Åhs, F., Fredrikson, M., Sollers, III, J. J., & Wager, T. D. (2012). A meta-analysis of heart rate variability and neuroimaging studies: Implications for heart rate variability as a marker of stress and health. *Neuroscience and Biobehavioral Reviews*, *36*(2), 747–756. https://doi.org/10.1016/j.neubiorev.2011.11.009

Thayer, J. F., & Lane, R. D. (2000). A model of neurovisceral integration in emotion regulation and dysregulation. *Journal of Affective Disorders*, *61*(3), 201–216. https://doi.org/10.1016/s0165-0327(00)00338-4

Thayer, J. F., & Lane, R. D. (2009). Claude Bernard and the heart-brain connection: Further elaboration of a model of neurovisceral integration. *Neuroscience and Biobehavioral Review*, *33*(2), 81–88. https://doi.org/10.1016/j.neubiorev.2008.08.004

Wang, S. (2005). A conceptual framework for integrating research related to the physiology of compassion and the wisdom of Buddhist teachings. In P. Gilbert (Ed.), *Compassion: Conceptualisations, research, and use in psychotherapy* (pp. 75–120). Routledge.

Wendt, J., Hamm, A. O., Pané-Farré, C. A., Thayer, J. F., Gerlach, A., Gloster, A. T., Lang, T., Helbig-Lang, S., Pauli, P., Fydrich, T., Ströhle, A., Kircher, T., Arolt, V., Deckert, J., Wittchen, H.-U., & Richter, J. (2018). Pretreatment cardiac vagal tone predicts dropout from and residual symptoms after exposure therapy in patients with panic disorder and agoraphobia. *Psychotherapy and Psychosomatics*, *87*(3), 187–189. https://doi.org/10.1159/000487599

Wendt, J., Neubert, J., Koenig, J., Thayer, J. F., & Hamm, A. O. (2015). Resting heart rate variability is associated with inhibition of conditioned fear. *Psychophysiology*, *52*(9), 1161–1166. https://doi.org/10.1111/psyp.12456

Winter, F., Steffan, A., Warth, M., Ditzen, B., & Aguilar-Raab, C. (2021). Mindfulness-based couple interventions: A systematic literature review. *Family Process*, *60*(3), 694–711. https://doi.org/10.1111/famp.12683

17
Compassion Focused Therapy and Heart Rate Variability

Chase S. Sherwell and James N. Kirby

The field of psychotherapy has long relied on self-report scales, client feedback, visual analogue scales, and behavioral indices to understand complex clinical phenomenon. Over the last twenty years, advances in neurophysiological approaches and measurements have spurred greater interest in how neural and physiological indicators can further enhance our understanding of clinical presentations (Förster & Kanske, 2021). The psychotherapy literature has also increasingly recognized the importance of understanding how physiology can impact threat processing and mood (Porges, 2007; Thayer & Lane, 2009). One therapy that adopts an integrative, evolutionary, contextual biopsychological approach is compassion focused therapy (CFT). Developed by Gilbert (2014), CFT primarily targets the self-criticism and shame that underpins many clinical disorders. One of the unique aspects of CFT is its emphasis on targeting physiology as a key factor in the therapeutic journey. Our work at the Compassionate Mind Research Group at the University of Queensland has been examining the links between compassion and physiology, along with examining the efficacy of CFT approaches to improve physiology. In this chapter we will discuss (a) conceptualizing compassion, (b) the physiological basis of compassion, (c) the links between compassion and heart rate variability (HRV), (d) current evidence on the efficacy of CFT in improving HRV, and (e) future research considerations for CFT and HRV.

Conceptualizing Compassion

Prosocial intentions and behavior are key to developing and maintaining positive interpersonal relationships (Reis et al., 2017). The underlying motives that lead to helpful actions towards others can vary in terms of how (e.g., what kind of action) and why (e.g., compassion or competitive self-interest), and are subject to both our internal states and traits (e.g., empathy), as well as external (e.g., time) and contextual (e.g., type of suffering) factors. The term compassion is often colloquially used to refer to any helpful act, blurring the lines between compassion and other helping behaviors such as kindness. And yet, individuals can readily and intuitively distinguish between acts that are kind and acts that are compassionate in nature (Gilbert et al., 2019). The defining feature of compassion is a sensitivity to suffering, with the intention to alleviate or prevent it (Gilbert, 2014). The underlying motive of compassion relies on the perceived or predicted presence of suffering, either in oneself or in others. This is in contrast to kindness, where the motive is to increase feelings of joy or happiness. Both kindness and compassionate acts incur some kind of personal cost. For example, offering to pay for a colleague's lunch may be an act of kindness in the absence of any necessity, whereas the same act would have a compassionate motive if said colleague could not afford lunch.

Albeit a subtle distinction, the underlying motives behind prosocial intent and actions interact with various internal and contextual factors that affect behavior. Our recent work has shown that, perhaps unsurprisingly, individuals report greater willingness to perform kind acts for people they like compared to people they dislike (Kirby et al., 2022). While our sample also showed a decrease in willingness to perform compassionate acts for disliked targets, the decrease in willingness was significantly less than what is seen for kind acts. It appears that compassionate motives are somewhat protected from likeability biases in our decisions to act. This illustrates that compassion is a distinct motivation, likely originating from unique evolutionary origins with distinct regulatory processes.

Through an evolutionary lens, compassion is rooted in mammalian caregiving. Evolutionary approaches argue that compassion evolved from caring behavior expressed in mammalian *K*-selected reproductive parental investment strategies (Kirby et al., 2017; Petrocchi & Cheli, 2019). Species with *K*-selected reproductive strategies typically have live birth, small numbers of young, and heavy parental investment post-birth (e.g., elephants, chimpanzees, humans) and are highly attuned to signals of distress from their young, form attachment bonds, and provide important sources of growth and physiological regulation for the infant (Mayseless, 2016). On the other hand, species with *r*-selected reproductive strategies, such as turtles and other egg-laying reptiles, typically have large numbers of young, are mobile and independent at birth and have rapid dispersal to avoid predation, and do not require parental investment for safety and attachment bonds (Mayseless, 2016). Compassion is believed to be an extension of the *K*-selected reproductive strategy, where the parental sensitivity to suffering of offspring is extended to other kinship members. Indeed, compassionate motives can extend the sensitivity of suffering to wider familiar and social circles, strangers, non-human animals, fictional characters, and critically, inwards to oneself (Gilbert, 2020). This evolved parental investment strategy has implications for the physiological infrastructure of mammals and humans, when dealing with aspects related to threat, safety, and safeness, which is critical for understanding compassion (Kirby et al., 2017).

Compassion can be further conceptualized into three main orientations depending on the agent and the target of compassion: compassion directed towards others, compassion directed towards the self (self-compassion), and receiving compassion from others. In all cases, compassion can be viewed as a *motivation*, which includes a signal detection to suffering, and a signal response to alleviate that suffering. Indeed, compassionate *intent* or feelings of compassion do not always necessarily result in compassionate action, and this can be one of the goals of CFT and compassionate mind training (CMT). In addition, CFT and CMT will not only aim to develop compassionate skills, but also to help facilitate the underlying compassionate motivation and reduce fears, blocks, and resistances (i.e., barriers) to translating compassionate intent into action.

The Physiological Basis of Compassion

The development of compassionate motives is thought to have been facilitated by the evolution of a range of physiological processes including the hormone interplay of oxytocin and vasopressin, and myelination of the tenth cranial nerve—the vagus nerve (Porges, 2007). As the largest nerve in the human parasympathetic nervous system (PNS), the vagus nerve innervates most organs in the body via efferent motor fibers (Brodal, 2010). In conjunction with afferent sensory fibers, the vagus nerve provides a direct circuit between the central and peripheral nervous systems enabling rapid adaptive physiological responses to physical and psychological stressors. Of particular interest to psychophysiology is the inhibitory control exerted by the vagus nerve over heart rate (Saul, 1990). Often broadly referred to as vagal tone, the regulatory influence of the vagus nerve on cardiac functioning, or cardiac vagal control (CVC), reflects adaptive regulation of autonomic arousal in response to current situational demands (Laborde et al., 2018). CVC can be estimated unobtrusively by quantifying HRV—the variation in timing of successive heart beats. While HRV has been used to examine the interplay between sympathetic and parasympathetic influences, several HRV parameters are thought to reflect vagal tone (and parasympathetic activity more broadly): the root mean square of successive differences between successive interbeat intervals,[1] the percentage of successive interbeat intervals that differ by more than 50ms (pNN50), and power in the high frequency range (0.15–0.4Hz), termed HF-HRV. Although there is no consensus on the ideal index of vagal tone (see Berntson et al., 2007; and J. J. B. Allen et al., 2007, for detailed discussions), collectively these metrics are typically referred to as vagally mediated HRV (vmHRV).

Vagal tone, or tonic CVC, is typically indexed via calculation of vmHRV at rest. Taken from a single point in time, measures of tonic vmHRV are typically used as an estimate of trait CVC (Di Bello et al., 2021). Several prominent neurophysiological models describe the reciprocal communication between the brain and heart that produces both psychological effects on autonomic function and physiological effects

---

[1] The interbeat interval is the distance in time between successive heartbeats, usually between successive R-waves, measured in milliseconds.

on psychological and behavioral processes (Laborde et al., 2017). Such frameworks also provide proposed mechanisms by which tonic CVC is predictive of psychological and behavioral outcomes. Polyvagal theory (Porges, 2007) posits that CVC enables prosocial behavior by regulating relevant physiological states, with higher CVC associated with improved social capacities. Supporting this view, higher vmHRV (indicating greater vagal tone) is associated with greater trait self-compassion (Svendsen et al., 2016) and reported social connectivity (Kok & Fredrickson, 2010). The neurovisceral integration model (Thayer & Lane, 2000) focuses on the role of the prefrontal cortex in regulating subcortical activity, and suggests CVC is a function of self-regulation and is associated with executive function. Meta-analytic findings indicate resting vmHRV is associated with greater prefrontal cortex activation, and more broadly activation of the central autonomic network that regulates autonomic physiology (Thayer et al., 2012). While these theories differ in terms of the neural mechanisms that lead to CVC, they generally agree that vmHRV is reflective of the functioning status of CVC and the role of the vagus nerve in mediating the rapid adaptation of autonomic states that enables flexible responsivity depending on current demands.

It is this adaptive flexibility that is thought to enable prosocial behavior in the context of suffering. Compassion can be conceptualized as an evolved algorithm that operates on a stimulus detection and response system (Gilbert, 2020). Stimulus detection involves being sensitive to signals of suffering and distress (e.g., threats, danger), and a stimulus response system enables behaviors which are congruent to the context of suffering that help to alleviate it. Vagal mediation is thought to be crucial in enabling approach behavior to contexts of suffering, as typically signals of threat, pain, or suffering can signal potential threats such as a predator or viral contamination (Di Bello et al., 2021; Gilbert, 2020). Physiological regulation is believed to suppress avoidant or scatter responses by downregulating sympathetic arousal in the face of potential threat, thus facilitating approaching suffering to help others in distress. Indeed, vmHRV has been shown to increase during compassion induction reflecting increased parasympathetic activity (Stellar et al., 2015).

While baseline vmHRV has been utilized widely as a physiological correlate of compassion, and more broadly prosocial behavior, executive functioning, and health (Di Bello et al., 2021; Thayer & Lane, 2009), this paints an incomplete picture. While tonic measurements of vmHRV (those measured over a particular point in time) may be predictive of psychological traits and behavior, they only provide an index of vagal tone at the time of measurement. It is critical to also consider *changes* in CVC in response to changing external factors, behavior, or changes in goal orientation. *Phasic* vmHRV refers to the relative change in measurements taken between two time points, providing a measure of adaptive capability depending on task demands, behavior, or context. Phasic measures of vmHRV are exemplified by the Three Rs experimental paradigm (Laborde et al., 2018), referring to *resting, reactivity*, and *recovery* (see Figure 17.1). Resting refers to (tonic) measures of HRV during rest that reflect the assumed general or trait CVC state of an individual. Similarly, in a

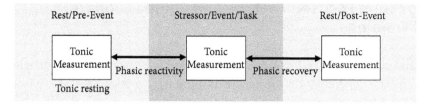

Figure 17.1 The rest, reactivity, recovery paradigm.

naturalistic context, this resting activity could be recorded during "typical" activity state or matched control task, sometimes called a "vanilla" control (Jennings et al., 1992; Parchment et al., 2016). Reactivity refers to the phasic activity or change in vmHRV between tonic measurements taken during the resting time period and vmHRV recorded during a specific experimental condition or task intended to elicit an autonomic response. Outside of laboratory conditions, this could also be any event of interest that is believed to elicit a physiological response. Recovery (or alternatively, vagal rebound) refers to the phasic change following a threatening event and reflects the return to baseline activity.

In the early stages of examining vmHRV and compassion, the emphasis was initially on examining the associations between resting vmHRV and self-reported compassion (Kirby et al., 2017). However, recent compassion science experimental work is examining phasic changes in vmHRV (Steffen et al., 2021). Possibly due to the early reliance on studying compassion and resting vmHRV, there was some confusion in the literature that compassion was almost like a chronic inflexible state of low arousal, associated with positive soothing emotions (Kirby & Petrocchi, 2023). The soothing function of compassion and resting vmHRV was thought to simply reduce the level of threat or anxiety experienced when engaging with suffering. However, new experimental paradigms are demonstrating the dynamic nature of vmHRV during compassionate engaging and action stages. For example, Di Bello et al. (2021) conducted a study with the intention to shed light on the complex nature of the relationship between compassion and HRV. They measured HRV in students exposed first to a video inducing empathic sensitivity (the first component of compassion—engaging with suffering) and then to a second video eliciting compassionate actions (the second component of compassion: behavior). Di Bello et al. (2021) found that HRV decreased after the first video but significantly increased after the second video, suggesting that it is simplistic to link the compassionate process with higher vmHRV. Indeed, compassion-focused interventions might often produce increased sensitivity to emotional pain, which is associated with empathic distress and lower HRV (e.g., Miller et al., 2016). However, such interventions are also associated with a concomitant increase in willingness to take actions to alleviate suffering, which is ultimately associated with increased vmHRV (e.g., Stellar et al., 2015). Thus, CFT adopts a nuanced perspective on the complex physiological regulation that underlies compassionate responding to suffering.

Compassion Focused Therapy and Compassionate Mind Training

Compassion is highly contextual, and the emotions, reasoning, and behaviors recruited will be dependent on the nature of the suffering encountered. CFT aims to improve the ability to recognize suffering in oneself and others, promote strategies to approach suffering with acceptance and understanding, and facilitate subsequent behaviors to alleviate suffering. As mentioned, CFT is an integrated biopsychosocial and contextual model of therapy informed by evolutionary approaches to psychology developed by Paul Gilbert (2014, 2020). One of the key aspects of the origin of CFT is the emphasis on "motivational focus," that is, the approach to CFT is to orient the therapeutic approach in compassion. Using this compassionate mindset, one can then engage in the therapeutic tasks necessary to help the specific difficulty (e.g., anxiety, depression). As a result, CFT is an integrated model which includes a range of different techniques and processes common among almost all therapies. For example, Socratic dialogues, guided discovery, inference chaining, psychoeducation, mindfulness, exposure, behavioral practice, which are common among many of the therapy schools (e.g., cognitive behavioral therapy, acceptance and commitment therapy, dialectical behavior therapy; Gilbert, 2020). There is a growing recognition by scholars in mental health and psychotherapies for the need to move to a more process-based approach to therapy, focusing on identifying the processes that give rise to better mental health, rather than staying fixed in separate schools of therapy (Gilbert & Kirby, 2019; Hayes et al., 2020; Hoffman & Hayes, 2019). As such, there should be increased convergence among the many schools of therapy as the science indicates which factors are more and which are less supportive of good mental health. This is already occurring with almost all therapies including identified therapeutic active ingredients such as exposure, mindfulness, breathing, imagery, behavior activation, and the inclusion of homework (Gilbert & Kirby, 2019). CFT includes these active ingredients as part of its approach, as empirical evidence indicates their efficacy in helping with life challenges (e.g., emotional difficulties, tragedies). However, where CFT might be unique relative to other therapeutic models is its definition of compassion as a motivation, and its emphasis on an evolutionary functional approach to compassion and emotions.

The aims of CFT are to address the key targets of self-criticism, shame, threat, fear, and trauma that underpin many mental health disorders by using a compassion-focused approach characterized by affiliative relating (both to ourselves and others) and behaviors to help alleviate suffering and improve quality of life and well-being. In CFT, core therapeutic tasks such as assessments and case formulations, along with the therapeutic bond, guide the therapy process. CFT has been used for a range of different clinical presentations, including, but not limited to, depression (Falconer et al., 2016; Noorbala et al., 2013; Savari et al., 2021), obsessive compulsive disorder (Petrocchi et al., 2021), psychosis (Braehler et al., 2013), personality disorder (Lucre

& Corten, 2013), anxiety (Cuppage et al., 2018; Gharraee et al., 2018), posttraumatic stress disorder (Daneshvar et al., 2020; Lawrence & Lee, 2014), eating disorder (Kelly & Carter, 2015; Kelly et al., 2017; Steindl et al., 2017), substance use disorder (Carlyle et al., 2019), chronic pain (Dhokia et al., 2020), problematic sleep (Eslamian et al., 2019), and intellectual disability (Clapton et al., 2018). The evidence in support of this approach is constantly growing, with a recent systematic review indicating greater support for CFT when delivered in a group format with at least twelve sessions (Craig et al., 2020). The systematic review also identified that CFT led to reductions in symptoms among difficult-to-treat clinical populations, such as forensic populations, eating disorders, and personality disorders.

CFT also has a specific skills-based program called CMT. The aim of CMT is the same as CFT: to help address core issues of self-criticism and shame by using a set series of compassion-focused strategies and exercises. CMT is time-limited and can be delivered in brief formats including a fifteen-minute audio guided exercise (Kim et al., 2020a), a two-hour brief seminar (Matos et al., 2017), six module sessions (Maratos et al., 2019), and a longer eight-session program (Irons & Heriot-Maitland, 2021). CMT is aimed for those in the community dealing with stress and self-criticism, but not necessarily meeting criteria for a clinical disorder. Unlike CFT, CMT does not include individual assessments and case formulations to guide the therapeutic process. Rather, CMT is a manualized program, which delivers set skills to the target group that aim to cultivate a compassionate mindset. In the delivery of CFT, these specific CMT exercises are used when needed, according to the CFT formulation. CMT/CFT are highly related, with the key point of difference being that the former is a manualized skills-based program aimed specifically at developing the compassionate-self to support well-being, whereas the latter is an open-ended therapy guided by assessment and formulation, using an array of active ingredients to help alleviate suffering for the specific life challenges presented in therapy.

How Does Compassion Focused Therapy Link to Physiology?

There are at least two pathways where CFT links specifically to physiology, first with the definition of compassion being rooted in evolved mammalian caregiving. The second is CFT's three-affect regulation model. As depicted below in Figure 17.2, the three-affect regulation model is informed by evolutionary principles with each system having important functions and associated emotions (Gilbert, 2014).

The function of the threat and self-protect system (Figure 17.2—# 3 *Threat*) is to protect the organism, and thus this system monitors dangers and threats to avoid harm. As a result, emotions such as anger, fear, anxiety, and disgust are associated with this system. The function of the drive system (Figure17.2—# 1 *Drive*) is to secure resources, such as status, shelter, food, reproductive partners. Emotions associated

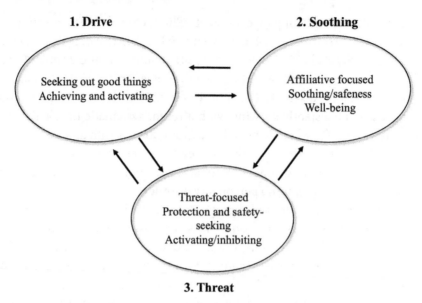

Figure 17.2 Three types of emotion regulation systems.

with this system include excitement, joy, and pleasure. Physiologically, the threat and drive systems are connected to the sympathetic system of the autonomic nervous system, as these systems rely on action. The function of the soothing/affiliative system (Figure 17.2—# 2 Soothing) is to slow the organism to complete important physiological tasks (e.g., rest and digest, repair and recover). Emotions associated with this system include contentment, safeness, and calmness. Physiologically, the soothing system is connected to the PNS, aimed to ground and slow the organism. Recent work by Sousa et al. (2021) has corroborated that physiological activity aligns with the related self-reported drive within each affective regulatory system in adolescents. According to Gilbert's (2014) model, all systems are necessary, but often there is an over reliance on the threat and drive systems to regulate emotional experiences and daily stressors (Irons & Heriot-Maitland, 2021). Thus, one of the major aims of CFT is to help stimulate the soothing system and develop the client's PNS, specifically as reflected in vmHRV.

Research Examining Compassion Focused Therapy, Compassionate Mind Training, and Vagally Mediated Heart Rate Variability

Over the last ten years there has been a growing number of evaluation studies examining whether CMT and CFT approaches can influence HRV in various populations, both clinical and non-clinical. These interventions include brief CMT interventions, as well as longer twelve-week CFT interventions.

Brief Compassionate Mind Training Interventions and Heart Rate Variability

One of the first randomized controlled trials examining CMT's impact on HRV was conducted by Matos et al. (2017). The CMT intervention was a brief two-hour seminar and included psychoeducation about compassion, as well as seven practices that are completed within the seminar, (a) body posture, (b) friendly voice tone and facial expression, (c) soothing rhythm breathing, (d) mindfulness, (e) cultivating the compassionate-self, (f) compassion for others, and (g) compassion for self. Participants were also provided a participant workbook which contained the exercises and were sent an email with a weblink to the recorded guided audio tracks that were used in the CMT seminar so participants could continue to practice the exercises. Matos et al. (2017) recruited a non-clinical sample of ninety-three participants, who were randomized to either the CMT ($n = 56$) or a waitlist control group ($n = 37$). The researchers examined intervention effects at two weeks post-intervention and found that CMT compared to the control condition had significant improvements in compassion, as well as positive emotions such as safeness and soothing. This supports the view that CMT is able to increase the soothing system of Gilbert's (2014) three-affect regulation model. In addition, CMT was able to reduce shame, self-criticism, and stress. Critically, the CMT group also had significant increases in baseline vmHRV at post-intervention compared to the control group, thus providing physiological evidence for the increase in the participants soothing system.

Importantly, in a further randomized control study, Matos et al. (2018) examined embodiment of these compassionate practices. Embodiment refers to what extent an individual perceives they can think, feel, and act as their compassionate-self. They found the more a participant felt they embodied their compassionate-self during CMT, the more beneficial the outcomes—greater embodiment was associated with higher levels of compassion, safeness, and reassurance. Unfortunately, embodiment was not examined in relation to HRV, which would be an important area for future research. In addition, the CMT seminars employed by Matos et al. in both studies included seven different practices, and it is uncertain which practice(s) are most important in cultivating vmHRV.

Regardless of whether the intervention is CFT or CMT, both include techniques to develop the "compassionate-self." The compassionate-self is conceptualized as including three specific qualities: wisdom (e.g., psychoeducation on flow of life), strength (e.g., from body posture and grounding), and commitment (e.g., taking actions to be helpful). Kim et al. (2020a) directly examined whether a compassionate-self practice would be sufficient to increase HRV over a two-week period with a non-clinical sample. Compassionate-Self practice was specifically isolated to determine its effectiveness at increasing vmHRV. The Compassionate-Self was a fifteen-minute guided audio practice that included three core elements: (a) body posture and grounding, (b) soothing-rhythm breathing, and (c) cultivating the compassionate-self (specifically cultivating wisdom, strength, and commitment to be compassionate). Participants came to the lab, completed a fifteen-minute resting state vmHRV assessment, and then listened to the Compassionate-Self practice for fifteen minutes while HRV was recorded. Participants were assessed at Time 1 and then again two weeks later at Time 2. Participants were also provided a unique link to a website with the compassionate-self practice and were encouraged to listen to the practice as often as they could over the two-week period.

The results from the Kim et al. (2020a) study revealed vmHRV significantly increased during the Compassionate-Self practice compared to resting state vmHRV at both Time 1 and Time 2 assessment periods. However, Time 2 baseline vmHRV did not significantly increase compared to the Time 1 baseline. Kim et al. (2020a) also examined dosage (frequency of listening to the audio tracks) and found that those who practiced more frequently benefitted significantly more in terms of increased vmHRV response to the Compassionate-Self practice compared to those who did not.

An additional feature of the Kim et al. (2020a) study was that they also examined participants' HRV in relation to proposed clinical thresholds for HRV. Research has found low HRV is associated with poorer mental health and physical health (Hartmann et al., 2019), and research by Jarczok et al. (2019) reported guidelines on what constitutes clinically-at-risk HRV. Applying these guidelines to the sample, Kim et al. (2020a) found the Compassionate-Self practice was able to shift four (pre-training) and seven (post-training) clinically-at-risk participants above the clinical cutoff of 25 RMSSD when engaged in the compassion intervention versus at rest. Moreover, using time series analysis Kim et al. (2020b) showed that at post-intervention participants were able to maintain increased vmHRV with less variation. This suggests the compassionate-self element of CMT can lead to sustained and stable effects post-training, even in light-touch interventions.

Higher Intensity Compassion Focused Therapy Twelve-Week Interventions and Heart Rate Variability

Moving beyond brief CMT interventions, there are now a growing number of longer CFT interventions with clinical populations, including university students enrolled in a counselling service (Steffen et al., 2021), those with body weight shame (Carter et al., 2023), and those with bipolar disorder (Gilbert et al., 2022).

All three studies used a recently developed protocol of CFT provided by Kirby et al. (2022). The structure of this protocol is included in Table 17.1. The CFT intervention is delivered in weekly two-hour modules. Each module includes (a) didactic presentation of material by facilitator, (b) guided meditation or imagery exercises, (c) pair exercises, and (d) large group discussions. As outlined in Table 17.1, the first five sessions of the program aimed at developing the participants' "compassionate-self." Thus, the program started with psychoeducation on defining compassion,

Table 17.1 A twelve-module compassion focused therapy intervention

Module	Content
1: Introduction to Compassion and the Tricky Brain	- **Aim:** To understand how individuals experience compassion, fears they have towards compassion and beginning psychoeducation of the evolved mind and how it functions. - **Module exercises:** Large group discussions, pair exercises, compassionate imagery, and the realities of life meditation.
2: Three Types of Emotion	- **Aim:** To introduce evolutionary functional analysis of emotion, assist individuals to understand the nature and function of threat-based emotions (anger, anxiety and disgust), drive-based emotions (happiness and excitement), and soothing-based emotions (safeness and contentment) and help individuals clarify compassion as a motive. - **Module exercises:** Large group discussions, pair exercises, and soothing rhythm breathing exercise.
3: Attention Training and Mindfulness	- **Aim:** To introduce individuals to the nature and function of attention (how to pay attention to attention), with introductions to mindfulness-based practices. - **Module exercises:** Large group discussions, pair exercises, connecting mindfulness skills with breathing, grounding, and body awareness skills such as use of body posture, facial expressions, and voice tones.
4: Safety/Safeness and Compassion from Others	- **Aim:** To introduce individuals to the concept of safeness (affiliative and exploratory focus) and how that differs to safety (threat focused). To explore how it feels to experience compassion from others. Discussions on how and why our relationships are important to us and support a range of physiological processes within us. - **Module exercises:** Large group discussions, pair exercises, breathing exercises, compassionate imagery, and safe place imagery.
5: The Compassionate Self	- **Aim:** To introduce individuals to the nature and concept of the compassionate self. The compassionate-self includes three key qualities: wisdom, strength, and commitment. These qualities are described and explored. - **Module exercises:** Large group discussions, pair exercises, breathing exercises, and cultivating the compassionate-self.
6: Multiple Selves	- **Aim:** To introduce group members to the concept of multiple selves, with a particular focus on threat-based emotions, examining specifically angry-self, anxious-self and sad-self. - **Session exercises:** Large group discussion, pair exercises, exploration and experiential practice of multiple-selves and responses, compassionate imagery, and breathing exercises.
7: Self-Criticism	- **Aim:** To help individuals understand the forms and functions of self-criticism and how to use the Compassionate-Self to work with disappointments, setbacks, and rejections. - **Module exercises:** Large group discussion, pair exercises, experiential exercises (self-monitoring), breathing exercises, compassionate imagery, and breathing exercises.

(*continued*)

Table 17.1 Continued

Module	Content
8: Shame and Guilt	- **Aim:** To help individuals understand the evolution of the threat, drive, and soothing systems in social relationships. Exploration of social rank systems and emotions: shame (external, internal), humiliation, and guilt. - **Module exercises:** Large group discussion, pair exercises, experiential exercises (experiencing shame and how the compassionate self works with shame), and breathing exercises.
9: Deepening Compassion for Self	- **Aim:** To help individuals deepen compassion for the self by facilitating broader abilities to opening and tolerating emotional and motivational experiences. - **Module exercises:** Large group discussion, pair exercises, experiential exercise (directing compassion towards others and self), compassionate letter writing, making compassion-focused flash cards, and breathing exercises.
10: Compassionate Assertiveness	- **Aim:** To help individuals understand assertiveness and how assertiveness is linked to strength and authority of compassion. Thus, allowing for individuals to express themselves confidently not aggressively or passively. - **Module exercises:** Large group discussion, pair exercises (unhelpfulness of aggressive, passiveness, and passive–aggressive responses), refection of compassionate self-identity, and breathing exercises.
11: Forgiveness	- **Aim:** To introduce individuals to exploring how to engage in the flow of compassion for others as well as forgiveness and how the suffering of others can influence us and what we feel in our body and what we do. - **Module exercises:** Large group discussion, pair exercises, practicing of perspective taking and empathy, and breathing exercises.
12: Envisioning a Compassionate Future	- **Aim:** To revisit the journey the group has been on and invite individuals to consider prevention and emergency strategies for future difficulties and envision what a compassionate future would involve. - **Module exercises:** Large group discussion, pair exercises (how to cultivate and strengthen compassion), acknowledgment of challenges, self-gratitude letter, compassionate imagery (compassionate wishes), and breathing exercises.

how the mind works, and the three affect regulation systems that underpin CFT. The program sessions then transitioned to active skills training by focusing on body posture, soothing-rhythm breathing, attention and mindfulness, and the development of the compassionate-self. The remaining seven sessions used the participant's compassionate-self to work on difficult emotions, specifically self-criticism, shame, self-compassion, assertiveness, and forgiveness. In each session there was a guided meditation or visual imagery exercise which was recorded and sent to the participants as part of personal practice between sessions. Participants also received a workbook with the key content covered across the twelve sessions. After each session, the participants received a standardized email summarizing the core components of the session, along with the live audio recording of the in-session meditation or imagery exercise.

The first examination of this twelve-week protocol using HRV was by Steffen et al. (2021). They examined the twelve-session protocol with thirty-one participants who were attending a university counselling center at pre- and post-intervention. They found the intervention improved levels of compassion, and reduced self-criticism and shame. In terms of HRV, they found no significant pre-post changes in baseline HRV at the group level. However, participants who reliably improved in self-compassion (as measured by the Compassion Engagement and Action Scale) also had a significant increase in HRV from baseline to post-intervention. Furthermore, they found those with secure attachment styles had greater HRV reactivity compared to those with insecure attachment styles. Steffen et al. (2021) suggested one method to help support continued practice of the exercises designed to increase vmHRV is to include vmHRV biofeedback within the sessions. As the study did not have a control group, it is recommended that future research integrating HRV biofeedback include an active comparator condition so that the effects can be attributed to the CFT protocol.

Extending on this groundbreaking work by Steffen et al. (2021), Carter et al. (2023) examined the same twelve-module protocol using a randomized controlled trial (RCT) design specifically to help those experiencing body weight shame. The study used an RCT design with participants randomized to the CFT ($n = 28$) or a waitlist control ($n = 27$) group. Participants were assessed at four time points (pre-intervention, post-intervention, three-month, and six-month follow-up) using both self-report and a physiological measure of PNS activity (i.e., HRV). Results indicated that CFT had a significant positive impact in both the short- and long-term at reducing body weight shame, increasing compassion, reducing self-criticism, and improving dieting behavior. However, CFT did not shift baseline HRV.

The authors provided three possible explanations for the lack of change in HRV. The first was that to achieve change in baseline HRV, practice and dosage between sessions are important, and these metrics were not assessed. The second possibility provided is that other lifestyle factors that are known to influence HRV, which were not controlled for, such as medication, sleep, and diet restricted the capacity for these compassion practices to improve baseline HRV (Licht et al., 2010). The third possibility provided was that baseline HRV may not have improved, but possibly HRV reactivity did, which we did not assess in this study.

Finally, Gilbert et al. (2022) applied the same twelve-week protocol for participants with bipolar disorder in an initial feasibility study. Six participants with a history of bipolar disorder took part in the evaluation. Although the twelve modules were used, these modules were administered over twenty-five sessions. The researchers examined a range of self-report factors, as well as HRV. Focus groups were also conducted for qualitative feedback on the feasibility of the approach. Significant improvements were found for four of the six participants in terms of self-reported compassion, self-criticism, and depressive symptoms. In relation to HRV, significant improvements in baseline HRV were observed between the first and second phase of the intervention. Clearly, more work is required to determine the efficacy of CFT compared to a control group for those with bipolar disorder, but initial feasibility evidence is promising.

CFT and CMT are showing growing evidence for their positive impact on both self-reported well-being and physiological improvement as measured by HRV. Critically, in comparison to other therapy approaches, cognitive behavioral therapy has been found not to change HRV (Mumm et al., 2019). In contrast, evidence to date suggests that compassion training can increase HRV in non-clinical groups with brief interventions (Kim et al., 2020a; Matos et al., 2017), as well as in longer twelve-module CFT applications with clinical populations (Gilbert et al., 2022; Steffen et al., 2021). Therapies must continue to harness the huge potential of HRV to help patients with a range of clinical disorders, and CMT and CFT offer a great possibility.

Future Research Considerations for Compassion Focused Therapy and Heart Rate Variability

We recommend incorporating vmHRV measures into future CFT research. Critically, vmHRV should be assessed beyond simple baseline trait indices. As mentioned, vmHRV is typically assessed either in terms of resting vmHRV (Kirby et al., 2017) or changes in resting vmHRV over time when completing compassion training (Kim et al., 2020a; Matos et al., 2017). Cardiac vagal control is a dynamic process that can reflect the nuanced changes in physiological state that accompany the shifts in affective and cognitive processes required to detect and respond to suffering. Future research should incorporate experimental designs that permit vmHRV testing across the Three Rs of resting, reactivity, and recovery. Collectively, this *vagal flexibility* (Balzarotti et al., 2017) is a powerful indicator of an individual's capacity for adaptive responsivity. We propose that vmHRV reactivity and recovery may be the most important dimension to assess for in compassion research, with the approach by Steffen et al. (2021) an example of how to incorporate such a method.

For example, an experimental paradigm could include four ten-minute blocks, with the first block assessing for baseline HRV, the second block examining HRV in a context of threat, the third block a recovery period, with the fourth block examining HRV during a compassion meditation practice. Such an experimental design allows for more nuanced testing of HRV in relation to compassion, and this has been adopted in our work, which is similarly being used by other labs (e.g., Steffen et al., 2021). Applying such a design to an evaluation of a CFT intervention could mean conducting this experimental HRV paradigm at pre- and post-intervention. This experimental design not only allows for testing for baseline change over time, but also for reactivity and recovery. Indeed, it could be that the benefits of compassion are that it helps individuals with the reactivity and recovery phases more than with the baseline stage. Indeed, if CMT and CFT interventions enabled quicker recovery of the vmHRV after threat this could be highly advantageous for mental health and well-being. Thus, more empirical research is needed that adopts such designs.

In such a paradigm, the blocks of rest and recovery are locked, however, what the threat block and compassion practice block include can vary. Previous research using a threat block has required participants to write about a recent setback in a self-critical way, which has been found to reduce vmHRV (Steffen et al., 2021). Including manipulation checks can be helpful at this point to ascertain just how distressing the participant found the self-critical writing task, and also asking how much they engaged with the task is important. For example, if the block is ten minutes, further instructions on how to continue writing about the set-back or disappointment in a self-critical way might be required. Our early piloting of this approach found some participants would only write self-critically for two to three minutes. Thus, we included further instructions, such that we first ask the participant to write about the setback, mistake, or disappointment, "*please write about the situation here, what happened? Please go into as much detail as you can.*" We then instruct, "Now that you have remembered a situation and connected it with it again, please write about how you were feeling about it at the time and what you thought about yourself? Please go into as much detail as you can, noticing the emotions you were feeling." Following this we ask on a scale from 1 (*not at all*) to 10 (*very much*), the extent to which they engaged with the self-critical writing task, how stressful/threatening they found it, and how difficult they found it to engage with the task.

Using a self-critical threat task is ideally suited to CFT/CMT evaluations, as one of the primary aims of the intervention approach is to target self-criticism. However, if you are recruiting a non-clinical sample it is highly possible that the self-critical writing task will not be experienced as particularly threatening. Thus, other threat tasks could include writing about a shame memory. Conversely, other threat paradigms could be adopted, such as the Trier Social Stress Test, which induces stress by requiring participants to make an interview-style presentation, followed by a surprise mental arithmetic test, in front of an interview panel who provide no encouragement or feedback (A. P. Allen et al., 2016). This threat task requires significantly more resources than the self-critical writing task, and in addition, is not necessarily the threat of concern by participants or clients seeking treatment or help from CFT/CMT. We would recommend trying to incorporate a threat task which is congruent to potential triggers or helpful to the population you are working with. For example, in a recent RCT of CFT for those with body weight shame (Carter et al., 2023), we included the threat task to be one where participants looked at photos of themselves for the ten-minute block. This is a highly threatening task for those with body weight shame. We asked participants to bring in a series of at least twenty photos, which had to meet specific guidelines (e.g., be a recent photo, where one can view whole body, not just face), these were then presented to the participants on a computer monitor whilst measuring HRV. We also included a manipulation check where we asked participants, on a scale from 1 (*not at all*) to 10 (*very much*), "*to what extent did you* like these photos" and "*to what extend did these photos make you feel bad about your body?*" Although in our RCT we did not observe baseline HRV increase from pre- to post-CFT intervention, we have yet to examine the reactivity and recovery blocks.

In terms of compassion-practice block, we have used the compassionate-self practice, which includes three components, (a) grounding and body posture, (b) soothing-rhythm breathing, and (c) cultivating compassion (specifically cultivating wisdom, strength, and commitment to be compassionate). This exercise has been found to improve HRV, reduce self-criticism, and improve compassion (Kim et al., 2020a). However, there are a range of other compassion practices within CMT/CFT which could be used, such as the ideal compassionate other, compassionate color, or safe place imagery. Moreover, other compassionate mantras, similar to Buddhist practices, could also be adopted, these typically include repeating a mantra such as, "*may you be free from suffering.*"

Another consideration for researchers is to begin to use ecological momentary assessments (EMA) to assess for dynamic changess in HRV in everyday life. There has been an explosion of research using EMA, with many arguing that a combination of lab-based experimental designs and EMA is ideal for studying psychological phenomena (Flake et al., 2020). Put simply, EMA involves repeated sampling of a participant's current or recent behaviors and experiences in real time in their natural environment. EMA aims to minimize recall bias, maximize ecological validity, and allow study of microprocesses that influence behavior in real-world contexts. EMA improves the ecological validity of studies examining prosocial constructs such as compassion (Schreiter et al., 2013), as contexts in the lab may or may not match the contexts in which compassion occurs in daily life. Di Bello et al. (2021) argued that to truly understand HRV and its links to compassion, continued monitoring of daily HRV is needed using wearable HRV devices. We are currently examining such a design which incorporates lab-based tasks with EMA using wearable HRV devices in an attempt to understand the experience of compassion in everyday life. In Figure 17.3 below we present the design of the experiment.

The experimental design tests the effectiveness of CMT and it integrates self-report trait measures of compassion, continuous daily HRV monitoring (using Firstbeat Bodyguard2 wearables), and EMA survey items on the experience of compassion in everyday life. In Session 1 the participant arrives and is shown how to use the Firstbeat Bodyguard2 wearable and given one for the duration of the study, as well as being shown how to complete the EMA survey items on their personal phone. Participants are randomized in Session 1 to a compassion condition or no intervention. The rationale for a no intervention condition is to examine compassion in daily life, whereas the compassion condition allows us to assess whether a daily compassion exercise leads to increased compassionate behavior in everyday life. The EMA period is a seven-day period where participants will receive seven signals a day between 10:00 a.m. and 10:00 p.m. on their phone. Survey signals will be sent semi-randomly (i.e., randomly within ninety-minute windows with minimum fifteen-minute gaps and expired after twenty minutes). Participants will then

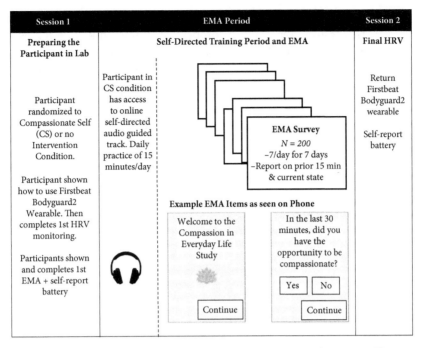

Figure 17.3 Our EMA study of compassion in everyday life, linking self-report and heart rate variability.

be asked a series of questions about their experience of compassion, for example, *"In the last fifteen minutes, did you have an opportunity to be compassionate?"* The participant is then presented with a series of forty items about their compassion experience (e.g., *How close are you with the person?*) and current psychological state (e.g., *Right now, I feel stressed*). This design will enable us to examine vmHRV leading up to, during, and after reported compassionate events in realistic contexts. In addition, we will be able to monitor and test whether dosage (how often listening to the compassionate-self practice) influences daily compassionate behavior and vmHRV over time. Our design will also allow us to examine for the associations between compassion and vagal flexibility in daily life. To date we have had over 100 participants through this design, which is pre-registered on the open science framework (https://osf.io/w3ujm/). We suggest such an approach can be tested with both clinical and non-clinical samples, as researchers recognize the usefulness of compassion to improve psychotherapy (Förster & Kanske, 2021).

Conclusion

There has been a significant advancement over the last ten years in our understanding of healthy physiological indicators and their integration into therapies to help in assessment and treatment. CFT and CMT have a theoretical model that integrates evolutionary and physiological principles, making HRV a core aspect of its approach and research. This chapter overviewed compassion and its links to HRV, as well as the evidence to date showing the significant links between HRV and compassion, and the potential for interventions to improve not only psychological but physiological health. The next ten years of research will uncover further nuanced aspects to HRV and its connection to compassion, possibly leading to new breakthroughs in how we develop therapies and help those who struggle with self-criticism, shame, and other mental health difficulties.

References

Allen, J. J. B., Chambers, A. S., & Towers, D. N. (2007). The many metrics of cardiac chronotropy: A pragmatic primer and a brief comparison of metrics. *Biological Psychology, 74*(2), 243–262. http://doi.org/10.1016/j.biopsycho.2006.08.005

Allen, A. P., Kennedy, P. J., Dockray, S., Cryan, J. F., Dinan, T. G., & Clarke, G. (2016). The Trier Social Stress Test: Principles and practice. *Neurobiology of Stress, 6*, 113–126. https://doi.org/10.1016/j.ynstr.2016.11.001

Balzarotti, S., Biassoni, F., Colombo, B., & Ciceri, M. R. (2017). Cardiac vagal control as a marker of emotion in healthy adults: A review. *Biological Psychology, 130*, 54–66. https://doi.org/10.1016/j.biopsycho.2017.10.008

Berntson, G. G., Cacioppo, J. T., & Grossman, P. (2007). Whither vagal tone. *Biological Psychology, 74*(2), 295–300. https://doi.org/10.1016/j.biopsycho.2006.08.006

Braehler, C., Gumley, A., Harper, J., Wallace, S., Norrie, J., & Gilbert, P. (2013). Exploring change processes in compassion focused therapy in psychosis: Results of a feasibility randomized controlled trial. *The British Journal of Clinical Psychology, 52*(2), 199–214. https://doi.org/10.1111/bjc.12009

Brodal, P. (2010). *The central nervous system: Structure and function* (4th ed.). Oxford University Press.

Carlyle, M., Rockliff, H., Edwards, R., Ene, C., Karl, A., Marsh, B., Hartley, L., & Morgan, C. J. A. (2019). Investigating the feasibility of brief compassion focused therapy in individuals in treatment for opioid use disorder. *Substance Abuse: Research and Treatment, 54*(5), 747–764. https://doi.org/10.1016/j.beth.2023.02.001 1178221819836726

Carter, A., Steindl, S., Parker, S., Gilbert, P., & Kirby, J. N. (2023). Compassion focused therapy to reduce body weight shame for adults categorized as obese: A randomized controlled trial. *Behavior Therapy, 54*(5), 747–764. https://doi.org/10.1016/j.beth.2023.02.001

Clapton, N. E., Williams, J., Griffith, G. M., & Jones, R. S. P. (2018). 'Finding the person you really are . . . on the inside': Compassion focused therapy for adults with intellectual disabilities. *Journal of Intellectual Disability, 22*(2), 135–153. https://doi.org/10.1177/1744629516688581

Craig, C., Hiskey, S., & Spector, A. (2020). Compassion focused therapy: A systematic review of its effectiveness and acceptability in clinical populations. *Expert Review of Neurotherapeutics, 20*(4), 385–400. https://doi.org/10.1080/14737175.2020.1746184

Cuppage, J., Baird, K., Gibson, J., Booth, R., & Hevey, D. (2018). Compassion focused therapy: Exploring the effectiveness with a transdiagnostic group and potential processes of change. *British Journal of Clinical Psychology, 57*(2), 240–254. https://doi.org/10.1111/bjc.12162

Daneshvar, S., Shafiei, M., & Basharpoor, S. (2020). Group-based compassion-focused therapy on experiential avoidance, meaning-in-life, and sense of coherence in female survivors of intimate partner violence with PTSD: A randomized controlled trial. *Journal of Interpersonal Violence, 37*(7–8), NP4187–NP4211. https://doi.org/10.1177/0886260520958660

Dhokia, M., Elander, J., Clements, K., & Gilbert, P. (2020). A randomized-controlled pilot trial of an online compassionate mind training intervention to help people with chronic pain avoid analgesic misuse. *Psychology of Addictive Behaviors, 34*(7), 726–733. https://doi.org/10.1037/adb0000579

Di Bello, M., Ottaviani, C., & Petrocchi, N. (2021). Compassion is not a benzo: Distinctive associations of heart rate variability with its empathic and action components. *Frontiers in Neuroscience, 15*, Article 617443. https://doi.org/10.3389/fnins.2021.617443

Eslamian, A., Moradi, A., & Salehi, A. (2019). Effectiveness of compassion focused group therapy on sleep quality, rumination and resilience of women in Isfahan City suffering from depression in summer 2018. *International Journal of Medical Investigation, 8*(4), 41–50. http://intjmi.com/article-1-445-en.html

Falconer, C. J., Rovira, A., King, J. A., Gilbert, P., Antley, A., Fearon, P., Ralph, N., Slater, M., & Brewin, C. R. (2016). Embodying self-compassion within virtual reality and its effects on patients with depression. *BJPych Open, 2*(1), 74–80. https://doi.org/10.1192/bjpo.bp.115.002147

Flake, J. K., & Fried, E. I. (2020). Measurement schmeasurement: Questionable measurement practices and how to avoid them. *Advances in Methods and Practics in Psychological Science, 3*(4), 456–465. https://doi.10.1177/2515245920952393

Förster, K., & Kanske, P. (2021). Exploiting the plasticity of compassion to improve psychotherapy. *Behavioral Sciences, 39*, 64–71. https://doi.org/10.1016/j.cobeha.2021.01.010

Gharraee, B., Tajrishi, K. Z., Farani, A. R., Bolhari, J., & Farahani, H. (2018). A randomized controlled trial of compassion focused therapy for social anxiety disorder. *Iranian Journal of Psychiatry and Behavioral Sciences, 12*(4), Article e80945. https://doi.org/10.5812/ijpbs.80945

Gilbert, P. (2014). The origins and nature of compassion focused therapy. *British Journal of Clinical Psychology, 53*(1), 6–41. https://doi.org/10.1111/bjc.12043

Gilbert, P. (2020). Compassion: From its evolution to a psychotherapy. *Frontiers in Psychology, 11*, Article 586161. https://doi.org/10.3389/fpsyg.2020.586161

Gilbert, P., Basran, J., MacArthur, M., & Kirby, J. N. (2019). Differences in the semantics of prosocial words: An exploration of compassion and kindness. *Mindfulness, 10*, 2259–2271. https://doi.org/10.1007/s12671-019-01191-x

Gilbert, P., Basran, J. K., Raven, J., Gilbert, H., Petrocchi, N., Cheli, S., Rayner, A., Hayes, A., Lucre, K., Minou, P., Giles, D., Byrne, F., Newton, E., & McEwan, K. (2022). Compassion focused group therapy for people with a diagnosis of bipolar affective disorder: A feasibility study. *Frontiers in Psychology, 13*, Article 841932. https://doi.org/10.3389/fpsyg.2022.841932

Gilbert, P., & Kirby, J. N. (2019). Building an integrative science for psychotherapy for the 21st century: Preface and introduction. *Psychology and Psychotherapy: Theory, Research and Practice, 92*(2), 151–163. https://doi.org/10.1111/papt.12225

Hartmann, R., Schmidt, F. M., Sander, C., & Hegerl, U. (2019). Heart rate variability as indicator of clinical state in depression. *Frontiers in Psychiatry, 9*, Article 735. https://doi.org/10.3389/fpsyt.2018.00735

Hayes, S. C., Hofmann, S. G., & Ciarrochi, J. (2020). A process-based approach to psychological diagnosis and treatment: The conceptual and treatment utility of an extended evolutionary meta model. *Clinical Psychology Review, 82*, 101908. https://doi.org/10.1016/j.cpr.2020.101908

Hofmann, S. G., & Hayes, S. C. (2019). The future of intervention science: Process-based therapy. *Clinical Psychological Science, 7*(1), 37–50. https://doi.org/10.1177/ 2167702618772296.

Irons, C., & Heriot-Maitland, C. (2021). Compassionate mind training: An 8-week group for the general public. *Psychology and Psychotherapy: Theory, Research, and Practice, 94*(3), 443–463. https://doi.org/10.1111/papt.12320

Jarczok, M. N., Koenig, J., Wittling, A., Fischer, J. E., & Thayer, J. F. (2019). First evaluation of an index of low vagally-mediated heart rate variability as a marker of health risks in human adults: Proof of concept. *Journal of Clinical Medicine, 8*(11), Article 1940. https://doi.10.3390/jcm8111940

Jennings, J. R., Kamarck, T., Stewart, C., Eddy, M., & Johnson, P. (1992). Alternate cardiovascular baseline assessment techniques: Vanilla or resting baseline. *Psychophysiology, 29*(6), 742–750. https://doi.org/10.1111/j.1469-8986.1992.tb02052.x

Kelly, A. C., & Carter, J. C. (2015). Self-compassion training for binge eating disorder: A pilot randomized controlled trial. *Psychology and Psychotherapy: Theory, Research and Practice, 88*(3), 285–303. https://doi.org/10.1111/papt.12044

Kelly, A. C., Wisniewski, L., Martin-Wagar, C., & Hoffman, E. (2017). Group-based compassion-focused therapy as an adjunct to outpatient treatment for eating disorders: A pilot randomized controlled trial. *Clinical Psychology & Psychotherapy, 24*(2), 475–487. https://doi.org/10.1002/cpp.2018

Kim, J. J., Parker, S. L., Doty, J. R., Cunnington, R., Gilbert, P., & Kirby, J. N. (2020a). Neurophysiological and behavioural markers of compassion. *Scientific Reports, 10*, Article 6789. https://doi.org/10.1038/s41598-020-63846-3

Kim, J. J., Parker, S., Henderson, T., & Kirby, J. N. (2020b). Physiological fractals: Visual and statistical evidence across timescales and experimental states. *Journal of The Royal Society Interface, 17*(167), Article 20200334. https://doi.org/10.1098/rsif.2020.0334

Kirby, J. N., Doty, J. R., Petrocchi, N., & Gilbert, P. (2017). The current and future role of heart rate variability for assessing and training compassion. *Frontiers in Public Health, 5*, Article 40. https://doi.org/10.3389/fpubh.2017.00040

Kirby, J. N., Gerrish, R., Sherwell, C., & Gilbert, P. (2022). The role of likeability in discriminating between kindness and compassion. *Mindfulness, 13*, 1555–1564. https://doi.org/10.1007/s12671-022-01900-z

Kirby, J. N., & Petrocchi, N. (2023). Compassion focused therapy: What it is, what it targets, and the evidence. In A. Finlay-Jones, K. Bluth, & K. Neff (Eds.), *Handbook of self-compassion* (pp. 417–432). Springer International Publishing.

Kok, B. E., & Fredrickson, B. L. (2010). Upward spirals of the heart: Autonomic flexibility, as indexed by vagal tone, reciprocally and prospectively predicts positive emotions and social connectedness. *Biological Psychology, 85*(3), 432–436. https://doi.org/10.1016/j.biopsycho.2010.09.005

Laborde, S., Mosley, E., & Mertgen, A. (2018). Vagal tank theory: The three Rs of cardiac vagal control functioning – resting, reactivity, and recovery. *Frontiers in Neuroscience, 12*, Article 458. https://doi.org/10.3389/fnins.2018.00458

Laborde, S., Mosley, E., & Thayer, J. F. (2017). Heart rate variability and cardiac vagal tone in psychophysiological research: Recommendations for experiment planning, data analysis, and data reporting. *Frontiers in Psychology, 8*, 1–18. https://doi.org/10.3389/fpsyg.2017.00213

Lawrence, V. A., & Lee, D. (2014). An exploration of people's experiences of compassion-focused therapy for trauma, using interpretative phenomenological analysis. *Clinical Psychology and Psychotherapy, 21*(6), 495–507. https://doi.org/10.1002/cpp.1854

Licht, C. M., de Geus, E. J., van Dyck, R., & Penninx, B. W. (2010). Longitudinal evidence for unfavorable effects of antidepressants on heart rate variability. *Biological Psychiatry, 68*(9), 861–868. https://doi.org/10.1016/j.biopsych.2010.06.032

Lucre, K. M., & Corten, N. (2013). An exploration of group compassion focused therapy for personality disorder. *Psychology and Psychotherapy, 86*(4), 387–400. https://doi.org/10.1111/j.2044-8341.2012.02068.x

Maratos, F. A., Montague, J., Ashra, H., Welford, M., Wood, W., Barnes, C., Sheffield, D., & Gilbert, P. (2019). Evaluation of a compassionate mind training intervention with school teachers and support staff. *Mindfulness, 10*, 2245–2258. https://doi.org/10.1007/s12671-019-01185-9

Matos, M., Duarte, C., Duarte, J., Pinto-Gouveia, J., Petrocchi, N., Basran, J., & Gilbert, P. (2017). Psychological and physiological effects of compassionate mind training: A pilot randomised controlled study. *Mindfulness, 8*, 1699–1712. https://doi.org/10.1007/s12671-017-0745-7

Matos, M., Duarte, J., Duarte, C., Gilbert, P., & Pinto-Gouveia, J. (2018). How one experiences and embodies Compassionate Mind Training influences its effectiveness. *Mindfulness, 9*(4), 1224–1235. https://doi.org/10.1007/s12671-017-0864-1

Mayseless, O. (2016). *The caring motivation: An integrated theory*. Oxford University Press. https://doi.org/10.1093/acprof:oso/9780199913619.001.0001

Miller, J. G., Nuselovici, J. N., & Hastings, P. D. (2016). Nonrandom acts of kindness: Parasympathetic and subjective empathic responses to sadness predict children's prosociality. *Child Development, 87*(6), 1679–1690. https://doi.org/10.1111/cdev.12629

Mumm, J. L. M., Pyrkosch, L., Plag, J., Nagel, P., Petzold, M. B., Bischoff, S., Fehm, L., Fydrich, T., & Ströhle, A. (2019). Heart rate variability in patients with agoraphobia with or without panic disorder remains stable during CBT but increases following in-vivo exposure. *Journal of Anxiety Disorders, 64*, 16–23. https://doi.org/10.1016/j.janxdis.2019.03.001

Noorbala, F., Borjali, A., Ahmadian-Attari, M. M., & Noorbala, A. A. (2013). Effectiveness of compassionate mind training on depression, anxiety, and self-criticism in a group of Iranian depressed patients. *Iranian Journal of Psychiatry*, *8*(3), 113–117. https://www.ncbi.nlm.nih.gov/pmc/articles/PMC3887227/

Parchment, A., Wohleber, R. W., & Reinerman-Jones, L. (2016). Psychophysiological baseline nethods and usage. In D. Schmorrow & C. Fidopiastis (Eds.), *Foundations of augmented cognition: Neuroergonomics and operational neuroscience. AC 2016* (pp. 361–371). Springer. https://doi.org/10.1007/978-3-319-39955-3_34

Petrocchi, N., & Cheli, S. (2019). The social brain and heart rate variability: Implications for psychotherapy. *Psychology and Psychotherapy: Theory, Research & Practice*, *92*(2), 208–223. https://doi.org/10.1111/papt.12224

Petrocchi, N., Cosentino, T., Pellegrini, V., Femia, G., D'innocenzo, A., & Mancini, F. (2021). Compassion focused group therapy for treatment-resistant OCD: Initial evaluation using a multiple baseline design. *Frontiers in Psychology*, *11*, Article 594277. https://doi.org/10.3389/fpsyg.2020.594277

Porges, S. W. (2007). The polyvagal perspective. *Biological Psychology*, *74*(2), 116–143. https://doi.org/10.1016/j.biopsycho.2006.06.009

Reis, H. T., Maniaci, M. R., & Rogge, R. D. (2017). Compassionate acts and everyday emotional well-being among newlyweds. *Emotion*, *17*(4), 751–763. http://dx.doi.org/10.1037/emo0000281

Saul, J. P. (1990). Beat-to-beat variations of heart rate reflect modulation of cardiac autonomic outflow. *Physiology*, *5*(1), 32–37. https://doi.org/10.1152/physiologyonline.1990.5.1.32

Savari, Y., Mohagheghi, H., & Petrocchi, N. (2021). A preliminary investigation on the effectiveness of compassionate mind training for students with major depressive disorder: A randomized controlled trial. *Mindfulness*, *12*, 1159–1172. https://doi.org/10.1007/s12671-020-01584-3

Schreiter, S., Pijnenborg, G. H. M., & aan het Rot, M. (2013). Empathy in adults with clinical or subclinical depressive symptoms. *Journal of Affective Disorders*, *150*(1), 1–16. https://doi.org/10.1016/j.jad.2013.03.009

Sousa, R., Petrocchi, N., Gilbert, P., & Rijo, D. (2021). HRV patterns associated with different affect regulation systems: Sex differences in adolescents. *International Journal of Psychophysiology*, *170*, 156–167. https://doi.org/10.1016/j.ijpsycho.2021.10.009

Steffen, P. R., Foxx, J., Cattani, K., Alldredge, C., Austin, T., & Burlingame, G. M. (2021). Impact of a 12-week group-based compassion focused therapy intervention on heartrate variability. *Applied Psychophysiology and Biofeedback*, *46*, 61–68. https://doi.org/10.1007/s10484-020-09487-8

Steindl, S. R., Buchanan, K., Goss, K., & Allan, S. (2017). Compassion focused therapy for eating disorders: A qualitative review and recommendations for further applications. *Clinical Psychologist*, *21*(2), 62–73. https://doi.org/10.1111/cp.12126

Stellar, J. E., Cohen, A., Oveis, C., & Keltner, D. (2015). Affective and physiological responses to the suffering of others: Compassion and vagal activity. *Journal of Personality and Social Psychology*, *108*(4), 572–585. https://doi.org/10.1037/pspi0000010

Svendsen, J. L., Osnes, B., Binder, P. E., Dundas, I., Visted, E., Nordby, H., Schanche, E., & Sørensen, L. (2016). Trait self-compassion reflects emotional flexibility through an association with high vagally mediated heart rate variability. *Mindfulness*, *7*(5), 1103–1113. https://doi.org/10.1007/s12671-016-0549-1

Thayer, J. F., Åhs, F., Fredrikson, M., Sollers, J. J., III, & Wager, T. D. (2012). A meta-analysis of heart rate variability and neuroimaging studies: Implications for heart rate variability as a marker of stress and health. *Neuroscience and Biobehavioral Reviews*, *36*(2), 747–756. http://doi.org/10.1016/j.neubiorev.2011.11.009

Thayer, J. F., & Lane, R. D. (2000). A model of neurovisceral integration in emotion regulation and dysregulation. *Journal of Affective Disorders*, *61*(3), 201–216. https://doi.org/10.1016/s0165-0327(00)00338-4

Thayer, J. F., & Lane, R. D. (2009). Claude Bernard and the heart-brain connection: Further elaboration of a model of neurovisceral integration. *Neuroscience and Biobehavioral Review*, *33*(2), 81–88. https://doi.org/10.1016/j.neubiorev.2008.08.004

18

Ethical Principles and Practice Standards in Psychophysiological Psychotherapy

Donald Moss

Introduction: Why Is There a Need for Ethical Principles and Practice Standards?

The Protection of the Patient

The first and obvious reason that ethical principles and practice standards are needed is for the protection of the patient. Unfortunately, there are frequent instances of therapists exploiting a patient or making errors in judgment causing harm to the patient. Clear ethical principles establish what actions are potentially harmful and should be avoided in clinical practice. Practice standards provide a minimal level of quality control, suggesting for example, that a thorough evaluation should precede treatment and that a patient who mentions chest pain should be referred to a qualified physician before stress management is attempted (Schwartz, 2016).

The Protection of the Professional

The second reason for the creation of ethical principles and practice standards is the protection of the professional delivering treatment. Patient dissatisfaction, complaints, and accusations can arise for any practitioner. Practitioners are better able to protect themselves against such complaints, if they can show that they have followed the published ethical principles in their field and have implemented interventions in accord with treatment protocols reported in journals and presented at professional meetings.

When seemingly groundless complaints are filed with a state licensing board, a state professional organization, or the insurance company covering a patient, it is stressful for the practitioner. However, if the practitioner can provide accurate documentation of a thorough assessment, careful treatment planning, and appropriate treatments, and the treatments closely follow protocols for evidence-based interventions for the patient's disorder, the complaint is often dismissed. A number of areas seem to be lightning rods for complaints, including sexual contact with patients, disclosure of information without patient consent, and counseling patients in the decision to separate from a spouse. Here too, however, careful adherence to published treatment guidelines and well-documented guidelines for release of information can protect the patient and the professional.

When practitioners enter new or less known fields of practice, such as applied psychophysiology and psychophysiological psychotherapy, it can easily be perceived that traditional ethical principles and practice standards are being violated. Psychologists, for example, are generally cautious about touching the patient, and yet physiological monitoring requires placing physiological sensors on the patient's body in order to record and display the biological signal. Hence the publication of specific ethical principles and practice standards for emerging specialty areas of practice is a priority.

The Protection of the Profession

The creation and dissemination of ethical principles and practice guidelines is also protective of the profession and the field of practice. Many potential patients and their families are cautious about behavioral health services, reflecting a variety of fears. Every time a practitioner abuses or carelessly harms a patient, and that case draws media attention, it does irremediable harm to the profession. The already anxious potential patient, who might greatly benefit from behavioral interventions, will now delay treatment longer or avoid treatment entirely.

Special Needs for Ethical Information in Psychophysiological Psychotherapy

Professional organizations, ethics committees, and licensing boards are in many respects conservative. Their mission is to implement codes and principles articulated over decades and to conserve the patient's well-being and professional practice standards. New developments in clinical practice, such as psychophysiological psychotherapy, push the envelope of past practice—for example, the usual psychological therapist's prohibition against touching the patient. As such, new practices are at risk for serving as lightning rods for complaints.

Practitioners in a newer area, or in a minority area, outside the mainstream, can best protect themselves by learning and implementing the best practices of the new field, as announced in professional journals and in training endorsed by professional organizations. Further, educating patients about the mechanisms and specific steps in the new specialized interventions is a priority, so that patients better understand the electrode placement and how physiological monitoring or feedback training is relevant for addressing their presenting problem. As Rains and Schwartz (2016) have observed, patients who understand the intervention and have a sense of ownership in the treatment plan, show more "adherence" and active participation in the treatment. They are also less likely to file a complaint.

Sources for Ethical Guidance in the Fields of Biofeedback, Physiological Monitoring, and Psychophysiological Psychotherapy

Behavioral health professionals are governed in their clinical practice by a variety of organizations and their practice standards and ethical codes. Practitioners are governed first, by their home discipline. The physician must adhere to American Medical Association ethical guidelines, the psychologist to the American Psychological Association's (2017a) *Ethical Principles of Psychologists and Code of Conduct*, and the nurse to American Nursing Association's (ANA, 2015) *Code of Ethics for Nurses*. In addition, practitioners are governed by ethical codes of conduct in any specialty professional organization to which they belong. Members of the Association for Applied Psychophysiology and Biofeedback (AAPB) must adhere to the AAPB Code of Ethics (AAPB, 2016), members of the International Society for Neuroregulation and Research (ISNR) must adhere to the ISNR Professional Standards and Ethical Principles (ISNR, 2020), and individuals certified by the Biofeedback Certification International Alliance (BCIA) must follow its Practice Standards and Ethical Principles (BCIA, 2016).

The psychotherapist who utilizes physiological monitoring and physiological skills training remains a psychotherapist. The APA's *Ethical Principles of Psychologists and Code of Conduct* (2017a) provide thorough discussions and guidelines on most aspects of psychotherapy, from advertising one's practice to informed consent to multiple relationships. This document is a useful starting point for any psychotherapist or counselor. In addition, a number of books provide thorough discussions of a broad range of ethical challenges facing the practicing mental health professional (Drogin, 2019; Knapp, 2012; Knapp et al., 2017; Koocher & Keith-Spiegel, 2016; Nagy, 2011).

Other Resources for Psychophysiological Psychotherapists

Where does the professional turn for more detailed training in ethics and practice standards matters? There are several sources that are of special value for our field. First of all, AAPB, ISNR, and BCIA regularly provide workshops on ethical principles through face-to-face workshops and webinars. Their websites and e-mail list regularly announce upcoming ethics programs. These same organizations provide extensive clinical training and workshops on biofeedback and neurofeedback practice. Regular continuing education workshops keep the practitioner aware of best practices. This is a strong support for clinical practice, because the practitioner can make treatment planning decisions informed by current best practices. Practitioners should regularly review major journals and magazines in psychophysiology, behavioral medicine, and psychotherapy. This list below provides only a small sampling given today's proliferation of journals, especially in counseling and psychotherapy:

American Journal of Psychotherapy
Annals of Behavioral Medicine
Applied Psychophysiology and Biofeedback
Biofeedback Magazine
Counseling and Psychotherapy Research
Frontiers in Neuroscience
Frontiers in Psychology
Health Psychology and Behavioral Medicine
International Journal of Behavioral Medicine
International Journal of Clinical and Experimental Hypnosis
International Journal of Psychophysiology
Journal of Behavioral Medicine
Journal of Consulting and Clinical Psychology
Journal of Psychophysiology
Journal of Psychosomatic Research
Psychology and Psychotherapy: Theory, Research, and Practice
Psychotherapy

Scholarly books in biofeedback and psychotherapy also provide updates on current practice standards and the research evidence on the therapeutic efficacy of biofeedback applications (Khazan, 2013; Khazan et al., 2023; Lehrer & Woolfolk, 2021; Moss & Shaffer, 2019; Schwartz & Andrasik, 2016; Tan et al., 2016).

Specific Issues in Psychophysiological Psychotherapy

Empathy and the Therapeutic Relationship

A key element in the success of any therapeutic intervention, in healthcare and mental healthcare, is the therapeutic relationship. Decades ago, Carl Rogers (1957) identified the necessary and sufficient conditions for positive therapeutic change: (a) the therapist and patient are in psychological/emotional contact, (b) the therapist sustains and exhibits a state of congruence and genuineness, (c) the therapist conveys an unconditional positive acceptance and regard for the client, and (d) the therapist sustains and communicates an empathic understanding of the patient's experience. Research continues to show that empathic rapport, communicative attunement, and personal empathy are common factors necessary for therapeutic benefit in psychotherapy, regardless of the therapeutic techniques utilized (Browne et al., 2021; Elliott et al., 2011; Norcross & Lambert, 2018). Research also shows that increased empathy in healthcare professionals improves patient satisfaction and increases the treatment effect for diabetes (Canale et al., 2012), cancer (Lelorain et al., 2012), gastroesophageal reflux disease (Dossett et al., 2015), obstetrics (Committee Opinion No. 480, 2011), and other conditions (Moudatsu et al., 2020).

The first task for the therapist in psychophysiological psychotherapy is to establish this relationship of empathy, understanding, and compassion with the patient. An empathic therapeutic relationship facilitates the patient's progress in treatment (Norcross & Lambert, 2018). In addition, practitioners should be aware that a relationship of mutual empathy and understanding may reduce the risk that patients will perceive mistreatment and pursue complaints (Kee et al., 2018).

Patient Education and Orientation to Therapy

Along with establishing a therapeutic relationship, the therapist has a responsibility to educate the patient to the process and techniques of psychophysiological psychotherapy (Schwartz, 2016). The therapist will introduce the mind–body link, the immediate impact of emotion and thought on physiology, and the use of sensors to monitor physiological processes during the therapy sessions.

Rationale for Physiological Monitoring

Initially, the patient may benefit from learning the so-called psychophysiological principle developed by Green et al. (1970), that:

> Every change in the physiological state is accompanied by an appropriate change in the mental emotional state, conscious or unconscious, and conversely, every change in the mental emotional state, conscious or unconscious, is accompanied by an appropriate change in the physiological state. (p. 3)

Monitoring physiology during psychophysiological psychotherapy sessions provides both patient and therapist with a window into emotions and conflicts that patients may not yet have admitted to themselves. Human beings can deny many emotions and desires to themselves cognitively, yet the body will disclose undeniable physical reactions when the subject is discussed. Increases in skin conductance, changes in rate and manner of breathing, increases in muscle tension, and sudden activations of cortical activity may all be a warning of such unrecognized emotional distress or conflicts.

Sensor Placement and Touch

Next, the purpose of each physiological sensor and the appropriate placement for each should be discussed and demonstrated. Placement of sensors should not begin until patients express both understanding and consent. Less intrusive placements should be chosen when options exist, to preserve patient modesty. In most cases, the ideal research sensor placement is not necessary for sessions of psychophysiological psychotherapy. Wrist to wrist placements will usually serve for electrocardiogram sensors, or blood volume pulse sensors with placement on a finger or earlobe may be used to monitor heart rate and heart rate variability. Frontal or cervical placement will usually suffice for monitoring muscle activity. In addition, when placing a respiratory band for monitoring breathing activity, the therapist can hold the band out for the patient to draw it across the navel (or chest) and around the torso, and the therapist can fasten the band behind the back. In this fashion, therapist contact with more sensitive areas of the body will be minimized, and the message of respect for the patient will be reinforced.

Once sensors are in place, the practitioner can more effectively demonstrate the mind–body link by alternately engaging in discussion with the patient, discussing sensitive topics, and calling the patient's attention to and discussing any instances of reactive physiological activation. In addition, the practitioner may invite the patient to relax and recover from any physiological activation, and then draw the patient's attention to and discuss the extent of recovery visible in the physiological line graph. Finally, a formal psychophysiological stress profile may be utilized to establish and communicate the patient's stereotypic responses to stress and recovery patterns (Moss & Shaffer, 2019; Sternbach, 1966).

Informed Consent

Informed consent is an essential element in today's healthcare. A signed written consent to treatment is a starting point for treatment. In any novel practice area, whenever a practitioner draws on interventions that are not widely familiar or have not yet been well supported by randomized controlled trials, it is advisable that the written consent form include a description of the treatment, parameters of the intervention, and the rationale. Patients will often consent to novel or experimental therapies, especially when they have had little benefit from mainstream therapies. Nevertheless, the patient is entitled to know that an offered treatment is not yet widely known or accepted or has not yet been subjected to extensive clinical trials.

Informed consent begins with a signed consent form but continues throughout the treatment process. Unrecognized patient problems may be identified during the assessment or during treatment sessions, requiring changes in the choice of treatment or extending the likely length of treatment. Patients may fail to respond to initial interventions requiring revision of the treatment plan. When such changes in the treatment plan occur, additional discussion is necessary to sustain the informed consent of the patient. These discussions and the changes in the treatment plan should be documented in the patient chart, along with a statement of the patient's consent. If another novel or unproven intervention is implemented, a revised written/signed consent form is recommended. It is also beneficial for the practitioner, with the patient's consent, to communicate the initial treatment plan, patient progress, and any revisions to the treatment plan to the patient's primary care physician and any referring medical specialist. This ensures better coordination of care, and often facilitates more physician support for the patient's behavioral care.

Scope of Practice and Competence for Practice

Scope of practice refers to which interventions practitioners are authorized to provide under their licensure and certifications. Psychologists, for example, are authorized to provide psychotherapy in all states, for patients with diagnosed mental health disorders and medical problems. Yet in many states, psychologists are not authorized to provide even rudimentary nutritional advice. Dentists may utilize biofeedback and various relaxation skills with patients with dental anxiety or other emotional issues that interfere with dental techniques. In spite of their skill and experience with biofeedback, however, their scope of practice does not allow dentists to treat individuals with post-traumatic stress disorder and other mental disorders.

Competence for practice is established by education, training, and experience (Knapp et al., 2017; Striefel, 2004, 2016). Even in areas where practitioners have the legal scope of practice and training in relevant techniques, practitioners should not take on treatment of unfamiliar patient populations without preparation. For example, neurofeedback is a relevant intervention for seizure disorders, but a certified neurofeedback practitioner should not commence treatment of a patient with seizures, unless either past training or current supervision/peer consultation prepare them to manage a seizure in the office.

Professionals who wish to practice psychophysiological psychotherapy should begin by reviewing their professional scope of practice, and then their competence. Does their licensure provide them with the legal scope of practice to conduct psychotherapy? Does their psychological training and experience prepare them to deliver competent psychotherapy with the patient groups under consideration? Does their psychophysiological training prepare them to competently apply sensors, understand the physiological processes being monitored, and translate the physiological signals into relevant information to inform psychotherapy?

Multicultural Awareness and Sensitivity to Diversity

Most professional groups have now established multicultural awareness, sensitivity to diversity, and recognition of the dynamics of power, privilege, and oppression as core competencies in ethical professional practice (American Counseling Association, 2014; APA, 2017b; BCIA, 2016; National Association of Social Workers, 2015). These guidelines remind us that behavioral professionals are cultural beings and may hold implicit attitudes and beliefs that negatively impact their perceptions of and interactions with individuals who are ethnically or racially different from themselves (Moss, 2019). Psychophysiological psychotherapists are encouraged to participate regularly in continuing education on diversity, cultural differences, and intersectionality. The purpose of such education is to increase sensitivity to diversity issues, and to enhance understanding of ethnically and racially different persons (Pedersen et al., 2008).

Diversity sensitivity and multicultural awareness include but go beyond avoidance of any discriminatory practices. Clearly, ethical practitioners cannot refuse services to clients because of sex, sexual orientation, sexual identity, race, religion, disability, or national origin. But of equal importance, ethical practitioners will pursue a detailed understanding of the special characteristics and needs of each community touched by their professional practice. Psychotherapists frequently encourage using online resources, community education, and home practices of self-care that may be impractical given the living conditions of specific patient groups. Any such interventions must be adapted to community realities to be practical.

Even usual ethical guidelines may have to be adapted in specific ways to comply with local standards, as in the case of health professionals living and serving in indigenous communities:

> The health professional in such instances may live in the indigenous village, participate in community religious ceremonials, and interact with patients and family members in everyday settings. Family and community acceptance of a provider may be limited if she or he does not participate in the rituals and celebrations of the village. Western concepts of maintaining confidentiality and avoiding dual relationships may need to be adapted as cultural norms require. (Moss, 2019, p. 324)

Conclusion

In summary, the professional engaged in psychophysiological psychotherapy is responsible for developing and maintaining an understanding of ethical principles and practice standards in the fields of both psychotherapy and applied psychophysiology, with attention to the ethical codes in each area. Effective treatment begins with the establishment of an empathic therapeutic relationship, with effective patient education to the parameters of psychophysiological monitoring during therapy, and with informed consent. The clinical practice of each psychophysiological psychotherapist is guided and limited by each professional's scope of practice and competence. Movement into the treatment of new diagnostic populations should be supported by continuing professional education and supervision/peer consultation. Finally, ethical practice in psychophysiological psychotherapy requires awareness and sensitivity to diverse populations and the living conditions in one's target communities.

References

American Counseling Association. (2014). *ACA code of ethics*. https://www.counseling.org/resources/aca-code-of-ethics.pdf

American Medical Association. (2001). *AMA code of medical ethics*. https://www.ama-assn.org/sites/ama-assn.org/files/corp/media-browser/principles-of-medical-ethics.pdf

American Nurses Association. (2015). *Code of ethics for nurses*. American Nurses Publishing.

American Psychological Association. (2017a). *Ethical principles of psychologists and code of conduct*. http://www.apa.org/ethics/code/

American Psychological Association. (2017b). *Multicultural guidelines: An ecological approach to context, identity, and intersectionality*. http://www.apa.org/about/policy/multicultural-guidelines.pdf

Association for Applied Psychophysiology and Biofeedback. (2016). *Association for Applied Psychophysiology and Biofeedback code of ethics*. https://aapb.org/Code_of_Ethics

Biofeedback Certification International Alliance. (2016). *Professional standards and ethical principles of biofeedback*. https://bcia.memberclicks.net/assets/docs/ProfessionalStandardsAndEthicalPrinciplesofBiofeedback.pdf

Browne, J., Cather, C., & Mueser, K. T. (2021). Common factors in psychotherapy. In T. Wykes (Ed.), *Oxford research encyclopedia of psychology*. Oxford University Press. https://doi.org/10.1093/acrefore/9780190236557.013.79

Canale, S. D., Louis, D. Z., Maio, V., Wang, X., Rossi, G., Hojat, M., & Gonnella, J. (2012). The relationship between physician empathy and disease complications: An empirical study of primary care physicians and their diabetic patients in Parma, Italy. *Academic Medicine, 87*(9), 1243–1249. https://doi.org/10.1097/ACM.0b013e3182628fbf

Committee Opinion No. 480: Empathy in women's health care. (2011). *Obstetrics and Gynecology, 117*(3), 756–761. https://doi:10.1097/AOG.0b013e3182147865

Dossett, M. L., Mu, L., Davis, R. B., Bell, I. R., Lembo, A. J., Kaptchuk, T. J., & Yeh, G. H. (2015). Patient-provider interactions affect symptoms in gastroesophageal reflux disease: A pilot randomized, double-blind, placebo-controlled trial. *PLoS One, 10*(9), Article e0136855. https://doi.org/10.1371/journal.pone.0136855

Drogin, E. Y. (2019). *Ethical conflicts in psychology* (5th ed.). American Psychological Association.

Elliott, R., Bohart, A. C., Watson, J. C., & Greenberg, L. S. (2011). Empathy. In J. C. Norcross (Ed.), *Psychotherapy relationships that work: Evidence-based responsiveness* (pp. 132–152). Oxford University Press. https://doi.org/10.1093/acprof:oso/9780199737208.003.0006

Green, E., Green, A. M., & Walters, E. D. (1970). Voluntary control of internal states: Psychological and physiological. *Journal of Transpersonal Psychology, 2*, 1–26.

International Society for Neuroregulation and Research. (2020). *Professional standards and ethical principles*. https://isnr.org/interested-professionals/isnr-code-of-ethics

Kee, J. W. Y., Khoo, H. S., Lim, I., & Koh, M. Y. H. (2018). Communication skills in doctor patient interactions: Learning from patient complaints. *Health Professions Education, 4*(2), 97–106. https://doi.org/10.1016/j.hpe.2017.03.006

Khazan, I. Z. (2013). *The clinical handbook of biofeedback: A step-by-step guide for training and practice with mindfulness*. John Wiley & Sons.

Khazan, I. Z., Shaffer, F., Moss, D., Lyle, R., & Rosenthal, S. (Eds.). (2023). *Evidence-based practice in biofeedback and neurofeedback*. Association for Applied Psychophysiology and Biofeedback.

Knapp, S. J. (Ed.). (2012). *APA handbook of ethics in psychology*. American Psychological Association.

Knapp, S. J., VandeCreek, L. D., & Fingerhut, R. (2017). *Practical ethics for psychologists: A positive approach* (3rd ed.). American Psychological Association.

Koocher, G. P., & Keith-Spiegel, P. (2016). *Ethics in psychology and the mental health professions: Standards and cases* (4th ed.). Oxford University Press.

Lehrer, P. M., & Woolfolk, R. L. (Eds.). (2021). *Principles and practice of stress management* (4th ed.). The Guilford Press.

Lelorain, S., Bredart, A., Dolbeault, S., & Sultan, S. (2012). A systematic review of the associations between empathy measures and patient outcomes in cancer care. *Psycho-Oncology, 21*, 1255–1264. https://doi.10.1002/pon.2115

Moss, D. (2019). Ethical principles, professional conduct, and practice standards. In D. Moss & F. Shaffer (Eds.). *Physiological recording technology and applications in biofeedback and neurofeedback* (pp. 320–331). Association for Applied Psychophysiology and Biofeedback.

Moss, D., & Shaffer, F. (2019). *Physiological recording technology and applications in biofeedback and neurofeedback*. Association for Applied Psychophysiology and Biofeedback.

Moudatsu, M., Stavropoulou, A., Pilalithis, A., & Koukouli, S. (2020). The role of empathy in health and social care professionals. *Healthcare, 8*(1), Article 26. https://doi.org/10.3390/healthcare8010026

Nagy, T. (2011). *Essential ethics for psychologists: A primer for understanding and mastering core issues*. American Psychological Association.

National Association of Social Workers. (2015). Standards and indicators for cultural competence in social work practice. https://www.socialworkers.org/LinkClick.aspx?fileticket=PonPTDEBrn4%3D

Norcross, J. C., & Lambert, M. J. (2018). Psychotherapy relationships that work III. *Psychotherapy, 55*(4), 303–315. http://dx.doi.org/10.1037/pst0000193

Pedersen, P. B., Draguns, J. G., Lonner, W. J., & Trimble, J. E. (Eds.). (2008). *Counseling across cultures* (6th ed.). Sage Publications, Inc. https://doi.org/10.4135/9781483329314

Rains, J. C., & Schwartz, M. S. (2016). Adherence. In M. S. Schwartz & F. Andrasik (Eds.), *Biofeedback: A practitioner's guide* (4th ed., pp. 233–248). The Guilford Press.

Rogers, C. R. (1957). The necessary and sufficient conditions of therapeutic personality change. *Journal of Consulting Psychology, 21*(2), 95–103. https://doi.org/10.1037/h0045357

Schwartz, M. S. (2016). Intake and preparation for intervention. In M. S. Schwartz & F. Andrasik (Eds.). *Biofeedback: A practitioner's guide* (4th ed., pp. 217–232). The Guilford Press.

Schwartz, M. S., & Andrasik, F. (Eds.). (2016). *Biofeedback: A practitioner's guide* (4th ed.). The Guilford Press.

Sternbach, R. (1966). Psychophysiological basis of psychosomatic phenomena. *Psychosomatics, 7*(2), 81–84.

Striefel, S. (2004). *Practice guidelines and standards for providers of biofeedback and applied psychophysiological services*. Association for Applied Psychophysiology.

Striefel, S. (2016). Ethical practice issues and concerns. In M. S. Schwartz & F. Andrasik (Eds.), *Biofeedback: A practitioner's guide* (4th ed., pp. 260–271). The Guilford Press.

Tan, G., Shaffer, F., Lyle, R., & Teo, I. (Eds.). (2016). *Evidence-based treatment in biofeedback and neurofeedback* (3rd ed.). Association for Applied Psychophysiology and Biofeedback.

Index

For the benefit of digital users, indexed terms that span two pages (e.g., 52–53) may, on occasion, appear on only one of those pages.

acceptance 263–64, 341–42
acceptance and commitment therapy 223–24, 337–50
  acceptance 341–42
  case example 346–47
  cognitive defusion 339–41
  committed action 345–46
  core principles 339–46
  heart rate variability biofeedback 341, 342, 343, 344, 345–46
  mindfulness 343
  observing self 344
  predicting response to 114
  values 344–45
adaptation 157–58, 175–76
addiction 69, 85, 194
adverse childhood experiences 59–60
affect 127–49
  adaptive 127–28
  balance of positive and negative affect for mental health 141–43
  cognition and 138–39
  core affect 127–28, 144–46
  current scientific theories 135–40
  definition 127
  excess of negative affect 128
  neural activation 137
  philosophical theories 130–35, 143–46
  psychophysiological barometer 137
  subjectivity 140
affiliative motivations 373, 374–76
agency 34–35, 282–83
allostatic load 60, 194, 280
American Psychological Association (APA), ethical guidelines 415
amotivation 20
amygdala 79, 80, 102, 103, 104–5, 113, 115
angiotensin-converting enzyme (ACE) 177
anterior cingulate cortex 71, 103, 106–8, 113–14, 138
anxiety disorders 81, 103–16
apoptosis 58, 59
approach 44, 157, 191, 194–95
archetypal image/value 21

arousal 158, 164, 198
arrested defenses 30–31
artificial intelligence 112–13
assertiveness training 294–95
attachment 21, 27–28, 31–32, 35–37, 250–52
attention
  bias 245, 260, 264–65
  networks 64
attunements 132–35
autobiographical memory 143
autogenic training 224, 233
autonomic nervous system 18–19, 27–28, 76, 79–80
autonomous motivation 20
avoidance 44, 128, 157, 191, 194–95

balance
  personality 191–96
  positive and negative affect 141–43
  stress response 175–76
baroreflex 233–34, 361
Barrett, Lisa Feldman 128
basal ganglia 64, 115
bed nucleus of stria terminalis 105
behavior
  behavioral activation system 194–95
  behavioral approach system 157
  behavioral inhibition system 157, 194–95
  behavior theory 223–24
  CFT competency 267
  evolved mind 43–44
  voluntary-involuntary behaviors 32
belief system 248–50
"better safe than sorry" 245
bifactor models of psychopathology 83–84
biofeedback
  blood flow control 231–32
  breathing control 232–33
  heart rate variability 72, 90–92, 233–34, 331–33, 337–38, 341, 342, 343, 344, 345–46
  historical background 225–26
  respiratory 331–33
  sources of ethical guidance 415–16
  "Trojan horse" 227–28

Index

biomarkers
  brain imaging and response to psychotherapy 111–16
  cardiac 72
  dimensional diagnostic approach 162–67
  see also heart rate variability
biopsychosocial model 13, 14, 15, 24–28, 135, 171
bipolar disorder 26
blood flow control 231–32
blood pressure 176, 177–79
Bohr, Christian 353
borderline personality 229
Bowlby, John 31–32, 195–96
brain
  imaging 71, 103, 111–15, *see also* functional magnetic resonance imaging
  networks 63–64
  plasticity, *see* neuroplasticity
  social brain 28
breathing
  breath-by-breath biofeedback 232–33
  heart rate and the breathing cycle 77
  heart rate variability 358–65
  mindful breathing 315–16, 326–27
  overbreathing 355–56
  psychotherapy 358–65
  resonance frequency breathing 362–65
  respiratory physiology 352–56
  retraining 87–88
  slow breathing 91–92
  teaching healthy breathing 356–58
brief compassionate mind training 399–400

Cannon, Walter 172
carbon dioxide 352, 353
cardiac biomarkers 72
cardiac vagal control 393–94, 404
cardiovascular system 175–76, 177, 178–82, 279–80
care/caring 13, 19–20, 22, 25–26, 27–28, 41–43, 250–57, 392
case studies 53–54, 72–73, 165–67, 311–22, 323–35, 346–47, 377, 385
categorical approach 153–55, 166
central autonomic network 81–82
cerebellum 115
chemical synapses 58–59
childhood adversity 59–60
choline 108–9
chronic inflammation 80–81
cognition
  affect and 138–39
  personality 197–98
  subjectivity 140

cognitive behavioral therapy (CBT)
  heart rate variability 87–88
  hypertension 182
  neuroplasticity 69–70, 71–72, 103–11
cognitive defusion 339–41
cognitive reappraisal 102–3, 182
communion 282–83
compassion
  affiliative motivations 373
  compassionate mind training 380–81, 397, 399–400
  Compassion Engagement and Action Scales 257–58
  competencies 41–43
  conceptualizing 391–93
  courage 252–53
  dyadic exchanges 384–86
  empathic resonance and 381–82
  enhancing therapy 382–84
  evolution of 392
  evolved algorithm 19–20
  fears, blocks and resistances 255–57
  flows of 254–56
  heart rate variability 18–19, 378–80, 381, 382, 395
  kindness and 391–92
  mindfulness 381
  motivation 392–93
  multifaceted process 257–69
  neurovisceral integration model 376–77
  pain perception 382
  physiological basis 393–95
  regulatory power 378
  self-compassion 256, 257, 382
  stimulus detection and response system 19–20, 394
  wisdom 253–54
compassionate mind training 380–81, 397, 399–400
compassion-focused therapy (CFT) 243, 391, 396–98
  arrested defenses 30–31
  attachment theory 35, 250–51
  attention 260, 264–65
  autonomic nervous system 18–19
  behavior 267
  brief compassionate mind training 399–400
  compassionate mind training 380–81, 397, 399–400
  compassionate-self practice 399–400, 406
  competence for practice 419
  competencies for action 264–68
  competencies for engagement 259–64
  cultivating compassion 259–60
  distress tolerance 261–62

empathy 262–63
evolved competencies 38–40
feeling 268
grieving 33
heart rate variability 397–407
higher intensity therapy (12 week) 400–4
imagery 265–66
knowing awareness and knowing intentionality 41
nonjudgement (acceptance) 263–64
physiology 246–48, 397–98
positive affect 34
reasoning 39–40, 266–67
sensory systems 267–68
social and non-social focused processes 21
social mentalities 22–23
stress management 294
sympathy 261
twelve competencies model 259–69
voice-hearers 23
voluntary-involuntary behaviors 32
competencies, evolved mind 37–43
competition for resources 25–26
competitive motives 21
complementarity principle 284–85
compulsive self-reliance 256
consciousness 133–34
  consciousness of 40
consent 418–19
consilience 14
controlled motivation 20
coping 174–75, 191, 194–95
core affect 127–28, 144–46
coronary heart disease 278–82, 284–86, 289–90
courage 252–53
culture-bound symptoms 221–22

Damasio, Antonio 128, 136
default mode network 64–65
default threat response hypothesis 78–80
defeat states 31–32
defensive action/immobility 79–80
depression 26, 28, 34, 66
Descartes, René 130–32
developmental processes 57–60
diagnosis
  categorical approach (*DSM*) 153–55, 166
  dimensional approaches 155–61, 166–67
Diagnostic and Statistical Manual (*DSM*) 153–55, 166
dialectical behavior therapy 229
dimensional approach
  diagnosis 155–61, 166–67
  personality 200–1
  psychophysiological biomarkers 162–67

dispositional negativity 162–63
dissociative identity disorder 334
distress tolerance 261–62
diversity sensitivity 420
dopamine system 66–68
dualism 54–55, 129, 130–32
dynamic equilibrium model 192
dysconnectivity hypothesis 85

ecological momentary assessments 406–7
electrical synapses 58–59
electroencephalography (EEG) 116–17, 162–63, 327–28
electrolytes 356
embodiment
  current scientific theories 135–40
  philosophical theories 130–35, 143–46
emotions
  adaptation 157
  brain regulation 102–3
  emotional journaling 326–27
  emotional resonance 262
  evolved mind 29–37
  mixed emotions 142
  muscle activation 314
  positive emotions 34–37
  psychophysiological event 313–14
  somatic marker hypothesis 136
  suppression 314
  threat emotions 30–34
  see also affect
empathy
  compassion-focused therapy 262–63
  empathic awareness 42, 43
  empathic resonance 381–82
  therapeutic relationship 416–17
enactivism 139
entrapment 31–32
environment of evolutionary adaptedness 195–96
epigenetics 16
ethical issues 413–22
event-related potentials 162
evolution
  caring behavior 22, 27–28, 250–57
  compassion 392
  four functions of evolved minds 16, *see also* mind
  personality 191, 195–96
  psychology 373
  social motivations 374
  stress response 172–74
executive function 82–83, 84–85
exercise interventions 89
exposure treatment 87

extinction learning 87

factor analytic methods 202–4
Fast Fourier Transform (FFT) 360–61
fear conditioning 78–79
feelings 30, 131–32, 134, 136, 137–38, 268
Ferenczi, Sandor 313
"fight or flight" 18–19, 76, 79, 172, 173–74, 179–80, 338, 354–55, 375
five-factor model 198–99
freezing behavior 79–80
Freud, Anna 314
Freud, Sigmund 14, 243–44
frontal lobe 71
functional magnetic resonance imaging (fMRI) 64, 103, 113–16, 345
fusion 339–41

Gellhorn, Ernst 225
General Hyperbolic Cosine Model (GHCM) 205
Generalized Graded Unfolding Model (GGUM) 205
glutamate 107
gratitude 256–57
Greek philosophers 130
Green, Elmer 417
grief 33–34
guided imagery 265–66
guilt 43

habituation, stress 176, 179–80
harm 17
Harris, Russ 339
Hayes, Steven C. 339
hearing voices 23
heart rate
  breathing cycle 77, 233–34
  monitoring 327–28
  sustained elevation 176
heart rate variability (HRV) 72, 75–100, 351, 375–76
  biofeedback 72, 90–92, 233–34, 331–33, 337–38, 341, 342, 343, 344, 345–46
  biomarker 163–64
  breathing 358–65
  brief compassionate mind training 399–400
  cardiac vagal control 393–94
  cognitive behavioral therapy 87–88
  compassion 18–19, 378–80, 381, 382, 395
  compassionate mind training 380–81
  compassion-focused therapy 397–407
  coronary heart disease 280
  determining vagally mediated levels 88–89
  ecological momentary assessments 406–7
  effectiveness of therapy 367–68
  higher intensity compassion-focused therapy 400–4
  indices of resting vagally-mediated 76–77
  integration with acceptance and commitment therapy 341, 342, 343, 344, 345–46
  interventions targeted at 89–90
  measuring 359–62
  neurovisceral integration model 78–83
  perseverative cognitions 77
  personality 199
  phasic 394–95
  physiological basis 76–77
  prefrontal function 81–85
  psychotherapy 365–68, 382–83
  psychotherapy research 86–88
  readiness for therapy 366–67
  sign of distress or health issue 366
  therapist influence 384–85
  three Rs paradigm 394–95
  training 362–65
  transdiagnostic marker of psychopathology 75, 83–85
Hebbian modification 60–63
hedonic treadmill 192
Heidegger, Martin 132–35, 144
Hierarchical Taxonomy of Psychopathology (HiTOP) 159–61, 167
hippocampus 71, 110
holistic models 135–36
hyper-affiliation 374–76
hypertension 177–78, 182
hyperventilation syndrome 232
hypnosis 224, 227–28, 330–31
hypocapnia 355–56

ideal-point models 202, 204–5
imagery 265–66
infant caring 27–28
inferior frontal gyrus 71
inferior parietal cortex 110
inflammation 80–81
information processing 244–45
informed consent 418–19
inhibition 80–83, 84–85, 87, 157, 194–95, 345–46, 376, 393
insomnia 62
insula 105–6
interoceptive systems 68–69
interpersonal circumplex 283–84, 287–88
interpersonal theory 282–90, 295

intracarotid sodium amobarbital test 82
item response theory 201–4, 205

Jacobson, Edmund 224–25
James, William 222–23

Kabat-Zinn, Jon 343
Kahneman, Daniel 128
knowing awareness and knowing intentionality
   40–41, 43
Konorski, Jerzy 56

Lang, Peter 226
late positive potential 116–17
Lazarus, Richard 226, 244–45
LeDoux, Joseph 30
Lilienfeld, Scott O. 154–55, 158
long-term potentiation 72
looming 17

machine learning 112–13
McEwen Bruce S. 60
meditation 182, 293–94, 315–16
memory 143
mentalizing 39
mesocorticolimbic system 69
Miller, Neal 225–26
mind
   algorithms 19–20
   behaviors 43–44
   competencies 37–43
   emotions 29–37
   mind–brain dualism 54–55, 129, 130–32
   motives 13–18, 20–28
   social minds 248–50
mindfulness 40, 89–90, 182, 264–65, 293–94,
   315–16, 326–27, 343, 380–81
monoaminergic systems 66–68
moods 132–33, 134
motives/motivation 157
   affiliative motivations 373, 374–76
   algorithms 19–20
   amotivation 20
   approach–avoidance 157
   autonomous/controlled 20
   biopsychosocial process 24–28
   compassion as 392–93
   competitive 21
   cultivating compassion 259–60
   evolved mind 13–18, 20–28
   social mentalities 21–24
   social motives 21–24, 374
motor (movement) systems 68

Mplus 209
multicultural awareness 420
muscle activation 314
muscle relaxation 224–25, 231
muscle tension 164–65

N-acetylaspartate (NAA) 107, 108–9
narcissism 28, 256–57
nausea 174
negative valence 157, 196–97
negativity bias 17, 78
networks, brain 63–64
neural development 57–60
neuroception 245, 337–38
neuroimaging 71–72, 103, 113–17, *see also*
   functional magnetic resonance imaging
neuroplasticity 55–70
   cognitive behavioral therapy 69–70, 71–
      72, 103–11
   definition 57
   Hebbian modification 60–63
   historical background 55–56
   interventions 69–70
   monoaminergic systems 66–68
   networks 63–64
   neural development 57–60
   prediction 66, 68–69
   psychopharmaceuticals 72
   psychotherapy 56–57, 103–11
   stress response 59–60
neuroticism 177, 180, 193–94, 195
neurotransmitters 66–68
neurovisceral integration model 78–83, 338–
   39, 376–77
nitric oxide 353
non-social reasoning 39
norepinephrine system 66–68
numbing 32–33

omega-3 fatty acid supplements 90
orbitofrontal cortex 109–10
overbreathing 355–56
oxygen 352–54

pain
   protective mechanism 174
   self-compassion 382
panic disorders 61–62, 71
parahippocampus 110
paranoia 26
parasympathetic system 18–19, 36, 76, 79–80,
   280, 374–75, 397–98
parental care 27–28

parietal cortex 110
Pavlov, Ivan 13–14
Pennebaker, James 327
perceptual networks 64
perseverative cognitions 77
personality
  allostasis 194
  balance 191–96
  coping 191, 194–95
  coronary heart disease 279
  dimensional models 200–1
  dominance approach 190, 198–99, 204–5
  dynamic equilibrium model 192
  evolution 191, 195–96
  factor analytic methods 202–4
  five-factor model 198–99
  heart rate variability 199
  hedonic treadmill 192
  heritability 189
  homeostatic regulation 191–96
  ideal-point models 202, 204–5
  intraindividual variability 193
  item response theory 201–4, 205
  measuring and analyzing 199–209
  nonlinearity 201–2, 208–9
  Personality Psychopathology-Five (PSY-5) 198–99
  psychological flexibility 193
  quadratic unfolding model 206–8, 209
  RDoC framework 189–90, 196–98
  reinforcement sensitivity theory 194–95
  set-point hypothesis 192–93
  stress response 171–72, 176–78, 179–80
  unified theory 191, 196–98
perspective-taking 262–63
pH 352–53
philosophical theories, affect and embodiment 130–35, 143–46
physiological monitoring
  case studies 317–18, 326, 327–28
  education of patients 417–18
  sources of ethical guidance 415–16
polyvagal theory 338–39, 374–75
Porges, Stephen W. 338–39
positive emotions 34–37
positive valence 157, 196–97
practice standards 413–22
prediction
  cognition 138–39
  default mode network 65
  neuroplasticity 66, 68–69
prefrontal cortex
  addiction 85
  general vulnerability for psychopathology 83–85
  heart rate variability 81–85
  mediating psychotherapy 102, 103
  plasticity in response to psychotherapy 108–10
  predicting outcome of psychotherapy 113, 114
  subcortical inhibition 80–81
progressive relaxation 224–25, 231
psychogenic polydipsia 69
psychological flexibility 193
psychopathology
  categorical approach 153–55, 166
  dimensional approach 155–61, 166–67
  heart rate variability as a transdiagnostic marker 75, 83–85
psychophysiological psychotherapy
  case studies 311–22, 327–34
  ethical issues and practice standards 413–22
psychosis 71–72
psychotherapy
  brain imaging biomarkers of response to 111–16
  breathing skills 358–65
  candidate brain systems 102–3
  cardiovascular reactivity 180–82
  emergence of psychophysiological contributions 224–26
  heart rate variability 365–68, 382–83
  historical reflection 243–46
  hypnosis-assisted 330–31
  interpersonal assessment 295
  neuroplasticity 56–57, 103–11
  physical intervention 54–56
  physiology and 246–48
  research 69–70, 86–88
  social mentalities 22–23
  treatment selection 117
  see also cognitive behavioral therapy

quadratic unfolding model 206–8, 209

racism 289
Ramón y Cajal, Santiago 56
Raynaud's symptoms 231–32
reasoning 39–40, 266–67
Reich, Wilhelm 224, 314
reinforcement sensitivity theory 194–95
relaxation therapy 224–25, 231
rescuing behavior 27
Research Domain Criteria (RDoC)
  personality 189–90, 196–98

psychopathology 155–59, 166
resonance frequency breathing 362–65
resources
    competition for 25–26
    seeking 17–18
respiratory biofeedback 331–33
respiratory physiology 352–56
respiratory sinus arrhythmia 77, 233–34, 361
reward system 64, 69
Rogers, Carl 416–17

sadness 33–34
safe haven 27–28, 35, 251–52
safeness/safety 18, 36–37, 375
satisfaction 18
schizophrenia 66–67, 69, 85
Schultz, Johannes 224
scope of practice 419
secure base 27–28, 35, 251–52
selective serotonin reuptake inhibitors (SSRIs) 67
self-compassion 256, 257, 382
self-concept clarity 262–63
self-consciousness 40
self-deception 134–35
self-to-self relating 23–24
sensorimotor system 68, 198
sensory system 138, 267–68
serotonin system 66–68
set-point hypothesis 192–93
shame 256, 257
Shapiro, David 225–26
sharing 25–26
shutdown 31–32
skin conductance 164–65
social anxiety 28
social brain 28
social mentalities 21–24
social minds 248–50
social motivation
    biopsychosocial processes 24–28
    evolution 374
    social mentalities 21–24
social rank 26
social reasoning 39–40
social support 36–37, 288
social systems 197–98
sodium amobarbital test 82
somatic marker hypothesis 136
spillover effects of treatment 228, 234
Spinoza, Baruch 132, 143–44
sports interventions 89
stimulus–response algorithms 19–20, 394

Stoic philosophers 130
stress 171–87, 277–309
    assertiveness training 294–95
    balance and adaptation 175–76
    biopsychosocial model 171
    cardiovascular reactivity 175–76, 177, 178–82, 279–80
    compassion-focused therapy 294
    coping and 174–75
    coronary heart disease 279–80, 289–90
    developmental neuroplasticity 59–60
    evolution of stress response 172–74
    habituation 176, 179–80
    health and well-being 175–76
    interpersonal theory 282–90, 295
    intraindividual variability of response 193
    management interventions 277, 281–82, 290–95
    mindfulness interventions 293–94
    personality and 171–72, 176–78, 179–80
    psychological flexibility 193
    respiration 354–55
Strosahl, Kirk D. 339
Structural Analysis of Social Behavior model 291–94
sympathetic system 18–19, 76, 78, 79, 374–75, 397–98
sympathy 261
synapses, electrical and chemical 58–59
systematic desensitization 224–25, 317–18

Thayer, Julian, F. 376
theory of mind 64
therapeutic relationship 416–17
threat
    attachment and threat regulation 35–37, 250–51
    default response to uncertainty 78–80
    emotions 30–34
    motive system 17
    vagus nerve 375
transactional cycle 285–86
transcendent self 344
treatment
    choice 117, 221–22
    history of 221
    models of 222–24
    multidimensional approach 228, 229–31
    spillover effects 228, 234
    symptom-treatment specificity 226–29
    see also psychotherapy
Trier Social Stress Test 287, 405–6
trophic factors 58

vagal flexibility 404
vagally-mediated heart rate variability, *see* heart rate variability
vagal tone 393–94
vagus nerve 18–19, 27–28, 36, 338–39, 374–76, 393
valence systems 157, 196–97
values 344–45
visual cortex 115–16

voice-hearers 23

Wada test 82
Wilson, Edward 14
Wilson, Timothy 128
wisdom 253–54
Wolpe, Joseph 224–25, 317

Zajonc, Robert 244–45